PENGUIN BOOKS
A HISTORY OF SRI LANKA

K.M. de Silva is Executive Director of the International Centre for Ethnic Studies (ICES), Kandy/Colombo, Sri Lanka, a post he has held since the establishment of the ICES in 1982.

Apart from his long association with the University of Ceylon (now the University of Peradeniya), Professor de Silva has held several distinguished positions including Smuts Visiting Fellow in Commonwealth Studies and Visiting Fellow of Clare Hall, Cambridge, President, International Association of Historians of Asia and Fellow of the Woodrow Wilson Center for Scholars in Washington.

Professor de Silva's publications include *Social Policy and Missionary Organisations in Ceylon, 1840–55* (1965), *Managing Ethnic Tensions in Multi-ethnic Societies: Sri Lanka, 1880–1985* (1986), *Regional Powers and Small State Security: India and Sri Lanka, 1977–1990* and *Reaping the Whirlwind: Ethnic Conflict and Ethnic Politics in Sri Lanka* (1998). He has been editor of *Ethnic Studies Report*, one of the editors of the *International Journal of Group Rights* and has been on the advisory board of *The Round Table*.

K.M. de Silva was selected as the Academic Prize Laureate (2002) of the 13th Fukuoka Asian Cultural Prizes. The Fukuoka Asian Cultural Prizes were established in 1990 by Fukuoka City, Japan, to recognize individuals who have made outstanding contributions to Asian scholarship and culture. Professor de Silva is the first Sri Lankan Fukuoka Laureate.

D1447655

A History of Sri Lanka

K.M. DE SILVA

PENGUIN BOOKS

PENGUIN BOOKS
Published by the Penguin Group
Penguin Books India Pvt Ltd, 11 Community Centre, Panchsheel Park, New Delhi 110 017, India
Penguin Group (USA) Inc., 375 Hudson Street, New York, New York 10014, USA
Penguin Group (Canada), 90 Eglinton Avenue East, Suite 700, Toronto, Ontario, M4P 2Y3, Canada (a division of Pearson Penguin Canada Inc.)
Penguin Books Ltd, 80 Strand, London WC2R 0RL, England
Penguin Ireland, 25 St Stephen's Green, Dublin 2, Ireland (a division of Penguin Books Ltd)
Penguin Group (Australia), 250 Camberwell Road, Camberwell, Victoria 3124, Australia (a division of Pearson Australia Group Pty Ltd)
Penguin Group (NZ), cnr Airborne and Rosedale Roads, Albany, Auckland 1310, New Zealand (a division of Pearson New Zealand Ltd)
Penguin Group (South Africa) (Pty) Ltd, 24 Sturdee Avenue, Rosebank, Johannesburg 2196, South Africa

Penguin Books Ltd, Registered Offices: 80 Strand, London WC2R 0RL, England

First published by C. Hurst & Co. 1981
This revised and updated edition first published by Penguin Books India 2005

Copyright © K. M. de Silva 2005

All rights reserved

10 9 8 7 6 5 4 3 2 1

Typeset in Sanskrit Palatino by S.R. Enterprises, New Delhi
Printed at Baba Barkhanath Printers, New Delhi

This book is sold subject to the condition that it shall not, by way of trade or otherwise, be lent, resold, hired out, or otherwise circulated without the publisher's prior written consent in any form of binding or cover other than that in which it is published and without a similar condition including this condition being imposed on the subsequent purchaser and without limiting the rights under copyright reserved above, no part of this publication may be reproduced, stored in or introduced into a retrieval system, or transmitted in any form or by any means (electronic, mechanical, photocopying, recording or otherwise), without the prior written permission of both the copyright owner and the above-mentioned publisher of this book.

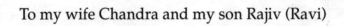
To my wife Chandra and my son Rajiv (Ravi)

Contents

Abbreviations

BP	Before Present Era
CHJ	*Ceylon Historical Journal*
CJHSS	*Ceylon Journal of Historical and Social Studies*
CLR	*Ceylon Literary Register*
CAN	Ceylon National Archives
CO	Colonial Office, despatches series
CRO	Commonwealth Relations Office, despatches series
DMK	Dravida Munnethra Kazhagam
ESR	*Ethnic Studies Report*
IESHR	*Indian Economic and Social History Review*
IPKF	Indian Peace Keeping Force
JCBRAS	*Journal of the Ceylon Branch, Royal Asiatic Society*
JRAS (GB & I)	*Journal of the Royal Asiatic Society of Great Britain and Ireland*
JRAS SL Branch	*Journal of the Royal Asiatic Society, Sri Lanka Branch*
JVP	Janatha Vimukthi Peramuna
KA	Koloniale Archief, the Archives of the former VOC (q.v.) now at the General State Archives at The Hague.
LSSP	Lanka Sama Samaja Party
MCS	*Modern Ceylon Studies*
MEP	Mahajana Eksath Peramuna
MP	Member of Parliament
MSLS	*Modern Sri Lanka Studies*
SLFP	Sri Lanka Freedom Party
SLNA	Sri Lanka National Archives
TULF	Tamil United Liberation Front

UCHC I (I & II)	The University of Ceylon, *History of Ceylon*, Vol. I, Parts I & II
UCHC III	The University of Ceylon, *History of Ceylon*, Vol. III
UF	United Front
ULF	United Left Front
UPHSL II	The University of Peradeniya, *History of Sri Lanka*, Vol. II
UCR	*University of Ceylon Review*
UNP	United National Party
VOC	Vereenigde Oost-Indische Campagnie

Glossary

accomodessan	:	land granted for duties rendered or offices held.
adigār	:	chief officer of state in the Kandyan kingdom. The *mahadigār* or first *adigār* took precedence over all others in the hierarchy of chiefs.
Ārannavāsins	:	forest-dwelling monks.
Äsala perahära	:	ritual or religious ceremonial procession.
aumildar/aumani	:	mode of collecting grain tax during the nineteenth century.
badda	:	tax.
basnayaka nilamē	:	principal lay officer of a shrine of gods (*dēvālē*).
bhikkhu	:	monk or priest, member of the Buddhist order.
cetiya, dāgäba, stupa, thūpa	:	edifice built over a relic, generally a dome-shaped monument.
chēna	:	forest land brought into cultivation by the slash and burn method (from the Sinhala *hēna*).
commandement, commandery	:	administrative division under the control of the Dutch.
dāgäba	:	see *cetiya*.
dakapathi	:	levy on water paid to the king and to others in control of water resources.
dēvālē	:	shrine of gods of the Buddhist pantheon.
dēvālēgam	:	people resident in villages attached to the *dēvālē*.
dēvālē land	:	land attached to the *dēvālē*.

divel	:	property granted to officials and functionaries in the employment of the state and of monasteries.
dhonies	:	small sailing vessels of south India; vessels with one mast.
disāvani, disāva, disāvony	:	provinces under the administration of a *disāva* in the Kandyan kingdom.
disāvē, disāva	:	governor of a province (*disāvani*) in the Kandyan kingdom; also in the maritime regions under the VOC; the title survived in British times and was conferred on native officials in the administrative hierarchy in the Kandyan provinces.
Durāva	:	a Sinhalese caste, toddy-tappers.
elu	:	the pure Sinhala, free from Sanskrit influence.
gabadāgam	:	royal villages in the Kandyan kingdom.
ganninānse	:	quasi-monk of early Kandyan times resident in a vihara, but who had not been admitted to the order of monks and was not necessarily celibate.
gansabhāva, gamsabhāva	:	village council.
Govikula	:	caste of farmers.
Goyigama	:	caste of farmers.
indaba	:	African tribal institution.
kachcheri mudaliyār	:	local official, aide to the government agent at the *kachcheri*.
kahavanu (kahāpana)	:	coins in circulation from about the first or second century AD. The standard coins of the early Anuradhapura period, they varied greatly in weight and with regard to the metal used.
kangānies	:	headmen, selected from among themselves or appointed by the employer of gangs of Indian immigrant labourers in the plantation sector.
kachcheri	:	provincial secretariat.

Karāva	:	a Sinhalese caste; fishermen.
kōlam	:	masked drama.
kōralē	:	an administrative unit of a *disāvani*.
kotikābadda	:	a tax on areca nuts.
kumbelamas	:	type of dried fish.
landraads	:	Dutch civil courts of law with cognisance over all land disputes of the local population.
lascarins	:	native militia.
mada idam	:	mud land or land on which 'wet paddy' is grown.
mahabadda	:	lit. great revenue, the Cinnamon Department.
mahākāvya	:	epic poem.
maha mudaliyār	:	native official, chief aide to the governor of the colony under British rule and the highest rank in the hierarchy of native officials.
mahanaduva	:	Great Court of Justice in the Kandyan kingdom.
marāla	:	death duties.
meriah	:	sacrifices of female infants.
mudaliyār	:	a chief headman; the administrator of a *kōralē* under the British.
muhandiram	:	title of rank, chief revenue officer in the Kandyan kingdom. The title was conferred on native officials in the administrative hierarchy under the British.
nādagam	:	a lyrical play consisting largely of verses and songs.
nikāya	:	a Buddhist sect.
nindagam	:	a village, or holdings in a village, in exclusive control of the proprietor.
nūrtiya, nūrti	:	drama of the same operatic character as a *nādagam* but with a greater proportion of prose dialogue.
pangu, panguva	:	share; thus *pangukāraya*, a peasant holder.
pansala	:	Buddhist temple, place of worship.
parangi	:	yaws.
paraveṇi, pamunu	:	hereditary property held in perpetuity.

pattu	:	sub-division of a *kōralē*.
perahära	:	procession; pageant.
pinkama	:	almsgiving.
piriveṇa	:	(Buddhist) educational institute attached to a temple (*vihara*).
plakaats	:	proclamations of the Dutch government.
police vidāna	:	native official, generally a village-level headman, responsible for the maintenance of law and order. There was no salary attached to the post.
purāna village	:	ancestral village or old, long-inhabited village, distinct from new village settlements in an area.
purāṇas	:	the earliest known Sri Lankan coins: small, square, oblong or oval pieces cut from a strip of silver and punch-stamped. Ascribed to the pre-Christian period, they were in circulation until about the second century. These punch-marked coins were very similar to the parallel coinage of India of the same period. Their weight ranged from 14.9 to 50.4 grains.
rājakāriya	:	lit. king's duty; this encompassed any service to the king, a lord or a temple in the Kandyan kingdom. In the colonial period, it denoted compulsory service rendered to the state as well as to a lord or a temple.
ratēmahatmaya	:	the chief of a district (*ratē*) in the Kandyan kingdom. This title was bestowed on native officials in the administrative hierarchy in the Kandyan provinces during the period of British rule.
Salāgama	:	a Sinhalese caste; cinnamon-peelers.
sāmanera	:	unordained monk.
sangha	:	Buddhist clergy; order of *bhikkhus*.
sāsana	:	the religion (Buddhism).
sannas	:	royal grants, usually inscribed on copper plates.

sokari	:	a form of dramatic entertainment where the story is enacted in mime with some, if not all, characters wearing masks.
stadholder	:	viceroy or governor of a province or town in the Netherlands.
stadholderate	:	chief magistrate of the United Provinces of the Netherlands.
stupa	:	see *cetiya*.
thägi, thegi	:	gifts.
thōmbo	:	register of lands.
topases	:	persons of mixed Portuguese–indigenous descent, could refer to persons who spoke two languages.
thūpa	:	see *cetiya*.
thunhavul land	:	late eighteenth-century Dutch land grants under which one-third of the land had to be cultivated with cinnamon.
uliyam	:	service to the state.
upasampadā	:	higher ordination of *bhikkhus*.
Vaddas	:	an aboriginal group whose ancestary is traceable to the pre-historic inhabitants of the island.
valauva	:	dwelling of the chief; manorial residence.
vanniyār	:	a vanni chief.
Vesak	:	second month of the Sinhalese calendar (May–June).
vidāne	:	village official with constabulary services.
vihara	:	a Buddhist temple.
viharagam	:	inhabitants of villages attached to *viharas*.
vihara land	:	land attached to the *vihara*.
vinaya	:	monastic discipline; disciplinary regulations.

Preface and Acknowledgements

There has been a good deal of new writing on the history of Sri Lanka published since the appearance of the first edition of this book in 1980. Much of this is, however, on early Sri Lanka and on the ethnic conflict in the late twentieth century. Some of my former colleagues at the University of Peradeniya and a few others connected with the International Centre for Ethnic Studies (ICES) have helped me with suggestions for changes and in the exhausting search for items for revision. Some changes emerged from discussions with colleagues on revisions of this volume; others have appeared from responses to the writings of critics, in books, journals and presentations at seminars. I am especially grateful to Professors Sirima Kiribamune, K.N.O. Dharmadasa and John Holt for their encouragement and help in revising this book. Many, if not most, of their suggestions have been incorporated in the revised text. Unfortunately, John Richardson's monumental volume of 764 pages, *Paradise Poisoned: Learning about Conflict, Terrorism and Development from Sri Lanka's Civil Wars* (ICES, Kandy, March 2005), appeared too late for me to benefit from a thorough reading.

This revision owes a great deal more to my wife Chandra than she will ever know. She kept insisting that the book was in need of revision and that it was something I owed to myself and the two institutions to which I was linked—the University of Peradeniya and the ICES. I started working on the revisions after my departure from the University of Peradeniya in July 1995. Although a substantial part of the revision was done before I fell ill in 2002, it was finally completed in 2004 after my recovery from the stroke.

The staff of the ICES has contributed more to the actual preparation of the revised text than any other group of persons. I am especially grateful to Ms Iranga Silva of the ICES for preparing two or more versions of the revised work on the computer, and to Kanthi Gamage, Librarian/Documentalist of the ICES, who has been enormously helpful in the search for published articles and for unpublished material whenever such material could be located, and in proofreading.

The maps in the book have been prepared by Dr Ram Alagan of the Department of Geography at the University of Peradeniya. Some of these maps are based on maps prepared in the 1970s for the original book and in the early 1980s for other publications by Professor G.H. Peiris. I am very grateful to all of them.

Kandy, Sri Lanka   K.M. de Silva
April 2005

Colonizers and Settlers

INTRODUCTION

The island of Sri Lanka, the southernmost part of the subcontinental mass of what is known today as south Asia, was separated from the subcontinent in recent geological times—c. 7000 BP.[1] This separation by a narrow and shallow sea, just 40 km in length at its narrowest point, is just as important a factor in the island's historical evolution, as the obvious proximity to the subcontinent and, therefore, its receptivity to a variety of influences—cultural, religious, political and economic—from there. In the earlier phases of the island's history the great north Indian empires of the Mauryas and the Guptas had a profound influence on it. This was followed in later centuries by the influence of kingdoms located further south in the subcontinent, like the Pallavas, and later on from the south Indian kingdoms of the Pāṇḍyas, Cheras and Cōḷas.[2] Less obvious than the Indian influence, but over the centuries just as important, was the influence of south-east Asia in trade, first of all, and next through the common religion, Buddhism.

The physical size of the island, 65,610 sq. km, was large enough to ensure that throughout much of its history, political pressure from the Indian kingdoms could be successfully resisted, and even in regard to cultural and religious influences these could be absorbed, assimilated, adapted and, in some instances, transformed. There was seldom any danger of being overwhelmed by these cultural influences and the island's Buddhist civilization, the most significant and enduring legacy of the north Indian empires, was retained, nurtured and protected long after Buddhism had ceased to be of any great significance in most parts of northern India.

Just as the proximity of Sri Lanka to India was an important factor in its historical evolution so too was its location in the Indian Ocean on the regional and transcontinental trade routes between south-east Asia and west Asia, and between China and these regions. Sri Lanka also had trade links with the great civilizations of Greece and Rome.[3] The profits derived from this international trade combined with the agricultural surplus from the production of rice and other commodities helped finance the multitude of religious and secular monuments, including the irrigation systems, in the principal cities of ancient Sri Lanka.

Apart from the beauty of the island, which has attracted comments from writers from ancient times to the present day, there are its physical attributes, the hills and mountains of the central and southern parts of the island, and the plains which surround them. These plains occupy nearly four-fifths of the land space in the island, ranging in height from near sea level to around 300 metres. The flatness of the plains is broken by scores of rocks and rounded mounds which rise occasionally to heights of 300 metres or more, the erosional remnants of an area levelled down over aeons of interrupted denudation and weathering.

The island has a variety of climatic zones. Temperatures range from between 25 °C and 29 °C in the plains to between 13 °C and 22 °C in the central hills and mountains. The diurnal variation in temperature is more pronounced in the hills and mountains than on the plains.[4] The island's location in the tropics—5° 55' to 9° 51' N—brings it within the influence of the north-east and the south-west monsoons. The northern, eastern and south-eastern parts of the island get rains mainly from the north-east monsoon from late October to the end of January, while the rest of the country benefits from both the north-eastern and south-western monsoons and is much wetter. Rainfall in most parts of the island is also convectional. Thus the annual rainfall over most of the island is over 1,250 mm.

The variety of climatic zones, distinct regional rainfall patterns, along with distinct physical features, result in a number of ecological systems, but the one that concerns us most in this history of the island, is the division into a wet zone and a dry zone, relative terms based on the amount of rain, its seasonal patterns and its effectiveness. The north-central and south-eastern parts of the dry zone form the physical stage on which the dramatic history of the island was played in the ancient and medieval times.

On the history of the island up to the end of the first millennium, and indeed for three centuries of the second, there is a wealth of historical data. Of these the first category consists of the Pali chronicles, the *Dīpavaṁsa* and *Mahāvaṁsa* with its continuation the *Cūlavaṁsa*,[5] which together provide scholars with a mass of reliable data, not available for other parts of south Asia[6] for most of the period under study. Next come the archaeological remains of the civilizations of Sri Lanka's dry zone, the magnificent array of religious and secular monuments written about in the chronicles mentioned earlier, and the irrigation works. The irrigation works consisted of reservoirs called 'tanks', many of them enormous in their capacity to carry water, and canals which carried water from the rivers to these tanks and supplied water to the fields for rice cultivation for centuries. Many of those tanks are still in use. They were repaired and reconstructed in the mid- and late nineteenth century and in the twentieth century. Third, there is the mass of inscriptional material mostly carved on rocks, painstakingly copied and collected by archaeologists over the nineteenth and twentieth centuries, and edited for the use of scholars.[7]

PREHISTORY

While the Sri Lanka chronicles contain a surprisingly full and reasonably reliable account of the early history of the island (they have no rival in India), their conception of its inhabitants at the time of the arrival of the Indo-Aryan colonizers and settlers, around the *parinibbāna* of the Buddha, as spirits, *yaksa*s and *nāga*s, is more useful as an index to the beliefs and perceptions of the literati of ancient Sri Lankan society than for the extraction of factual information on the island's prehistory and proto-history. Faxian, a Chinese traveller who lived on the island for some time, was not much more helpful when he

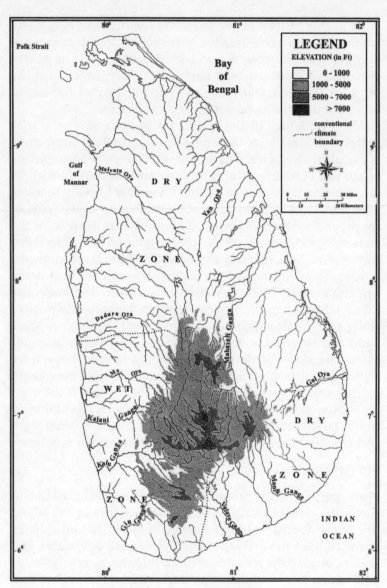

Sri Lanka : Physical Features

wrote in the fifth century AD that Sri Lanka 'originally had no human inhabitants, but was occupied only by spirits and *nāgas* with which merchants of various countries carried on a trade'. Our present state of knowledge of the prehistoric and proto-historic inhabitants of the island is a little clearer thanks to the research of archaeologists—especially those of the mid- and late twentieth century.[8]

While archaeological evidence on the prehistory of Sri Lanka is still rudimentary, it is possible for us to attempt the bare outlines of the beginnings of human society on the island, using data relating to India which affords a convenient, though not entirely reliable, point of comparison, and through recent archaeological discoveries in the island. The first appearance of Homo sapiens on the island could have occurred by about 125,000 BP. The evidence of human settlements is much stronger from about 34,000 BP onwards. The data on this comes from cave excavations in the lowland wet zone. These anatomically modern prehistoric humans belonged to what are called the Balangoda cultures.

A few quartz and bone implements are the only surviving traces we have of mesolithic man's presence on the island. The stone-working technology of the Balangoda cultures appears to continue into proto-historic times. The neolithic or pottery phase saw the technique of producing stone implements by abrasion and the solid core drill.

The Balangoda cultures, in their mesolithic phase, seem to have had an island-wide distribution. There are indications of a rudimentary knowledge of agriculture, probably during the neolithic phase. Evidently Balangoda man—a cave-dweller—knew how to produce fire. The scarcity of calcined bones among his food remains suggests, however, that flesh was generally eaten raw and there is a hint too of cannibalism.

In physical characteristics, Balangoda man was predominantly Australoid with Neanderthaloid overtones. The Vadda aboriginals of Sri Lanka are physically closest to Balangoda man from among the ethnic groups who still live on the island today.

The transition from the mesolithic Balangoda culture to the proto-historical Early Iron Age is not well-documented in

Sri Lanka. The earliest manifestation of the Iron Age in Sri
Lanka is believed to be about 1000–800 BC. With the Early Iron
Age came cattle, horses, paddy cultivation and pottery. Iron
technology greatly increased the capacity of the land to provide
a living to larger number of humans. It was now easier to
clear the equatorial rainforests.

The submergence of Balangoda man and his physical and
cultural attributes under pressure of the early colonizers from
India would very likely have postdated 500 BC, with possible
survivals into a much later period in the rainforests of
Sabaragamuva, which were not penetrated by civilized man
to any considerable extent until the end of the first millennium
AD. The early colonizers from India found the island an attractive
proposition for settlement; there was, for the most part, adequate
water from convectional and seasonal rains; the dense tropical
forests could be cleared using iron technology the colonists
had brought to the island. Apart from these, pearl fishery was
well-established in the north-western part of the island and a
major source of copper was available at Seruvila on the eastern
part.[9] In addition, the island was strategically located on the
trade routes between south-east Asia and west Asia.

THE INDO-ARYAN COLONIZATION

In the *Mahāvaṁsa*, that irreplaceable literary source for the
reconstruction of the early history of the island, the story of
man in Sri Lanka begins with the arrival there, sometime in
the fifth century BC, of Vijaya (the legendary founding father
of the Sinhalese) and his turbulent companions—700 in all—
who had been banished for misconduct from the kingdom of
Sīhapura in northern India by Sīhabāhu, Vijaya's father. After
a long and eventful voyage they landed near the present site
of Puttalam on the north-west coast and set about the business
of establishing a foothold on the island. Beneath this charming
exercise in myth-making lurks a kernel of historical truth—
the colonization of the island by Indo-Aryan tribes from northern
India.[10] The original home of the first Indo-Aryan immigrants
to Sri Lanka was probably north-west India and the Indus region.

There was, very likely, a later immigration from the east around Bengal and Orissa. The *Mahāvaṁsa* story of Vijaya has it that towards the end of his reign he invited his younger brother to come to Sri Lanka as his successor. This the latter was unwilling to do but he sent his youngest son, Panduvasudeva, instead. He landed at Gokanna (now Trincomalee) towards the north-east of the island with thirty-two followers and was subsequently enthroned at Upatissagāma, thus ensuring the continuity of the Vijayan dynasty. Gokanna was a natural port of disembarkation for boats arriving from the Bay of Bengal and thus this account of the arrival of Panduvasudeva affords evidence of the possibility of a second wave of colonization, a hypothesis strengthened by the linguistic affinities between the Sinhala language in the early phase of its development and the prakrits of eastern India.

The Pali chronicles referred to earlier were the work of *bhikkhus* and, naturally enough, were permeated by a strong religious bias and encrusted with miracle and invention. The central theme was the historic role of the island as a bulwark of Buddhist civilization and in a deliberate attempt to underline this, a synchronizing of the advent of Vijaya with the parinibbāna (the passing away) of the Buddha is contrived.

> When the Guide of the World, having accomplished the salvation of the whole world and reached the utmost stage of blissful rest, was lying on the bed of his *nibbāna* in the midst of the great assembly of gods, he the great sage, the greatest of those who have speech, spoke to Sakka who stood near him: 'Vijaya, son of King Sīhabāhu, is come to Laṅkā from the country of Lāla together with 700 followers. In Laṅkā, O Lord of gods, will my religion be established, therefore, carefully protect him with his followers and Laṅkā.'[11]

This was to become in time the most powerful of the historical myths of the Sinhalese and the basis of their conception of themselves as the chosen guardians of Buddhism and of Sri Lanka as a 'place of special sanctity for the Buddhist religion'. This intimate connection between the land, the 'race' and the

Buddhist faith foreshadowed the intermingling of religion and national identity which has always had the most profound influence on the Sinhalese.

The traditional accounts of the colonization of the island lay great emphasis on conquest by tribes of conquerors led by a warrior nobility. But while their contribution was important enough in its own way, this would have formed just one element in the Indo-Aryan migration. There is, for instance, the possibility that traders reached the island while sailing down the Indian coast and that the natural products of Sri Lanka, gems in particular, may have provided the incentive for some of them to found settlements there. The early settlers either absorbed, swept away or pushed into the remoter regions of the island the original inhabitants whom they encountered.

These Indo-Aryan settlements were established and developed in several parts of the island from about the fifth century BC. The earliest settlers were those on the west-central coast who pushed inland along the banks of the Malvatu Oya and founded a number of riverbank settlements. Their seat of government was Upatissagāma where the first 'kings' of the Vijayan dynasty reigned. The settlers on the east coast would have moved inland along the Mahaveli River. Somewhat later, there was perhaps an independent band of immigrants who settled in Rohana in the south-east, on the mouth of Valave River, with Māgama as their chief seat of government. The settlers came in numerous clans[12] or tribes, the most powerful of whom were the Sinhalese.

Their settlements were all in the dry zone, were riverine in character and rice was the staple crop. These migrants introduced the use of iron to the island. The iron axe and the iron plough, which they brought with them, revolutionized the pattern of life in their new environment. The earliest colonists were dependent on the north-east monsoon for cultivating a single annual crop of rice. The climate was rigorous if not harsh, the rains seasonal but not reliable. With the expansion of the settlements, provision of a regular supply of water for cultivation became a matter of vital concern to the community. Two general solutions applied together were used: irrigation by means of channels cut from rivers and the construction of tanks or reservoirs. Irrigation and the use of iron implements in clearing forests and in agriculture would have ensured fairly rapid changes in this proto-historic period.

When the first Indo-Aryan immigrants formed villages, there was very likely some general idea of tribal union, with every member of the clan entitled to an allotment of land sufficient for his wants. But joint family tenure was not a regular feature in the land tenure system of ancient Sri Lanka and we have no evidence at all of collective ownership of land. In Sri Lanka, as in India, the myth that the village was self-sufficient in its economy and self-governing and self-regulating in its social and political life, dies hard,[13] even though it seems evident that the extension of the area under cultivation and habitation through the process of expanding irrigation facilities would by its very nature have emphasized the interdependence of villages rather than their self-sufficiency.

By 250 BC, there is evidence of a recognizably literate culture in the main areas of settlement—a contribution, no doubt, of the early Indo-Aryan settlers—even though the outlying communities may have remained pre-literate. Indeed, it is believed that the first appearance of writing in the Brahmi script was as early as c. 600–500 BC.[14]

BUDDHISM

It is very likely that the early Aryans brought with them some form of Brahmanism. By the first century BC, however, Buddhism had been introduced to the island and was well established in the main areas of settlement. According to the *Mahāvaṁsa*, the entry of Buddhism to Sri Lanka occurred in the reign of Devānampiya Tissa (250–210 BC), a contemporary of the great Mauryan Emperor, Aśoka, whose emissary, Mahinda (Aśoka's son, as some authorities would have it, or his brother, as is suggested by others), converted Devānampiya Tissa to the new faith. Once again the *Mahāvaṁsa's* account of events conceals as much as it reveals and what it hides in this instance is the probability that Buddhists and Buddhism came to the island much earlier than it suggests.

The Buddha (or the Enlightened One) was born in north India around 563 BC. The son of the Kshatriya chief of the republican Śakya tribe, his youth and early manhood were passed in ease and luxury. But in time he became increasingly dissatisfied with this life and as a comparatively young man he abandoned his home and family and opted for a life of asceticism in a search for salvation. Six years of this austere existence left him profoundly disillusioned with it and quite convinced that asceticism taken to exaggerated lengths was not the path of salvation. This realization spurred him on to a single-minded search for a more satisfying means of salvation. On the fortieth day of a long spell of meditation, an understanding of the cause of suffering dawned on him. He had attained enlightenment.

At the Deer Park at Sarnath (near Varanasi) he preached his first sermon and gathered his first five disciples. This sermon, the 'Turning of the Wheel of Law' as it was called, incorporated the Four Noble Truths (suffering, the cause of suffering, cessation of the cause, and the path leading to cessation), which form the nucleus of Buddhist teaching. The Buddha explained that the world was full of suffering, that this was caused by human desire, that the path to salvation lay in the renunciation of desire through the Eight-fold Path consisting of eight principles of action: right views, resolves, speech, conduct, livelihood, effort, recollection and meditation, the combination of which was described as the Middle Way, the basis of a life of moderation and equipoise. Salvation lay in achieving nirvana, or freedom from the wheel of rebirth. The doctrine of karma was essential to the Buddhist conception of salvation, but in contrast to the Brahmanical view of karma it was not used to buttress the prevailing caste structure, since Buddhism was basically opposed to caste. Buddhism was, if not atheistic, at least non-theistic in as much as the emphasis on causality as the basis of analysis left nothing to divine intervention and in the Buddhist system God was not regarded as essential to the universe. Despite the severely rational undertone of its arguments, its simplicity and freedom from complicated metaphysical thinking contributed to its immediate appeal to those who heard it.[15]

About a hundred years after the Buddha's parinibbāna the *sangha* split in two—the *Sthaviras* (Elders) and the *Mahāsanghikas* (members of the Great Order). According to tradition there were three Buddhist councils, the first of which was held at Rājagŗha after the Buddha's parinibbāna. It was at the second council, which took place at Vaishali a century later that the split occurred. At the third council in Pataliputra in 250 BC, during the reign of Aśoka, the Sthaviras emerged as the orthodox or Theravada sect (the Sthaviravāda School). The more sectarian Buddhists succeeded in excluding the dissidents and innovators—the heretical Mahāsanghikas—the Sthavira or Theravada faction. This paved the way for the later schism of Buddhism into the Little Vehicle (Theravada) or more orthodox branch, and the Greater Vehicle or Mahayana branch with its stress on the compassionate bodhisattva, intent on enlightenment for himself and the liberation of others. Though Buddhist sources have naturally endeavoured to associate Aśoka with the third council, he does not refer to it anywhere in his inscriptions, not even in those relating specifically to the sangha.

Aśoka's conversion to Buddhism occurred after his famous Kalinga campaign of 260 BC.[16] Remorse-stricken at the carnage and fearful destruction he had caused when he utterly routed the Kalingas, he found himself attracted to Buddhism in his effort to seek expiation. After a period of two-and-a-half years he became a zealous devotee of Buddhism, but he would not permit his personal commitment to Buddhism conflict with the duty—indeed, the practical necessity—imposed on him as ruler of a vast empire to remain above the religious rivalries and competition within it. Thus the restraints of kingship in a multi-religious empire may have prompted the decision not to participate actively in and associate himself with the third council. However, he could and did lend his patronage to the missionary impulse which emerged from this council's deliberations where the decision was taken to send missionaries to various parts of the subcontinent and to make Buddhism an actively proselytizing religion, which in later years led to its propagation in south and south-east Asia. One such mission was that sent to Sri Lanka in the time of Devānampiya Tissa.

The Mauryan Buddhist mission to Sri Lanka found itself preaching to a receptive audience. No doubt, the conversion of Devānampiya Tissa was decisive in ensuring its success. At a time when the authority of the kingdom of Anuradhapura over other 'kingdoms' in the island was on the increase, its patronage of Buddhism would have greatly hastened the acceptance of that religion by the people at large. According to both epigraphic and literary sources, the spread of Buddhism over the island's settlements was swift. But as it expanded its sway, Buddhism was transformed by the assimilation of pre-Buddhistic cults and rituals and ceremonials of an exorcist character. Buddhism was coming to terms with its Sri Lankan environment.

The rapid spread of Buddhism was not without political implications. For one thing, religious sentiment strengthened the friendly links established between Sri Lanka and the Mauryan empire. The Buddhist mission to Sri Lanka had been led, as we have seen, by Mahinda who was either Aśoka's son or brother; following on his success came Sanghamittā, a kinswoman of Aśoka, to establish the order of Buddhist nuns on the island. Apart from frequent exchanges of gifts and envoys between the two countries, Aśoka also sent a branch of the bo-tree[17] under which the Buddha had attained enlightenment. This tree still survives at Anuradhapura in Sri Lanka, while its parent was cut down in later centuries by an anti-Buddhist fanatic. A close link was also forged between the state and Buddhism. Devānampiya Tissa himself granted a royal park in the capital city of Anuradhapura as a residence for the ordained priesthood. This was the beginning of the Mahāvihara, the historic centre of Buddhist orthodoxy in ancient Sri Lanka. Within a short time of Mahinda's mission, Buddhism emerged as the established religion of the country. Finally, at this time, the level of development of Sri Lanka's agricultural economy did not yet provide an adequate foundation for a unified and centralized state. But settlements spread all over the island were evidently speaking a common language and were soon found using a common script. The rapid spread of Buddhism was a potent factor of unification, primarily cultural no doubt, but one which strengthened the process of political unification within the island.

THE DRAVIDIAN INFLUENCE

Sri Lanka's close proximity to southern India has been the basis for the assumption that there were Tamil settlements on the island in the early years of its history. Certainly, Tamil and other literary sources point to substantial urban and trading centres in south India in the third century BC. Very probably, there were trade relations between them and Sri Lanka and it is also highly probable that the island's trade with the Mediterranean world could have been through these south Indian ports. By the third century BC, Dravidian intrusion into the affairs of Sri Lanka became more marked. In 177 BC, two south Indian adventurers usurped power at Anuradhapura and ruled for twenty-two years, to be followed ten years later (in 145 BC) by another, Elāra, who maintained himself in power for a much longer period—for forty-four years, according to the *Mahāvaṁsa*—and earned an enviable reputation for justice and impartial administration. These Dravidian attempts at establishing control over the Anuradhapura kingdom appear to have been motivated partly at least by the prospect of influence over its external trade.

Apart from this, there is evidence from archaeological investigations conducted at Pomparippu in the north-west of the island in 1956 and 1957 of a culture which bears some resemblance to the south Indian megalithic culture;[18] the similarities are most noticeable in the Adichchanallur site just across the water from Pomparippu.[19] There are striking similarities in the style of urn burials and the characteristics of the pottery and the associated objects found at these two sites.

The settlement at Pomparippu and a possible one at Katiraveli in the east of the island need to be treated as isolated occurrences, not as evidence of widespread Tamil settlements.[20] These two settlements could be dated between the second century BC and the third century BC. For many centuries thereafter there is no inscriptional or other archaeological evidence, or literary evidence, of Tamil settlements in the country. There were, of course, Tamil mercenaries who were brought to the island occasionally from about the fifth century

AD, but more particularly from the seventh century AD onwards. Their presence in the early stages was for short periods and served a political purpose. They fought on behalf of aspirants to the throne and on behalf of rulers whose position was insecure. Thus, Sri Lanka from very early in its recorded history had seen groups of persons from southern India enter the island as traders, occasionally as invaders and as mercenaries but their presence was of peripheral significance in the early demography of the island.

The evidence available at present would tend strongly to support the conclusion that Indo-Aryan settlement and colonization preceded the arrival of Dravidian settlers by a few centuries. An expert on the subject, a Sri Lankan Tamil scholar, has pointed out that 'on the basis of the present evidence we could say that it was only by about the tenth century that permanent settlements of Tamils began.... [These] settlements were by no means extensive but their importance lies in the fact that they formed the nucleus of the later settlements that covered the greater part of northern Sri Lanka'.[21]

STATE BUILDING

The next theme that needs to be reviewed in this chapter is the process of political evolution which led to the emergence of a kingdom unifying the whole island under its sway. How this process of political unification came about and the main phases in it are matters on which no firm conclusions are possible. The account of these events in the *Mahāvaṁsa* is at once too bold in its outlines and too simple in its narration.[22] While the *Mahāvaṁsa* treats all kings of Sri Lanka since the mythical Vijaya as rulers of the whole island, the inscriptional evidence points to quite a different situation, with the Anuradhapura kingdom (tradition attributes its foundation to Pandukābhaya, the third king of the Vijayan dynasty) as merely the strongest, if that, among several in the northern plain[23] and in the Malaya[24] and Rohana regions, as well as in other parts of the country.

This structure had not changed substantially during the rule of Devānampiya Tissa. He held a consecration ceremony, for which the wherewithal was supplied by Aśoka, somewhat more elaborate than that performed for Aśoka himself, and assumed the title of Devānampiya Tissa maharaja. This was in a purposeful bid to transform the prestige accruing to him from his recently established political and religious links with Aśoka and the Mauryan empire into the hard reality of overlordship over the whole island. In spite of this, other rulers on the island did not readily acknowledge his sovereignty.[25] Certainly such influence as he had in the southern kingdom of Rohana was both minimal and temporary and this was despite the establishment of a kingdom at Māgama in Rohana by Mahānāga, his brother.

This collateral branch of the royal house at Anuradhapura eventually unified Rohana and thereafter established control over the whole island as well. It took them a century and a half to achieve it. The key figure in the unification of the south was Kāvantissa, during whose rule the authority of Māgama began to be felt throughout Rohana. In a sense, Kāvantissa was only accelerating a process of unification begun by his father, but very likely the threat posed by Elāra's rule in Anuradhapura made it more urgent than ever before to impose Māgama's hegemony over Rohana.

The phases in Māgama's ascendancy in Rohana are worth noting because of its profound importance for the eventual unification of the island under a single ruler. The annexation of the tiny 'kingdom' of Giri ruled by Siva, Kāvantissa's brother-in-law, was the first step. Eased out of Giri, Siva merely moved further north to the 'city' of Soma close to the Rohana kingdom of Seru. Since Soma and Seru lay on the frontier between Rohana and the Anuradhapura kingdom, Māgama could scarcely risk their continued existence as independent political entities. But it was impolitic to use force to achieve their subordination since it could attract the attention of the ruler of Anuradhapura and afford him an opportunity for intervention. Kāvantissa, therefore, sought to achieve his purpose—and did so—without resort to war: he merely moved into the area on the pretext of building a religious monument dedicated to the Buddha in apparent fulfilment of a prophecy of the Buddha himself. With the absorption of Soma and Seru, Māgama's authority extended to the Mahaveli River which thus became the northern boundary of Rohana. Rohana was now poised for battle with the Anuradhapura kingdom, but Kāvantissa, cautious as usual, did not take the offensive against Elāra. This, his son and successor Dutthagāmani did with decisive effect.

The long—fifteen-year—campaign waged by Dutthagāmanī against Elāra, which culminated in a duel fought in accordance with Kshatriya rules of chivalry and the latter's death, is dramatized as the central theme of the later chapters of the *Mahāhvaṁsa* as an epoch-making confrontation between the Sinhalese and Tamils, and extolled as a holy war fought in the interests of Buddhism. Dutthagāmanī's triumph was nothing less than the consummation of the island's manifest destiny, its historic role as the bulwark of Buddhism: the southern kingdom ruled by the Sinhalese Buddhist had prevailed over the northern kingdom ruled by a Dravidian usurper who, despite all his admirable qualities as a man and ruler, was nevertheless a man of 'false' beliefs.

The *Mahāvaṁsa's* account of these events glosses over facts and events which were inconvenient to its prime consideration of immortalizing the honour and glory attaching to Dutthagāmanī. Kāvantissa's shrewd statecraft, which laid the foundations for his son's success, receives scant attention. The *Mahāvaṁsa* depicts Elāra as the ruler of the whole northern plain and Dutthagāmanī's family as kings of the whole of Rohana ever since Mahānāga established himself in Māgama; this was not historically accurate, for Elāra was not the ruler of a united northern kingdom, nor were Dutthagāmanī's forbears kings of the whole of Rohana. Besides, the facile equating of Sinhalese with Buddhists for this period is not borne out by facts, for not all Sinhalese were Buddhists, while on the other hand, there were many Tamil Buddhists. There were, in fact, large reserves of support for Elāra among the Sinhalese and Dutthagāmanī, as a prelude to his final momentous encounter with Elāra, had to face the resistance of other Sinhalese rivals who appear to have been more apprehensive of his political ambitions than they were concerned about Elāra's continued domination of the northern plain. Nor did Dutthagāmaṇī's campaigns end with the capture of Anuradhapura after the defeat of Elāra. He brought the northern plain under a single political authority for the first time, and Elāra was only one, if still the most formidable, of his adversaries. There are references in the chronicles to Dutthagāmaṇī's battles with as many as thirty-two rulers in the course of his campaigns in this relentless quest for domination.

All this, however, is not to underestimate Dutthagāmaṇī's achievement. He accomplished what he set out to do, to establish control over the whole island. It was, in fact, the first significant success of centripetalism over centrifugalism in the island's history.

The capital of the kingdom at the time of Dutthagāmaṇī was, of course, Anuradhapura. It had been the principal urban centre in the north-central plains for two or three centuries prior to Dutthagāmaṇī's time (161–137 BC) as ruler of the island. The archaeological evidence available would appear to suggest that Anuradhapura's emergence as an important urban centre preceded the establishment of an island kingdom by several centuries. By about 800 BC, Anuradhapura was as large as 10 hectares (ha) in extent and had expanded to 50 ha or so in the period 700–600 BC. In the time of the Mauryan ruler, Aśoka, in the third century BC, it was nearly 100 ha in extent, making it the tenth largest city in the Indian subcontinent at that time and perhaps the largest south of Ujjain and Sisupalgahr.[26] Anuradhapura was linked to a port city, Mahatittha (Mantota) on the north-west coast, an important centre in the Indian Ocean trade.[27]

By the time of Devānampiya Tissa, the city was an elegant and populous urban centre, part administrative centre, part trade centre and part religious centre. Early irrigation systems linked the city with its hinterland and some of the early tanks provided the water required for its expanding population. This was Dutthagāmaṇī's legacy and he expanded his inheritance by constructing or beginning the construction of some of the most celebrated religious edifices of ancient Sri Lanka. Anuradhapura had the unusual distinction of serving as the capital city for close to 1,500 years, a length of time unmatched by any other city in the Indian subcontinent.

The Anuradhapura Kingdom I
Aspects of Political History from Saddhātissa
to the Cōḷa Conquest

INTRODUCTION

The kingdom of Anuradhapura, the classical Sinhalese kingdom, lasted nearly 1,500 years and the city of Anuradhapura lasted just as long as the capital city. In the earliest phase of its history, Anuradhapura was the capital of the principal kingdom on the island; it was the capital of the island kingdom since the time of Dutthagāmaṇī (161–137 BC) to the end of the tenth century, a longevity unmatched by any other capital city in south Asia.

This present chapter provides a brief survey of some of the principal features of the political history of the Anuradhapura kingdom from the time of Dutthagāmaṇī's successor, Saddhātissa, to the Cōḷa conquest, a thousand years of history with all the vicissitudes of fortune that such a long period of time would normally bring. In Chapters 3, 4 and 5, we review some of the principal features of the life of this classical Sinhalese kingdom, beginning with the network of irrigation systems, the backbone of its economy, its external and internal trade and its economy. Chapter 5 reviews the history of Anuradhapura as a Buddhist kingdom, the oldest Theravada Buddhist kingdom in existence.

The political history of the kingdom can be divided into three distinct phases or periods. The first phase is the early Anuradhapura period, the kingdom's first seven centuries to the reign of Dhātusena in the fifth century, the principal feature of which was the rise and consolidation of its power. The middle

Anuradhapura period saw the maturation of the kingdom, a phase in which one saw considerable instability, particularly in the seventh century, and the regular entry of Tamil mercenaries brought into the island by Sinhalese kings to help prop up their power, or by aspirants to the throne. The mercenaries formed the nucleus of a Tamil element in and around the court. The late Anuradhapura kingdom saw two centuries of political stability (the eighth and ninth centuries) followed by a century of increasing stress and instability as the Sinhalese kingdom struggled to cope with external threats from south Indian kingdoms. Those threats became more formidable in the tenth century and culminated in the absorption, if not of the kingdom itself, of at least most of it, under the Cōḷa empire, while the great city of Anuradhapura ceased to be the capital city.

From the tenth century onwards, Anuradhapura's past glories remained part of folk memory and traces of that glory were visible in its role as a city of pilgrimages. For many centuries, the city lost its battle with the jungle tide. Not till the 1870s, nearly a thousand years later, did it begin to enjoy a new political status, but only as the administrative capital of a province, during the years of British colonial rule.[1]

Throughout its history, there were three factors conducive to instability in the Anuradhapura kingdom. These were: dynastic conflicts, succession disputes and pressures from south India. The first two, dynastic conflicts and succession disputes, were more prevalent in the first two phases of its history, while the third was more significant in the late Anuradhapura kingdom. There were incursions and interventions from south India in the first two phases as well, but these were relatively brief and not very threatening to existing institutions and structures or as destructive as the invasions of the late Anuradhapura period, in particular, the Cōḷa invasion of the tenth century.

DYNASTIC CONFLICTS

The dynasty of Devānampiya Tissa became extinct in the first century AD. We do not know how this happened. One significant feature of the subsequent political history of Sri Lanka was that the right to the throne appeared to lie with one of two powerful clans, the Lambakannas and the Moriyas. By the beginning of the first century AD, the Lambakannas were established in power, enjoying by far the most prestige of all the clans. Their claims to this position of primacy did not go unchallenged. The opposition came mainly from the Moriyas, who became in time their chief rivals for power. Their periodic struggles for the throne are a conspicuous feature of the history of this period. The Lambakannas were more successful than their rivals, as the following brief summary of the dynastic history of this period would show.

The first Lambakanna dynasty[2] (established by Vasabha, AD 67–111) retained its hold on the throne at Anuradhapura[3] till the death of Mahānāma in AD 428, when the dynasty itself became virtually extinct. In the confusion that followed his death, there was a south Indian invasion and Sinhalese rule—such as it was—came to be confined to Rohana. The Moriya Dhātusena led the struggle against the invader and for the restoration of Sinhalese power at Anuradhapura. His success brought the Moriyas to power but not to a pre-eminence such as that achieved by the Lambakannas in the past few centuries. Indeed Dhātusena (455–73) had hardly consolidated his position when he was murdered by his son Kassapa, who usurped the throne at Anuradhapura at the expense of Moggallāna I, Kassapa's brother, whom Dhātusena had been grooming as his legitimate successor.

Despite a political structure that was prone to instability, there was—as Chapters 3, 4 and 5 will show—enormous creativity in irrigation technology and extraordinary agricultural progress and the establishment and expansion of a Buddhist civilization along with the architecture and arts of such a vibrant civilization, in the early Anuradhapura kingdom. The kingdom's political institutions which had evolved over the centuries demonstrated great resilience during periods of crisis, but occasionally there were times when the structure as a whole was revealed to be rather brittle. Yet, productive effort in the economy, inventive genius in technology and inspiration in cultural activity seemed to be unaffected by these periods of instability.

Indeed the history of the early Anuradhapura period reveals a political structure at odds with itself, confronting the challenges of dynastic rivalries, succession disputes and the accompanying political crises, generally coping adequately with them, but occasionally almost overwhelmed by them. Often these political crises were themselves a reflection of a crucial flaw in the form of administrative and political structures unable to keep pace with the productive energies of an expanding economy, or, for that matter, with the political ambitions of rulers who sought control over the whole island without acquiring the requisite administrative machinery, which alone could have converted this aspiration into a hard political reality.

In the middle Anuradhapura phase, beginning with Upatissa II (517–18) and his successors, there was a return of the Lambakannas to power, but the re-establishment of Moriya control came just over fifty years after the death of Upatissa II, through Mahānāga (569–71). His immediate successors, Aggabodhi I (571–604) and Aggabodhi II (604–14), managed to maintain the Moriya grip on the Anuradhapura throne but not to consolidate their position, for the Lambakannas were, in fact, always a formidable threat, and under Moggallāna III (614–19), they overthrew Sanghatissa II (614), who proved to be the last of the Moriya kings.

It took nearly six decades of frequent episodes of turmoil for the Lambakannas to re-establish their supremacy. Once they had done so they maintained their pre-eminence once again over a very great length of time. Indeed, the second Lambakanna dynasty established by Mānavamma (684–718) gave the island two centuries of stable government. In the last phase of the dynasty's spell of power, the severest tests that confronted it came from south Indian invaders and not local rivals, a theme to which we shall return later in this chapter.

Once the Moriya challenge to the Lambakannas petered out by the end of the seventh century AD, competition between them was replaced by a Lambakanna monopoly of power. But the comparative political stability of the period of the second Lambakanna dynasty owed less to the disappearance of the

Moriya threat to their power than to other factors. Of these latter, the most important had to do with the law of succession to the throne.

In the early Anuradhapura kingdom, there appears to have been no clearly recognized law of succession to the throne. What mattered were the wishes of the ruling monarch[4] who generally chose a favoured member of the royal family, a son or a brother, whose title, however, was seldom unchallenged by others who felt they had as good a claim to the throne. With the establishment of the second Lambakanna dynasty, succession to the throne came to depend more on custom and well-established practice and kings followed each other in the succession from brother to brother and on to the next generation. In combination with a stable and accepted mode of succession to the throne, the sanctity that now surrounded the king—due to the spread of Mahayanist Buddhist ideas, in particular the belief that kingship was akin to divinity—made it much more difficult for pretenders to the throne and rivals in general to command a politically viable following even when weak kings ascended the throne. Disputed successions had contributed as much to political instability in the Anuradhapura kingdom before the accession of the second Lambakanna dynasty as dynastic conflicts.

The most celebrated of these succession disputes was that between Moggallāna and Kassapa, an important feature of which is linked with one other contributory cause of political instability at this time. The reliance of Moggallāna I (491–508) on an army of Indian (largely south Indian) mercenaries[5] to dislodge Kassapa proved in the long run to be more significant than his victory over the latter. These auxiliaries became, in time, a vitally important, if not the most powerful, element in the armies of Sinhalese rulers some of whom, notably Aggabodhi III (628, 629–39) and Dāthopatissa I (c. 639–50), showed them great indulgence and favour because they owed their position largely to their support. From serving the strictly limited purposes for which they had been hired—fighting on behalf of aspirants to the throne, or sustaining a ruler in power—they became, in time, kingmakers, a volatile and unpredictable group and a turbulent element who were in themselves, quite often, the greatest threat to the stability of the realm. They were also the nucleus of a powerful Tamil influence in the court.[6]

When Mānavamma seized the throne, he curbed the powers of the Tamil army commanders and courtiers, removed many of them from the high positions they held and in general established a stricter supervision over their activities. He achieved considerable success in his avowed policy of reducing Tamil influence in the affairs of state. His successors sought to continue this policy, but were less effective in this for they could never do without these mercenaries.[7] Indeed, a reduction of Tamil pressures on the Sri Lankan polity was impossible in view of the political situation in south India.

These south Indian pressures constituted a very powerful element of instability in the politics of the late Anuradhapura kingdom. The flourishing but vulnerable irrigation civilization of Sri Lanka's northern plain was a tempting target for south Indian powers across the narrow strip of sea which separated it from them, and while ever so often it came under the influence, if not control, of one or other of them, it could still retain its independence by setting one of them against the other or others, which in effect meant that Sri Lanka was generally wary of the predominant power in south India. Sri Lanka was drawn into the political struggles of south India as a necessary result of her geographical position, but her entanglement in them was not always intrinsically defensive in intent.

With the rise of three Hindu powers in south India—the Pāṇḍyas, Pallavas and Cōḷas—in the fifth and sixth centuries AD, ethnic and religious antagonisms bedevilled relations between them and the Sinhalese kingdom. These Dravidian states were robustly Hindu in religious sentiment and quite intent on eliminating Buddhist influence in south India. In time, south Indian Buddhism was all but wiped out by this aggressive Hinduism and, as a result, one supremely important religio-cultural link between south India and the Sinhalese kingdom was severed. Besides, the antipathy of these south Indian states to Sri Lanka normally whetted by the prospect of loot, was now for the first time sharpened by religious zeal and ethnic pride. One important consequence flowed from this: the Tamils in Sri Lanka—the mercenaries being the most important element among them over the years—became increasingly conscious of their ethnicity, which they sought to assert in terms of culture and religion, Dravidian or Tamil and Hindu. Thus the Tamils on the island, in particular the mercenaries, became sources of support for south Indian invaders, an unpredictable fifth column at the outset but a much more predictable one in time.

PARTICULARISM

Rulers of the Anuradhapura kingdom sought to establish control over the whole island, but generally this was more an aspiration than a reality.[8] The more powerful of them succeeded in unifying the country, but such periods of effective control over the island were rare and no institutional structure capable of surviving when royal power at Anuradhapura was weakened—especially at times of disputed succession—appears to have been devised.

With the passage of time, the number of administrative units within the island increased. By the first quarter of the sixth century, there were already three of these. Silākāla (518–31) handed over the administration of two of the provinces of the kingdom to his elder sons, retaining the rest for himself. To his eldest son, Moggallāna, he granted the division to the east of the capital; Dakkhinadesa, which was the southern part of the Anuradhapura kingdom, went to his second son, together with the control of the sea coast. Within two decades of his death there were four units:[9] Uttaradesa (northern division), Paccimadesa (western division), Pachinadesa (eastern division) and Dakkhinadesa (southern division). Of these, Dakkhinadesa was the largest in size. From the time of Aggabodhi I, its administration was entrusted to the mahapā or mahayā, the heir to the throne, and so came to be called the Māpā (Mahapā) or Māyā (Mahayā)-rata as opposed to the Rājarata (the king's division). It soon became so important that along with Rājarata and Rohana it was one of the three main administrative divisions of the island.

In seeking to establish their control over the whole island, the Anuradhapura kings confronted formidable difficulties, not the least of which was the particularism (one might even say a well-developed sense of local patriotism) which made rulers of outlying regions, in particular Rohana, jealously protective of their local interests and identity. Needless to say, the dynastic and succession disputes and, in time, repeated invasions from south India were hardly conducive to the strengthening of any administrative machinery for the control of these provinces from Anuradhapura. Dakkhinadesa itself could on occasion pose difficulties, but never on the same scale or regularity as Rohana, and was easier to bring to heel when resourceful and ambitious kings ruled at Anuradhapura.

Particularism then was a perennial issue and Rohana—the home of lost and potentially viable causes, the refuge of Sinhalese kings overthrown by foreign invaders and a bridgehead for a reconquest or the liberation of Anuradhapura from foreign rule—was the crux of the problem. During most of the period covered in this chapter, its rulers behaved as though they were independent potentates and Rohana's status varied from time to time from that of a mere administrative division of the Anuradhapura kingdom to a principality and a semi-independent or independent kingdom. To take one example at random: throughout most of the reign of Silākāla (518–31) and his successors, Mahānāga had effective control over Rohana first as a rebel, then as an accredited governor of the province and finally as an independent ruler. When he in turn became king at Anuradhapura (569–71), he united the whole island under his rule. It is likely that with the two Aggabodhis who succeeded him to the throne, the authority of the rulers of Anuradhapura prevailed in Rohana, but during the troubled century that followed, Rohana's local rulers appear to have reasserted their independence.

In the early centuries of the Anuradhapura kingdom, there is little or no evidence of a regular army, except for a small body of soldiers who guarded the palace and the capital city. Though a regular force was established with the passage of time with foreign—largely south Indian—mercenaries as a

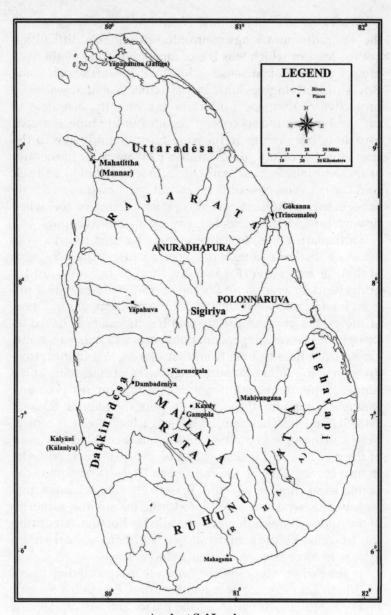

Ancient Sri Lanka

component element in it, this was still far from being a standing army which could have been used on a regular basis to impose the will of the 'central' authority over recalcitrant provinces far from the capital. Nor was the administrative structure adequate for the purpose of serving as an efficient mechanism of control over such provinces from Anuradhapura. The inscriptions of this period reveal the existence of a sabha or council of ministers. It is impossible to determine whether this developed from the earlier institution known as the *āmati pajaha* or whether it was something completely new. Nor have we any clear picture of the functions of this council. In the early centuries of the Anuradhapura kingdom, the main officials were few: the *sēnāpati* (the chief of the 'army'), the *bhaṇḍāgārika* (treasurer), a few *adhyaksas*, *mahāmātra*s and a *purohita*. By the tenth century, there was a regular hierarchy of officials with a wide range of titles. Evidently a complex administrative structure had emerged; its writ ran in many parts of the country and affected many aspects of the lives of the people (especially in the vital field of irrigation). But it is impossible to reach any firm conclusions about the precise functions of the bulk of these officials, or to assess the nature of their impact on the outlying provinces. Clearly, the relationship between Anuradhapura and Rohana was governed not so much by formal administrative structures or institutional links as by the more volatile and unpredictable give-and-take of personal ties.

One important theme emerges from this: the comparative weakness of the central authority vis-à-vis the outlying provinces under the Anuradhapura kings generally. Thus the Sinhalese kingdom was not a highly centralized structure but one in which a balance of political forces incorporated a tolerance of particularism. This held true for the whole history of the Anuradhapura kingdom.

There is also the position of the *paramukha*s (from the Sanskrit *pramukha*, chief or notable) or the *kulīṇa* gentry closely connected with the clan structure of Sinhalese society. They were clearly people of standing and importance, a social elite of distinctly higher status than the village headmen (*gamika*) and others. Kinship ties linked some of them to the ruling elite—

high officials in the court and elsewhere—and in some instances to the royal family itself. It is very likely that they had special privileges in terms of land and their claims to 'proprietary' rights over land and irrigation works go back to the earliest inscriptions. In the political struggles of the Anuradhapura kingdom—and in the succeeding centuries when the capital was at Polonnaruva—they were a factor to be reckoned with by the rulers of the day and foreign invaders as well. More to the point, they were among the prime beneficiaries of the dynastic conflicts of these centuries and the struggles for power within the royal family; their bargaining power and influence were thus at a premium and this too militated against the concentration of authority in the hands of the ruler.

The consequences that flowed from this weakening of royal authority and from the tolerance of particularism were not always or necessarily harmful: they gave great scope to local initiatives at the district and village level[10] and these appear to have been strong and resilient enough to cope with turmoil during power struggles at the centre, or during foreign invasions. During much of the history of the Anuradhapura kingdom they could have been, and indeed they often were, more enduring than the institutions controlled, if one could use that term, from the centre. This probably explains how a political structure, at the centre, prone to instability in periods of crisis could have sustained the magnificent irrigation system that was one of the glories of the Anuradhapura kingdom. No doubt the maintenance of the system in good repair, quite apart from its expansion, required a sophisticated machinery under some form of central control. But it was the permanent institutions rooted among the people at the village level that ensured the survival of the system during periods of turmoil, which were such a regular feature of the Anuradhapura kingdom.

PRESSURE FROM SOUTHERN INDIA

The accession of Mānavamma and the establishment of dynastic stability in the period of the Lambakanna monopoly of power in the seventh to the tenth centuries saw a consolidation of the political structure whose main features we have analysed here. The succession disputes which disturbed the politics of the early Anuradhapura kingdom so frequently had largely disappeared. There was an enlargement and greater sophistication in the administrative machinery; royal authority was augmented and particularism was at a discount when powerful rulers controlled Anuradhapura, as they did with greater frequency in the late Anuradhapura period. The strengthened monarchy and institutional structure confronted other and more powerful challenges in the form of pressure from south India. This had been one of the factors of instability of the early Anuradhapura kingdom, but it assumed much more serious proportions and eventually overwhelmed Sri Lanka in the late tenth and eleventh centuries. It is to this theme that we now turn our attention.

We have seen how Mānavamma sought to impose restraints on Tamil mercenaries and courtiers. But he himself had seized power with Pallava assistance. While his accession to the Anuradhapura throne marked the beginning of a long period of dynastic stability, the association, if not alliance, with the Pallavas was to bring political perils in its train. When the Pāṇḍyans were building their first empire and were in confrontation with the Pallavas for supremacy in south India, Sri Lanka was inevitably opposed to the Pāṇḍyans. By the middle of the ninth century, the Pāṇḍyans had prevailed over their rivals and set about settling scores with the latter's allies, including the Sinhalese kingdom. There was a devastating Pāṇḍyan invasion of the island during the reign of Sena I (833–53) under Sri Māra Sri Vallabha (815–60), during which they found ready support from the island's small Tamil population. They sacked Anuradhapura and imposed a substantial indemnity as the price of their withdrawal.

Shortly after the Pāṇḍyan withdrawal, the Sinhalese were afforded an opportunity for intervention in Pāṇḍyan affairs. A Sinhalese army invaded the Pāṇḍya country in support of a rebel Pāṇḍya prince and during their successful campaign they ravaged the city of Madurai. Meanwhile, the Pallavas and their allies harassed the Pāṇḍyans on their northern frontier. The result was a distinct weakening of Pāṇḍya power but not to the advantage of the Pallavas, for this occurred at a time (the last quarter of the ninth century) when the Cōḷas[11] were emerging as a formidable threat to both the Pāṇḍyans and the Pallavas. The latter were the first to be absorbed by the Cōḷas, who then proceeded southward to Pāṇḍyan territory.

Disturbed by the prospect of a Cōḷa hegemony over south India, the Sinhalese, in a remarkable but totally understandable reversal of policy, threw their weight behind the Pāṇḍyans in a desperate attempt to sustain them as a buffer state between the expanding Cōḷa empire and Sri Lanka. A Sinhalese army was sent to south India in 915 in support of the Pāṇḍyan ruler Rājasimha II against the Cōḷas, but to little effect, for Parāntaka I (907–55) inflicted a crushing defeat on the Pāṇḍyans whose king now fled to Sri Lanka carrying with him the Pāṇḍyan regalia. The Cōḷas never subdued the Pāṇḍyan territories as completely as they had the Pallava kingdom. The Sinhalese now had to face the wrath of the victors, for whom the desire— and need—to capture the Pāṇḍyan regalia was an added impetus to a retaliatory invasion of Sri Lanka. There were other compelling political reasons as well: the Sinhalese kingdom was a threat to the security of the southern frontier of the Cōḷa empire, as a refuge for defeated Pāṇḍyan rulers and as a base for potential invasions of the mainland. In short, the consolidation of Cōḷa power in the Pāṇḍyan kingdom was incomplete so long as Sri Lanka remained independent. Apart from these, there was the prospect of loot,[12] of control over the pearl fisheries of the gulf of Mannar and the gems for which the island was famous, as well as its trade.

Up to the middle of the tenth century, the Cōḷa military expeditions to Sri Lanka were in the nature of brief but destructive incursions and once the immediate objectives of the missions had been achieved, the Cōḷa armies withdrew to the mainland. Under Rājarāja the Great (983–1014), however, the Cōḷas embarked on a more aggressive and ambitious programme of conquest which devastated the city of Anuradhapura and the Sinhalese kingdom and the Rājarata, the heartland of the defeated Sinhalese kingdom, became part of the Cōḷa empire. Mihindu V, who ascended the throne in 982, the last Sinhalese king to rule at Anuradhapura, was captured by the invading Cōḷas in 1017 and died in captivity in south India. The island had barely recovered from the devastation of the Pāṇḍyan invasion of the ninth century when it faced the more cataclysmic effects of the Cōḷa invasion and occupation. The conquest of the island was completed under Rājarāja's son Rājendra. Resistance to the Cōḷas began very early and southern parts of the island slipped out of Cōḷa control but the Rājarata continued to be ruled by the Cōḷas as a *mandalam* or province of the Cōḷa empire. The mandalam was subdivided into *valandūs* (which were mostly named after Cōḷa royalty), *nādus* and *ūrs*.

A more significant—and permanent—change introduced by the Cōḷas was the decision to shift the capital from Anuradhapura to Polonnaruva—a move determined, in this instance, by considerations of security.[13] The Mahaveli itself afforded some protection to this city. The main threat to the Cōḷas in the Rājarata came from Rohana, and Polonnaruva was well placed to guard against invasions from that quarter since it lay near the main ford across this river which an invading army from Rohana needed to force. There were other advantages as well. Proximity to the Mahaveli, the longest river in Sri Lanka, enhanced the economic value of Polonnaruva's location, an important consideration, given the development of commercial relations with south-east Asia and China in which the port of Gokanna (modern Trincomalee) on the east coast was an important centre. Indeed it has been argued that the transfer of the capital to Polonnaruva reflected 'the dynamics of Indian Ocean' trade.[14]

Within a few years of Rājendra's completion of the conquest of the island, Rohana became the centre of a protracted resistance movement against the Cōḷas. There was opposition to them in the Rājarata as well. Early attempts at dislodging the Cōḷas by organizing raids from Rohana had foundered badly, partly on account of divisions among aspirants to the Sinhalese throne, and the Cōḷas were able occasionally to recruit support for themselves from among local notables in Rohana. While the particularism for which Rohana was notorious was an obstacle in the early stages to a concerted bid to expel the Cōḷas from the island, that obstacle was eventually overcome. A successful resistance movement drove the Cōḷas out of Sri Lanka under the leadership of Vijayabāhu I (1055–1110).

The Anuradhapura Kingdom II
An Irrigation Civilization

INTRODUCTION

No people in any age or country had so great practice and experience in the construction of works for irrigation...

Tennent, *Ceylon* (1859)

> It is possible that in no other part of the world are there to be found within the same space, the remains of so many works for irrigation, which are at the same time, of such great antiquity and of such vast magnitude as in Ceylon...
>
> In, Egypt, Syria, Persia, and in India, there are remnants of far greater works, and in these countries, works of far greater antiquity, as well as magnitude, but probably no other country can exhibit works so numerous and at the same time so ancient and extensive, within the same limited area, as this Island...
>
> Bailey, *Report on Irrigation in Uva* (1859)

Thus did two awestruck British officials of the nineteenth century view the most distinctive achievement of the people of the Anuradhapura kingdom—their masterly organization and maintenance of an irrigation network spread over the dry zone, a network that was remarkably attuned to coping with the geological and geographical peculiarities of its location: 'Problems of intermittent streams, gross yearly variations, undulating relief, high evaporation some 8^0 from the Equator, poor groundwater resources, indifferent soils and marked seasonal concentration of rainfall with its risk of disastrous floods....'[1] The dry zone afforded excellent conditions for the cultivation of rice: the high constant temperatures and received solar radiation, as well as the comparatively gentle relief of the region in contrast to the more rugged terrain of the wet zone of the south-west quadrant. But as against this, the rainfall was largely restricted to the period between September and January, less reliable and less 'effective' than in the wet zone. The topography of the dry zone with its gently undulating plains, the succession of small shallow stream valleys and low interfluves made irrigation more difficult than in a single great river basin or on a really flat plain. Besides, 'the irrigation problem' is much more formidable in an area with alternate wet and dry periods and a vanishing water table than in one with perennial streams and wells and a more even rainfall pattern.

THE IRRIGATION NETWORK CONSTRUCTED

The earliest projects were no doubt directed more at conserving than at diverting water on any large scale. But by the first century AC, large-scale irrigation works were being built. The reign of Vasabha (67–111) is regarded as a period of prolific activity and he is credited with the construction of twelve reservoirs and canals.[2] Most of these that can be identified are located in the Anuradhapura area. The construction of tanks, canals and channels which this involved exhibited an amazing knowledge of trigonometry and the design of the tanks a thorough grasp of hydraulic principles.

In 1979, there was a demonstration of how skilled the ancient engineers had been. Canadian engineers, making an aerial survey searching for the most appropriate spot to build a dam for the Madura Oya Project in the Polonnaruva region in the eastern part of the dry zone, identified such a spot only to find after preliminary investigations at the ground level that it had been the very spot chosen by Sinhalese kings centuries earlier. When the forests were being cleared they found, not far below the surface, a well-preserved sluice and part of a dam. The Canadians moved to a site some short distance away, leaving the old site undisturbed for archaeologists to study.

The tanks had broad bases which could withstand heavy pressures and at suitable points in the embankment there were outlets for the discharge of water. A British engineer working in Sri Lanka in the late nineteenth century and early twentieth century pointed out that the Sinhalese were the 'first inventors of the valve pit' (bisokotuva)[3] counterpart of the sluice which regulates the flow of water from a modern reservoir or tank. He went on to claim that the engineers of the third century BC or earlier who invented it had done their work with a sophistication and mastery that enabled their successors of later centuries merely to copy the original device with only minor adaptations or changes, if any.[4] Sri Lanka owes more to the unknown inventors of this epoch-making device than to all but a handful of kings whose virtues are extolled in the Mahāvaṁsa and Cūlavaṁsa. Without the technological breakthrough which the bisokotuva signified, irrigation works on the scale required to sustain the civilization of ancient Sri Lanka—the construction of artificial lakes of outsize dimensions like the Minneriya Tank attributed to Mahāsena (AD 274–301) and the Kalāvāva built by Dhātusena (AD 455–73) where vast expanses of water were held back by massive dams—would have been all but impossible. During the early Anuradhapura period, the agricultural surpluses made available by the multitude of irrigation tanks scattered in rich profusion over much of Sri Lanka's dry zone, along with the profits from external trade, made possible, in substantial measure, the enormous investment which the architectural and sculptural splendours of Anuradhapura required. That same agricultural surplus and the profits of external trade provided the capital for investment in irrigation works, dams, tanks and canals. Indeed, the early Anuradhapura period was the most creative and dynamic era in the history of irrigation in ancient Sri Lanka.[5]

A variety of seemingly intractable technical and physical problems were confronted and overcome, and the skills acquired and experience gained in this period were a rich lode mined by future generations. In the first century AD, the main problem had been that the water resources of the Kalā and Malvatuoyas, dry-zone rivers which dwindled to a mere trickle of water for much of the year if they did not dry up altogether over long stretches, were unequal to the demand for an abundant and dependable supply of water set off by population growth in a vigorous civilization. This could only be ensured by the diversion of water from rivers like the Mahaveli and others closer to the wet zone south of Anuradhapura which carried a perennial supply of water. The most notable of the irrigation projects of this early period was the Älahära Canal which took the waters of the Ambanganga, a tributary of the Mahaveli to the Anuradhapura region. This canal, first mentioned in the Mahāvaṁsa's account of the reign of Vasabha,[6] stretched about 48 km from a weir across the Ambanganga. Its length was testimony to the maturity and competence of the irrigation engineers of ancient Sri Lanka. During the reign of Mahāsena, the Älahära Canal became the main source of water supply for the Minneriya Tank which he built, and which was by far the largest tank up to that time. Mahāsena is credited with the construction of sixteen tanks and canals, four of which are in the Anuradhapura area and one in the Puttalam district.[7]

Three notable trends in the development of irrigation facilities during Mahāsena's reign were: a resolute endeavour to harness the waters of the Mahaveli and the Ambanganga, the most important project being the massive Minneriya Tank; the improvement of facilities for water conservation in the north-western part of the island; and the attempt to develop the south-western part of the dry zone on the periphery of the wet zone. Together they accelerated agricultural development in the vicinity of Anuradhapura and opened up new areas for cultivation in the east and south-west. All the major irrigation projects initiated by him were achieved by a prodigious investment of labour resources on an unprecedented scale and they reflect, too, a notable advance in irrigation technology on the island.

The reign of Dhātusena (455–73) matched, if it did not surpass, the achievements of Mahāsena and Vasabha in the extension of the island's irrigation network. He is said to have added to the irrigation works in the Mahaveli region by building a dam across that river. But the main focus of attention in irrigation activity during his reign seems to have been the development of water resources in the western part of the dry zone. By far the most impressive achievement by this period is the construction of the Kalāvāva, which tapped the Kalā Oya and helped to supplement the supply of water to Anuradhapura and the area around the city.[8]

The Kalāvāva was an outstanding technological feat on its own. It had an embankment 5.2 km long and rose to a height of about 12.2 m, with a bund constructed of blocks of dressed granite mortised together to enable a very close fitting. Even more amasing was the 86.4 km Jayaganga linking it to the capital city to augment the waters, in its environs, of tanks such as the Tissa, the Nagara and the Mahādāragatta. Apart from irrigating an area of about 466 sq. km, the gradient in the first 27.4 km of its length was a mere 15.24 cm in 1.6 km (6 inches to a mile). R.L. Brohier, the historian of Sri Lanka's irrigation systems, points out:

> The Jayaganga, indeed an ingenious memorial of ancient irrigation which was undoubtedly designed to serve as a combined irrigation and water supply channel, was not entirely dependent on its feeder reservoir the Kalaweva for the water it carried. The length of bund between Kalaweva and Anuradhapura intercepted all the drainage from the high ground to the east which otherwise would have run to waste. Thus the Jayaganga adapted itself to a wide field of irrigation by feeding little village tanks in each subsidiary valley which lay below its bund. Not infrequently it fed a chain of village tanks[8] down these valleys—the tank lower down receiving the overflow from the tank higher up on each chain.[9]

There was also the Yodavāva in the Mannar district, attributed to Dhātusena, formed by building an embankment about 11.3 km long. Fed by a 27.4 km canal from the Malvatu Oya, the Yodavāva covered a vast area. It was a shallow reservoir and its efficiency in water storage must have been severely affected by the heat and aridity of the region, but the topography of the area made it impossible to construct a tank with a greater depth without resorting to techniques of lift irrigation. Carefully laid-out canals flowing at a low gradient distributed the water from the Yodavāva to a multitude of village tanks around it. Together with the Pānankulam, this tank was a vitally important asset in an area— Mannar—which records some of the lowest rainfall on the island.[10]

THE NETWORK EXPANDED

By the end of the fifth century, two major irrigation complexes had been developed, one based on the Mahaveli and its tributaries and the other on the Malvatu Oya and Kalā Oya. The skill with which these were elaborated further in subsequent centuries into a web that linked the Mahaveli and dry zone rivers, tributaries of the Mahaveli, and irrigation canals from coast to coast was demonstrated by Brohier in 1937.[11] The two cities of Anuradhapura and Polonnaruva, the vital centres of political power and cultural activity which contained the most impressive monuments of Sinhalese civilizations were the cores of this network. Anuradhapura was much the larger of the two, and necessarily so, for during the first ten centuries AD it was, with brief interludes, the capital of the island.

There was the third core of Sinhalese civilization apart from the Anuradhapura and Polonnaruva areas, located in the dry zone of the south-east in Rohana where the climate was more severe and the rainfall much less reliable. Rohana was settled by the ancient Sinhalese nearly as early as the Anuradhapura region itself and was just as dependent on irrigation as the latter, with the difference that instead of the large tanks which dominated the landscape of the Rājarata, it had a distinctive irrigation pattern, a multitude of small and medium-sized projects, most if not all of which were the product of local initiatives. Apart from a few small tanks in the reign of Dhātusena, and the building of a weir across the Valave River in the ninth century, there is hardly any recorded evidence of kings of the Rājarata devoting as much attention to the development of irrigation in the south-east of the island as they did to the main centres of civilization in the northern plain.

In the Rājarata, the Mahaveli complex provided the more dependable and abundant source of water, and while contributing substantially to the prosperity of the Anuradhapura region its prime function was to nurture the well-being of Polonnaruva and the outlying zone in its vicinity. The irrigable land area around Polonnaruva was further extended by Moggallāna II by the construction of the Padaviya Tank which utilized the waters of the Mā Oya.

As we have seen in the previous chapter, proximity to the Mahaveli, the longest river in Sri Lanka, increased the economic potential of this region. Mahāsena had built the famous Minneriya

Tank there and between the fourth and ninth centuries, a number of smaller tanks in the region helped sustain a considerable local population whose agriculture produced a substantial surplus for the state to extract. With the growth of commercial relations with China and south-east Asia, in which the port of Gokanna (modern Trincomalee) would have played a prominent part, the economic importance of the region was further enhanced. Thus the adoption of Polonnaruva as the capital of the Sinhalese kingdom by four kings of the period between the seventh and tenth centuries, and the final abandonment of Anuradhapura in its favour, were determined as much by considerations of economic benefit as by strategic and military factors.[12]

A thriving civilization dependent on irrigation for its sustenance has an insatiable demand for water and the search for a dependable and permanent supply of water is a never-ending one. Breakdowns caused either by some structural fault or by the depletion of water supply in periods of drought were inevitable, with the result that not every unit or link in this chain of interconnected tanks and channels was working at peak efficiency (or for that matter working at all) at any given phase of the island's history in these centuries. Quite apart from essential repairs and maintenance, renewal was vitally important, as too were extensions of the irrigation network. Major initiatives in irritation activity called for a tremendous burst of energy, and these were not very frequent. Most rulers were content with keeping the tanks and channels which formed the country's stock of irrigation works functioning at a reasonable level of efficiency.

By the end of the seventh century, there was a vast array of irrigation works spread over a substantial part of the dry zone of the country. The monumental scale of the large tanks is compelling evidence of a thriving economy and of a state structure which had the resources from an agricultural surplus and the profits from trade to invest in these projects as well as on religious and public buildings designed on a lavish scale.

It would be appropriate at this point to quote C.W. Nicholas's assessment of this achievement.

The Anuradhapura Kingdom II   39

This achievement, accomplished by the seventh century, is a very notable and distinguished one because many of these projects, if put in hand today [1960] would still be regarded as major undertakings. The chief engineers responsible for planning designing and construction were undoubtedly men of the highest technical ability as well as men of vision. We have no knowledge of what gaugings they made, what formulae they employed in their calculations and what instruments they used. All that information which must have been imparted orally, is irretrievably lost. We know, from surveys carried out in recent times for the restoration of ancient schemes, that the instruments they used were capable of the same accuracy as modern instruments. In some sections of the ancient canals the fall was only six inches to a mile, in most sections one foot to a mile.[13]

There were fewer new irrigation projects initiated in the eighth, ninth and tenth centuries than in the past. Many explanations have been made for this apparent lull, including the argument that it was all due to a sharp drop in the profits of external trade.[14] This contention is too facile. By the end of the seventh century, the system was already nearly a thousand years old and there would have been a multiplicity of factors at play for this lull, of which an apparent fall of revenue from external trade would have been just one. Explaining that the reasons for this decline in activity are not easily discernible, Nicholas goes on to add:

It may be that what had been already accomplished was, with occasional extensions, sufficient: perhaps these earlier works did not begin to be utilised to the full extent of their productivity till the ninth century. Then apparently, if we may so infer from the references to famine and scarcity in the inscriptions of Kassapa V and Mahinda IV...food crises could occur if the irrigation system failed to function to the full through natural causes or neglect, and the time for constructing great, new schemes was approaching: but these undertakings would have been delayed by the invasions, disturbances and conquest during the second half of the tenth century.[15]

By itself the irrigation network of ancient Sri Lanka was a tribute to the ingenuity of her engineers and craftsmen and the organizational skills of her rulers. Nowhere else in south Asia does one find such a multiplicity of irrigation works as in the dry zone of Sri Lanka. The scale of comparison is not with the Indian subcontinent, but with the major hydraulic civilizations of the ancient world, the fertile crescent of west Asia and China itself. Despite its diminutive size, Sri Lanka belongs to this super league in regard to irrigation technology and creative achievement in irrigation works, for nowhere else in 'the pre-modern world was there such a dense concentration of irrigation facilities at such a high technical level'.[16]

A HYDRAULIC CIVILIZATION

Ancient Sri Lanka was the example par excellence of a hydraulic civilization, but it does not figure at all in Wittfogel's massive work[17] on the theme. This was just as well, for Sri Lanka's hydraulic experience, dispassionately reviewed, would have provided a refutation of some of the vital component elements of his theoretical framework.[18]

No part of Sri Lanka's dry zone conformed to Wittfogel's model of 'full aridity', and while it could be argued that in the two core areas of Sinhalese civilization in the Rājarata— the Anuradhapura and Polonnaruva regions—transfer of water from a distant locality was an essential prerequisite for the development of agriculture, the other part of the Wittfogelian theorem that 'government-led hydraulic enterprise is identical with the creation of agricultural life' has less validity for Sri Lanka. Irrigation projects were among the most important public works undertaken by the state in ancient and medieval Sri Lanka,[19] but despite their crucial importance for economic development they were not 'identical with the creation of agricultural life' in any part of the dry zone. Certainly, the role of 'government-led hydraulic enterprise' in sustaining agricultural development in Rohana was comparatively minor, and even in substantial parts of the dry zone of the Rājarata outside the two focal points of civilization there, regional initiatives were just as important as state enterprise in sustaining the system. Indeed, in all parts of the dry zone, while major irrigation schemes were largely matters of state enterprise, such local initiatives—

communal, institutional (especially monastic) and even individual—were responsible for the construction of a multitude of smaller reservoirs and village tanks which conserved water from the seasonal rains for agricultural development in their locality and which existed concurrently with and often independent of the main irrigation complexes.[20]

Nor did the state retain ownership of all the major irrigation works constructed under its direction. Dhātusena ceded half the income of the Kalāvāva to his brother. The long Älahära Canal was granted to a monastery not long after its construction. Monasteries, indeed, often had the resources to maintain irrigation works in their charge or control in good repair. Immunity grants of the Anuradhapura period record the transfer to the monasteries of the control of sections of the population together with the right to exact taxes and *corvée* labour from them; apart from these fiscal rights, administrative and judicial powers traditionally enjoyed by the king were also delegated to them by such grants. Similar immunities came to be enjoyed by the kulīna gentry who claimed proprietary rights over some irrigation works and land.

Lists of officials which occur in inscriptions of the ninth and tenth centuries, when the irrigation network of Sri Lanka was most extensive and highly developed, have been cited as evidence of the existence of a hydraulic bureaucracy. Quite clearly the services of men with a high degree of technical skill were necessary for the construction of large and complex irrigation works, for their maintenance in good repair and for the regulation of irrigation water to fields. But this is not conclusive evidence of an irrigation bureaucracy on the Wittfogelian model, of a phalanx of technically competent officials who formed the key ingredient in an authoritarian political structure in which power was concentrated in the king and his bureaucracy. On the contrary, hydraulic society as it developed in Sri Lanka was not a centralized despotism, rigidly authoritarian and highly bureaucratic, but a structure and society in which power was shared between the monarch and other groups in society, including the gentry and monastic institutions.

The more important state-sponsored irrigation works boosted the island's agricultural economy by enabling extension of the area under cultivation and habitation and facilitating more intensive exploitation of agricultural resources without upsetting the balance between land and population. Instead of a single annual crop, large-scale irrigation works ensured the production of two or three crops a year. The resulting agricultural surplus was adequate to maintain a large section of the population not engaged in food production and to sustain a vibrant and dynamic civilization. It provides an effective demolition of yet another of the key features of Wittfogelian theory—*stasis* as a characteristic of hydraulic civilization.

We need to end this brief survey of the hydraulic civilization of ancient Sri Lanka on a more sombre note. Irrigation civilizations by their very nature are critically vulnerable to natural disaster and foreign invaders. For such a society is like a complex machine with an extraordinarily delicate mechanism. It could function with amazing efficiency but could break down just as easily if maintenance were neglected or as the result of some seemingly manageable damage to the mechanism. With increasing complexity, inertia and negligence could be as insidiously detrimental to its smooth functioning as the more palpable threats from natural disaster or foreign invasion.

As we shall see in later chapters of this volume, the irrigation system was repaired, indeed reconstructed, and expanded by the Polonnaruva kings once Anuradhapura was abandoned after the Cōḷa invasions. Thereafter it lay damaged and neglected, and under a crushing cover of forests and jungles for six centuries, when some repairs were initiated under British rule in the 1860s and thereafter. The reconstruction was sustained with greater commitment and enthusiasm in the 1930s and 1940s. The first new major irrigation work since the days of the Polonnaruva kings came in the 1950s, in the early years of independence. Thirty years later came the dams and canals of the Mahaveli Scheme, whose magnitude and spatial reach matched, if not surpassed, those of the Sinhalese rulers who constructed similar works in the heyday of irrigation activity in the Anuradhapura kingdom. By this time Sri Lanka was no longer a hydraulic civilization, but the latter had left an enduring legacy for posterity, a legacy which had a powerful appeal for politicians and the people.

The Anuradhapura Kingdom III
The Political Economy

TRADE

Chapter 3 dealt in some detail with the central feature of Sri Lanka's economy, the elaborate network of irrigation reservoirs ('tanks') and canals, which sustained the island's agrarian system. The literati of this period of the island's history placed much higher value on irrigation works than on trade, as we can see when we read the chronicles, the *Mahāvaṁsa* and the *Cūlavaṁsa*. There is very little mention of trade in them, either external trade or internal trade, although external trade was of considerable importance for Sri Lanka.

There have been many more publications on Sri Lanka's external trade in recent times by archaeologists[1] and historians[2] than in the past.[3] Through these publications we have a somewhat clearer picture than we had two or three decades ago about the role of external trade in the island's economy. Nevertheless, it is still difficult to reach any firm conclusion on two issues, namely, the extent to which the expansion of the irrigation system was dependent on revenues from external trade or indeed how much of the revenues from that source went into the construction of the architectural and sculptural features of Anuradhapura, considering that some of the religious edifices in and around the city were truly colossal, matching the pyramids of Egypt in scale.

Was the agricultural surplus provided by the irrigation system and the fields it supported adequate for regular investment in the expansion of the system itself and for the sculptural and architectural features it constructed? Or were these dependent too on the revenues extracted by the rulers

from external and internal trade? Recent research, which we
have relied on for this section of the present chapter, does not
provide adequate data for a reasonably accurate answer to
these and other questions.

Since Asia was such a large part of the geography of those
times, the regional ramifications in the scale of operations in
international trade amounted to a transcontinental enterprise
rather than a regional one, as they would be today, ranging as
it did from the Arabian peninsula at one end to China on the
other, and from India to what is now known as Central Asia.[4]
We know a great deal more today about the major players on
this expansive trade arena; and we know much more on the
growth of Sri Lanka's ports, especially Mahātittha, the principal
port of the Anuradhapura kingdom, thanks as much to
archaeologists as to traditional literature. Among the other
ports was Gokanna (modern Trincomalee) on the east coast
about which we know less than we know about Mahātittha.
Recent and current archaeological work provides exciting
glimpses of trade at the ports of the southern coast, especially
those of the present Hambantota region.[5]

Sri Lanka's location in close proximity to the Indian
subcontinent and athwart the trade routes of the Indian Ocean
was its principal point of advantage and one which ensured that
the island was an important link in the maritime networks of the
Indian Ocean from very early times. Writers such as Ptolemy viewed
Sri Lanka as a country of great importance in regard to trade
with the East. It is evident from his work that western sailors
had circumnavigated the island as early as the second century AD.

A recent scholar has pointed out:

Sri Lanka's outstanding significance for external trade has been
recognised through the ages, and has been attributed to its central
position in relation to the countries of the East and West. Cosmas
Indicopleustes, who realised this fact as early as the sixth century
AD, called the island the 'mediatrix' between the countries of
eastern and western Asia. His observations, however, are only
the climax of a long series of notices of the island by Greek
and Roman authors, most of whom show some awareness of
the commercial significance of Sri Lanka's natural resources.[6]

D. P. M. Weerakkody, whose views we have quoted here is only one of these scholars. There is also Osmund Bopearachchi who asserts that 'In the fifth century Sri Lanka became the main centre of trade in the Indian Ocean,'[7] and

> ...Sri Lanka occupies a central position, in the Indian Ocean between East and West, in the middle of sea routes that link the shores of the Persian Gulf, Red Sea and Southwest Asia with Southeast Asia and the Far East. This island is furthermore gifted with numerous bays, natural harbours, estuaries and navigable rivers to facilitate both sea borne and inland trade.[8]

From the earliest times, merchants were attracted to the island by the prospect of trade drawn by reports of potential profits. Very likely the earliest settlements on the north-west coast were trade settlements, with pearls (from the pearl banks close by), gems from the south-west interior and ivory and other articles forming items in their trade. Throughout the period reviewed here, these commodities, essentially luxury goods, formed vitally important components of Sri Lanka's external trade and were valuable sources of revenue to the island's rulers. Other commodities traded included spices and elephants. There are also occasional references to cotton.

The island's trade with south India was always of crucial importance; it formed part of the latter's flourishing commerce with the Roman empire.[9] In the early stages traders from the Mediterranean world were content to receive the island's products in south Indian ports and did not come to the island themselves. Thus the Indian connection was most crucial for the great port of Mahātittha or Māntota, separated from the subcontinent by only a narrow stretch of water and at the same time inevitably linked to east–west maritime trade.

The maritime networks that gave Mahātittha the strategic importance it acquired had a great deal to do with links with the east coast of south India. Eventually, these had wider implications for Sri Lankan commerce not only in the vicinity of south India but in the entire Bay of Bengal region and with south-east Asia. While the Indian connection gave northern ports like Mahātittha a decisive advantage over others, the merging of the east, west and south Asian trade at Mahātittha gave it pre-eminence over the other ports of north-west Sri Lanka.[10]

There was another important factor in the rise of Mahātittha—a direct response to the growth of western trade in the Indian Ocean. The growth of Roman maritime commerce in Asia and the discovery of the monsoon winds in the first century AD led to the rise of numerous trade centres along the western and south-western coast of India. Mahātittha appears to have provided a convenient link between the two Indian coasts. By the sixth century AD, Sri Lanka had become the most important centre for the east–west entrepôt trade, a trade which provided Sri Lankan rulers with substantial resources over and above the traditional agricultural surplus.

Just as critical were Mahātittha's links with Anuradhapura. No other Sri Lankan port had this advantage and the growth of the port city and the capital were inextricably linked. Anuradhapura itself as the capital city became increasingly important as a commercial centre. Apart from indigenous merchants there was, from very early times, a colony of *Yavanas* (Greeks) and by the fifth century AD a colony of Persian merchants too. Faxian refers to the imposing mansions of resident merchants and states that one of them probably had the office of 'guild lord'. There were also Tamil merchants in the capital. The only other towns of commercial importance were the ports of the north-west, in particular, Mahātittha. Trade in all these centres, it would appear, were mainly in luxury goods, foreign and local.

There are gaps in our sources on the island's trade with south India in the period from about the fifth century to the seventh century AD. After the seventh century evidence of trade with the west becomes negligible. This appears to be the result of the rise of a new trade emporium in east–west trade, Sri Vijaya in Sumatra, which in time overshadowed Mahātittha.

The seventh century not only marks the beginning of Sri Vijaya as a maritime power in south-east Asia, but also the ascendancy of the Pallavas on the east coast of India, who became important in the trade between India and south-east Asia. The Sri Lanka rulers themselves cultivated very close ties with the Pallavas.[11] With the emergence of Sri Vijaya and the Pallavas, regional trade in the Bay of Bengal rose in importance and was very rapid.

In addition, the rise of Islam in the seventh century and the expansion of the Arab empires beyond the Arabian homeland into the fertile crescent resulted in far-reaching changes in Asian commerce. Muslim traders began to play an important role in the Indian Ocean. By the ninth century, the Muslims were the dominant traders along the entire maritime route from the Red Sea and the Persian Gulf on to Canton in China. Moreover, direct trade with Canton made it possible for Muslim merchants to buy silk and other goods at their source, thus reducing the importance of Sri Lanka as an entrepôt and Sri Lankan traders as middlemen.

By the ninth century, Muslim traders had established themselves in the ports of Sri Lanka. They were to form the nucleus of the country's Muslim community of the present day.

As a parallel development with wide implications in the trade of the Indian Ocean, Chinese traders made their entry as early as the eighth century. The Indian Ocean had become a major trade channel between China and the Middle East when the Tang dynasty consolidated its power in China. Soon Chinese merchants were looking beyond the land and sea frontiers of China for opportunities in trade. With the use of monsoon winds capable of driving ships directly over the ocean between the Persian Gulf and China, the Indian Ocean trade was accomplished in dramatically shortened periods of time and consisted of single voyages from one end to the other of the Eurasian system.

Chinese interest in and links with Sri Lanka had been determined in the past by an interest in Buddhism. Now these links were superseded by concerns of trade. By the eighth century, Chinese porcelain and stoneware were important items of export. Once China had been unified under the Song dynasty, ceramics became a major export commodity and part of the trade with Sri Lanka.

A major change occurred in AD 878 when a Chinese rebel organized a massacre of genocidal proportions reportedly killing as many as 120,000 foreigners in Canton—Arabs, Christians, Jews and Persian Muslims. One of the predictable results was that Arab ships stopped going to Canton. Instead they turned to Indian and south-east Asian ports. This made the Bay of Bengal a more lucrative trading area than ever before but once again Sri Vijaya gained more from this than Sri Lanka.

The ninth century AD was a time of tension between Sri Lanka and the Pāṇḍyans and while this began to affect Mahātittha's position adversely, the more important factor in this latter process continued to be Sri Vijaya's commanding position in the trade of the Indian Ocean. There was a focus on the east coast of Sri Lanka and away from Mahātittha. In a period of 200 years, well before the Cōḷa conquest, four Sinhalese kings left Anuradhapura to rule from Polonnaruva: Aggabodhi IV (667–83), Aggabodhi VII (772–77), Udaya I (797–801) and Sena I (833–53).[12] This was well before the Cōḷa conquest. It was also a time when there was a visible growth of Mahayanist Buddhist centres along the east coast of the island with Mahayana Buddhism emerging as a factor which linked Sri Lanka with Bengal under the Palas[13] and with south-east Asia. The Cōḷas themselves entered into the rivalries in the Bengal trade and it was the entry of Cōḷas that led to the eventual eclipse of Mahātittha's position as a major commercial centre and of Anuradhapura as the capital.

Nevertheless, recent archaeological excavations at Mantai have revealed that the ancient port of Mahātittha continued to be an integral part of the trading network which linked Persian Gulf ports with India and Sri Lanka during the Sassanian period and the period of Arab ascendancy. Middle Eastern ceramics, which have been dated around the eighth and eleventh centuries AD, and corresponding Chinese ceramics have been found at Mahātittha.

Up to the eve of the Cōḷa invasions of the tenth century, internal trade, at least, had been largely in the hands of Sinhalese merchants who dominated the main market towns and were granted special charters by the kings. During the period of Cōḷa rule in the tenth and eleventh centuries, Indian merchant alliances displaced these Sinhalese merchants, especially along the principal trade routes of the Rājarata. But their ascendancy was of limited duration and did not survive the restoration of Sinhalese power.

Part of the story of external trade has to do with a variety of sea-going vessels, of the construction of vessels and with sailors and seafarers.[14] There are references in the traditional literature to Sri Lankan or, to be more precise, Sinhalese merchants and sailors. Sri Lankan vessels evolved over the centuries from frail craft such as rafts, to outrigger canoes and catamarans, suitable for the passage through the Palk Straits to southern India. When, in time, it became necessary to build boats capable of travel over the Indian Ocean, much more spacious ships were built, sailing crafts with an outrigger—the *yatra oruva*.[15] These ships were constructed for sailing to other parts of south Asia and on to what is called South-east Asia today.

As early as the fifth century AD, trade routes linked the ports of south Sri Lanka with those of south-east Asia and China. In the sixth century AD, Sri Lankan ships were important in the trade of the Indian Ocean. Later on, such vessels moved to the Chinese ports; indeed, Chinese ships did not reach the Persian Gulf at this stage and the largest ships in that trade came from Sri Lanka. In the time of the Tang dynasty, Sri Lankan ships were among the largest and most imposing in the maritime trade of Asia.

The tradition of expertise in shipbuilding and of complicated voyages across the Indian Ocean continued in the twelfth and thirteenth centuries under the Polonnaruva kings.

Trade, as it touched the mass of the people, was of a humbler kind, principally the exchange by barter, or by a limited use of currency, of the surplus grain at their disposal, of services and of manufactured goods. From the very early years of the Anuradhapura kingdom, there is evidence of the use of currency.

There were two types of coins which were legal tender: local issues and coins from outside the country, brought in by foreign traders and accepted as a means of exchange.[16] Indeed, the earliest epigraphical evidence on the circulation of the punch-marked *karshapana* from northern India was at the end of the

third century BC. Buddhist Jataka stories refer to these coins
as *kahāvanas*. Reliable data on the circulation of currency is
difficult to get, apart from statements in literary works of
kings making payments in thousands of *karshapanas* either in
donations to monasteries or for the construction of religious
monuments.

The entry of foreign coinage to Sri Lanka was the necessary
result and function of external trade. South Indian coins—
some from the Pāṇḍyan kingdom, for instance—came to the
island because merchants from that part of the Indian
subcontinent served as intermediaries between Sri Lankan
merchants and Roman traders. The appearance of late imperial
Roman coins seems to coincide with the rise of eastern trade in
the fourth and fifth centuries AD. These are fewer in number
than the hordes of such coins found in parts of India. On the
other hand, despite the popularity of trade with China, there
was an absence of Chinese coins prior to the tenth century,
virtually the end of the Anuradhapura kingdom.

There are occasional references in the *Mahāvaṁsa* to caravan
traffic to and from the central highlands in search of spices
and commodities such as ginger. These caravans consisted of
wagons and pack animals. Apart from trade in these items,
there must have been some limited local trade in cloth, salt
and a few luxury articles.

By the end of the fifth century, the economic activity of
these indigenous traders was sufficiently advanced to sustain
a system of commerce in grain, in particular seed grain, which
came to be deposited as capital on which interest was charged.
The grant of some of this grain for religious purposes—the
performance of the *āriyavaṁsa* festival—was recorded in
inscriptions which show that at the gates of Anuradhapura
and some of the other towns were important business centres,
the *niyamatanas*. There merchants received grain to be
deposited as capital (*gahe*) to be lent—not sold—to cultivators,
who had to return the capital with interest (*vedha*) added. The
interest, which was taken periodically by the depositor or the
person to whom the donation had been made, was usually
specified and varied with the type of grain. The people who

engaged in this activity, namely, those who stored and lent grain, were bankers of sort, evidence no doubt of the increasing sophistication in economic activity. Among the donors of caves to bhikkhus for residence and other purposes in the early inscription are guilds (*pugiyana*) and members (*jete* and *anujete*) of such guilds.

LAND TENURE AND TAXATION[17]

Trade, both external and internal, dealt with in the first part of this chapter, amounted to no more than foothills in a Sri Lankan economy in which the mountain ranges were its agrarian sector. In this second part of the present chapter we need to examine the importance of land as a determinant of social and economic relations. We do see some similarities to a feudal system, but other features make the applicability of the term 'feudal' rather troublesome. Thus while relations between some agricultural workers and landholders in Sri Lanka during these centuries could be judged 'feudal', there is as yet no evidence of a contractual relationship between lord and 'vassal', or of peasants working as serfs on the lord's estate. However, there was—in common with European feudalism—an obligation to service as a condition of holding land, whether from secular or religious 'landlords', but with one vital difference in that, here the nature of that obligation was, during much of this period, determined by caste as well.

No doubt the king had some claims over most of the land in his kingdom, but this did not amount to anything approaching 'fixed proprietary exclusiveness'. Implicit in the land grants of these centuries is the recognition of the 'rights' of individuals with regard to land.[18] In none of these grants is there mention of the king's prior consent being a condition to alienation of land by individuals while, on the contrary, some inscriptions provide evidence of kings actually buying 'property' for the purpose of subsequent donation.

The direct relationship between taxation and the protection afforded by the king to his people could not have been unknown in Sri Lanka in ancient times. This service would have entitled him to a portion of the produce of land in the kingdom in return and also quite naturally put him in a position to exercise some control over land. The limits of this control would depend on his own sense of what was right and, above all, on the customs and traditions of the kingdom.

Income-producing irrigation units, such as tanks and canals and the fields fed by them paid a tax—*bojakapathi*—probably in kind.[19] This the king sometimes granted to individuals as remuneration for services rendered to the state. Such grants were also made to the sangha. In a society in which irrigation was of such crucial significance, water was treated as a precious commodity which could be bought and sold as it passed through the tanks, the canals and fields, with the 'owners' of tanks (*vāpi-hamika*) imposing a charge for the water that passed through and in turn paying for the water that came in.[20] Because he had the largest of the tanks as his special preserve and a controlling interest in the whole irrigation system, the king was the prime beneficiary of this levy on water. Until the beginning of the seventh century AD, this payment was called *dakapathi*. It was paid to the king as well as collected by private 'owners' of small reservoirs and canals. In the ninth and tenth centuries, the payment for the share of water made to the king was called *diyadedum*, and it was termed *diyadada* in the twelfth and thirteenth centuries under the Polonnaruva kings.

In addition to the right to dakapathi,[21] the king claimed a share of the produce from all occupied and cultivated land. Unoccupied wastelands, both fallow and cultivable, were regarded as being in the king's 'possession' and over these forests and wastelands, cleared and cultivated, he could grant virtually complete 'proprietary' rights to any individual or institution, if he so wished. Wasteland and land newly developed by the state became royal property as there was no antecedent right of a private individual. The king's prerogative of laying claim to waste or jungle land must have served a number of purposes including the vitally important one of developing new areas, or extending those already settled; another was the rehabilitation of deserted settlements or those devastated by war—invasions and civil wars—and natural disasters such as droughts and floods. Abandoned and ownerless land, it would appear, belonged to the king; that is to say, where land was not cultivated or occupied, the king had prior rights to forests and timber, animal life for the chase, natural resources such as mines and gem pits and treasure troves in such lands. This did not necessarily mean, however, that the people had to 'buy' land from the king to open up new cultivation.

With the maturing of Sri Lanka's hydraulic civilization, 'private' property rights seem to have become more conspicuous. Inscriptions, mainly after the ninth century AD, contain references to a type of tenure known as *pamunu* or *paraveni* which, in the context of the land tenure system of that time, conveyed the meaning of heritable right in perpetuity. Religious and charitable institutions received pamunu property through royal and other benefactors. Individuals could acquire pamunu property in at least three ways, namely, royal grant, purchase and inheritance (inheritance of land was normally within a framework of kinship). The king also granted pamunu rights to individuals, usually as rewards. Pamunu tenures were subject to no service except in cases where the king stipulated at the time of the grant that a comparatively small payment was to be made to a religious or charitable institution. Here we come up against the crucially important question of how officials in the king's service were paid. It would seem that during much of the period covered by this chapter they were permitted, in return for their services, to retain part of the revenue they collected. This is not to suggest that revenue was farmed or that these officials became hereditary revenue collectors with overt political power, but only that the system of land tenure was used to eliminate to a large extent the payment of emoluments in cash, an important consideration since specie was in short supply. Because there was no binding linkage between the revenue allotted to them and their official duties as administrators of a unit of territory, the king's officials had few opportunities for an independent political role. The result was that while the corps of officials in the bureaucracy and in the court kept increasing in number, they did not, for much of the period of the Anuradhapura kings, develop into a baronial class, a feudal aristocracy, with very large areas of the country's agricultural land parcelled out among them.

By the ninth century, however, this picture begins to change. The inscriptions of this period refer to a form of tenure known as *divel*—property granted to officials or functionaries in the employment of the state or of monasteries. (A divel holding from a monastery would be no more than the grant of the revenue of the land allotted to a functionary.) Divel holdings were, in effect, property rights bestowed on an individual as subsistence in return for services rendered to the grantor and were terminable on the death of an employee or at the will of the granting authority. The recipient of a divel holding got the revenue which the king or a monastery had enjoyed earlier.

As for the king's officials, the size of their divel holdings varied with their status—the higher they were in the hierarchy, the larger the holding. The revenues enjoyed from such landholdings were significant enough in terms of their implications, not only for the economic strength bestowed on these officials but for other considerations as well, for over and above this revenue from land there could also quite often be the grant of the services of the people living on it, and the transfer of land revenue to the king's officers carried with it, unavoidably, some administrative power over these plots of land or villages. Besides, rights held on land in consideration for services to the king could be transferred by individuals who held them. (The transfer of land, however, did not entail transfer of services. These latter had to be continued by the original recipient of the grant.) Divel tenure was thus doubly significant; it marked a strengthening of rights to private property and the emergence of a trend towards something amounting to feudal rights, and of a class of landlord officials who became a powerful group of intermediaries between the cultivators and royal authority. Since the office by virtue of which divel was held could often in time become hereditary, the relationship between divel holders and their tenants, though inherently deferential on the part of the latter, could well develop into one of mutual respect and cordiality, and when the connection remained unbroken for several generations there could also be a strong sense of attachment and loyalty.

From divel tenure we now turn to compulsory services or, what came to be known in later centuries as, *rājakāriya*, service for the king. The inscriptions of the ninth century and after offer us a glimpse of this system of compulsory services. There is very little evidence, however, on how rājakāriya worked in the Anuradhapura kingdom. There was a close link between compulsory services and divel holdings and between the former and caste: the duties performed were dependent on an individual's caste. We are not certain whether every layman in the country (unless specially exempted) was bound to turn out for service in the militia in times of war, and in general to perform gratuitous services on public works such as the construction of roads, bridges and tanks, which was the key feature of the rājakāriya system in its maturity in the seventeenth and eighteenth centuries. There is more evidence, however, about exemptions from compulsory services. Temple lands were generally exempt from royal service and, as in later centuries, those landholdings not liable to service tenure were generally exempt from the demands of the rājakāriya system. Inscriptional evidence from the ninth century and after reveals that one of the immunities granted to some lands and villages was that royal officials could not exact various types of labour from people living in them.

The closest approximation in ancient times to absolute ownership of 'private property', that is, property not belonging to the state, were monastic holdings and estates with their proclivity for expansion unhampered by fragmentation. Monastic wealth accumulated gradually but steadily through donation and exchange as well as by purchase. Inscriptional evidence of the fourth and fifth centuries AD shows that monasteries could purchase property. Property held by religious establishments could not be alienated by sale and no villages or land belonging to them could be mortgaged or gifted away. By about the ninth century AD, monasteries had come to own, apart from movable possessions, a vast extent of property in estates, irrigation works and even salterns, some of them situated at considerable distances from the institution that owned them.

While monasteries held land under a variety of tenures, they had over certain plots of land—in particular grants made by kings out of their private landholdings and the donations of plots held by individuals under pamunu tenure—the most unrestricted rights of ownership possible within the tenurial system. In most cases, a grant to the sangha would mention the monastery for which the donation was intended. Some grants were more specific than this and indicated a particular institution within a monastery such as an image house or a *piriveṇa* as the beneficiary. Lands granted to individual monasteries belonged to them alone and not to the sangha as a body, a fact brought into focus by the not infrequent boundary disputes between some of the most renowned and powerful monasteries of ancient Sri Lanka.

Religious establishments used in their landholdings a form of service tenure similar to that of the king: a share of the produce from the plots of land permanently held by them was given to those who worked for and in the monasteries. Some of the temple lands, however, were cultivated by serfs or slaves belonging to the monasteries and there was no tenurial contract between such serfs and slaves and the monastery.

Most of the inscriptions which recorded immunities granted by the king to religious establishments show that the peasants cultivating such lands were not expected to provide services to the king. The grant of immunities from services due to the king implied that these obligations were to be performed for the monastery instead. Service in temples took three main forms—occasional, continuous and periodical. It seems likely that land was given for maintenance mainly in consideration for continuous and periodic services.

We need to consider, at this stage, the implications of these developments. A form of monastic landlordism evolved and the monasteries themselves developed into largely self-sufficient economic units, their lands were cultivated by tenant farmers while a multifarious assortment of craftsmen provided specialized services in return for land allocated to them. Some of the labour on monastic lands was performed by slaves but this was of limited scope and significance.[22] One of the most conspicuous immunities enjoyed by certain monastic properties was the *brahmadeya* status. The increase in income which inevitably followed from this was less significant than the fiscal and judicial authority over the tenants of such properties and the virtual exclusion of royal officials from them. As a result, such monasteries enjoyed 'the most complete property rights known in early medieval Sri Lanka...'; while there are instances of similar transfers of authority to the laity, these were rare.[23]

CASTE

Despite the significance of caste in relation to land tenure, and in particular service tenure, there has been very little research on the subject in relation to ancient Sri Lanka. As with other significant features of the island's social system, caste[24] too had an Indian origin, but developed its own peculiar characteristics on this island. One great difficulty that confronts us in our efforts to trace the evolution of the caste system in Sri Lanka is that terms such as *jāti*, *kula* and *gotra* used so frequently in the inscriptions and in the chronicles have a multiplicity of meanings. They could no doubt refer to caste groups, but they could also mean family, tribe or 'race'. There is no record of any caste system in Sri Lanka in the period before the conversion of Devānampiya Tissa and the rapid spread of Buddhism on the island. Nevertheless, it would seem that many if not all the elements that were to constitute the caste system in later times were there in some form. Buddhism in the early years of its expansion may well have retarded if not arrested the growth of caste in Sri Lanka, for some time at least, but still could not prevent it from eventually becoming the basis of social stratification in Sinhalese society.

While most castes had a service or occupation role, the distinctive feature of the Sinhalese caste structure in contrast to its Indian prototype was that there was no religious sanction from Buddhism for caste. Thus while caste endogamy and taboos against association with persons of some castes— regarded as 'low'—also existed, endogamy and taboos did not cover the whole range of social relations and, significantly, there was no category of 'untouchables' in Sinhalese society except the numerically insignificant *rodi*.

Brahmanism was the religion of the ruling elite groups before the conversion of Devānampiya Tissa to Buddhism changed the situation. Despite the rapidity with which the new religion spread on the island in the next few centuries, and despite its status as the official religion, the tolerant atmosphere of a Buddhist society ensured the survival of Hinduism with only a marginal loss of influence. Brahmans retained much of their traditional importance in society both on account of their learning and their near monopoly over domestic religious practices.

There is little or no evidence of a pure Kshatriya varna on the island in proto-historical and early historic times. In later centuries, the Sinhalese royal families declared themselves to be Kshatriyas and claimed descent from the so-called solar and lunar dynasties. It seems most unlikely that any of Sri Lanka's rulers in the early Anuradhapura period and before were scions of a recognized north Indian Kshatriya clan. But they were the de facto rulers on the island and the ruling families sought to maintain themselves as a distinct group. Royal princes and princesses were given the titles *aya* and *abi*. The general Vaisya varna, however, had its counterpart in Sri Lanka in the peasantry organized in families and in the specialized professions and trades. These latter, in the early centuries of the Anuradhapura civilization, were incipient 'occupational' groups. The only evidence we have of a Sudra varna in the early centuries of the Anuradhapura kingdom is the reference to *Candāla*s who lived just on the outskirts of Anuradhapura and did the scavenging work of that city. We do not know whether or not the Candālas were aboriginal people who had been degraded to Sudra status.

In Sri Lanka, as in India, the emphasis was on the vocational and service aspects of caste much more than ritualistic ones. Caste groups were brought into a service system in which an individual's role and function depended on birth status. The higher castes and those considered to be low in caste status had their mutual obligations, but the more onerous of these were quite obviously those of the latter towards their caste superiors. Tenurial obligations to the king and the state were also determined by caste status as for that matter were those of the various groups of functionaries, craftsmen and others in the service of monasteries. Thus, there was a connection between landholding and service obligations to both secular and religious authorities with the fundamental difference, however, that in Sri Lanka, caste status was an additional consideration or factor in the determination of these services. Caste services, however, were not always attached to land. They were tied to landholdings only in relation to certain services performed for the king or his officials and for religious and charitable institutions. In other cases, members of lower castes received some payment, mostly in kind but sometimes in cash, from members of the higher castes in return for their services or caste obligations.

Caste evolved into a more elaborate system under the Polonnaruva kingdom in the twelfth and thirteenth centuries.

The Anuradhapura Kingdom IV
A Buddhist Civilization

Buddhism was, to use modern parlance, the 'established' religion of the Anuradhapura kingdom. The conversion of Devānampiya Tissa was the momentous event from which this link between state and religion emerged and thereafter, over the centuries, it became formalized or institutionalized, with Buddhism and royal authority supporting each other and drawing strength from their association.[1]

Of the formal obligations of the ruler to the established religion, three were of special importance. First of all, there was a provision, by the state and its citizens, of the wherewithal for the maintenance of the sangha. Second, part of the state's economic resources were used for the construction of religious edifices and monuments, with the architectural and sculptural embellishments associated with these—a theme reviewed in detail in the second part of this chapter. And third, it was the king's duty to protect the established religion. This obligation taxed the ruler's resources of statesmanship to the full because of the need to steer a wary course between the defence of Buddhism and an entanglement in the doctrinal disputes of the day and in the prolonged struggle between the orthodox Theravada school and its persistent Mahayanist rivals. Closely linked with the obligation to defend the established religion was the onerous responsibility, which devolved on the ruler of the day, of overseeing if not initiating a purification of the sangha when increasing wealth and luxury inevitably led to corruption and indiscipline among bhikkhus. However, monarchical intervention to cleanse the sangha proved to be rarer in the period covered by this chapter than thereafter.

The third section of this chapter is a brief sketch of the salient features of language and literature in the Anuradhapura kingdom.

According to the vinaya rules which governed the lives of the sangha, its members were expected to live on the charity of the people. However, with the rapid increase in the number of bhikkhus, this became increasingly precarious and unrealistic as a source of sustenance. Thus, from the beginning, monasteries became dependent on the state for their maintenance and pious kings regarded it their sacred duty to divert part of the resources and revenues at their command for the maintenance of the sangha. As a result, monasteries came to own vast temporalities and in the course of time they became the biggest landholders in the kingdom. Some of the social and economic implications of the emergence of monastic landlordism have been discussed in the previous chapter. Suffice it to say, at this point, that the wealth they controlled afforded the sangha a more durable and indeed an enduring protection of their own interests and existence, quite apart from increasing their authority over the community at large.

We turn next to a review of the king's role as protector of the established religion. This theme can only be analysed in terms of and against the background of the sectarian squabbles within the sangha which erupted in ancient Sri Lanka. Inevitably, this discussion will take us beyond the narrow confines of the study of the ruler's role as protector of the established religion into the wider theme of the evolution of Buddhist doctrine and practices in the kingdom of Anuradhapura.

The teachings of the Theravada school were marked by a remarkable blend of clarity, simplicity and compassion. There was an emphasis on the uniqueness of the Buddha, the Enlightened One, who showed the way to salvation and a stress on individual effort as the means to this end: one reached salvation by one's own efforts. A bhikkhu, for instance, would attain nirvana by a single-minded dedication to the demands of his chosen vocation as a disciple of the Buddha, and the ideal set for him was the status of an *arahānt*, one who achieves nirvana and is not reborn thereafter.

Theravada doctrine had the defects of its virtues: generally clear, simple, compassionate and restrained, it was at the same time a trifle too abstract and lacking in emotion, passion and vehemence, if not enthusiasm. At the core of Mahayanist teaching was its conception of the bodhisattva, a compassionate figure who forgoes nirvana to work for the salvation of all beings. A bodhisattva seeks enlightenment to enlighten others, continues in the cycle of rebirths and uses his piety and spiritual attainments to guide all living things in their quest for salvation. Theravada sensibilities were offended by the Mahayanist contention that the status of a bodhisattva was a more altruistic ideal to strive for than the attainment of nirvana for oneself.

Through their cult of the bodhisattva, the Mahayanists provided Buddhism with a new mythology. More significantly the Buddha himself came to be regarded and worshipped as a god and was placed in a cosmic view in which a succession of Buddhas was distributed through infinite time and space. In Mahayanist teaching, the accumulation of merit through one's own endeavours and spiritual attainments, although essential in the quest for salvation, was not the only means to this end. There was also the emotional aspect of devotion and divine grace through worship of the heavenly saviour Buddhas and bodhisattvas. A central feature of Mahayanist religious practice was the worship of images of the Buddha and later of bodhisattvas.

The greatest name associated with these new developments in Buddhist thought was Nāgājuna and his principal disciple, Āryadeva. The latter, an original thinker himself, is believed to have been a scion of the Sinhalese royal family. And this brings us to the point that Mahayanist doctrine was soon preached in Sri Lanka. The Mahāvihara bhikkhus rose in opposition to these, but there was a sympathetic reception for Mahayanism by the Abhayagiri sect, which had been founded in the reign of Vattagāmani Abhaya (c. 103 BC). It had seceded from the Mahāvihara and had established itself as a rival and independent sect. There were frequent disputations between the Mahāvihara and the Abhayagiri sect on matters relating to monastic discipline and doctrinal interpretation, ranging from truly significant issues to the very trivial. These polemical wranglings and sectarian disputes became more frequent and

sharper in tone with the development of the cleavage between
Theravada orthodoxy and heretical versions of Buddhism.[2]
The third century AD saw a historic confrontation between
the orthodox Theravada school and the intrusive and dynamic
Mahayanist doctrines (the Mahayanists were called
Vaitulyavādins and Vitaṇdavādins in the *Mahāvaṁsa*), which
began, as is usual in such encounters, with the orthodox school
on the offensive, urging the ruler to fulfil his traditional
obligation to the 'establishment' of using the resources of the
state for the enforcement of religious conformity and, if need
be, to crush heterodoxy before it could stabilize itself. This is
what happened under Vohārika Tissa (209–31) when the
Mahāvihara bhikkhus convinced him that the new teachings
were incompatible with the true doctrines of Buddhism. These
repressive measures were only temporarily successful and the
Mahayanists were too resilient and resourceful to be kept
down forever. Within a generation, the struggle was renewed,
but this time the Mahāvihara woke up to the limits of its
influence on the ruler of the day, Gothābhaya (249–62), who
could not be persuaded that coercion on behalf of religious
orthodoxy was the answer to the problems stemming from
doctrinal dissonance in the sangha. On the contrary, he was a
little sympathetic to Mahayanism himself. Under Mahāsena, the
tables were turned on the Mahāvihara sect. Orthodoxy now
faced the ruler's wrath, which was manifested with a virulence
that far surpassed Vohārika Tissa's suppression of Mahayanism.
Indeed, some of the magnificent edifices of the Mahāvihara
complex were pulled down and the material from them used
for the extension of the Abhayagiri. Mahāsena founded the
Jetavana monastery and the institutions affiliated to it formed
a congregation generally partial to the Abhayagiri and its
doctrines. Thus the third of the sects into which the sangha
was divided in ancient Sri Lanka had emerged.[3]
    Orthodoxy was not so easily dislodged. It had links, strong
and intimate, with all sections of the population, but above all
with the nobility. These loyalties were strong enough to restrain
Mahāsena and to compel him to stop well short of a complete
destruction of the Mahāvihara sect. Under his successor, the

Mahāvihara sect recovered much of its former privileges. It had weathered the storm and re-emerged as the centre of orthodoxy, largely through the indefatigable energies, scholarship and piety of monks such as Buddhaghosa (fifth century AD), although a great deal of its original prestige and power was irretrievably lost in the struggle against Mahayanism.

The *Cūlavamsa* would have us believe that there was no substantial change in the position of the Mahāvihara in the later centuries of the Anuradhapura kingdom; that it remained the centre of the 'official' version of Buddhism; that kings continued as its patrons and, as defenders of the faith, suppressed heterodox sects whenever these appeared to offer a challenge to the Mahāvihara. But the fact is that the position of the Mahāvihara was much weaker and less influential than this.

Though the Mahāvihara had survived the worst effects of Mahāsena's purposeful hostility, the sectarian strife of the third century and early fourth century had demonstrated the limits of its powers. It neither received the exclusive loyalty of the rulers of the day and the people at large nor did it dominate religious life as it had done in the early centuries of the Anuradhapura kingdom. Every now and then new sects representing some fresh interpretation of the canon would emerge and the Abhayagiri and Jetavana viharas continued to be receptive to these heterodox sects and ideas.

Indeed, it would seem that for much of the Anuradhapura period, the Abhayagiri had a more numerous following than its more illustrious rival. The Abhayagiri complex covered a larger area than that of the Mahāvihara, while its edifices rivalled if they did not surpass those of the latter in grandeur and variety. Besides, the bhikkhus of the Abhayagiri enjoyed a reputation for spiritual attainment and learning both in Sri Lanka and abroad. The equating of heterodoxy with sinfulness, which the Mahāvihara and its adherents put forward in their criticisms of the Abhayagiri, was one which had no basis in fact or acceptance among the Buddhists of the island.

Though it was never able to displace Theravada Buddhism from its position of primacy, Mahayanism had a profound influence on Sri Lankan Buddhism. This it achieved by the response it evoked among the people, in the shift of emphasis from the ethical to the devotional aspect of religion. To the lay Buddhist, Mahayanist ritual and ceremonies had a compelling attraction and they became a vital part of worship. The anniversary of the birth of the Buddha became a festive occasion celebrated under state auspices. Relics of the Buddha and of the early disciples became the basis of a powerful cult of relic worship.[4] Of these the most significant and popular was the tooth relic[5] of the Buddha which was brought to Sri Lanka in the reign of Sirimeghavanna (AD 301–28) under Mahayanist auspices and housed in the Abhayagiri, since the Mahāvihara would have nothing to do with it, in the early stages at least.[6] But the lack of enthusiasm on the part of the Mahāvihara could not prevent the cult of the tooth relic from becoming an important annual Buddhist ceremony whose appeal became progressively more contagious to the point where, after some centuries, the possession of the tooth relic became essential to the exercise of sovereignty in Sri Lanka.

The Mahayanist influence[7] was also seen in the increasing popularity of images of the Buddha and of bodhisattvas in Buddhist worship. As a result, an image house became, in time, an essential feature of the complex of structures that formed a vihara. There was also—evidence once more of Mahayanism's persuasive appeal—a profound change in the Theravadin concept of the Buddha, one feature of which had significant political implications—the belief that a righteous king could attain Buddhahood in a future birth. This latter was an irresistible attraction for royal patrons of Buddhism. They could hardly demonstrate any enthusiasm, much less passion, for suppressing a religious doctrine the effect of which was to confer an element of divinity on kingship.

One other point needs emphasis. Mahayanism was not the only influence at work in softening the pristine starkness of Theravada Buddhism. There were others too: pre-Buddhistic cults, Hinduism and Tantric Buddhism, in chronological order.

The belief that one's life was affected by good and evil spirits, that is, disembodied souls or incorporeal beings, who needed to be propitiated by prayer and ritual, was one of the ritual elements of the pre-Buddhistic folk religion to survive in the face of the more rational outlook which Buddhism encouraged. Eventually, Buddhist rites were developed to cater to this pre-Buddhist survival and a ceremony called *pirit* was evolved. This consisted of the public chanting by bhikkhus of extracts from the Buddhist scriptures in times of general calamity such as drought, epidemic or famine, for the purpose of exorcizing evil spirits from a place or person. Sorcery and magical arts, generally pre-Buddhistic in origin, remained as strongly rooted among the people after their conversion to Buddhism as before and indeed continued to exercise their sway with virtually undiminished power. This accommodation between Buddhism and pre-Buddhistic cults and practices became a feature of Sinhalese religious beliefs lasting up to modern times.

Although the spread of Buddhism on the island was at the expense of Hinduism, the latter never became totally submerged, but survived and had an influence on Buddhism which became more marked with the passage of time. Vedic deities, pre-Buddhistic in origin in Sri Lanka, held their sway among the people, and kings who patronized the official religion, Buddhism, supported Hindu temples and observed Brahmanical practices as well. Hinduism was sustained also by small groups of Brahmans living among the people and at the court.

It was in the later centuries of the Anuradhapura kingdom that the Hindu influence on Buddhism became more pronounced as a necessary result of political and religious change in south India. The early years of the Christian era saw Buddhism strongly entrenched in south India. Nagarjunakonda (in Andhra) and Kanchipuram were famous Buddhist centres there. Close links were established between these south Indian Buddhist centres and Sri Lanka. There was a Sri Lanka vihara at Nagarjunakonda and the introduction and establishment of new heterodox Buddhist sects in Sri Lanka was primarily the work of visiting ecclesiastics from India or of Sri Lankan students of famous Indian theologians.

After the sixth century all that remained of south Indian Buddhism, inundated by the rising tide of an aggressive Hindu revivalism, were a few isolated pockets in Orissa, for example, maintaining a stubborn but nonetheless precarious existence. There was no recovery from that onslaught. The intrusive pressures of south Indian kingdoms on the politics of Sri Lanka carried with them also the religious impact of a more self-confident Hinduism. All this was especially powerful after the Cōḷa invasions and Cōḷa rule.

There was, for instance, the influence of Hindu rituals and modes of worship; faith in the magical effect of incantations, a great Vedic phenomenon and, more importantly, in bhakti (devotion as a means of salvation), which was an important part of Hinduism from about the seventh century AD. This strengthened the shift from the ethical to the devotional aspects of Buddhism initiated by Mahayanism. Hindu shrines came to be located close to viharas. The assimilation of Hindu practices in Buddhism, of which this was evidence, was reinforced by the gradual accommodation in Buddhist mythology of Hindu deities such as Upuluvan, Saman and Nātha. This latter occurred by the tenth century.

Tantric Buddhism had established itself and indeed had begun to flourish in India from about the eighth century, especially in the land of the Palas. As with every Indian religious movement of the time, its influence began to be felt almost immediately in Sri Lanka, so much so that when two well-known exponents of Tantrism, Vajrabodhi and Amogharajra, arrived on the island sometime in the eighth century, they were able to collect a large number of Tantric texts as well as learn some of the Tantric ritual practices prevalent there. In the ninth century, Tantrism had an even stronger impression on Sri Lanka. Two Tantric schools or sects were introduced, the Nīlapatadarśana and the Vajravāda, the latter in the reign of Sena I (833–53) by a bhikkhu from the Viramkara monastery at Anuradhapura. Sena I himself became an adherent of Tantrism. Tantric incantations or *dhāranis* in the Indian Devanagari script of the ninth century, inscribed on stones, clay tablets and copper plaques, as well as Tantric images, for example, those of the Goddess Tara, in bronze and copper, have been found in a number of places in the old Rājarata.

Thus, Sri Lanka's Theravada Buddhism accommodated a variety of religious influences—pre-Buddhistic cults and practices, Mahayanism, Tantric Buddhism and Hinduism—but was not overwhelmed by any or all of them.

One last theme needs to be reviewed in this section of the present chapter—Buddhism as a link between Sri Lanka and other parts of Buddhist Asia. There were, in the early stages, links with China, but in time the closest and most intimate ties were with the Buddhist kingdoms of south-east Asia, especially with lands where the prevalent form of Buddhism was Theravadin, namely, modern Myanmar (Burma), Thailand and Cambodia. Thus there were frequent exchanges of pilgrims and scriptural knowledge with Rāmaṇṇa in Myanmar. These links became much stronger after the tenth century under the Polonnaruva kings. As we shall see in a later chapter, resuscitation of the Sinhalese sangha after the destructive effects of the Cōḷa conquests owed a great deal to bhikkhus from upper Myanmar sent over for this purpose by its king at the request of Vijayabāhu I.

Relations with Cambodian Buddhism hinted at in the chronicles were very probably more tenuous than those with Myanmar Buddhism. Whether this was because Cambodian Buddhism, unlike its Rāmaṇṇa counterpart, was Mahayanist we are in no position to say. There is evidence too that Sinhalese nuns went to China in the fifth century AD and helped in the ordination of women there. In 411, the famous Chinese Buddhist traveller Faxian visited the island and stayed there for two years. But contacts with Chinese Buddhism, generally, were occasional and had few long-term effects.

ARCHITECTURE AND SCULPTURES[8]

The concept of Buddhism as state religion had as one of its essential features the obligation assumed by the ruler to divert some of the state's economic resources at his command for the construction of religious edifices, which became in time more magnificent in scale and visual impact. The earliest Buddhist shrines in Sri Lanka were based on Indian models, and in the wake of the Mauryan Buddhist mission to the island came the arts and crafts of India as well. But after an initial period of Indianization, which tended to imitate the parent culture, a distinctive Sri Lankan style in art and architecture was evolved, bearing the stamp of its Indian origin no doubt, but not identical with that of any particular region of India. The most constant feature of Buddhist Sri Lanka is the stupa or *cetiya* which came to the island from northern India.[9] These stupas generally enshrined relics of the Buddha and the more celebrated illuminati of early Buddhism, and were on that account objects of veneration. They dominated the city of Anuradhapura and the landscape of the Rājarata by their imposing size, an awe-inspiring testimony to the state's commitment to Buddhism and to the wealth at its command. The stupa, generally a solid hemispherical dome, gave a subdued but unmistakable expression to the quintessence of Buddhism—simplicity and serenity.

There were five important stupas at Anuradhapura. The first to be built was the small but elegant Thūpārāma. Dutthagāmanī built two, the Mirisaväti and the Ruvanvälisäya or the Mahāstupa. Two stupas subsequently surpassed the Mahāstupa in size, the Abhayagiri and the largest of them all, the Jetavana. The scale of comparison was with the largest similar monuments in other parts of the ancient world. At the time the Ruvanvälisäya was built it was probably the largest monument of its class anywhere in the world.[10] The Abhayagiri was enlarged by Gajabāhu I in the second century AD to a height of 85.3 m or more, while the Jetavana rose to over 121.9 m.[11] Both were taller than the third pyramid at Giza and were the wonders of their time, with the Jetavana probably being the largest stupa in the whole Buddhist world.

Thūpārāma around 1900

Abhayagiri around 1900

Jetavana as it is today

Smaller stupas were also built in the early Anuradhapura period at Mihintale, Dighavapi and Mahagama.

Those of the later Anuradhapura period such as the Indikatusaya at Mihintale and the stupa at the Vijayarāma at Anuradhapura were of modest proportions. Their domes were elongated in shape and the three basal terraces[12] were reduced to mouldings. These seem to have been inspired by the Mahayanists.

One feature of the colossal stupas merits special mention: the frontispieces which project from their bases. The exuberant architecture of these frontispieces—*vāhalkaḍas*, as they were called—with their ornamental sculptures are in agreeable contrast to the stark simplicity, if not monotony, of the lines of the stupas. The best examples of vāhalkaḍas are those of the Jetavana and Abhayagiri *dāgābas* at Anuradhapura and the Kantaka-cetiya at Mihintale. These sculptures bear evidence of the influence of the Amaravati school but with a restraint which makes up for a lack of vitality.

Among the architectural features of this period is the *vatadāgē*, a shrine enclosing a small stupa. The largest of the vatadāgēs is at the Thūpārāma at Anuradhapura, which had four circles of stone compassing the stupa, while each of those of Medirigiriya and Polonnaruva has three circles of pillars, those of Tiriyay and Mihintale having two each. Though the vatadāgēs all follow a common design, each has some distinctive feature of its own. The earliest extant vatadāgē to which a date can be assigned is that at Medirigiriya from the reign of Aggabodhi IV.

The Lovāmahāpāya or the Brazen Palace is unique among the ancient monuments of Anuradhapura. Designed to house the monks of the Mahāvihara, it was begun by Dutthagāmanī and is believed to have risen on completion to nine storeys in all. The bhikkhus were accommodated on the basis of rank, with some floors being reserved for the most senior and, presumably, the most venerable among them. All that remains of this early skyscraper are some 1,600 weather-beaten granite pillars which are a haphazard reconstruction of the twelfth century, with some of the pillars upside down and not even on the original site.

Literary works refer to the splendid mansions of kings and nobles, but few traces of these have survived since they were built mostly of wood. There are no traces at all of the habitations of the common people. Stone played only a limited role in Sinhalese architecture and was usually restricted to ornamental details and ancillary features. But these latter have survived, while the woodwork which was the basis of Sinhalese architecture, domestic and public, has not. An example of this are the stone-faced baths, various in shape and dimension but elegant in design, located within the precincts of the monasteries and royal parks. These have survived.

The abundance of timber suitable for building purposes and the lack of a type of stone which was at once durable and easy to work, appear to have hindered the development of stone architecture in Sri Lanka. When such a style did emerge, the inspiration came once more from an Indian source, from south India this time, where the earlier architecture of brick and wood was yielding place, so far as religious edifices were concerned, to one solely of stone. This had its influence on Sri Lankan architecture. The best example of stone architecture of this period is the *galgē* at Devundara, the southernmost point of the island. The shrine was built to house the image of Upuluvan, the ancient Varuna, the protector of the island. The simplicity and lack of ornamentation in this shrine was in striking contrast to the exuberance of the Dravidian style that was developing about the same time in south India.

Both in terms of its variety and artistic achievement, the sculpture of the Anuradhapura kingdom is as rich and impressive as its architecture. Some of the outstanding features of this sculptural heritage are reviewed here, beginning with the moonstones which many scholars regard as the finest product of the Sinhalese artist.

At a time when the Buddha image came to be regarded as a regular feature of a Buddhist shrine in Sri Lanka, the moonstone was central to the theme of worship.[13] Its decorative features were intended to communicate symbolic significance to the worshipper. The motif appears to have come to Sri Lanka from Andhra, but it had its fullest development in Sri Lanka. There are six moonstones at Anuradhapura, each one a masterpiece.

The earliest Buddha images found in the island go back to the first century AD. Thanks to the research and recent publications of Ulrich von Schroeder,[14] much more is known about Sri Lankan Buddha images, the Sri Lankan contribution to Buddhist art and the role of Sri Lanka in the diffusion of the Buddhist art system in south-east Asia than in the past.

Moonstone, Anuradhapura

There is, of course, the early influence of India, especially Andhra Pradesh, on the Buddha image on the island, as seen in a standing Buddha of Amaravati marble, which is about 1.8 m high and was probably imported from Amaravati (Guntur District, Andhra Pradesh). It was discovered almost intact at Mahā Illuppallama in Anuradhapura. Fragments of Buddha images in the Amaravati style and in the distinctive marble of that school have also been found. In time, Buddha images were carved and sculpted in Sri Lanka and developed peculiarly Sri Lankan characteristics, without, however, effacing all traces of the Indian prototype on which they were modelled. Buddha images in bronze of characteristically Sri Lankan workmanship have been found in western Java, Celebes, Vietnam and Thailand, thus demonstrating 'that Sri Lanka represents to a certain extent the missing link in the dissemination of Buddhism from India to Southeast Asia'.[15] Images of the Buddha in a sedentary position, from the early period of Sinhalese sculpture, are perhaps more exciting and impressive than the more stately statues of the Buddha in a standing posture— the very simplicity of the conception is singularly successful in its dignified and elegant evocation of the concept of samadhi.

Some of the standing Buddha images are of colossal proportions and are, consequently, awe-inspiring. The most remarkable and famous of these is the 12.9 m high Buddha image at Avukana. The group of colossal images carved on the face of a rock at Buduruvāgala near Vallavāya comprises a Buddha image in the centre, attended by a bodhisattva on either side. These figures at Vallavāya may be dated to the ninth and tenth centuries, to which period may also be attributed the stylistically interesting bodhisattva figure at Väligama on the south coast. Buddha images in the recumbent position, of similar proportions, are found at Älahära and Tantrimalai. At Māligāvala in the Buttala area a Buddha image nearly 12 m high has been fashioned completely in the round, probably brought from the quarry to the site, and set up in position in the shrine. This colossus which had fallen and lay on the ground, badly damaged, was repaired and restored to its pedestal in the early 1980s.

Images of similar size and bulk carved on rock faces have not been found in India. However, there were figures of larger dimensions carved on rock faces by Buddhists in what is now Afghanistan, of which the group at Bamiyan was the most spectacular till it was destroyed in March 2001 in a fit of Islamic fundamentalism by the Taliban rulers of that country.

The Indian influence is prominent in other features of the sculptural achievements of the Anuradhapura kingdom. The dvārapalas or guardians of the four directions—usually in the form of a nāga king in human form[16] attended by a grotesque pot-bellied dwarf, the guard-stones at Buddhist shrines—bear the distinct mark of the Amaravati school. The rock-cut Isurumuniya vihara below the bund of the Tissavāva at Anuradhapura is renowned for its sculptural embellishments, the most celebrated of which are two reliefs carved on rock outcrops: the lovers—a young warrior on a stone seat with a young woman on his lap—and a man seated in the pose called royal ease with the head of a horse behind him. The first of these, the lovers, has characteristics of the Gupta school of India of the fourth and fifth centuries, while the second is in the Pallava style of the seventh century.

Guard-stone, Anuradhapura

There is also that most astounding monument of them all, the rock fortress of Sigiri, a complex of buildings, part royal palace (with superbly designed ornamental gardens), part fortified town, which together constitute a magnificent and unique architectural tour de force. Sigiri is remembered today for the exquisite frescoes in a rock pocket some 12.2 m above the access pathway. Who these female figures are has always been a matter of debate among scholars.[17] H.C.P. Bell argued that they were the wives of King Kassapa, but a more recent theory—propounded by Paranavitana—is that Sigiri was devised less as a fortified town than as a symbolic representation of the palace of Kuvera, the god of riches, who dwelt on the summit of Mount Kailasa, and that the females are 'Lightning Princesses' attended by 'Cloud Damsels'.

Guard-stone, Anuradhapura

The paintings at Sigiri are the earliest surviving specimens of the pictorial art of Sri Lanka that can be dated; they are approximately the same age as those of Ajanta in India with which they bear comparison. Though no paintings of an earlier era than those at Sigiri have survived, the inscriptions and literature of the early Anuradhapura period show that painting as an art form had as long a history as sculpture and architecture and was as extensively practised. Its techniques and artistic theory are likely to have been based on Indian traditions modified to suit the local milieu. Thus the Sigiri paintings represent a sophisticated court art with centuries of experience behind it.

Fragments of paintings dated to the seventh or eighth centuries have been discovered in the lower relic chamber of the stupa to the east of the Kantaka-cetiya at Mihintale. They comprise figures in outline, of divine beings rising from clouds in four directions. Paintings have also been noticed in the eastern vāhalkaḍa of the Ruvanvälisäya, the eastern vāhalkaḍa of the Jetavana; at a site named Gonapola in the Digāmādulla district (Gal Oya) and in some caves at Sigiri. In addition to these, there were until very recently the remains of paintings, of the same vintage as the Sigiri frescoes, in the rock temple at Hindagala near Peradeniya.

LITERATURE

Buddhism was, without doubt, the greatest stimulus to literary activity among the ancient Sinhalese. The Theravada Buddhist canon was brought to the island by Mahinda and his companions and handed down orally. These scriptures were in Pali and it was in this language that they were committed to writing for the first time, at Aluvihara near Mātale in the first century BC. The preservation of the Theravada canon, which had been lost in India at a comparatively early date, is one of the landmark contributions of the Sinhalese to world literature.

Around these scriptures grew a considerable body of writing in Pali and old Sinhalese, consisting of exegetical works, religious texts and historical accounts. The Mahāvihara bhikkhus compiled an extensive exegetical literature in Pali. No doubt its rivals, the Abhayagiri and Jetavana, matched the achievement of the Mahāvihara in this field, but nothing of their work has survived. Not that very much of the body of material produced by the Mahāvihara has survived either but these works together formed the basis of the extensive canonical and commentarial literature in Pali,[18] and the chronicles in that language in the fifth century AD and later. The oldest Pali chronicle surviving today is the *Dīpavaṃsa*, which provides an account of the history of the island up to the time of Mahāsena, with scattered references to developments in India when these had some bearing on Sri Lanka. The Pali commentaries and canonical literature, a systematic compilation of the fifth century AD by Buddhaghosa,[19] Buddhadatta and Dhammapala, none of them a native of the island, demonstrate greater literary skill. Buddhaghosa, whose most famous work is the *Visuddhimagga*, is much the most celebrated of these scholars. His work was intended mainly for Buddhist missionary activity overseas in south-east Asia.

One notable feature of Sri Lanka's Pali literature needs special mention: the remarkable tradition of historical writing among the Sinhalese. The earliest historical work is the *Dīpavaṁsa*, a compilation, very probably, of the fourth century AD. The *Mahāvaṁsa*, also in Pali verse and covering the same period of history, is a much more sophisticated accomplishment and one which succeeding generations used, quoted with pride as the definitive work on the island's history, and felt compelled to update. Its continuation—the *Cūlavaṁsa*, attributed to Dhammakitti in the twelfth century—surveyed the island's history up to the reign of Parākramabāhu I (1153–86). A subsequent extension by another bhikkhu took the story to the fourteenth century and it was concluded by yet another in the late eighteenth century.

These chronicles, notwithstanding their flaws and gaps, provide a remarkably accurate chronological and political framework for the study of the island's history. But their scope is by no means limited to Sri Lanka, for events and personalities on the Indian subcontinent are often mentioned. These references have provided scholars with data to determine the chronologies of Indian kings and empires as well, the classic case being the identification, in the nineteenth century, through the *Mahāvaṁsa* of the great Indian emperor, Aśoka.

Sinhala as a distinct language and script developed rapidly under the joint stimuli of Pali and Buddhism. Indeed, it would be true to say that the art of writing came to Sri Lanka earlier than Buddhism. By the second century AD Sinhala was being used for literary purposes and thereafter a body of religious writing explaining the Pali canon was accumulated, primarily for the purpose of conveying its ideas to those not conversant with Pali. The Sinhala language was also enriched by translations from Pali. But Pali did not remain for long the only or even the dominant influence on Sinhala. Sanskrit, the language of the Mahayanist and Hindu scriptures, which was richer in idiom, vocabulary and vitality, left a strong impression on the Sinhala language in the later centuries of the Anuradhapura era. There was also a considerable Tamil influence on the vocabulary, idiom and grammatical structure of Sinhala.

Very little of the Sinhala work of this period has survived, and most of it seems stilted, pedantic and lacking in originality and vitality. This is not surprising since much of it was written for scholars and conformed to rigid literary conventions. The earliest known Sinhala work was the *Siyabaslakara*, a work on rhetoric, a Sinhala version of the well-known Sanskrit text on poetics, the *Kāvyādarśa*. Its author was probably Sena IV (954–56). There were also exegetical works and glossaries, but none of them had any literary pretensions. Some of the inscriptions of the first and second centuries BC appear in verse. Much more interesting, as examples of a lively and sensitive folk poetry, are the verses written on the gallery wall at Sigiri by visitors to the place in the eighth and ninth centuries, of which 700 stanzas have been deciphered.[20] These verses are a poignant reminder of how rich this vein of folk poetry must have been. Almost all of it is now irretrievably lost.

Nothing of the more formal poetry has survived. Moggallāna II, for example, apart from being a great builder of tanks, was a man of letters and is said to have composed a religious poem, of which, however, there is now no trace.

Just as Pali was the language of Sinhalese Buddhism, Sanskrit was the sacred language of the Brahmans (and Hinduism) and of Mahayanism. With the spread of Mahayanism in Sri Lanka, the more erudite bhikkhus turned to the study of Sanskrit since most of the Mahayanist scriptures were written in that language. Sanskrit studies became more popular in the island with the influence of the Pallavas who were great patrons of that language. Some of the more famous Sanskrit works were known on the island and Sanskrit theories of poetics and rhetoric were studied. But Sri Lanka's contribution to Sanskrit literature was both meagre and imitative. The one notable work was that of Kumāradāsa (a scion of the Sinhalese royal family but not a king), who composed the *Jānakīharaṇa* in the seventh century AD. Its theme was the Ramayana. There were also a few inscriptions in Sanskrit and some minor writings in that language.

All in all, therefore, the major contribution of the Sinhalese in the period of the Anuradhapura kings was in Pali. Creative writing in that language reached a level of competence far above that in either Sinhala or Sanskrit.

6

The Polonnaruva Kingdom
Indian Summer of Sinhalese Power

The two centuries surveyed in this chapter present every element of high drama. There was, first of all, the expulsion of the invading Cōḷas from the Rājarata after a long war of liberation and the restoration of a Sinhalese dynasty on the throne of Sri Lanka under Vijayabāhu I. This restoration had hardly been consolidated when there was a relapse into civil war and turmoil, but before anarchy had become all but irreversible, a return to order and authority took place under Parākramabāhu I. There was such a tremendous amount of constructive achievement in administration, economic rehabilitation, religion and culture in the reigns of Parākramabāhu I (1153–86) and Niśśaṅka Malla (1187–96) that it could easily have taken place over a much longer period of time and still deserve to be called splendid and awe-inspiring. But in retrospect, the activity appears to have been too frenetic, with an over-extension of the island's economic resources in the restoration of its irrigation network and the architectural splendours of the city of Polonnaruva, and of its political power in overseas adventures.

THE POLITICAL HISTORY OF THE POLONNARUVA KINGDOM[1]

In his campaign against the Cōḷas, the odds against Vijayabāhu had been a little short of overwhelming till he established a secure base in Rohana. The improvement in his strategic position vis-à-vis the Cōḷas in Sri Lanka coincided with a weakening of Cōḷa power in peninsular India during the reign of Vīrarājendra I (1063–69). Confronted by a vigorous Cālukya challenge from the Deccan, the Cōḷas were increasingly on the defensive on the mainland and this certainly affected their response to the attacks which Vijayabāhu now launched on their colony in the Rājarata. What had been for long a war of attrition now entered a new phase with an energetic two-pronged attack on the Cōḷa-occupied Rājarata, with Anuradhapura and Polonnaruva as the major targets. Anuradhapura was captured quickly but Polonnaruva, the Cōḷa capital, only fell after a prolonged siege of the now isolated Cōḷa forces there. But faced with total defeat, Vīrarājendra I was obliged to despatch a relief expedition from the mainland to recapture the Rājarata and if possible to carry the attack back into Rohana. Nevertheless, the respite which the Cōḷas in Sri Lanka gained by this was brief, for the will to struggle on in the face of determined opposition was eroded even further with the death of Vīrarājendra I. His successor Kulottunga I, a Cālukya prince, came to the throne after a period of acute crisis in the Cōḷa court, and his attitude to the Cōḷa adventure in Sri Lanka was totally different from that of his immediate predecessors Rājādhirāja, Rājendra II and Vīrarājendra—all sons of Rājendra I—for whom it had been a major interest and commitment. Unlike them, his personal prestige was not involved in the fate of the Cōḷa colony in Sri Lanka, and he could—and did—quite dispassionately end the attempt to recoup Cōḷa losses there. What mattered to him above all else was the security of Cōḷa power on the mainland. Thus by 1070, Vijayabāhu had triumphed and the restoration of Sinhalese power was complete.

Vijayabāhu's role in the prolonged resistance to Cōḷa rule, which culminated eventually in their expulsion from the island, would by itself have ensured his position as one of the greatest figures in the island's history, but his achievements in the more humdrum fields of administration and economic regeneration were no less substantial. Infusing fresh energy into the machinery of administration, he established firm control over the whole island and presided over both a rehabilitation of the island's irrigation network and the resuscitation of Buddhism. The established religion had suffered a severe setback during the rule of the Cōḷas who, naturally enough, had given precedence to Saivite Hinduism.

On his death, a disputed succession jeopardized the remarkable recovery from the ravages of Cōḷa rule which he had achieved in his reign of forty years. His immediate successors proved incapable of consolidating the political unity of the island, which had been one of his greatest achievements, and the country broke up once more into a congeries of warring petty kingdoms and principalities. There was an extended period of civil war from which, in time, the remarkable figure of Parākramabāhu I emerged.

Parākramabāhu I had the distinct advantage of being closely related to the royal dynasty at Polonnaruva and was therefore in a position to stake a claim to the throne. Once he captured power, his legal status as sovereign was accepted, unlike the claims of his two predecessors at Polonnaruva, Vikramabāhu II and Gajabāhu II. Three clear phases in Parākramabāhu's rise to power can be demarcated. The first of these was the establishment of control over Dakkhinadesa and his consecration as Mahādipāda, a title usually adopted by the heir to the Polonnaruva throne. In the second phase, the tripartite struggle between him as ruler of Dakkhinadesa and the rulers of Polonnaruva and Rohana, Parākramabāhu's aim was not so much to capture Polonnaruva as to secure his own recognition as heir to the Polonnaruva throne, and this he achieved. In the harsh conflict that ensued, Parākramabāhu's victory was at first by no means certain, but it ended with him very much in control over the Rājarata and Dakkhinadesa, though not of Rohana which still maintained a defiant independence. The third and longest phase began after he took control of Polonnaruva and found his position threatened by the ruler of Rohana. For Parākramabāhu, intent on establishing his control over the whole island, Rohana was the last and most formidable hurdle to clear. Its ruler was quite as determined as his predecessors in the days of the Anuradhapura kings to protect Rohana's particularist interests against the central authority in the Rājarata. One of the crucial factors in Parākramabāhu's success in this struggle was his capture of the Tooth and Bowl relics of the Buddha which had by now become essential to the legitimacy of royal authority in Sri Lanka.

Once the political unification of the island had been re-established, Parākramabāhu followed Vijayabāhu I in keeping a tight check on separatist tendencies on the island, especially in Rohana where particularism was a deeply ingrained political tradition. Rohana did not accept its loss of autonomy without a struggle and Parākramabāhu faced a formidable rebellion there in 1160, which he put down with great severity (there was a rebellion in the Rājarata as well in 1168 and this too was ruthlessly crushed). All vestiges of its former autonomy were now purposefully eliminated, and as a result there was, in the heyday of the Polonnaruva kingdom, much less tolerance of particularism than under the Anuradhapura kings. As we shall see, the country was to pay dearly for this over-centralization of authority in Polonnaruva.

Parākramabāhu I was the last of the great rulers of ancient Sri Lanka. After him the only Polonnaruva king to rule over the whole island was Niśśaṅka Malla, the first of the Kalinga rulers, who gave the country a brief decade of order and stability before the speedy and catastrophic break-up of the hydraulic civilizations of the dry zone. The achievements of the Polonnaruva kings Vijayabāhu I, Parākramabāhu I and Niśśaṅka Malla, memorable and substantial though they were, had their darker side as well. The flaw had to do with a conspicuous lack of restraint, especially in the case of Parākramabāhu I. In combination with his ambitious and venturesome foreign policy, the expensive diversion of state resources into irrigation projects and public works—civil and religious—sapped the strength of the country and thus contributed to the sudden and complete collapse which followed so soon after his death.

At the death of Parākramabāhu I, the problem of succession to the throne arose once more and was complicated by the fact that he had no sons of his own. The inevitable confusion and intrigue were cut short by the success with which Niśśaṅka Malla (who introduced himself as a prince of Kalinga, chosen and trained for the succession by Parākramabāhu himself) established his claims, although it was conceded that Vijayabāhu II had precedence over him by virtue of seniority if not for any other reason. As the scion of a foreign dynasty,

Niśśaṅka Malla was less secure on the throne than his two illustrious predecessors. If he was not overwhelmed by the problems inherent in maintaining intact the political structures fashioned by Vijayabāhu I and Parākramabāhu I, two of the most masterful rulers the island had seen, his successors clearly were. With his death, after a rule of nine years (how he died is not known), there was a renewal of political dissension within the kingdom complicated now by dynastic disputes.

The Kalinga dynasty maintained itself in power with the support of an influential faction within the country. But their hold on the throne was inherently precarious and their survival owed much to the inability of the factions opposing them to come up with an aspirant to the throne with a politically viable claim, or sufficient durability once installed in power. In desperation they raised Lilāvatī, a queen of Parākramabāhu I, to the throne on three occasions. The ensuing political instability inevitably attracted the attention of Cōla and Pāṇḍya adventurers bent on plunder. These south Indian incursions culminated in a devastating campaign of pillage under Māgha of Kalinga, from which the Sinhalese kingdom of the Rājarata never recovered.

Māgha's rule and its aftermath are a watershed in the history of the island, marking as they did the beginning of a new political order. From then on, instead of a single ruler for the island there were two, and sometimes three, till the time of Parākramabāhu VI (1411–66) who established control over the island. He was the last Sinhalese ruler to do so.

Three short extracts from the *Cūlavaṁsa* capture the essence of the tragedy as near contemporaries saw it:

> But since in consequence of the enormously accumulated, various evil deeds of the dwellers in Lankā, the *devatās*, who were everywhere entrusted with the protection of Lankā, failed to carry out this protection, there landed a man who held to a false creed, whose heart rejoiced in bad statesmanship, who was a forest fire burning down the bushes in the forest of the good, that is generosity and the like—who was a sun whose actions closed the rows of night lotus flowers—that is the good doctrine—and a moon destroying the grace of the groups of

the day lotuses—that is of peace—(a man) by name Māgha,
an unjust king sprung from the Kaliṅga line, in whom reflection
was fooled by his great delusion, landed as leader of four and
twenty thousand warriors from the Kaliṅga country and
conquered the Island of Lankā. The great scorching fire—
King Māgha—commanded his countless flames of fire—his
warriors to harass the great forest—the kingdom of Lankā.[2]

From the wider picture of the fall of the Sinhalese kingdom
the author of the *Cūlavaṁsa* turns to details in the processes of
destruction:

While thus his great warriors oppressed the people, boasting
cruelly everywhere, 'We are Kerala warriors,' they tore from
the people their garments, their ornaments and the like,
corrupted the good morals of the family which had been
observed for ages, cut off hands and feet and the like (of the
people), destroyed many houses and tied up cows, oxen and
other (cattle) which they made their own property. After they
had put fetters on the wealthy and the rich people and had
tortured them and taken away all their possessions, they made
poor people of them. They wrecked the image-houses,
destroyed many *cetiyas*, ravaged the *viharas* and maltreated
the lay brethren. They flogged the children, tormented the five
(groups of the) comrades of the Order, made the people carry
burdens and forced them to do heavy labour. Many books
known and famous they tore from their cord and strewed
them hither and thither. The beautiful, vast, proud *cetiyas* like
the Ratanāvalī (*cetiya*) and others which embodied as it were,
the glory of the former pious kings, they destroyed by
overthrowing them and alas! Many of the bodily relics, their
souls as it were, disappear. Thus the Damila worriers in
imitation of the worriers of Māra, destroyed in the evil of their
nature, the laity and the orderī.[3]

From there the author of the *Cūlavaṁsa* turns to what he treats
as a particularly serious offence:

The monarch caused the people to adopt false views and
brought confusion into the four unmixed castes. Villages and
fields, houses and gardens, slaves, cattle, buffaloes and

whatever else belonged to the Sihalas he had delivered up to the Keralas. The *viharas*, the *parivenas* and many sanctuaries he made over to one or other of his warriors as dwelling. The treasures which belonged to the Buddha and were the property of the holy Order he seized and thus committed a number of sins in order to go to hell. In this fashion committing deeds of violence the Ruler Māgha held sway in Lankā for twenty-one years.[4]

Polonnaruva ceased to be the capital city after Māgha's death in 1255 and two new centres of political authority evolved. The heartland of the old Sinhalese kingdom and Rohana itself were abandoned. The Sinhalese kings and people retreated further and further into the hills of the wet zone of the island in the face of repeated invasions from south India. They sought security primarily, but also some kind of new economic base to support the truncated state they controlled.

The second political centre was in the north of the island. Tamil settlers occupied the Jaffna Peninsula and much of the land between Jaffna and Anuradhapura known as the Vanni; they were joined by Tamil members of the invading armies, often mercenaries, who chose to settle in Sri Lanka rather than return to India with the rest of their compatriots. It would appear that by the thirteenth century, the Tamils too withdrew from the Vanni and thereafter their main settlements were confined almost entirely to the Jaffna Peninsula and possibly also to several scattered settlements near the eastern seaboard. By the thirteenth century, an independent Tamil kingdom had been established with the Jaffna Peninsula as its base. The turbulent and confusing history of these two kingdoms is reviewed in greater detail in Chapters 7 and 8.

FOREIGN RELATIONS: CŌḺAS AND PĀṆḌYAS

At the beginning of this period the Cōḷas were still the dominant power in south India, with the Pāṇḍyas struggling to maintain themselves as a distinct political entity. As for Sri Lanka, the predominant south Indian state sought to assert its authority over the island, or at least to influence its politics.

Sri Lanka's rulers on their part endeavoured to support the rivals of the dominant power in order to protect their own interests. In brief, they attempted to maintain a balance of power in south India. Thus, for as long as the Cōḷas was the dominant power, Sri Lanka's alliance with the Pāṇḍyas continued.

The early rulers of Polonnaruva were far too preoccupied with the internal politics of the island to pursue a dynamic foreign policy. But the situation changed when Parākramabāhu I had consolidated his hold on the island's affairs. His first venture in foreign affairs, the participation in what is known as the 'war of Pāṇḍyan succession' was the inevitable result of Sri Lanka's alignment with the Pāṇḍyas. This proved to be a long-drawn-out involvement, beginning as it did a little before his seventeenth regnal year and dragging on till the end of his reign. While there was some initial success, the Sri Lanka armies were eventually defeated. Nevertheless, they were able to sustain a determined and prolonged resistance against the Cōḷas, despite the latter's military superiority. Parākramabāhu often succeeded in negating a Cōḷa victory, even an overwhelming one, by diplomatic intrigue, for Pāṇḍyan rulers who secured their throne with Cōḷa backing subsequently turned to Parākramabāhu for assistance, thus rekindling a war which appeared to be fading away, as the Cōḷas reacted by seeking to replace such a ruler with a more reliable and pliant protégé. Thus Parākramabāhu I achieved what he set out to do, to prevent the establishment of a Cōḷa hegemony over south India. Had the Cōḷas been left unopposed, they could have been a greater threat to the security of Sri Lanka than they were, and may even have endangered Parākramabāhu's own position by espousing the cause of Sri Vallabha,[5] an aspirant to the Sri Lanka throne who was living in exile in the Cōḷa country. As it was, when Sri Vallabha did organize an invasion, it proved to be a dismal failure.

If this prolonged entanglement in south Indian politics ended in military failure and severely strained the island's economy, it nevertheless contributed substantially to the impairment of Cōḷa power. Thus while the successors of Parākramabāhu I inherited a legacy of Cōḷa hostility to Sri Lanka, the Cōḷas were by then on the verge of being eclipsed by their rivals, the Pāṇḍyas.

The last Sri Lankan ruler to intervene in the affairs of south India was Niśśaṅka Malla, who despatched a Sri Lanka expeditionary force to the mainland and, unlike Parākramabāhu I, accompanied his troops on their mission. His activities there, about which he makes exaggerated claims in his inscriptions, were no more successful militarily than those of Parākramabāhu's generals.

By the mid-thirteenth century, the most menacing threat to the enfeebled Sinhalese kingdom came from the Pāṇḍyas, their traditional allies against the Cōḷas. The prolonged crisis in the Sri Lankan polity naturally attracted the Cōḷas, but not any longer with the same frequency or effectiveness as the Pāṇḍyas who, as the predominant power in south India, now sought to establish their influence, if not domination, over Sri Lanka. Pāṇḍyan princes on the Polonnaruva throne, and Pāṇḍyan intervention during the period of Māgha's rule on the island, bear testimony to the persistence of the traditional pattern of the dominant power in south India seeking to establish its influence on the governance of the island.

The range of Sri Lanka's political and cultural links with Indian states was not limited to south India. As we have seen, the Sinhalese kingdom had very close ties with Kalinga in the Orissa region, but surprisingly there is little or no Indian evidence bearing on this. On Sri Lanka's ties with the Cālukyas of the Deccan, some information is available. There was indeed a natural convergence of political interests between Sri Lanka and the kingdoms of the Deccan, prompted by the common desire to keep the Cōḷas in check.

FOREIGN RELATIONS: SOUTH-EAST ASIA

Under the Polonnaruva kings an exciting new dimension of politics emerged—links with south-east Asia, in particular with Burma (then known as Rāmaṇṇa) and Cambodia.[6] Because of her strategic position athwart the sea route between China and the west, there had been, from the very early centuries of the Christian era, trade links between the island and some of the south-east Asian states and China. Now, the principal driving force was religious affinity—a Buddhist outlook, Theravada or Mahayanist—which strengthened ties that had developed from association in trade. Till the eleventh century the cohesion which comes from strong diplomatic and political ties was still lacking. In the eleventh and twelfth centuries, at a time of unusual ferment in the politics of the south-east Asian region, with many kingdoms then engaged in a self-conscious search for a new identity, and reaching out for new political ties, formal political relations were established between some of these states and Sri Lanka. The Polonnaruva rulers responded eagerly to these initiatives for they relished the new and attractive vistas in politics, trade and religious and cultural ties which links with south-east Asian kingdoms held out.

In time the religious and cultural ties marked the beginning of Sri Lanka's powerful cultural influence on south-east Asia. The Polonnaruva period was the heyday of that Sri Lankan cultural influence. For Vijayabāhu I, engaged in a grim struggle against the Cōḷas, there were immediate advantages from this in the form of economic aid from Anauratha of Pagan. The alliance with Pagan appears to have continued after the expulsion of the Cōḷas, and it was to Pagan that Vijayabāhu I turned for assistance in reorganizing the sangha in Sri Lanka, thus underlining the connection between political ties and a common commitment to Buddhism.[7]

But just as important in the development of political relations between Sri Lanka under the Polonnaruva kings and south-east Asia was the commerce of the Indian Ocean. Kenneth Hall has shown how 'the upper Malay peninsula became the centre of multi-partite interaction among the Sinhalese of Sri Lanka, the Burmese and the Khmers as the regional trade developed'.[8] Conflicting commercial interests led to war between Parākramabāhu I and Burma.[9] Intent on expanding his country's stake in the maritime trade of the Indian Ocean, Parākramabāhu I sought to establish close ties with the powerful Khmer kingdom of Cambodia. This aroused the suspicions of the Burmese King Alaungsithu, who viewed it as a potentially serious threat to Burma's own maritime trade. To protect this latter, he resorted to a policy of obstructing Sri Lanka's trade in south-east Asia, resulting in strained relations between Burma and Sri Lanka, and eventually war. Parākramabāhu I despatched an expedition to lower Burma.[10] But once this indecisive encounter was over there was a speedy restoration of friendly relations between the two countries.

Between the death of Parākramabāhu I and the collapse of the Polonnaruva kingdom there are only two instances of Sri Lankan rulers seeking political links or contacts with southeast Asia. These were Vijayabāhu II and Niśśaṅka Malla; the first maintained friendly relations with Burma, and the latter with Cambodia as well. But Niśśaṅka Malla's claims in this regard are a matter of some controversy.

In a curious way, all these various strands which made up the politics of the island in the last days of the Polonnaruva kingdom were linked together by the only recorded southeast Asian invasion of Sri Lanka. The invasion, which occurred in 1247 when Parākramabāhu II (1236–70) was the Sinhalese king ruling at Dambadeniya, was led by Chandrabhānu of Tāmbralinga, a petty kingdom in the Malay Peninsula which had established itself as an independent state in the last days of the Sri Vijaya empire in the thirteenth century.[11] Parākramabāhu's forces defeated Chandrabhānu, who fled to the Jaffna kingdom, then under Māgha. There he succeeded in securing the throne for himself (how he did so we do not know for certain) and was the ruler in Jaffna at the time of the Pāṇḍyan invasion.

This latter stemmed from Pāṇḍyan rivalry with the Cōlas, who supported Māgha's regime in Sri Lanka. Indeed Māgha, as the ruler of the northern kingdom, was no more than a satellite of the Cōlas. When, by the middle of the thirteenth century, the Pāṇḍyas had established themselves as the dominant power in south India, they were inclined to support the Sinhalese kings against the newly established kingdom in the north of the island.

Their intervention in the affairs of Sri Lanka, if more restrained in its objectives than that of the Cōlas, was, however, no less governed by considerations of realpolitik. They invaded Jaffna and forced Chandrabhānu to submit to Pāṇḍya power, but at the same time there was no inclination on their part to permit the Sinhalese to re-establish their control over Jaffna. Chandrabhānu was allowed to remain on the throne at Jaffna as a tributary of the Pāṇḍyas. It became evident that one of the limitations imposed on him was that there could be no disturbance of the balance of political power on the island at the expense of the Sinhalese ruler. When Chandrabhānu embarked on a second invasion of the Sinhalese kingdom, and Parākramabāhu II appealed to the Pāṇḍyas for help, an expeditionary force was despatched to bring the Jāvaka ruler to a realization of the limits of his power. The combination of Pāṇḍyan and Sinhalese forces won an overwhelming victory and Chandrabhānu himself was killed in the confrontation. Instead of handing over control of the Jaffna kingdom to Parākramabāhu II, the Pāṇḍyas preferred to install a son of Chandrabhānu as ruler of Jaffna. When he in turn became a threat to the Sinhalese, the latter once more sought the help of the Pāṇḍyas, who intervened with decisive effect; but Sinhalese control of the Jaffna kingdom was still equally unacceptable to the Pāṇḍyas, and so Āryacakravarti, the leader of the Pāṇḍyan army of invasion on this occasion, was installed as ruler of Jaffna under their overlordship. When the Pāṇḍyan empire in turn collapsed as a result of Muslim inroads into south India, Jaffna became an independent kingdom under the Āryacakravartis.[12]

ECONOMIC AND SOCIAL STRUCTURE

The economic and social structure of the Polonnaruva kingdom, like its art and architecture, was a natural development from, if not a continuation of, those of the Anuradhapura kingdom. It was a hydraulic civilization and a primarily agricultural economy made more prosperous from profits from internal and external trade.

Its astonishing creativity in irrigation was all the more remarkable for the brief period of time over which it was achieved and the massive efforts at restoration which preceded any attempts at expansion. Repair and restoration, by themselves, called for a prodigious expenditure of resources. Most of this work was concentrated in the reigns of three kings, Vijayabāhu I, Parākramabāhu I and Niśśaṅka Malla, the

outstanding contribution being that of Parākramabāhu I whose reign marked the peak of Sinhalese achievement in hydraulic engineering.[13]
The Polonnaruva kings were the heirs to several centuries of experience in irrigation technology. But they themselves—and especially Parākramabāhu I—made a distinctive contribution of their own in honing these techniques to cope with the special requirements of the immense irrigation projects constructed at this time. There was, for instance, the colossal size of the Parākrama Samudra (the sea of Parākrama) which, with an embankment rising to an average height of 12 m and stretching over its entire length of 13.7 km, was by far the largest irrigation tank constructed in ancient Sri Lanka. This stupendous project incorporated two earlier tanks, the Tōpāvāva and the Dimbutuluväva. Fed from the south by the Angamädilla Canal, it was linked on the north-west with the Giritale Tank and through it with the Älahära System. The earthworks involved in this project were unprecedented in scale and the stonemasonry of this and other irrigation works of this period involved the handling of stone blocks of up to 10.7 metric tonnes in weight.[14]

Parākrama Samudra, Polonnaruva

Refinement of irrigation technology was demonstrated also in the three weirs built across the Daduru Oya, the only river in the western part of the dry zone to provide anything like a perennial supply of water. The second of these diverted water to the Mahagalla Reservoir (which had been built by Mahāsena) and was a masterly engineering feat whose special feature was the amazing precision with which the large stone blocks of its outer walls were fitted, their joints only 0.64 cm in width.[15]

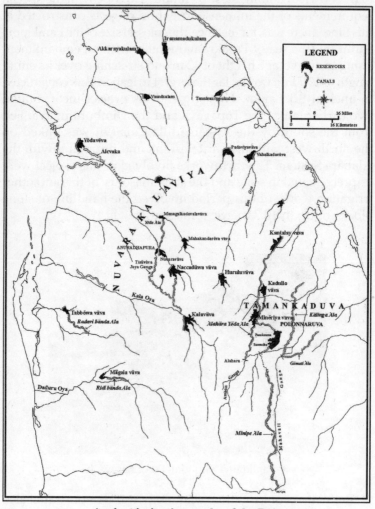

Ancient irrigation works of the Rājarata

The *Cūlavaṁsa*'s account of the reign of Parākramabāhu I contains an extensive catalogue of irrigation works repaired, restored, expanded or constructed in his reign. The impression of tireless devotion to this crucial aspect of governmental enterprise in Sri Lanka's hydraulic society could hardly be described as inaccurate. But it is essential to remember that it was no truer than in the Anuradhapura era that every link and every unit in this intricate irrigation network was working pari passu for any great length of time. They could not have done so, and, in fact, did not. If this perspective appears somewhat to limit the achievement of that era, one must remember that this was the last major phase in the development of irrigation in ancient Sri Lanka. Nothing on this scale was attempted, much less achieved, till the second quarter of the twentieth century, when the Gal Oya Scheme in the present Eastern Province, the first irrigation scheme to be constructed in the very early years of independence from British rule, easily overshadowed the Parākrama Samudra. And so the chronicler's account can be seen for what it was, evocative and even poignant, for he was lamenting, in a later and more cramped era, the passing of an age of creativity, when the island's irrigation tanks were no more than stupendous ruins, but yet

> ...the proudest monuments...of the former greatness of their country when the opulence they engendered enabled the kings to lavish untold wealth upon edifices of religion, to subsidise mercenary armies and to fit out expeditions for foreign conquest.[16]

We turn next, and briefly, to the caste structure of Sri Lankan society under the Polonnaruva kings. Two points are of special interest. There is, first, much stronger evidence of a hierarchical arrangement of castes, though it is difficult to determine the exact or even approximate place of each caste in that structure. The segmentation of Sinhalese society into some of the numerous castes which exist today began before this period, but the process appears to have been accelerated in it. Second, there was increasing rigidity in the observance of caste duties, obligations and rights on the basis of custom and usage. For instance, a Tamil inscription of 1122 reveals that washermen were required to perform their customary duties to members of certain other—presumably 'higher'—castes and that there would be no remission of this obligation. A rock inscription of Vijayabāhu I at Ambagamuva shows that he had constructed a special platform on Adam's Peak below the main terrace of the 'sacred' footprint for the use of persons of 'low' caste. More significantly, there are Niśśaṅka Malla's repeated references to, and ridicule of, the aspirations of the *Govikula* (the *Goyigama* caste, then as now very probably the largest caste group among the Sinhalese, though possibly not at that time the most prestigious) to kingship in Sri Lanka. Quite clearly, this was regarded as a monopoly of the Kshatriyas. This hardening of caste attitudes is attributed to the burgeoning influence of Hinduism on religion and society in Sri Lanka.[17]

Land tenure in the Polonnaruva kingdom was as much a multi-centred system as it was earlier and its pattern was just as complex.[18] There was a wide variety both in the number of individuals and institutions sharing land and rights accruing from land as well in their tenurial obligations. The king had definite claims over most of the land in the kingdom, but these were no obstacles to private individuals in buying and alienating land. To a much greater extent than in the Anuradhapura kingdom, the 'immunities'—various concessions and privileges in regard to land—granted during this period strengthened the position of the hereditary nobility.

The conferment of these immunities—which were very much in vogue in this period—was a special privilege of the king or someone in a position of similar authority, such as heirs apparent or regional rulers with considerable power such as those of Rohana. In general, immunities guaranteed freedom from interference by royal officers and ensured exemption from taxation. Pamunu (or paraveṇi as it was called after the fourteenth century) and divel holdings were now a conspicuous part of the tenurial system in a period when, paradoxically, there was a positive efflorescence of royal authority, in terms of its grandeur and majesty. As in the late Anuradhapura period, however, the most salient manifestation of such immunities were those granted to the monasteries. These now extended beyond the conventional rights to labour and the whole or part of the revenue of the block or blocks of land or village thus granted to the transfer of fiscal as well as administrative and judicial authority over the lands thus held. As a result, the monasteries and their functionaries came to be entrusted with much of the local administrative duties traditionally performed by the king's officials. It would appear that some new administrative structures were developed to cope with this significant enlargement of the role of the monasteries in the social system.

The principal source of the king's revenue in the Polonnaruva kingdom was the land tax with taxes on paddy contributing the major portion; there were smaller yields from levies on other crops. There was also the *diyadada* (the equivalent of the *diyadedum* of the Anuradhapura kingdom), the tax on the use of water from irrigation channels which no doubt yielded a very substantial income. There was, in addition, revenue from certain valuable items in the country's external trade—gems, pearls, cinnamon and elephants—extending from a share of the profits to monopoly rights. Thus the mining of gems seems to have been a royal monopoly, which was protected by a prohibition on permanent settlement in the gem-producing districts. Individuals were permitted to mine for gems on payment of a fee. Mining was carried out seasonally under the supervision of royal officials, with the king enjoying prerogative rights to the more valuable gems. Pearl fishery too was a royal monopoly conducted on much the same basis. Finally, the king's own lands were also a quite notable source of income for him. These taxes were collected by a hierarchy of officials. At the base of the structure were the village authorities—possibly village headmen—who were entrusted with the collection of taxes due to the king from each village; these were delivered to the king's officials during their annual tours.

The fact that these taxes were paid partly at least in grain and other agricultural produce—which, being more or less perishable, could not be stored indefinitely by the officials who collected them—may have been a guarantee against extortionate levies on the peasantry. A tax of one-sixth of the produce was regarded as an equitable land tax, but in practice there was no uniformity in the rate of taxation, a flexibility which could often be to the disadvantage of the peasant. It is significant that Vijayabāhu I, on his accession to the throne, should have directed his officials to adhere to custom and usage in the collection of taxes, and that Niśśaṅka Malla himself claims to have reduced taxes presumably because they had become burdensome.

One of the notable features in the economic history of the period extending from the ninth century to the end of the Polonnaruva kingdom was the expansion of trade within the country. The data available at present are too meagre for an analysis of the development of this trade, or indeed for a detailed description of its special characteristics, but there is evidence of the emergence of merchant 'corporations', the growth of market towns linked by well-known trade routes and the development of a local, that is to say, regional coinage. Tolls and other levies on this trade yielded a considerable income to the state.

There was at the same time a substantial revenue from customs dues on external trade although the data we have are too scanty to compute with any precision the duties levied on the various export and import commodities. Sri Lanka was a vital link in the great trade routes between the east and the west, of importance in 'transit' trade due to her advantageous geographical location and in the 'terminal' trade on account of her natural products such as gems, pearls and timber. Apart from the traditional ports of the north and north-west of the island and on the east coast, those of the west coast too became important in this trade. Besides, the island's numerous bays, anchorages and roadsteads offered adequate shelter for the sailing ships of this period.

Trade in the Indian Ocean at this time was dominated by the Arabs, who were among the leading and most intrepid sailors of the era. The large empires at both ends of the route— the unity imposed on the Muslim world by the caliphs and the peace enjoyed by China during the Tang and Sung dynasties—helped increase the tempo of the trade between

China and the Persian Gulf. The countries of south and south-east Asia lying between these two points shared in this and indeed derived a considerable profit from it. Luxury articles were the main commodities in this inter-Asian and international trade and to this category belonged Sri Lanka's gems and pearls. The competition for this Indian Ocean trade was not always peaceful. Behind the Cōḷa expansion into south-east Asia lay a determination to obtain greater control over the trade and trade routes of the Indian Ocean. Although powerful political motives spurred them on to a conquest of Sri Lanka, the Cōḷas were always aware of the economic advantages of this—her valuable foreign trade and her strategic position athwart the maritime trade routes of the Indian Ocean. While Sri Lanka herself seldom resorted to war in defence of her trade interests, Parākramabāhu I's expedition against Burma, though somewhat exceptional, was nevertheless a significant demonstration of how commercial rivalry could undermine a long-standing alliance based on a common religious outlook.

Though most of the vessels used in her external trade were generally of foreign construction, seaworthy craft were built in Sri Lanka as well and are known to have sailed as far as China. Perhaps some of the latter may even have been used to transport Parākramabāhu I's troops to Burma.

Foreign merchants were attracted to the island because of its importance as a centre of international trade. The most prominent of the merchant groups settled in Sri Lanka were the Moors, descendants of Arab traders to the island. These Arab merchants and their agents had established settlements in south India as well, as early as the tenth century. They were a dominant influence on the island's international trade in the period of the Polonnaruva kings, a position which they retained till the early decades of the sixteenth century when the Polonnaruva kingdom itself was no more than a memory. However, the foreign trade of that kingdom was by no means a Moor monopoly. There were other foreigners living on the island for reasons of trade, and among the more interesting of these were Cambodian bird-catchers. The feathers of exotic birds were an important item in international trade at this time.

Although trade, external as well as internal, had grown substantially in Sri Lanka during the Polonnaruva era, domestic agriculture continued to be the predominant economic activity of the kingdom. And the role of money in the economy appears to have been, as in the days of the Anuradhapura kingdom, of merely peripheral significance.

RELIGION AND CULTURE

The inevitable result of the Cōḷa conquest was the intrusive impact of Hindu-Brahmanical and Saiva religious practices, Dravidian art and architecture and the Tamil language itself on the religion and culture of Sri Lanka. The period of the south Indian invasions of the Anuradhapura kingdom in the ninth and tenth centuries coincided with the decline of Buddhism in India and the collapse of important centres of Buddhist learning as a result of Muslim invasions. These processes proved to be irreversible. South Indian influence on Sri Lanka thereafter became exclusively Hindu in content.

It is against this background that the recovery of Buddhism under the Polonnaruva kings needs to be reviewed. The most substantial contributions came from Vijayabāhu I and Parākramabāhu I. The unification of the sangha in the latter's reign was one of the most significant events in the history of Sinhalese Buddhism. Traditionally, this has been viewed in terms of the triumph of the Mahāvihara, and the discomfiture if not suppression of the Abhayagiri and Jetavana nikāyas. But recent research has shown this to be quite inaccurate. The loss of property by the monasteries during the period of Cōḷa rule, and again in the interregnum between Vijayabāhu I and the accession of Parākramabāhu I had had a deleterious effect upon all the nikāyas. Their disintegration had, in fact, led to a new grouping of the sangha under eight *mula*s or fraternities. Parākramabāhu I brought these eight fraternities together under a common leadership—a process of unification which was at once much more and much less than imposing the authority of the Mahāvihara over the other two nikāyas. It did not end sectarian competition, but appears to have had a tonic effect on both evangelistic and scholarly activity.[19]

The resuscitatory zeal of these two monarchs in particular demonstrated afresh the remarkable resilience of Sri Lankan Buddhism. Sinhalese bhikkhus maintained contacts with distant centres of Buddhism like Nepal and Tibet; they also made vigorous but unsuccessful attempts to spread their teachings in Bengal,[20] apart from engaging in spirited disputes with their Theravadin colleagues in south India on questions relating to the interpretation of the canon. It was south-east Asia, however, that was most receptive to their teachings, and the expansion of Sinhalese Theravada Buddhism in that region—Burma and Thailand—was an important trend in its cultural history during this period.

Two other developments in Sri Lankan Buddhism need mention. First, there was the increasing popularity of the *Ārannavāsins*, the forest-dwelling monks in the latter part of this period, who gained prominence in scholarly activities and took the lead in reformist movements. Second, there was an increasing involvement of monasteries in secular activity, which stemmed mainly from the large land grants donated to the sangha and the transfer of administrative authority over the temporalities to the monasteries, a significant extension of the privileges normally implied in the immunities granted with such donations of land.

One of the distinctive features of the literature of the Polonnaruva period was the continued vitality of Pali as the language of Sinhalese Buddhism. The tradition was still very much in favour of writing in Pali rather than Sinhala. The Pali works of this period were mainly expositions or summaries of works of the Pali canon. There were also the *tīkā*s explaining and supplementing the commentaries composed in the Anuradhapura era. The *Dāthavaṁsa*, a history of the tooth relic, was one of the more notable literary contributions in the Pali language. Its author, Mahānāma, is also credited with the first part of the *Cūlavaṁsa*, the continuation of the *Mahāvaṁsa*. The Pali literature of this period bears the impression of the strong stimulating effect of Sanskrit, which had a no less significant influence on contemporary Sinhala writing. The bulk of the Sinhala works of this period are glossaries and translations from the Pali canon. There were also two prose works by a thirteenth-century author, Gurulugomi, the *Amāvatura* and the

Dharmapradīpikāva, of which the former was more noteworthy; and two poems (of the late twelfth and early thirteenth century), the *Sasadāvata* and the *Muvadevadāvata*, both based on Jātaka stories, and both greatly influenced by the Sanskrit works of Kālidāsa and Kumāradāsa.

The literature of the Polonnaruva era that has survived is neither substantial nor exceptionally distinguished. Indeed, all of it shares the flaws of the literature of the Anuradhapura period without its compensating virtues, and they do not compare, in creativity or originality, with the writings of the succeeding period of Sri Lanka's history.[21]

In architecture and sculpture the performance was memorable. Apart from the restoration of ancient edifices, Vijayabāhu I's major contribution was the construction of the Temple of the Tooth (now represented by the ruin called the *Atadāgē*). There was a considerable setback to this artistic recovery in the instability and turmoil that followed his death. With Parākramabāhu I the great period of artistic activity of Polonnaruva began, and was continued under Niśśaṅka Malla during the brief decade (1187–96) of order and stability which his reign represented and during which Polonnaruva reached the zenith of its development as a capital city.

The Gal Vihara sculptures (in the reign of Parākramabāhu I) are the glory of Polonnaruva and the summit of its artistic achievement. The four great statues of the Buddha which comprise this complex, representing the three main positions— the seated, the standing and the recumbent—are cut in a row from a horizontal escarpment of streaked granite. Each of these statues was originally sheltered by its own image house. The consummate skill with which the peace of the enlightenment has been depicted in an extraordinarily successful blend of serenity and strength has seldom been equalled by any other Buddha image in Sri Lanka. Of similar nobility of conception and magnitude is the colossal figure (of a sage, as some scholars would have it, or a monarch, as others insist) overlooking the bund of the Tōpāvāva. The dignity, puissance and self-reliance of the figure have been rendered with amazing economy and restraint.

Sage, Polonnaruva

Of the architectural monuments attributed to the reign of Niśśaṅka Malla the most unforgettable is the collection of temples and viharas in the so-called Great Quadrangle, which has been described as among the 'most beautiful and satisfyingly proportioned buildings in the entire Indian world'.[22] The Niśśaṅka-latā mandapaya is a unique type of Sinhalese architectural monument: a cluster of granite columns shaped like lotus stems with capitals in the form of opening buds, within a raised platform, all contributing to a general effect 'of extreme chastity and Baroque fancy [unsurpassed] in any Indian shrine'.[23]

The Hätadāgā was certainly begun and completed during Niśśaṅka Malla's reign. The embellishments on the pillars of

Buddha image, Gal Vihara, Polonnaruva

the Atadāgē have no rival in the decorative art of the Sinhalese, and stand comparison with the best examples of such work elsewhere. The beautiful vatadāgē, 'one of the loveliest examples of Sinhalese architecture,'[24] has its name associated with Niśśaṅka Malla but it is doubtful if he did much more than construct its outer porch. The Satmahalprāsāda and the stupendous Rankot Vihara (or, to give its ancient name, the Ruvanväli), with the frontispieces and chapels at its base, were the work of Niśśaṅka Malla.

Although there is a striking continuity between the art and architecture of Polonnaruva and that of Anuradhapura, the distinctive feature of Polonnaruva's architectural remains is the mingling of Buddhist and Hindu decorative elements, a fusion

Buddha image, Gal Vihara, Polonnaruva

Ruvanvelisaya as it is today

which extended far beyond the mere stylistic plagiarism of
Hindu and Dravidian forms. It reflected the powerful influence
of Mahayanism and Hinduism in the lives of the people.

Siva dēvālē No. 2 is the earliest in date of all the monuments
now preserved in Polonnaruva. Built entirely of stone, it dates

Tisawewa, Anuradhapura

Twin ponds, Anuradhapura

from the time of Cōḷa rule and is a representative example of Dravidian architecture at its best. Later in date and more ornate is Siva dēvālē No. I. Both are smaller, one might even say miniature, versions of the towering Cōḷa architecture of south India.

The Satmahalprāsāda, a stupa with an unusual pyramid-like form in seven levels or storeys, is much more of an enigma.

Was this monument yet another derived from an Indian prototype[25] or an outstanding example of south-east Asian—Cambodian and Burmese—influence on Sri Lankan architecture? The latter seems more likely because of the peculiar shape of this monument and in view of the very close religious ties at this time between Sri Lanka and the Buddhist countries of south-east Asia.[26]

As at Anuradhapura, few secular buildings have survived in Polonnaruva. Of Parākramabāhu's palace only the foundations remain today, but Niśśanka Malla's audience hall is in a better state of preservation.

As for painting, what is now preserved is a very small fraction of the work executed by the artists of the Polonnaruva kingdom. Of the secular paintings nothing has survived, although the evidence suggests that the walls of palaces—like those of shrines—were decorated with paintings. Those on religious edifices have fared slightly better. The Lankātilaka bears traces of paintings on both its exterior as well as interior walls. The walls of the Tivanka-pratimāghara (erroneously called the Demalamahasāya) carry more paintings than any other monument at Polonnaruva or indeed on the island, but the date of these paintings is a matter of conjecture, for though this shrine was built in the reign of Parākramabāhu I, it has evidently been renovated and possibly altered at a later date.

These paintings are the work of artists who had centuries of tradition behind them and who belonged to a school which, in its heyday, had ramifications throughout the subcontinent of India and beyond it. The famous cave paintings of Ajanta and Bagh are its most mature products. By the twelfth century, this artistic tradition was almost extinct in India, but the fragmentary remains of the Polonnaruva paintings afford proof that it had been preserved in Sri Lanka long after it had lost its vitality in the land of its origin. Nevertheless, like the earlier Sigiri paintings, these latter are distinctly provincial in comparison with the Indian prototype.

Indeed, all the later work in Polonnaruva, whether in art or architecture, appears archaic if not atavistic, the result very probably of a conscious effort at reviving and imitating the artistic traditions of the Anuradhapura kingdom. The moonstones of Polonnaruva are inferior to those of Anuradhapura in vitality and aesthetic appeal, just as the baths which adorned the palaces and monasteries were smaller in size and, with the single exception of the exquisite lotus bath, less elegant in design.

The transformation of Polonnaruva into a gracious cosmopolitan city[27] was the work of three kings—Vijayabāhu I, Parākramabāhu I and Niśśaṅka Malla. This development could be measured in generations if not decades and not, as in the case of the cognate process in Anuradhapura, in centuries. Polonnaruva had a smaller area than Anuradhapura, but its compactness was conducive to a remarkable symmetry in the location of its major edifices, all of them like so many links in some gigantic creation of a celestial jeweller who used the Parākrama Samudra to the best possible advantage to set them off.

The comparatively short period in which the architecture and sculptural splendours of Polonnaruva were created is no doubt testimony to the dynamism and creativity of its rulers and people. But it had its sombre side as well, for in retrospect the activity seems febrile, and this conspicuous investment in monuments must have impaired the economic strength of the kingdom and contributed greatly to the rapid decline that set in after the reign of Niśśaṅka Malla.

The Fragmentation
of the Sri Lankan Polity
From c. 1250 to the End of the Fifteenth Century

The collapse of the ancient Sinhalese kingdom of the dry zone is one of the major turning points in Sri Lanka's history.[1] Traditionally, Māgha's invasion and the orgy of destruction in which his cohorts indulged are regarded as the climacteric in the deracination of Sri Lanka's hydraulic civilization. Yet the fact remains that many of the invasions of preceding centuries, notably that of the Cōḷa ruler Rājarāja, were just as destructive as those that followed on the death of Niśśaṅka Malla. The irrigation network had been resuscitated after these tribulations and the population returned to the productive regions of the dry zone. The questions we need to answer are why it was that after the mid-thirteenth century Sri Lanka's hydraulic civilization did not demonstrate a similar resilience and why the processes of destruction proved to be irreversible.

One needs to guard against exaggerating the extent of the recovery from the destructive effects of the Cōḷa invasions of the tenth century, for its key feature had been the shift of the capital from the traditional centre of Sinhalese power, Anuradhapura, to Polonnaruva. This was in itself an admission of weakness for it was the abandonment of Sri Lanka's classical urban centre, its capital for nearly 1,500 years. No other city in south Asia has had a longer period as the capital city. The events of the mid-thirteenth century demonstrated that Polonnaruva was just as vulnerable to attacks from the mainland. By now the proverbial resilience of the Sinhalese kingdom of the dry zone was gone, because the latter's resources of vitality had been impaired beyond replenishment by the feverish activity of the three major rulers of the Polonnaruva kingdom—Vijayabāhu I, Parākramabāhu I and Niśśaṅka Malla. The centralization of power at the capital city, which was a feature of their administration—and their swift and ruthless suppression of particularist aspirations of the outer provinces—eroded the traditional autonomy of these regions to the point where they lost their ability to serve their time-honoured function as a refuge for Sinhalese kings confronting invasions from the mainland, as well as their ability to sustain a viable core of resistance once the Rājarata itself had succumbed. Above all, there was a distinct diminution of the strength of the Sinhalese kingdom vis-à-vis its rivals on the Indian mainland and hence a greater vulnerability to attack. The age-long pressures from the Indian mainland assumed a more forbidding dimension with the establishment, consolidation and expansion of a Tamil kingdom in the north of the island and the emergence of the Vanni chieftaincies as a buffer between this northern kingdom and what was left of Sinhalese power in Sri Lanka.

Polonnaruva was abandoned after Māgha's rule and the next three kings ruled from Dambadeniya. One ruler made Yapahuva his royal residence. These were both rock fortresses; so was Kurunegala, another site of royal power in this quest for safety against invasion from south India and the threat from the north.

The last occasion when Polonnaruva served as the capital city was in the reign of Parākramabāhu III (1287–93), but this only illustrated the perilous position to which Sinhalese power was reduced: he ruled at Polonnaruva because of his subservience to the Pāṇḍyas.[2] But not all the Sinhalese monarchs of this period were content with being the rulers of a client state or to relinquish the natural aspiration of Sinhalese kings to establish control over the whole island even if the resources to achieve this were grievously limited. Parākramabāhu II almost achieved this: his power extended over Rohana, the central hills and the Vanni and he annexed Polonnaruva, but could not establish control over the Tamil kingdom in the north of the island. He held his coronation at Polonnaruva and attempted to restore that city to its former status as the centre of Sinhalese power, but was compelled to return to

Dambadeniya which remained his capital for the rest of his reign in recognition of the persistent danger of a Pāṇḍyan invasion of the island.

As we shall see in the next chapter, Sinhalese power shifted from Kurunegala to the central mountains further to the south, a region which had never in the past been well-developed or highly populated or a centre of civilization, although it was an excellent refuge for defeated causes and a bridgehead for resistance movements. And it was there in the fourteenth century that a kingdom was set up with Gangasiripura or Gampola on the Mahaveli River as its capital. The capital was shifted to Senkadagala, modern Kandy or Mahanuvara. It was probably the southward expansion of the northern kingdom which compelled this shift to Gampola which was much more easily defensible than Kurunāgala and far less accessible as well to intruders from the north.

At much the same time that the Sinhalese kingdom of Sri Lanka's dry zone began its slide to oblivion, hydraulic civilizations in Cambodia, northern Thailand and the Pagan region of Burma, in all of which a rich agricultural surplus served as the highly productive basis of complex societies and cultures of great vitality, were losing their vigour and drifting to irrevocable decline.[3] None of these regions was reoccupied.

A hydraulic civilization is like a highly efficient and robust machine with a sophisticated but delicate, even brittle, controlling mechanism—the intricate network of tanks, weirs and channels and the institutional machinery devised for its maintenance. The fact that these civilizations all declined at about the same time has been the basis of the argument that this controlling mechanism and especially institutional machinery for its maintenance tends to weaken in time from some inherent structural fault, quite apart from the invasions of the sort that plagued Sri Lanka in the tenth and thirteenth centuries.[4] The contention that the breakdown in hydraulic civilizations comes remorselessly with age carries conviction. The irrigation network which sustained the Polonnaruva kingdom, for instance, represented fifteen centuries of development. But by itself it is inadequate as an explanation for the fall of Sri

Lanka's hydraulic civilization and we need to turn once more to the political problems of the mid-thirteenth century.

A complex irrigation network such as that of the Polonnaruva kingdom requires a high level of organization and efficiency in administration. The comprehensive disintegration of the political system bequeathed by Parākramabāhu I would have paralysed the administrative machinery which kept this irrigation network in running order. Under the Anuradhapura kings, village institutions and regional administrations had ensured the survival of some parts of the irrigation system at least during periods of turmoil at the capital—succession disputes and periods of civil war—and invasion. But the over-centralization of administration in the Polonnaruva kingdom appears to have had a deleterious effect on local initiatives, with the result that when royal authority collapsed at Polonnaruva, administrative units in the outlying regions were no longer capable of maintaining their sections of the irrigation network in good repair.

There seems to be another factor which made the thirteenth century different from earlier periods of crisis. This was malaria,[5] which, it must be emphasized, was not the cause of the abandonment of the heartland of ancient Sri Lanka. Very little is known about when it took root in the island, but it would appear to have spread to Sri Lanka well before the sixteenth century. The anopheles mosquito would have found ideal breeding places in the abandoned tanks and channels, and, in fact, malaria has often, in other parts of Asia, followed the destruction or abandonment of irrigation works. Within a century of its spread to this island it would have added a further and insuperable obstacle to the reoccupation of the once productive areas of the dry zone; indeed it defeated all attempts at large-scale resettlement of the dry zone till the late 1930s. Thus malaria, coming in on the heels of the destructive invasions of the mid-thirteenth century and thriving on disused irrigation works, played a critically important part in multiplying obstacles to resettlement.

The drift of Sinhalese power to the south-west was no doubt actuated by a search for security, but there was the attraction of economic potential as well. The coastal regions of the western and northern seaboard had from the early years of the Anuradhapura kingdom supported scattered but economically viable trade settlements. Through the centuries these settlements not only survived but also expanded with the increase in the volume of trade transacted between Sri Lanka and the states of the Indian Ocean. They would have attracted people— especially traders—from the main centres of population. With increasing political instability at the centre of Sinhalese power, these settlements would have had a more compelling attraction. Thus the shift of Sinhalese population to the south-west was not a movement to some unknown and unexplored regions of the island but to familiar localities which offered not merely security but also potential for a more than modest livelihood.

In the second half of the fourteenth century, the fortunes of the Sinhalese reached their nadir. True, the writ of the Gampola kings appears to have run in Rohana as well as on the western seaboard, but for a short period in the fourteenth century, Jaffna under the Āryacakravartis was the most powerful kingdom on the island. As we shall see in the next chapter, when Sinhalese power on the island declined, the Tamils moved southwards to exact tribute from the south-west and central region—their tax collectors were at work on parts of the Gampola kingdom. The Tamil kingdom maintained a steady and relentless pressure on the Sinhalese, especially in the border territories which now extended as far south as the Four Kōralēs, close to Gampola itself but not easy of access because of its rugged hills and forests.

By the middle of the fourteenth century, the Jaffna kingdom had effective control over the north-west coast up to Puttalam. After an invasion in 1353, part of the Four Kōralēs came under Tamil rule and thereafter, over the next two decades, they probed into the Mātale district and naval forces were despatched to the west coast as far south as Panadura. They seemed poised for the establishment of Tamil supremacy over Sri Lanka and were foiled in this by the defeat inflicted by the forces of the Gampola kings in 1380. They were also embroiled with the powerful Vijayanagar empire in a grim struggle for survival against the latter's expansionist ambitions across the Palk

Straits. Indeed, the impact of south India on the Tamil kingdom of the north was not restricted to culture and religion but deeply affected its political evolution as well, for it was drawn irresistibly into the orbit of the dominant south Indian state of the day.

As the next chapter will show, the Gampola kingdom[6] presented an air of decrepitude, especially in its political structure in contrast to the vigour and dynamism of its northern adversary. There was, for instance, a curious system of sub-kings or co-rulers: when Bhuvanekabāhu IV (1341–51) was king at Gampola, his brother Parākramabāhu V (1344–59) ruled at Dadigama less than 30 miles away as the crow flies; and in 1359, Parākramabāhu V and Vikramabāhu III (1357–74) were co-rulers. This division of authority could scarcely have improved prospects of successfully protecting the border districts of the kingdom from incursions from the north, even if the diffusion of power was a calculated response to the latter. But nothing illustrated more vividly the parlous position to which the Gampola kings had been reduced than the rise in importance of influential chief ministers, who became in time more powerful than the kings they served. The first of these was Senādhilaṅkāra in the time of Bhuvanekabāhu IV. The exploits of Senādhilaṅkāra link the fortunes of the Gampola kings in the Kandyan Hills with those of their northern adversary. They also laid the foundations of the kingdom of Kotte, soon to be the principal Sinhalese kingdom.

His career paved the way for the later rise of the Alagakkōnāra family to eminence. The Alagakkōnāras were traders who had migrated to the island from Vanchipura in south India—one of several such families to migrate—in the wake of the Muslim invasions.[7] The first phase in their 'Sinhalization' would appear to have been through their conversion to Buddhism. By the middle of the fourteenth century, this family wielded considerable political power and had kinship ties with the Gampola kings when Alakeśvara, a descendant of Niśśaṅka Alagakkōnāra, married a sister of Vikramabāhu III. Their status and political influence reached its peak when Alakeśvara organized the successful resistance against the threat from the north in the reign of Bhuvanekabāhu V (1371–1408). Undeterred by the panic-stricken flight of their king, the Sinhalese army, rallied by Alakeśvara, attacked and dispersed the Tamil forces. As a result, he became the de facto ruler of the kingdom although Bhuvanekabāhu V remained on the throne.

The Jaffna kingdom's expansion southwards had been checked, but the Sinhalese had no reason to believe that this had been halted for good. On the contrary, they assumed that pressure from the north would persist. The capital of the Sinhalese kingdom was moved once more, this time from the mountains to the west coast near Colombo, where Niśśanka Alagakkōnāra had built the fort of Jayavardhanapura (Kotte). Once again the shift of the capital was evidence of the continuing weakness of the Sinhalese kingdom, and once more the reasons for the move were essentially defensive: to protect the west coast with its rich cinnamon resources, which the Tamil kingdom was so anxious to gain control of.

For the Sinhalese, the sudden abatement of the pressure from the north, which coincided with the shift of the capital to the western littoral, was an unexpected bonus. But their respite was brief and this time the danger came from a distant land across the seas—China under the Ming emperors.

In the early fifteenth century, seven powerful naval expeditions, great fleets of junks, under the command of Zheng He visited the ports of the Indian Ocean in both the eastern and western seas demanding tribute and obedience to the Chinese emperor.[8] On Zheng He's first visit to the island in 1405, the Sinhalese king was Vīra Alakeśvara who had succeeded Bhuvanekabāhu V—the last ruler of his line. Zheng He's objective was to take back the *daladā*, the tooth relic. Chinese interest in the daladā was nothing new. In 1284, the great Kublai Khan himself had despatched a mission to the island for the same purpose;[9] it had returned to China with its main aim unaccomplished but, seemingly and fortunately for Sri Lanka, without a sense of grievance. Zheng He was no more successful in his quest than the representative of Kublai Khan but unlike the latter he went back aggrieved by the treatment he had received and five years later he led another expedition which seized the Sinhalese king, Vīra Alakeśvara, his queen and some of the notables of the kingdom and took them as prisoners to China. Quite apart from their political and religious objectives, Zheng He's expeditions had commercial ones as well: they reflected the importance attached by the Chinese to Sri Lanka as a centre of inter-Asian and international trade.

Vīra Alakeśvara was eventually released and returned to the island but there was never any serious hope of his recovering the throne after the humiliation of a foreign captivity. (No Sri Lankan ruler of the past, save Mihindu V, had suffered a similar fate but in his case it was the consequence of a staggering military defeat at the hands of a powerful invading army.) In 1414, the captives returned to the island—among them the Chinese emperor's nominee to the Sinhalese throne—but they came back to a more settled and tranquil political atmosphere than anyone had the right to expect after Zheng He's telling demonstration of Chinese strength and Sinhalese weakness.

In 1411, Parākramabāhu VI began what was to be a very long reign of fifty-five years. In its first phase, his capital was at Rayigama, close to Kotte but somewhat towards the interior. By 1415, he established himself at Kotte—having in the meantime speedily eliminated the protégé of the Chinese emperor—and founded what came to be called the Kotte kingdom.[10] The fifty-five years of his reign were rich in incident and achievement. We are concerned here with its political aspects. His greatest achievement was to check what seemed to be a well-nigh irreversible trend—the break-up of the Sri Lankan polity. He was the first Sinhalese king since the days of Parākramabāhu I and Niśśaṅka Malla to bring the whole island under his rule, and the last ever to do so. But in retrospect, the half-century of his rule was no more than a sudden eruption of flame from a dying fire, for Parākramabāhu VI, the founder of the Kotte dynasty, was also its sole great figure. Within forty years of his death, the Kotte kingdom, weakened by internal disputes, faced the formidable challenge of the Portuguese in the first phase of Sri Lanka's long encounter with Western colonialism, an encounter that lasted till the middle of the twentieth century.

In the early years of his reign, Parākramabāhu VI was confronted with a dual threat from the traditional adversaries of the Sinhalese, the Jaffna kingdom in the north and from south India in the form of the expanding Vijayanagar empire. The Vijayanagar thrust was successfully repulsed in about the twentieth year of his reign and from that he moved on to an invasion of Jaffna which was by this time a Vijayanagar satellite. The Vanni principalities, a buffer zone between the kingdom of Jaffna and Kotte, the northern part of the old Rājarata, were first subdued in order to prevent any possibility of an attack from the rear once his forces had reached the Jaffna kingdom. Tradition has it that the Sinhalese population in the Jaffna kingdom rose in revolt against their Tamil rulers before Parākramabāhu VI's invasion. Nevertheless, invasion of the northern kingdom was a daunting proposition and the first such was repulsed. The second achieved its objective: it succeeded in putting to flight the Jaffna king, who sought refuge in south India and did not return for two whole decades. By the middle of the fifteenth century, the Jaffna kingdom was under Sinhalese rule. Sapumal Kumāraya, the adopted son of Parākramabāhu VI, was installed on the throne of Jaffna.

The mountainous core of the island—the nucleus of the Gampola kingdom—was virtually under the control of Parākramabāhu VI. But in the last years of his reign he faced an insurrection there led by Jōtiya Sitāna. Although this insurrection was comprehensively crushed—a prince of the Gampola royal house was appointed in place of Jōtiya Sitāna to administer the area on behalf of the Kotte king—it is nevertheless significant for being the first expression of a Kandyan claim to autonomous status and distinct identity.

The administrative arrangements made for the central region—the Udarata—after the rebellion there brings us to the crucial flaw in Parākramabāhu VI's system of government. There was no innovation in or expansion of the machinery of government to consolidate the re-establishment of an island polity. What Parākramabāhu VI did was to place subjugated regions under their former rulers who then acted as vassals of Kotte, or installed new rulers with wide powers falling just short of semi-independent status. The fact is that the Kotte kingdom under Parākramabāhu VI was an inherently brittle structure in which centrifugal forces were kept in check by the personal influence and authority of a gifted ruler.

As happened so often in Sri Lanka's history, a disputed succession—following Parākramabāhu VI's death—destroyed the life's work of an extraordinarily resourceful ruler. His nominee to the throne—his grandson—succeeded him at Kotte, but could hardly hold his own against the more dynamic Sapumal Kumāraya who moved in to do battle for the throne. The struggle was short and decisive. Parākramabāhu VI's grandson was killed and Sapumal Kumāraya took over at Kotte with the title of Bhuvanekabāhu VI. But this struggle for the throne led inevitably to a relaxation, if not the disappearance, of control over the outer provinces of the kingdom.

The first to benefit from this were the northerners. Jaffna successfully re-established itself as an independent kingdom under Pararājasēkaram (1479–1519). The Tamil kingdom developed a more distinct and confident Hindu culture that drew its inspiration from south India. More ominous, however, was a determined bid by the Udarata—the Kandyan region— to stake a claim to an independent political role of its own. As we shall see, the foundation of the Kandyan kingdom may be traced back to the last quarter of the fifteenth century. The absorption of the Kandyan region into the Kotte kingdom under the energetic Parākramabāhu VI did not extinguish separatist tendencies among the Kandyans; on the contrary it may have helped to transform these into a proto-nationalism. With his death and the rapid decline of the power of Kotte in the late fifteenth and early sixteenth centuries, in the wake of disputed successions and prolonged political instability, the Kandyans were afforded the opportunity to assert their independence from the control of the ruler at Kotte.

When Bhuvanekabāhu VI died in 1477, the authority of Kotte was restricted to the south-west and a small area of the north-west. The Jaffna kingdom was independent and Kotte was in no position to re-establish its control over the Udarata. Parākramabāhu VI's legacy had been spent within a decade of his death.

ASPECTS OF ECONOMIC AND SOCIAL CHANGE

Political instability, the bane of Sri Lanka's history throughout this period, had an inevitably debilitating effect on the economy. In the Sinhalese kingdom of the south-west and the central mountainous core of the island, rain-fed agriculture—the cultivation mainly of rice—was the norm and this subsistence agriculture was the bedrock of the economy. The agricultural surplus available to the state would seem to have been quite modest in comparison with that of the more expansive epochs of the hydraulic civilizations of the past. This and the instability and insecurity so characteristic of these centuries could hardly have been conducive to the irrigation works in the parts of the dry zone still under the control of the Sinhalese kingdom being maintained and kept in repair. The meagre evidence[11] available to us would appear to indicate that there was at this time a distinct decline in agricultural production.

Economic activity did, however, develop on new lines. In general, trade rose higher in the scale of the ruler's priorities than ever before. For instance, with the increased demand for spices in Europe after the Crusades, the island's cinnamon, which grew luxuriantly in the forests of the south-west littoral, became an important item in its export trade. By far the larger share of the profits of the cinnamon trade was absorbed by the state, which as a result became less dependent on revenue from grain than in the past. One needs to guard against the danger of exaggerating the importance of cinnamon as a source of revenue. Before the sixteenth century, and indeed even at the end of that century, the yield from this source was well below that from other items of export such as elephants and areca nut, while the export trade as a whole, despite its increasing importance, was much less productive than the traditional sources of revenue such as land taxes and revenue from grain.[12]

The land tenure system of this period was, in fact, another point of continuity with the past. The description of its features contained in previous chapters is by and large valid for this period as well, with one notable and obvious difference: water rates ceased to be a source of revenue.

The island's foreign trade had three significant features. Sri Lanka was still a lucrative and strategically important location in the east–west trade of this period. Second, there were the island's own direct commercial links with Malacca, which controlled much of the south-east Asian and China trade. (Zheng He's incursions into the Indian Ocean appear to have been motivated, in part at least, by a desire for some leverage in this Asian maritime trade and his expeditions to Sri Lanka had, as we have seen, commercial objectives quite apart from religious and political considerations.) There was next the island's Indian trade, its commerce with Calicut, the Coromandel Coast, Gujarat—itself a major trade centre—and Bengal. Sri Lankan merchants were engaged in trade along the coasts of India from Cambay to Bengal.

This external trade was conducted largely through the ports of the west coast: Kalpitiya, Puttalam, Salavata (Chilaw), Kammala, Negombo, Colombo, Kalutara, Beruvala and Galle. The main items of export were areca nut, elephants, gems and cinnamon, and the principal imports were cloth and dry fish.

The east–west trade of the period was dominated by the Arabs and their international trade links gave the Arab settlers resident in Sri Lanka an advantage over their potential competitors, including of course, the island's indigenous traders in Sri Lanka's external trade. Their most formidable rivals for this latter were the Chetties, the bankers of south India. The Arab traders were also, on occasion, advisers to Sinhalese rulers on foreign trade; in 1283, for instance, Bhuvanekabāhu I's mission to the Egyptian court was planned and carried through by Arabs living in Sri Lanka.

One significant consequence of the growing importance of trade was a slow but perceptible increase in the use of money in the economy. By the end of the fifteenth century, the economy's monetization was already under way.[13] No doubt the process was facilitated by the profits which came to the indigenous traders. Equally, if not more important, was the cash which the people at large earned by the sale of areca nut, the most important item in terms of value in Sri Lanka's foreign trade.

As foreign trade grew in importance, Arabs appear to have settled in larger numbers in the coastal areas and the ports whence they gradually moved into the interior in pursuit of their trading interests. They maintained their identity largely through their religion and the customs associated with it,[14] but as a result of intermarriage between them and the local population, they became Indo-Arab in 'ethnic' character rather than purely Arab.

If this expansion in the Moorish population added one more element to Sri Lanka's plural society, the accommodation of groups of recent immigrants from south India and their absorption into the caste structure of the littoral saw the emergence of three new Sinhalese caste groups—the *Salāgama*, the *Durāva* and the *Karāva*. They came to the island, in this period, in successive waves of migration which continued well beyond it into the eighteenth century. The disparity in the extent to which segments of each of these castes have been assimilated within the social system would suggest that the length of their contact with Sinhalese society has varied. The process of assimilation was facilitated by their adoption of the culture of the region to which they had migrated.

Their position in the caste hierarchy has varied with the times. Similarly, there were also notable changes in occupational roles, though all three of them had the common characteristic of very tenuous links, if any, with traditional agriculture. Thus in the *Jeyavansa*, a Sinhalese poem believed to have been written in the fifteenth century, the Salāgamas are referred to as weavers, but with the passage of time their caste occupation came to be that of peeling cinnamon and preparing it for the market. How and when this transformation came about we do not know, but the easy accommodation of these migrant groups and their indigenization underlines the resilience and remarkable flexibility of the caste structure of the Sinhalese areas of the littoral region.

RELIGION AND CULTURE[15]

A study of Buddhism during this period reveals the operation of two seemingly contradictory trends. There was, first of all, a very noticeable deterioration in the morale and discipline of the sangha, and Buddhism itself confronted surprisingly powerful pressure from Hinduism. The efforts of a number of kings and ministers, including the Dambadeniya kings Vijayabāhu III (1232–36) and Parākramabāhu II, the ministers

Senādhilankāra and Alakeśvara under the Gampola kings and Parākramabāhu VI of Kotte, the greatest of the rulers of this period, failed to stem the rot. Indeed, Senādhilankāra took the drastic step of purging the sangha of worldly and corrupt bhikkhus, and during the period of the Gampola kings the post of *sangharāja*, chief of the bhikkhus or the primate of the Buddhist order, was created as a means of restoring harmony within the sangha and instilling a sense of dedication among the bhikkhus. That none of these measures was really effective was due mainly to the political instability and turmoil of these centuries.

Significantly too, doctrinal disputes had little or nothing to do with the tensions among the bhikkhus of this period. The struggles between orthodoxy and the Mahayanists had long since been resolved by the absorption within the 'official' form of Buddhism of some of the doctrines, rituals and deities of heterodoxy. The cult of the tooth relic, for instance, retained the importance it had acquired in the Polonnaruva period. Indeed the possession of the tooth relic was regarded as essential to the legitimate exercise of sovereignty over the island. Special shrines were built to house it and customs evolved to regulate the ritual and public celebrations in its honour. Every year the tooth relic was taken out and carried in procession round the capital city and it was exhibited to the people on auspicious days.

Along with the veneration of Mahayanist deities, the worship of Vedic and post-Vedic Hindu deities was firmly established as part of the religious practice of Sri Lanka Buddhism. Thus the shrine of Upuluvan (Varuna) at Devinuvara, originally built in the seventh century AD, was restored by Parākramabāhu II, who also celebrated the annual Äsala festival of that god. A new centre of the cult of Upuluvan, which became well-known in later centuries, was established at Alutnuvara in the Four Kōralēs by Parākramabāhu IV (1302–26). By the fifteenth century, Upuluvan had been elevated to the status of the national god of the Sinhalese. There were at the same time three other major deities—Saman, the God of Adam's Peak; Vibhīṣaṇa, and Skanda. The shrine at Kataragama, dedicated to Skanda, had by the end of this period become one of the major centres of religious worship on the island. Its fame had spread beyond the shores of the island, as far away as Thailand. The inscriptions of the fourteenth century refer to these four gods—Upuluvan, Saman, Vibhīṣaṇa and Skanda —as the guardians of the island and their images, along with those of some other minor deities, were installed at Lankatilaka and Gadalādeniya as attendants of the Buddha. The Pattini cult, an important part of the religion of the Sinhalese up to recent times, is referred to for the first time in the reign of Parākramabāhu VI.

This Hindu influence in Sri Lanka was nurtured by groups of Brahmans, whose numbers increased during these centuries. They enjoyed the patronage of the rulers (they enjoyed special favour with Parākramabāhu VI) and the support of the people. In contrast, the sangha's influence with the kings and nobility of Kotte declined steadily after the death of Parākramabāhu VI and the upper crust of Sinhalese society was fast becoming Hindu in outlook. Hindu shrines proliferated in the Kotte kingdom. The shrine of Munnesaram near Salavata (Chilaw) received the support of Parākramabāhu VI. There were also the famous Hindu shrines in the areas under Tamil control—the Kandaswamy Kovil at Nallur, Jaffna, and the one at Trincomalee.

For Buddhism, then, this was a period of trouble. As the 'official' religion it shared in the vicissitudes of the state, with recurrent episodes of accelerated deterioration coinciding more or less with periods of political instability and intermittent revivals when strong rulers imposed their authority on the country. The most notable examples of the latter were Parākramabāhu II and ParākramabāhuVI. During the small patches of stability against a large canvas of political decline, unstable conditions and a general loss of vitality, dynamic rulers could infuse the official religion with renewed vigour. But the limits of this renewal must be emphasized: it was a series of intermittent flashes rather than a sustained or prolonged effort; and the official religion had long since ceased to be purely Theravada.

Despite all this, however—and this is the second trend—Sri Lanka enjoyed enormous prestige abroad as the home of Theravada Buddhism. Buddhism had disappeared in India, its original home, and its holy places there were no longer accessible to devotees on account of the Muslim invasions. Sri

Lanka, thus, came to be regarded by the Buddhists of Myanmar, Thailand and Cambodia as a second—one might even say, surrogate—holy land of Buddhism because of the relics of the Buddha preserved at the island's major centres of Buddhist worship.

Of the art and architecture of this period very little has remained. There are the ruins at Yapahuva, with fortifications surpassed only by those of Sigiri in their refinement and power. The most impressive of the remains of this massive rock fortress is a porch leading to a building on a terrace at the foot of the rock on the eastern side (which is believed to have been the palace) and the stairway giving access to the porch. In its design this stairway has much in common with those of the Khmer pyramids in Cambodia. There is evidence also of south Indian—Dravidian—influence.

The two most notable monuments of this period are the temples of Lankatilaka and Gadaladeniya, both completed around 1344 in the time of Bhuvanekabāhu IV of the Gampola dynasty. The former is a natural development from the Polonnaruva architecture. Gadaladeniya, not far from Lankatilaka is in the Dravidian style of south India, but with a stupa in place of a śikhara. Apart from its base and door frames, Lankatilaka is entirely a brick construction. At Gadaladeniya the inner shrine is built almost entirely of stone, while brick is used only for the śikhara. Both shrines, each in its own way, embody the syncretistic nature of the official religion of the day. Nowhere else is the intrusion of Hindu practices, with their tolerant accommodation within the 'official' version of Buddhism, more acutely demonstrated than in these shrines.

If the fragmentation of the Sri Lankan polity had a deleterious effect on religion and was not conducive to any remarkable achievement in art and architecture, it scarcely affected development in literature. Indeed, Sri Lanka in these centuries provides one more example of that paradoxical situation, seen so often in history, of literature thriving amidst conditions of political turmoil. Two themes are noteworthy, poetry flowered after some stolid, unimaginative work in prose literature; and second, and more significantly, religious prose gave way to secular poetry—the sandeśa kāvya.

The first phase in this literary achievement was in the reign of the Dambadeniya kings, Vijayabāhu III and Parākramabāhu II, but more especially under the latter who was a scholar in his own right. During his reign there was a resolute effort to foster Buddhism and promote learning. The king himself is regarded as the author of the *Kavsilumina*, an extensive poem based on the Kusa Jātaka story and conforming in large measure to the requirements of a *mahākāvya*. The *Pūjāvaliya* (written around 1266) is the earliest classical Sinhalese prose work whose date of composition can be definitely fixed. Belonging to the same period but probably earlier than the *Pūjāvaliya* was the *Saddarma Ratnāvaliya*, a compendium of Buddhist stories based mainly on the Pali *Dhammapadatthakathā*; the author retells the stories of the Dhammapada commentary in the language and idiom of the people. In doing so he captures the imagination of his readers and listeners as much by a delightful lucidity of style and charming humour as by the moral tone of the stories and their didactic purpose.

The reign of Parākramabāhu IV at Kurunegala was marked by the appearance of literary works of a historical and legendary character, based on popular objects of veneration such as the tooth relic and the sacred bo-tree. The *Daladā Sirita*, the story of the sacred tooth relic, was composed at the request of Parākramabāhu IV. The translation of the Jātakas in the form of the *Pansiya-panas-jātaka pota*, is by far the most powerful and pervasive single influence in the literature of this period and probably the greatest single literary achievement of the century. The thread woven through all the stories in this collection is the working of the karmic law, how the bodhisattva perfected himself in a series of births. These stories have remained an endless source of moral edification and pleasant diversion to successive generations of the Sinhalese people.

In the Gampola kingdom a new literary genre, marking a departure from traditional poetry, came into its own: this was the *sandeśa kāvya*,[16] the origins of which are to be found in Kālidāsa's celebrated *Meghadūta* (the Cloud Messenger) in northern India. It gained popularity in south India around the fourteenth century and there it developed its own special characteristics. The Sinhalese *sandeśas* were composed about the same time, among the earliest of these being the *Tisara* and *Mayura sandeśas*. The sandeśa poems reached their maturity in the Kotte kingdom in the cultural efflorescence of the reign of Parākramabāhu VI. Sri Rāhula Mahā Sthavira, the most distinguished bhikkhu in the kingdom, and the foremost scholar of his day, was the author of the *Paravi* and *Sälalihini sandeśas*, the latter a work of greater elegance and refinement than the former. The *Girā* and *Hamsa sandeśas* (authorship unknown) also belong to the Kotte period. The sandeśa poems were manifestly secular in spirit and tone, in contrast to the conspicuous religiosity of earlier literary works and, as a result, they are a useful source of information on the social and political conditions of the country.

The *Kāvyaśekhara,* a full-fledged mahākāvya and a work of considerable distinction, also belonged to the Kotte period, but the Crowning achievement in its poetry was the *Guttila dā kava*—traditionally attributed to Vättāvē thera—the story of the Guttila Jātaka. Although it contains some features of the traditional ornate poem, it is its mellifluous simplicity that has made it a thing of enduring joy.

In striking contrast to poetry, prose works as a whole were both undistinguished and unimaginative. Even the *Saddharma Ratnākaraya,* which represents the last substantial work in the *Pūjāvaliya* tradition, showed a decline in literary skill.

The Kotte period, especially the reign of Parākramabāhu VI was the high-water mark of achievement in Sinhala literature. Thereafter, for several centuries—indeed till the eighteenth century—there was nothing of any significance.

The Periphery Stakes a Claim

INTRODUCTION

One of the consequences of the disintegration and disorder in the principal Sinhalese kingdom following the destructive invasion of Māgha of Kalinga was the emergence of two kingdoms in the periphery, each making a bid for an independent existence, each challenging the authority of the principal kingdom and its successors. These were the Tamil kingdom in the north of the island and the Kandyan kingdom in the central hills. The latter had a much longer and very distinguished history in the seventeenth century and after, while the former established itself in the thirteenth century, prospered in the early part of the fourteenth century and maintained its independent existence till it was conquered by the principal Sinhalese kingdom, Kotte, under its most dynamic ruler, Parākramabāhu VI. After a decade or so from his death, it recovered its independence and survived till 1620 when the Portuguese conquered it and its independence was extinguished for good.

These two kingdoms of the periphery were not without some influence on each other, especially that of the kingdom in Jaffna on what later became the Kandyan kingdom. By the late fourteenth century, however, the kingdom in Jaffna was too weak for anything more than a single-minded concentration on its survival. Few Sri Lankan kingdoms have seen such remarkable changes in status and size during their existence as the short-lived kingdom of Jaffna.

To the historian, the two kingdoms had little in common, apart from being part of the periphery seeking and, in the case of the kingdom in Jaffna, actually securing an independent existence of its own. What they had in common was a paucity of reliable historical evidence, literary or archaeological, on the early phases of their histories. There is, in fact, much more evidence on the early years of the Kandyan kingdom, extracted by scholars from the meagre literary, inscriptional and archaeological source material available than on the kingdom in Jaffna. The principal scholar on the early history of the Kandyan kingdom has been Professor T.B.H. Abeyasinghe.[1] On the kingdom in Jaffna we have more scholars but relatively less evidence. The scholars are Professors Karthigesu Indrapala[2] and Sirima Kiribamune,[3] both of whom, and more particularly the former, have thrown considerable light on the position of Tamils in ancient Sri Lanka. On the later years of the kingdom in Jaffna we have a magisterial survey[4] by the archaeologist and historian Senarat Paranavitana published in 1961 which is still to be superseded by subsequent research.

THE EARLY YEARS OF THE KINGDOM IN JAFFNA

This section of the present chapter begins with an extract from the introduction to the unpublished doctoral dissertation 'Dravidian Settlement in Ceylon and the Beginning of the Kingdom of Jaffna' by Dr Karthigesu Indrapala:

> Until about the thirteenth century A.D., the history of [Sri Lanka] was the history of the Sinhalese people. From about the middle of the thirteenth century, it has been the history of the Sinhalese and Tamil people in the island. From that time for over three centuries, the majority of Tamils were concentrated in a kingdom of their own in the northern part of the island. In 1620, the last of the Tamil rulers was executed by the Portuguese conquerors who brought the Tamil areas under their rule.[5]

This extract conveys very effectively some of the essential features of the history of the island.

In another work first presented in 1965 but published in 2000, Dr Indrapala pointed out that from the meagre evidence available 'commercial interests, political adventure and the prospect of military employment had led Tamils to come to Sri Lanka in the early centuries of the island's history. The question 'is whether this led to the rise of permanent and widespread Tamil settlements in the island'.[6] His own answer to this question begins with the comment that

> Considering the numbers of Tamil invasions and the number of occasions when Tamil mercenaries were enlisted, it appears that more Tamils came to Sri Lanka as invaders and hired soldiers than as traders. Since most of the invasions succeeded in ousting the Sinhalese rulers and in paving the way for rule by Tamils for short periods, the invading troops must have remained in the island on such occasions till the Sinhalese princes regained the throne. Whether these armies stayed behind after they were defeated is something regarding which there is no evidence.[7]

A decisive change came in the seventh century. Prior to that there were only three instances, each separated from the others by about two centuries, recorded in the Pali chronicles, of mercenaries from the Indian mainland being brought to Sri Lanka. In the seventh century, mercenaries from the Indian mainland were brought to the island on several occasions and in large numbers. The *Cūlavaṁsa* records eight instances of mercenaries being brought to the island at that time. The frequency with which mercenaries entered the island would appear to suggest that not all of them went back and that they may have had small settlements in and around Anuradhapura and possibly other strategic places. Nevertheless, it is not till the tenth century that there is any significant literary or epigraphic evidence regarding any Tamil settlements.[8]

As against this, there is a body of archaeological evidence of probable Tamil settlement much earlier than the tenth century AD—a group of megalithic burials at Pomparippu in the north-western littoral of Sri Lanka, dated between the second century BC and second century AD. The Pomparippu region could be taken as one of the earliest settlement areas of the Tamils in Sri Lanka. There is, in addition, a similar but smaller settlement in Kathirvelu (on the east coast).

The location at the Pomparippu site, near the mouth of the Kala Oya and close to the pearl banks of the north-western coast, suggests that it is probable that it originated as a

settlement of pearl-divers, fisherman and other peaceful
settlers. Whether the pioneer Tamil settlers of this region actually
survived as a distinct group till later times cannot be determined
with any certainty. In later times—we do not know when this
actually happened—Pomparippu became known as a Tamil
area. The proximity to, as well as the continuous relations with,
the Tamil country across the seas may have helped the settlers
to maintain their ethnic identity or, on the other hand, they
may have assimilated with or been assimilated by the larger
Sinhalese population, but these are all matters of speculation.[9]

After a careful survey of the sparse evidence available,
Indrapala reaches the conclusion that:

> Looking back on the whole body of evidence that is available...we
> have to conclude that there was no widespread Tamil settlement
> before the tenth century. The settlements at Pomparippu and
> the possible settlement at Kathirvelu (on the east coast) have
> to be treated as isolated earlier settlements.[10]

In his article Indrapala returns to a theme referred to earlier
in this present chapter, the paucity of historical sources for a
study of the early history of the Tamils, and more importantly,
the dubiousness of those that exist. Describing these sources
as 'wholly unreliable' he explains that:

> On the Tamil side the chronicles that are extant are those
> written nearly three centuries after the foundation of the Tamil
> kingdom in the island in the thirteenth century.

> The sections of these works dealing with the period prior to the
> thirteenth century, i.e., the period during which the earliest Tamil
> settlements were established—are full of legendary material
> and are wholly unreliable. The Tamil works of South India have
> no notable allusions to the activities of the Tamils in Ceylon.

The second significant point he makes, relating to the earliest
Tamil settlements in Sri Lanka, has been discussed earlier in
this chapter. His conclusion in regard to these is unambiguous.

> ...on the slender evidence at our disposal it would be
> rather far fetched to claim that there were permanent or

widespread settlements of Tamil trading communities in the first millennium AD.[11]

He reiterated this in his paper presented in 1965 when he stated: 'But evidence for extensive settlement bearing the signs of a date earlier than the tenth century is lacking'.

THE JAFFNA KINGDOM—ITS RISE AND FALL

On the basis of the evidence Dr Indrapala has set out in his work, one could say that it was

...only by about the tenth century that permanent settlement of the Tamils began and the Cōḷa conquest of the Anuradhapura kingdom in the late tenth century seems to have given an impetus to the migration of Tamils into the island.[12]

These settlements 'became fairly extensive early in the eleventh century.' The location of these Tamil settlements in this first phase were

...still outside the Jaffna district. Of the present day Tamil areas only the upper half of the Eastern Province and parts of the western coast had Tamil settlers in the eleventh and twelfth centuries. The main stage in the process of Tamil settlement which led to the transformation of the present Northern Province into an exclusively Tamil speaking area had not yet been reached in the twelfth century. That stage was reached with the conquest of Māgha and it is doubtful that the Tamil settlements of the period before the thirteenth century would have resulted in the division of the country into two linguistic regions.[13]

Dr Indrapala explains that the 'second and most important stage of the Tamil settlements are covered by the whole of the thirteenth century'[14] with the establishment of a Tamil kingdom in the northern part of the island. Even as regards this phase, Dr Indrapala believes that 'no genuine traditions of the Tamil settlement or invasions were preserved by the Tamils until they established a stable kingdom in the thirteenth century.'[15]

Far more important for our purposes is his assessment of the destructive political impact of the invasion of Māgha of Kalinga:

The invasion of Māgha [of Kaliṅga] with the help of Tamil and Kerala mercenaries was far more violent than the earlier invasions. Its chief importance lies in the fact that it resulted in the permanent dislodgement of Sinhalese power from north Ceylon, the confiscation of lands and properties belonging to the Sinhalese by the Tamil and Kerala mercenaries and the consequent migration of the official class and several of the common people to the south western regions. These factors more than any other helped the transformation of northern [Sri Lanka] into a Tamil region and directly led to the foundation of a Tamil kingdom there. In the second phase, with the foundation of an independent Tamil kingdom, a deliberate policy of settling Tamils in the Jaffna district and the Vanni regions was followed by the first rulers of the Tamil kingdom. This led to a migration of peaceful settlers from the Tamil country [in Southern India]. It was this peaceful migration that was largely responsible for the Tamil settlement of the Jaffna district. It was a deliberate and organised process....[16]

The first phase of the evolution of the Jaffna kingdom is associated with Māgha of Kalinga who moved to that region after his expulsion from Polonnaruva. His successors ruled the Jaffna region as a subordinate principality of the Pāṇḍyan kingdom. The Āryacakravarti dynasty which ruled till it was overthrown by the Portuguese, was of Pāṇḍyan descent.

Chapters 6 and 7 of this volume have shown that in the second half of the fourteenth century, the fortunes of the principal Sinhalese kingdom reached their nadir. As Sinhalese power in the island declined, the Tamils moved southward to exact tribute from the south-west and central regions and the Tamil kingdom kept up a steady and purposeful pressure on the Sinhalese especially on the border regions. For a brief period of about twenty-five years in the middle of the fourteenth century, the Jaffna kingdom's territorial claims stretched to the north-west coast of the island up to Puttalam. In the last quarter of the fourteenth century, its ambitions for greater influence on the island were thwarted primarily because of the successful resistance from the Sinhalese kingdom in the central hills, the Kandyan kingdom. Indeed the severe defeat inflicted on the

Jaffna kingdom in 1380 proved to be decisive in this regard. The Jaffna kingdom—or the kingdom of the Āryacakravarti rulers as it was called—was also embroiled with the powerful Vijayanagar empire in a struggle for survival against the latter's expansionist ambitions across the Palk Straits. The Tamil kingdom of Jaffna, whatever its strength within the island, was drawn irresistibly into the orbit of the dominant south Indian state of the day, and to the status of a satellite, whether of Pāṇḍya in the early years or of Vijayanagar in its later stages.

The previous chapter of this book would have shown how the Kotte kingdom, under Parākramabāhu VI, successfully resisted the establishment of Vijayanagar control in the north of the island and then proceeded to bring the Jaffna kingdom under its sway. His control lasted for over two decades, but on his death his political legacy was rapidly exhausted by his successors. Although the Jaffna kingdom recovered its independence in the last quarter of the fifteenth century, its survival owed much more to divisions within the main Sinhalese kingdom—the kingdom of Kotte—and the rise of the Kandyan kingdom than to any inherent strength of its own. Over the next two centuries the Kandyan kingdom inherited the mantle of Kotte and became in time the last surviving Sinhalese kingdom in the island's history.[17] It was an age of political instability with the boundaries of these several states constantly shifting, sometimes expanding and sometimes contracting, in response to the pressures of rivals. Nevertheless, it would be true to say that by the beginning of the sixteenth century the Jaffna kingdom was the smallest and weakest of them all.

The Jaffna kingdom survived, beleaguered and more vulnerable to force majeure than the others, till the early years of the seventeenth century when it succumbed to the Portuguese and was never to recover its independence again. At the time of its conquest by the Portuguese it controlled the Jaffna Peninsula and its periphery. It was thus reduced in size to what it had been prior to its rapid and brief expansion in the early and middle parts of the fourteenth century.[18]

Between the Jaffna kingdom and the Sinhalese kingdoms lay the Vanni chieftaincies which were collectively a buffer between the first and the second. Their emergence was the direct result of the breakdown of central authority with the collapse of the Polonnaruva kingdom in the thirteenth century. Dispossessed Sinhalese nobles, as well as south Indian military chiefs in Māgha's army, were able to establish control over parts of the Vanni in the dry zone. The Sinhalese chieftaincies of the Vanni lay on the northern borders of the Sinhalese kingdom, while their Tamil counterparts controlled the areas immediately bordering the northern kingdom and the remoter areas of the eastern littoral region outside the control of the two major kingdoms. In their own territories the Vanni chieftains[19] functioned very much like feudal lords, offering military protection, at a time of great political instability, to those who came under their authority, and they owed allegiance to one or other of two kingdoms, depending on the political situation which, during much of the late fourteenth and early fifteenth centuries, could often mean an accommodation with the Tamil kingdom or with the principal Sinhalese kingdom. Most of what is today the Eastern Province lay beyond the effective control of the Jaffna kingdom and was not part of it.

THE EARLY BEGINNINGS OF THE KANDYAN KINGDOM

The central mountainous region of Sri Lanka had never been a well-developed, highly populated area or a centre of civilization in the past. This region, known as the Malayarata, was important only as an occasional centre of resistance against foreign invasions and as a haven for insurrectionists and outlaws. The earliest phase in the emergence of a kingdom in this region was in the fourteenth century, with Gangasiripura or Gampola, on the river Mahaveli as the capital; in the fifteenth century the capital was shifted to Senkadagala Nuvara, modern Kandy. The Kandyan kingdom referred to by historians is this kingdom with Senkadagala as its capital. But as the Gampola kingdom too was situated in the hills of the Kandyan region, or the Udarata as it was called and as it was one of the Gampola kings who shifted his capital to Senkadagala, the Gampola phase of this process of development needs to be reviewed here.[20]

Previous chapters have shown how the capital of the Sinhalese kingdom was at Kurunāgala at the beginning of the fourteenth century. The reasons for the shift to Gampola are not really known, but there is some literary evidence to suggest that the king left Kurunāgala because of internal strife in the kingdom. This was also the period when the Āryacakravartis of the northern Tamil kingdom were attempting to expand their frontiers. Gampola, because of its natural barriers of forests and rivers, would have been selected to meet this challenge from the north.

Inscriptional and literary evidence show that the first king of Gampola was Bhuvanekabāhu IV who began his reign in 1341. His brother Parākramabāhu V ruled at Dedigama in the Four Kōralēs, three years after this date in a system of co-rulers, a feature of this period. There is evidence that Buvanekabāhu IV ruled up to at least 1353–54 and that Parākramabāhu V ruled till 1359. The next king of Gampola was Vikramabāhu III, referred to as Sirisangabo-Sri Vikramabāhu in inscriptions, who became king in 1356 and for at least three years he and Parākramabāhu V were co-rulers. Vikramabāhu reigned for at least eighteen years, that is, up to 1374–75.

In reviewing the main features of the political history of the Gampola phase of Sri Lanka's history, the reigns of these three kings, that is, the period from 1341–42 to 1374–75, need to be considered together. During this period the power of the Gampola kings spread to the southern parts of the island. The connection between the Rājarata and Rohana had been broken as a result of the numerous foreign invasions which took place towards the end of the Polonnaruva period. The attention of the Dambadeniya kings was directed only towards the Māyārata and the Rājarata. All their schemes were based on the ancient centres of civilization in the northern plain and Rohana was not an important part in these schemes. But this state of things changed as the centre of the Sinhalese kingdom shifted to the Kandyan Hills.[21] The chief minister of Buvanekabāhu IV and Parākramabāhu V, Senādhilankara constructed religious edifices at Devinuvara and Väligama in the south of the country, evidence that the power of the Gampola ruler was recognized in that region. One could even assume that Rohana became part of the main Sinhalese kingdom, again, during this period.

As we have seen, one reason for the choice of Gampola as capital was the threat of the Āryacakravartis from the northern Tamil kingdom. Before long, there were incursions into the Udarata kingdom. Inscriptional evidence provides some interesting details on these incursions and their consequences. The Kotagama and Lahugala inscriptions refer to one Ariyan of Singai Nagar who invaded the Four Kōralēs and that rather than confront the invader, Parākramabāhu of Dedigama fled. An inscription of 1359, found near a bo-tree at Medawala in Harispattuva, reveals that a person named Marthandan Perumal appointed Brahmins to collect taxes from the villages of Sinduruvana, Balawita, Mātale, Dumbara and Sagama Thunrata which belonged to the Gampola kingdom, in the time of Vikramabāhu III. T. B. H. Abeyasinghe argues that Marthandan Perumal was none other than Ariyan of Singai Nagar of the Kotagama inscription and that as a result of his incursion the Four Kōralēs as well as some other sections of the Udarata kingdom came under the control of the northern kingdom. The *Rajāvaliya* too refers to the fact that the Āryacakravartis collected taxes from the Udarata kingdom and the southern lowlands.

We need to turn briefly to the system of co-rulers that developed as a notable feature of the politics of the of the Gampola kingdom. As we have seen when Bhuvanekabāhu was king of Gampola his brother Parākramabāhu V ruled from Dedigama. From 1356–57 to 1359, Parākramabāhu V and Vikramabāhu III were co-rulers. We do not know how this custom, which existed up to the middle of the sixteenth century, originated. Since this practice was prevalent in the Cōḷa empire, it could have come to Sri Lanka from there and may have been adopted here as conditions were favourable for it, one of the consequences of the inability of the Gampola rulers to withstand threats from the northern kingdom. In such a situation it was natural that regional rulers would seize the opportunity to stabilize and expand their powers. The prevailing decentralization was a reflection of the weakness of the Gampola kingdom.

It was not only a period of co-rulers, but also a period when 'chief' ministers became more powerful than kings. The first of such 'chief' ministers was Senādhilankara in the time of Bhuvanekabāhu IV. There is evidence that Senādhilankara was born in Singuruvana, close to Peradeniya. At his request Bhuvanekabāhu IV donated substantial extents of land to the new Lankatilaka Vihara, one of the principal architectural legacies of the Gampola kings to their eventual successors as rulers of the Kandyan kingdom. The *Nikaya Sangrahaya* mentions that Senādhilankara constructed a three storeyed image house at Devinuvara and another image house at Akbo Vehera and that he carried out a purification of the sangha. An image house that he constructed at Kanchipuram in south India is also mentioned in the same book. But the fact is that by 1360 his power had declined and that he was second among officers of state is evident from the Vigulavatta inscription. Perhaps it was Senādhilankara who paved the way for the rise of the Alagakkonāra family to power later on. After Vikramabāhu, the kingdom of Gampola passed on to Bhuvanekabāhu V who became king in 1371. Vikramabāhu was still alive and according to data available in inscriptions he ruled for at least thirty-five years, up to 1407. The most important political development during his period of rule was that the Sinhalese kingdom freed itself from the grasp of the king of Jaffna. During the invasion of 1359, Māyārata and a number of Kandyan districts had passed into the hands of the Jaffna ruler. It was Alakeśvara who assumed the leadership of the struggle against the Tamils by organizing action to free these areas from their domination. The first step in this campaign was the clearing of some marshlands near Colombo and the construction of the fortress of Sri Jayavardanapura. Next, when his forces were ready, he drove out the tax collectors of the king of Jaffna, attacked the Tamil encampments in the Sinhalese kingdom and drove out the soldiers from them. Faced with this threat to their campaign of expansion, the Āryacakravartis, who obtained foreign aid, sent an army overland up to Mātale and a naval force up to Panadura. As we have seen, rather than confronting this menacing challenge the Sinhalese king had fled leaving Alakeśvara to carry on the struggle against the Tamil forces. Despite the apparent cowardice of the king, the Sinhalese army

fought and defeated the Tamil forces which had camped at
Mātale. The Tamil army which had penetrated into the coastal
regions around Kotte was defeated by Alakeśvara and as a
result the regions controlled by the Sinhalese kings were freed
from pressure from the rulers of the kingdom of Jaffna.
Alakeśvara[22] was a descendant of Niśśaṅka Alagakkōnāra
who came to Sri Lanka from Kanchipuram in south India. Some
south Indian families moved to the island first as refugees
and then as settlers as a result of the Muslim invasions of
south India in the fourteenth century. They also embraced
Buddhism. The Alakeśvara family was probably one of these.
Although they originally were a trading family, they had
accumulated considerable political power. Naturally,
Alakeśvara's power reached a climax when the forces he led
against Jaffna were triumphant; he was the saviour of the
Sinhalese. No wonder then that he overshadowed the ruler
and the latter felt it necessary to accept this uncomfortable
relationship as a pragmatic accommodation to a harsh reality.

After the death of Bhuvanekabāhu V, power passed into
the hands of a number of kings who were not consecrated
and in their hands sovereign power was more informal than
real. In a parallel development, after Alakeśvara's death, there
was a struggle among the members of his family, to occupy
the position he had held. Kumara Alakeśvara seemed to be in
control from 1386–87, and during the next four or five years,
Vīra Alakeśvara. In 1391, Virabāhu Epa, a relative of
Bhuvanekabāhu defeated Vīra Alakeśvara and captured
power. He remained in power for five years during which
time he is believed to have driven out the Tamils once again.
In the meantime, Vīra Alakeśvara obtained foreign help and
recaptured power in 1399. His rule ended in 1411 when he
was captured by the Chinese Admiral Zheng He and taken
prisoner to China. Throughout this entire period,
Bhuvanekabāhu V seemed to have been the king in name only.

The eventual beneficiary of the successful campaign of
resistance against incursions from the kingdom of Jaffna was
not the kingdom of Kandy so much as the kingdom of Kotte
on the south-west coast. Towards the end of the reign of

Bhuvanekabāhu V, the Kotte kingdom with its capital Jayavardanapura Kotte was clearly the principal Sinhalese kingdom. The rise of the Kotte kingdom to this position of primacy has been referred to in previous chapters of this book. Under Parākramabāhu VI, Kotte had absorbed the kingdom of Jaffna. During the period when the Alakeśvaras were the unCrowned kings, the centre of Sri Lankan power shifted to the western coastal region and the Kandyan kingdom, which had up to then been a separate unit, lost this position.

During the reign of Parākramabāhu VI, the Kandyan kingdom became a subordinate unit of the Kotte kingdom, administered by an official appointed by him. The Medawala inscription shows that in 1458 this official was Jothiya Sitana or Divanawatte Lanka Adhikarin. According to the *Rājavaliya*, Jothiya Sitana neglected or refused to pay tribute to Kotte and did not send people to perform rājakariya, thus challenging the authority of the Kotte ruler. We know that Sēnāsaṃmata Vikramabāhu started ruling an independent Kandyan kingdom in or around 1469. It is possible that during the period of confusion following the death of Parākramabāhu VI, the Kandyans took advantage of the struggle for succession in Kotte and freed themselves from Kotte domination.

Nevertheless, from the time of Parākramabāhu VI, the rulers of Kotte regarded the Kandyan kingdom as a subordinate unit of the Kotte territories, administered by a ruler or prince appointed by the king of Kotte, on his behalf. The Kandyans were called upon to pay dues as tribute to Kotte and also to send people to perform rājakariya. Deviations from this form of political subservience were treated as unacceptable behaviour meriting either forceful admonition or political or military intervention. But there were also more artful, more subtle, means of ensuring control. Parākramabāhu VI, realizing that maintaining the loyalty of the Udarata was a delicate question, married a princess from the Udarata. Having suppressed the revolt initiated by Jothiya Sitana, he appointed a descendant of the Gampola kings as ruler of the Udarata. Bhuvanekabāhu VI sought to follow the policy of Parākramabāhu VI by marrying a princess of the Udarata. Through deft diplomacy and an occasional resort to force, the Kandyan kingdom was reduced in status to a semi independent principality. The Kandyans, for their part, never abandoned their aspirations to independence.

It was Sēnāsaṃmata Vikramabāhu who established the Udarata as an independent kingdom, after fifty years of domination by the Kotte kingdom. The capital of this kingdom was Senkadagala (modern Kandy). Why Senkadagala was preferred to Gampola as the capital is not known but a century before it became politically significant, it was important for religious reasons. According to tradition, Sēnāsaṃmata Vikramabāhu constructed the city of Senkadagala. Not content with freeing the Udarata from Kotte, he seems also to have been successful at annexing a border district belonging to the Kotte kingdom. According to the Alutnuwara inscription the chiefs as well as the people of the Four Kōralēs, agreed to support the Udarata kingdom against its enemies, as long as the Udarata kings did not harm their interests. That he was able to win the support of the Four Kōralēs, even though certain conditions had been insisted upon and accepted, could be seen as a victory for the king of the Udarata. The loyalty of the people of the Four Kōralēs was very important as any army from the lowlands had to pass through the Four Kōralēs before it came to the Udarata. Vikramabāhu's inscriptions show that it did not recognize the authority of Kotte and that the Udarata aspired to complete independence.

Historians feel that there is some special significance in the title 'sēnāsaṃmata' used by Vikramabāhu. The Udarata army, which was able to repel the Āryacakravarti forces, even without the leadership of the king and which played an important part in the declaration of independence in the time of Parākramabāhu VI, was probably instrumental in the rise of Vikramabāhu. He may have used the title 'sēnāsaṃmata', a hitherto unused title, because he was indebted to the army. It may also have been due to this feeling of indebtedness that, in the Gadalādeniya inscriptions, he made a promise that no harm would ever come to the army from the chiefs of the Udarata.

It is possible that the Udarata reverted to the status of a subordinate state paying tribute to the Kotte kingdom after his death. According to the *Rājavaliya*, when the Udarata ceased to pay tribute and assumed the status of an independent kingdom, during the reign of Dharma Parākramabāhu of Kotte (1489–1513), the army which was sent by the Kotte ruler succeeded in bringing back tribute of substantial value, as well as the king's daughter. The history of the period shows that the independence that the Udarata gained with the accession of Bhuvanekabāhu VI lasted less than fifty years and that whenever possible the Kotte kingdom attempted to regain its control over the Udarata.

As we shall see in later chapters of this book, the kings of the Udarata attempted to counteract threats to their kingdom in a number of ways. Whenever there was internal strife and a possibility of civil war in the Kotte kingdom, they took advantage of the situation and backed one side or another in an attempt to weaken that kingdom. It was this policy which Jayaweera Bandara of the Udarata followed when he helped Bhuvanekabāhu, Māyādunnē and Rayigam Bandara—the three sons of Vijayabāhu of Kotte—in the *Vijayabā-Kollaya*, the assassination of Vijayabāhu, and the partition of Kotte in 1521. Thereafter, with the sons of Vijayabāhu fighting each other for supremacy in the Kotte kingdom, the Kandyan king shrewdly shifted his support to the person or group least likely to harm the interests of his kingdom.

None of these attempts of subtle and not so very subtle interference in the troubled politics of Kotte saved the Udarata from the threat of reconquest by the rulers of Kotte later on. Plans for the recapture of the Udarata were prepared; attempts were made sometimes with success, but the success, as we shall see, was often limited, till the 1580s when the Kandyan kingdom lost its independence for a brief period. By the 1540s, the Kandyan kings had to face another threat—the Portuguese— and the successful resistance to the Portuguese and the Dutch in the seventeenth and eighteenth centuries forms a vitally important part of Sri Lanka's history in that period, a theme that is discussed in detail in later chapters of this book.

The Crisis of the Sixteenth Century

The area under the direct authority of the Kotte ruler varied from time to time, but at the beginning of the sixteenth century that kingdom was still the largest and most powerful of the island's political entities. Within its boundaries, which extended from the Malvatu Oya in the north to beyond the Valave River in the south and from the mountainous core of the island in the east to the sea on the west, lived the major portion of the island's population. It was there that trade and agriculture were most developed.

We need to reiterate, at this stage, a point which is often missed, namely that the principal source of royal income in Kotte was land revenue and not trade.[1] The Kotte kings were the biggest 'landowners' in the country, and the *gabadāgam*—the king's villages—were also quite often the richest of them all. The annual income from the gabadāgam alone exceeded three million *fanam*s at a time when the total income of the Kotte ruler was just over four million fanams. Indeed, customs duties yielded less than one-tenth of the annual income derived from the gabadāgam.

It was an economy in which barter was the principal mode of exchange. Yet there was, significantly, an annual payment of over 600,000 fanams to the king, in cash, from the gabadāgam, striking evidence that the monetization of the economy of the littoral region was not an eighteenth- or nineteenth-century phenomenon, but had its roots going back at least as far as the fifteenth century.

The main source of cash income for the peasant was areca nut. The areca palm grew in almost every village in the Kotte kingdom save in the dry zone. There was, moreover, a flourishing export trade in this commodity with supplies obtained from within Kotte as well as from the Udarata—the Kandyan kingdom—and with the profits channelled largely to the royal treasury. Coconut too was a cash crop of some significance, but neither as a medium of barter nor as a source of cash income was it by any means a rival to areca. Nor for that matter, at least not yet, did the cinnamon trade seriously compete with areca as a source of cash income. In terms of the revenue it yielded to the royal treasury, the cinnamon trade at this stage was still relatively insignificant compared with traditional agriculture. Cinnamon had two other limitations. Its benefits, such as they were, went largely to the Salāgamas, the cinnamon peelers as a caste group; the emergence of this new caste occupation was a gradual process stretching over a few centuries and in response to the increasing demand for cinnamon as an item of export trade. The business was strictly limited to the excess they delivered over their obligatory free supply in return for the lands they held. The surplus was sold in the open market. The profits derived from these sales could hardly be described as considerable, but they were apparently a sufficient inducement to produce a surplus. In any case, these profits gave the peelers a coveted cash income.

The traditional land tenure system of the Sinhalese described in earlier chapters—with the king as the main source of land grants and service tenure a key feature—was like some vast natural phenomenon seemingly impervious to change. In fact, while its structure remained without fundamental variation in form, it had a remarkable capacity to accommodate itself to social and economic pressures and stresses.

While the successors of Parākramabāhu VI continued to regard themselves as chakravartis or emperors of the whole island, in practice their effective power was limited to Kotte proper. Not that the Kotte ruler's authority was unchallenged within his own kingdom—there were occasional revolts such as the one that erupted in Pitigal and Alutkuru Kōralēs during the reign of Vīra Parākramabāhu VIII (1477–89). This long-drawn-out rebellion was brought under control by his successor Dharma Parākramabāhu IX.

The most persistent cause of fissiparous tendencies in Kotte was neither popular revolt nor foreign pressure but succession disputes. Brothers of the king ruled portions of the kingdom and each of them had the title raja or king, though all were subordinate to the emperor of Kotte. It is possible that this practice originated from a desire to keep princes who had some claim to the throne in good humour by giving them positions of responsibility. There was perhaps the belief as well that the presence of loyal relatives of the monarch in these outlying districts afforded some security. In the long run, however, it led inevitably to the weakening of Kotte's political structure, for those princes who could do so transformed the areas they administered into virtually autonomous principalities.

The most eventful of the succession disputes of this period was the Vijayabā-Kollaya, or the assassination of Vijayabāhu in 1521. Vijayabāhu VI married twice, and had three sons by his first queen and one by the second. When the king sought to secure the succession for his youngest son, the three elder princes obtained the assistance of the Udarata ruler, killed their father and shared the kingdom among themselves. With this partition of Kotte, the Sri Lankan polity appeared to have reached a state of fragmentation which seemed well beyond the capacity of any statesmanship to repair. Kotte's aspirations to overlordship over the rest of the island had never really been capable of fulfilment. With the death of Parākramabāhu VI those aspirations seemed no more than a cruel joke.

The role of the ruler of Udarata in the Vijayabā-Kollaya is significant. It was a cynical and shrewd move to aggravate the political instability in Kotte and thus ensure full scope for the separatist ambitions of the Udarata—the future Kandyan kingdom. By the 1470s, Sēnāsammata Vikramabāhu (1469–1511) seems to have made use of the disturbed political conditions in the lowlands to make himself the autonomous ruler of the highlands. He endeavoured to increase his own authority whenever Kotte was facing internal problems. Vikramabāhu's son and successor, Jayavīra (1511–52) readily aided the three princes of Kotte when they appealed for assistance against their father in 1521. The Kandyans saw in this turmoil the opportunity to assert their independence from the control of Kotte. Thus the decline of Kotte proved to be a necessary condition for the rise of the Kandyan kingdom.[2] The northern kingdom of Jaffna, with its capital at Nallur, had successfully reasserted its independence soon after the death of Parākramabāhu VI. The new ruler, Pararājaśekaram (1478–1519), content with control over the Jaffna Peninsula and the neighbouring coastlands, was not inclined to challenge the authority of Kotte south of Mātota. For their part, the kings of Kotte, who were preoccupied with their own problems, made no attempt to regain the north, although they continued to assert claims to overlordship over Jaffna. The Jaffna kingdom was by now small and weak, although it received the allegiance of a few chieftains who ruled the Vanni.

The Vanni principalities extended from the borders of the Jaffna kingdom and along the eastern coast to Yala and Panama in the south. The term vanniyār—a Vanni chief—appears at this time to have embraced a wide category of persons ranging from appointees of the kings of Kotte, who administered outlying districts, to autonomous rulers of large though somewhat undeveloped and sparsely populated areas. Apart from a few principalities near Jaffna, the vanniyārs in general seem to have paid tribute to the kingdom of Kotte.

THE PORTUGUESE INTRUSION: THE FIRST PHASE

It is against this background that one needs to review the entry of the Portuguese upon the Sri Lanka scene. The first contact of the Portuguese with the Kotte kingdom in 1505–06 was largely accidental, and it was not until twelve years later that the Portuguese sought to establish a fortified trading settlement. The building of the first fort near Colombo aroused popular hostility, fanned no doubt by the Moorish traders established on the island who largely controlled its external trade, and the fort had to be given up. But the Portuguese attempt to establish control over the island's cinnamon trade continued. Their trade in Sri Lanka was conducted from an unfortified factory at Colombo.

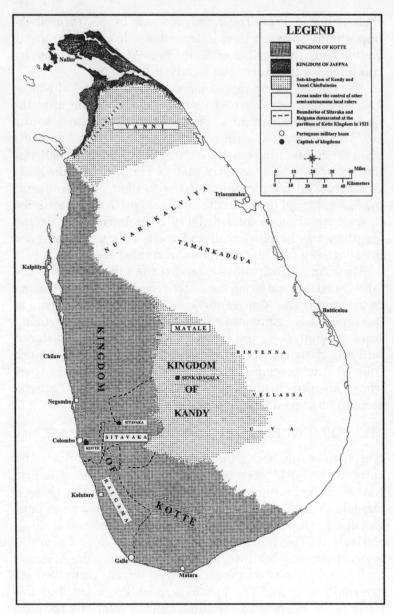

Sri Lanka in the Early Sixteenth Century

One striking feature of Portuguese activities in Asia and Africa was that they did not aim at territorial conquest so much as the control of commerce by subduing and dominating, by means of naval power, the strategic points through which it passed. At no stage did they establish a dominance over the politics of south Asia. What they did was to use their sea power and superior technology at points of weakness or where there were sharp divisions and thus they attained an influence out of proportion to their real strength.[3] They were drawn into the politics of Sri Lanka, and particularly of the Kotte kingdom, in their anxiety to establish a bridgehead for control over the island's cinnamon trade. Part of Vijayabāhu VI's unpopularity among his subjects stemmed from his seeming subservience to the Portuguese. But it was after the partition of Kotte into three distinct political entities that Portuguese intervention became a permanent feature of the island's politics.

While the ruler of Kotte, Bhuvanekabāhu, lost a considerable amount of territory when that kingdom was partitioned in 1521, the region left to him was by far the richest and largest of the three with resources adequate to maintain his position as the most important if not the most powerful monarch on the island. But Bhuvanekabāhu was no match for his more daring and ambitious younger brother Māyādunnē, the ruler of Sītāvaka, who aimed at control over the whole of the Kotte kingdom as it stood before the partition. The Kotte ruler hoped that Portuguese protection would preserve his kingdom against Māyādunnē and willingly accepted the status of a Portuguese satellite. Over the rest of the century, the major trend in the history of the truncated kingdom of Kotte was its increasing dependence on and subservience to the Portuguese.

Portuguese involvement in the affairs of Sri Lanka was not limited to the south-west littoral; it stretched to the Udarata (the Kandyan kingdom) and to the Tamil kingdom. The circumstances in which Portuguese interference in the politics of these kingdoms developed varied markedly and so for that matter did the success they achieved.

Although the Kandyan ruler regarded himself as one of the principal beneficiaries of the partition of Kotte in 1521, his relief at what seemed to be the weakening of the main source of danger to the Udarata was shortlived, for out of the chaos of the partition emerged the vigorous and aggressive Sītāvaka kingdom, a much more serious threat to Kandy than Kotte had ever been. Faced with this disturbing prospect, the Kandyan ruler did in the early 1540s what Bhuvanekabāhu had done in similar circumstances: he turned to the Portuguese and willingly accepted the status of a satellite state. The symbols of this voluntary subordination were the presence of a small Portuguese force in Kandy and the entry there of Roman Catholic priests. The two parties—the Kandyan ruler and the Portuguese—failed to gain the objectives they had set out to attain and their association led instead to misunderstandings, mutual suspicions and complications. The Kandyan ruler adopted another line of approach, a marriage alliance with the ruling family of Kotte— the Kotte connection—which, like that with the Portuguese, was later to cause immense difficulties for the Kandyan kingdom. But neither singly nor in combination could these connections ensure the security of the Udarata against Sītāvaka.

Portuguese interest in the Tamil areas in the north of the island stemmed from two considerations. First, the Jaffna Peninsula was strategically important in securing control of the seaborne traffic from the Malabar coast to Sri Lanka; and second, there was the pearl fishery. The Portuguese intrusion in the affairs of the Jaffna kingdom began in the 1540s, as part of the process of extending Roman Catholic missionary activity on the island. The missionaries had crossed over from south India and by 1544 had made heavy inroads, especially among the fisherfolk of Mannar and Jaffna. The Hindu ruler of the kingdom reacted angrily and violently and killed a large number of Roman Catholic converts. The Portuguese, especially the missionaries, were anxious to avenge these killings, but it was only in 1560 that a retaliatory expedition was despatched. Although at first this achieved some success, the Portuguese were forced to retreat to Mannar in the following year. But this setback was merely temporary and very soon Portuguese influence over the affairs of the Jaffna kingdom was so well established that they were even able to levy tribute from the ruler. The fact that another Portuguese attack on the Jaffna kingdom was launched in 1591 is evidence, however, that there was still some resistance to them. On this occasion the king of Jaffna was killed and a Portuguese protégé was placed on the throne.

THE WARS OF THE KOTTE SUCCESSION

In the period 1521–39 Kotte and Bhuvanekabāhu could not escape the consequences of the Portuguese connection which had developed under Vijayabāhu and had contributed greatly to the latter's unpopularity at the time of his assassination. Portuguese pressure at this stage was economic rather than political, an attempt to gain a monopoly of the cinnamon trade of the country and to establish a fort in the vicinity of Colombo for trading purposes. This second objective was regarded as being much less important than the first.[4] Nevertheless, they were both viewed with unconcealed distaste in Kotte and Bhuvanekabāhu himself was not inclined to cooperate in them. But he was powerless to sever the Portuguese connection which circumstances were to drive him into strengthening.

The initiative in concerting action against the Portuguese in these matters was taken by the Muslim traders resident in Kotte and their co-religionists in Malabar, who resented the loss to the Portuguese of their trade on the island. Although they were primarily interested in defending their own trading interests, their initiatives evoked a sympathetic response from among the people against the Portuguese. Bhuvanekabāhu himself was drawn into this conflict, but he was unwilling to risk an open confrontation with the Portuguese and as a result he responded eventually in a manner which only served to underline his increasing subservience to them. He would not lend his aid to the Muslims; worse still, in 1526 he was compelled under Portuguese pressure to expel them from Kotte. This proved to be an unpopular measure and Māyādunnē and the ruler of Rayigama stepped in to champion the cause of the Muslims. The ruler of Sītāvaka was the principal beneficiary of the hostility which was building up in Kotte against the Portuguese connection. He secured a formidable ally in the zamorin of Calicut, whose navy, though not the equal of the Portuguese, was to be of great assistance to him over the next decade.

In the late 1530s, Māyādunnē stepped up the pressure on Kotte. Bhuvanekabāhu had no sons by his chief queen, and Māyādunnē and the ruler of Rayigana—his two brothers— had reason, therefore, to regard themselves as heirs apparent to the Kotte throne. In 1538, when the ruler of Rayigana died, Māyādunnē seized his territories. Bhuvanekabāhu acquiesced in this and even gave it his formal approval in the hope, no doubt, that this would mitigate Māyādunnē's hostility to him. However, Māyādunnē had set his sights on control over Kotte and would not be distracted from this aim by his brother's calculated gestures of appeasement. Where Bhuvanekabāhu was conciliatory Māyādunnē was bellicose and awkward. Repeated provocations eventually precipitated an armed conflict between them in which the Portuguese backed the Kotte ruler and Māyādunnē secured the support of the zamorin of Calicut.

Although in the early stages of the conflict the advantage was with Māyādunnē—indeed, a decisive victory lay within his grasp—the superior military technology of the Portuguese saved the day for Kotte. Māyādunnē was forced to sue for peace. The terms imposed on him were utterly humiliating and none more so than the requirement that he execute the leaders of the Malabari forces who had come to the island to assist him and send their severed heads to the Portuguese. Māyādunnē complied with this demand to the disgust of the zamorin and as a result the Sītāvaka–Calicut entente was never to be revived.

The first war of Kotte succession thus ended in a humiliating setback for Māyādunnē, but no sooner had the Portuguese expeditionary forces departed than he began winning over many of the provincial chiefs of Kotte. His success was remarkably rapid and by 1541 large areas of the Kotte kingdom were under the de facto control of Sītāvaka,[5] although there was still a nominal allegiance to Bhuvanekabāhu. Nothing contributed more to the rapid erosion of Bhuvanekabāhu's hold over large parts of his kingdom than the conduct of his Portuguese allies: contumacious Portuguese factors and overbearing Portuguese settlers undermined his authority and alienated him from his subjects.

By this time, Bhuvanekabāhu, intent on excluding Māyādunnē from the Kotte throne, had taken a fateful decision.

He had two sons by a junior queen, but they were not entitled to the throne while his only child by the chief queen was a daughter named Samudra Devi who had married Vīdiyā Bandāra and had a son Dharmapala by him. In 1540, an envoy was sent to Lisbon to secure a guarantee of Portuguese support for a move to have this grandson—Dharmapala—declared Bhuvanekabāhu's rightful heir and successor. By solemnly Crowning a golden statue of the young prince in 1543, Joao III of Portugal pledged support for this unusual enterprise. By doing so he ensured that the struggle for the Kotte succession would embroil his country in a bitter conflict with Māyādunnē. The succession from grandfather to grandson was atypical. The fact that it was to be effected under the auspices of the Portuguese made it even more unpalatable to Māyādunnē and to the people of Kotte.

Bhuvanekabāhu's problems increased with the arrival in Kotte of a group of Franciscan missionaries. They came at his invitation as part of the price exacted for Portuguese recognition of the right of succession of Dharmapala to the Kotte throne. The Sinhalese envoys had exceeded their brief in giving the impression that Bhuvanekabāhu himself would be a willing convert to Roman Catholicism. But while the king readily welcomed the missionaries and gave them permission to build churches and preach in Kotte, he categorically repudiated his envoys' promise of his own conversion. The Franciscans were not put off: they aimed at converting the king himself in the certain knowledge that if they succeeded they would pave the way for the conversion of a large number of his subjects. Bhuvanekabāhu, for his part, realized that there was no more certain way of alienating the affection of his people than by changing his religion. But despite his obvious opposition to the attempt to convert him, Franciscan pressure continued. In time Bhuvanekabāhu became less favourable to Christian missionary activity and there was a marked deterioration in relations between the Portuguese and the king of Kotte as a result. Nevertheless, much of the resentment against the Portuguese settlers and missionaries rubbed off on the king and from this nobody benefited more than Māyādunnē.

However, the relationship between the Kotte and Sītāvaka rulers was not always a straightforward one of sworn enmity and consistent hostility. In the early 1540s, they forgot their differences for long enough to pursue a common policy of opposition to the pretensions of the Udarata ruler, Jayavīra (their erstwhile ally against their father in 1521), to the status of an independent ruler. Māyādunnē was the driving force in this campaign against the Udarata. An independent Kandyan kingdom in alliance with the Portuguese would pose a formidable threat to the Sītāvaka kingdom, for it would mean that two frontiers, the western as well as eastern, would be under pressure. A joint Sītāvaka–Kotte attack on the Udarata came in 1545 and the Kandyans were compelled to accept the terms of peace imposed by the victors. Portuguese assistance for the Kandyans came too late, and once it did arrive the Kandyans had reason to regret it for their would-be rescuers annoyed and irritated the people by their insolence and offended the ruler by their incessant demands for rewards despite the fact that they were too few in number to assure him and his kingdom any security against its enemies. Thus the first attempt at an alliance between the Portuguese and the Udarata ended unhappily.

This was a period of shifting loyalties and rapidly changing alliances, with an attempt first of all at restoring friendly relations between Kotte and the Udarata. More surprising still, Māyādunnē, fearing the isolation of his kingdom as a result of such a move, sought an accommodation if not alliance with the Portuguese, directed against Kotte. But before these could develop further, the old Portuguese–Kotte axis was revived—primarily against Sītāvaka but, on the insistence of the Portuguese and despite the obvious reluctance of Kotte, against the Udarata as well.

The Portuguese–Kotte invasion of Kandy in 1546 which followed ended in disaster and led to great bitterness between the two defeated parties. Although Māyādunnē's attempt to benefit from this by allying himself with the Portuguese did not succeed, Portuguese relations with Kotte were severely strained. Nevertheless, when towards the end of 1550 fighting between Kotte and Sītāvaka erupted again, the Portuguese stepped in to support Kotte once more. In the course of this campaign Bhuvanekabāhu died under very strange circumstances: he was killed by a shot fired by a Portuguese soldier. Although the Portuguese claimed that this was an unfortunate accident, it is impossible to exclude the suspicion that it was an assassination of which the Portuguese viceroy, de Noronha, who had led the Portuguese expeditionary force to Sri Lanka, had prior knowledge.[6]

With the death of Bhuvanekabāhu, the second war of the Kotte succession began, infinitely more complicated than the first because of Bhuvanekabāhu's son-in-law Vīdiyā Bandāra. When Māyādunnē proclaimed himself king of Kotte and advanced down the Kelani River, the Portuguese, supported by a section of the Kotte nobility, proclaimed Dharmapala king, with his father Vīdiyā Bandāra as regent. Evidently there were reserves of popular support for Dharmapala within Kotte, but this would have been of little avail had Vīdiyā Bandāra not proved to be the energetic and dynamic man he was. The credit for organizing a successful resistance to Māyādunnē must go to him. The Sītāvaka forces were driven back from the Kotte kingdom. The Portuguese intervened at this stage— 1551—with the largest army they were ever to land on the island, and joined in the attack on Sītivāka. Māyādunnē had hardly regrouped his forces after the initial setback at the hands of Vīdiyā Bandāra when the joint Portuguese–Kotte army moved into Sītāvaka itself. Mayādunnē was forced to flee to Deraniyagala in the interior, leaving Sītāvaka at the mercy of its enemies. Surprisingly, his adversaries returned to Kotte without administering the coup de grâce. This was partly because de Noronha realized that it would have involved a hard campaign in mountainous territory. There were more sordid considerations as well—the Portuguese seemed more intent on plundering the Kotte treasury in the aftermath of Bhuvanekabāhu's death than in pursuing Māyādunnē in the wilds of Sabaragamuva.[7]

Though Māyādunnē lived to fight another day, he had little reason to believe that the balance of political forces on the island would shift in his favour as quickly or as comprehensively as it did. In the beginning the odds seemed to favour his rivals in Kotte and the Udarata. In the Udarata, Karaliyaddē Bandāra, elder son of the ageing Jayavīra, raised a revolt once more, executed his step-brother and rival, and expelled his father from Kandy. Jayavīra now sought refuge in Sītāvaka. The clash between Sītāvaka and the Udarata that followed was indecisive, but Sītāvaka now had a hostile Udarata in its flank. The main problem, however, was still Kotte and the redoubtable Vīdiyā Bandāra.

From the beginning of 1552 to the end of 1555, Vīdiyā Bandāra was a volatile and wholly unpredictable factor in the island's politics. For the Portuguese, intent on a swift transformation of Kotte into a Roman Catholic client state, he was a singularly inconvenient barrier between them and their undisputed control over the youthful king. Moreover, his success against Māyādunnē encouraged him to cherish the hope of a less restricted role in Kotte's affairs than that contrived for him by the Portuguese, a stop-gap regent with little independent power. The Portuguese treated him with considerable suspicion even though he embraced Roman Catholicism in late 1552. The suspicion soon matured into hostility and the Portuguese proceeded to imprison him. Yet the resourceful Vīdiyā Bandāra escaped from prison in 1553 and raised a revolt against the Portuguese. Māyādunnē, sensing the prospect of advantage in this situation, came to Vīdiyā Bandāra's assistance and between them they launched a vigorous onslaught against the Portuguese in Kotte and pushed them back to the coast, confining them to the area in the immediate vicinity of Kotte and Colombo. The extent and speed of their success in this campaign owed much to a shrewd exploitation of the powerful undercurrent of anti-Portuguese feeling among the people, exasperated by a reaction against Roman Catholicism.

Vīdiyā Bandāra's daring escapades and military skill alarmed Māyādunnē no less than the Portuguese. As a result, by 1555 there was a cynical realignment of forces with the two inveterate enemies, Māyādunnē and the Portuguese, coming together in a temporary alliance against an unusually gifted adversary. Each needed the other's help against Vīdiyā Bandāra; each no doubt gambled on winning the larger share of the spoils with the elimination of their common enemy; but on any dispassionate assessment the odds clearly favoured Māyādunnē rather than the Portuguese. When Vīdiyā Bandāra was defeated, Sītāvaka emerged as the largest and strongest kingdom on the island. With Vīdiyā Bandāra out of the way, the momentum of events pushed Sītāvaka to the threshold of a new era of dominance in the south-west. The Portuguese contributed greatly to this by their single-minded pursuit of saving souls, a policy that was intrinsically detrimental to their political interests. Their most memorable success—the conversion of Dharmapala in early 1557—was politically a disaster. With all the enthusiasm of the recent convert, he proceeded to the unprecedented and gravely provocative step of confiscating all the lands owned by the sangha and the devālās (Hindu temples) in his kingdom and gifting them to the Franciscans. From then on, Dharmapala was nothing more than the creature of the Portuguese and his main, if not his only, indigenous support came from the Roman Catholics in Kotte. And almost immediately Māyādunnē marched against Kotte, confident that the king's subjects, antagonized by his conversion to Roman Catholicism and embittered by the confiscation of temple properties, would rally to the side of the invading Sītāvaka armies. In the prolonged fighting that now ensued, stretching into the early 1560s, Dharmapala and his Portuguese mentors were saved from complete defeat because the Sītāvaka forces lacked cannon sufficiently powerful to demolish the fortifications of Kotte and Colombo; and in the first few years the presence of strong Portuguese forces in Colombo was a deterrent against any attempt to storm the fort. Nevertheless, the Portuguese themselves took the decision, in 1565, to abandon Kotte and concentrate their forces in Colombo. Dharmapala and his Sinhalese followers deplored this decision, but the Portuguese were intent on cutting their losses. Though damaging to Portuguese prestige, it was a tactically wise move, for they were no longer burdened with the defence of Kotte. Dharmapala was now a ruler without a kingdom, for Colombo was, in fact, a Portuguese fort, no more, no less.

THE DOMINANCE OF SĪTĀVAKA

Over the next twenty-five years, Sītāvaka came into its own. In Māyādunnē's son Rājasimha I the Portuguese confronted a more implacable enemy and one whose opposition to them was more consistent. When barely sixteen years of age he had been the nominal head of the army that defeated Vīdiyā Bandāra at Palanda and had been known since then by the name Rājasimha. His reputation as a soldier had been greatly enhanced in the campaigns of 1557–65. Although Rājasimha did not succeed to the Sītāvaka throne till 1581—on Māyādunnē's death—he more often than not led the Sītāvaka forces in battle during this interlude.

A determination to complete their mastery of the old kingdom of Kotte by expelling the Portuguese from their stronghold of Colombo dominated the strategy and tactics of the Sītāvaka rulers over the next two decades. The Portuguese, for their part, were not content to accept their reduced position without a struggle. They resorted to the tactics—successfully used against them earlier by Sītāvaka—of harrying villages in the vicinity of Colombo which now owed allegiance to Sītāvaka. Above all else they spurned any suggestion of a truce with Sītāvaka and used their naval power with great effect over the next decade against the more vulnerable coastal regions under the control of Sītāvaka. In 1574, on the death of Dharmapala's queen, the Portuguese took the initiative in obtaining a bride for him from the Udarata. For Rājasimha this was doubly provocative: it held out the prospect of a political link between Dharmapala and his Portuguese mentors, on the one hand, and the Udarata, which could threaten Sītāvaka's eastern frontier; on a personal level, there was an element of humiliation because Rājasimha himself had unsuccessfully sought the hand of this very same Kandyan princess. In 1574, Sītāvaka launched an attack on Kandy, upon which the Portuguese moved into the offensive with destructive forays into the coastal regions of the south-west in which, apart from the usual incendiarism, harassment of the civil population and destruction of crops and livestock, they engaged in a calculated policy of vandalism and iconoclasm directed against the traditional religions: they destroyed the

Rājamaha Vihara at Kelaniya near Colombo, the Hindu temple at Munneswaram, as well as viharas elsewhere on the north-west coast and in the interior. The key to Portuguese survival in the age of Sītāvaka's dominance in the affairs of Sri Lanka was naval power. It enabled them to establish new centres of influence in the littoral region, in Jaffna primarily but in other areas as well. Thus they constructed a fort at Galle in the south of the island between 1571 and 1582 and in this same period obtained tribute from some of the Vanni chiefs—those of Trincomalee and Batticaloa in the east and of Puttalam in the north-west. But for Sītāvaka the most ominous feature of this clever use by the Portuguese of their one element of strength was the prospect of an Udarata–Portuguese entente which the events of 1574–76 had foreshadowed.

Rājasimha's attack on the Udarata in 1574 had been more a punitive raid than a concerted bid to bring that kingdom under Sītāvaka rule. In 1578, Rājasimha decided to take the offensive against the Kandyans to bring them securely under Sītāvaka's control if not its rule. Although he captured the strategically important Balana Pass, which secured access to the capital of the Udarata, his expedition failed insofar as its main objective was concerned. Once again the Udarata was saved by Portuguese intervention in the form of naval forays on the south-west and north-west coasts, which compelled the Sītāvaka forces to abandon their Kandyan venture and to concentrate their attention on the Portuguese.

This Rājasimha did with redoubled energy and for over two years from 1579 the city of Colombo was under siege. The Portuguese were driven to desperate straits in contriving to survive this relentless pressure, but endure it they did, and naval power—Rājasimha was unable to prevent the arrival of reinforcements from Goa—was once more the key to their survival. When the siege was raised in 1581 there was no Portuguese counter-offensive. Because of a severe shortage of Portuguese manpower in the east, they could not afford to concentrate large forces in Colombo. As for Sītāvaka, they kept up the pressure by establishing their military headquarters at Biyagama, less than ten miles from Colombo. The Portuguese were confined to the city and its environs.

In 1580, at a time when his fortunes and that of the Portuguese in Sri Lanka could scarcely have been at a lower ebb, Dharmapala took the decision to bequeath his kingdom on his death to the Portuguese monarch Dom Manuel. This was the final phase in the subservience of the Kotte monarchy to the Portuguese. Dharmapala's grandfather had been a protégé of the Portuguese, a pliant ruler of a satellite state; he himself ended as a *roi fainéant*.

Māyādunnē died in 1581 and Rājasimha succeeded to the throne though not without opposition. For nearly two decades Sītāvaka had been engaged in almost continuous warfare and there was naturally a longing for a respite and for a reduction in the high taxation which had been the inevitable result of these wars. If these campaigns had brought glory to Rājasimha and Sītāvaka, inevitably he was identified also with the burdens they imposed on the people. Significantly, there was considerable opposition from the sangha as well. Whether this was the cause or the result of his conversion to Hinduism we are in no position to say. But Rājasimha easily crushed this opposition.

Once he had consolidated his position—which he did quite swiftly—he turned almost at once to another—and this time, successful—Kandyan campaign. The Udarata was absorbed in the Sītāvaka kingdom. Sītāvaka was now relieved of anxieties about its eastern frontier and Rājasimha was in direct control of a larger extent of territory in Sri Lanka than any ruler had been since the days of Parākramabāhu VI. More important, Rājasimha I gained valuable additional resources in men and material for use against the Portuguese.

It was obvious to the Portuguese that this successful Kandyan campaign would be the prelude to another attack on Colombo. They expected this attack in 1582 and in anticipation of it rebuilt the walls of the Colombo fort. It was five years before the attack was launched Rājasimha was making careful preparations for what was to be the coup de grâce against the Portuguese. But he also had to cope with disturbances within his kingdom, in Sītāvaka itself, and a movement against him in the Udarata in favour of Weerasundera Bandāra. Rājasimha crushed the latter. Weerasundera was killed and with it any prospect, for the time being, of a prolonged uprising against Sītāvaka. But Weerasundera's son Konnappu Bandāra escaped to the Portuguese and was later known as Dom Joao of Austria. Rājasimha's last siege of Colombo, in 1587–88, was also the best known. Once again he came close to victory and was only thwarted by his inability to prevent Portuguese reinforcements from coming in from India. In 1587–88, Sītāvaka's power had reached its zenith: few could have predicted that within five years Sītāvaka itself would be destroyed beyond any hope of recovery.

The train of events which was to culminate in Sītāvaka's uprooting was precipitated by a rebellion in the Udarata, triggered by the seizure of men and the capture of material for the siege of Colombo. But the crucial factor that led to the loss of support for Rājasimha in the Udarata was clearly the execution of Weerasundera. The success of the Kandyan revolt in 1590 encouraged Rājasimha's enemies within Sītāvaka. The Seven Koralās rose in rebellion and when Rājasimha withdrew his men from the Udarata to meet this threat the Portuguese moved in and destroyed the Sītāvaka stockades at Biyagama and Kaduwela. His immediate reaction of beheading the commanders of these two stockades only aggravated the discontent in Sītāvaka.

Rājasimha regarded the tumult in the Seven Kōralēs as a minor irritant compared to the Kandyan 'rebellion'. He led his army to the Kandyan Hills determined to crush this revolt. But his campaign failed and on his way back to Sītāvaka he died of a septic wound caused by a bamboo splinter piercing his foot.

His death in 1593 left a power vacuum in Sītāvaka. There were too many contenders for power, none capable of bending the bow of Ulysses. Within two years Sītāvaka had caved in, destroyed by a combination of self-inflicted wounds and Portuguese arms and almost the whole of the old kingdom of Kotte, as it existed in 1521 prior to its partition, acknowledged the sovereignty of Dharmapala and the authority of the Portuguese.

Sītāvaka's achievement was considerable. Within two generations, despite a continued struggle against the superior manpower resources of Kotte and the military technology of the Portuguese, to say nothing of the Udarata, it was one of the most powerful kingdoms on the island. Portuguese forces, many times the size of those that freely devastated the Kandyan kingdom in the seventeenth century, were successfully confined by Rājasimha I within the fort of Colombo. More than once Sītāvaka nearly succeeded in driving the Portuguese out of Sri Lanka and only the lack of a navy or naval support to match that of the Portuguese prevented a complete success. Indeed, during the brief period of its existence of about seventy years, the Sītāvaka kingdom established a record of resistance to foreign rule which has never been matched in the history of Western rule in Sri Lanka.

Sītāvaka's greatest legacy to Sri Lanka, then, was this tradition of resistance, to which the Kandyan kingdom became the legatee. But a comparison between Sītāvaka and the Kandyan kingdom as defenders of Sinhalese independence would show that Sītāvaka's achievement was the more creditable of the two. For one thing Sītāvaka did not have the advantage of easily defensible frontiers; no mountain chains protected it, and the Kelani River—unlike the Mahaveli in the Kandyan area—was navigable almost up to the capital city of Sītāvaka by river crafts which could transport men and arms for the Portuguese. What the two kingdoms had in common were the forests, and the men of Sītāvaka were as skilled in guerrilla warfare as the people of Kandy were to be. But the rulers of Sītāvaka were also adept in the arts of conventional warfare, the open confrontation between armies on a battlefield. Very early, they had mastered the techniques of modern warfare and military technology, and in conventional warfare they proved to be a match, and often more than a match, for the Portuguese. In this sense no Sinhalese rulers of the future bore comparison as warriors with Māyādunnē and Rājasimha, nor did they confront the same heavy odds as those which the rulers of Sītāvaka faced.

The rapidity with which the area controlled by Sītāvaka expanded from the late 1550s created formidable problems of administration, especially in regard to the consolidation of control over the new acquisitions. They were, of course, assessed for revenue purposes and efforts were made to develop areas depopulated as a result of the prolonged warfare of this period; but these wars left little time for innovation in government machinery.

Rājasimha of Sītāvaka was remarkably attuned to the
changes that had occurred in the sixteenth century, especially
with regard to the economy and most especially with regard
to the cinnamon trade. Most, if not all, of the cinnamon lands
of the littoral region were under the control of Sītāvaka after
1565. The processed cinnamon was collected and stored in
royal warehouses and sold to traders, at the market price, on
the king's authority. Cinnamon was a key source of state
revenue under the Sītāvaka kings, particularly during the rule
of Rājasimha when some of the measures he adopted showed
a radical departure from the traditional practice of the Sinhalese
kings. Thus, to keep prices high he emulated the Portuguese
in burning excess stocks of cinnamon and as a result the rise
in price was spectacular. It would be true to say, however,
that Māyādunnē and Rājasimha were more adept in the martial
arts than in the prosaic business of peacetime administration.
Prolonged warfare exacted a fearful price from the people
and the military prowess of the Sītāvaka kings was in the end
a crushing burden on the economy.

The collapse of Sītāvaka was even more dramatic and
precipitate than its rise and expansion had been. Rājasimha,
on whom it can largely be blamed, was only about fifty years
old at the time of his death in 1593. He had eliminated almost
every potential rival so that there was no successor capable of
consolidating his achievements or holding the kingdom
together against its enemies. His intolerance of opposition in
the last years of his rule served to elevate a number of self-
seeking adventurers to key positions in the armed forces.
When he died he left his army almost intact, but there was no
one to take his place in inspiring its loyalty and without his
leadership its morale was easily undermined.[8]

Within a few years of Rājasimha's death, Portuguese control
over the south-west littoral region was extended, consolidated
and stabilized. The crisis of the sixteenth century, which began
with the decline of Kotte, culminated in the collapse of Sītāvaka
and with Portuguese dominance, if not control, over two of
the three kingdoms that had existed when the century began.
In Kotte, Dharmapala was a mere figurehead and in Jaffna a

protégé of the Portuguese was on the throne. Only the Kandyan kingdom survived, the last of the independent Sinhalese kingdoms. The dramatic collapse of Sītāvaka with Rājasimha's death enabled it to assert its independence once more. But with the release from Sītāvaka's domination came renewed danger from an old enemy—the Portuguese.

Portuguese Rule in the Maritime Regions, c. 1600–58

A t the close of the sixteenth century, the Estado da India had reached the zenith of its prosperity. The Portuguese had been absorbed into the state system of Asia where their naval power and their usefulness as trading partners had enabled them to establish a seemingly stable position. Then in 1595–96 there appeared in Asian waters an ominous threat to the Portuguese in the shape of Dutch ships: indeed, for the Portuguese the effect of their arrival can only be described as catastrophic. After 1585, when Philip II with increasing rigour banned their trade with Iberian ports, the Dutch were better prepared than the English to undertake a hazardous sea voyage to the Spice Islands by way of the Cape of Good Hope. In financial strength, administrative skills and naval experience they were well ahead of the Portuguese and the English. The formation of the Vereenidge Oost-Indische Campagnie (VOC) in 1602 coordinated the Dutch efforts and gave them the backing of what, for over a century, was the greatest commercial company in the world. It received extensive state support and monopolist privileges, and deliberately set out to challenge the Portuguese position in the East. Despite initial reverses in attacks on Portuguese forts and settlements, the Dutch had ousted the Portuguese from the Spice Islands, besieged Mozambique and Malacca and blockaded Malacca and Goa all within four years of the foundation of the VOC. Thereafter, the VOC steadily expanded its factories and its influence from the Red Sea to Japan. The establishment of the Dutch headquarters at Batavia after 1619 meant that Portuguese vessels could only use the neighbouring straits of

Malacca at great risk to themselves. In the wake of the Dutch came the English but the Hollanders had done much of their work for them by breaking the back of Portuguese sea power in the Far East. In the Persian Gulf and off the west coast of India, however, it was the English who bore the brunt of the attack, at any rate in the first quarter of the century.

Ironically, it was in this period, when Portuguese power was on the decline in almost all parts of Asia, that there was a notable extension of their authority and influence in Sri Lanka: in Kotte and Jaffnapatam.

Portuguese control over the Kotte and Jaffna kingdoms, established in the last decade of the sixteenth century, was consolidated over the first third of the seventeenth century. Sri Lanka's maritime regions and the Zambezi river valley in Africa were the only two regions in which the Portuguese extended their control beyond the range of their coastal forts. The rapid collapse of Sītāvaka and the facile restoration of Kotte had shown the Portuguese that the military resources available to them on the island were adequate for the expansion of their power there. The strategic value of Sri Lanka was underlined with the arrival of the Dutch in eastern waters, for Dutch vessels bound for the East Indies sailed round the southern coast of the island. Besides, the growth of Mughal power in the Deccan under Akbar in this same period posed a threat to the Portuguese in Goa.

THE EXPANSION OF PORTUGUESE POWER IN SRI LANKA

Till 1597, the reality of Portuguese power in Kotte had been camouflaged somewhat. Dharmapala was still, nominally at least, its ruler. But the aged and expendable Dharmapala never took up residence in his old capital, and seldom asserted his rights to his kingdom; much less did he attempt to share its administration with the Portuguese. In 1580, he had bequeathed his kingdom to the Portuguese monarch, and this bequest—confirmed and clarified by subsequent documents—furnished the Portuguese with a sufficient and exclusive claim to the kingdom of Kotte. This legal title they proceeded to proclaim within two days of Dharmapala's death on 27 May 1597. The proclamation was an occasion for much solemnity and ceremony. Dom Jeronimo de Azevedo, the Portuguese captain-general in Sri Lanka, summoned to Colombo Dharmapala's principal officers, as well as representatives of the provinces, and delegates chosen by those assembled there took an oath of allegiance to the Crown of Portugal on behalf of the people of Kotte.[1]

From the beginning, however, there was resistance to Portuguese mastery over Kotte. While Dharmapala was alive, there had been two major revolts, one led by Akaragama Appuhamy in 1594 and the other by Edirille Rāla in 1594–96. In the first two decades of Portuguese rule after Dharmapala's death there were four major revolts—those of Kāngara Ārachchi in 1603, Kuruvita Rāla in 1603 and 1616–19, and Nikapitiyē Bandāra in 1616–17.[2] There were minor revolts in the Seven Kōralēs in 1616 and in the Matara *disāvony* in 1619.

In the last years of the sixteenth century, the main centres of rebellion were the Kelani and Kalu River basins and in particular the Siyanē, Hevagam, Salpiti, Rayigam and Pasdun kōralēs. By 1600, Portuguese mastery over these regions had been consolidated and thereafter it was in the periphery[3]— the border regions where their authority was not yet secure— that Sinhalese resistance persisted. Nevertheless, once resistance erupted into rebellion in these parts, there was a tendency for the rebels to move into the Kelani Valley to confront Portuguese power there. As the Portuguese tightened their grip over the Kotte kingdom, potential rebels faced heavier odds, but once a rebellion broke out, the insurgents were able to hold out for much longer than in the first decade.

There were two basic driving forces in these resistance movements—the desire to be rid of the foreigner, to which was connected a hostility to the Roman Catholic religion. The second factor had to do with discontent among the people at large arising from the rigours of Portuguese land policy, the lawlessness of officials and the government's increased demands for services and goods from the people.

Resistance movements against the Portuguese received aid primarily from the Kandyan kingdom. Jaffnapatam aided the rebels once, but that was in 1617, a year of acute crisis when the Portuguese were faced with a major rebellion in the lowlands of the south-west.

The kingdom of Jaffnapatam was the weakest of the three major units into which Sri Lanka was divided in the sixteenth century; it was the poorest and, because it was easily accessible by sea, vulnerable in a way that the Udarata and Sītāvaka never were. Moreover, with the establishment of Portuguese control over the lowlands of the south-west, Sinhalese *lascarin* troops were used against the Jaffna Tamil forces, without fear of desertion to the ranks of the enemy.

A Portuguese expeditionary force under Andre Furtado de Mendoça in 1591 had consolidated the Portuguese hold in Jaffna. The new king, Ethirimanna Ciṅkam, owed his throne to the Portuguese and was pledged to favour Christianity. The disturbed political situation in Jaffnapatam during the three preceding decades had seen the power and influence of the Jaffna nobility increase at the expense of the king, while some of these nobles became Christians and looked to the Portuguese for advancement, the bulk of them remained steadfastly Hindu and resented Portuguese interference with their cultural and trade ties with Tanjore. The ruler's commitment to Christianity alienated the majority of his subjects as well because of their fidelity to the traditional religion.

The weakness of the king's position became evident within a year of de Mendoça's expedition when discontent in the Jaffna kingdom compelled Ethirimanna Ciṅkam to abandon his palace and seek refuge in the Portuguese township of Jaffna. After a brief struggle Ethirimanna Ciṅkam re-established his control over the northern kingdom, but he found it politic to move away from his Portuguese mentors and to make an ostentatious demonstration of his independence of them. Partly, this was a shrewd move to win the support of his subjects; but there were other reasons as well. Some of the Portuguese in Jaffna scarcely concealed their contempt for him and openly insulted him when he disagreed with them. He had suffered financial losses on account of variations in the tribute demanded from him by the factor of Mannar—elephants in one year and cash in another without prior warning. Besides, the Portuguese *ouvidor* or judge of Mannar sought to extend his authority to the Jaffna kingdom as well. Above all, there were the complications caused by the proselytizing zeal of the missionaries.

The Portuguese themselves were dissatisfied with Ethirimanna Ciṅkam—indeed they had begun to have doubts about his loyalty to them as early as 1595—but while relations between the two parties kept deteriorating, neither felt inclined to make a move against the other. In 1614, however, the Portuguese king sent definite instructions to depose Ethirimanna Ciṅkam and only the lack of means for the task prevented the captain-general of Sri Lanka from embarking on this enterprise. As it was, they were spared the necessity because of Ethirimanna Ciṅkam's death in 1616.

The Portuguese viceroy at Goa soon found himself faced with the complications stemming from a disputed succession to the throne of Jaffna and a seizure of power by a faction led by Caṅkili Kumara, a nephew of Ethirimanna Ciṅkam, who killed all princes of the blood save the legitimate heir—Ethirimanna Ciṅkam's three-year-old son and Caṅkili's own brother-in-law. Then Caṅkili as well as a rival sought recognition from the Portuguese as regent of Jaffnapatam. Faced with Nikapitiyē Bandāra's formidable rebellion, the Portuguese had no aversion to Caṅkili acting as regent on condition that he would not give assistance or refuge to Nikapitiyē Bandāra.

But Caṅkili had little popular support in Jaffnapatam and his position there soon became insecure. In August–September 1618, a revolt was organized by a Christian group and Caṅkili was driven to seek refuge in Kayts whence he applied to the Portuguese for assistance but found them reluctant to support him against their co-religionists. It was at this stage that Caṅkili appealed to the powerful nayak of Tanjore who promptly obliged him with a force of 5,000 men which easily crushed the rebellion. Nevertheless, his position remained as unenviable as it had been previously. In Jaffnapatam, Caṅkili was dependent on troops from Tanjore, many of whom remained behind under their commander to serve in the Jaffna forces; on the other hand, he could not break with the Portuguese. He continued to pay them tribute and allowed freedom of movement to their settlers and priests within the kingdom even while they were urging the authorities in Goa to conquer Jaffna.

It was under Filipe de Oliviera in 1619 that the Portuguese made their move, for reasons which were defensive in intent. They had found that Cankili, despite assurances to the contrary, was permitting mercenaries and supplies to move into territory held by anti-Portuguese forces at a time of great danger to their position in Sri Lanka. The Jaffna ruler was making efforts to get the Kandyan king—Senarat—into renewed opposition to the Portuguese and had already sought aid from the Dutch at Paleacat. In March 1619, de Sa, the Portuguese captain-general on the island, received news from Mannar that a cousin of the last Kunjali admiral of Calicut had appeared off Jaffna with five armed vessels—presumably at the request of Cankili—and that this fleet was attacking Portuguese ships.

Although the Portuguese expedition was speedily successful and Cankili was captured and taken to Colombo as a prisoner, throughout 1620–21 there were pockets of opposition to the Portuguese in Jaffnapatam. The Portuguese had to wage two major campaigns, each more arduous than that by which the kingdom of Jaffnapatam had been conquered in 1619, before they consolidated their position. In both cases, sizeable invading forces from Tanjore were joined by local Tamil recruits in an attempt to oust the Portuguese—who nonetheless held out successfully.

One of the key factors in the success of the Portuguese in Jaffnapatam in 1619–21 was the presence of a pro-Portuguese Christian minority in Jaffna. During and after the conquest this minority provided a source of strength in Jaffna, which may well have tipped the scales in favour of the Portuguese on crucial occasions.

Two points about the conquest of Jaffna are worth noting. First, it provided a useful accession of strength to the Portuguese at a time when their fortunes were on the wane in the East. It strengthened their control over pearl fishery and, by giving them greater influence over the supply of elephants from the Vanni, increased their domination over the island's elephant trade. Jaffna was the main market for elephants captured in the island.

There was the advantage too that Portuguese soldiers could be rewarded with grants of land in Jaffnapatam. But most important of all, at a time when their command of the sea was being challenged, Portuguese communications between the Malabar and Coromandel Coasts were made safer than before once they had control over Jaffna. Second, the subjugation of the Jaffna kingdom was one of the most lasting effects of Portuguese rule. The Dutch and the British after them continued the policy of treating Jaffnapatam as a mere unit of a larger political entity.

For two decades after regaining its independence, the Kandyan kingdom was confronted by a concerted Portuguese attempt to bring it under their rule and thus complete their domination over the whole island. As legatees of the Kotte kings, the Portuguese sought to reassert Kotte's overlordship over the Udarata. Moreover, through the process of conversion to Roman Catholicism, the Portuguese had pliant protégés whose claims to the Kandyan throne were as good as, if not better than, those of any other aspirant. These claims they now advanced in support of an extension of Portuguese power to the Udarata. Pedro Lopes de Souza led a Portuguese expeditionary force for this purpose in 1594 taking with them the Sinhalese princess, Kusumāsana Devi, or Dōna Catherina as she was called, who had the strongest claims to the Kandyan throne. The aim quite explicitly was to install her there in the Portuguese interest. But they were outwitted by Konappu Bandāra, an erstwhile protégé of theirs (he had fled to them on the execution of his father Weerasundera Bandāra by Rājasimha I) who was to be the legatee—quite unexpectedly— for the Portuguese of the successful guerrilla campaign directed against de Souza's force. He captured the prized Kusumāsana Devi and married her, thus securing solid claims to the Kandyan throne, even though the Portuguese would not recognize them. Konnappu Bandāra reigned in Kandy as Vimala Dharma Sūriya till 1604.[4] The Portuguese would neither grant him recognition in this position nor abandon their claims, as heirs to Kotte, to suzerainty over the Udarata. Indeed, Portuguese anxiety to subjugate Kandy increased with the arrival of the Dutch in Asian waters.

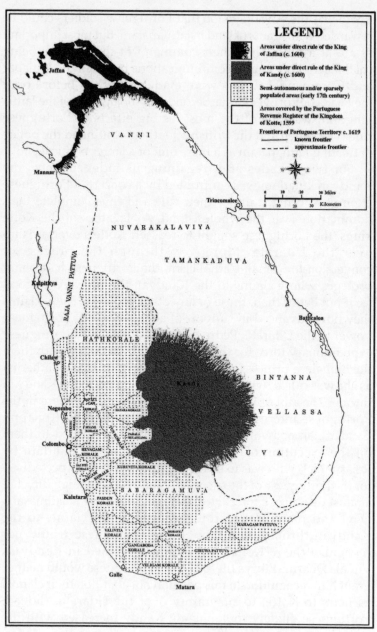

Sri Lanka in the Early Seventeenth Century

Vimala Dharma Sūriya and his successor Senarat[5] (1604–35) between them re-established the kingdom of Kandy. Their aims were modest and starkly limited: survival was all and peace on any terms which the Portuguese were prepared to grant. But the latter (especially when de Azevedo was captain-general) were not interested in peace with the Kandyans and were intent on the systematic destruction of parts of the Kandyan kingdom through regular forays. The Kandyan kingdom retained its independence only because the Portuguese could not muster the manpower (in terms of Portuguese soldiers) necessary to subjugate it. But Kandyan policy towards the Portuguese did not change; it remained one of détente. This they achieved to some extent by the treaty of 1617, under the terms of which the Portuguese at last recognized Senarat as ruler of the Kandyans. The latter in turn acknowledged the authority of the Portuguese to rule over the maritime districts of the Sinhalese. The Kandyans agreed to pay tribute to the Portuguese and promised to deny entry to any of their enemies.

The annexation of Jaffna in 1619 worked to the disadvantage of the Kandyans by depriving them of a potential ally and a bridgehead for communication with other rulers in south India. One result of the annexation was that the only ports which the Portuguese did not control in Sri Lanka were on the east coast, which was acknowledged as being part of the Kandyan kingdom. Despite this, they soon set about gaining control of the two major ports of Batticaloa and Trincomalee; the latter they captured quite easily and in 1628 they seized and fortified Batticaloa. Despite these blatant infringements of Kandyan sovereignty, Senarat would do nothing to precipitate a confrontation with the Portuguese.[6]

By 1628, however, the signs of a change in the Kandyan policy towards the Portuguese were manifesting themselves. Senarat's son Rājasimha—the future Rājasimha II—anxious to take on the mantle of Sītāvaka and of his namesake Rājasimha I, in resolute opposition to the Portuguese—was largely responsible for the change. The Kandyans now resorted to a more aggressive policy and organized incursions deep into Portuguese-held territory. The Portuguese, in turn, reverted to the old policy of attempting an armed invasion for the subjugation of Kandy. In 1630, a Portuguese expedition under Constantine de Sa set out for this purpose, but it was routed at the battle of Randenivela near Vellavaya. Once again, as under the Sītāvaka kings, the Portuguese were harried and pushed back to the security of their forts. Once again, in imitation of Māyādunnē and Rājasimha I, the aim was to drive the Portuguese out of Sri Lanka.

THE EXPULSION OF THE PORTUGUESE

The change of policy from détente to vigorous resistance was sustained over the next twenty-eight years. But in the meantime a respite came in 1633—a temporary truce, a peace of exhaustion. A Luso-Kandyan treaty signed in 1633 was, curiously, more favourable to the Portuguese in that their control over the ports of the eastern coast was recognized. It required the threat of the renewal of war to get the Kandyans to accept the treaty as a disagreeable but temporary necessity. And they began to look earnestly for foreign assistance against the Portuguese, the objective being the prevention of reinforcements from abroad for Portuguese forces in forts on the seafront. Time and again, in the past naval power had been the decisive factor in the survival of the Portuguese in Sri Lanka.

Negotiations between Rājasimha II and the Dutch were conducted over a long period, but were successfully concluded in 1638. Each side hoped to use the other for its own ends. For Rājasimha II the sole objective was the expulsion of the Portuguese and he was willing to pay a heavy price for this. For the Dutch the primary interest was in the cinnamon trade which they desired to control, and if possible monopolize. Rājasimha was prepared to assign them a monopoly of the spice trade of the island in return for aid against the Portuguese, as well as reimbursement of the costs of the campaign. This latter provision was nothing more than a trap for the Kandyans, a sordid essay in chicanery which was to poison relations between the two parties in the future.[7]

The treaty came into effect immediately and almost at once it led to misunderstandings and bickering between the allies.

In 1639, Trincomalee and Batticaloa were captured from the Portuguese and handed back to the Kandyans, but when the ports of Galle and Negombo were taken in 1640, the Dutch[8] retained them under their control on the grounds that the Kandyan ruler had not paid them the expenses incurred in these expeditions.[9] It is not without significance that while the east coast was not a cinnamon-producing area, the ports of Galle and Negombo afforded control over some of the richest cinnamon lands on the island.

Meanwhile, the diplomatic and political affairs of Europe also intruded into the conflict in Sri Lanka. At this time—1640—a native Portuguese dynasty was raised to the throne (by a very popular rebellion) after a period of eighty years during which Portugal was under Habsburg rule. One of the immediate effects of this was to put an end to hostilities between the Dutch and the Portuguese in Europe. However, not till 1645 did this armistice apply to the conflict between them in the eastern seas. For a period of about seven years, there was a lull in which the Portuguese in Sri Lanka were afforded a breathing space. During the same period disagreements between Rājasimha II and the Dutch nearly broke up their alliance and there seemed every prospect of a triangular conflict in Sri Lanka, but when hostilities between the Dutch and the Portuguese were resumed in 1652, Rājasimha returned to support the Dutch in what proved to be the final phase in the expulsion of the Portuguese. In May 1656, their fort of Colombo surrendered after a long and heroic resistance. It took the Dutch two more years to eliminate the Portuguese presence from the island; their capture of Jaffna, the last Portuguese stronghold in the island, in 1658 gave the coup de grâce.

After the surrender of Jaffna in June 1658, the Dutch fleet crossed over to the south Indian mainland to attack the Portuguese strongholds there. The capture of Tuticorin and Nagapattinam gave them control over the narrow straits between Sri Lanka and the Indian mainland, ensuring at the same time greater security for their forces in Sri Lanka. The Dutch conquest of the Portuguese provinces in Malabar was completed by 1663, and with that Portuguese rule in southern India came to an end.

The success of the Dutch over the Portuguese was a reflection of the substantially superior resources available to them.[10] Their economic strength was so much greater than that of the Portuguese since the Hollanders and Zeelanders had established a mastery amounting to a near-monopoly over the carrying trade of Europe and commanded between them the largest mercantile fleet in the world at that time. Besides, although the populations of the two countries were about the same, the Dutch could draw on Germany and Scandinavia for as much additional manpower as they needed, while the Portuguese, who had no such external resources at their disposal, found themselves dragged into wars in Flanders, Italy and Catalonia in the wake of the Habsburgs.[11] Native-born Portuguese liable to military service in the Estado da India never amounted to more than 6,000 to 7,000 at any one time. The conquest of the Kandyan kingdom, for instance, was attempted with less than 1,000 Portuguese troops. De Azevedo's army, for instance, had only 800 Portuguese troops and 300 *topases*.[12] Indeed, it is difficult to see how the Portuguese, with a population of a little over one million, could have successfully vied for colonial supremacy against the Netherlands, France and England, all of which had far greater resources. Besides, Portuguese reliance on 'gentlemen of blood and coat armour' as military or naval leaders placed them at a disadvantage with officers in the service of the VOC, where great merit and not birth was the criterion for promotion.

Dutch resources in the way of shipping, munitions and equipment, far superior to those of the Portuguese, were directed with greater effect and purpose. The Portuguese made a desperate bid to defend their far-flung possessions without having adequate naval forces to maintain communications between them, and by grasping at too much they lost all, or nearly all, when they might have done better to have concentrated their forces on a few places. Nevertheless, when we consider the fact that the Portuguese were also engaged in fighting a bitter (and ultimately, largely successful) war against the Dutch West India Company in Brazil and West Africa from 1624 until 1654, it is in many ways remarkable that they were able to hold out in Asia for as long as they did.

Considerations of prestige militated against any policy of cutting their losses. The Portuguese confronted desperate expedients and agonizing choices as they sought to defend the whole sprawling territorial and commercial structure of the Estado. And when, at last, a choice had to be made, it was Brazil that was preferred to the possessions in Sri Lanka and Malabar. As for Sri Lanka, it was of vital significance that the shift of Portuguese interest from India and the Indian Ocean to Brazil and the Atlantic took place in the mid-seventeenth century and not merely after the discovery of Brazilian gold in 1690. The councillors of Joao IV accorded a clear priority to the saving of Brazil over saving the Estado da India, a choice equivalent to that of letting the Dutch overrun Sri Lanka and their possessions on the Malabar Coast. Moreover, the local interests of those Portuguese who identified themselves with Goa rather than Lisbon were antithetical to the metropolitan interests of the Crown of Portugal. These Goan interests severely impaired the Portuguese effort to save Ceylon after the renewal of war with the Dutch in 1652. Within sixty years the Estado was destroyed as an imperial structure and was reduced to some East African footholds, Goa and the western Indian settlements, Timor and Macao.[13]

THE IMPACT OF PORTUGUESE RULE

Portuguese rule in Sri Lanka was limited in area and duration. Area-wise it was limited to the old Kotte kingdom and to the Jaffna kingdom. The Portuguese ruled for nearly sixty years in Kotte and just under forty years in Jaffna. Even in these regions, but more especially along the border with the Udarata, their control was not unchallenged by indigenous forces. But despite these limitations their governance of the maritime region was significant for the wide range of changes they initiated, and all in all their imprint on Sri Lanka was more marked than that of the Dutch who had a far longer period of control. We have very little information on the Portuguese in the Jaffna kingdom. Jaffnapatam was a comparatively small area of peripheral importance to the Sri Lankan polity of this period—our main interest. The focus of attention, in this chapter will thus be on Portuguese rule in Kotte, the Sinhalese areas of the littoral.

Under the Portuguese there was little or no interference with the existing administrative structure of the territories they controlled; they used the native administrative hierarchy for their own purposes and left it much as they found it. Even the high-ranking mudaliyārs were seldom displaced provided that they made the necessary change in religious affiliation. Again, the Portuguese preferred to use revenue farmers to collect taxes rather than relying entirely on officials. The renters were required to pay fixed sums of money to the government for the right to collect the taxes. The Portuguese did make an attempt to encourage *fidalgos* to settle in the island as landlord tax-collectors, but not many were attracted there for this purpose. At the same time, officials, whether Sinhalese or Portuguese, were given land grants called *accomodessans* in the traditional Sinhalese manner, instead of salaries. There was also one notable contribution of the Portuguese in the sphere of administration, the compilation of *thōmbos*[14] or registers of agricultural holdings. The revenues due to the state were set out in detail in the thōmbos. The Portuguese countenanced, continued and sustained the caste system, using it for their own purposes, where necessary with subtle and significant modifications in its working such as for instance in regard to the cinnamon-peelers.

The first twenty years of Portuguese rule saw the introduction of several important modifications in the traditional land tenure system, the most significant being the trend towards the substitution of quit rents for service tenure at the village holders' level.[15] This again was not so much an innovation as the extension to the people at large of what had been a privilege of the thin upper crust of the social structure whose *nindagam* holdings were subject to such a payment.

A second departure from tradition—the entry of Portuguese settlers to the ranks of village landholders, and the gradual alienation of royal villages (gabadāgam) to Roman Catholic missionaries and Portuguese settlers—had more far-reaching consequences, not only for the traditional society but also for the Portuguese themselves. The evidence suggests that these changes in landholding did not, as a rule, result in any displacement of cultivators, which, however, seems to have been due to the chronic shortage of agricultural labour in early seventeenth-century Kotte rather than to any solicitude for the indigenous peasantry.[16] On the other hand, when a gabadāgam was granted to an individual,[17] he became entitled to all payments and services from it and the treasury was left with only the quit rent, which was fixed at 12 per cent of the assessed income of the landholder. The state thus sustained a heavy loss of revenue from each so alienated, a loss which kept increasing with the number of gabadāgams transferred to the Portuguese; the tendency to make such transfers was as marked in Kotte as it was in Jaffna. The implications in terms of loss of revenue of such transfers could be gauged from the fact that Portuguese-held villages constituted one-fifth of the land area of Kotte. *Viharagam* and *dēvālēgam*, when transferred to Roman Catholic missionaries, made no payment to the state in cash or service.[18]

The first phase of Portuguese rule saw a steady decline in the number of villages reserved for the state and a corresponding contraction in the revenue from this source. As a result, the Portuguese administration on the island was in great financial difficulty in the first two decades of the seventeenth century and was forced to adopt unpopular and oppressive measures such as the compulsory purchase of areca. Had the gabadāgam been left in the hands of the state, the Portuguese would have had fewer financial worries.[19]

By the 1630s, moreover, the Portuguese administration faced an equally disturbing circumstance—village-holders were beginning to buy and sell villages. Under the Kotte kings the sale of villages was prohibited by royal decree, and this restriction had been adhered to, right up to the early 1620s. So long as the unit bought and sold was the village the peasant or *pangukāraya* was not seriously affected. By the 1620s, however, the sale of individual holdings or *pangu*s within the village became a regular feature. Though this right to sell individual holdings had existed in Sri Lanka since very early times, there had been few such sales during the disturbed times of the sixteenth century. With the return of peace such land transactions had increased and by the 1630s there was, as a result, a small but growing class of landless peasants. The Portuguese sought to check these sales of pangus for a more practical and selfish reason: they found that even those who held land on service tenure and especially categories of service which the state regarded as essential to its interests (cinnamon-peelers, elephant-hunters, woodcutters and carters), were selling their lands. In 1634, it was decreed that all lands bought from these categories of service-holders were to be restored to their previous owners and by the mid-seventeenth century the Salāgamas were forbidden to sell their land.[20]

During the years 1621–28, the Portuguese administration in Sri Lanka (in both Kotte and Jaffna) was at last able to meet all expenses from the revenue received from local sources and ceased to be a financial burden on the Estado da India. The war with Kandy did lead to a deficit once again over the next six years, but with the restoration of peace in 1633–34, their financial position improved to the point where local resources, in fact, provided a surplus over and above the costs of administration, and this began to be used for Portuguese ventures elsewhere in Asia.[21] The solvency of the Portuguese regime in Sri Lanka, after a long period of budgetary deficits, was, in fact, a reflection of a fundamental change in the economy of the Sinhalese areas of the littoral, the increasing importance of cinnamon as a source of state revenues, and from the 1630s an unprecedented improvement in the prices this commodity fetched in international trade. With the Portuguese hegemony began an era in which the sale of a commercial product, cinnamon, rather than dues from land became the chief source of revenue for the state.[22]

Cinnamon thrived in the forests of the Kelani Valley and on the coastal stretches of the Kotte kingdom from Chilaw to the Valave River. When the Portuguese obtained de facto control of the cinnamon lands of Kotte in the early 1590s they also inherited the system of open trade in this commodity that had prevailed previously.[23] There were no restrictions on the production of cinnamon. The export of the spice—except the quantity specifically delivered to the state—was in the hands of private individuals who had obtained licences for the purpose.

Almost from the beginning, Portuguese officials urged that a closer control of the cinnamon trade was desirable from both an economic and a political point of view. For example, there was the need to prevent the loss of revenue incurred by the sale of cinnamon through ports outside Portuguese control. Several measures designed to promote greater control over the cinnamon trade were promulgated in the 1590s; Colombo was declared the only port through which cinnamon could be legally exported and in 1595 its export was made a private monopoly of the captain of Colombo who was required to sell a fixed proportion of his stocks at cost to the state. But while these measures ensured more efficient control over the trade, they failed to check the fall in prices of the commodity. This latter trend continued into the first decade of the seventeenth century. In the hope of reversing this, the Portuguese resorted to various means of restricting the supply of cinnamon and when these proved unsatisfactory it was decided in 1614 that the trade in cinnamon would be a royal monopoly. It was the Portuguese who first established a state monopoly of overseas trade in cinnamon. Not that this immediately had the desired effect; throughout the period 1615–28 the main objective— that of raising prices—was not achieved. But from 1629, prices began to rise and this lasted over the next decade.

For the production of cinnamon the Portuguese used the traditional Sinhalese machinery—the caste system—but characteristically with innovations which stopped well short of its transformation in basic structure, habitual character or disposition. There was, in fact, a purposeful restriction of change to meet the peculiar requirements of the Portuguese. The demands of the state on the Salāgamas grew inexorably— arguably a modification rather than the metamorphosis which the recruitment in increasing numbers of non-Salāgama Sinhalese for cinnamon peeling in the first half of the seventeenth century would seem to signify. By 1650 these included people of the Karāva, Hunu and Padu castes. The change of occupation did not either improve or detract from their status vis-à-vis the Salāgamas. Worse, still, once this obligation was foisted on a group, there was little or no hope of its being released from it. At the same time, a fundamental change in the basis of the services due from the peelers was introduced. Where earlier these were based on the extent and quality of the land held by them, by the end of the period of Portuguese rule they were associated with the person rather than the land. By the middle of the seventeenth century it had become the standard practice to impose on every Salāgama aged more than twelve years the obligation to supply a fixed quantity of cinnamon, and the nature and extent of a landholding had little or nothing to do with the labour extracted by the state from him.

Areca nut, an article of commercial value long before Portuguese rule began, was a mainstay of local trade in the Kotte kingdom and peasants had grown accustomed to bartering it for their cloth and salt. When the Portuguese gained control over Kotte, the state's entitlement to areca was confined to the produce paid as dues in kind by those who lived in the gabadāgam, the levy known as the *kotikābadda*. Under the Portuguese, every village in which the areca palm grew, and not merely the gabadāgam, was obliged to contribute a share of the produce from this source to the government; payment for it was at a fixed rate, generally well below the market price. The Sinhalese were bitterly opposed to this unprecedented compulsory purchase of areca and regularly urged on the government the need to abolish the system. But these protests were futile. Not merely that, but the fixed price at which purchases were made was rigidly adhered to regardless of market conditions and invariably to the detriment of the peasants. The areca collected by the government very probably found its way to south India to pay for the purchase of rice which was imported from there. Sri Lanka and south India still formed a trading unit and the trade with south India was indeed vital to the economy of the littoral under Portuguese control for south India supplied rice and cloth and bought areca in exchange.

The coming of the Portuguese to Sri Lanka thus certainly led to greater commercial activity, increasing monetization of the economy and higher prices for its products. Because commodity prices were artificially but rigorously restrained after 1597, the producers' share of the sale value of these remained static while the benefits of higher prices were retained by the state, or Portuguese officials, civil and military, and Portuguese residents engaged in trade.

RELIGION

Perhaps the most notable legacy of the Portuguese on the island was the introduction of Roman Catholicism. In their zeal for proselytization, they ruthlessly destroyed Buddhist and Hindu temples and handed viharagam and dēvālēgam over to the Roman Catholic orders. The policy of preventing the worship of religions other than Roman Catholicism had begun in the days of Dharmapala. At the same time, various inducements were held out to potential converts to Roman Catholicism by way of reward, honour and advantage. Thus converts were assured of preferential treatment under the law, as well as exemption from certain taxes. In brief, these converts came to be regarded and treated as a privileged group. As the religion of the establishment, Roman Catholicism would have had a potent appeal to those at the apex of the Sinhalese caste hierarchy (and probably their counterparts among the Tamils as well) who aspired to high office, or at least to the retention of their traditional position under the new dispensation. For them, adherence to the established church was a necessary qualification. For the humble and lowly, Roman Catholicism was a means of gaining the standing denied them under the traditional religions.

The bonds of the traditional society, already strained by the movement of refugees from the south-west coast to the highland regions, were further weakened by the fanaticism and bigotry of the Portuguese which deprived the people living in the regions under their control of their religious mentors. Perhaps the Tamils of the north suffered more than the Sinhalese, since the bhikkhus found a convenient and congenial refuge in the Kandyan kingdom. Bigotry, even fanaticism, had not been unknown in Sri Lanka's past—nor for that matter had persecution on grounds of religious beliefs. But instances of this had in general been rare, and in the case of Buddhism, not since the distant past. By the sixteenth century, tolerance of other faiths was a well-established Buddhist tradition. In

Sri Lanka, the Portuguese record of religious persecution, coercion and mindless destruction of places of worship sacred to other faiths was unsurpassed in its scale and virulence.[24] The establishment of Roman Catholicism was achieved at the cost of tremendous suffering and humiliation imposed on the adherents of the traditional religions and on Islam.

Yet, the impact of Roman Catholicism was not entirely destructive. It is to the credit of the Portuguese that conversions to Roman Catholicism stood the test of harassment and persecution under the Dutch and the indifference of the British. In sharp contrast, Calvinism, which the Dutch propagated with much the same zeal if not quite the same means as the Portuguese did Roman Catholicism, developed no strong roots among the people, and its influence evaporated with the collapse of Dutch power. Moreover, the conversion to Roman Catholicism of a large proportion of the people in the areas under Portuguese control opened the way for the absorption of new social concepts such as monogamy and the sanctity of marriage, and certainly the disappearance of polygamy and polyandry from the lowlands owes much to the influence of the new religion.

Their period of rule was too short for the Portuguese to have left any real mark on the island's architecture and sculpture. Their forts and churches were either demolished or renovated by the Dutch. But the Portuguese as the first builders in Sri Lanka of dwelling houses of any substantial or permanent kind contributed most of the words associated with the building craft to the Sinhalese language. The rounded Sinhalese roofing tile of the coastal areas bears a strong resemblance to that of southern Europe. The possibility that this was introduced to the island by the Portuguese is strengthened by the fact that the traditional roofing tile of the Kandyan areas is flat rather than rounded.

A Portuguese dialect was spoken in Sri Lanka till well into the twentieth century. Portuguese was indeed the lingua franca of maritime Asia and many of its words have been absorbed into the Sinhalese and Tamil languages. Portuguese influence on female dress survived in the lowlands, especially among the Sinhalese, till the nineteenth century. Indeed they left a greater cultural imprint on the people of the lowlands than the Dutch who ruled for a much longer time. All this is striking testimony to the remarkable foresight of Joao de Barros who predicted in 1540:

> The Portuguese arms and pillars placed in Africa and in Asia, and in countless isles beyond the bounds of these continents, are material things, and time may destroy them. But time will not destroy the religion, customs and language which the Portuguese have implanted in those lands.[25]

The Kandyan Kingdom
at Bay, 1658–87

The elimination of Portuguese power in Sri Lanka aggravated rather than solved the problems that confronted Rājasimha II vis-à-vis the maritime regions of the island. He viewed the Dutch forces as mercenaries he had hired, and he hoped, quite unrealistically as it turned out, that after his aims had been achieved, the Dutch would return whence they had come, leaving behind a few officers and stores for trade purposes. As for the Dutch, their policy in the East was always that of gaining political control over spice-producing areas and where possible securing a complete monopoly of trade. In Sri Lanka their aim was nothing less than the control of the cinnamon-producing areas of the island, which they had no intention of handing over to Rājasimha II.[1]

The Dutch claimed that the lowlands were being held as collateral security till the Kandyan ruler repaid the costs incurred in the expulsion of the Portuguese from Sri Lanka under the terms of the treaty of 1638. When, after the fall of Jaffna in June 1658, the Dutch presented their bill, it was evident that it had been computed with cynical disregard for equity. For one thing, the value of the cinnamon, areca, elephants and land revenue they had obtained from the lands they controlled was calculated, unilaterally, at far below their true commercial value. Once this artificially low valuation of benefits derived was set against their expenses, the balance due was stated to be 7,265,460 guilders which, considering the Kandyan ruler's resources, was a staggering sum far beyond his capacity to pay. Besides, the king's liability kept increasing with every day the Dutch forces were stationed in the island. Such, in brief, was the sum total of the title which the Dutch could lay claim to, and realizing its intrinsic weakness they did not make much of it. And not surprisingly, Rājasimha II firmly refused to consider, much less recognize, the legality of Dutch rule in the maritime regions of the island. However, except in regard to Jaffnapatam where the Dutch took over the Portuguese possessions in their entirety, their control in other parts of the island extended to about the half the land area which the Portuguese had possessed.[2]

Confronted with overwhelming evidence of Dutch duplicity, Rājasimha II retaliated by resorting to frequent and destructive raids on the territories under their control. The Wallalaviti, Pasdun, Rayigam, Salpiti and Alutkuru Kōralēs were systematically devastated and denuded of their population, thus creating a belt of wasteland which served as a 'natural' frontier between the king's dominions and those of the Dutch. But this frontier was nevertheless an artificial one, for the king's influence permeated the border regions under Dutch rule and was not without importance in the other areas controlled by them. The loyalties of the Sinhalese to the Kandyan ruler were kept alive.

In the first two decades of Dutch rule in the maritime regions of the island, the dominant influence in shaping their response to the challenge posed by Rājasimha's militant hostility was Admiral Ryklof van Goens, who in 1656 had been given charge of the attack on the Portuguese possessions in south Asia. After the expulsion of the Portuguese from the island, he was stationed in Colombo as commissary and superintendent over the Coromandel Coast, Surat, Sri Lanka, Bengal and Malacca. The immediate need in Sri Lanka, as he saw it, was to erect a powerful defensive ring on the frontiers with the Kandyan kingdom, especially on the more populated western and southwestern sides. Van Goens, no believer in defence per se, soon emerged as the most forceful and consistent advocate of a forward policy in Sri Lanka. His first move was to seize, in 1659, the Kandyan port of Kalpitiya, which fell after a brief assault. He viewed it as the first of a series of such attacks devised for the purpose of encircling and weakening the Kandyan kingdom and compelling it to come to terms and recognize Dutch sovereignty over the lowlands. In addition to a purposeful bid to gain control over Sabaragamuva, the Seven Koralēs and Four Kōralēs, van Goens sought to occupy the Kandyan ports on the east coast and thus impose an economic blockade on the Kandyan kingdom.

This forward policy did not receive the support of van Goens's superiors in Batavia, who were quite content to leave Rājasimha II in occupation of the lands he controlled provided he left the Dutch in peace to exploit the economic resources of the parts of the island which they held. As a commercial organization, their primary concern was the extraction of the maximum possible profits from the lands under their control. But to do this it was necessary to show the people that the Dutch were there in Sri Lanka to stay and to persuade them of their good intentions. Above all, they had a realistic understanding of the fact that the success of the seasonal cinnamon harvest, the trading commodity that had been the original cause for Dutch involvement in the affairs of the island, depended greatly on the goodwill of the king and the people. The Dutch administration on the island was expressly forbidden to embark on any territorial expansion at the expense of the Kandyan ruler and van Goens was directed to pursue a conciliatory policy in order to restore good relations with Rājasimha II. As a result, Kalpitiya, where the trade had been closed to the Kandyans after its occupation, was now opened to their traffic and routes to the Kandyan kingdom were reopened in the hope that commercial and other contacts would be re-established. This reluctance to extend Dutch territory in the island was part of a policy of restraint involving south India as well. With the conquest of the Portuguese possessions in Malabar in 1663, Batavia felt that the limits of Dutch territorial expansion in south Asia had been reached.

It was one thing for Batavia to formulate a policy of restraint but quite another to get van Goens to implement it, especially in a situation where the initiative lay so much with the man on the spot. Van Goens was a man of great influence (with the directors of the VOC in the Netherlands, to whom he appealed over the heads of the Batavian authorities) and vision. He was impressed by the island's potential as a centre of Dutch interest

in south Asia; he regarded Sri Lanka as being superior to Java
and felt that Colombo and not Batavia should be the chief seat
of Dutch power in the East. What he had in mind was the creation
of a major sphere of Dutch interest in south Asia based on Sri
Lanka (as its core) and the south Indian coast. For the moment,
however, he gave in to Batavian pressure and desisted from
any significant moves to extend the land frontiers of the Dutch
possessions on the island. But these restraints did not extend
to plans to expand the VOC's influence along the sea. The
Dutch had laid claim to the exclusive possession of the littoral
of Sri Lanka and the right to keep out all other Europeans.
Extensive tracts of the coast, however, were under Kandyan
control, and this was especially significant as regards the east
where Trincomalee and Batticaloa as well as smaller ports
served as centres of a thriving trade with India and beyond.

The most menacing prospect for the Dutch lay in the trade
conducted by English and Danish merchants who from 1650–
55 were sailing into the port of Kottiyar in Trincomalee Bay in
their port-to-port small-scale trading in the Bay of Bengal;
the Kandyan ruler, for his part, actively encouraged this. The
Dutch, on the other hand, were apprehensive about his control
over ports on the east coast, not merely because it threatened
their economic and trading interests: they realized that trade
links could mature into political ones and that it was through
these ports that these would be established. All these questions
assumed much greater urgency when the English East India
Company began to show interest in acquiring a trading
settlement on the east coast of Sri Lanka. The English East
India Company wanted a station in the island which would
serve a dual purpose: it would enable them both to break into
the monopoly of the island's cinnamon trade which the Dutch
had established and to participate in the flourishing Indo-Sri
Lankan trade. Well aware of the rift between the Dutch and
the Kandyans, the English East India Company was encouraged
to open negotiations with Rājasimha II to acquire a trading
station and concession in or around Trincomalee. Besides, in
1659–60, the crew of two English vessels which had touched
on the east coast had been captured by the Kandyans.[3] The

English East India Company's officials in Madras were urged
to establish contact with Rājasimha II for the purpose of securing
trade concessions and also to obtain the release of these captives.
The Dutch soon came to know of these plans and tightened
their naval watch on the Kandyan ports. Although both the
English and the Kandyans went ahead with their negotiations,
eluding the Dutch blockade as best they could, no official
English mission could be sent to Kandy. And nothing came of
these negotiations, largely because the English were unable
to give the Kandyan ruler the quid pro quo he wanted most—
the promise of armed support against the Dutch. The Dutch
used their superior naval power in Asian waters to keep English
vessels out of Kandyan ports. Nevertheless, the English refused
to concede to Dutch claims of monopoly and sought to exercise
the freedom of the seas and free mutual relations with Asian
rulers. But their attempt to gain entry on the east coast of Sri
Lanka served to strengthen the hands of Dutch officials like
van Goens, whose advocacy of further territorial expansion
on the island became more persuasive in consequence. They
now kept pressing for the occupation of the east coast ports—
for Trincomalee at least and, if permitted, Batticaloa as well.
Batavia was at last persuaded of the danger of leaving the
east coast unoccupied and convinced of the need to maintain
a presence there to keep out other European nations.

Then in 1664, there came quite unexpectedly an opportunity,
which van Goens grasped with alacrity, to embark on something
much wider in scope than this limited programme of expanding
Dutch control over the ports. A major rebellion broke out that
year in the Kandyan kingdom against Rājasimha II, led by
Ambanvala Rāla, and although the king got the better of his
adversaries, he nevertheless felt compelled in 1665 to seek
Dutch assistance against the rebels. He asked for a detachment
of Dutch troops in Kandy and for naval patrols in the east
coast waters. In making this appeal Rājasimha II played right
into the hands of van Goens, who had come back in September
1664 to assume the office of governor for the second time.
These unforeseen developments in the Kandyan kingdom
strengthened him in his conviction that he was dealing with a
weak adversary, who was no match for the Dutch.

In April 1665, three months after Rājasimha's first appeal
for assistance, two Dutch companies marched into the Kandyan
kingdom, one from Colombo and the other from Galle, and
occupied the two strategic strongholds of Ruvanvella and
Bibilegama. The aim was not to save Rājasimha but to expand
Dutch power and this latter objective they proceeded to
accomplish; the territory held by the Dutch in the western
and south-western parts of the island was soon almost doubled
in area. A mass emigration of people was encouraged from
the king's lands to the Dutch possessions, to settle in and
cultivate unoccupied land; all the while the impression was
sedulously created that this was no aggrandisement at the
expense of the king, nor a challenge to his authority. By 1667,
Dutch power extended to the Four Kōralēs, and then up to
Alawwa on the Maha Oya, which gave them a controlling
position over the Seven Kōralēs. There was at the same time
an infiltration of Dutch power on the east coast: in 1665, an
expedition occupied and fortified Trincomalee, and by 1668
Batticaloa and Kottiyar were under their control. As in the
west, these Dutch strongholds were used as nuclear areas to
establish a dominance over the surrounding countryside.

All in all, the Dutch position on the island improved
immeasurably in the period 1665–70. The area they now occupied
was more than double what they had held before 1665; they
had established a firm control over the entire coastline of the
island. This not only gave them much greater security against
the prospect of trespassing by other European powers through
the ports of the east coast, but also gave the Dutch a position
of complete dominance over the trade and traffic of the island.
At the same time the fact that they now had a larger population
under their control meant that the problem of labour supply
would be less acute than previously, just as the acquisition of
rice-producing lands in the west improved their position with
regards to food supply. The cinnamon resources under Dutch
control were substantially augmented by the expansion of
Dutch power in the west of the island.

The extension of Dutch control over all the ports of the island
had an economic motive which was just as compelling as the

political one we have discussed so far—to establish dominance over the trade of the island. As we have seen, Kalpitiya was occupied and fortified in 1659 and the ports of the east coast had been brought under Dutch control between 1666 and 1668. With the construction of a lookout post in Panama and Magama in the south-east, the whole coastline was dotted with strategic points of control and inspection. And then in 1670, a decision was taken to establish a commanding position in the island's trade. Cinnamon had been successfully and exclusively controlled almost from the very moment of the establishment of Dutch rule. The export of elephants, areca, chanks (the spiral shell of a gastropod) and pearls was now declared a monopoly of the company, as was the import of cotton goods, pepper, tin, zinc and other minerals. Rice was the only major item of import left out. What they wanted above all was the control of the import market in textiles and the export trade in areca.

A series of regulations was introduced to put this monopoly into effect. All vessels sailing to the island had to secure passes from the nearest Dutch factory in India; these were given only to the large well-policed ports of Colombo, Galle and Jaffna where the visitors could be placed under surveillance. Boats were checked on the high seas. Apart from these restrictive measures, efforts also were made to keep the country supplied with textiles and to collect and export all areca in Dutch vessels. Capital was released for investment in cotton goods for the Sri Lankan market in Madura and Tanjore.

These measures had consequences that were not entirely beneficial to the Dutch. Within ten years they contributed to a sharp rise in import prices and led inevitably to the organization of a flourishing smuggling trade in textiles and areca. To combat this an expensive cruising operation, with armed sloops, had to be mounted, and continued well into the eighteenth century.

These, however, were long-term effects. Meanwhile Batavia was alarmed by van Goens's repeated requests for reinforcements to support the extension of Dutch control into the border districts of the Kandyan kingdom on which he had embarked. These requests came at a time when Dutch territorial expansion was proceeding apace in many parts in south-east

Asia. Batavia repeatedly sought to restrain the Dutch administration in Sri Lanka; it was increasingly critical of the expansion of Dutch power far into the interior and was always cautioning against arousing the hostility of Rājasimha II. Van Goens, on the other hand, worked on the assumption that the Kandyan kingdom was crumbling through internal discord and was too weak to survive for long against determined Dutch pressure. He believed that the whole island could be annexed if the Kandyans were defeated. But the crucial flaw in van Goens's policy was his facile underestimation of Kandyan resilience and strength, and events were soon to demonstrate the sagacity of Batavia's insistence on restraint.

In September 1668, there came sporadic, localized uprisings against the Dutch in the Meda, Kadawata and Atakalan Kōralēs, which compelled them to withdraw from the interior military strongholds of Sabaragamuva and Arandara, but resistance was not sustained and they were able to reoccupy these places. This, however, was a temporary respite, since the Kandyans were waking up to the perils of acquiescence in the decisive shift in the balance of power in Sri Lanka in favour of the VOC. They were especially uneasy about the zealous pursuit of a trade monopoly, and these economic pressures served to aggravate Kandyan anxieties over the policy of territorial expansion adopted by the Dutch since 1665. When the Kandyan counterattack came in August 1670, it was a massive one, with the heaviest blows directed at the western and south-western frontiers. There were simultaneous attacks on Kottiyar, Batticaloa and Panama on the east as well.

More ominous, for the Dutch, was the appearance of a French squadron under Admiral de la Haye off the east coast of the island with which the Kandyans soon sought an anti-Dutch alliance. This French squadron had as its main objective the establishment of a central base of French power in the East, preferably in Sri Lanka or in Banca at the Bantam coast. Encouraged by the eager response they had evoked from Rājasimha II, the French sailed into Kottiyar near the Dutch fort of Trincomalee and gradually entrenched themselves there. Rājasimha II for this part now increased his pressure on the Dutch and intensified his attacks on a number of fronts. Besides, the Sinhalese under Dutch rule were incited to rebel against them, and once resistance broke out into riot or rebellion, the Kandyans extended their support to the rebels. The Kandyan army attacked the Dutch on the east coast, doubtless in the hope that the French could be drawn into the conflict. This the French refused to do being still at peace with the Dutch. This was to the great disappointment of the Kandyans, who had ceded Kottiyar under any circumstances, however discreet the French might have been, for they were deeply perturbed by Rājasimha's bold diplomatic initiative in negotiating with the French for assistance against them. The French were easily driven out of Kottiyar, and not content with that, the Dutch proceeded to the Coromandel Coast with a reinforced fleet and forced the French to surrender at San Thomé in September 1672.

The Dutch were less successful against the Kandyans. A vigorous trade blockade of the Kandyan kingdom was essayed, but to no visible effect. Although by the end of 1673 the Kandyan offensive appeared to have been contained, guerrilla activity continued sporadically and Dutch control over the interior remained tenuous. And then in 1675 the Dutch suffered a heavy blow to their prestige when Bibilegama, an important fortified stronghold in the south, fell to the Kandyans. Once again this reverse was accompanied by massive desertion of lascarins and increasing guerrilla activity deep into the Dutch lowlands.

Rājasimha II had demonstrated over 1670–75 that he was not an ineffective ruler without resource as portrayed by the Dutch officials on the island. He had shown great shrewdness in his choice of targets for attack and had been successful in eliminating Dutch authority over much of the newly conquered area. Nor had the Dutch policy of expansion undertaken after 1665 brought the economic benefits which had been anticipated. On the contrary, it had burdened its authors with recurring and growing annual deficits. Worse still, the prolonged hostilities of these years had made it difficult for them to meet the annual target for cinnamon collection, while other economic activities were even more grievously curtailed. Nor, for the same reason, had it been possible to organize the civil administration in the interior. Moreover the widespread simultaneous uprisings against them took their toll on manpower. Dutch military resources were spread thin over several fronts. When Batavia received urgent pleas for reinforcements, it was in no mood, or indeed in any position, to supply them at a time when there were major military involvements in the Archipelago and when the Netherlands itself was facing a difficult war in Europe. Rājasimha II, in fact, compelled the Dutch to reappraise their policies on the island, for the events of 1670–75 served to convince the Batavian authorities of the wisdom of their opposition to van Goens's forward policy in Sri Lanka. But Batavia's review of the VOC's policy on Sri Lanka was nothing if not deliberate and long-drawn-out. In the end, the council finally decided as late as August 1677 that the only way out of the impasse on the island was to offer Rājasimha II the return of all lands seized from him since 1665 and to abandon all the fortifications that had been erected there.[4] The Dutch administration on the island was asked to make this offer in a letter to Rājasimha II.

However, the implementation of this policy was resolutely and successfully undermined. Ryklof van Goens was succeeded as governor of the Dutch possessions in the island in 1675 by his son, who was fully in empathy with his father's views. The father became Governor General at Batavia in January 1678 and with his son as governor in the island was able to reassert his influence over Sri Lanka policy. Between them, the two men saw to it that matters reverted to the status quo ante 1675. But not for long, for the younger van Goens vacated his post in 1680 and was succeeded by Laurens Pyl (confirmed as governor in 1681), who was much less enamoured of a forward policy than his predecessors and more realistic in his assessment of the Kandyan problem.

The crux of the problem, as Pyl saw it, was that Rājasimha II was strong enough to paralyze economic activity in the lowlands if he so wished, by preventing the peeling of cinnamon and threatening the coastal towns. Indeed, he viewed the contest between the Dutch and the Kandyans as an unequal one because the latter were able to field much larger forces. The cogency of his arguments strengthened the position of Ryklof van Goens's critics on the Batavian council and a fresh review of Sri Lanka policy was initiated in 1681. The Governor General refused to participate in these discussions, but his influence was now at an end. He retired from office in November 1681, a sick and broken man. As the council saw it, the raison d'étre of Dutch power in Sri Lanka lay in the island's cinnamon resources and all other considerations were not merely subordinate to this, but, they should emphatically not be allowed to get in the way of the smooth functioning of the cinnamon monopoly. Territorial control of the island and its attendant expenditure were justified only insofar as it was needed for the maintenance of this monopoly. The aims of the policy were pitched low in the hope that the basic minimum could be achieved without much expenditure. The council resolved to reiterate the decision made in April 1677 to return to Rājasimha II the lands taken over since 1665. They took the precaution of naming in the resolution the districts to be returned, which were identical to those named in the 1677 resolution. At the same time, the council urged upon its Sri Lankan officials the importance of coming to terms with Rājasimha II during his lifetime and, if possible, entering into a peace treaty with the Kandyan ruler recognizing the pre-1664 frontiers.

If this resolution too was not implemented, it was because of the changing political situation within the Kandyan kingdom. Rājasimha II was not inclined to begin negotiations with the Dutch for as long as they held lands captured from him and were thus in a position of strength from which to drive a hard bargain. This was less important, however, than the reports reaching the Dutch in Colombo of the king's increasing debility and these tempered their eagerness to negotiate terms with him. For the king was now in his eighties, no longer active and vigorous in the pursuit of a forceful policy against the Dutch. It seemed sensible to watch events in the Kandyan kingdom, especially with regard to the succession to the throne. Thus the Dutch themselves lost interest in the attempt to remodel their relations with the Kandyans and were reconciled to an unsatisfactory but tolerable stalemate. Pyl and the council of Sri Lanka had reached the conclusion that the territorial status quo on the island should not be upset. In the event of a strong successor to Rājasimha II emerging, the Dutch would be in a formidable bargaining position with him. This consideration also ruled out any change in the boundaries during the last years of Rājasimha II's reign. The Dutch preferred a policy of inactivity, blended with constant vigilance. They were in favour of opening the ports for the trade of the Kandyans as a gesture of goodwill to pacify them; the Batavian authorities were persuaded to endorse this line of action.

In the meantime, while Rājasimha II lived, they followed a policy of tactful and prudent restraint and of seeming submissiveness. Frequent missions were sent to Kandy with presents for the king and his permission was sought before the peelers were despatched to the forests to collect cinnamon. This permission he generally granted and the peeling of cinnamon was seldom obstructed. In the last years of his reign, Rājasimha II appears to have been anxious to foster good relations with the Dutch so that he might leave behind a legacy of goodwill to his successor.

The Struggle for Mastery over Sri Lanka, c. 1680–1766

THE KANDYAN KINGDOM

Rājasimha II was something of an exception among Kandyan rulers in his commitment to a policy of resistance to the westerners in control of the littoral. No Kandyan ruler before or after him pursued such a policy so consistently. During the period reviewed in this chapter, resistance to the VOC erupted with remarkable persistence in the Sinhalese areas of the lowlands, owing little to the initiative or encouragement of the Kandyan rulers. No doubt on many occasions the rebels were aided by the Kandyan ruler, and no doubt too the rebels generally regarded themselves as his 'subjects' and the Kandyan kingdom itself as the last bastion of Sinhalese independence. Nevertheless, the sporadic turbulence and spirited resistance of the low country was a striking contrast to the quiescence of the Kandyan kingdom vis-à-vis the VOC during these decades.

The internal politics of the Kandyan kingdom during this period were surprisingly uneventful. This was partly because the succession to the throne was unusually orderly and peaceful—so much so that even the accession of the Nāyakkar dynasty to the Kandyan throne in 1739 was accommodated with the minimum of disturbance. In that year, with the death of Narendrasimha, the last Sinhalese king of Sri Lanka, the throne passed to his chief queen's brother, Śrī Vijaya Rājasimha, a Nāyakkar. The Nāyakkars belonged to the Vaduga caste, a Telegu-speaking group originally hailing from Madurai in south India. When their home territory was overrun by the Muslims they had moved to the Coromandel Coast, which formed part of the Vijayanagar empire. In the seventeenth century, they had established marriage ties with the Kandyan royal family—the wives of both Vimala Dharma Sūriya II and Narendrasimha were Nāyakkars—and these links certainly improved their position in south India, where they themselves were of no great account. Their status as the ruling dynasty in the Kandyan kingdom after 1739 would, no doubt, have enhanced their standing considerably.[1]

The ease with which the Nāyakkars established themselves on the Kandyan throne affords a sharp contrast to the earlier turbulent succession disputes in the Sinhalese kingdoms—Anuradhapura, Polonnaruva and Kotte. It is generally believed that the accession of the Nāyakkars led to increasing tension between the chiefs and the Kandyan ruler, and that this represented the challenge of indigenous forces to a set of foreign kings. It is true that the Kandyan chiefs were an influential factor in the internal politics of the Kandyan kingdom under the Nāyakkars, but this was not unusual and, more to the point, they seldom seemed capable of concerted joint action sustained over any great length of time. Family squabbles and factional disputes kept them deeply divided and suspicious of each other. Nor is it without significance that the one major rebellion against a Kandyan ruler of the seventeenth and eighteenth centuries occurred in 1664, in the reign of Rājasimha II, long before the Nāyakkar accession. Apart from an abortive rebellion against Kīrti Śrī Rājasimha, the only Nāyakkar ruler to face serious opposition was the last of the dynasty, and the last king in Sri Lanka's history, Śrī Vikrama Rājasimha, in the early nineteenth century. The fact, however, is that the Nāyakkars blended with the Kandyan background with remarkable ease, and their success in this owed not a little to their calculated but enthusiastic support of Buddhism. The 'aristocratic' opposition to the Nāyakkars was largely a matter of wishful thinking on the part of the Dutch.

By its survival in the face of heavy odds, the Kandyan kingdom provided a link, indeed a continuity, in political institutions, social structure and religion, if not in its economy, with the Sinhalese kingdoms of the past from Anuradhapura to Kotte. In the Kandyan version of a 'feudal' polity all political and economic rights originated, theoretically, from the king whose authority extended to religion as well. He was the 'lay head' of the Erastian religious system of the Sinhalese and the chief patron and economic support of the sangha. In practice, however, monarchical authority was considerably less pervasive than it appeared to be, hedged in, as it was, by safeguards and softened by *sirit*—tradition, custom, convention and the example of 'good princes'. A third constraint on the operation of an efficient despotism was fear of rebellion, no minor consideration in a situation where the king had no standing army at his disposal.

Of the institutional checks on royal authority the most conspicuous was the *amātya mandalaya* or the royal council, to which important matters of state were delegated from time to time. Its influence and authority depended as much on subjective factors such as the personality and prestige of the councillors as on the skill with which their advice reflected the collective wisdom of the community embodied in custom and tradition. This council consisted of the two *adigārs*[2] or *maha nilamēs*—the chief administrative authorities of the kingdom—the *disāvas*, the *rate-rālas* and the *maha mohottāla* or chief secretary. It would appear that the king generally abided by the decision and advice of the council,[3] especially when there was unanimity.

The nucleus of the kingdom consisted of the *Kanda-uda-pasrata* which during much of this period was divided into nine[4] administrative units or ratas all situated within the mountains and plateaux in close proximity to the capital. There were also the disāvonys,[5] more extensive in area, sloping away from the central hills and plateaux towards the Dutch border or the sea: the exceptions were Valapane and Udapalatha which lay within the mountainous core of the kingdom. The nine ratas were generally more populous and fertile than the disāvonys, but their administrators—the rate-rālas or rate-mahatmayās—had less power and influence than their counterparts in the disāvonys, the disāvas, for the simple reason that these latter were close to the capital and kings were generally very sensitive to the possibility of the power and pomp of the disāvas encroaching on royal authority. Of these administrative units, the Four Kōralēs, the Seven Kōralēs, Mātale and Uva were the most important in terms of political status, the most lucrative to their disāvas and the most prestigious as well.[6] At the other end of the scale were the Vanni districts of the north-central and eastern parts of the dry zone generally ruled by Vanni chiefs, tributaries of the Kandyan kings. Effective authority in the Vanni districts lay with the vanniyārs rather than the disāvas appointed by the king.

Nuvarakalaviya, the heartland of the hydraulic civilizations of ancient Sri Lanka, was a special case. There the village communities were to all intents and purposes acephalous administrative entities. Control by the central government was minimal and the office of disāva of Nuvarakalaviya was symbolic of rank but conferred neither real power nor any considerable revenue. The decay of the hydraulic civilization of the dry zone left some of the villagers—who remained there—in conditions of appalling poverty; they had abandoned settled cultivation, were increasingly dependent on the produce of the jungle for their sustenance and were often ignorant of the techniques of wet rice cultivation. Like Nuvarakalaviya, the remoter provinces 'below the mountains'—Velassa, Bintenna and Tamankaduva—situated on the periphery of the Kandyan kingdom, were little subject to the control of the central government and brought no considerable revenue either to the king or to the minor disāvas appointed over them.

In their disāvonys, the disāvas were virtual rulers: they were responsible for the collection of revenue, exacted the labour service due to the king, enjoyed judicial powers, communicated with the ruler through the adigārs and, in general, saw to the good governance of the territory under their control. The method of conscription was such that military authority too was concentrated in their hands. The disāvas could, with the help of local officials in the provinces, rally the peasants for war. No king after Rājasimha II is known to have led the troops into battle, and in the wars with the Dutch it was the adigārs who took the leadership. In war and in ceremony the people followed the disāva of the province. The disāva normally resided in the capital as a pledge of the fidelity of the people under his command and visited his disāvony only when state business so demanded. Administrative authority and the right to collect revenue were delegated to local officials, generally members of the local aristocracy of the disāvony, selected from among the *rate ātto*, the equivalent of a yeomanry.

A disāvony like a rata was divided into kōralēs (comprising a group of contiguous villages) and a kōralē into *pattus*. The disāva appointed his subordinates from among the Govikula in each of these, a kōralē (an office of trust and considerable remuneration) for a pattu, a *muhandiram* in charge of each caste group in a specified territorial division, and under the muhandiram were the *vidānes* responsible for such caste groups in a village. Since almost every inhabitant possessed some land, he had a tenurial obligation to make a contribution to the state in cash or kind and to render personal service. The link between the cultivator and the state, in the collection of these taxes and the performance of services (rājakāriya), was the vidāne or headman. There were also the *baddas*, formed on the basis of caste groups, which cut vertically across the territorial system without regard to regional boundaries and divided the population into functional groups. The authority of each badda over the caste group and its services was all-embracing. During the eighteenth century, the badda system was highly centralized and functioned under separate departmental heads. However, during the last few years of the kingdom's existence, the baddas tended to come under the control of the disāvas.

Concentration of authority in the hands of the disāvas—especially those in charge of the principal disāvonys—was always a potential danger to royal authority, and for that reason a policy of checks and balances was resorted to. There were, of course, the obvious but crude devices of setting aristocratic families against each other and seeking to win support by rewarding loyal service with gifts in the form of land grants. Great care was taken to see that the disāvas were not appointed to their home or ancestral territories. In the remoter parts of the country where the disāva's authority was potentially at its greatest, the *basnāyaka nilamēs* of dēvālēs (lay trustees of dēvālē property) were a powerful countervailing force, especially because some of the more important dēvālēs had very large extents of land in these remote regions.

CASTE

Kandyan 'feudalism' was an association of land tenure with a system of endogamous occupational castes, which enabled a complex system of labour specialization to operate without the use of money. Through the baddas caste services were channelled to the benefit of the state. Each caste was economically privileged in the sense that it alone had the right to supply a particular kind of labour. Every separate craft had its own headmen and all the craftsmen held land in return for the services they rendered so that the craftsmen, like everyone else, were cultivators but provided the specialized service demanded of their caste.

Three points about the caste system of the Kandyan kingdom need special emphasis. First, it was a more rigid, or rather, less flexible system than that of the Sinhalese areas of the littoral. But this was not always so. Early in the seventeenth century, Antonio Barretto (Kuruvita Rāla), a Karāva, was made disāva of Uva. The eighteenth century provides no such example of a non-*Goyigama* in so exalted a position. Similarly, in later times there is greater strictness in regard to concubinage of women of lower castes. The evidence then is of increasing stratification of Kandyan society in the eighteenth century, in contrast to the greater mobility and social change within the caste system in the Sinhalese areas, apparent under Dutch rule.

Second, as in the caste system of the littoral region the dominant element was the Govikula or Goyigama (which formed almost half the population). Since the entire population lived in part by farming, and everyone had a share of land, it was the Goyigama exemption from 'professional' services as craftsmen or artisans that set them off from other castes. Besides, the Goyigamas in the higher administrative services did not till the soil at all, but derived their income from the land by employing others.

The Govikula, like other castes, was divided into sub-castes. The sub-caste was strictly endogamous, the organized unit with which individuals were mainly identified. Not all subdivisions within the Govikula could strictly be called sub-castes, however, and there was considerable social mobility within the lower ranks of the Govikula. The *Radala* and the *Mudali* were the highest of the sub-castes of the Govikula. They were strictly endogamous and formed the real aristocracy of the Kandyan kingdom, although the rest of the Goyigamas were also considered honourable. The Radala preserved its status by frequent intermarriage within its own ranks. Secondary wives of the kings were always selected from the nobility and collateral members of the royal family found spouses from among the nobles. Political power tended to concentrate in their hands since they controlled the key posts in the administration, manned the court and had considerable social control, epitomized in the personal retinue which formed part of their privileges. Besides, they had much land which gave them substantial wealth. This landed wealth conferred not only economic security in the sense of its continuity from generation to generation, but also enormous prestige. Some of the posts in the administrative hierarchy were hereditary for almost 150 years: thus the Ähälēpola family were high in the king's service from the time of Rājasimha II, if not earlier. Among the other families of similar hereditary influence were the Pilima Talavēs, Leukēs, Māmpitiyas and Galagodas.

The selection of all administrative officers and the whole economic structure had caste as its foundation. While the Radala and Mudali formed the apex of the administration, other subdivisions of the Govikula had distinctive official positions within the bureaucracy. All official posts within the central government or in the provinces depended on the rank of the officer within the Govikula. All other castes were regarded as *hīna jāti*. While the position of the Govikula at the top of the caste hierarchy was never in doubt, there was no fixed order of precedence among the non-Goyigama castes of the Kandyan kingdom. Their rank and status may have changed in the seventeenth and eighteenth centuries, but the process could not be compared with the corresponding one in the maritime regions.

All social relationships between the various castes and overt caste symbols were fixed by custom (it was in regard to marriage that caste rules were most rigidly observed). A person's caste was something quite unalterable. His social life, his conduct and his position in society, as well as his legal rights and liabilities (including the taxes he paid and the services he performed), were all determined by caste. Inveterate custom, rather than religious sanctions, held the caste system together. And here we come to the third point: the ultimate controlling authority of the caste system was secular and it continued as a vigorous force in a Buddhist society because state power was vitally involved in maintaining it.[7] The sangha too was not averse to upholding the caste system in its sphere of activity, thus helping in its own way to legitimize the social order.

THE ECONOMY

The economic basis of the Kandyan kingdom was subsistence agriculture in which paddy cultivation was the central feature. Paddy cultivation was at all times an enormously disciplined culture but more so in hilly terrain where terraces had to be constructed. It was also generally a communal activity around which the social and economic life of the village revolved—the preparation of the fields for sowing and the harvesting and thrashing of the crop all required the active support of the cultivator's neighbours in the village. A prime requirement was a plentiful and well-regulated supply of water, which was provided by the heavy monsoonal and convectional rains of the wet zone in which much of the Kandyan kingdom lay. In the drier areas, the water supply was supplemented by village tanks. Shifting agriculture—*chēna*[8] cultivation—was an integral part of the village economy, its role being especially important in the dry zone. The unique feature of chēna cultivation in Sri Lanka was that it was practised by a peasantry who were also engaged, simultaneously or otherwise, in settled forms of cultivation. Because of the abundance of forest land—the greater part of the Kandyan kingdom was covered with forests—and low population density, chēna cultivation, far from being a wasteful form of agriculture[9] as the Dutch and later the British regarded it, was, in fact, 'an economically justifiable form of land usage'.[10] All paddy lands in the kingdom were subject to both compulsory services[11] (these services were attached to the land and not the individual so that whoever enjoyed the use of a plot of paddy land had to supply the labour due from it or provide a substitute for that purpose) and taxes paid in kind *(kada rājakāriya)*, while some of them had in addition the obligation of specialized services. These latter were generally professional services organized under the baddas and performed by non-Goyigama castes specially in various crafts: potters, carpenters, goldsmiths, painters, wood and ivory carvers and weavers.[12] Lands held by the Govikula were not subject to services of this nature. There was also an annual rate, which varied with the size of the holding, paid in grain at harvest time. The basis of all these imposts and services was the *mada bim*, the paddy field proper; neither the cultivator's *goda bim* (garden) nor his *hēna* (chēna) were liable to any taxes. The *marāla* or death duty[13] was paid in kind, generally in grain, but in the sixteenth and seventeenth centuries more often in cattle. And the king had the exclusive rights to precious stones.

The king obtained the services and ensured the loyalty of the higher officers in his administration by generous grants of rights over land. The disāvas were granted what were known as *saramāru nindagam* lands, which they held during office. But such lands were not heritable. When the king gave a gabadāgama or royal village to a chief, it became a nindagama, and the produce of the *muttettu* or the proprietor's share went to the *gambadda* or grantee. The rest of the village was divided into pangus or shares and the shareholders now performed services or paid dues to the grantee instead of to the king. Thus as long as he held office, the grantee of a saramāru nindagama had the usufruct of the muttettu and rights to enjoy services of its tenants and certain dues from them, to fine or eject them for non-performance of services and finally to settle disputes among them. Nindagam, given to disāvas in paraveni on the basis of a royal sannas, conferred the highest rights in land, amounting in effect to hereditary estates, which in certain special cases were declared free of all services to the Crown. These paraveni nindagam, as they were called, gave a family a sense of identity from generation to generation and greatly enhanced its prestige.

The king's cash income was very limited. Indeed, specie was scarce in the Kandyan kingdom and paddy was frequently resorted to as a medium of exchange, while many economic transactions were on the basis of barter. This was partly because considerations of security—the threat of invasion from the littoral—hampered the development of trade; since the kingdom's security depended on its inaccessibility, the construction of roads and bridges was deliberately discouraged. Communications within the kingdom were at all times very difficult on account of the forests, the mountainous terrain and the heavy rains. Thus districts and, for that matter, villages developed as distinct economic entities with little surplus production and no means of disposing of any surplus—in brief, as congeries of local economies rather than as a truly cohesive 'national' economy.

The VOC's economic activities contributed greatly to this contraction of the Kandyan economy. For a long time there had been considerable trading activity between the Kandyan kingdom and Madurai–Tanjore in south India. This trade, a vitally important one for the Kandyan economy, was disrupted from around 1665–70 when the Dutch annexed a number of Kandyan ports and established a trade monopoly. As we have seen, Kandyan products had to be exported through the VOC or its agents at prices fixed by them well below their real market value. The Kandyan villager suffered a heavy economic loss, for the VOC paid him a paltry sum for his areca which would have fetched considerably higher prices if direct sales had been permitted. Again, once the VOC became the sole importer of cloth the Kandyans were the losers. Thus, throughout the greater part of the eighteenth century the external trade of the Kandyan kingdom was crippled, resulting inevitably in the shrinking of the Kandyan economy during this period.

THE CONSOLIDATION OF DUTCH POWER IN SRI LANKA

The VOC's relations with the Kandyan kingdom in these decades are reviewed here in terms of three themes: Dutch anxiety to gain recognition of their sovereignty over the regions they controlled, which the Kandyans steadfastly refused to concede but which they were compelled to do by the treaty of 1766; Kandyan opposition to the trade monopoly imposed by the Dutch; and, over most of this period, the recognition by both the Kandyans and the Dutch of the limits of their power and, stemming from this, the acceptance of their interdependence in regard to certain key areas of activity.

After the death of Rājasimha II, the aim of Dutch policy was to revise the treaty of 1638 and to negotiate a new one which would reflect more accurately the political situation that existed, and above all, which would recognize Dutch sovereignty over the coast and seas of the island. They were especially anxious to obtain secure title to their possessions in order to guard against foreign intrusions. Protracted negotiations with Kandyan officials over the period 1688 to 1697 brought no results and this cooled the enthusiasm of the Dutch for a new treaty.[14] For forty years thereafter they were less concerned about securing recognition from the kings of Kandy of their possession of the maritime lands. Instead, the Dutch were content to base their claims on a right of conquest from the Portuguese and the fact of effective possession since then. This, the Kandyan rulers refused to accept. Specific issues of conflicting interest arose and developed around this question of legal title, the most potent of these being with regard to Kandyan external trade in the context of Dutch insistence on monopoly rights.

Although most of the commodities of trade which came within the trade monopoly claimed by the Dutch originated in the coastal areas, the Kandyan region was the source of areca, pepper and cardamoms—which grew abundantly there, and formed important items in the once flourishing trade between the Kandyan kingdom and the Indian coast. Similarly, textiles and salt were essential items of import for the Kandyans. Once the Dutch established their monopoly in trade, all transactions in these commodities had to be conducted through the company or its approved 'agents' and at prices fixed by the Dutch authorities, generally disadvantageous to the Kandyan producer and consumer. The monopoly resulted in a considerable loss of revenue to the court as well as to the chiefs.[15]

Under Vimala Dharma Sūriya II, the successor of Rājasimha II, both the court and the chiefs urged the Dutch to relax the rigours of their monopoly by opening some of the ports to Kandyan trade. Although at first the Dutch were inclined to be conciliatory and to grant these requests, the realization that it would be detrimental to the economic interests of the company compelled them to stand firm against any relaxation. The chiefs had tried unsuccessfully to send boats on their behalf through Puttalam. Vimala Dharma Sūriya II, a diffident and altogether pacific character felt obliged to demonstrate his displeasure at the commercial policy of the Dutch by ordering the closure of the lines of communication between his kingdom and the Dutch territories. The Dutch retaliated by tightening their monopoly after 1703. Although the Kandyan kings did not follow a consistent policy of hostility to the Dutch, nevertheless, the closure of the 'roads' was one option that was available to them and which was used to considerable effect. It was not a positive act of aggression and the Dutch could hardly regard it as such, but it did have an impact on them since it often resulted in an inconvenient dislocation of the island's trade. This pattern of an onerous monopoly provoking the closure of the 'roads' in retaliation was to be repeated throughout much of the eighteenth century.

Narendrasimha, Vimala Dharma Sūriya II's son and successor, was confronted with these problems almost from the time of his accession in 1707. There was a considerable loss of revenue in areca and a shortage of textiles on account of the Dutch trade monopoly. In retaliation the 'roads' from Kandy were closed in 1716 and this caused a noticeable shortage of areca in the Dutch ports as well as a reduction in the sale of cloth. The Dutch, however, were not to be deflected from their policies. They would not consider any possibility of opening the ports. In 1720, the frontier gates were opened once more and the trade between the Kandyan kingdom and the lowlands was resumed. But the pressure for a relaxation of the monopoly and the opening of the ports continued. Those most restive on this issue were the Kandyan chiefs in their anxiety to get a better price for the areca and pepper bought by the Dutch in Kandy. They took up the position that there was no justification for the closure of the ports when there was no threat of a foreign attack. In 1732, the pathways of the kingdom were closed again and this continued for two years, much longer than on previous occasions. It caused a dearth of areca and cardamoms. Nevertheless, the Dutch decided to put an end to any expectation of free trade and the Batavian Council instructed Governor Pielat (1732–34) to send a letter to the court, declaring firmly and pointedly that the ports would not be reopened for Kandyan trade in breach of the Dutch monopoly under any circumstances.

Governor van Imhoff was sent to the island in July 1736 to rebuild, if possible, good relations with Kandy. He began on a conciliatory note. There was a refreshing tone of moderation and realism in his analysis of the situation of the island. The keynote was his emphasis on the interdependence of the Kandyans and Dutch, and the need to share the country's trade on a more equitable basis: the major share would continue to remain with the Dutch, but he was willing to give up the trade monopoly at least to the extent of granting the Kandyans some limited benefits in trade on their own. In 1736, he attempted to secure a peace treaty with the Kandyan kingdom, recognizing the legality of Dutch sovereignty over the lowlands in return for some limited trading concessions—the Kandyans were to be offered the right to send three vessels from Puttalam for purposes of trade (in goods that were not monopolized by the Dutch) to the Indian coast. He regarded such concessions as a means of binding the Kandyan rulers to the Dutch in perpetual friendship. When this compromise was rejected by both the Kandyans and the Batavian government, van Imhoff's thoughts quickly turned to a more rigorous and hostile line of action—a swift expedition to Kandy, a seizure of the king and enforcement of a peace treaty incorporating the terms desired by the Dutch. Narendrasimha was ailing and not expected to live long. Since he had no male heir the Dutch rightly anticipated a disputed succession and political instability on his death, conditions which could be exploited to their advantage. But Batavia recognized these recommendations for what they were— a revision to van Goens's policies—and strongly opposed them. There was no objection to appeasement of the Kandyans provided van Imhoff could do it within the framework of existing policy and with the expedients available to him.

Pressure on the Dutch eased substantially with the breakdown in the king's health in 1737 and his death in 1739.

A POLICY OF COEXISTENCE

For most of the period covered by this chapter the two parties—the Kandyans and the Dutch—preferred a policy of coexistence to one of prolonged tension. Neither was strong enough to gain a decisive advantage over the other, while each in its own way needed the other's support in some matters of vital importance. Thus the Kandyans, while fully aware of their own influence among the Sinhalese under the rule of the VOC, seldom resorted to incitement of them against the Dutch, and even when they did so there was a very noticeable element of cautious restraint in such activities. The Dutch, for their part, despite provocations, were circumspect in dealing with the court. They took care not to offend it in any way. There was, in fact, a scrupulous and consistent adherence to formalities and civilities and a remarkable tolerance of court etiquette even when it was tediously exhausting if not positively degrading. Above all, both parties were keenly aware of their mutual dependence.

Dutch assistance in the form of boats and ships was required by the Kandyans in regard to two issues principally, and regularly, and since neither of these had to do with trade or politics, the Dutch were willing to help. The Kandyan royal family, as the only ruling house in the island, had to look to south India for its spouses. The Dutch readily accommodated requests for aid in sending missions to south India for this purpose, as well as in bringing the bridal party to the island. The Kandyan monarchs, Narendrasimha, Śrī Vijaya Rājasimha and Kīrti Śrī Rājasimha were afforded this facility in 1710, 1739 and 1751 respectively. Again, Dutch aid in the form of ships was vital, if not indispensable, in helping Kandyan rulers to maintain contact with the Buddhist states of south-east Asia—Burma and Thailand principally—to revitalize Sinhalese Buddhism, and to re-establish the *upasampadā* and the purity and strength of the sangha in Sri Lanka.[16] Indeed because of the distances to be covered and the hazards of the long voyages, these missions could never have

been undertaken without the active help of the Dutch. Three
such missions were sent. The first two in 1741 and 1747 both
failed, though not for the same reasons; while the third, which
left in August 1750 and returned to the island in the middle of
1753, was a pronounced success and a landmark in the history
of Buddhism in Sri Lanka.[17]

The Dutch, for their part, were equally dependent on Kandyan
goodwill in matters of vital importance to them—the successful
collection of cinnamon for export and the transport of elephants
to Jaffna. The first of these was by far the more important and as
regards this the king's permission was required for peeling
cinnamon within Kandyan territories. His influence was not
confined to these regions. He could, if he wished, impede the
smooth functioning of the Dutch machinery for cinnamon
production in the lowlands under the control of the VOC by virtue
of his leverage with the Salāgamas. Generally, the peeling of
cinnamon in the Kandyan kingdom as well as the transport of
elephants to Jaffna was permitted, except on occasions when
relations between the two parties were more than ordinarily
strained. At least up to the end of the 1720s the Kandyan king
did not as a rule seek to subvert the loyalty of the salāgamas and
thus disorganize the peeling of cinnamon in the regions under
Dutch control. Even during the administration of Petrus Vuyst
(1726–29), when the Dutch were under severe stress on account
of internal problems in the lowlands, Kandyans did not seek to
turn these to their advantage. But this reluctance disappeared
over the next decade.

In the early 1730s, the efforts of the VOC administration to
extract a larger portion of the agricultural production of the peasants
for its coffers led to widespread discontent in the low country.[18]
The discontent ripened into unrest and the Kandyans smarting
under the restraints of the Dutch trade monopoly were afforded
an opportunity for embarrassing the Dutch by inciting the people
of the low country to resistance. The chiefs took the initiative in
this. The Kandyan kingdom served as a refuge for malcontents
facing punishment and as a bridgehead from which they would
sustain their opposition to the Dutch. As we have seen, the
'roads' linking the low country with the Kandyan kingdom

were closed on the king's instructions in 1732. In 1733, the peeling of cinnamon in the Seven Kōralēs was forbidden on the king's orders, as was the transport of elephants through the kingdom. The situation in the low country deteriorated further under Governor Domburg (1734–36). The VOC's demands on the service castes—especially the Salāgamas—kept increasing and the Kandyans gave the latter secret encouragement in their opposition to the Dutch when not openly inciting them to rebellion. Disaffected elements in the low country used the king's name to rally support for themselves against the Dutch. The king's influence was very vividly demonstrated, and in a manner most damaging to the Dutch, when the salāgamas were persuaded to desert or to slacken the pace of collection of cinnamon.

If the Kandyans anticipated that a policy of fanning the flames of discontent in the low country would yield the result they most desired—a relaxation of the trade monopoly and the opening of the ports—their hopes were quickly and resolutely dispelled by the Dutch. As we have seen, neither in Sri Lanka nor in Batavia would the VOC make any concession on this. True, this continued manipulation of agrarian discontent in the lowlands to the discomfiture of the VOC largely explains the initiatives attempted by van Imhoff which were discussed earlier in this chapter. But while Batavia would countenance appeasement and conciliation, it continued to insist on a maintenance of the trade monopoly.

The pressure on the Dutch eased considerably in the early 1740s. This is explained to some extent by the internal politics of the Kandyan kingdom—the accession, in 1739, of the Nāyakkar dynasty to the Kandyan throne.[19] While their kinship ties with south Indian states were to pose considerable dangers to the Dutch in later years because of the potential these held of political links with their European rivals and competitors in south India, the establishment of the Nāyakkar dynasty caused no immediate change in Kandyan–Dutch relations. The 'roads' were opened once again and internal trade between the two regions was resumed. This respite did not last long. By the time van Gollenesse took over as governor in 1743, the Kandyans began stepping up their pressure on the Dutch in the low country. The Salāgamas, still very loyal to the Kandyan ruler, often took their complaints to him, and time and again van Gollenesse had to appeal to the Kandyan chiefs to use their influence with the salāgamas to persuade them to fulfil their tenurial obligations to the VOC. With the accession of the Nāyakkar dynasty to the Kandyan throne, the chiefs began to play a greater role in policy making.

Much more serious and ominous for the future were the incursions being made regularly into Dutch territory by the Kandyans. In 1743, for instance, there was a raid into Siyanē Kōralē, as well as sudden attacks on Dutch outposts in the Trincomalee district. Although a show of firmness by van Gollenesse sufficed to repulse most of these, it was not possible to guard against all such forays. Van Gollenesse had a shrewd grasp of the intricacies of the political and power structure of the Kandyan kingdom and sought to exploit the divisions and factions within the court by a mixture of flattery and bribery— the disbursement of gifts to some of the factions—to the advantage of the Dutch. But he was in no position to sustain this initiative because of a succession of natural disasters— floods, crop failures and epidemics of smallpox and 'pestilential fevers' (probably malaria) in 1747–48. The advantage was now once more with the Kandyans and van Gollenesse found that their pressure for free trade continued unabated and was, in fact, intensified with the settlement of increasing numbers of Nāyakkar relatives of the king in the Kandyan court.[20] Some of the Kandyan chiefs entered into partnerships with south Indian Muslim merchants in a potentially profitable smuggling trade through the Kandyan ports. It would appear that the Nāyakkar kinsfolk of the king, with their south Indian connections, took the initiative in this. Van Gollenesse had to take rigorous measures to curb this smuggling trade. But the pressure for free trade continued.

Kandyan incursions into Dutch-controlled territory in the lowlands continued during the administrations of van Gollenesse's successors, Loten (1752–57) and Schreuder (1757–62). And since Dutch land policies, especially under Schreuder, became even more rigorous in their impact than those of the 1730s, in a single-minded effort to extract an ever-increasing share of the produce of the land from the peasants, opportunities for the Kandyans to meddle in the affairs of the lowlands kept proliferating and were eagerly exploited. It became increasingly difficult to maintain the restraints observed by both parties in this war of nerves and two decades of intermittent tensions, pressures and irritations led directly to open warfare in the early 1760s during van Eck's administration (1762–65) for the first time in more than a century.[21]

THE ENGLISH EAST INDIA COMPANY ENTERS THE PICTURE

It was in 1762 that the Madras establishment of the English East India Company sent its first diplomatic mission to Sri Lanka under John Pybus. The English had long hesitated in seeking to develop contacts with the Kandyan kingdom for fear of offending the Dutch, whose neutrality in the Seven Years War, which was then raging, was advantageous to them. But the initiative on this occasion had come from the Kandyan ruler who was desperately seeking the friendship of other European powers as a counterpoise to the Dutch. Although the English were conscious of the island's strategic value in the Anglo-French struggle for supremacy in India, they had no definite plans with regard to Sri Lanka and no policy to apply. Thus the Pybus mission was basically an intelligence project to gain an understanding of the political situation on the island, and to assess the military and problems that confronted the Kandyan rulers. The British diplomats had no intention of being drawn into a commitment to the Kandyans which could in any way be interpreted as a formal offer of assistance against the Dutch.

In striking contrast, the Kandyans, faced with the prospect of war with the Dutch, expressed a positive desire for British assistance and they hoped that the Pybus mission would treat this as the central point of the negotiations it was to conduct in Kandy. But Pybus had no authority to make such an offer, and keeping to his instructions he was deliberately vague and hesitant whenever this theme emerged in the course of his discussions with the Kandyans. He did produce the articles of a draft treaty for discussion, but these were more in the nature of a manoeuvre designed to extract information on what potential benefits the Kandyans were inclined to offer to the British than a serious attempt at negotiating an agreement conferring benefits on both parties. Thus Pybus's request for a territorial foothold for the English East India Company on the king's territory on the coast, in return for which nothing substantial was on offer, was far from being an optimistic attempt to get something for nothing. The offer was a cynical device to test the Kandyan reaction to the prospect of a British bridgehead on the island. It is important at this point to emphasize that Pybus, in his request for a territorial foothold on the coast, was not thinking exclusively of the port of Trincomalee and that it was not the primary aim of his mission to ask for British control of that port. The British had a working arrangement with the Dutch which allowed them to use the harbour as a refitting port for the British Eastern fleet whenever necessary.

The discovery that the Pybus mission was in Sri Lanka and negotiating with the Kandyans came as a great surprise to the Dutch. But by the time the discovery was made they were already at war with Kandy. The news of the Pybus mission served to harden the Dutch attitude towards the Kandyan kingdom and to spur them on to a total reversal of their tactics and policies with regard to their position in Sri Lanka. The legal fiction that they administered the territories they controlled as servants of the Kandyan king had been maintained for too long partly because the expenses of a protracted war against the Kandyans, which was the only means of converting this fictitious position into the hard reality of effective sovereignty, acted as a deterrent to the Dutch. In 1762, reluctance to embark on a war, even a long one, against the Kandyans melted away and an expedition was despatched to the Kandyan Hills to bring the Kandyan kingdom to heel. It was routed as comprehensively as the Portuguese invading forces had been in the past. But the Dutch were too perturbed by the Pybus mission and its implications to let this defeat deter them from renewing the effort to compel the Kandyans to accept the fact of Dutch sovereignty over the island's maritime regions. A second expedition despatched in 1765 was successful because it was better planned, and the Dutch were able to extract from the Kandyans a settlement and a treaty which gave them all they desired.

The clauses of the treaty of 1766[22] spelled out the realization of what had lately become the major objectives of Dutch power in Sri Lanka. The Dutch were now the paramount power in Sri Lanka and the Kandyan kingdom was reduced to the position of a landlocked state dependent on the Dutch for supplies of some essential items of food (such as salt and dry fish), with its external trade under Dutch control and with severe limitations on the conduct of its foreign relations. Very few concessions were made to Kandyan sensibilities despite the fact that the Dutch success on the battlefield was more apparent than real and that the treaty had been extracted by the use of prolonged diplomatic pressure and threats of a renewal of war. In reality, the treaty was a hollow triumph for it did not represent an accurate expression of the real balance of political forces in Sri Lanka. The Kandyans were too resentful and humiliated to reconcile themselves to the new situation and the Dutch lacked the power to compel the Kandyans to a strict adherence to the essential features of the treaty if they were recalcitrant. The rigorous terms imposed on the Kandyans by the treaty of 1766 spurred them on to a feverish search for foreign assistance in expelling the Dutch from Sri Lanka.

The Kandyans' passionate pursuit of a policy of revenge against the Dutch coincided with the eruption of the penultimate phase of the Anglo-French conflict for the control of India. The British were anxious to prevent the French from filling the power vacuum caused by the waning of Dutch power in Asia. As a result, the Dutch were soon embroiled in the Anglo-French struggle for the control of south India. From this emerged the threat to the Dutch in the maritime regions of Sri Lanka and British interest in the island. Since many of the south Indian rulers were connected by kinship and marriage ties to the Nāyakkars, they could easily act as brokers in a Kandyan–English East India Company alliance and thus link Sri Lanka with the politics of the Madras region. The link was attempted during the Seven Years War. If the role of the south Indian states in this was much less than decisive, it was because—as we shall see—the operation of more powerful forces, which pulled Sri Lanka into the power struggle in south India, had made their mediatory role superfluous.

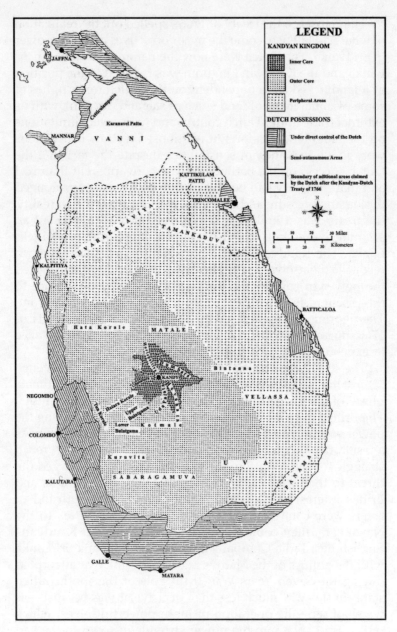

Sri Lanka in the Mid-Eighteenth Century

Trade and Agriculture
Under the VOC

The lure of cinnamon brought the VOC to Sri Lanka and throughout the period of its rule in the island's maritime regions, the protection of the cinnamon monopoly was its great passion. Occasionally, it showed some interest in other cash crops—coffee, pepper and cardamoms, for instance—but this, as we shall see, was only for brief periods when the supply from the traditional sources of these commodities within the far-flung eastern possessions of the VOC was inadequate to meet the demand for them in the markets of Europe and Asia. In the wider perspective of the VOC's international trade, Sri Lanka's role was that of its main producer of cinnamon.

CINNAMON

As the sole suppliers of cinnamon in the European and Asian markets, the Dutch were in a position to dictate the price at which it was sold. This was a freedom the Dutch seldom had with regard to other commodities. This was reflected in the extraordinary increase in the price of cinnamon in Europe as well as in the East from the 1660s, when the VOC established its control over Sri Lanka's littoral and its cinnamon trade. From an average of 1.50 guilders a pound in 1660, the price moved up to 3 guilders over the rest of the seventeenth century. In the mid-eighteenth century, the price reached 6 guilders and stood at a quite exceptional 8 or 9 guilders a pound in the 1780s before returning to an average of 6 or 7 guilders in the 1790s, the last years of Dutch rule on the island. Sri Lanka's cinnamon was superior to that of its overseas competitors, but only three or four out of about ten types of the island's cinnamon were of fine quality, and sufficient quantities of the finest cinnamon required for the European market could never be found. What was most remarkable was that Sri Lanka did not benefit from the consistently high prices which its most valued export commodity commanded in the markets of the world, nor for that matter did the VOC administration on the island, for the profits from cinnamon did not appear in its accounts.[1] The profits from sales in Europe went directly to the Netherlands chamber of the company, and those at Asian ports remained there. The result was that neither the regions in Sri Lanka which produced the spice nor the people engaged in its production derived any substantial advantage from this trade.[2] The VOC monopolized both the trade and the profits from it.

The history of Sri Lanka's cinnamon trade during the period of the VOC's rule of the island's maritime belt has three distinct phases, with the administrations of Governor van Imhoff and Governor Falck serving as convenient dividing lines. Some aspects of this first phase have been reviewed in earlier chapters and therefore will not be dealt with at any great length here. Common to all these phases are some distinctive features. First, because the Salāgamas were under a service obligation to deliver fixed quantities of cinnamon gratis and were paid a bare pittance for that which was supplied in excess of this quota, the company's production cost was next to nothing. The cinnamon department—the mahabadda under a Dutch official (the captain of the mahabadda)—was entrusted with the administration of the very rigorous *plakaats* designed to preserve cinnamon as a Dutch monopoly.[3] The main function of the department was mobilization of all able-bodied Salāgamas to peel the cinnamon and make it ready for export. The mahabadda maintained lists of Salāgamas, which were regularly scrutinized and revised to check absenteeism and avoidance of this service obligation.[4] The peeling of cinnamon in the forests was inordinately rigorous and unpleasant, and quite understandably the Salāgamas resorted to all manner of ruses to avoid the service. Pressures, relentlessly maintained, on the Salāgamas to bring in ever-increasing quantities of cinnamon—to exceed their quotas and not merely meet them—imposed on them a crushing burden of tenurial obligations.

Second, despite their control of the major cinnamon-producing areas of the south-west, the Dutch could never do without supplies obtained from the Kandyan kingdom as well. In combination with the influence the Kandyan ruler had with the Salāgamas, this dependence on the Kandyan kingdom for supplies of cinnamon underlined the vulnerability of the VOC to diplomatic and political pressure from the Kandyans. There was, third, the central feature of Dutch land policy in the littoral under their control: the protection of the cinnamon producing forests—they were content to leave potentially productive land lie idle rather than allow it to be cultivated if there was the slightest chance of harm to the cinnamon plants that grew so luxuriantly in the forests. This singularly restrictive land policy left extensive tracts of cultivable land beyond the reach of the people. The VOC justified these restraints by the arguments that slash and burn agriculture would lead to soil exhaustion; that the clearing of land for chēnas would inevitably result in the destruction of cinnamon plants; and indeed that cinnamon seeds scattered by the wind and birds would not take root in chēna lands cleared of their forest cover. In the nineteenth century, the British, who succeeded the Dutch in control of the island, would be just as rigid in their opposition to chēna cultivation, although the rationale in that instance was composed of a different set of arguments, with the charge of soil exhaustion serving as the single common factor. But this is to anticipate events.

These three factors, each in its own way, and in combination, kept the Sinhalese areas of the littoral in a state of incipient tension during much of the eighteenth century. In terms of its relative importance in provoking opposition to the VOC, the third was the most significant. The more perceptive of the Dutch officials were aware of this, but till van Imhoff appeared on the scene nobody of any importance was willing to disturb this holy cow—the cardinal principle of Dutch land policy of leaving large areas of land unproductive in order to protect the cinnamon that grew there—much less to slaughter it. Van Imhoff could see neither logic nor equity in this and persuaded the company directors that some of this land could be put to better use, for example, for the cultivation of coconut, which held out the prospect that arrack—a product of the coconut palm—could become a major source of income for the VOC. He took the initiative in granting land for other 'secondary' crops as well, coffee among them, a line of policy which his successor van Gollenesse was inclined—initially, at least—to continue and expand by including pepper in the category of crops for which such lands were available. Later van Gollenesse began to have reservations about this policy because the VOC suffered a loss of revenue when high land was converted to gardens; however, he did not stop these land grants altogether, but made sure that full rights of alienation would be given only after the company's share of revenue had been paid.[5]

In 1746 came a more notable departure from established practice when van Gollenesse decided to permit Muslims and Chetties to own and cultivate land. Hitherto aliens living in Dutch territory—Muslims and Chetties were so regarded— had been prohibited from land ownership. They appear to have been engaged in occupations other than agriculture and were obliged to work for the company at its various establishments for three months of the year (*uliyam* service), an obligation which they could commute for a fixed sum of money each year if they wished. This liberalization proved to be short-lived; it did not survive the sudden and prodigious increase in the price of cinnamon in the mid-eighteenth century—from 3 guilders to more than 6 guilders a pound—a doubling in price stimulated by the upsurge in the demand for cinnamon in Europe. There was now, naturally, tremendous pressure, to step up cinnamon production, and in its wake came a sharp and deliberate reversal of the trends initiated by van Imhoff and van Gollenesse and a return under Loten and Schreuder to the conventional policy of rigorous restraints on the use of unproductive lands for agriculture in order to protect the cinnamon plants that lay scattered in them.[6]

Loten reimposed the VOC's policy of restraining the extension of traditional subsistence agriculture into forests and wastelands which had potential for the extraction of cinnamon bark.[7] Schreuder refined these restraints through a series of aggressively stringent measures into a harsh, even iron-handed, regime which heeded neither equity nor custom; he ordered the destruction of peasant holdings—gardens, in particular—if the cultivator could produce no legal title;[8] not even service tenure lands which people had held without disturbance for generations were exempted, while long-established villages were relocated in areas deemed unsuitable for cinnamon if the original site contained cinnamon in commercially exploitable quantities.

In the context of growing population pressure[9] on existing agricultural lands, the effects of Schreuder's measures were disastrously explosive. Agrarian discontent was normally synonymous with Salāgama restiveness at their service obligations which kept them for up to eight months of the year in the forests peeling cinnamon. Now exasperation and restlessness had a much wider base, although the Salāgamas reacted most violently of all because they confronted burgeoning pressures in the form of increasingly burdensome quotas and harsh punitive measures if these were not met. They responded as they usually did where pressures became intolerably severe, by deserting in large numbers to the Kandyan kingdom. But this traditional escape valve could no longer cope with the hostility generated by Schreuder's harsh measures. The entire south-west of the island erupted in rebellion in 1757 and this was not put down entirely till the early 1760s.

The Salāgamas figured prominently in sustaining the rebellions, but there were other factors at work too. The Kandyans moved in to aid the rebels and set about doing it without the restraints they had observed in the 1730s. For Governor Schreuder the villains of the piece were the headmen between whose economic interests and those of the VOC there were now unmistakable signs of conflict. Their resentment at the reduction of their *accomodessan*s was aggravated by the losses, actual and potential, they sustained because of the land policies of Loten and Schreuder. Cinnamon grew best on land that was also suitable for coconut cultivation in which the headmen and others had an increasingly important stake. But neither their grievances nor their machinations in inciting the peasants to rebel were responsible for the outbreak of rebellion on this occasion. Schreuder believed, or chose to believe, that the peasants had been goaded to rebellion by the misdeeds of the headmen rather than the policies of the VOC. While there were indeed some complaints against the headmen on this score during the Galle and Matara uprisings of 1757–60, these were a peripheral rather than a fundamental issue and to focus attention on them as Schreuder contrived to do was an exercise in explaining away rather than explaining the causes of these upheavals. Schreuder's successor, van Eck (1762–65), took a more realistic attitude in 1762 by relaxing some of the harsher aspects of the land policies which had provoked resistance, and he did so because they could not be implemented without serious opposition from the people. No alternative policy was immediately forthcoming. Indeed, one did not appear till 1767 in the aftermath of the wars with Kandy in the 1760s and the treaty of 1766.

Surprisingly, the last decades of the VOC's administration were full of new, one might even say radical, innovations in the organization of export agriculture, and in new initiatives with regard to traditional agriculture. All this is hardly consistent with the reality of an organization facing a bleak and uncertain future in an international situation which threatened its very existence, and confronting an acute economic crisis, at a time when retrenchment and paralysis in administration would have seemed more natural than innovative departures from established patterns. Two of these latter concern us here, and both came with Governor Falck (1765–85).

The first of these was the experiment begun in 1769 of cinnamon cultivation on a plantation basis. As late as 1768, Falck himself had gone on record as sharing the conventional belief that cinnamon could not be cultivated in plantations and that it thrived only in the jungles. The first experimental plantation was begun at Maradana near Colombo. By 1771, there was positive evidence of its economic viability, with the result that within a short time cinnamon plantations were established in other parts of the south-west littoral as well. Besides, the principle of plantation production was extended to other crops, to coffee for instance, and during the administration of de Graaf (1785–94) the company turned to cotton and indigo plantations when it became difficult to obtain cloth from the Coromandel Coast, the traditional source of import to the island.[10]

Once Falck was firmly convinced that cinnamon could be promoted as a successful plantation crop throughout the south and south-west, the full rigour of Dutch land policy was at last relaxed. The decision taken to grant *thunhavul* lands to the inhabitants on the understanding that one-third of it should be planted with cinnamon and the rest with any crops they wished was significant both because it was a positive attempt to meet the needs of the people on their own terms by a liberalization of land policy, as well as marking a real breakthrough in cinnamon exhumation. The most liberal extension of thunhavul lands occurred during the early years of de Graaf's term of office, and the unbroken coconut belt from Matara to Chilaw is evidence of its remarkable success on a long-term basis. Second, Falck was responsible for a reversal of the traditional attitude of exploiting the labour of the Salāgamas without commensurate compensation in kind or cash. This departure by Falck from Dutch practice was continued by de Graaf throughout the last years of Dutch rule, and it survived well into the early years of British control in the nineteenth century.[11]

Falck gave Salāgamas a wide range of concessions, most of which were not available to other castes: special consideration in the grant of lands, exemptions from land dues and tolls at ferries; the right of plying vessels without paying anchorage dues; free collection of salt and the right to trade in it and, even more important, exemption from the jurisdiction of the ordinary courts. As a result of these privileges, the last quarter of the eighteenth century marked the rise of the Salāgamas as a caste group—these concessions were available to all Salāgamas and not merely to their caste headmen—in social and economic status to the point where non-Salāgamas were anxious to get their children, and themselves if possible, registered as Salāgamas to enjoy these benefits. The privileges conceded to the Salāgamas provoked the envy of other castes, but from the point of view of the Dutch the new policy paid rich dividends. There was now hardly any disruption to the peeling of cinnamon. The Salāgamas became so attached to the company that they reported on the felling of jungle for chēna cultivation, served on the commissions that reported on the suitability of lands which could be converted into chēnas and supervised the destruction of garden crops found in cinnamon lands.

Ironically, while these changes were to have far-reaching consequences, the Dutch found that they made no impact on the main question that concerned them—that of increased production of quality cinnamon. Between 1764 and 1792 there was actually a fall in the quantity obtained. In fact, annual collections of cinnamon hardly reached former levels and it was with great difficulty that sufficient quantities to meet the requirements of the directors were found. Nor did these two innovations confer any special immunity against agrarian unrest and rebellion in the Sinhalese areas of the littoral.

SUBSIDIARY CROPS

There was always the possibility of a flourishing trade in coffee had the VOC not stifled its growth in its territories in Sri Lanka. The company decided to introduce coffee as a garden crop in its possessions in 1722, but coffee culture did not catch on for some time and its production was quite negligible till the 1730s, when Amsterdam instructed the Sri Lankan administration to collect as much coffee as possible on the island. By the end of the decade, substantial quantities were gathered for export, and this trade became part of the company's general trade monopoly. Coffee from Sri Lanka was shipped to Indian and Persian ports where it competed successfully with Arabian coffee. But soon Javanese coffee production increased enormously and the Dutch were oversupplied, and from 1738 onwards the company instructed its officials in Sri Lanka to discourage its production. These instructions were adhered to over the next two decades.

The same kind of outlook and policies governed the Dutch attitudes towards pepper and cardamom. In regard to both these products, however, there was a complicating factor: the main centre of production was the Kandyan kingdom, and there were attempts, therefore, to encourage cultivation of these crops in the Dutch territories in order to be independent of Kandyan supplies. This was most evident with regard to pepper, one of the island's traditional minor crops. Even though the Dutch did not regard the island as a major producer of this commodity, they were nevertheless able to collect relatively large quantities of it. While there were some doubts expressed about the desirability of promoting its cultivation in the island, the official policy of the company during much of the eighteenth century was in favour of encouraging the expansion of pepper culture, within the Dutch territories, as a garden crop. During the early part of the eighteenth century there was a steady increase in the demand for Sri Lanka cardamoms in Europe. It would appear that the company collected cardamoms for its Asian trade as well. Most were obtained from the Kandyan kingdom, but some also grew in the company's lands in the Matara disāvony. Traders from the low-country travelled to the Kandyan kingdom to collect the produce sold to the company.

In the second half of the eighteenth century, with its pepper trade in Malabar and cardamom trade in the Indonesian Archipelago facing difficult times, the company showed much greater interest in obtaining supplies of these from Sri Lanka. But it continued to blow hot and cold: thus in 1765 Dutch officials on the island received instructions to promote the cultivation of coffee (in 1760 under Schreuder the VOC had declared itself ready to buy as much coffee as was available), pepper and cardamoms, but in the very next year they were ordered to restrain coffee production and to accept only the coffee actually delivered to them. Dutch officials on the island were hopeful that after the treaty of 1766 there would be an abundant supply of cardamoms from the Kandyan kingdom, thus obviating the need to stimulate its cultivation in the company's territories, but characteristically, the prices offered by the VOC were niggardly, and as a result the Kandyans were not interested. Rather than offer a higher price, the company preferred to incur the expense of promoting its cultivation in its own territories on the littoral. As for pepper, the decision was taken in 1770 to bring all lands alienated for pepper cultivation under cinnamon cultivation.

By the 1780s, however, the Dutch had lost their hold on their once flourishing Malabar trade, and with alternative sources of supply of pepper and coffee urgently called for, the VOC looked once more to Sri Lanka. Its officials on the island were urged to give vigorous support to the production of coffee (the directors hoped to obtain about 453,597 kg to 680,396 kg), pepper (production was to be stepped up until the quantity obtained from Sri Lankan sources could replace that normally obtained from Malabar) and cardamom. De Graaf enthusiastically supported this policy, but the drive to boost production of these commodities proved to be too vigorous. It provoked a major rebellion in 1789–90 in the areas in which the efforts were concentrated. From Matara the rebellion spread to other parts of the littoral (especially Chilaw and Puttalam) and to the Hapitigam and Alutkuru Kōralēs. A chastened Batavian government soon urged de Graaf to halt his energetic bid to stimulate production of coffee, pepper and cardamom, and to return to the more conventional priorities of Dutch agricultural policy in which cinnamon took pride of place.

One important point about these subsidiary crops needs special emphasis: coffee, pepper and cardamom were an important source of money income for the people of the littoral. Sinhalese officials in the provincial administration and headmen of various castes often derived considerable cash incomes from their lands as well as from trade in subsidiary crops such as cardamom. (Sinhalese headmen of the border districts and Muslim traders served as agents of the VOC for the purchase of cardamom from the Kandyan kingdom.) As a result, not only was the monetization of the economy accelerated but also the greater familiarity of the Sinhalese with cash transactions— in combination with the capital that had accumulated in the hands of some of their number in the littoral under Dutch rule— gave them a decided advantage in exploiting the opportunities in trade and plantation agriculture that came their way in the early nineteenth century under British rule.

TRADITIONAL AGRICULTURE

As early as 1656, the Dutch in Batavia had issued a set of instructions—the first of their kind—to the VOC in Sri Lanka in which great emphasis was placed on the promotion of subsistence agriculture and rice cultivation. The aim avowedly was the attainment of self-sufficiency in food on the littoral. In the first few decades of Dutch rule, disturbed political conditions and particularly the prolonged tension on the border with the Kandyan kingdom were hardly conducive to the attainment of this objective. One problem was the depopulation of large tracts of territory, especially on the disputed borders. The Dutch encouraged people to return to these regions in the knowledge that this would certainly help increase productivity in traditional agriculture within the Dutch territories. This was in any case a long-term perspective dependent on political conditions beyond the control of the VOC. The first governor, van Goens, had resorted to a more unorthodox solution: he imported slaves from south India and settled them on the south-west littoral. This experiment did not increase the production of rice in the Dutch territories; the focus of attention was and continued to be cinnamon almost to the exclusion of all else, and encouragement of traditional agriculture was sporadic, inadequate and unsystematic.

In the drier parts of the littoral under the company's control—in the Batticaloa and Matara districts, for instance—the expansion of rice cultivation depended on the restoration of the irrigation works there. The compulsory services available to the Company were seldom used for this purpose, or for the maintenance of village tanks, dams and sluices; in short they were rarely directed to work to the benefit of subsistence agriculture. Their one notable achievement in irrigation was the construction of the Urubokka Dam in the south. It was the first new irrigation project on the island since the days of the Polonnaruva kings. The Urubokka Dam was an impressive engineering feat which successfully surmounted the disadvantages of a climatic barrier which left one side of a mountain range plentifully supplied with rain and the other side subject to long periods of drought. A reliable supply of water was provided for several thousands of hectares of paddy lands as far as Ranna in the parched Giruve-pattu Plains. Apart from this one successful project in Rohana, the Dutch did more to restore irrigation works at Akkarai-pattu on the east coast than elsewhere in their territories. There were plans for the restoration of the Yodaveva at Mannar and the Kantalai Tank, as well as irrigation works on the Pattipola Aar (Gal Oya) in the east, but nothing came of these.

In fact, the very substantial achievement of the Dutch in canal building completely overshadowed their work in irrigation. These canals were among their most notable contributions to the island's economic development. We digress, at this point, for a brief look at this canal system. The first canal was the one from the Kelani River just north of the fort of Colombo through the Muturajavala Swamp to Pamunugama. By the eighteenth century, this had been extended by way of lagoons, backwaters and rivers to the Maha Oya on to Puttalam and 24 km across the Puttalam Lake to Kalpitiya. The development of inland river and canal communications over the low country south of the Kelani River was stepped up during the administration of van Imhoff.[12] A canal connecting Nedimala and Kotte provided a continuous waterway from the Kelani River to the Kalu River, while the latter was linked southwards to the Bentota River by a canal joining the Moran Ela and the Kaluvamodera Ela. Alternative inland communication between the Kalu and Bentota Rivers was provided a link between the Galvaka Ela and the Palawatta River. The suburbs of Galle and Matara were also canalized to facilitate transport of agricultural produce and for floating timber down from the forests of the hinterland. Further south, a canal system of about 48 km was based on the Polvatta River at Veligama and the Nilvala River which flows past the Matara Fort. The Colombo rendezvous of all canal traffic was Grandpass, the old ferry on the bend of the Kelani north of Colombo. The most valuable of these canals commercially was the San Sebastian from Grandpass through Bloemendhal by the base of Hulftsdorp Hill to the Beira Lake and thence to Colombo's waterfront.

The Dutch also developed a canal system north and south of Batticaloa in the east, a region which afforded an excellent combination of advantages for water navigation. There was a 50-km stretch from Batticaloa to Samanthurai in the south, while in the north a canal linked Batticaloa with Vanderloos Bay, 42 km away, thus making possible a continuous line of inland water transport extending to 92 km. Parts of these canal systems served also as flood protection schemes: on the east coast between Batticaloa and Kalmunai, the Nilvala River in Matara and the northern suburbs of Colombo. The Mulleriyava Tank in the lower reaches of the Kelani River was an example of a combined flood protection and irrigation scheme. These canals were not without some benefit to indigenous agriculture: the Mulleriyava Tank, for instance, was in part at least an irrigation project; and most of the others provided easier facilities for the transport of rice from areas which had a surplus to regions in need of it.

To return to the theme of traditional agriculture, the Dutch territories on the island, taken as a whole, needed to import rice. They grew ever more dependent on external sources of supply for much of their requirements of rice, a pattern of reliance on imports which continued throughout the period of Dutch rule and beyond it into the nineteenth and twentieth centuries. The only way of expanding rice production to the point of eliminating the need for imports from India would have been by liberalizing the VOC's land policy, but as we have seen, during the first hundred years of their control over the island's littoral there was, except for a brief period under van Imhoff and van Gollenesse, a reluctance to make any concessions in regard to land for peasant agriculture. On the contrary, there was an obsessive interest in protecting land suitable for cultivation from encroachment by the peasants, for fear of harm to cinnamon plants growing on such lands.

With the treaty of 1766, the area under Dutch rule was substantially expanded. The new territories acquired— Puttalam and Chilaw in the north-west, Magam-pattu in the south and nearly 5,000 sq. km from the Kumbukkan Oya in the south-east to the Mahaveli in the east—were potentially rich rice-producing areas. Falck himself realized that the development of these regions could help cut imports of rice and grasped that an essential preliminary to their development was the restoration of the irrigation works there. Had his energies not been concentrated so intensely upon an attempt to drain the Muturajavala Swamp close to Colombo, he might

230 A History of Sri Lanka

have achieved a significant breakthrough in the littoral of irrigation in the parts of the dry zone under Dutch control. But the draining of this swamp was beyond the technological capacity of the day and the financial resources of the VOC. Lack of success in this venture doomed other, and possibly more viable, projects in which Falck was interested—such as the restoration of the Yodaveva in Mannar—to failure as well,[13] for neither capital nor administrative energies were available for them on a scale which would have ensured success.

In the 1780s, the need to make the Dutch territories on the island self-sufficient in rice was more urgent than ever before; the price of rice from the Coromandel rose sharply on account of disturbed political conditions there. From 1780, the company found increasing difficulty in providing the foreign exchange to finance imports of rice, and by 1785 other factors—a shortage of sailors to man the ships required to import rice and the higher priority given to rice imports to Surat and Malabar—made it even more difficult to obtain rice from abroad. Within the Dutch territories on the island, the need for the import of rice was greater because of recent decisions to expand the cultivation of cinnamon and to revitalize the production of coffee, pepper and cardamom. Surprisingly, Batavia, far from encouraging the VOC establishment on the island to pay greater attention to rice cultivation, was inclined to regard capital expenditure—especially on irrigation works—for this purpose as a luxury beyond the capacity of the VOC in its parlous financial position. Its emphasis was on retrenchment and reduction of expenditure.

Despite the obvious lack of encouragement from Batavia, Falck's successor, de Graaf, persisted in attempts to expand rice production in the Dutch territories. One reason for his decision to impose the direct rule of the VOC on the Vanni territories[14] was the belief that this would permit the company to exploit the agricultural resources of this region more efficiently. Although Batavia approved this move, it did so, significantly, because of the political advantages anticipated from this, rather than in the hope of potential economic benefits. There was no support from Batavia for a more interesting proposal to import Chinese agriculturalists to help improve techniques of rice cultivation and productivity by training the local peasants in the art of transplanting rice. The VOC argued, not without justification, that this was too radical a departure from the traditional agricultural practices of the people and was likely to be a disturbing influence, if not provocative in its impact, rather than beneficial in terms of improved output. Above all, de Graaf was anxious to expand the irrigation facilities of the Giruve-pattu— the one success story in the Dutch attempts to revitalize the disused and neglected irrigation works of Rohana—and began work there without Batavia's prior permission. But when Batavia learned of these initiatives, it was severely critical and ordered de Graaf to stop work. Similarly, they rejected his proposals for the restoration of the Yodaveva in Mannar and the Kantalai Tank in the north-east of the island. And finally, there were his attempts to induce people from Matara to colonize the deserted lands of the Magam-pattu further south. What the people wanted was land in the vicinity of their homes, not in Magam-pattu, and they reacted to this attempt to shift them there with a violence that surprised de Graaf. A fierce outburst of peasant rebellion engulfed the Matara disāvony in the years 1783–90, and spread to other parts of the Dutch territories on the island. It was indicative of the persistence of agrarian discontent, despite the liberalization of land policy initiated by Falck.

There were a number of factors which precipitated this outbreak of violence against the company. One has been referred to earlier in this chapter, namely, that the peasantry were disturbed by the unusually aggressive measures taken by de Graaf to boost the production of coffee, pepper and cardamom in the Dutch territories. The second has to do with one of the unforeseen consequences of the successful completion by Falck of the cadastral survey of the Dutch territories. When population expanded beyond the capacity of a village to cope with it, the traditional remedies were the expansion of the village or the establishment of a new one in its vicinity. The thōmbos defined the boundaries of village holdings with a precision to which the local population was not accustomed and the opening of new holdings in the village or the establishment of new villages became much more difficult as a result.[15] Third, the speed with which de Graaf moved in seeking to implement this colonization project appears to have upset the potential beneficiaries of the scheme. Fourth, the Kandyans, smarting under the humiliation of the treaty of 1766, were more than ordinarily diligent in inciting the peasants to rebellion and in their assistance to the rebels once the rebellion broke out. The border was so porous that rebels and Kandyan agents moved in and out with the utmost ease.

The rebellion of 1789–90 had one significant consequence for de Graaf. It discredited him in the eyes of his superiors in Batavia who had a plausible excuse and good reason thereafter to distrust his judgement in matters relating to agriculture and the peasantry. Thus his initiatives in traditional agriculture were thwarted as much by his own impulsiveness as by Batavia's opposition and excessive caution.[16]

THE ISLAND'S TRADITIONAL OVERSEAS TRADE

The Dutch brought the whole island—not merely the territories under their control—within the wider network of international trade conducted by the VOC's eastern trading enterprises.[17] Under the VOC, the island's trade had a monopolistic sector and a competitive sector, distinct from each other and without many mutual links. The monopoly sector, which was dominated by the Dutch, embraced all the island's valuable cash crops and the VOC enjoyed the lion's share of the profits from these. Sri Lanka became a unit in the well-knit trade system of the VOC's eastern enterprises. Nevertheless, the traditional trade of the island showed remarkable resilience and power of survival for two main reasons: first, the island's geographical position and second, the complementary nature of the economy of the whole Indo-Sri Lanka region. The island produced goods, which were in great demand in the Indian mainland and the most desirable imports could easily be secured from there.

At the time of the Dutch conquest of the Portuguese possessions on the island, Sri Lanka had well-established trade links with three Indian regions: the trade of the Bay of Bengal, of which Sri Lanka's was a unit, the west coast of India and the south (the entire coast of the southernmost parts of India from Travancore through Madras to Fort St George). This pattern of trade persisted throughout the seventeenth and much of the eighteenth century. Sri Lanka, and particularly the regions under Dutch control, imported rice from all these regions, but especially from Bengal and Coromandel since it was cheaper there than elsewhere. The Bengali traders also brought in textiles (silks and muslins), butter, sugar, vegetable oils and a few other commodities, and in return they took in a wide assortment of the island's produce. During the seventeenth century and the early eighteenth century, this included a considerable number of elephants. There was a brisk demand for those animals in that part of India. The sale of elephants, in fact, provided much of the foreign exchange necessary for the purchase of rice, leaving the trade with a balance in Sri Lanka's favour. The other commodities bought by these traders were areca, chanks, cowries, pearls and spices in controlled quantities. Rice was one of the major items of import from the west coast of India, and the main exports to it included areca, coir and ropes. The southern trade was perhaps the most important of all, being the lifeline to the peasant economy of the Kandyan kingdom. The major article of import from this region was textiles, particularly the coarser varieties within the reach of the peasant consumer, as well as rice, salt and salted fish which were sent to those parts of the island which lacked them. In exchange, these traders took mainly areca, a commodity in great demand in the whole of south India. The regular trade between Sri Lanka and the Maldive Islands continued without interruption throughout the whole period of Dutch rule in the maritime regions of the island. The Maldives supplied Sri Lanka with *kumbelamas* and cowries (these were used in its trade with India and also exported to Europe), and took back in return spices, areca and some rice. In recognition of a traditional obligation, the sultan of the Maldives sent the Dutch, as sovereigns of coastal Sri Lanka, a tribute of cowries. One other aspect of the traditional trade of India needs mention—that between Jaffna and Travancore in which a principal item was the tobacco grown in Jaffna for which the raja of Travancore held a monopoly.[18]

The trade with India was in the hands, largely, of foreigners—some Tamils, Malabari Muslims and Chetties. The Chetties and other Hindus were, perhaps, the largest group numerically. Many of them had long been settled in the ports of Colombo, Galle and Jaffna, and were an important link with the Indian traders. Tamil Hindus in Jaffna also functioned as brokers and agents. The Malabari Muslim traders had blood relations living in Mannar, Galle and Batticaloa, while some of them had a dual domicile.

The political disturbances of the early and mid-seventeenth century had not caused any interruptions of this trade; indeed it had adjusted to these conditions by avoiding the larger ports which were also the centres of military and naval activity, and moving into smaller ports. There was also a definite shift of operations to the relatively peaceful east coast—the ports of Kottiyar and Batticaloa—where, moreover, there was the advantage of easy communication with the Kandyan kingdom. From the 1650s, the VOC had control of the major ports of Colombo, Jaffna and Galle, and in the period 1659–70 they extended their authority to the ports in other parts of the island as well, thus effectively reducing the Kandyan kingdom to the position of a landlocked state. In 1670, the decision to monopolize the predominant part of the island's trade was taken. Cinnamon was from the outset a Dutch monopoly, but now all the important items, with the significant exception of the import of rice, became company monopolies. The three items which it sought to dominate were the import of textiles and the export of areca and elephants, the first two of which directly affected the Kandyan kingdom and the third indirectly.[19]

The adverse effects of the trade monopoly introduced by the VOC in the 1670s were seen within a decade, with a decline in trade and a general shortage of food and clothing in the community at large. Rising prices encouraged the development of a flourishing smuggling trade in textiles and areca. To combat this smuggling trade an expensive cruising operation with armed sloops had to be mounted, which went on well into the eighteenth century. From the point of view of the Dutch, the interruption of the large-scale traffic from Bengal and north Coromandel—these traders ceased to come as regularly and in as large numbers since their operations were hampered by the monopoly—had more drastic consequences in the form of a shortage of rice, to relieve which the Dutch were compelled to transport rice in their own vessels. A relaxation of some of the restrictions in 1694 marked the beginning of a partial liberalization. Most important of all, the Bengal shippers were encouraged to resume sailing to Jaffna and Galle, given greater freedom to deal with indigenous private traders and were granted permission to bring in certain types of textiles. The requirement that these traders sailed only to the major ports was set aside and, as a result, trade at the smaller ports was reactivated once again. These reforms had the desired effect: the Bengal traffic was resumed and the Coromandel and Madura boatmen came back in larger numbers, although their freedom was still restricted. Rice and textiles were more freely available than before.

From the experience gained in these years the Dutch adopted a policy of selective restrictions and incentives affecting the Indian traders. While the Bengal, Surat and north Malabar traders were offered incentives as an encouragement to trade with the island, restraints—though not as severe as those of 1670—were imposed on the south Coromandel traders. The VOC regarded the boat traffic with south India as being especially harmful to its interests and was, therefore, intent on keeping it under control. These boatmen had an expert knowledge of the coast of the island and the Dutch cruisers had virtually no success in hampering them in their efforts to beat the restrictions. Above all, they resorted to bribery, corruption being endemic among Dutch officials. The collusion between them and the traders enabled the latter to escape the full rigour of the company's trade monopoly, to say nothing of the duties due on their goods. Governor Becker found that the senior officials of the company at Galle had formed a partnership to engage in illegal private trade in cloth. Such corruption was the chief reason why the smuggling of cloth continued until the end of the eighteenth century. Thus the company's profits from textiles never matched their true potential, and their profits from areca too kept declining.

The policy of liberalization was given greater emphasis under Governor van Imhoff in an attempt to encourage Indian traders and even other European competitors of the Dutch. This trend was continued by van Gollenesse and led to some recovery of trade in Sri Lanka. The liberalization which van Imhoff introduced was indeed minute in comparison with what he had proposed—the transformation of the Dutch possessions on the island into a major emporium of trade in south Asia. He wanted freedom to sell a wide variety of merchandise in the ports of Sri Lanka so that traders from all over the subcontinent might be attracted there. The island would thus become a centre for the exchange of goods from many regions of Asia. Van Imhoff even envisaged a reduction of the company's expensive establishments on the Indian mainland and in Persia, since their functions could well be performed from Sri Lanka. But these proposals were too far-reaching in that they implied a comprehensive restructuring of the VOC's Asian commercial policy, which the directors scarcely considered, much less endorsed.

The VOC in Sri Lanka:
The Last Phase, 1767–96

During much of the period covered by this chapter, the Anglo-French struggle for the control of India cast a long and ominous shadow across Sri Lanka. The losses inflicted on France in the Seven Years War had not put an end to her ambitions for the recovery of her overseas empire. Indeed, from about 1771, France entertained plans for the invasion of India. As a result, Trincomalee became a matter of vital interest to the two contenders for supremacy in peninsular India, but more especially, to the British.

The importance of Trincomalee in the days before the steamer was that it satisfied the needs of naval power in two ways. During the monsoons a squadron defending India had to lie to the windward of the subcontinent; it required a safe harbour in which to shelter during the violent weather occasioned by the inter-monsoonal storms in October and to a lesser extent in April. Only Trincomalee could fulfil these requirements adequately, hence its importance for the defence of India—it commanded both the Malabar and Coromandel Coasts of India. The British Eastern fleet faced the north-east monsoon in Indian waters on forty occasions between 1746 and 1795. On fifteen of them it used Trincomalee for this purpose, and eleven of these were during April in the period of the south-west monsoon. All these were apart from the frequent calls made at Trincomalee for repairs, wood and water.[1] These statistics assume even greater significance when one considers the question of the availability of these facilities at Trincomalee during periods of war. During the closing stage of the War of Austrian Succession, the Dutch had been Britain's allies and

the British had been free to use the port. But they did so even
before the Dutch entered the war. During the Seven Years
War the Dutch had been neutral, but the British navy had
continued to visit Trincomalee and to use its facilities.

But what of the future? Would Trincomalee remain what it
had been up till that, namely a neutral port readily accessible
to the British in times of peace and war? It was because events
of the late 1770s and early 1780s were to reveal that the answer
to this question was not a simple, straightforward 'yes' that
the VOC in Sri Lanka became embroiled in the Anglo-French
struggle in India. The treaty of 1766 was too much of an affront
to their pride for the Kandyans to accept it in anything other
than a mood of deep resentment.[2] Not unnaturally, they showed
no interest in cooperating in its implementation and this
attitude was made evident from the time the treaty was ratified.
Thus the advantages of the treaty to the VOC, such as they were,
were bought dear in terms both of the increased cost of defending
the coasts and borders and continued difficulty in collecting
cinnamon in the Kandyan kingdom. Nor did the treaty of 1766
do much to ensure the security of the VOC in Sri Lanka in
relation to potential threats from abroad. If in the first decade
after its ratification such threats seemed to have receded
somewhat, the relief was temporary. Once a breakdown on
the European diplomatic front occurred again, the Dutch in
Sri Lanka were wide open to attack from their European rivals.
They were no match for the French or the British.

Falck, the craftsman who fashioned the treaty of 1766, was
nothing if not circumspect in his handling of its implementation,
no doubt realizing that it did not accurately reflect the relative
strengths and weaknesses of the two powers, the VOC and the
Kandyans. What he wanted most urgently was to bring under
the VOC's control all the coastal territories ceded to it and to
do this with the cooperation of the Kandyans if possible. The
alternative, he realized, was to do this without their cooperation,
which always carried the danger that it would require the use
of force—something which Falck was reluctant to consider. Thus
he resolved on a policy of winning the Kandyans over to an
acceptance of the treaty through a mixture of cajolery, bluff and

firm determination, always stopping well short of a resort to arms or of provocative action which might compel the Kandyans to do the same. The latter, however, saw this as obvious evidence of weakness, which gave them greater confidence in facing up to the VOC. A diplomatic mission was sent to Kandy in January 1767 as part of Falck's campaign. Although this mission did not achieve its purpose of bringing the Kandyans to an acceptance of the consequences of the treaty they had signed in 1766, it set the tone in maintaining a surprising cordiality in relations between the two estranged parties. A Kandyan mission set out for Batavia later in 1767 in the hope that the treaty might be renegotiated, but this mission was entirely fruitless. The Dutch would make no such concession; they hoped that they would wear down the Kandyans by refusing to consider any possibility of a departure from the treaty.

For the VOC in Sri Lanka, the treaty of 1766 was a meaningless exercise if the boundaries of the territories conceded to them were not demarcated. More to the point, the Kandyans had to be persuaded to cooperate and to accept compensation for the loss they had incurred. But this the Kandyan ruler refused to do. Falck took as much comfort as he could from the fact that the Dutch were in de facto possession of these areas. In keeping with instructions from Batavia, he sent a mission to Kandy every year thereafter, seeking the king's formal approval for the cession of the coastal regions. These requests were firmly rebuffed and the Kandyan ruler, convinced that the Dutch persisted in this policy only because they were too weak to resort to arms again, began to demand from 1770 onwards that the coastal lands be returned to the Kandyan kingdom. By 1773 Falck's—and Batavia's—patience had worn thin and the decision was taken to demarcate the boundaries unilaterally. In so doing, the company allocated to itself more territory than it was allowed by the treaty especially in the eastern coast— far beyond the limits of their own definition of the extent of a Sinhalese mile. This demarcation of boundaries, without their participation or consent, deeply offended the Kandyans.

The VOC evidently believed that its control of the island's littoral would be sufficient guarantee against any possibility of Kandyan rulers making contacts with the European rivals of the Dutch. But it was not too difficult to elude the Dutch coast patrols, and the Kandyans sought the assistance of the French against the VOC

France's intervention on the side of the beleaguered Americans in their War of Independence may be viewed as part of an ambitious plan to launch a concerted attack on the British overseas empire.[3] This plan included a scheme for an onslaught to be delivered in Asia in the form of a joint military and naval offensive against British possessions in India. Britain's defeat in America provided the opportunity to put it into operation. In the meantime, prolonged trade rivalries between the Dutch Republic and Britain, and British insensitivity to Dutch interests, had placed the Dutch increasingly under the influence of France and moved them to join an armed neutrality against Britain in 1778, and in 1780 into a declaration of war. Because these developments coincided with the loss of Britain's American empire and the preparations by France for the invasion of India, Britain was faced with the urgent task of concerting plans for the security of her eastern possessions. With the outbreak of war between the British and the Dutch in 1781, the latter's overseas possessions, including strategic points such as Trincomalee and the Cape of Good Hope, became potential bases for the French for the prosecution of their designs against the British possessions in Asia.

By 1781, the position of Trincomalee in relation to British interests had undergone a sharp change; from being a neutral port accessible to the British it was converted overnight into a viable base for French attacks on India. And once the British were denied the use of Trincomalee by the Dutch in 1781, the urgent need for a British base on the eastern side of India was underlined. Plans were devised for the capture of Trincomalee for the purpose of preventing its use as a base by the French for their projected invasion of British India. The plan of operation devised at this time had, in its original form, the limited objective of seizing Trincomalee and the Dutch possessions on the Coromandel Coast, but in October 1781 it was amplified into a grandiose project for the capture of all Dutch settlements in Ceylon. Trincomalee remained the prime target and the British captured it in January 1782. Its subsequent loss to the French under Admiral Suffren in August 1782 was a notable blow to British prestige. Very soon thereafter the British lost Madras and their position in Asia appeared to be seriously threatened. Only the failure of Bussy's expedition and the dogged resistance offered by Admiral Sir Edward Hughes to the dynamic and imaginative forays launched by Suffren saved the British and foiled what was to be the last resolute effort of the French to retrieve their declining fortunes in India. Trincomalee in the meantime remained under French control till the end of the war in 1783.

A second diplomatic mission to Kandy despatched by the English East India Company coincided with the attack by the English on Trincomalee early in 1782. The passage of time had done little to alleviate the resentment of the Kandyans over the Pybus fiasco and thus Hugh Boyd's task in 1782 was the unenviable one of conducting delicate negotiations against the background of deep-rooted suspicion. Boyd's instructions were to negotiate with the Kandyan king, 'to conciliate him to our interest' and to impress upon him the good faith of the Company and its desire to cultivate his friendship. This time the British were prepared to enter into a mutually beneficial treaty of alliance with the Kandyans. In return for British military assistant against the Dutch, the Kandyans were asked to furnish provisions for British troops left behind on the island (presumably after the capture of Trincomalee). These terms, which would have delighted the Kandyans if Pybus had offered them in 1762, seemed much less attractive in the changed circumstances of 1782 and the offer was not accepted. The new king, Rājadhi Rājasimha, had succeeded to the Kandyan throne on the death of his brother, Kīrti Śrī Rājasimha, in December 1782 after a long reign of thirty-four years. In the years 1780–82, British power in south India seemed to be tottering in the face of attacks by the French and Hyder Ali; Suffren's capture of Trincomalee in August 1782 and the fall of Madras would have provided seemingly undeniable signs of the decline of British power. Thus Rājadhi Rājasimha needed much more convincing proof of British good faith and of the basic viability of British power before committing himself to a treaty which would have the inevitable effect of precipitating war with the Dutch.[4] Although the purpose of the Boyd mission was to make a bid to have Trincomalee as a British-controlled port, the British were generally more interested in a political arrangement that would deny its use to the French than in obtaining effective control over it in their own right. Thus at the peace negotiations of 1783–84, the British were content to let the Dutch retain Trincomalee.

By rejecting these overtures from the English East India Company the new king was signalling his readiness to normalize relations with the VOC. In permitting the peeling of cinnamon in his territories he gave further evidence of his friendly intentions. Falck was ready to meet him halfway. Realizing that the question of the coastal lands was the key to good relations between the VOC and Kandy, he urged Batavia to make some concession to Kandyan sensibilities in this regard. But he was baulked by Batavia's intransigence. Thus when Falck died in early 1785 after an extraordinarily long tenure of office (twenty years) he left the problem of relations with the Kandyan kingdom as intractable as ever. His successor de Graaf (1785–94) was in every way a contrast to him.[5] Where Falck had been conciliatory and restrained, de Graaf was aggressive and expansionist. Falck's open diplomacy with the Kandyans gave way to intrigues in the Kandyan court directed by de Graaf's mahā mudaliyār with the governor's blessings; the hatching of plots with some of the courtiers was in the hope of using them to extend the influence if not dominance of the VOC over Kandy. When de Graaf took over the administration, he had before him a Batavian directive that the return of the coastal lands—so often requested by the Kandyan ruler—was never to be considered, much less conceded. In urging de Graaf to remain adamant on this, Batavia was preaching to the converted. Yet in this both Batavia and de Graaf were totally unrealistic and short-sighted. The VOC was attempting to do in its decline what would have taxed its energies in its prime—not merely to hold the coastal territories without concessions to the Kandyans but to extend the frontiers further inland. De Graaf was the more culpable in thus misjudging the situation within the island.

He first moved against the vanniyārs, the bulk of whom generally acknowledged the overlordship of the VOC and paid tribute to it. There had been frequent suggestions from Dutch officials in Trincomalee and Jaffna that the company should absorb these Vanni districts so that their agricultural potential could be better exploited, but little heed had been paid to such proposals till de Graaf took office as governor. Earlier, his predecessor Falck and the Batavian authorities had refused to make any such move, Falck because he regarded it as dishonourable and impolitic to abrogate the agreements entered into with the vanniyārs, and Batavia—characteristically—for fear of the heavy expenses likely to be involved in the extension of Dutch control into these regions. De Graaf, unconcerned by such considerations, moved with decisive effect, despite much opposition, to annex these miniscule 'chiefdoms' and to bring much of the Vanni under the direct control of the VOC.

All this was part of a general policy of extending Dutch control well beyond the limits established in 1766. What de Graaf had in mind was the annexation of all the low-lying territories of the Kandyan kingdom, leaving a truncated state, consisting largely of mountainous territory, without the resources to challenge the VOC's hold over the rest of the island and unable to maintain contact with the outside world except through the Dutch authorities. By 1791–92, he was ready for war against the Kandyans and prepared to provoke an incident to precipitate a conflict. His Kandyan policy was an essay in gullibility—wrong-headed, unrestrained and unrealistic. The VOC could not have embarked on such a venture with the human and economic resources at its disposal. Batavia awoke to the dangers inherent in de Graaf's 'forward policy' and ordered him to abandon all his plans for a Kandyan expedition and to seek a reconciliation with Kandy. This latter de Graaf was unwilling to do and he resigned his post. The expedition never set forth, but the damage done to Kandyan relations under de Graaf was more or less irreparable—this at a time when the VOC's position in the east was becoming increasingly and obviously vulnerable.

The War of American Independence and the Anglo-French War in Asia had underlined the importance of Trincomalee for the future of Britain in Asia, and this too led to a decisive change in British policy on Trincomalee. In the period 1788–95, the desire to gain possession of Trincomalee became one of the dominant themes in Britain's relations with the Dutch. There was no cordiality in the relations between the two countries in this period. Britain's overbearing attitude contributed to the increase of French influence in Dutch affairs. The ascendancy of the pro-French Patriot Party in Holland culminated in the conclusion in November 1795 of a defensive alliance between the French and the Dutch Republic, which posed the distinct threat of a Franco-Dutch attack on Britain's eastern possessions, especially those in India. There was also the imminent prospect of the Dutch possessions in Sri Lanka being a bridgehead for French support to Tipu Sultan in India, the most formidable of the native rulers who opposed the British. No wonder then that Sri Lanka, and Trincomalee in particular, loomed large in the calculations and schemes of British statesmen. Pitt himself took the precaution of authorizing Cornwallis in 1787 to occupy Trincomalee in case of war with the Dutch. At the same time, the British persisted in diplomatic negotiations with the Dutch over the control of Trincomalee. These negotiations had begun around 1784 and continued intermittently till about 1791 when it became clear that no progress was possible. They had the effect of aggravating the suspicion and mutual recriminations which were the feature of Anglo-Dutch relations at this time. Nevertheless, when the British fleet returned to eastern waters in 1789 it again used Trincomalee as a refitting port.

With the outbreak of the revolution in France, the ideological gulf between the stadholderate and its adherents and the Patriot Party widened. While popular support for the Patriot Party increased, there was a corresponding decline in the influence of the stadholder. For the British, the most alarming feature of this development was the subservience of the province of Holland—through the Patriot Party—to revolutionary France. The occupation of Dutch territory by the French revolutionary armies in January 1795 and the establishment of the Batavian Republic brought the shape of the new politics in the country into sharper and clearer focus and underscored the threat which it posed to British interests, European and colonial. What concerned Britain most were the Jacobin implications of the French occupation of the Dutch Republic, the fear that with the establishment of the Batavian Republic, Dutch overseas territories would be stimulated to organize political insurrections on the same ideological pattern. To forestall the danger of such insurrections, which would have made the Dutch colonies an easy prey to the French, the British were compelled to take precautionary measures. Early in 1795 the Dutch stadholder sought asylum in England, where he was installed in Kew Palace. A document (which came to be known as the Kew Letter) was extracted from him in his capacity as captain-general and admiral of Holland, enjoining all governors of colonies and commanders to deliver possession of forts and installations under their command to the British forthwith. An assurance was given that these would be restored to the Dutch on the return of independence (presumably from the French) and of the country's ancient constitution and established forms of government. This letter was used by the British as authority to mount a comprehensive operation to gain control of about a dozen Dutch territories. The occupation of the Dutch possessions in Sri Lanka was the most protracted—it took more than six months from July 1795 to February 1796—and the most eventful of the operations undertaken on the basis of the Kew Letter.

The Madras establishment of the English East India Company was in immediate charge of the negotiations that preceded the conquest of the Dutch possessions in Sri Lanka. The company made no secret of its determination to use force in case the stadholder's letter was not accepted by the Dutch authorities in Sri Lanka, and an ultimatum to this effect was issued by Hobart in Madras. The Supreme Government of the English East India Company, reflecting the views of Governor General Sir John Shore, disapproved of the threat to use force and argued that Hobart should have employed conciliatory methods at the outset. Hobart's memorandum was nevertheless sent. The Dutch authorities in Sri Lanka attempted nothing more than a show of resistance. They had neither the military (or naval) strength nor the financial resources for such an undertaking. There were, besides, sharp ideological divisions within the council and between them and the rank and file, with many of those in positions of authority anxious to accede to British demands to hand over the Dutch possessions to their control. At every stage they sought to prevent the organization of meaningful resistance to the British. When, after such hesitation, the decision was taken to offer resistance, influential groups in the leadership made certain that it would be merely perfunctory. All this was in sorry contrast to the obstinate and prolonged struggle which the Portuguese in Sri Lanka had put up against the Dutch in the seventeenth century.

For the British, however, the Dutch resort to hostilities altered the whole complexion of the enterprise because it violated the terms of Hobart's letters (which accompanied the stadholder's Kew Letter) and freed them from the obligation to treat the Dutch possessions in Sri Lanka as protectorates taken on trust. Military action against the Dutch had been preceded by the initiation of diplomatic negotiations with Kandy, for which purpose the third of the English East India Company's missions to the Kandyan kingdom during this period was despatched. A senior official, Robert Andrews, was chosen for this purpose. This time the Kandyans were far more receptive to British requests and offers than they had been in 1782. Kandyan relations with the Dutch had reached their nadir during the administration of de Graaf and there seemed little prospect of an improvement under his successor (and father-in-law) van Angelbeek (1793–96). Andrews was instructed to explain to the Kandyans that British actions against the Dutch in Sri Lanka in 1795–96 had been taken with a view to averting a civil war in the Dutch possessions and to prevent their capture by the French. He was urged to impress upon the Kandyan monarch the dangers of French revolutionary ideology, especially its virulent antipathy to monarchical rule. This was apart from instructions to obtain detailed information about Dutch–Kandyan relations, along with copies of treaties between the Kandyans and the Dutch. There was also a formal request for the Kandyan king's permission for the English

East India Company to set up a factory in some convenient part of the king's territories for purposes of trade and to build fortifications for the factory's protection.

In his discussions with the Kandyans, Andrews found that they sought guarantees against the return of the maritime regions to Dutch control and treated this as the most vital feature of any treaty to be negotiated. The British, on the other hand, were more interested in the short-term advantages of obtaining the king's assistance against the Dutch and not inclined to give the categorical undertaking demanded by the Kandyans that the maritime regions should not revert to Dutch control. Although these two positions were in a sense irreconcilable, Andrews succeeded in persuading the Kandyans to send ambassadors to Madras to continue the negotiations. In Madras, Hobart took up the position that the British were entitled to all the Dutch possessions in Sri Lanka by virtue of conquest from the Dutch and dismissed without reservation the claim, made in the fourth clause of the draft treaty presented by the Kandyans, that the British were entitled merely to what the king of Kandy offered them out of his gracious pleasure. Hobart, nevertheless, offered the Kandyans a trade outlet on the coast which they could use for obtaining an adequate supply of salt and fish, with the right to employ ten ships for this purpose. The Kandyan ambassadors, reluctant at first, were persuaded by Andrews to sign a draft treaty on these lines, and Andrews himself returned to Sri Lanka in August 1796 to secure the king's ratification of the treaty, but there he was faced with demands for an increase in the number of ports to be conceded to the Kandyans. He had no authority to concede these demands, nor was he inclined to do so. Thus the treaty was never ratified.

The draft treaty was far less rigorous than that imposed on the Kandyans by the Dutch in 1766. Not only did it provide for a source of supply for salt and fish under Kandyan control, but the Kandyans were also offered a base and outlet for their external trade. Thus the treaty was not without advantage to the Kandyans, although they persisted in their endeavour to get the British to concede—as the Dutch had done till 1766— the principle, which was no more than a legal fiction, of

Kandyan sovereignty over the maritime regions of the island formerly under effective Dutch control. By the time negotiations over the treaty finally collapsed, the British were in command of the former Dutch possessions in Sri Lanka, without any substantial assistance from Kandy. And they soon came to know of the treaty of 1766 and recognized the strength of their legal position as successors to the Dutch by virtue of conquest of the coastal belt extending around the entire island, in depth seldom stretching more than 20 miles into the interior.

The traditional Kandyan policy of seeking foreign assistance to oust the European power established in the maritime regions had on this occasion led to the substitution of a very powerful neighbour for a weak one. Should this new neighbour ever decide that the independent status of the Kandyan kingdom was in any way an obstacle, let alone a threat to its territorial ambitions in south Asia, it had the resources—unlike its predecessors, the Portuguese and the Dutch—to subjugate that kingdom.

The Impact of Dutch Rule

In terms of the extent of territory and the number of people directly ruled, the Dutch possessions in Sri Lanka were the largest of the outer administrations of the VOC, that is to say, outside the Indonesian Archipelago which formed the core of its overseas empire. It ruled these regions of the island for a much longer period of time than the Portuguese. Yet, its impact on the country was seemingly much more limited than that of the Portuguese whose language and religion—especially the latter—showed remarkable powers of survival. In economic policy, which we have reviewed here in earlier chapters, there was, apart from one significant innovation which came in the last phase of Dutch rule (the concept of plantation agriculture), a continuity between Dutch and Portuguese practice. And so too in other spheres of activity such as the system of administration,[1] to which we now turn, where new departures, with the single exception of the Dutch contribution in law, the introduction of Roman–Dutch law, were overshadowed by this same element of continuity.

ADMINISTRATIVE STRUCTURE

Like the Portuguese before them, the VOC took over the indigenous administrative structure, adapted it for its own purposes and left it much as they found it. Thus the traditional division of each disāvony into kōralē, pattu and village was maintained with mudaliyārs, kōralēs and atukōralēs as the chief administrative officials. In each village there was a vidāne in whom was vested the day-to-day management of village affairs.

The enforcement of service obligations on behalf of the government lay with the headmen. They enjoyed wide judicial authority at the local level and had a general superintendence of all agricultural activity as well as the maintenance of irrigation facilities. From the outset, the Dutch sought to win over the native headmen, believing no doubt that they would be invaluable as supports of the new regime. Generally, these officials were Sinhalese Christians while in the Jaffna commandement the mudaliyārs and muhandirams were appointed from wealthy Tamil Christian families. Native headmen who had served the Portuguese were not displaced provided that their loyalty to the Dutch was beyond doubt and they made the necessary change in religious affiliation from Roman Catholicism to Calvinism, which, it would appear, caused no great difficulty for almost all of them.

The disāva, a Dutch official, had supervisory control over the indigenous administrative structure. There were three such officials on the island, one each at Colombo, Jaffna and Matara. As head of this administrative structure, the disāva was in constant touch with these native officials and was the link between the company and the people. The range of administrative functions performed by the disāva was remarkably comprehensive. This made him a very powerful individual in the eyes of the people, but not, it would seem, an effective check on the headmen.[2] The Dutch, in fact, could never be sure of the native chiefs and had to be constantly on their guard against them. There were frequent complaints about the excessive influence and authority these officials wielded at the local level as well as charges of corruption, oppression and illegal exactions. What was most disturbing to the Dutch were the divided loyalties of the chiefs and their collusion—actual or potential—with rebels in the Sinhalese areas of the littoral and with the Kandyans at times of strained relations or war between the Dutch and the Kandyan kingdom.

Part of the problem lay in the fact that the native officials were recompensed for their services by the traditional form of payment, accomodessans—the grant of revenues of productive land in villages—a system which lent itself to a great deal of corruption and maladministration by powerful and unscrupulous officials who deprived the company of much revenue to which it was entitled, quite apart from abusing their authority over tenants on such lands. But, above all, it enhanced the power and influence of the native chiefs, because accomodessans, though originally attached to a particular office and reverting to the state when the holder vacated his office, increasingly became hereditary (accomodessan lands could not be sold by the recipient) with the tendency for offices to pass from father to son. In the eighteenth century, the Dutch sought to restrict to a minimum the extent of land given as accomodessans, as well as to put an end to the hereditary nature of appointments to office. There were, at the same time, attempts to reduce the number of these native officials.[3] Van Gollenesse, in particular, trimmed the indigenous administrative cadre rigorously, but despite this it continued to remain top-heavy and privileged in terms of rights to land through accomodessans.

The VOC kept certain castes—whose services were of vital importance to its interests—directly under European officials rather than the traditional supervision of the Goyigama disāvas. The solution they resorted to—caste headmen with distinct caste jurisdictions—was less an innovation than a modification of the machinery of administration then in existence. The consequence of its introduction was a distinct diminution of the area of authority of the Goyigama disāvas and kōralēs. The Salāgamas, not surprisingly, were the first to be given caste headmen of their own with a jurisdiction extending well above a mere village or locality. During the administration of van Gollenesse came a totally new development, the appointment of a muhandiram from the Durāvas.

The Sinhalese headman system was a very complex one, and no comprehensive study of it has yet been attempted. But from the information now available it would appear that one of its features was that these officials, especially at the village level, generally had caste rather than territorial jurisdictions. There were single-caste villages, usually smaller and less important than their multi-caste counterparts. These latter appear to have had several headmen, the number varying with the distribution of castes, and their jurisdiction was limited to certain areas and localities, especially in the ports where, apart from several caste groups, ethnic minorities and aliens also lived. Thus, these large villages generally had many headmen, some of them with just a dozen or even fewer families under their charge.[4] The Karāva had their headmen and the Salāgamas their own vidānes (as they were organized in a separate badda). The Portuguese had tried to simplify this system and to reduce the number of headmen. Whether they succeeded in this we do not know, but one point seems clear enough: the jurisdiction of Goyigama headmen at the village level (the lowest in the hierarchy) seems to have been limited in Dutch times. Nevertheless, all headmen, irrespective of caste, were under the control of Goyigama disāvas and kōralē vidānes. When the VOC introduced caste headmen with wider powers and areas of authority than under the traditional system, the Salāgamas, Karāvas and Durāvas no longer came under the jurisdiction of the Goyigama disāvas and kōralē vidānes. It meant also that the Goyigamas were excluded from a limited number of higher positions in the traditional hierarchy. To this extent the appointment of caste headmen was consistent with the general policy of curbing the influence and authority of the indigenous administrative hierarchy.

The headmen's influence was too pervasive and well established to be dislodged by anything short of a relentlessly pursued and purposeful course of action extended over several decades. But the VOC did not display that sort of tenacity. On the contrary, changes introduced by the Dutch actually strengthened the power of the headmen, while attempts to erode their influence led to the precisely opposite effect. The entry of headmen as renters of taxes was an example of the first, and the consequence of preparing registers of dues, obligations (the thōmbos), illustrates the second. The VOC collected a wide range of taxes, of which those on paddy were the most lucrative. Like the Portuguese before them, they preferred to farm these rents. The company was also entitled to a medley of dues which varied extensively within the territories they administered. Variety in this instance was governed by the peculiar economic resources of each area, as well as the caste composition of the population. These dues too were farmed annually. A scrutiny of the lists of renters in the eighteenth century shows that the predominant group was the headmen, especially in the most important and lucrative of them of all, the paddy rents. To some extent this was due to the fact that an economically significant section of the population of the south-west of the island, the Muslims, were debarred from appointment as renters during the period of Dutch rule.[5]

The emphasis on the maintenance, without substantial change, of the traditional tenurial structure had one significant corollary—the need to understand and keep a record of the traditional service obligations. But in regard to these latter the Dutch came up against a formidable obstacle—the reluctance of the native headmen to provide them with adequate, much less comprehensive, information on the complicated system of land tenure in the areas under Dutch control. The headmen realized that their own personal power and influence would be seriously undermined once Dutch officials obtained a fair understanding of the complexities of the system of land tenure. For the VOC this information was vital: without it they could not fully exploit the revenues to which they were entitled as the government of the day. They found a solution in a device the Portuguese had introduced—the thōmbos or registers setting out systematically the labour services and other dues from the inhabitants of the territories they controlled. The earliest Dutch thōmbo, that of Jaffnapatam, dates from 1677. Some portions of the Galu kōralē were registered, on a rather makeshift basis, in 1698. The systematic compilation of thōmbos for all Dutch provinces of the south-west was only initiated during the administration of van Imhoff, and made very slow progress. The registration of the Colombo disāvony was completed in August 1759, while in the Galu kōralē and Matara disāvony this work was still unfinished as late as 1767.[6] Governor Schreuder attributed the lack of progress in the work of registration to the opposition of the native headmen. No doubt the project suffered greatly from the lack of cooperation from them, but that was not the only reason for the delays. The turmoil in the low country in the late 1750s and early 1760s was hardly conducive to progress in ventures of this sort.

The cadastral survey of the VOC's territories in the south and south-west of the island was resumed and brought to a successful conclusion during Falck's long (1765–85) administration. The exhaustive details of the survey, coupled with the mode of registration chosen, inevitably delayed its completion. Work on the survey of the Colombo disāvony was completed in 1770 and on that of the Galle Commandery in the early 1780s. The successful completion of this project owed much to the victory in the war against the Kandyans in 1765 and their recognition of Dutch sovereignty in the littoral with the treaty of 1766, which had the long-term effect of a politic—and reluctant—acceptance of the reality of Dutch authority by the native headmen.

These thōmbos immeasurably strengthened the position of the Dutch vis-à-vis the people by placing at the government's disposal comprehensive and reasonably accurate data on tenurial obligations, as well as a precise definition of the extent of lands held under various tenures within its territories. The VOC believed that the thōmbos would help reduce their dependence on the native headmen in regard to administration. But this hope was not realized for the reason that the efficient supervision of headmen by Dutch officials was not forthcoming. The cooperation of the headmen at various levels of administration was just as vital in collecting the revenues and dues and exacting the labour services due to the state in accordance with the thōmbos, as it had been in the compilation of these registers. Their cooperation was indispensable also for the periodic revision of the thōmbos to bring them up to date. Thus, far from their power and influence over the inhabitants being reduced in any way, both were substantially enhanced as a result of a measure—the compilation of the thōmbos—which was designed, in part at least, to have precisely the opposite effect.

THE ADMINISTRATIVE MACHINERY
AND THE LEGAL SYSTEM

The VOC's administrative machinery proved inefficient and— the company would have added—expensive, while its officials were corrupt even by the standards of the day. The establishments in Sri Lanka and Malabar were reputed to be the most expensive of all and were looked upon as being responsible for bringing the company to a state of indebtedness by the end of the seventeenth century. In the case of the VOC's establishment in Sri Lanka, there was an element of unreality in this charge since the profits of the enormously lucrative cinnamon trade were excluded from this computation.

The corruption ranged from the alienation of unoccupied land and the assignment of revenues to high-ranking Dutch officials,[7] to participation by these officials in smuggling and the illegal private trade; the latter included the smuggling of cinnamon—despite the regulations introduced to protect the company's monopoly—and of areca (to south India) and textiles (to Sri Lanka), in collaboration with Indian traders. The textile trade was especially lucrative in view of the company's monopoly of the market on the island in the eighteenth century. Illegal private trade was well entrenched in the eighteenth century and survived all attempts to eradicate it. These abuses could hardly have survived if later governors, especially those of the early eighteenth century, had maintained the standards of efficiency and integrity set by the earlier ones. Certainly, by the end of the seventeenth century, the decline in efficiency and personal integrity at the highest level of the administration on the island was a serious cause for concern for the VOC. Proceedings were instituted against Governor Becker (1707–16) after he left the island. Maladministration, even misrule, continued in the first three decades of the eighteenth century, the nadir being reached under Petrus Vuyst (1726–29) when the judiciary too was affected by the prevailing malaise. At Vuyst's instigation, a number of persons, including Dutch officials and 'free' burghers (Dutch settlers), were sentenced to death on trumped-up charges and executed. Vuyst was dismissed from office in 1729 and summoned to Batavia, where he faced a trial for these 'judicial' murders and on other serious charges. He was found guilty and executed in 1732. Reforms introduced by van Imhoff in 1736–40 restored respect for the office of the governor, and the zest for efficiency in administration and probity in personal conduct demonstrated by van Gollenesse, Loten and Schreuder was sustained over the rest of the eighteenth century.

In the sphere of judicial administration, the most constructive achievement of the Dutch lay not so much in the courts they set up as in the laws they introduced.[8] Wherever possible these courts applied the customary laws of the people. The position was made clear in a memoir left for his successor by Commandeur A. Pavilioen of Jaffnapatam in 1665: 'The natives are governed according to the customs of the country if these are clear and reasonable, otherwise according to our laws.'[9] While the laws and customs of the Tamils of Jaffnapatam were codified for the first time in the *Tēsavalamai*, and the Muslims had their own Islamic law, the position with regard to the Sinhalese under Dutch rule is less clear. Significantly, no such code of customary laws was compiled for the Sinhalese who formed a clear majority of the people in the territories under the control of the VOC. Evidently Sinhalese customary law had not the resilience and cohesiveness of that of the Hindus and the Moors. Why was this so? Was it that the link between customary law and religion was stronger and closer among the latter than with the Sinhalese? Or could this be explained on the basis of two small ethnic-religious minorities safeguarding their identity by a stronger commitment to their distinctive cultures, of which their customary laws formed an integral part? By the last decade of the eighteenth century, the obsolescence of Sinhalese customary law was an established fact; Roman–Dutch law had superseded it.[10] In many ways Roman–Dutch law was the most lasting contribution of the Dutch to Sri Lanka.[11]

The application of Roman–Dutch law to the Sinhalese consolidated social changes such as monogamy and emphasis on the sanctity of marriage, which had their origins under Portuguese rule. But its strongest influence was on inheritance of property and indeed on the concept of private property. Innovations in regard to the instruments for transfer of property gave a legal stamp to private landholdings.[12] From the late seventeenth century onwards, the VOC had endeavoured to bring the transfer of property, movable and immovable, under their direct supervision, and the manner in which such transfers should be made was specified. But no great success in this was achieved till Schreuder's administration, when a more purposeful bid was made to bring about the desired change. The transfer of property by sale, gift or inheritance now had to be effected by means of official forms provided by the secretariat under the supervision of authorized officers. By this time there was a greater readiness on the part of the Sinhalese to accept this requirement. The regulations devised by the VOC brought the instruments for the transfer of private property in line with Roman–Dutch law. Landed property acquired a new and firmer legal status. The headmen benefited from this most of all for it opened out opportunities to them for strengthening their claims to land. They became holders of large extents of landed property, privately held. This in turn led to greater inequalities in landholding as a result of which the dependence of the peasantry on the headmen was substantially reinforced.

On Schreuder's instructions, a comprehensive survey of the lands belonging to the VOC in the south-west of the island was conducted. The main aim was to obtain as accurate a picture as possible of the existing cinnamon resources in and around villages and to locate sites with potential for expansion in the future. The data provided by the survey, which eventually covered 1,197 villages in the Colombo disāvony and was published in August 1758, was used to establish a much tighter government control over lands suitable for cinnamon. As a result, even service tenure holdings which people enjoyed for generations came under attack. What followed from this was a fundamental change in the pattern of landholdings in the south-west of the island, from one in which the dominant features were service tenure holdings, which were not alienable by the holders and where ultimate rights of deposition lay with the sovereign, to one in which freehold rights with their owners enjoying full rights of alienation became predominant. This change with regard to the status of private landholdings was among the most far-reaching introduced by the Dutch.[13]

RELIGIOUS POLICY

In the first few decades of the VOC's administration in Sri Lanka's littoral, the Dutch Reformed Church, having supplanted the Roman Catholic Church in the role of the 'established' religion, embarked enthusiastically on a policy of hostility to

Roman Catholicism[14] and on a concerted bid to proselytize among the Sinhalese and Tamils. Neither of the processes was maintained for long, especially the latter. The VOC's hostility to Roman Catholicism was motivated as much by political considerations as by religious conviction, for Portuguese power and the Roman Catholic Church in the island had been so closely linked that the destruction of one was impossible without the elimination of the other's influence. Roman Catholic worship was now prohibited by law, with severe penalties for any breach. Priests were forbidden entry to the island and all Roman Catholic churches were taken over and converted into chapels. There were, not surprisingly, many defections from Roman Catholicism to Protestantism, but a substantial number of Catholics appear to have remained steadfast. They were ministered to by priests smuggled in at great risk from India. The harried Roman Catholic clergy found a haven in the Kandyan kingdom much the same way in which Muslim victims of Portuguese persecution had found earlier. By the beginning of the eighteenth century this exercise in religious persecution was abandoned because it had proved ineffective in practice. Many of the anti-Catholic plakaats, although they remained in the statute books, were seldom if ever observed in practice.

The Dutch were rather more tolerant of the indigenous religions than the Portuguese had been. While they did not actually harry the Buddhists (for fear of offending the Kandyan ruler, who regarded himself as the trustee of Buddhist rights on the island) they did not officially countenance Buddhism, and harassment of Hindus and Muslims continued—though not with the same virulence as under the Portuguese. Buddhist and Hindu worship was prohibited in towns but, it would appear, not in the villages. The extensive temple properties confiscated by the Portuguese were not returned to those who originally controlled them.

While the VOC encouraged the people over whom they ruled to adopt Calvinism,[15] and membership of the Dutch Reformed Church was a prerequisite for high office under the Dutch, this enthusiasm for conversion was not sustained for long. As time went on their aim was 'the narrow one of holding together the native converts of the seventeenth century and of keeping the Dutch community on the straight and narrow path of godly devotion'.[16] The Dutch Reformed Church in Sri Lanka was not particularly well equipped for anything more than that. All its ministers were company servants and the church itself did not enjoy the status of an independent mission. To the VOC, religion was a matter of secondary importance and its officials seldom gave their church much more than perfunctory assistance, although they kept a tight control over its activities. As a result, the Dutch Reformed Church had limited financial resources and suffered from a paucity of ministers. There was, therefore, scarcely any possibility of a resolute campaign of proselytization among the people at large. Moreover, few of its ministers knew Sinhalese or Tamil. Nevertheless, the Dutch Reformed Church did not lack converts. The material benefits anticipated from association with the established religion were a powerful attraction to elite groups seeking continuation in high office. But converts were by no means confined to the elite: in 1743, the church had a membership of 53,219 in Colombo, and 200,233 in Jaffna in 1758 (there were thirty-seven churches in the consistory there). The bulk of these, as the Dutch records admit, were Calvinists and Christians only in name.[17] Calvinism, in fact, did not develop any strong roots among the people, and its influence, in sharp contrast to that of Roman Catholicism vis-à-vis the Portuguese, did not survive the collapse of Dutch power.

The link between proselytization and education established by the Portuguese was maintained by the Dutch. They took over the schools begun by the Portuguese, revitalized them and added to their number by their policy of attaching schools to each church. The schoolmaster in charge maintained a register of students and fines were imposed to ensure pupils' regular attendance. Fines were also imposed on Christian adults for not attending church. The rigours of these requirements had been relaxed somewhat by the eighteenth century, but the regulations were reimposed during van Gollenesse's administration.[18]

The schools provided a simple system of instruction with reading and writing in the vernaculars and arithmetic. Regular inspections by the local minister of religion and by civil officials ensured satisfactory standards in the schools. The schoolmasters were paid by the state. They also acted as registrars of births, marriages and deaths. The introduction of a regular system of registration in the villages was a major innovation of the VOC. Indeed, the registration of marriages re-emphasized the concept of monogamy which Roman Catholic Christianity had introduced under the Portuguese and gave it greater significance and formality. Two seminaries were established in Jaffna and Colombo for higher education and the more talented pupils from all over the island were sent there to be educated. They also maintained them at their expense. The first of these was established at Nallur in 1690 and lasted till 1709 when it was closed down and its students and teachers were transferred to Colombo.[19] These seminaries trained students as teachers and catechists in the expanding school system, and as clergymen. Instruction was largely in the vernaculars, but some Latin and Dutch were also introduced. Towards the end of the eighteenth century, the practice of sending a few students for higher education to the Netherlands was begun.

In 1737, during van Imhoff's administration, a printing press was established in Colombo with the avowed intention of making Christian literature available in the vernacular languages—a prayer book in Sinhalese (1737), translations of the Gospels (1739) and simple catechisms—for schools, churches and other institutions. This was the foundation for more sophisticated polemical work in the next decade, and greater technical competence in printing and in the production of books. Under van Gollenesse the translation of the New Testament into Tamil was begun. This major undertaking was completed during Schreuder's administration. The education programmes initiated by the VOC achieved only limited success in the intended aim of spreading Calvinist Christianity among the youth of the country, but it had the profoundly important consequence of helping the spread of literacy in the lowlands—in the south-west and the north—an advantage which has been maintained and indeed consolidated throughout the nineteenth and twentieth centuries.

Calvinist polemics against Roman Catholics, and indeed
Calvinist tracts and other religious works were generally
fewer in number than, and inferior in literary skill to, Roman
Catholic literature of the same genre in the indigenous
languages. In the seventeenth century, the Roman Catholic
propagandists had begun by using the island's traditional folk
drama for their evangelical work with translations into
Sinhalese and Tamil from, and adaptation of works in,
European languages for this purpose.[20] Quite obviously, the
visual impact of this art form and the spoken word were
regarded as being more effective for proselytization than
tracts and pamphlets in a society in which literacy was limited
to a tiny elite. But by the end of the seventeenth century, the
Roman Catholics had a substantial oeuvre of literary works
to their credit, largely due to the efforts of Fr Jacome Gonçalves,[21]
a Konkani Brahman from Goa. Arriving on the island
surreptitiously to minister to the Roman Catholics in the littoral,
Gonçalves found a convenient refuge in the Kandyan kingdom
from which to conduct his operations. Very soon he mastered
both Sinhalese and Tamil and, during, his stay on the island,
made an outstanding contribution to Christian literature in
both languages. His works covered a wide range of themes—
scripture and theology, devotional hymns, lexicography
(Sinhalese–Portuguese, Portuguese–Sinhalese and Portuguese–
Sinhalese–Tamil dictionaries) and even anti-Buddhist
polemics[22] (a curious way, this, of repaying the hospitality and
tolerance of the Kandyans). Gonçalves's Tamil writings—on
the doctrines of the Roman Catholic church and refutations of
heretical beliefs—were the largest in number, in that language,
produced by a single author.

The introduction of the printing press no doubt gave the
Calvinists a considerable advantage in their campaigns against
Roman Catholicism and the indigenous religions, but this was
not sustained for long, because towards the end of the
eighteenth century the VOC's religious policy was becoming
less intolerant if not yet consistently liberal. Even opposition
to their traditional enemy—the Roman Catholics—abated
somewhat, and the latter were able to begin resuscitating the

morale of their dwindling and demoralized flock. At the same time, the resurgence of Buddhism in the Kandyan kingdom was to have a considerable impact. Although this was felt mainly among the Buddhists, the Hindus themselves were inspired by it to a revival of their religion after the long period of decline which had set in with the struggle against the Portuguese. Indeed, the Tamil kingdom of the north had been a bastion of Hindu civilization and Tamil culture, with a library at Nallur and poets resident at the court. The rule of the Portuguese had been much more destructive in its impact on Hinduism in the north of the island than on Buddhism in the areas under their control even though they were harsh and intolerant enough in regard to the latter. The decline of Hinduism had continued under the VOC, but now in the late eighteenth century one saw at last the glimmer of a revival.

Largely because they ruled the littoral for much longer than the Portuguese, the Dutch left a more substantial legacy in architecture.[23] Despite a proclivity (which they shared with all colonial powers) to introduce to their dependencies the styles and fashions in vogue in the metropolitan country, the architecture of the VOC in Sri Lanka was a more successful adaptation of European modes to the requirements of a warm climate than that of the British during their rule in Sri Lanka. This was seen to the best advantage in the simple and solid architecture they introduced in their forts and in their town planning.[24] Few traces remain of the castle-fort of Colombo today. The ramparts of the old Dutch fort of Galle and part of the wall which enclosed the town under the VOC are still the dominant architectural features of this southern town. Also in the south is the fort of Matara—its walls constructed in the shape of a six-pointed star—built by Baron van Eck in 1763–65. This structure is better preserved than most others. A picturesque gateway still exists, its pediment decorated with the monogram of the VOC in an ornamental setting. Over the arch (carved in wood) are the arms of Baron van Eck. Few monuments of Dutch rule on the island weathered better than the ramparts, battlements and picturesque stone sentry boxes of the castle-fort of Jaffna destroyed in the 1980s; it was also by far the best of the military works of the Dutch.

VOC Emblem, Galle

Dutch Fort, Galle

Ramparts of Galle

The churches built during the rule of the VOC are beautifully proportioned, yet simple in outline and plain if not severe in form. A closer look at them shows considerable variety in the ornamental fanlights over the lintels of doorways, and more important, the gables. The gable was an inspiration of the Renaissance, which the Dutch used in their homeland and in all their colonies with every possible variation in detail. The Dutch architects relied on the gable to soften the overpowering sternness and solidity of the churches they built. The best examples of such gables may be seen to this day in churches they erected in their principal stations, Colombo (the Wolvendaal Church), Galle and Jaffna. From the date of its dedication up to the end of Dutch rule in Sri Lanka the Wolvendaal Church (built between 1749–57) was their principal place of worship. The most distinctly Dutch building, with the best example of the Dutch gable, is the church built by the VOC in Galle. One other feature of these churches merits mention: the pulpit with its stair and handrail. The ribbons and tassels decorating the canopy over the pulpit are carved in wood with exceptional skill and sensitivity in style.

This brings us to the point that the Dutch introduced to the island a wealth of furniture in a variety of designs then popular in the metropolitan country, worked in ebony, nedun and calamander. Devoid of the rococo embellishments inspired by Chinese decorative art which the Dutch copied, this was the oldest European furniture style to be introduced to the island.[25]

In the larger towns under Dutch control the settlement within the walls sometimes overflowed out to the suburbs which came to be called the *pettah*. Clean and shaded streets were laid out in a rectangular grid and usually showed, in perspective, two long receding rows of slender wooden pillars on either side. The pillars fronted deep verandahs or *stoeps* and one-storeyed buildings with low-pitched roofs. A wooden trellis separated the verandahs from the road; the gardens of the houses were at the back. Through these houses the Dutch left a lasting impression on the domestic architecture of the Sinhalese,[26] not to mention that of the British in the nineteenth century.

Religion, Literature and the Arts in the Kandyan Kingdom

RELIGION

With the establishment and consolidation of Portuguese rule in the Sinhalese areas of the littoral, the Kandyan kingdom became the sole surviving link in the age-long connection between Sinhalese power and the Buddhist religion. It was the heir to the traditional relationship between the state and religion. The two most treasured relics of the Buddha, the tooth relic and the alms bowl, always kept in the possession of the king at the chief administrative centre on the island and associated with the continuity of Sinhalese kingship, passed into the hands of the Kandyan rulers after the 1590s.

Throughout much of the eighteenth century, however, Buddhism was in a state of debility, worn out and almost moribund, to the extent that valid ordination of bhikkhus was a perennial problem. Both Vimala Dharma Sūriya I and Vimala Dharma Sūriya II made special efforts to revive the *sāsana*, and sent missions to Arakan in Burma to obtain bhikkhus from there to help restore the *upasampadā*, the higher ordination, in Sri Lanka. Any success achieved through this process was no more than temporary, and by the end of the eighteenth century it had become practically impossible to hold a valid ordination ceremony. The result was that those who entered the Buddhist order did so without the prescribed rites. They came to be called *gaṇninānse*, an indeterminate status, part layman, part monk; at best they were a parody or caricature of the bhikkhus, at worst a travesty. They retained their lay names, continued to engage in secular activities, wore a white or saffron-coloured cloth rather than the traditional saffron robes of the bhikkhu, and few if any were celibates. Indeed, the prospect of a comfortable living on temple properties was very often the main attraction for entry into the Buddhist order in the form of ganninānses. Few of them had mastered the Buddhist texts, most were content to indulge in magic, sorcery, astrology and divination and were, in fact, priests or magicians rather than bhikkhus in the ideal and doctrinal sense.[1]

The most remarkable and purposeful effort at Buddhist reform came, surprisingly, from within the sangha itself in the mid-eighteenth century with the formation of the *Silvat Samāgama* (the brotherhood of the pious) by Välivita Saranankara (1698–1778), a *sāmanera* (unordained monk).[2] The Silvat Samāgama called for a return to more exacting standards of conduct for the sangha, where piety, devotion and a sound knowledge of the scriptures rather than family influence and connections would be the qualifications for admission to the order, and where the ideal of poverty was juxtaposed with the reality of the ganninānses' devotion to the affairs of a householder's life. Narendrasimha, the last Sinhalese king of the Kandyan kingdom, was less than enthusiastic about fostering a Buddhist revival of the sort that Saranankara had in mind; the Kandyan *radala*, who had a vested interest in temple property controlled by scions of their families in the role of ganninānses, did not view such a reformist movement with much kindness either. But the situation changed dramatically when the Nāyakkar dynasty assumed the Kandyan throne. In their eagerness to compensate for their marginal political status as a foreign dynasty, the Nāyakkars extended the most lavish patronage to the regeneration of the authentic religious and cultural traditions of the people.[3]

The first priority, as the Buddhist reformers saw it, was the restoration of the upasampadā, and Śrī Vijaya Rājasimha was persuaded to take the initiative in this by sending a mission to Thailand for this purpose under his auspices. Three missions were despatched, and the third, sent in 1750 in the last year of his reign, was eventually successful. In 1753, a group of Thai monks reached Sri Lanka and in that year the upasampadā was restored. While the restoration of the upasampadā was the greatest contribution of the Thai monks to the Buddhist revival in Sri Lanka in the second half of the eighteenth century, the monks were also instrumental in reasserting the primacy of Buddhist symbols and practices over those of Hinduism which had gained ascendancy during Buddhism's period of decline. It would appear that the annual Äsala perahära owes its present form to their initiative. Under the Sinhalese rulers of the Kandyan kingdom this festival was celebrated as an occasion for the ceremonial worship of Hindu gods, and had no connection with the Temple of the Tooth or with any other Buddhist temple. The Thai monks persuaded Kīrti Śrī Rājasimha to reorganize the perahära and to introduce a new daladā (tooth relic) perahära into the general ritual complex of this annual ceremony, with a position of primacy over all the other perahäras in it. The Äsala perahära in this form symbolically underlined the primacy of Buddhism within the Sinhalese religious system, even if it did not restore or re-establish it.[4]

We turn next to the institutional aspects of this revival of Buddhism. There was first of all the establishment of the Siyam Nikāya, the most important of the modern Buddhist sects; and next the development within it of the Malvatta and Asgiriya chapters, both adhering to the same doctrinal tenets and each of equal status. When Kīrti Śrī Rājasimha decreed in 1765 that the upasampadā ceremony could only be performed at Malvatta and Asgiriya, they came to have exclusive rights over the admission of novices to higher ordination, not merely within the Kandyan kingdom but in the Sinhalese areas of the littoral under the control of the VOC. The title of sangharāja was conferred on Saranankara, but was discontinued after his death. All this formed part of a process of centralizing the affairs of the sāsana, and the development of a strong establishment with close links with the state.

The king appointed the chief bhikkhus, and the latter in turn, the incumbents of smaller pansalas. He endowed the important temples, as the disāvas did, with land grants. (Since the bhikkhus were generally recruited from the Govikula, the endowment of family temples by pious nobles led to close

ties of kinship between the chiefs and the bhikkhus.) The
inhabitants of villages attached to Buddhist temples (viharagam)
came under the authority of its chief bhikkhu, while the dēvālēs
dedicated the services of, and collected dues from, the people
resident in villages attached to the dēvālē (dēvālēgam). Apart
from services due to the viharas or the basnāyaka nilamēs,
temple tenants were also liable to unpaid public service,
especially at the important national festivals in the capital city.
As in the past, the king intervened in disputes regarding
incumbencies of viharas; he was, in fact, the final arbiter in
them. Again, the king appointed incumbents, at his discretion,
to newly built viharas and pansalas, as well as to restored
and re-endowed temples.[5]

The overriding authority of the ruler in religious affairs
was demonstrated most starkly in Kīrti Śrī Rājasimha's decree,
promulgated after the establishment of the Siyam Nikāya, which
restricted its membership to the Govikula alone. Saranankara
acquiesced in this, although it went against the Silvat Samāgama's
well-established practice of ignoring caste distinctions among
its membership. With Kīrti Śrī Rājasimha's decree, the non-
Goyigama bhikkhus were rigorously excluded from the
sangha; indeed, a large number of them were even prohibited
from performing the ceremony of higher ordination. This caste
exclusiveness in the sangha was nothing new either in the
Kandyan kingdom, or in the Sinhalese kingdoms of the past;
indeed, it was well established in the days of the Dambadeniya
kings in the thirteenth century. What was significant in Kīrti
Śrī Rājasimha's decree was that it ostentatiously legitimized
caste exclusiveness. Equally important, the acquiescence of the
Siyam Nikāya leadership in this demonstrated afresh the
strength of traditional values in the Buddhist revival.

The reaction to this appeared within a generation, not in
the Kandyan kingdom but in the low country where, in the
last years of the eighteenth century and the first decade of
the nineteenth, a predominantly non-Goyigama fraternity of
bhikkhus, the Amarapura Nikāya, was established on the
refusal of the Siyam Nikāya to grant upasampadā to non-
Goyigamas.[6] The authority of the exclusively Goyigama Siyam
Nikāya was still unchallenged within the Kandyan kingdom.

LITERATURE AND THE ARTS

Saranankara's work was as much a landmark in the world of Sinhalese learning and literary activity as it was in the history of the sangha. It arrested a decline that was well-nigh complete, and although the vigour of the revival he initiated subsided considerably by the turn of the eighteenth century, the resuscitated tradition was kept alive by a system of pupilary succession, to undergo further refinement in a second wave of revivalism in the latter half of the nineteenth century.

The last substantial figure in the classical literary tradition[7] of the Sinhalese, which had reached its peak in the Kotte kingdom and the reign of Parākramabāhu VI, had been the sixteenth-century poet Alagiyavanna. But his poetry revealed a decline in literary skill; control of the classical idiom was poor and the poetic idiom was forced and artificial. The panegyrics of the seventeenth and early eighteenth centuries represented a further degeneration of the classical tradition. A refreshing contrast was a more popular literary form: a balladic type of narrative verse, its imagery drawn from the poet's environment and its highly evocative language based on folk speech instead of an archaic poetic diction and conventional literary stereotypes. Among the significant prose works of the mid-seventeenth century were the *Rājaratnākāraya* and the *Rājāvaliya*, a chronicle surveying the story of Sri Lanka from its earliest beginnings—from the time of Vijaya—to the accession of Vimala Dharma Sūriya II. All these works were a blend of myth and historical fact. More down-to-earth are the *Kadayim-pot* and *Vittipot*—of which there were a large number in this period—compendia of traditional lore depicting the history of royal lineages and the prestigious Kandyan families, with descriptions of important landmarks in the country and territorial boundaries. Although these were generally prose works, they were sometimes interspersed with verse. However, the sum total of these literary works did not amount to an outburst of creativity or originality. On the contrary, they underlined the collapse of the classical literary tradition of the Sinhalese.

The classical languages, Pali and Sanskrit, were essential ingredients of traditional scholarship, and Pali in particular had a special significance in the context of Saranankara's age; the revival of the study of this, the language of the Buddhist scriptures, was essential for the revitalization of that religion. Saranankara and his disciples rescued the classical tradition from the demise to which it had seemed inevitably destined. For all its vitality, this literary revival was intrinsically atavistic in outlook and its keynote was formalism. The prose and poetry of this era were lacking in full control of the classical idiom and displayed little originality.

The literature of the period was not all in this classical mould, or merely that of a learned elite. The tradition of folk literature, especially folk poetry, was still alive and very active. Among its features were attempts at biographies (including a eulogistic one of Saranankara) in prose and verse and some impressionistic and rather stereotyped surveys of contemporary events. The erotic poetry of the period was an offshoot of the panegyric—panegyrics contained among other things descriptions of the erotic appeal and sexual prowess of the hero—but there were models for imitation in Tamil literature as well. This new genre, for all its flaws,[8] had one outstanding quality: a robust secularity which set it off from the classical tradition of the day, in which the subject matter of verse and prose was religious in content and outlook.

The seventeenth and eighteenth centuries are a period of modest achievement in architecture and the arts in general. This partly reflects the meagreness of the economic resources of the Kandyan kingdom, to which the Portuguese forays of the early seventeenth century and the Dutch economic policy as well as their invasions of the 1760s, contributed in no small measure.

The town of Senkadagala (modern Kandy), like most cities and towns of ancient Sri Lanka, was more or less square in layout, with its streets running north–south and east–west. Senkadagala consisted, in fact, of two square enclosures with the smaller one containing a number of temples and the one on the east dominated by the king's palace which faced east. The Daladā Māligāva or the Temple of the Tooth was attached to the king's palace and the complex of shrines associated with the former was in the same locality. Vimala Dharma Sūriya I is said to have built his palace in Senkadagala in the Portuguese style. After it was burnt down by de Azevedo, and the replacement built by Senarat had suffered a similar fate, not much attention was paid in the later years to the embellishment of the royal palace at Kandy. The Kandyans were ready to abandon it at short notice, or even to burn it down in the face of invaders. Rājasimha II's position was altogether stronger, and in the more settled political conditions of the day he built a new palace in the capital and another later at Hanguranketa. His palace at Kandy, more elegant and substantial than those of his predecessors, was enlarged by Kīrti Śrī Rājasimha, ironically to be burnt down by the Dutch shortly afterwards. The rather unpretentious structure that survives today is the palace as rebuilt by Kīrti Śrī Rājasimha and renovated by his successors. The walls of its central hall had originally been decorated in fine taste with stucco reliefs and terracotta plaques of which little survives today. Of the palace at Hanguranketa there is hardly a trace.

One important manifestation of the revivalist spirit of the second half of the eighteenth century was the great interest shown in rehabilitating the ancient temples and places of worship neglected or abandoned in the past, such as those of Anuradhapura and Polonnaruva[9], or vandalized by the Portuguese, such as the shrines on the littoral. The reigns of Kīrti Śrī Rājasimha and his successor Rājādhi Rājasimha are especially distinguished in this regard. Of the former, it has been said that there was 'hardly a *vihara* of any importance in the Kandy district which was not restored by him or newly built by him'.[10] The ruined cities of Anuradhapura and Polonnaruva were in the grip of two immensely powerful forces—an impenetrable forest cover and malaria—far beyond the capacity of the Kandyan rulers to overcome. As a result, their efforts at restoring the shrines there were futile exercises without any prospect of success. But the reconstruction of shrines on the littoral destroyed by the Portuguese was easier to accomplish. Indeed, Rājasimha II had shown how this could be done. In 1588, Thomé de Sousa had devastated the celebrated dēvālē at Devundara. After the Portuguese had been forced to relax their grip on the Matara district, Rājasimha II had erected a devāle there dedicated to Vishnu; it was the precursor of a distinctive Kandyan type of architecture. Kīrti Śrī Rījasimha restored the devāle at Munneswaram near Salāvata (Chilaw), which had suffered great damage at the hands of the Portuguese.

The oldest of the temples in Kandy, as old as the town itself, is the Nātha Dēvālē built by Narendrasimha, who also constructed the present Temple of the Tooth. This two-storeyed structure replaced an earlier one of three storeys, built by Narendrasimha's father, which had been for some time on the verge of collapse. Kīrti Śrī Rājasimha renovated the Temple of the Tooth in his day and decorated its walls with paintings from the Jatakas. No traces of these paintings remain today. Of the two major Buddhist viharas in Kandy, Malvatta was built by Kīrti Śrī Rājasimha, while the Asgiriya complex was the work of the Pilima Talauvē family. Kīrti Śrī Rājasimha was responsible for the construction of two temples on the outskirts of Kandy, the Gangārāma and Degaldoruva, the latter celebrated for its beautiful frescoes. Work on the audience hall in Kandy began in 1784 in the reign of Rājādhi Rājasimha and the project was completed early in the following century by Śrī Vikrama Rājasimha, who also built the elegant *pattiruppuva* of the Daladā Māligāva and constructed the decorative lake in the heart of the town.

The strongest influence on the architecture of the Kandyan kingdom appears to have been south Indian, in particular, the Malabar region—a natural development in view of the close links between it and the Kandyan kingdom in this period. As in Malabar, wood rather than stone was the basis of Kandyan architecture. The audience hall, for example, was supported on either side by two rows of richly carved wooden pillars. This design was adapted and worked in stone in the Daladā Māligāva. Second, one of the more interesting features of Kandyan architecture—the long verandah supported on pillars of wood, stone or masonry—was also derived from the same south Indian source. The peaked roofs of these structures rose one above the other (as, for example, in the Lankātilaka Vihara), the walls protected from the weather by overhanging eaves.

One of the distinctive Kandyan contributions to Buddhist architecture was the *tämpath viharagē*, a special type of image house built on piles. Buddhist temples of this period generally had a pansala or residence for the bhikkhus, a vihara or image house, and a stupa or dāgäba as well, although there were some temples without dāgäbas. Attached to almost every temple was a dēvālē dedicated to a Hindu deity and often an image of this god was housed under the same roof as the statue of the Buddha. In some of the Kandyan temples the stupa is replaced by the tämpath viharagē, a much more indigenous structure which may have originated from the need for protection from the weather and insect pests as well.

We have more information on the domestic architecture of the Kandyans than on that of the people of previous centuries.[11] The houses of the people were very simple one-storey structures—the humblest had just one room—with walls of mud beaten into a timber framework, a thatched roof and floors made smooth by a mixture of mud and cow-dung. The *valauva*s, the houses of the elite, were more elegant structures, but they too were generally dark with unglazed windows on the inside only, the rooms generally being arranged around an inner courtyard *(hatarās midula)* open to the sky.

The sculpture of these centuries was intrinsically imitative and, when compared with that of the past, quite undistinguished. None of the images or statues of this period bears comparison with the masterpieces of Anuradhapura and Polonnaruva. The decline in artistic standards is best seen in the moonstones: its symbolism was forgotten and it was treated merely as a piece of ornamentation, with a variety of motifs and shapes. The moonstones of the Daladā Māligāva are typical of this development, with their elongated ends and rather mechanical and highly conventionalized ornamentation.

There seems to have been no connecting link between the artistic traditions of Sigiri, Polonnaruva and the Kandyan kingdom. Nevertheless, all aspects of Kandyan painting— measurement, proportions, choice and arrangement of colours, composition of figures and the relative position of figures to one another—were based on tradition formulated by generations of masters. Kandyan art is, in fact, stylized, its motifs and subjects are traditional and its style is rather two-dimensional with an emphasis on line (this does not disappear under daubs of paint but remains visible) and colour. Although the palette was limited, this had its advantages in the sense that the colours stand out brilliant and unadulterated. The best examples of traditional Kandyan art are the frescoes at Degaldoruva and at the Ridī Vihara at Kurunegala, the work of an unordained monk Devaragampola Silvatänna in the years 1771–76. The Dambulla Rock Temple was redecorated in the eighteenth century in much the same style. The paintings of the temple at Kaballalena in the Kurunegala district were also the work of the school of painters of which Devaragampola Silvatänna was the most distinguished exponent. On the littoral too, in the eighteenth and early nineteenth centuries, artists of this school painted the shrines at Mulkirigala in the Hambantota district, the Totagamuva Rajamahāvihara at Telvatta and the Sailabimbārāmaya in Dodanduva, both in the Galle district. The difference in style in these paintings suggests that they could have been the work of three different artists.

Even the best work of this period—at Degaldoruva and at Dambulla—although interesting in terms of colour, pattern and religious feeling was rather naive and inferior in technique and sensitivity compared to the works of the past. They are, very likely, offshoots of a school of Indian painting which flourished at Lepakshi near Vijayanagar and were thus of Dravidian derivation rather than of the Deccan or the Ganga Basin.

The English East India Company
in Sri Lanka, 1796–1802

The uncertain political future of the territories in Sri Lanka that came under the control of the English East India Company in 1795–96 was reflected in the devices adopted for their administration. Although Dundas was inclined towards permanent British control from the outset, a decision on this was postponed and in the meantime the administration was placed under the Madras government of the English East India Company, which proceeded to adopt a variety of expedients to recoup from these territories the costs of their conquest and military expenditure. The keynote was improvisation.

With the failure of the peace negotiations at Lille, the British government in November 1797 resolved to place the former Dutch possessions in Sri Lanka more emphatically under the Crown than before. Although it was at first intended that they should become a Crown Colony entirely independent of the East India Company, the court of directors, egged on by Lord Wellesley, who had succeeded Sir John Shore as Governor General, protested against it, urging the necessity for preserving a united authority in India.[1] The final decision was left to Henry Dundas, President of the Board of Control for India, who settled upon a compromise under which the company shared the administration of these territories with the Crown, and was in turn guaranteed a monopoly of trade, the most coveted portion of which was the cinnamon trade of Sri Lanka, once a flourishing enterprise but now yielding merely a moderate profit. This system of dual control lasted from 12 October 1798, with the appointment of the Honourable Frederick North as governor, until 1 January 1802 when these territories became the British Crown Colony of Ceylon. During these years the most consistent advocate of the establishment of permanent British control on the island was Wellesley, under whom British power in India had emerged clearly beyond any possibility of successful challenge from the French and, after the destruction of Tipu Sultan's power, from any combination of native states.

This transformation of the British position in India had a curious effect on Dundas, who came to believe that British power in India could rely safely on naval supremacy to meet any possible future threat from the French. The determination to keep the maritime regions of Sri Lanka as a Crown Colony weakened considerably. What Dundas wanted was consolidation, not expansion, of British power, and Wellesley's initiatives and ambitions came to be viewed by him as an irresponsible and expensive over-extension of resources. As a result, they were now at cross-purposes, Dundas being increasingly suspicious of Wellesley's motives.[2] He found it easier to thwart Wellesley in his ambition to control the maritime regions of Sri Lanka from India, as part of the process of establishing a unity of authority in India, than over the more vital issue of securing the confirmation of Sri Lanka as a British possession at the peace conference. Over the latter, Dundas was now lukewarm, but he was not influential enough to have his views endorsed by the government.

When the English East India Company began its administration of Sri Lanka's littoral, the continuity of British control over these territories was by no means assured. Nevertheless, not all its officials on the island (or in India for that matter) believed that British rule had necessarily to be temporary, and some very influential men worked on the assumption that it need not be so. Following the British practice in conquered territories, the laws, customs and institutions prevailing in the former Dutch 'colony' were allowed to continue. There was no reluctance to use the services of VOC officials who chose to remain in Sri Lanka. The only ones displaced were those who had held high office under the VOC and some native officials, especially the headmen who had formed an integral part of the Dutch administrative machinery. Some south Indian officials, who belonged to the indigenous section of the civil establishment at Fort St George, were brought in too. The major premise in all these decisions was that there was no certainty that British rule on the island's littoral would be permanent. By their very nature, these decisions were improvisations designed for a situation in which long-term plans were impossible. But at least two of them created problems for the new regime. The introduction of the *aumildars*, the most important of these south Indian officials, and their subordinates aroused the resentment of their Sri Lankan counterparts and eventually provoked their undisguised opposition. As for the VOC officials who continued in service, there was always the hope—if not the expectation—of a restoration of Dutch rule at a peace settlement. As a result they demonstrated an understandable reluctance to commit themselves unreservedly to the British cause.[3] In this uncertain situation the presence of these Dutch officials served to revive the flagging loyalty of headmen and schoolmasters to the VOC and to remind them that there was always the possibility of a restoration of Dutch rule.

There was, at the same time, another strand in the policies of the new regime, based on the belief that Sri Lanka's littoral would not be returned to the Dutch. This is seen in the efforts taken to cultivate the friendship of groups in the local population whom the Dutch had treated with suspicion or hostility. The most notable among them were the Roman Catholics and the Muslims. The restrictions imposed on them by the VOC were substantially moderated if not relaxed. The concessions offered to the Roman Catholics included the right to marriage and burial services performed by their own priests and to the burial of their dead in their own churchyards, all of which had been prohibited during the Dutch regime. Muslims had been suspect to the VOC on account of their religion, while their expertise in trade and commerce had made them feared and envied as well. Thus the disabilities imposed on them covered both fields, the religious and the economic. The English East India Company relaxed the religious laws affecting the Muslims, eliminated the curbs imposed on their commercial activities and gave them entry to the lucrative rents of government revenue.[4]

Within a few months of the conquest, Robert Andrews, one of the senior officials in the new administration, outlined a set of far-reaching social and economic reforms which he intended to introduce. His superiors in Sri Lanka and Madras had misgivings about them, those in Sri Lanka were apprehensive that the reforms might provoke opposition among the people and those in Madras felt that reforms of this nature should not be attempted until these territories were acknowledged as British possessions in law. Neither thought it necessary to repudiate or countermand the reforms or to reprimand Andrews when he went ahead with their introduction. In initiating the reforms Andrews hoped to ensure that British rule in Sri Lanka's littoral would not be a temporary episode between two periods of Dutch rule.[5] The reforms affected all strata of society and every ethnic group in the population. They provoked immediate and widespread opposition. The native headmen were antagonized by the decision to withdraw their accomodessans. The abolition of rājakāriya (and uliyam[6] and capitation taxes[7]) would not by themselves have had any disturbing effects, had they not been accompanied by an ill-considered attempt to introduce some uniformity into the farrago of land taxes then in force, which in practice meant, as it often does in matters of this nature, an increase in the taxation level. To complicate and confuse matters even further, there was also a series of new and irksome levies, ranging from a vexatious one on personal ornaments to a potentially productive but no less irritating tax on coconut palms and other trees.

A radical transformation of the traditional tax structure of this nature would, at the best of times, have caused some dissatisfaction and grumbling. To attempt it at very short notice and without the support of the headmen—the intermediaries between the government and the people—made this whole sequence of operations exasperating and provocative. In December 1796, the rebellion which Colonel (later General) James Stuart, Andrews's superior on the island, had predicted as the likely outcome of introducing the reforms, erupted and remained alive throughout 1797 although the full range of the armed forces available to the British in Sri Lanka were used to quell it. Although the epicentre of the disturbances was the Colombo disāvony, and in particular Rayigam, Hevagam, Siyana and Salpiti kōralēs, tremors were also felt in Jaffna, Batticaloa and the Vanni. The Kandyans lent the rebels their aid and Dutch officials resident in Sri Lanka and possibly some French agents helped to fan the flames. The rebellion began to peter out in the first quarter of 1798, but only after the Madras government in desperation gave an undertaking to revoke Andrews's reforms and to restore the old system of taxes. Only once thereafter were the British faced with a rebellion equally formidable, namely, in 1817–18. But the rebels of 1797–98, unlike those of 1817–18, achieved their aims and were not defeated.[8]

In the meantime, a Committee of Investigation consisting of Brigadier General de Meuron, Major Agnew and Robert Andrews himself had been appointed. It was granted extraordinary powers to investigate the causes of the rebellion, recommend measures of reform and redress grievances. The committee was given executive powers as well and entrusted with responsibility for the administration of the territories captured from the VOC. It administered these territories from June 1797 to 12 November 1798. The investigations of the committee revealed that while there had indeed been abuses and malpractices, the inevitable consequence of the precipitate introduction of a series of far-reaching reforms, the discontent that ensued was not due to any exceptional rapacity on the part of the pre-reform regime. The critical flaws lay in the novelty of the taxes introduced, the administrative devices adopted and, most important of all, the powers conferred on the south Indian officials which encroached on those of the native headmen and extended to some of the most sensitive aspects of the lives of the people, such as caste. It was easy, therefore, to misconstrue decisions taken in ignorance of custom and tradition as evidence of studied insensitivity to these, and the native headmen, chafing at the presence of the aumildars and their south Indian subordinates, were able to exploit popular opposition to the taxes to discredit the new administration among the people at large.

In these circumstances, the committee felt that it had no alternative but to recommend the restoration of the status quo, wherever that was possible, as the most logical and practical solution to the problems that confronted it. There was virtual unanimity in the committee over recommendations to restore rājakāriya and uliyam, and to reinstate the headmen to office, such posts being restricted to men from the Goyigama and Vellala castes. In the committee's view, a restoration of the status quo included the continued employment of Dutch officials who had served the former regime. These Dutch officials, however, could not reconcile themselves to British rule and the belief which prevailed among them that the Dutch would regain control of their possessions on the island appeared to have been strengthened by the outbreak of this rebellion. The committee had hardly begun the process of implementing its policies of reconstruction and restoration when Governor North took over the administration under the system of dual control.[9] When he reached Colombo peace had been restored. He found that de Meuron's Committee had analysed the causes of the rebellion and recommended remedial measures and it was to the latter that North turned his attention.

In the three years of his administration under the system of dual control, North was intent on ensuring that British authority over the former Dutch possessions in Sri Lanka should become permanent. On this—but on little else—he was supported by the government at Fort St George and by many of its officials in Sri Lanka. The restoration of the old order which de Meuron's Committee had recommended was entirely in accordance with North's own conservative instincts.

His first act was to restore the headmen to office. In so doing he implemented one of the committee's principal recommendations, on which they had deferred a decision when they learnt of the new arrangements for the administration of the maritime regions of Sri Lanka. The re-establishment of rājakāriya and uliyam was decisive in the restoration of the old order; but this was complicated now by the fact that after two years of freedom from them the people were reluctant to see them resumed, and once the restoration of rājakāriya was attempted there was widespread evasion of such services. North sought to resolve this by trying to make rājakāriya acceptable, and this proved to be more difficult than a straightforward abolition. He began with an attempt to get all those holding land under rājakāriya to register themselves, with the family as the unit for registration. When this failed to yield the results he anticipated, he responded by embarking on an even more ambitious project—registering title to holdings on the basis of single ownership. This more sophisticated venture in registration began on 20 February 1800, and a special administrative structure was created for this purpose with an improvised survey department as its core. Two advantages were anticipated from this radical departure from the traditional system: obscurity of title to land would be eliminated and single ownership would be an incentive to more efficient production in agriculture. Registration on a single-owner basis became one of North's most cherished projects, but it made little or no headway in the face of people's reluctance to embark on so radical a departure from custom and tradition.

There were, however, aspects of rājakāriya which were more amenable to control. Under a proclamation of 3 September 1801, all rājakāriya lands were made liable to taxes of one-fifth of the produce on lowland and one-tenth on highland. This was in conformity with existing practice. But there was also a new tax of one-tenth of the produce on dry grain, in place of a medley of land taxes which had not brought in much revenue and which generally varied from region to region. It did not take North long to realize that the restoration of the old order and old institutions which he was attempting benefited the headmen more than the people or the government. He moved now to reduce their powers. By the proclamation of 3 September 1801, they were deprived of their accomodessans and were to receive salaries instead. A fresh limitation of the scope of headmen's duties was introduced by deliberately excluding them from the registration of holdings under rājakāriya. North realized that rājakāriya had to be enforced on the basis of caste and that the headmen had made themselves dispensable in this because of the information and local knowledge which they had accumulated. A solution to this problem was sought in a codification of caste law, which, however, was easier suggested than done; in fact, it was never done. North hoped that once a code of caste law was compiled, the *landraad*s would adjudicate in caste disputes.

North's reforms in these spheres were less visionary and revolutionary than those attempted by Andrews; besides, they were, to a greater extent than Andrews's, a continuation of trends initiated in the last years of Dutch rule. Indeed, most of the changes North attempted to bring about in the Sinhalese areas had been in operation there already; and they were not applicable in Jaffnapatam where the headmen received one-tenth of the paddy collection as their remuneration instead of accomodessans, and where, moreover, the uliyam obligation had already been dissociated from the land. North's conservatism was best demonstrated in his policy on caste. He was in total agreement with the de Meuron Committee and the Madras government on the necessity of upholding the caste system as it existed. The codification of caste law which he envisaged was designed with this end in view. As part of his commitment to this same objective, he took the unusual—and illogical—step of declaring himself head of the Salāgama caste and making Robert Arbuthnot, a senior civil servant, head of the Karava caste. Very soon, under North's instructions, government institutions—including schools and hospitals—began to pay fastidious attention to the caste sensibilities of the people who came within their purview. Similarly, within the administrative hierarchy persons of inferior caste were prevented from assuming authority over persons of 'high' caste, which meant in effect the restriction of the most influential posts within the reach of native officials to the Goyigama and Vellala castes. The privileges conferred upon the Salāgama caste by the Dutch at the very end of their rule in Sri Lanka were rescinded. This meticulous sensitivity to the caste system and the attempt to bolster it by administrative and legal means were clearly intended to win the support of the people at large for the new regime.

At the same time, under North, conciliation of sections of the population with a grievance against the Dutch was pursued with even greater vigour than in the past. Once again the main beneficiaries of this policy were the Muslims. The number of Muslim renters increased substantially due partly to the growth in the renting process, but also partly to North's high regard for their enterprise in trade which was believed to have augmented government revenues. He refused to reimpose the uliyam tax on them and evidence of its previous payment was treated as a complete commutation of service obligations. This exemption from all such burdens was an advantage and a privilege denied to others. The favours shown to the Muslims extended to other areas of activity as well. Thus the men appointed to recruit soldiers for the new native regiments raised by North were Muslims, as were all the *subidars* and *janidars* (the only commissioned grades to which the indigenous population were eligible). Also, North was anxious to set up a special school for Muslim children in recognition of the fact that they regarded attendance at existing schools with distaste.[10]

The generosity shown to the Muslims was in sharp contrast to the treatment meted out to other religious groups, including the Roman Catholics. Although the latter were now in a much more advantageous position than they had been under the Dutch and the policy of tolerance of Roman Catholicism was continued under North, not all the obnoxious regulations imposed on them by the Dutch were abolished. The Buddhists and Hindus were not so fortunate. Their requests for licences to erect temples and places of worship were not granted as of right and they certainly do not seem to have been granted licences to establish schools, for North was anxious that their children should attend government schools. The rationale behind this and behind North's religious policy was the belief that the great majority of the people of the maritime regions were Protestant Christians. This was based on a ridiculously uncritical acceptance of the opinions of Dutch officials resident in Sri Lanka and of the native headmen and schoolmasters. In the government schools established by the VOC the curriculum was fundamentally religious in orientation, and Sinhalese and Tamil were the media of instruction. These were given a new lease of life. North was keenly interested in the spread of Christianity and he treated the Dutch Reformed Church and the Church of England as belonging alike to the government's religious establishment. State funds were used for the repair of dilapidated churches and the construction of new ones. Clergymen were encouraged to tour the country to minister to the spiritual needs of their adherents and to propagate the faith among the people at large. The requirement imposed by the Dutch that headmen in the government service should be Protestant Christians was strictly enforced.

The keynotes of North's internal policy were stabilization, pacification and reconstruction after the turmoil of the first two years of British rule. He realized that the re-establishment of peace and order could not, by itself, convince the government in Britain that these territories were worth keeping as a British possession. North sent glowing accounts of the island's potential in trade and commerce in order to remove any fears about the likelihood of its becoming a drain on British resources. When the decision was taken to convert the former VOC possessions in Sri Lanka into a British Crown Colony, North's sanguine reports on its economic prospects carried much less weight than a careful assessment of its strategic importance to the British empire.

In October 1798, when the system of dual control was established, Dundas still had doubts about the severance of the link between the English East India Company and the administration of Sri Lanka's maritime regions. Within a year these doubts had disappeared and he was inclined to see the former Dutch territories on the island as a distinct political entity, independent of India. In reaching this decision he was guided as much by a resolution to curb Wellesley's ambitions as by more mundane considerations—a desire to obtain another outlet for patronage. It was also guided by North's difficulties with the English East India Company's civil servants. North and Wellesley were agreed on the retention of the maritime regions of Sri Lanka as a British possession. Despite North's great admiration for

Wellesley and the latter's influence over him, the course of events in Sri Lanka drove him irrevocably to policies which amounted to an advocacy of its separation from India. The crux of the problem lay in his relations with his civil servants.

The Madras Presidency of the English East India Company resented the loss of patronage which it suffered by the introduction of the system of dual control. North, for his part, obliged by order of the directors of the East India Company to fill most of the vacancies in the island's administration with civil servants of Madras, protested vigorously against this but to no avail. From the moment of his arrival on the island he faced the unconcealed hostility of the Madras civil servants and these strained relations continued throughout the period of dual control, although there was some improvement when North's own men (who had come with him from Britain) were found to be just as prone to corruption and inefficiency as the men from Madras. Salaries and prospects of promotion in Sri Lanka were so inferior to those in Madras that no civil servant of ability or ambition sent to the island from that Presidency was willing to remain there for long. Moreover, the languages and customs of the people of Sri Lanka's littoral were so totally different from those of Madras that service in the one was almost useless as preparation for the other. North strongly urged that the only solution to this problem was the creation of a separate civil service for Sri Lanka, but this was impossible for as long as the system of dual control was in operation. Nor was he any more successful in the measures of administrative reform which he initiated in this phase; the Madras civil servants gave him little support.

In late 1800, Dundas informed Wellesley: 'have wrote [sic] a private letter to Mr North to inform him of what is nearly decided in my mind. I mean to take the government of Ceylon again [sic] into the King's hands, and separate it from the government of the Company. The junction has done no good, and a good deal of mischiefī.'[11] Wellesley was adamantly opposed to it but his protests were in vain, although the same communication would have given him the satisfaction of learning that Ceylon becoming a Crown Colony was now almost certainly a reality.

The former Dutch possessions in Sri Lanka were finally ceded to the British at the Peace of Amiens in March 1802. The Amiens settlement merely ratified the preliminary peace concluded in London on 1 October 1801. Dundas opposed the treaty and resigned office; thus the retention of British control over the maritime regions of Sri Lanka at the Peace of Amiens owed more to Pitt and Lord Grenville, the foreign secretary, than to him.[12] A British Crown Colony was established in Sri Lanka, largely, if not entirely, for reasons of imperial strategy.

From the brief but unfortunate association with Madras and the East India Company, Sri Lanka gained one inestimable benefit. In later years, whenever it was suggested on the island, in India or in Whitehall that for the sake of economy or administrative convenience the colony of Sri Lanka should be treated as an integral part of the Indian empire, the memory of these unhappy years served as a reminder of the attendant perils.

The Fall of the Kandyan Kingdom[1]

The British conquest of the Dutch possessions in the maritime regions of Sri Lanka shifted the balance of power on the island decisively against the Kandyans, with the substitution of a very powerful neighbour for a weak one. The success of the Kandyan resistance to repeated Portuguese and Dutch encroachments and the continued survival of the Kandyan kingdom as an independent state in the face of these threats engendered among the Kandyans a feeling of self-confidence that bordered on a complacent assumption of invincibility. Yet, the survival of the Kandyan kingdom as an independent state was due much more to the inadequacy of the resources of the Portuguese and of their successors, the Dutch, for the purpose of subjugating the Kandyan kingdom than to the inherent military strength of the latter. The British were an altogether more formidable proposition. Under Wellesley, the process of expanding their power in the Indian subcontinent at the expense of all rivals, indigenous and foreign, progressed with remarkable rapidity to the point where they emerged as the dominant force in south Asia.

In the early years of their rule in Sri Lanka, the British had no real anxiety to round off total control over the island. They were not seriously alarmed even when they discovered that the Kandyans, in pursuit of their traditional policy, were giving encouragement to rebels in the lowlands during the rebellion of 1797. On the contrary, Andrews had begun a policy of relaxing the rigid curbs on the external trade of the Kandyans which the Dutch had imposed and permitted the Kandyans to develop trade contacts across the seas in the hope of thus demonstrating that British control over the island's littoral was much less irksome to Kandyan interests than Dutch rule there had been. Moreover, so long as there was the prospect that the maritime regions of Sri Lanka might revert to the Dutch at a European peace conference, it was politic to maintain a policy of non-interference in Kandyan affairs.

But the disputed succession to the Kandyan throne which followed on the death of Rājādhi Rājasimha in August 1798 offered opportunities for intrigue. Within three weeks of his arrival in Colombo, North turned his attention to the Kandyan problem. When Śrī Vikrama Rājasimha ascended the Kandyan throne, North sent the usual letter of greeting in the conventional terms of formal flattery. One aspect of the Kandyan policy of the British had already been determined before North's arrival— that no encouragement would be given to the Kandyans in their attempts to reopen the question of the treaty with the British which the Kandyans had refused to ratify in 1796. There was a sense of relief that the Kandyan refusal to ratify the treaty had rendered it void; the British were thus spared the irksome disadvantages to their interests on the island which would have followed had the treaty been ratified. North needed little encouragement to stand by this decision, and all endeavours on the part of the Kandyans to reopen this question were firmly rebuffed. At the same time, the concessions on external trade which Andrews had introduced were continued by North in the hope of persuading the Kandyans that British rule in the littoral was likely to benefit the Kandyans more than Dutch rule.

When Rājādhi Rājasimha died of fever (like his predecessor he was childless) there was no obvious successor to the throne. The most powerful person at court was the first adigār, Pilima Talauvē, a man of supposed royal descent himself, who had signed the Preliminary Treaty of 1795 and maintained the most cordial relations with the British. He held several offices and had enjoyed enormous influence which he now used with decisive effect to install a protégé as king. This latter was a youth of eighteen, without the benefit of a formal education, a Sri Lanka-born Nāyakkar named Konnasāmi, the son of a sister of one of the queens dowager. At Rājādhi Rājasimha's death, however, Muttusāmi, a brother-in-law (he was a brother of three of the late monarch's queens), claimed to have been nominated by the late king as his successor. He and his sisters were promptly placed by Pilima Talauvē in confinement. However, Muttusāmi was not the only potential disputant. It has too easily been assumed that Pilima Talauvē's aim in placing Śrī Vikrama Rājasimha on the throne was to eliminate him as soon as an opportunity offered and to re-establish a Sinhalese dynasty with himself as king. But his ambitions were more limited and realistic. He had no personal ambition to gain the throne, but merely the desire to control matters from behind the scene, to wield influence and a measure of power without personal responsibility, and without the odium which would inevitably follow upon misrule. The Nāyakkar dynasty, especially under Kīrti Śrī Rājasimha and Rājādhi Rājasimha, had identified itself with the Kandyan national interest and blended the Nāyakkar personality into the Kandyan background with consummate skill. Its policy of transforming itself into an indigenous dynasty whose claims to that status were accepted by the people had proved so successful that a restoration of a Sinhalese dynasty was not a viable policy even against the background of a disputed succession such as that of 1798. Besides, even assuming that such a restoration was possible, there is little reason to believe that Pilima Talauvē was an acceptable choice. An overt attempt by him in this direction might well have set off a revolt of other potential Kandyan claimants and torn the country apart.

Pilima Talauvē soon discovered that his protégé, far from being pliant as he had seemed, was adopting an attitude of independence which the kingmaker had not anticipated. Pilima Talauvē became increasingly resentful of this and began almost at once to plot Śrī Vikrama's downfall. It is impossible to determine with any accuracy what Pilima Talauvē's plans were when he began his intrigues with North, apart from the primary aim of eliminating Śrī Vikrama Rājasimha from the throne. That done, the next phase of the problem would emerge—who would succeed to the throne of Kandy, and on what terms? The British claimed that Pilima Talauvē's objective was to ascend the throne himself, but there was no convincing evidence of this: he could well have been thinking of a more satisfactory and pliable protégé who would permit him to wield the power and influence he sought. This protégé too could have been a Nāyakkar. But if the British were brought in to help dethrone a recalcitrant Śrī Vikrama Rājasimha, this by itself could complicate the situation and raise a number of questions for which the answer or answers would no longer be within Pilima Talauvē's power to fashion. It would certainly involve a redefinition of the relationship between the new ruler and the British. Would their relationship reflect the new balance of forces in Sri Lanka and south Asia; that is to say, would the Kandyan kingdom be reduced to the level of a satellite state, its foreign policy controlled by the British, its defence in British hands and its independence confined to matters of social and economic policy? Pilima Talauvē would have known that British assistance would be forthcoming only on terms to be determined by them and that the compensation or advantages they sought in exchange for support in this venture would have been anything but satisfactory to the Kandyans. What is more likely is that he calculated that he could use British help for his immediate purpose, and once this had been achieved, British influence could be drastically reduced, or eliminated altogether, by the dextrous use of the traditional Kandyan policy of creating trouble for them in the form of sporadic but planned acts of harassment or through the assistance of yet another foreign power. The effectiveness of this traditional Kandyan policy in the past must have encouraged hope in its continued applicability now. Thus it seems likely that Pilima Talauvē had nothing more precise in mind beyond the elimination of Śrī Vikrama Rājasimha; beyond that he would trust to luck, and to his undoubted skill as a master manipulator of persons and forces, to devise solutions to each succeeding problem as it arose.

Like their predecessors in control of the island's littoral, the British regarded the long and indistinctly defined frontier as an irritating and expensive item of military expenditure, while being at the same time an irksome and formidable obstacle to trade. Besides, it was impossible to develop plans for the economic regeneration of the British colony in isolation from the larger island-wide framework and the independence and aloofness of the Kandyan kingdom would impede the development of the British possessions in Sri Lanka, especially in their administration and communications. At the same time, the island was small enough for effective control without any serious drain of human and financial resources for the purpose. There was the additional advantage that the conquest of the Kandyan kingdom would eliminate a cumbrous internal frontier, leaving only the sea as a line of defence.

These, in brief, were the compelling reasons which a man on the spot would have given in justification of a policy of interference in the affairs of the Kandyan kingdom. North saw in Pilima Talauvē's overtures an opportunity for the establishment of a controlling British interest in Kandy. Dundas himself was thinking on much the same lines but with a greater awareness of the limits to be observed in the implementation of such a policy. Nothing should be done 'by force or concussion of any kind'. On the other hand, 'if by conciliation and fair treaty we obtain a substantial right of interference in the Government of Candia [sic]...,' 'it would be important to see that [the] sword must be exclusively ours, and the civil government in all its branches must be virtually ours—but through the medium of its ancient organs'. North kept Dundas informed of a scheme for getting the Kandyan ruler to accept a treaty whereby his kingdom would become a British protectorate.[2] British troops would be guaranteed a regular supply of victuals and a road connecting Colombo with Trincomalee would run through the Kandyan territory. The inspiration behind this policy was Wellesley himself and his subsidiary alliance system which had been the means of establishing British paramountcy over the whole of the subcontinent of India.

Dundas's cautious endorsement of a policy of 'limited' interference in Kandyan affairs, made in 1799, before his disenchantment with Wellesley's ambitions had begun to suffuse his policy on south Asia, could not be regarded as a firm sanction of what North was attempting in regard to the Kandyan kingdom in 1800. Neither Dundas nor the East India

Company gave any official approval for North to embark on negotiations with the Kandyans, although Wellesley gave the project his warm approbation. Thus North had nothing to offer Pilima Talauvē or the king. Pilima Talauvē, on the other hand, was an opportunist playing a double role with the British and his own king and hoping to extract as much benefit as he could from the resulting confusion. The king was the more difficult problem since he had no enemies (save Pilima Talauvē) from whom he needed to be protected; thus he was hardly likely to jeopardize the independence of his country by entering into a sort of treaty which a subsidiary alliance entailed. Nevertheless, he considered it politic to yield to North's entreaties and accepted an embassy under General MacDowall which was to bring these proposals to Kandy. MacDowall's mission had two purposes in view: it was undertaken in the hope of gathering 'intelligence' on the Kandyan kingdom and it sought to negotiate the terms of a treaty on the lines mentioned earlier. The latter project was turned down by the king and his ministers, but the mission was more successful in gathering 'intelligence'. But North's primary aim had been to obtain a treaty and the failure in this venture made him more receptive than ever before to the prospect of removing the king and his 'perfidious ministers' as the only means by which he could have his way.

North's Kandyan policy had demonstrated from the beginning a cynical disregard for the niceties of diplomatic conduct. For he had begun a complex plot with the obviously disaffected chief minister of a ruler whose title he had recognized and who had given him no cause for quarrel. Nor was the use of an embassy for these purposes any less reprehensible. North realized that Pilima Talauvē's purpose was the deposition and assassination of the king, yet he persisted in his intrigues confident that his intervention would be the means of preserving the king's person and dignity, and believing that he could avoid the hostilities which Pilima Talauvē more than once hinted were imminent. North was supremely confident that, whatever happened, he would be in control of the situation. Like Pilima Talauvē he was playing off one antagonist (the chief minister) against the other (the king) in the hope that he would pick up the pieces. But North had underestimated the personal influence and power of the king and the degree of support which he could generate among his people. He chose to believe the stories sedulously spread by Pilima Talauvē and corroborated by the host of spies whom the British employed, about the unpopularity of the king and the widespread disaffection in the kingdom. Thus North was confident that should war break out, a short decisive campaign would ensue, and that to the chiefs and people British control would be an acceptable alternative to Śrī Vikrama Rājasimha's rule.

Once the basic decision to engage in hostilities had been taken, it was not at all difficult to find a cause for war, especially with Pilima Talauvē more than willing to provide one. By the end of 1803, MacDowall advanced with an expeditionary force to Kandy.[3] He reached the city to find it evacuated. A puppet ruler, Muttusāmi, was formally installed as king, but it was soon evident that the people held him in contempt and were in no way inclined to rally to his support. The Kandyan forces had merely withdrawn from the capital to regroup in preparation for the prolonged guerrilla campaign which was their customary tactic against invading armies. They had not been defeated. In a very short time the British forces were isolated among a sullenly hostile population and were already in difficulties about food. When the monsoon set in, the elements, combined with disease, brought about the destruction of the British forces who attempted to evacuate the capital they had occupied. MacDowall himself recommended this course of action, but his own ill health soon compelled him to retire to Colombo and the command fell to a Major Davie, an officer lacking the experience or competence for an undertaking of this magnitude and delicacy. In May, the British position was no longer tenable and Davie decided to abandon Kandy even before North's formal order to retire was received. On 24 June 1803, the remnants of the British army and the pretender Muttusāmi were intercepted by Kandyan forces at Vatapuluva on the banks of the Mahaveli. The pretender was handed over to the Kandyan ruler and was speedily executed. As for the

British officers and men, they were almost all killed in the encounter or executed subsequently. Some may even have killed themselves rather than fall into the hands of the Kandyans; even the sick left behind at the hospital in Kandy were put to death. Only Davie and three others escaped this fate.

The first Kandyan war had gone the way of earlier Portuguese and Dutch attempts to conquer Kandy. The Kandyan country, with its rugged terrain, malarial climate and lack of roads, could not be held by inadequately supplied European troops against Sinhalese guerrilla tactics. North had not devised an efficient commissariat for his Kandyan expedition. The campaign was ill-planned and the troops were ill-equipped for the rigours of a Kandyan war. Above all, the British had seriously miscalculated a matter of the utmost importance—the support of the people. They had believed that the people would cooperate against the seemingly unpopular and inexperienced ruler, but on the contrary they were confronted with a great reserve of popular support for the king. North sought to extricate himself as well as possible from the consequences of the Kandyan disaster and found a convenient scapegoat in Pilima Talauvē. But the real cause of the disaster was the inadequacy of his own planning for an expedition of this magnitude.

The Kandyan war dragged on for two years. North, like some latter-day de Azevedo, persisted in a policy of harassment, mounting regular forays into the border provinces with the sole purpose of destruction and pillage in an attempt to intimidate the Kandyan people. The chiefs, in the meantime, continued to intrigue with the British, while the resources of the kingdom were thus being systematically destroyed. Indeed, within a dozen years of winning a victory over an invading force from the littoral which was as notable if not as comprehensive as any of their past victories over the Portuguese and the Dutch, the Kandyan kingdom lost its independence. The fall of the last Sinhalese kingdom was a case of political suicide, and the king and the chiefs share the blame in this essay in self-destruction. Neither could see how close they had all come to disaster in 1803. On the contrary, their victory had made them—and particularly the king—dangerously complacent about their powers of survival and the continuing viability of the kingdom as an independent political entity against pressure from the coast. They were quite oblivious to the fact that the events of 1803 had not shifted the balance of power on the island in their favour.

As for the king it was natural that he should use the prestige accruing to him from the defeat inflicted on the British to make himself master of the country. Almost immediately, he set about asserting his authority within the kingdom, which in effect meant a consistent attempt to curb the chiefs and restrict their privileges. Pilima Talauvē's career at court received a setback from the Kandyan campaign of 1803, but he contrived to salvage something from the wreck and persisted in his intrigues with the British. By 1810, the king was strong enough to move against him and deprive him of all his offices, which perhaps goaded him into the desperate course of raising a revolt against the king and plotting his murder. The plot failed and he paid the penalty for failure. He was executed and it is significant that his execution did not result in any political convulsion in the country.

Nevertheless, the impression this may have given of the king's undisputed hold over the country was deceptive. His vigorous measures against the nobles—of which the execution of Pilima Talauvē was a very notable one—provoked a powerful aristocratic counter-offensive which, within a few years, alienated him from the majority of the chiefs who were now readier than ever before to accept British intervention. The processes of aristocratic opposition to the king were given greater momentum with the alienation of some of the more prominent bhikkhus. Whether this was due to disenchantment with the king's religious policies or to the close kinship ties of these bhikkhus with the aristocracy cannot be determined with any certainty. The execution of Pilima Talauvē had been followed by the appointment of his nephew Ähälēpola as first adigār. Soon Ähälēpola, like almost all Kandyan noblemen, was intriguing against the king and sounding the British about the prospects of intervention. But the British were now chary of being drawn into another Kandyan adventure on the promises of any chief.

The alienation of the Kandyan aristocracy was soon to reach the point of no return. Open hostility developed between the king and his first adigār. Ähälēpola, deprived of his disāvony and his honours in early 1814 because he refused to present himself at court at the king's command, tried to raise a rebellion in Sabaragamuva and, when this failed, crossed into British territory. He left his wife and children in the king's power to suffer the penalty meted out by Kandyan law to relatives of traitors. The precise mode of the execution of Ähälēpola's wife and children has been transformed by legend into a story of incredible horror. The defection of Ähälēpola marked a decisive phase in the subversion of the Kandyan kingdom. The disaffection of the nobles had given momentum to forces which were clearly beyond the king's control. Ähälēpola was followed into exile by other chiefs, all of whom offered their aid to the British for the overthrow of the king. But Governor Robert Brownrigg was wary of any impulsive bid to intervene, especially because he had received no instructions from Whitehall and because he was not yet certain of any substantial measure of Kandyan support against the king.

There had been a change in the British policy towards Kandy since the arrival in 1805 of General Sir Thomas Maitland, Brownrigg's predecessor as governor of the British colony of Ceylon. The punitive raids on the border districts, which North had initiated after the debacle of the invasion, were abandoned since they had accomplished little more than devastation of outlying areas without in any way inflicting a mortal wound. Besides, the Kandyans were far from being defeated and Maitland realized that the financial and military resources for a conquest of the Kandyan kingdom were not yet available to him. More important, he believed that a war with Kandy was not only expensive but pointless, for the Kandyan forces were too weak to pose any serious threat to the British possessions on the island. Maitland decided to remain strictly on the defensive; but he was willing to make peace on condition that the British survivors of the Kandyan expedition of 1803 were returned and the British were allowed to retain everything they had held before the war. He would not consent, however, to involving the British government in the despatch of an embassy to Kandy and without this a formal treaty of peace (and consequently, the release of Davie) could not be secured. In any case, negotiations were unlikely to be successful. The Kandyan terms for a formal treaty included the cession of a seaport, something which the British regarded as not negotiable under any circumstances. By tacit agreement hostilities between the two parties ceased and the British for their part lost nothing from letting things remain as they were.

Nevertheless, as the opposition of the aristocracy to Śrī Vikrama Rājasimha mounted, it became almost certain that the British would seek to exploit the situation in their own interest. By this time they had in John D'Oyly an expert on Kandyan affairs. He had built an efficient intelligence network and was in communication with the disaffected chiefs; but he nevertheless viewed coldly and dispassionately any 'feelers' the Kandyan nobility made with regard to British intervention in the affairs of the Kandyan kingdom. All such propositions were subjected to a searching and rigorous examination. By 1814, D'Oyly had come to the conclusion that the alienation of the Kandyan aristocracy from Śrī Vikrama Rājasimha had reached a point where the British could intervene with decisive effect. With the assistance of his spies and contacts, he was conducting negotiations with the Kandyan chiefs and by the end of 1814 all preparations for an invasion had been completed. Every chief of importance was in league with the British, and most notably Molligoda, Ähälēpola's successor as first adigār. All that was necessary now was some convenient pretext for the British to move in and there were many in the Kandyan kingdom who would gladly contrive to provide one. Brownrigg would have liked to use as a casus belli the punishment meted out to some traders taken in Kandyan territory under suspicion of being British spies, but Whitehall was averse to punitive action unless British territory were invaded.

Brownrigg, however, had already decided to invade Kandy himself; his plan of campaign, prepared with Ähälēpola's assistance, was ready. The technical aspects of the invasion plan bore the stamp of an able staff officer, Major William

Willerman.[4] As the man on the spot the governor could determine what constituted an invasion of British territory. When the king's troops chased a band of insurgents across the Sabaragamuva border into British territory, Brownrigg chose to treat this as an invasion. No opportunity was given to the king to apologize for the incident and this 'violation of British territory' was treated as a sufficient cause of war. The odds were in his favour and he moved against the king's forces with two British and five locally recruited regiments which he commanded in person. In a proclamation dated 10 January 1815 (issued on 13 January), he announced that the war was being undertaken on behalf of the oppressed Kandyan people who were to be protected from the depredations of their ruler. This proclamation has been justly described as 'a clever if self-righteous and magniloquent piece of propaganda'.

The second Kandyan war was over in forty days, without any notable military engagements. The most distinguished performance on the British side belonged to the military engineers for their technical skill and ingenuity in transporting artillery through the forests and mountains of the Balana Pass to Kandy. The British army marched unopposed to Kandy because the king's forces under Molligoda (who was in communication with the British) showed little inclination to resist. A semblance of opposition was maintained till Molligoda could safely cross over to the British, which he did once his wife and family were secure from the king's wrath. The British forces reached the city to find that the king had fled with his family, leaving the city open. With the king's capture on 18 February 1815 formal arrangements had to be made for the administration of his kingdom.

The Kandyan chiefs, in their intrigues against the king, had failed to realize that it was almost inevitable that the British should seek complete control over the whole island, if not possession of it. With a power as strong as the British in possession of the coast, the position of the isolated Kandyan kingdom was delicate and precarious. And whatever the reluctance of Whitehall to give formal encouragement to a further augmentation of British territorial possessions in south Asia, there was bound to be ready acquiescence in the face of a fait accompli, especially where the territorial gains were made in response to local pressure. The fate of the Kandyan kingdom was a case in point. The contribution of the chiefs gave momentum to local pressure for British intervention and this was a factor of vital importance in the transfer of power to the British.

Śrī Vikrama Rājasimha himself was not without blame. Had he shown greater flexibility in the pursuit of his prime objective of keeping the chiefs under control, he might have achieved his aims without any formidable opposition. But the ruthlessness with which he pursued his enemies was his own undoing. Crucial to the king's discomfiture, however, was his failure to retain the support of at least one of the factions of the aristocracy. The support of the people at large whom he sought to protect from the nobles was not an effective substitute for a bloc of aristocratic loyalists. By exacting rājakāriya, without due regard to conventions and practices governing such labour, in constructing the Kandy Lake and improving the palace, he ended up alienating the people as well. Despite this erosion of support for the king among the people, it is significant that they did not rise against him in support of either Pilima Talauvē (in 1810–11) or Ähälēpola (in 1814), first adigārs both, when they sought to raise a rebellion against the king. Both attempts failed dismally and this in a country where the record of resistance to unpopular rulers was almost as significant as the long tradition of resistance to foreign invaders. Śrī Vikrama Rājasimha's rule was singularly and significantly free of any such demonstration of the people's dissatisfaction. The people gave little or no support to the advancing British army in 1815 and demonstrated no enthusiasm at the cession to the British of the Kandyan kingdom. Thus the political turmoil in the kingdom in 1814–15 can by no stretch of the imagination be called a rebellion of the people. Nor can it be described as a civil war. It was a conspiracy hatched by the aristocracy against a ruler whose government was a threat to their interests as a social group; but the conspiracy achieved its purpose only because the British saw in it an opportunity to achieve their own objectives.

There was no real decline of the Kandyan kingdom in the sense of a deep-rooted crisis of society, nor an economic breakdown which affected the people, but only a running-down of the political machinery of the state in the face of a prolonged confrontation between the king and the chiefs in the ruling hierarchy. The pressures built up by this confrontation led to an irreparable breakdown in the political sphere and the Kandyan kingdom, divided against itself, became a tempting prey to the British who already had an iron grip on the coast and were not disinclined to round off total control over the island now that a suitable opportunity had presented itself. On 2 March 1815, the Kandyan kingdom was formally ceded to the British by its leaders, secular and religious. The terms of the convention signed on that date by Brownrigg on behalf of the British and by the chiefs on behalf of the Kandyans had been drafted largely by John D'Oyly. The document was read to the assembled chiefs and to the headmen of the districts gathered outside. The people took no part in the ceremony and indeed the townsfolk showed not the slightest interest in the proceedings.

The Kandyan Convention of 1815 reflected the political factors operating at that time. The concessions made to Kandyan interests on that occasion were granted because the political situation suggested these as essential to the purpose of conciliating groups that had rendered valuable assistance to the British. Thus the Kandyan Convention preserved intact the powers and privileges of the chiefs, the laws, the customs and institutions of the country and what in the eyes of the Kandyans was more important than all else—the Buddhist religion. The fifth clause of the convention, employing language described by Brownrigg as being 'more emphatical than would have been my choice', declared that 'the Religion of Buddhoo, its rites, ministers and places of worship are to be maintained and protected'. When he sent a copy of the convention to the Colonial Office, Brownrigg explained that he had been obliged to consent to 'an article of guarantee couched in the most unqualified terms', because it was vitally important to quiet the apprehensions of the Kandyans about their religion. Only by making it clear that the fifth clause of the convention would be scrupulously observed could the British gain the adherence of the bhikkhus and chiefs. The convention was approved by the home government with some reluctance, since the guarantees on religion were considered too emphatic. In the eyes of the Kandyans the connection between the state and Buddhism in Ceylon was hallowed by tradition and was therefore worth maintaining as an end in itself. This connection had very seldom been broken and the Kandyans in 1815 hoped that their new alien rulers would accept this responsibility as the Nāyakkar dynasty had done. One other point of importance regarding the convention needs mention here—its legal status became a controversial theme, not least in the twentieth century in view of the claims made by spokesmen for Kandyan interests who came to regard it as fundamental law, immutable and almost sacrosanct. But the British took their stand on English constitutional law and treated the Convention as little more than an ordinary treaty capable of amendment by subsequent legislation.

The rebellion of 1817–18 had its roots in the fact that the Kandyans had called in British help in 1815 for the sole purpose of eliminating an unpopular ruler. They had not contemplated the prospect of the establishment and continuation of British rule and when they awoke to the reality of foreign control they found it extremely irksome and unpalatable. Although the British established a separate administrative structure for the Kandyan provinces and maintained intact most of the fundamental features of the traditional system, this did little to reconcile the Kandyans to British rule. The cession of the Kandyan kingdom to the British stemmed not from some deep-rooted crisis of confidence in the institutional and ideological structure of Kandyan society but from a political conflict which was in the main confined to the king and the aristocracy. Whatever gloss the British, or the Kandyans for that matter, placed on the undertakings given and obtained in 1815, the substitution of British control for Nāyakkar rule had the effect of reinforcing and deepening the commitment to the old society and to the institutions, secular and religious, associated with it. All strata of Kandyan society were involved. Nostalgia for the traditional monarchical forms, the one element of the old system, which the British quite deliberately eliminated, affected far more

than merely the aristocracy. There was little popular enthusiasm
for the version of monarchy introduced by the British into the
Kandyan provinces and it required the rumblings of rebellion
for British officials to understand the strength of the Kandyan
yearning for a monarchical restoration. Yet this was precisely
the point on which the British could make no concession.

The passion for monarchical restoration rekindled the old
Kandyan tradition of resistance to the foreigner and the sense
of loss felt by the Kandyans at the removal of the indigenous
monarchy became—shortly after the establishment of British
rule—a powerful and combustible political force which needed
only a spark or two to be ignited. British administrators in the
Kandyan provinces, though not deliberately insensitive to
Kandyan feelings, nevertheless gave adequate cause for
dissatisfaction by not paying sufficient attention to tradition
and custom in the processes of administration. That the
bhikkhus were among the first to be alienated is not surprising,
because the categorical undertaking given by the British to
maintain and protect Buddhism was difficult to implement
given even the best of intentions. It required an extraordinary
sensitivity to the nuances of tradition and custom, and with
regard to these a British Resident was clearly no substitute
for a Kandyan ruler in fostering and protecting the national
religion. At the same time, a mood of disenchantment with
British rule affected a substantial number of the most influential
nobles. By the beginning of 1817 there was unmistakable evidence
of popular discontent and the prospect of a rebellion. At the
centre of the gathering storm were Uva and Vellassa, sparsely
populated and the most isolated of the Kandyan provinces.
Under Kandyan rule, their remoteness and the difficulty of
communications had ensured them a substantial measure of
independence from the control of the king's government.
Although the British in 1815 had met with little or no resistance
in this region, they had never properly subdued it and the people
remained aloof from and hostile to the new rulers. They found
little reason subsequently to reconcile themselves to the British,
whose soldiers and administrators were especially heedless of
their sensitivities. Loyalty to the old regime was strongest here.

It was in this region that a pretender appeared in the middle of 1817, in the guise of a Nāyakkar prince. This was Vilbāvē, an ex-bhikkhu posing as Doraisāmi, a member of the deposed royal family. That the pretender claimed to be a Nāyakkar prince is a point worth noting, both as evidence of the Nāyakkar dynasty's continuing popularity among the Kandyans and as an acknowledgement of their status as indigenous rulers. Vilbāvē had made his entry at the shrine of Kataragama in July 1817 soon after the annual festival there had been brought to a close. He made a declaration that he had been chosen by the god of Kataragama to be king of Sri Lanka. A population discontented with British rule was immediately receptive to his appeal. The rebellion which broke out in Uva in September 1817 took the British by surprise. It erupted at a time when their forces in Sri Lanka were depleted and when there was in addition a shortage of native auxiliaries. Besides, this was the rainy season in Uva and communications were hampered by swollen rivers, while the interception of the mail service by the rebels made coordinated action by the British forces even more difficult. At the outset, the British took energetic measures to localize the rebellion and confine it to Uva.

If the outbreak of rebellion took the British by surprise, the chiefs too were caught unawares, but they soon seized the opportunity it provided for a concerted attempt to drive the British out. The first influential chief to defect was Käppitipola, disāva of Uva, who went over to the rebels in November 1817. He was Ähälēpola's brother-in-law and his family was connected with most of the important chiefs. His defection was ominous in two ways: it marked the beginning of an aristocratic commitment to the cause of the rebels, giving it a leadership and a more precisely defined sense of purpose; and it was a sign that the rebellion could not be contained within the confines of Uva. Käppitipola soon assumed the leadership of the rebellion. He came to know the deception practised by the pretender in claiming Nāyakkar connections and princely status, but he nevertheless chose to conceal this both from his fellow aristocratic conspirators and from the people. His intention was to use the pretender as a puppet, perhaps to be subsequently discarded when he had served his purpose. The solemn ceremony of initiation of the pretender which took place in May 1818 at Vellavaya was under Käppitipola's auspices.

The British efforts to confine the rebellion to its original centre in Uva and Vellassa succeeded up to the end of January 1818. But thereafter it spread to the provinces in the vicinity of Kandy. Dumbara rose under its disāva, Madugalle (who became one of the principal rebel leaders); Hevaheta followed suit and in the same month the rebels reached Sabaragamuva, in some parts of which they received enthusiastic support. The Seven Kōrāles were next to go over to the rebels and soon almost all the Kandyan provinces, with the exception of lower Sabaragamuva, the Three and Four Kōralēs, Udunuvara and Yatinuvara, had joined the resistance movement. By April–May 1818, British power in the Kandyan provinces was so gravely imperilled that withdrawal from the interior, with the exception of the few loyal western provinces was contemplated. In Uva and Vellassa, all posts, save those required to preserve communication between Badulla and Batticaloa, were abandoned. Every chief of any importance except Molligoda had either joined the rebellion or was in custody. Ähälēpola was seized on 2 March 1818 and sent down to Colombo where he was kept in custody. There were no charges against him, no accusation even of disloyal conduct and it was not intended to charge him as rebel. Nevertheless, the British regarded him as a potential convert to the rebels and someone whose defection would be especially damaging to their interests. Molligoda's loyalty was of crucial importance to the British because his influence kept the Four Kōralēs loyal and it was through this district that the vital communications between Colombo and Kandy passed.

The rebellion assumed the proportions of a truly 'national' uprising; the threat posed to the British by this traditional 'nationalism' in the Kandyan areas sprang from the tremendous reserve of spontaneous support it evoked from all strata of the Kandyan people. In the Kandyan provinces only the Moors, a small minority group, remained staunchly loyal to the British. The rebellion was spasmodic, irregular and local, and the scanty British forces were spread too thin to cope with it successfully.

The only answer to the guerrilla tactics adopted so skilfully by the Kandyans was to starve into submission those villages which harboured guerrilla bands and to terrorize the population in the hope of cutting off support for the guerrillas. These tactics were resorted to in the beginning not so much for strategic reasons as because it seemed the only possible retaliatory measure the British could take, given the scanty human resources at their disposal. But even after reinforcements reached the island from India, these scorched-earth tactics were continued and their scope widened. These 'search and destroy' missions caused dire privation among the people and their effect eventually was to sap their morale. Had the Kandyans been able to inflict any telling losses on the British, any military defeats of note, there might have been a means of sustaining their hopes. But there were no such military victories and the sheer superiority of British firepower and military resources began to tell. The tide had turned against the Kandyans by mid-1818 and with each successive reverse the morale of the guerrilla bands cracked beyond the hope of repair. By September, Uva and Vellassa were subdued and the revolt was confined to Mātale, Dumbara and Nuvarakalaviya. The arrival of a full complement of reinforcements from India enabled the British to penetrate these provinces as well.

The rapid collapse of the rebellion which then set in was due as much to shortcomings in the rebel leadership as to British tactics and policies. The rebel leaders could never quite submerge their personal differences and rivalries for the common cause. An influential section of the Kandyan aristocracy remained faithful to the British and their loyalty was rewarded by the grant of very substantial material benefits. The British were able to expose Vilbāvē for the impostor he was and this had disastrous effects, not least because some of the rebel leaders resented Käppitipola's influence over Vilbāvē and his connivance in the imposture. But the demoralization caused by the revelation that Vilbāvē was an impostor was nothing in comparison to the effect of the recapture of the tooth relic by the British—it had been spirited away from the Daladā Māligāva by certain bhikkhus at an early stage of the revolt.

Brownrigg reported that its recovery was regarded by Kandyans of all classes as 'a sign of the destiny of the British people to rule the Kandyans'. Molligoda is reported to have said that '...in his opinion, and in that of the people in general, the taking of the relic was of infinitely more moment' than the capture of Käppitipola and Madugalle.

The great rebellion of 1817–18 was the most formidable insurrection during the whole period of British rule in Sri Lanka. When, after a long and ruthless campaign, the resistance of the Kandyans was broken, the British were masters of the whole of Sri Lanka at last. For the first time in several centuries—since the days of Parākramabāhu I and Vijayabāhu I in the eleventh century—the island was under the control of a single power. From then until 1818 only Parākramabāhu VI of Kotte (1411–66) laid claim to a similar all-island control. Between 1815 and 1818, the British achieved that in which Kotte, the Portuguese and the Dutch had so signally failed—the conquest of the Kandyan kingdom. Thus the year 1818 marks a real turning point in the history of Sri Lanka. It took the British two decades or more from 1818 to accomplish the absorption of the old Kandyan kingdom into the Crown Colony of Ceylon. Although the proclamation of 21 November 1818 greatly reduced the privileges of the chiefs and slightly changed the guarantees on religion given in 1815, the unification attempted in 1818 was merely political. The British did not set up a unified administrative system for the whole island till 1832 and two administrative systems were maintained, one for the maritime regions which had been subjected to the influence of western rule since the sixteenth century, and another for the old Kandyan kingdom which had preserved, to a much greater extent, the social and cultural patterns of the traditional Sinhalese society. It was Governor Barnes's system of roads which first broke the isolation of the Kandyan region and brought it securely under British control. The Colebrooke–Cameron reforms of 1832 provided the legislative and administrative (including judicial) framework for Sri Lanka's unification. The successful establishment and expansion of plantation agriculture in the Kandyan provinces consolidated this unification by providing an economic basis for it.

Economic and Social Change in the Early Nineteenth Century, 1802–32

Although its political power was eliminated when the maritime regions of Sri Lanka became a Crown Colony in 1802, the English East India Company still retained a monopoly of the trade of the new colony and, with the colonial government itself, was one of the two forces which shaped the colony's economy. The East India Company's influence operated through its control of the colony's external trade, in particular the cinnamon trade. In the first three decades of the nineteenth century, cinnamon was the staple of the colonial economy and revenue from this source was the mainstay of the colonial finances.[1] In 1802, the East India Company was given the sole right to buy cinnamon from Sri Lanka for the European market, the quantity being fixed beforehand. The terms of these contracts, which the colonial government accepted under pressure from Whitehall, were more advantageous to the company than to the colony. The market in Europe for Sri Lanka cinnamon was buoyant throughout these years and the company obtained quite substantial profits. When the contract came up for renewal in 1814 there was considerable pressure in the colony for the colonial government to become the direct supplier of cinnamon to the European market. Although it did not succeed in this, the judicious application of pressure did result in better terms for the colony,[2] while no great hardship was caused to the company which continued to enjoy substantial profits from the trade. In 1822, when the contract expired, the colonial government took up the position that it should not be renewed. The Colonial Office was still hesitant to support such a stand, but the pressure from the colonial government was too strong on this occasion. From 1822, the sale of cinnamon overseas was brought directly under its control.

The island reputedly produced the finest-quality cinnamon in the world. This enabled it to dominate the market and obtain a monopoly in Europe. On the complacent assumption that there would be no difficulty in retaining these markets, the colonial government resorted to restricting production and maintaining artificially high prices. It soon became evident that Sri Lanka's 'natural monopoly' was due as much to proper management as to the fine quality of its cinnamon. High prices stimulated severe competition from cinnamon grown in Java and in parts of India, especially the Coromandel Coast and Malabar. Though coarser than the Sri Lanka product, these were substantially cheaper. An even more formidable rival was cassia (*Cassia lignea*) which grew widely in south India, the Philippines, the Dutch East Indies and above all in southern China. In the face of increasing competition, the price of Sri Lanka cinnamon dropped sharply as did the quantity sold, although the situation improved somewhat in the later 1820s when the stocks of the East India Company dwindled and cassia began to lose its attraction.

The economic relations between Sri Lanka and the East India company ranged over the whole field of the island's external commerce, for Sri Lanka lay within the area in which the company's chartered privileges were in operation. Besides, some of the company's Indian territories were traditionally Sri Lanka's trading partners. Thus the company could, almost single-handedly, determine the pattern of the colony's external trade, a point clearly demonstrated when—after it had lost its monopoly status as the sole buyer of the island's cinnamon—it introduced its own cinnamon as a competitor against the Sri Lanka product. Cinnamon was perhaps a special case, but the same pattern of activity may be observed in relation to other products as well, particularly arrack and tobacco produced on the island. If further proof were needed one could turn to the coastal trade between the south-west of Sri Lanka and the Malabar and Coromandel Coasts, which from early times had formed a component part of the trade of the Indian subcontinent. This had survived, in a clandestine form, despite all the VOC's efforts to eliminate it[3] and in the early nineteenth century was an important element in the colonial economy. It was mainly controlled by the south Indian mercantile communities, who had long dominated the coastal trade of the Indian Ocean. Since the capital investment involved was not very substantial, Sri Lanka traders living in and around Jaffna and Galle—the main ports concerned with the trade—and Colombo were able to obtain a small share of this trade; Europeans settled in Madras, Pondicherry and Cochin, as well as those in the colony, occasionally invested their capital in it. The profits obtained were substantial and in terms of volume it was variously estimated at between two-thirds and four-fifths of the entire foreign trade. Successive governors of the colony recognized its importance in the colonial economy and made determined attempts to convert it from a clandestine to regular trade free of the discriminatory duties and restrictions which were the inevitable consequence of the monopoly practices of the East India Company. But in this they had little success, since opposition of the East India Company to any relaxation of these restrictions was unshakable.[4]

The island's trade with Europe and especially Britain was slow to develop and at first it was almost entirely in the hands of the government, which exported cinnamon (through the East India Company), arrack, coconut oil and other articles and imported all articles of necessity for its European servants and for the elite in Colombo. The local merchants engaged in the coastal trade lacked capital and the organizational resources to enter this trade. European agency houses established on the island won a major breakthrough in this trade in 1824, when in response to their agitation, Governor Sir Edward Barnes decided to halt importing on account of the government. By 1830, the trade was well established if not flourishing, with eleven firms engaged in it in Colombo, Galle and Trincomalee. But it soon came up against the monopoly structure of the colonial government's economic activities and the East India Company's resolute defence of its own interests.

The most valuable items of export were in the hands of the government and thus a two-way trade was almost impossible. Imports required for Sri Lanka were shipped first to Madras, Bombay or Calcutta, which functioned as entrepots for the island. Since the customs policy of the East India Company did not favour an entrepot trade, re-exporters in India profited excessively at the expense of importers in Sri Lanka. The situation within the colony was not much better: high port dues and customs duties as well as unfavourable rates of exchange hampered this trade. The one item of external trade in which European firms established on the island had secured a foothold was in the export of coffee, but here again the East India Company's privileged position in Britain was a serious obstacle. Exports of coffee to the English market from Sri Lanka faced discriminatory duties; exporters agitated to get these removed by the home government. They also sought markets elsewhere and found one in Mauritius, but an Act of Parliament prohibited the importation there of coffee produced within the area where the East India Company's charter operated and so exporters turned their attention in the 1820s to having this manifestly unfair provision repealed. But once again they were thwarted by the influence exerted by the company. Only one area of the colony's external trade was unaffected by the interests of the East India Company: the trade with countries in south-east Asia, mainly the Malay Peninsula and the Dutch East Indies, but it was not of any great importance in terms of volume and value.

The claim was often made in public statements that the economy was liberalized under the British administration, but far from that being true, the basic policies of the successor regime were very much like those of the Dutch; indeed the monopoly structure was if anything much more thoroughgoing than that of the VOC. There was at the same time a mutually incompatible and often conflicting policy of fostering private enterprise. Where such conflicts arose, the monopoly structure generally prevailed, the one exception being coffee culture. Also, although successive governors recognized that a spirit of individualism was emerging among the indigenous population, a process which they wished to encourage, yet they refused to come to terms with similar developments, largely initiated by Europeans in the sector of the economy in which the government held sway, with coffee culture being, once again, the one notable exception to this pattern.

The contradictory nature of these policies is seen with regard to a decision taken by Whitehall at the time when the former Dutch possessions on the island became a British Crown Colony: it was not to be modelled on the West Indian 'plantation' type. Europeans were prohibited from holding land outside the confines of the town of Colombo. While the early governors of the colony themselves viewed the island as a military station with a mercantilist economic tradition, they were nevertheless unhappy with the decision to restrict European landholding. They believed this to be detrimental to the economic development in the colony and by judicious application of pressure succeeded in getting the Colonial Office to rescind the ruling. From 1812 onwards, Europeans and their descendants were permitted to purchase or receive as grants up to 4,000 acres of land. Maitland, who was largely instrumental in persuading Whitehall on this matter, believed that it would help transform the colony's economy. This did not mean that Maitland and his successors were intent on giving freer rein to individual enterprise; the current ambivalence on this matter continued to bedevil the government's economic policies.

The island was regarded as a potentially attractive field for European investment, if not settlement (several writers advocated European colonization), with cinnamon still the main attraction for prospective European investors. But with the government insistent on the maintenance of its monopoly, the investors turned their energies to other crops. Although many of these crops seemed to have real promise, the one positive success, by the end of the 1820s, was coffee, which owed much to the interest taken by the government and in particular by Governor Sir Edward Barnes. Investors in coffee were readily accommodated in regard to loans and wastelands (that is, jungle or scrub jungle). Coffee holdings were exempted from the prevailing taxes on land and the export duty on coffee was abolished—all these measures originated from Barnes who deliberately devoted the resources of the state to promote coffee culture. The government itself opened an experimental coffee plantation of 200 acres attached to the Botanical Gardens at Peradeniya. While the success of coffee—isolated though it was—pointed the way to a viable economic base for the future, the state was so firmly entrenched in the economy that few envisaged the triumph of private enterprise over monopolies, even though these monopolies were neither more efficiently run as enterprises nor less damaging to the economy as a whole than under the Dutch.

The most conspicuous feature of this economic system was cinnamon, the base of the colony's mercantilist structure. A complex set of regulations, largely inherited from Dutch times, rigidly enforced the monopoly, with little heed given to the adverse effects these had on the economy. Two aspects of this require emphasis. The regulations protected the cinnamon plant, but their effect was to depress the value of land on which cinnamon was found growing, quite apart from retarding the development of such lands. Second, in a concerted bid to obtain ever-increasing quantities of cinnamon, the government drove the Salāgamas to the utmost limits of their capacity. However, this proved economically wasteful, for the Salāgamas generally deserted in large numbers while many died of fever contracted when peeling cinnamon in the jungles and the government was forced to depend more and more on less efficient labour. Besides, despite this reliance on compulsory labour, the expenses of the cinnamon department kept increasing and the profits from the monopoly were much less than anticipated at the beginning of British rule.

To turn to another state monopoly, the high price of salt— the government's margin of profit was estimated to be as high as 1,100 per cent—not only caused hardship to the average consumer, but also hindered the development of a potentially valuable fish-curing industry on the coastal belt. Indeed, the harsh enforcement of this monopoly was responsible for the desolation of the once thriving Magam-pattu, the premier salt-producing area.

One of the crucial features of the colonial government's direct intervention in the economy was the use it made of rājakāriya. The Portuguese and the Dutch had been content to maintain and exploit it for their own purposes and such changes as they saw fit to introduce did not materially alter its character. The British adopted a strikingly different course of action: although many officials viewed rājakāriya as basically obnoxious to British principles of justice and deleterious in its effects upon the people, they still continued to rely on it and to make more efficient and profitable use of it to further their policies, all of which changed its character and transformed it into the true compulsory service system it became under the British. There were two features of rājakāriya which British officials regarded as being of crucial importance: the personal service rendered to the 'king' or his agents by landholders who enjoyed lands granted by him; and the liability of all landholders, irrespective of the nature of their tenure, to provide labour services on public works. During the last phase of Dutch rule, one saw the beginnings of a trend towards dissociating service tenure from rājakāriya. In Andrews's impulsive reform of rājakāriya during the early years of the Madras administration, this trend was accelerated and taken to its logical conclusion, although Andrews himself did not see a continuity between his reforms and anything that had happened under the Dutch. Despite the jaundiced view North took of Andrews and his reforms, his own attempts at improving the rājakāriya system showed that, at bottom, his attitude towards it was much the same. This time, however, there were no disturbances but there were other disconcerting consequences: the monetary loss sustained by the state and the difficulty which the state faced in obtaining voluntary labour.

Maitland, although an unfriendly critic of North's reforms of rājakāriya, did not reject them in their entirety. He restored service tenure, but as land continued to pay tax, rājakāriya was not placed on its original footing. Significantly, he did not abrogate the right of the state to extract service on the basis of caste and the performance of duties in connection with public works was made, as under the kings, a gratuitous service. A significant modification of the system of labour services was developed, attuned to the peculiar requirements of the colonial administration, namely, compulsory services proper. After the suppression of the Kandyan rebellion of 1817–18, a form of neo-rājakāriya similar to that of the littoral was introduced there, without its traditional sanction— expressed in the ancient adage, 'king's duty is greater than service to the gods'—and this perhaps made compulsory services doubly distasteful to the people. The colonial officials, in fact, acknowledged that theirs was a fundamentally different system—one in which the ideological framework of the past was to a great degree superseded by a newer and more pragmatic concept of service viewed as no more than a personal tax owed by the individual to the state.

With these changes, caste became firmly established as the basis of personal service. Although this affected all castes, the most repressive effect was upon the castes who were called upon to perform services considered economically vital to the state. Of these, the Salāgamas suffered most because the cinnamon monopoly was the pivot of the mercantilist system operated by the British.

One other point needs special mention: the extensive use of rājakāriya in public works, which under the British meant roads to the exclusion of almost all else. Their construction and maintenance in the difficult terrain of the interior, especially in the Kandyan provinces, made for unusually heavy demands on the services of the people. The colonial government most notably under Barnes, found rājakāriya the cheapest and most effective means of accomplishing this. To the people at large, however, this emphasis on the use of rājakāriya services for road construction was perhaps the most obnoxious feature of the British administrative system.

Money and markets were of little significance in the Kandyan provinces. The economy of the maritime regions was also largely based on subsistence agriculture, although trade was of greater significance there. Most villages could obtain many essential food items—especially salt—and textiles only from outside, while many were not self-sufficient in rice. A fair proportion of the population was dependent for rice on 'imports' (that is, from outside the village boundaries); indeed the whole country was not self-sufficient in rice and the colony's customs returns showed a considerable import of rice, principally from south India. This reliance on imports was the continuation of a trend which began under the Dutch. Chēnas formed an essential part of village agriculture and the dry grains produced on them were a necessary supplement to, if not a substitute for, rice.

The peasants, on the whole, had only a precarious return for their labours on their paddy fields at the best of times. They were often compelled to fall back for their sustenance on other occupations as well—not all of which were necessarily associated with agricultural work within the village. There is evidence of the increasing resort to wage labour by the government (despite the existence of compulsory services), by European capitalists and even by the local inhabitants themselves. On the coast, trade was, on a modest scale, another avenue of sustenance.

The general picture is one of stagnation in agriculture and this was attributed to the scarcity of capital and the absence of industry. In the early years of British rule various remedial measures were considered. There was the belief that capital formation would be stimulated by compelling the people to pay their taxes in cash instead of in kind. Others stressed the need for improvements in agricultural techniques. In an age when so much hope was placed on the possibilities of rapid development through colonization and immigration, it was inevitable that proposals should be made for the introduction of European colonists and Indian and Chinese immigrants. The former, it was argued, would invest their capital in agriculture while the latter would set an example of industry to the proverbially indolent natives. Again, there were demands for a more positive role by the government in responding to the needs of agriculture. The neglect of irrigation was highlighted, and it was argued that rājakāriya should be utilized, as in earlier times, for restoring and maintaining the country's irrigation network, as much as it was used for road construction.

Barter was of great importance in the lives of the people, both within a village and on a wider regional basis. The Kandyans, for instance, bartered dry grains, areca and jaggery for salt, salt fish and cloth, which they obtained from traders on the coast, while the inhabitants of the Jaffna Peninsula exchanged salt, tobacco and cloth for areca, cotton and beeswax from the south-west coast. To some extent the resort to barter was made necessary by the scarcity, if not absence, of circulating specie, but, more important, it had behind it the sanction of custom and tradition. There was, however, a slow but quite perceptible departure from this system in the early years of British rule, although once again this was a continuation of trends which had their origins in the last phase of the Dutch administration in the maritime regions of Sri Lanka. Trade was the main agency of this transformation. The removal of internal trade barriers— especially after the cession of the Kandyan kingdom—also contributed substantially to the growth of trade, as did the political stability which followed upon the establishment and consolidation of British rule and the new markets and economic opportunities which emerged from these. By the 1820s the beginnings of a market economy were clearly discernible.

The new economic opportunities were exploited mainly by the people of the maritime regions, not only in their own areas but also in the Kandyan provinces. Men from the low country established themselves as traders and engaged in wage labour—in the Botanical Gardens at Peradeniya, for example. This pattern was to continue throughout the nineteenth century. The Kandyans themselves were not entirely insensitive to economic stimulation as was demonstrated by the eager participation of the peasants in cultivating coffee as a garden crop. While these developments and the network of roads that was built, had the effect of integrating the Kandyan provinces into the larger economy of the island, they were nevertheless not powerful enough to prevent the Kandyans from continuing to maintain a separate identity. Indeed, the distinctions between the coast and the Kandyan areas were given greater emphasis in the next few decades by the economic and educational advances achieved by the people of the littoral.

Economic stagnation continued to affect the country till the 1830s, when the gradual success of coffee culture had a profound effect on the economy. Moreover, by the 1830s the British, as undisputed masters of the Indian seas, were in the process of consolidating their possessions in India and had more time to ponder the possibilities of profitably developing the island's economy and settling its major internal political problems. The appointment of the Commission of Eastern Inquiry—the Colebrooke–Cameron Commission—was a clear indication that the Colonial Office had decided that a new phase in the colony's development should begin. Once the value of the island as a strategic station had begun to wane with the end of the Napoleonic Wars, Whitehall no longer viewed its financial difficulties—the persistent failure of all efforts to equalize revenue and expenditure—with an indulgent eye. Indeed, the recurrent deficit in the colony's finances prompted Whitehall to initiate this searching scrutiny of Sri Lanka's affairs. But the problem of the deficit could not be treated in isolation from the wider issues of colonial administration. It was recognized that the time had come for a thorough evaluation of economic policy. The choice was between the 'tropical system of compulsion' and the principle of economic freedom. Reduced to the basic realities of the situation in Sri Lanka in the 1830s, it meant a choice between the continuation of the Dutch pattern of mercantilist restrictions and monopolies and the use of native devices such as rājakāriya, or a clean break from these in favour of what may be termed laissez-faire economics.

The Colebrooke–Cameron Commission introduced an integrated and in many ways radical set of reforms[5] designed to establish in Sri Lanka the superstructure of the laissez-faire state. They had much in common with Bentinck's reforms in India, but were more far-reaching in their impact and more consistent in the application of current liberalism. As adherents of laissez-faire and free trade, the commissioners saw little to commend in the pattern of economic activity then prevailing in the colony with its mercantilist structure, discriminatory administrative regulations and the overwhelming importance of the state monopolies in the economy. Not surprisingly, they gave very high priority to the abolition of the cinnamon monopoly, which was by far the most conspicuous of them all and the embodiment—as they saw it—of all the deficiencies of the mercantilism which they portrayed as the main obstacle to economic growth in the colony. In their view, the state should restrict itself to creating an environment conducive to the growth of private enterprise. It should encourage the entry of foreign capital (mainly British) to invest in plantation agriculture— primarily cinnamon—and in the production of rice on a commercial basis. Their sharpest criticisms were directed at the rājakāriya system. Colebrooke and Cameron objected to it primarily on humanitarian grounds—they regarded it as an intolerable and oppressive relic of feudalism—but these were by no means the only consideration in their forthright insistence on its abolition. Rājakāriya was an obstacle to the free movement of labour and to the creation of a land market, both of which were vitally important in the establishment of the laissez-faire state.

Economic improvement and the growth of educational opportunities were the most powerful stimuli of social change in the nineteenth century. But in the period covered by this chapter it was the elite, those in the higher rungs of the caste, social and administrative hierarchy—the headmen belonging to the Goyigama caste—that profited most from them. While this was especially so with regard to educational opportunities, it was equally true of economic ones. Thus the lists of renters (of revenue) of both the Madras and Crown governments contained a substantial number of headmen, many of whom had accumulated wealth by the efficient manipulation of the system of compulsory labour for personal ends. When shares in the newly opened stage coach service were available for purchase, many of the headmen, including some who had made money by supervising compulsory labour employed in the construction of the Colombo–Kandy road invested in them. Thus, the new economic and educational opportunities were used by the headmen and their families to strengthen their position in local society.

The entrenchment of caste in the compulsory services system, and through the courts as well, protected the Goyigama headmen from their most likely competitors for these economic and educational opportunities—the emergent castes of the littoral, the Salāgamas, Karāvas and Durāvas. In the last phase of their rule, the Dutch had conferred great and unprecedented privileges on the Salāgamas in recognition of their value in regard to the cinnamon monopoly. They were exempted from certain land dues, tolls and taxes and from rājakāriya outside the Cinnamon Department. Besides, the care and respect which the natives were taught to bear for the cinnamon plant had the effect of raising among the Salāgamas a pride in the caste and service. The situation changed considerably under the British, beginning with North. Calls on their labour, under service tenure, increased inexorably within the Cinnamon Department and without, while the privileges they had received from the Dutch were gradually removed. Indeed, they had become so accustomed to these privileges that they complained in a petition to London that the changes effected under British rule reduced them 'to the same equal footing with natives of other castes'. The changes in their status in the economy and, in particular, the loss of their privileges were reflected in attempts to avoid service in the Cinnamon Department, when Salāgamas once more resorted to the tactic of registering their children under the names of persons who were not attached to that department. This was in marked contrast to the last phase of Dutch rule when attempts were made by non-Salāgama people to register themselves as Salāgamas to take advantage of the privileges conferred on cinnamon-peelers.

The struggle for caste mobility was diverted to the one field which lay beyond the government's influence and pressure, namely indigenous religion. Here we need to turn to the revival of Buddhism in the maritime regions which derived its impetus from the invigorating influence of Vālivita Saranankara's activities in the Kandyan kingdom. One feature of the revival—Kīrti Śrī Rājasimha's decision to restrict the upasampadā to the Goyigama caste—was a great setback to the aspirations of the three main non-Goyigama castes of the littoral, the Salāgamas, Karāvas and Durāva. The Kandyan hierarchy itself recognized the strength of the processes of social mobility in the maritime regions of the south-west by a politic—and grudging—acceptance of the need to make exceptions to this rule in the case of prominent bhikkhus of those castes when appointments were made to temples in the maritime regions under the control of the VOC. But these concessions proved quite inadequate and the growing dissatisfaction with the Siyam Nikāya sect on account of its restrictive caste outlook in the matter of ordination spurred Salāgama bhikkhus in 1802 to send a mission to Burma to obtain valid higher ordination there. In the first decade of the nineteenth century, five delegations from the Salāgama, Karāva and Durāva castes travelled to Burma for this purpose. The Amarapura Nikāya, which emerged from these endeavours, was the only significant development in Buddhism in the first half of the nineteenth century; it was open to all castes, in defiance of the Kandyan practice which restricted ordination to those of the Goyigama caste.[6] The Amarapura Nikāya was to make considerable headway in the first half of the nineteenth century; its influence spread into the Kandyan areas, much to the chagrin and consternation of the Kandyan bhikkhus. At this time it appeared to possess a vitality that the more conservative Kandyan Buddhism lacked, but it soon settled into a groove of its own. Nevertheless, it left its mark on the Buddhism of the littoral, which in contrast to Kandyan Buddhism came to be distinguished by its greater flexibility and receptivity to the forces of change and social reform.

The recovery of Buddhism, of which the emergence of the Amarapura Nikāya was one of the most notable features, owed not a little to the more relaxed religious attitudes of the British.[7] The great majority of the people of the maritime regions shed their allegiance to the Dutch Reformed Church and identified themselves as Buddhists. But Buddhism was soon faced with the problem of survival in the face of the challenge offered by the British missionary societies. The struggle might have been a more unequal one had the new rulers shown greater enthusiasm for the propagation of Christianity, but in the first two decades of British rule the administration was always inhibited by a fear that religious controversies might provoke political difficulties. This was more noticeable with regard to the Kandyan region where, apart from other problems, there was the treaty obligation under the terms of the Kandyan Convention of 1815 to protect and maintain Buddhism. The government's attitude to Buddhism was one of reluctant neutrality rather than open hostility. Thus, left largely to their own resources, the missionary organizations made slow progress in their efforts to make inroads among the adherents of the traditional religions of the country.

At the same time, from the beginning of British rule there was an attempt to alleviate the lot of the Roman Catholics. They obtained a great measure of religious freedom, especially under a regulation of 27 May 1806 which removed the religious disabilities affecting them. But in the early years of the nineteenth century, the Roman Catholic Church in Ceylon was in no position to consolidate the gains it had derived from this measure. There were, besides, limits to the liberalization that followed on the establishment of British rule on the island. British officials in Ceylon were not immune to the anti-Catholicism which influenced the behaviour of all classes in English society in the nineteenth century. Significantly, it was with the passage of the Catholic Emancipation Act in Britain that the position of the Roman Catholic Church in Sri Lanka improved. By the end of the period surveyed in this chapter, the resilience of Roman Catholicism on the island had been demonstrated and the recovery from its desperately poor position under the Dutch appears to have been complete by then.

Neither the Buddhists nor the Roman Catholics at this time matched the vigour and vitality of the British Protestant mission which sought to establish themselves on the island. The Dutch Reformed Church deprived of state support (when most of its clergymen refused to swear allegiance to the new rulers), lost the vast majority of its flock, thus demonstrating the essential superficiality of conversions to Protestant Christianity under the Dutch. Not that the scandal of 'Government Christians' or 'Christian Buddhists' did not linger on in British times. In the first two decades of British rule, there was no consistent support for British missionary societies from the state, although they were welcomed by the colonial authorities with formal correctness. Apart from Governor North, there was a general reluctance on the part of the British to encourage their activities, especially in the Kandyan areas where mission work was severely restricted. This was in keeping with the practice in India where the East India Company discouraged missionary activity for fear that the work of the missionaries might provoke religious strife and thereby create embarrassing political problems for the company. Thus in Sri Lanka too, during this period, the colonial government endeavoured to adopt and maintain an attitude of neutrality in religious affairs, but most of the influential officials of the day were sympathetic to the missionaries and assisted them in many ways.

In the first three decades of British rule the one consistent agent of change was the missionary. Much more than the soldier and the administrator, he was committed to the advocacy of change, the more so because he had seldom to bear the consequences of impulsive attempts at evangelization and was much less concerned than the administrator and the soldier with the maintenance of political stability. Despite the government's reluctance to commit itself to offering them any support on a formal basis, British missionary organizations on the island grew in strength and confidence during this period. Their increasing influence as pressure groups in the metropolitan country served to guarantee the successful establishment and expansion of missionary activities in the colonies.

From the beginning of their activities in Sri Lanka the British missions used the school system for evangelization.[8] The Dutch had left behind a rudimentary network of parish schools in the maritime regions, in which children were taught reading, writing and Christianity. The Madras administration maintained these schools and did not allow them to fall into ruin. North was more positive in his endeavours to continue the ecclesiastical and education system of the Dutch, but he received scant support from Whitehall and indeed from many of his subordinates on the island. As a result, despite North's enthusiasm, the parish schools made no substantial progress; their survival was due to the efforts of the Revd James Cordiner,

North's confidant and associate in the enterprise. The situation changed somewhat with the arrival of Governor Maitland. It was not that he was enthusiastic for the propagation of Christianity or for the support, much less expansion, of the system of parish schools. But the evangelical pressure of Whitehall was too strong to resist and Castlereagh, the Secretary of State for the Colonies, wrote to Maitland explaining that the government was being censured for discouraging Christianity. He enjoined on Maitland the necessity of promoting education. Thus it was because of evangelical pressure that the parish schools in Sri Lanka survived. They owed much to Sir Alexander Johnston, then chief justice of Ceylon, and to other officials, but above all else to the missionary societies who undertook their management.

When the Kandyan provinces came under British control, Brownrigg was reluctant to permit evangelism there and discouraged the Wesleyan missionaries who sought to establish a mission station in Kandy. But with the expansion of the civil and military establishments in Kandy, he appointed the Revd Samuel Lambrick as chaplain to the forces there in 1818. Lambrick extended his activities to evangelistic work among the Kandyans and eventually opened a vernacular school in the district. The Church Missionary Society moved in to continue this work and by 1823 the Kandy mission station controlled five schools. Brownrigg's successor, Barnes, did not wish to maintain the parish schools. He thought that the existing education system was expensive, inefficient and far from useful, and he imposed rigorous cuts in expenditure on education. Nor was he at ease about teaching children the tenets of Christianity, believing as he did that an attempt to force these on others merely led to the thwarting of one's own beliefs. In his view the reading and writing of the native tongue should be the first requirement.

In the years before 1832 there was no coherent policy on education, which was not regarded as a service normally provided by the state. As a result, the government's contribution in this sphere was both slight and sporadic. But if the state was lukewarm, if not actually hostile, to the expansion of education, the missions became increasingly well equipped to continue their own educational work. Although their financial resources were still meagre, their administrative skills and their zeal for evangelization more than made up for this. Since the state lacked the administrative machinery for the purpose of running and maintaining a school system, the missions that had a rudimentary organizational structure which could be adapted for this purpose stepped in. Indeed, the distinctive feature of the first phase of missionary activity in nineteenth-century Sri Lanka is the single-minded struggle of the missionaries to build up a school system at a time when the government itself was disinclined to do so. Through the years they devised the guiding principles that were to govern educational development in Sri Lanka for decades thereafter, and from their experiments emerged the system of denominational schools which prevailed on the island for more than a century.

The view that education was a legitimate sphere of state activity was strongly endorsed by W.M.G. Colebrooke, the senior member of a two-member Commission of Eastern Enquiry (the other member being C.H. Cameron), whose reports and recommendations (1831) were to be major landmarks in British policy in Sri Lanka. Colebrooke observed that the schools maintained by the government were 'extremely defective and inefficient'. He acknowledged unhesitatingly the superiority of the schools run by the missionaries and was not inclined to encourage the establishment of government schools in areas served by the missionary schools. To 'facilitate the reform of the government schools', he recommended that they be placed 'under the immediate direction' of a school commission composed of the Archdeacon of Colombo and the clergy of the island, as well as the government agents of the provinces and other civil and judicial officials. A notable change in government policy on education became evident with the implementation of Colebrooke's recommendations on education in 1832. With the establishment of the school commission the state had indeed acknowledged its responsibility for the supervision, if not organization, of education. State intervention in education now assumed a regular and definite form.

Crown Colony Government, 1802–32

THE ADMINISTRATIVE FRAMEWORK[1]

British experience in North America in the last quarter of the eighteenth century served to underline the increasing disenchantment with representative institutions in colonial government and set in motion a trend towards concentration of power in the hands of colonial governors. Since the British possessions in Sri Lanka were regarded mainly as a strategic outpost, this pattern was evident there as well. Indeed, the pattern of colonial administration which the British had inherited from the Dutch in combination with rājakāriya, which placed at the governor's disposal a massive pool of labour, strengthened the governor's powers beyond the limits set by Whitehall.

In the advisory council established in 1802 was the germ of a legislative authority. But this council was clearly subordinate to the governor, just as the colonial government was subordinated to the imperial government. A more effective check on the governor's autocracy lay in the Supreme Court of Judicature and the new High Court of Appeal set up by the Judicial Charter of 1801. The charter establishing the Supreme Court prescribed its jurisdiction and laid down rules governing its exercise; these were a close approximation to English law and legal practice, more liberal and humane in temper than those established by the VOC. At the end of North's tenure of office there was an elaborate if somewhat expensive system of courts; the use of the English language in the courts was well established and the process of anglicization of the system of judicial administration had been set in motion. More significant, however, was the emergence of a conflict between the judiciary and the military, the forerunner of a prolonged and bitter confrontation between the executive and the judiciary under North's successor, Maitland.

Faced with a challenge to his authority by Chief Justice Lushington, Maitland sought to bolster his own position by instituting a reform of the judicial structure. Ironically, the Charter of Justice of 1810 strengthened the position of the chief justice vis-à-vis the governor and the instructions accompanying the charter enhanced it still further. And Sir Alexander Johnston (newly knighted), the guiding influence behind the new charter, returned to the island as chief justice. (There was one other notable feature of the reforms of 1810: the introduction of trial by jury in the criminal sessions of the Supreme Court, which also owed much to Johnston's persuasive advocacy.) Maitland regarded the relegation of the governor to a position which in some ways was inferior to that of the chief justice as an unacceptable development and although he was due to leave the island soon and thus had no personal interest at stake, he nevertheless took it upon himself to make his objections to the scheme known in Whitehall. He did this with a vigour and cogency which yielded fruit in an almost immediate reappraisal of the situation. A new charter issued on 30 October 1811 was much more favourable to the executive and restored much of the governor's power and influence in the administration of justice. But the conflict between the Supreme Court and the governor continued unabated till the introduction of the Charter of Justice of 1833, which established a more satisfactory relationship between the executive and the judiciary.

Those conflicts emerged from conditions inherent in the constitutional structure of the colony, which gave the executive a degree of power and influence over the minor judiciary and the lower courts which the judges of the Supreme Court, as the only members of the judiciary who were really independent of the governor, viewed with displeasure. Nor was this resentment at what was regarded as unwarranted interference by the executive in the administration of justice confined to the judges of the Supreme Court. In the Kandyan provinces the governor established an even greater control over the judicial authorities. The normal restraints on executive authority and interference with the judiciary which existed in the littoral did not operate in the Kandyan areas since the Supreme Court was denied any jurisdiction there. Every attempt by the Supreme Court to extend its jurisdiction to the Kandyan provinces was successfully repelled by the governor. The governors, for their part, were just as resentful of the independence of the judges of the Supreme Court and showed scant respect for their rights. All other officials in the country were very much under the governor's control.

One of the most conspicuous features of British administrative policy in this period was the Europeanization of the higher bureaucracy. In this they departed from the Dutch and Portuguese practice where much greater use had been made of the traditional indigenous machinery of administration. The new policy inevitably made for steeply rising administrative costs; the structure regularly expanded despite sporadic attempts at retrenchment. The revenue did not keep pace with the increasing costs of administration and coupled with the clear failure to devise a new financial base for the colony, this was the fundamental reason for the recurrent deficits in the government's financial account. Recruitment to the covenanted civil service established in 1802 was on the basis of patronage under the control of the Secretary of State for the Colonies, while the regulation and control of the service was very much the purview of the governors—a division of responsibility which did not always operate smoothly. Since patronage was the sole determinant and educational qualifications were not insisted upon, the result was that the 'writers'—as these recruits were called—were young and immature. The exercise of the secretary's patronage had the effect of making the covenanted service an almost exclusively European one. In making these appointments, the secretaries of state were rarely guided by the needs of the colony, as regards either the number of apprentices or their suitability.

After a period of apprenticeship under a collector in the provinces, or at a government department in Colombo, these recruits were appointed to their substantive posts. It was at this point that the elite status of the covenanted service really emerged. A number of posts in the establishment were reserved exclusively for them and their basic emoluments were fixed and maintained at a very high level without regard to the financial state of the colony. The salary structure of the Ceylon Civil Service was the highest in the empire outside India and there was the additional inducement of liberal pensions obtainable after a relatively brief period of service. Despite these advantages and attractions, the civil service could hardly be described as an efficient body. When Maitland sought in 1808, for the first time, to introduce the principle of merit in civil service promotion, he met with strong resistance from a powerful lobby of civil servants who were quite happy with the existing system of promotion by seniority.

The Ceylon Civil Service was, from the outset, prohibited from engaging in private trade. This restraint was reaffirmed by Maitland and Brownrigg, but it would appear that there was some laxity in its enforcement; besides, it did not extend to agricultural pursuits, which were separated from trade by a very thin line indeed. It was also stipulated that cadets should acquire a competent knowledge of the local languages—Sinhala and Tamil. This was seldom observed in the spirit of the original regulation. The higher bureaucracy, with their exclusive and privileged status in the official hierarchy, were an administrative elite and a virtual ruling caste in the colony. It was the heyday of the belief that a civil servant should be a jack of all trades and master of all. It was also the heyday of the view that the technical expert should be subordinate to the administrator. Although the covenanted civil servants tended to think of their service as synonymous with administration, there were other categories of officials who were equally vital for the working of the administrative machinery. A considerable body of Europeans of various but supposedly inferior skills and quality manned the lower echelons of the official hierarchy. The clerical service which assisted the civil servants was composed largely of Burghers—the descendants of the Dutch—who elected to remain on the island after the British conquest: clerical service became a tradition with them.

More important, despite the hostility of the British towards them, it was clear that the native headmen were an indispensable

link between the rulers and the people. Thus they continued
to perform functions which had traditionally fallen within their
purview; but the government's policy was one of curbing their
powers, reducing their privileges and bringing their activities
under the supervision of British officials. Their duties were
closely defined, they were paid a fixed salary instead of being
granted accomodessans as had been the former practice and
some of the powers they had enjoyed in the past, especially
their judicial powers, were transferred to British officials. None
of these measures really succeeded in meeting the twin aims
of the government, namely, eroding the headmen's influence
among the people and integrating them within the administrative
structure as a set of cogs in an increasingly complex machine.
Their authority rested on their influence and respect in local
society rather than on their legal or political position, and this
influence and respect remained more or less stable.

North left much less of a mark on the civil service and the
administration than did his successor Maitland. The
reorganization of the administration and the reforms initiated
by Maitland were some of the most constructive achievements
of this period. They survived unchanged till 1832 (and well
beyond that date in some respects) but the high standards of
administrative efficiency which he set fell considerably after
his departure from the island. Perhaps his outstanding
contribution lay in his definition of the scope of the powers
and functions of the official hierarchy in the provincial structure.
It was in the collector that British rule was manifested at the
local level. Originally appointed with the management of
revenue in mind, he and his assistants soon grew in power and
prestige because they were often the only British officials in
the provinces. And in the collector of the province came to be
concentrated the major administrative, financial and revenue
powers of the provincial administration. The collector exercised
supervision over all officials in his district, including those
attached to departments with specialized duties. The military
was beyond his control and the emphasis on security often—
and certainly at the beginning of this period—elevated the
commandants of the local garrisons into a special position,

with the result that there were numerous clashes between the civil and military authorities in some districts over their respective spheres of authority. Maitland, the soldier–administrator, devised a solution to this problem by defining the spheres of authority of the two services.

Because of a deliberate policy of combining executive and judicial authority in the hands of the collectors, the conflicts between the executive and the judiciary which existed at the centre were largely absent at the provincial level. The collectors were responsible for policing their districts through various grades of headmen; they acted as fiscals and justices of the peace, and from North's time they were entrusted with powers of magistracy which conferred on them a limited jurisdiction in minor criminal offences. It was also a common practice for the collectors to hold the chief judicial office in the province. This combination of executive and judicial authority was repeatedly criticized by the judges of the Supreme Court, firm believers in the theory of the separation of powers, but the government persisted with this policy, pointing out, first, the overriding consideration of security, second, that the primary duty of revenue collection was hampered by the absence of judicial authority in the collector and finally, that only the civil servants could acquire a sufficient understanding of the people's habits and customs to enable them to deal knowledgeably with their litigation. The collector was the agent of the executive in the provinces, but despite every effort to establish regulatory and supervisory devices, the inadequacy of communications made these ineffective, and the greater the distance from Colombo the more independent the collectors were. There was clear evidence too, in the first half of the nineteenth century, that the administrative structure was more efficient in the provinces than the central establishment at Colombo.

Throughout this period the chief secretaryship—the principal office in the official hierarchy—was held by the incompetent John Rodney during whose long tenure of office (1806–33) this crucial post fell in importance and did not function with the efficiency demanded of it as the nerve centre of the colonial administration. That it did not fare worse and that it provided some measure of coordination at the top was due entirely to the efforts of those who held the post of deputy secretary. Rodney's successor, Philip Anstruther, who held the post from 1833 to 1845, was in every way a contrast to him. He revitalized the office and demonstrated its effectiveness as a coordinating centre in the hands of a dynamic personality. The governor was treasurer ex officio, but the duties of that office were handled by others. All government auditing and accounting were in the hands of the auditor general and the accountant general, the latter office being often combined with the former or with that of the vice-treasurer.

From the beginning there was an attempt to differentiate revenue collection and disbursement from purely administrative work at the centre: this led to the growth of administrative departments with specialized functions. Here again one notes the energy and initiative of Maitland. North had assigned the collection of the inland revenue to a board of senior officials. This was no more than a supervisory body, the revenue collection proper being undertaken by the collectors. Maitland, who believed in centralized financial control, found this board ineffective for the purpose and replaced it with a commissioner of revenue with wide powers, to whom was also assigned the duty of control and supervision over the collectors and subordinate officials in their revenue duties. Initially, the customs revenue was collected by customs masters stationed at Colombo, Galle and Jaffna, but with Maitland's reorganization, the duties of these officials were transferred to collectors. The deep involvement of the government in the colonial economy necessitated the creation of a number of separate establishments to conduct specific economic activities. Chief among these was the Cinnamon Department, closely modelled on the mahabadda of old. Like the Portuguese and the Dutch, the British too found that they could not devise a better system for the collection of cinnamon than the traditional mechanism. Other establishments concerned with economic activities did not develop into fully-fledged departments, although they generally functioned as separate bodies.

Several new departments were created in this period. Most notable of these was the registrar general's department, established by North for the registration of lands after the introduction of his tenurial reforms. Maitland, however, preferred to revert to the Dutch practice of assigning this task to schoolmasters, who were also responsible for the registration of births, baptisms, marriages and deaths. Another office created by North, that of the surveyor general, was retained but Maitland combined it with the post of civil engineer, the official who superintended public works. Neither this new department nor that of the land registrar developed into key branches of the administrative machinery in this period. So long as the economic environment discouraged free enterprise and rājakāriya was used for the construction and maintenance of public works, this picture could hardly change.

The most complex administrative problem that confronted the British was the absorption of the old Kandyan kingdom into the Crown Colony of Ceylon. Under the terms of the Kandyan Convention, the British consented to the continuation of the traditional administrative system, without much change, 'according to the laws, institutions and customs established and in force amongst them'. Nevertheless, the traditional system was not unreservedly guaranteed and the British retained the right and power to introduce changes as and when they deemed fit. Carefully embodied in the convention was a declaration of the inherent right of government to redress grievances and reform abuses in all instances whatever, whether particular or general, where such interposition shall become necessary. This latter clause of the convention became in effect 'the source of British jurisdiction' in the Kandyan provinces and the means of superseding Kandyan law and judicial institutions in many respects. While the customary law of the Sinhalese had disappeared in the maritime regions, a version of it existed in the Kandyan provinces as part of a living tradition and the British themselves recognized it and continued to apply it there. But a process of superseding Kandyan law began very early and was well established by 1830. Where the Kandyan law was silent or not clear, principles of English law considered relevant in the circumstances were applied. By 1830, the legal principles and formalities prevailing in the Sinhalese areas of the littoral came to be applied in the Kandyan provinces in the field of criminal law and procedure, civil procedure and the law of evidence. The Kandyan law survived chiefly in regard to inheritance, caste, marriage, land tenure and personal service for land.

At the time of the cession of the Kandyan kingdom to the British, the traditional machinery of justice had come to a virtual standstill. There was no noticeable improvement under D'Oyly in the first year of British rule. The Board of Commissioners of Kandyan Affairs was established on 23 August 1816 and among its functions was the administration of justice. While the principal and subordinate chiefs continued to exercise judicial functions, the Board of Commissioners as a body was constituted as another court of law. The collective board with the chiefs associated in its deliberations replaced the *mahanaduva* of old. More substantial changes were effected after the suppression of the rebellion of 1817–18. Under the belief that English legal procedure was superior to the Kandyan procedures, British officials were entrusted with an increasing personal control and authority over the judicature in the Kandyan provinces. The new machinery was still a compromise between the indigenous and the foreign and it became increasingly evident that it was an unsatisfactory compromise with some of the worst features of both systems. Unfamiliar formalities and technicalities were enforced in an alien language, while traditional institutions—such as the *gamsabhāvas*—and traditional laws and customs were devalued.

The administrative machinery devised for the control of the Kandyan provinces had the twofold effect of buttressing the governor's autocracy and of bringing it at the same time into sharper focus. Within this region there were no restraints on the governor's autocratic powers: there was no advisory council and the jurisdiction of the Supreme Court did not extend there. Instead, the whole judicial machinery was under his control and for the Kandyan provinces he was in effect the court of final appeal. He exercised his executive power through his personal representative, the Resident and the Board of Commissioners. Within this structure the Resident had responsibility for political affairs, the second commissioner was invested with authority in judicial matters, while the third was placed in charge of revenue collection and allied matters. With the suppression of the great rebellion of 1817–18, the judicial and revenue commissioners were now explicitly vested with the powers and responsibilities of the high-ranking chiefs of the old order. The changes brought into effect after the rebellion and with the proclamation of 21 November 1818 did not alter the constitutional position of the governor, who continued to wield supreme legislative, executive and judicial powers. If there was some semblance of a separation of executive and judicial authority in the littoral, this was wholly absent in the interior. In the Kandyan provinces military and executive authority was combined in the same official and the security factor was emphasized with the appointment of the officer commanding the forces in the interior to the board in 1819 and his elevation to the presidency with the death of the Resident, Sir John D'Oyly, in 1824. Like the frontier regions of India, the Kandyan region drew the best administrative talent that was made available in Ceylon.

The two fundamental issues in the administration of the Kandyan provinces were: first, the position of the chiefs and, second, the question of security. With the suppression of the rebellion of 1817–18 the British were able to devise means of reducing the power and status of the chiefs by requiring them to function completely subordinate to and under the direct supervision of British officials. It was Brownrigg's hope to reduce the chiefs to the status of stipendiaries charged with carrying into effect the regulations and orders of the government and to establish British officials as 'the real organs of power'. Agents of government with wide exclusive and judicial authority were appointed in every outlying district, while those close to Kandy were brought under the control of the Board of Commissioners. But this loss of their former power and privileges did not result in any appreciable decline in the influence of the chiefs over the people so long as they were and continued to be 'the only medium of communication between the government and the people'. Second, the national consciousness of the Kandyans was the most formidable problem that confronted the British in Ceylon in the three decades following the cession of the Kandyan kingdom. In the 1820s, Barnes's network of roads, built with the help of the traditional rājakāriya system, placed the military control of the Kandyan provinces firmly in British hands. The secret of Kandy's long and successful survival in the face of over two centuries of western attempts at subjugation lay in the fact that most of the country was a wilderness suited to guerrilla warfare of which the Kandyans were masters. Now guerrilla tactics could no longer cut communications between garrisons or hold up troop movements. It is a measure of the success of Barnes's policies that in 1831 a significant step in the establishment of a uniform administrative structure for the island was taken. With the appointment of Sir Robert Wilmot Horton as governor in 1831, the governor's constitutional position changed somewhat. The advisory council was formally established and its powers were extended to the Kandyan provinces; this foreshadowed more far-reaching changes that came two years later with the Colebrooke–Cameron reforms.

Perhaps the most valuable contribution of Colebrooke and Cameron to the island's future political development was to give it a more liberal form of government than that which had prevailed before 1833. This latter bore the stamp of Dundas's concern for a strong executive. Colebrooke sought to reverse this trend. In place of the advisory council, he proposed the creation of two councils—the executive and the legislative councils—to assist the governor. The Legislative Council was to serve a limited purpose. The Colonial Office, like Colebrooke, did not regard it as a representative assembly in embryo, but looked upon it as a check upon the governor in the sense that it was an independent and fairly reliable source of information for the Secretary of State who would otherwise be dependent on the governor alone for information with regard to the colony and its affairs.[2] In brief, it was introduced to make Whitehall's control over the colonial administration more effective. This concept of the role of the Legislative Council was too restrictive. For the really remarkable feature of the Legislative Council established in

1833 was not so much the existence of an official majority within it as the presence of unofficials. And the presence of unofficials served to underscore the validity of the comment that the '... essential purpose of establishing a legislative body has always been to give representation to the inhabitants of the dependency...'. Implicit in this was the assumption that the principle of representation necessarily involved acceptance also of the concept of the Legislative Council as a representative legislature in embryo. From the start, the unofficial members of the Legislative Council—and some of the local newspapers of the day—tended to look upon the Legislative Council as the local parliament.

The chief significance of Colebrooke's recommendations was not merely that they reversed the trend towards concentration of authority in the governor, but that as a measure of constitutional reform they were far ahead of anything prevalent at that time in India or the non-white colonies. The British colony of Ceylon was very much 'the constitutional pioneer' of the non-European dependencies of the British empire over the period from 1833 until about 1870. Hence this was perhaps Colebrooke's most notable recommendation and the one by which he deserves to be remembered. Cameron's contribution to this process of liberalization lay in the Charter of Justice of 1833, based on his report on the judiciary. James Stephen, the permanent undersecretary at the Colonial Office, described this charter as '...a pure invention...based on speculation (chiefly those of Bentham)'. Cameron was, in fact, a dogmatic Utilitarian unlike Colebrooke. One of the flaws of the judicial system established in 1833 was that it was not rooted in the country's legal traditions. It did not give the people what they needed most, a system that would 'investigate disputes and administer justice...in a plain and summary manner'. Nevertheless, it was the foundation of the island's modern judicial system and the most lasting contribution of the Utilitarians to Sri Lanka.

Colebrooke's approach to the Kandyan problem resembles in some ways that of Durham to the comparable problem of French Canada. In 1833, his proposals were accepted and the separate administrative system for the Kandyan provinces was abolished and amalgamated with the territories on the littoral acquired from the VOC, in a single unified administrative structure for the whole island. The existing provincial boundaries within the two administrative divisions—the Kandyan and maritime provinces—were redrawn and a new set of five provincial units, of which only the Central Province was Kandyan pure and simple, was established. The new provincial boundaries cut across the traditional divisions and placed many Kandyan regions under the administrative control of the old maritime provinces. An administrative (including judicial) and legislative unification was imposed on Sri Lanka and a policy of absorbing and assimilating the old Kandyan kingdom within this structure was initiated as a means of obliterating the sense of nationality among the Kandyans.

For all their earthiness and practicability these reforms possessed more than a tinge of genuine idealism. At the Colonial Office some of their more liberal and enlightened aspects were diluted if not eliminated altogether, while the civil servants on the island who actually implemented them had no sympathy for the liberalism which lay beneath the reforms. As a result, the reforms became a much more pedestrian business than they might have been if the recommendations of the two commissioners, accepted by the Colonial Office, had been implemented in the spirit in which they were conceived. Nevertheless, the Colebrooke–Cameron reforms were the first well-integrated system of reforms introduced after the establishment of British rule on the island. They marked the first systematic and successful attempt to break away from the Dutch pattern of colonial administration and to reject its basic assumptions in favour of a more enlightened form of government.

An Era of Reform and Reconstruction, 1833–50

The reformist zeal generated by the Colebrooke–Cameron reforms and a passion for change affected every sphere of activity—political, economic and social—for nearly two decades. Never before, and seldom thereafter under British rule, was there the same warm support in official circles for policies designed to transform society.

SOCIAL REFORM

The most powerful influence on the social policy of this period was religious sentiment. This was partly due to evangelical influence (mainly through James Stephen) at the Colonial Office, men like Governor Stewart Mackenzie (1837–41) and a host of subordinate officials in Sri Lanka who believed in the urgency of converting the 'heathen' to Christianity. It was also partly due to the agitation of missionary organizations for a redefinition of the relationship between Buddhism and the colonial government on the island.[1] During his brief tenure of office as Secretary of State for the Colonies in the late 1830s, Lord Glenelg had laid it down that the conversion of the people to Christianity should be a vital aspect of state policy in Sri Lanka. His successors during this period shared this belief to a greater or lesser extent. The new policy naturally implied active state support of missionary enterprise and it was significant that the state supported all Christian missions on the island alike. The determined application of this policy resulted in bitter sectarian strife, because the Anglicans fought tenaciously in defence of their privileged position in education, the registration of births, marriages and deaths, and state-subsidized church construction.

In Sri Lanka at this time, missionary organizations were the dominant influence in education. The medium of instruction in most schools was the English language, and with the 'filtration theory' very much in vogue, the aim was to educate the elite. It was accepted without question that education should aim primarily at conversion to Christianity. Not the least significant of Mackenzie's achievements was his success in breaking the hold of the Anglican establishment on the school commission. He was less successful in his attempts to have the vernaculars used in instruction in schools and to bring education to the masses, both of which challenged the current orthodoxies on education in the eastern empire and were for that reason rejected by the Colonial Office. But in the years 1843–48, one aspect of Mackenzie's policies, vernacular education, was officially adopted mainly because of the tactical skill and administrative ability of a Wesleyan missionary, the Revd D. J. Gogerly. Education was a sphere of state activity in which missionary influence on policy making was most marked. Had there been fewer sectarian squabbles that influence would have been even stronger.

In Sri Lanka, unlike India, there were no glaring social evils associated with the indigenous religions—no sati, *thägi, meriah* sacrifices, or rituals such as those of the temple of Jagannath. There was thus less scope for the social reformer. The problems that attracted attention were far less intractable than those in the Indian subcontinent. The mild form of slavery then existing on the island was gradually abolished, with the government taking the initiative in this; the state also took a paternal interest in the aboriginal *Vaddas*, protecting them, civilizing them and attempting to convert them to Christianity. Although the missionaries had little influence on the actual formulation of these policies (especially, that on slavery), they sympathized with and actively supported them, since they coincided with their own aims. They served as auxiliaries of the government in various projects of social reform, the Vaddah [*sic*] Mission of the Wesleyans being the most significant of them.

No policy of social reform could ignore the problems posed by the caste system, for caste in a sense was the most awkward impediment confronting the social reformer. Neither the administrators nor the missionaries had a clear policy on caste except a vague egalitarianism. Had there been something as morally and socially repugnant as untouchability, it might have been possible to focus attention on it and thereby compel the adoption of a positive programme of action; but untouchability scarcely existed in Sri Lanka, where caste was too amorphous to be tackled by a precise and deliberate policy. Nevertheless, at this stage the government was against caste without knowing very much about it except that it hampered their programmes of reform. They were convinced that caste was both obnoxious and intolerable and were opposed to any positive recognition of caste distinctions.

Two decisions of the government, the abolition of rājakāriya in 1833 and the reform of the jury system in 1843, focussed attention as never before on the state's attitude to caste. While the abolition of rājakāriya was perhaps the most telling blow against the caste system in the first half of the nineteenth century, there was no positive declaration on that occasion explicitly directed against caste discrimination as there was in 1843–44 in the controversy over the reform of the jury system. There was a third, and no less significant, development—the appointment of non-Goyigamas as mudaliyārs of the Governor's Gate.[2] These posts had been the preserve of the Goyigama elite and were the most prestigious positions available to a Sinhalese. In the 1840s, the Goyigama monopoly of these coveted posts was breached for the first time with the appointment in 1845 of Gregory de Zoysa, a Salāgama. The second to be appointed was Mathew Gomes, a mudaliyār of the washers since 1814. He was appointed in 1847 but his tenure of office was short (he was dismissed for embezzlement in 1848). These two appointments were a prelude to a more significant one—that in 1853 of Jeronis de Soysa of the Karāva caste, the wealthiest Sinhalese of the day. The Goyigama establishment opposed the appointment and endeavoured to get the government to give de Soysa a position of lower status, namely that of mudaliyār of Moratuva, the village from which he hailed. But Governor George Anderson, stood firm.

In no aspect of policy was the impact of evangelicalism and missionary influence felt more strongly than on the question of the severance of the connection of the state with Buddhism.[3] The connection of the state with Buddhism stemmed from the terms of the Kandyan Convention of 1815. Until 1840, this association with Buddhism had been maintained without much protest, but thereafter the whole question was reopened in the wake of the successful missionary campaign in India against the connection of the East India Company with Hinduism. When pressure from missionaries for a total dissociation of the state from Buddhism emerged, the Sri Lanka government, aware of the unpopularity of any such move and fearing that this religious agitation would result in civil strife, refused to be stampeded into hasty and indiscreet action. The missionaries, however, succeeded in imposing their views on the Colonial Office where James Stephen became the ardent advocate of their contentions and where under his influence successive Secretaries of State in the 1840s called upon the colonial government to sever the state's connection with Buddhism. The crucial policy decision with regard to this was taken by the Secretary of State, Lord Stanley, in 1844 and was reaffirmed by Earl Grey in 1847.

Despite these peremptory instructions from London, officials in Colombo were reluctant to implement this policy with the rigour and precision which the despatches (written by Stephen) called for. They had doubts about the morality of abrogating the solemn undertaking to protect Buddhism given in 1815 and reaffirmed (though less categorically) in 1818. Besides, there was the vital question of determining to whom the functions and traditional obligations of the state in regard to Buddhism should be transferred. Crucially important in this regard was the question of temple lands and the protection of the property rights of the viharas and dēvālēs; should the severance of the state's connection with Buddhism be effected without a settlement of this question of temple lands, the whole legal position of the temples over their lands and tenants would be undermined. Higher church dignitaries in Europe had a corporate legal status; there was nothing comparable to this in Sri Lankan Buddhism and legal enforcement of the most elementary property rights of viharas and dēvālēs would be impossible without some form, which the courts could recognize, of accrediting an ecclesiastical dignitary or temple trustee. For a long time, however, the Colonial Office, under James Stephen's influence, treated Buddhism as though it had a centrally organized structure akin to Christianity and did not see the need to establish such a body to inherit the state's obligations and duties in regard to the protection and maintenance of that religion. Nor were they conscious of any moral obligation in this regard. Faced with this uncompromising attitude of the Colonial Office, the Sri Lankan officials had no alternative but to proceed apace with the dissociation from Buddhism. They took a more practical and pragmatic position, however, and endeavoured to evolve some administrative machinery to which the ecclesiastical responsibilities vested in the government by the Kandyan Convention could be transferred. Their pleas for caution and moderation fell on deaf ears; the Colonial Office under Stephen would not yield an inch. Completely convinced of the justice of his policy, he obstinately refused to recommend any concessions to the Buddhists on this matter.

THE TRANSFORMATION OF THE ECONOMY

Perhaps the most remarkable feature of the 1840s was the invigorating effect which the success of plantation agriculture, especially coffee[4] culture, had on the economy of the colony. A period of experimentation in plantation crops began in the mid-1830s and within fifteen years the success of one of the crops, coffee, had radically changed the economy. There were, in the late 1830s, two centres of coffee cultivation on the island—the Udugama Hills about 26 km from Galle, where several Colombo-based commercial houses had opened coffee plantations, and Gampola, Peradeniya and Dumbara in the Kandy district. The Galle ventures failed, but the Dumbara plantations were a pronounced success and even more of a breakthrough to sound commercial profitability than those at Gampola and Peradeniya. The effect of the proven viability of the Kandyan plantations was the suspension, to a large extent, of planting operations in the Southern Province. The Central Province, the heartland of the old Kandyan kingdom, was henceforth the focus of plantation activity.

In the six years from 1838 to 1843 no fewer than 130 plantations were opened up in the Central Province, almost all of them in districts within 50 km of Kandy. By 1846, there were between 500 and 600 coffee plantations on the island, the great majority of them in the Central Province. Indeed the area under coffee nearly doubled between 1 January 1845 and 31 December 1847, from 10,205 hectares to 20,278 hectares.[5] Knowledgeable contemporaries estimated that nearly £5 million was invested in coffee, both by individuals (many of whom operated on the proverbial shoestring) and by agency houses. The stimulus to this unrestrained expansion of cultivation ('the coffee mania', as it came to be called) was provided by a steep rise in the consumption of coffee in Britain and western Europe and, to a lesser extent, the protection afforded to colonial as against foreign coffee in the British market.[6]

A fall in coffee prices in 1845 jolted the more perceptive investors and planters into a more realistic assessment of the industry's prospects. Nevertheless, it did seem as though economy and retrenchment could stabilize the island's coffee industry. Commercial credit was still relatively sound and capital was still forthcoming to support coffee properties in this period of trial, although it was already apparent that a large amount of capital was buried in the soil with little prospect of recovery. The island's coffee industry might have held its own, had not the commercial crisis of 1847–48 in Britain intervened. The depression in Britain set in motion a train of events which culminated in the near collapse of the island's coffee industry. A fall in the consumption of coffee, accompanied by overproduction, had the inevitable consequence of a sharp drop in prices. This soon revealed the inherent weakness of Sri Lanka's apparently booming coffee industry. The coffee disaster of 1847–48 brought down the great agency house of Ackland Boyd and Company (which at the height of the coffee mania controlled as many as thirty-five plantations in the Central Province), smaller houses such as Hudson, Chandler and Company and scores of individual proprietors and small investors.

The coffee industry was nevertheless more resilient than gloomy contemporary observers anticipated. Indeed, by 1849 signs of recovery were already noticeable; in the early 1850s many of the abandoned plantations were made viable again and then new plantations were opened after confidence had been gained from the rehabilitation of the old ones. A shrewd observer of the contemporary scene pointed out that some of the new proprietors had started off with an advantage of inestimable value—during the financial crisis of 1847-48, scores of estates had changed hands at very low prices and their new owners were able to start without the crippling burden of their predecessors' debt. But the recovery of coffee in Sri Lanka owed almost as much to improving market conditions in Britain. Although coffee prices never attained the heights reached in the spacious days before 1845, they nevertheless afforded an adequate if not substantial margin of profit, so much so that although the protection enjoyed by colonial coffee in the British market was entirely removed in 1851, it did not in any way check the recovery of the island's coffee industry.

The extraordinary success of coffee in this period should not divert attention from the fact that it did not establish a distinct ascendancy till the mid-1840s and that plantation activity in the two decades from about 1820 to 1840 was notable for experimentation in several plantation crops in various parts of the island. In the 1820s, indigo cultivation was unsuccessfully attempted near Veyangoda in the wet zone lowlands. Between 1833 and 1843, in fact, there was every prospect that the island would have developed several agricultural industries, instead of relying exclusively on cinnamon or coffee. An attempt was made, whether consciously or not, to recreate in Sri Lanka the economic pattern of the West Indies with its emphasis on sugar and coffee as major industries and cotton and tobacco as subsidiaries. Until the end of 1845, there were as high hopes of sugar as there were of coffee. In the wet zone lowlands, sugar plantations were opened at Negombo, Kalutara and in the Galle district at Baddegama and Udugama; in the Kandyan provinces there were two centres of sugar production, one at Peradeniya and the other in Dumbara. These ventures had all failed by the mid-1840s, which contemporaries attributed to factors such as climate, soil and location. A few experimental ventures in cotton cultivation were attempted in the east of the island, in what became the Eastern Province after 1833, and on a comparatively large scale in the Jaffna Peninsula, but none of these ventures were even modestly successful to attract the attention of European capitalists at this time. Indeed, cotton culture never really got going. There was, in fact, a very limited amount of capital available for investment in Sri Lanka's plantations, and this capital tended to concentrate on the one successful enterprise, coffee.

Contemporary with this there was a parallel development— the decline of the cinnamon industry, till then the staple of the island's export economy. The speed with which the abolition of the cinnamon monopoly was effected in the early 1830s introduced an element of uncertainty and instability into an already declining industry. Besides, the British Treasury, calculating that the implementation of Colebrooke's recommendations would result in a fall in government revenues, insisted on the imposition of an export duty of 3 shillings a pound of cinnamon, which had the most disastrous consequences, for it quickly made the island's cinnamon practically uncompetitive in foreign markets. Pressure from the colonial government and the cinnamon trade led to reductions of this duty in 1841 (to 2 shillings a pound), 1843 (to 1 shilling) and 1848 (to four pence) and the duty was finally abolished in 1855. But every reduction in duty had failed to make cinnamon competitive with cassia *(Cassia lignea)*, a cheap substitute which was capturing an increasing share of the market. Every reduction of duty had come too late. Had more capital been pumped in and more scientific techniques of production been used, the cinnamon industry might have recovered much earlier than it eventually did. Colebrooke, however, even as late as 1840, was convinced that cinnamon could remain the staple of the island's economy and continue to yield a substantial revenue to the state. But in the early 1840s few were inclined to invest in an obviously declining cinnamon industry when coffee yielded such high profits. Cinnamon never recovered the position it enjoyed in the years before 1833; it survived as a minor crop controlled by Sri Lankan plantation owners and smallholders and was subject to widely fluctuating market conditions.[7]

Thus, by the mid-nineteenth century, there was every appearance that the island's economic development in the immediate future would be characterized by monoculture in its plantation sector, for only coffee had survived and only coffee gave promise of permanent success. But the overwhelming predominance of coffee as a plantation product did not survive for long. By the 1860s, coconut had emerged as a plantation crop with a great potential for expansion. Indeed, European planters had begun to cultivate coconut on a commercial scale from the early 1840s; the early plantations were located in the Jaffna Peninsula and on the east coast near Batticaloa, with a few properties in the south-west as well. However, the depression of the late 1840s put a severe brake on the extension of coconut cultivation and it was not till the early 1860s that production began to expand again.

One other feature of the economic development of the island in the 1830s and 1840s did not survive into the mid-century. Prominent among the pioneers of planting enterprise were British civil servants (and military officials) stationed on the island. These men were there on the plantations because Colebrooke, with amazing lack of foresight, had reduced their salaries, curtailed many of their financial privileges (including their right to an attractive pension) and eliminated many avenues of normal promotion, while encouraging them to engage in plantation activity. And very soon they were paying attention to their plantations to the neglect of their official duties. The decline in civil service standards and morale became a persistent theme in official despatches to and from Colombo in the early 1840s. But purely from the point of view of economic development, the civil servants of this period served a useful if somewhat unusual function as pioneer planters at a time when there were few entrepreneurs either among the small band of Europeans resident on the island or among the local inhabitants. The civil service reforms of 1844–45, in which Anstruther, Colonial Secretary of the Sri Lanka government and a pioneer coffee planter himself, played an important role, put an end to the civil servants' involvement in trade and plantation agriculture.

But several features of this phase of plantation activity survived into the second half of the nineteenth century. There was, for instance, the close reciprocal relationship between the expansion of plantations and the growth of communications. One of the vital preliminary steps in this relationship was the development of the road linking Colombo to Kandy. This was open to rough cart traffic by 1823 and fully bridged and completed by 1832. Although undertaken primarily for administrative and strategic (that is, political) reasons, this vital link came to have great economic advantage. Several roads were undertaken or sponsored by the government in response to the needs of the plantations and these roads in turn enabled the extension of coffee cultivation into new regions. Next there was the crucially important role of the agency houses, both in their managerial function and as credit institutions. The early planting enterprises, whether individual proprietors or partnerships, had little capital of their own and were dependent on outside sources of capital to a remarkable extent. Many of the small capitalists who purchased land in the early 1840s were only able to carry on by borrowing money from England or Colombo through agency houses.

Producers of coffee were confronted with the fact that it took nearly a year between the harvesting of the annual crop and its sale in London for them to get the money for the coffee exported. Again, although wages were generally low, the volume of current expenditure in coffee estates was nevertheless large and consumed a significant portion of the money available. Also, coffee was more vulnerable than other crops to variations in rainfall and, therefore, coffee production involved unusual risks: since the crop for the whole year was often dependent on the weather during a single month, a week's—or a day's—untimely or unseasonal rain might well destroy the chance of an adequate return for a whole year's labour. Apart from these hazards, fluctuating exchange rates and delays and difficulties in shipping posed formidable difficulties for those engaged in plantation agriculture at this time. British commercial banks were generally reluctant to purchase long-term securities, or to advance money on land or fixed equipment, because they regarded foreign plantations as 'the most objectionable of all fixed securities'. As a result, the agency house became almost

Road to Colombo from Kandy through Kadugannawa Pass
—Nineteenth Century. Source: *Ceylon* by Emerson Tennent, Vol II.

the only source of liquid capital funds for the plantations. In sharp contrast to their principals in London, the agency houses regarded plantations as good investments. The fact is that their loans to planters on the security of plantations, factories and even crops were relatively safe ventures whereas they would have been quite unsafe for a bank. This was because of their knowledge of every circumstance connected with the markets and the power of superintendence which they often retained.

Nothing was more exasperating to the British planters in Sri Lanka at this time than the fact that with the great majority of their plantations established in the old Kandyan kingdom, they were still as dependent on immigrant Indian labour as their contemporaries in the West Indies or Mauritius. A pioneer coffee planter explained that the Kandyans had no incentive to work on the plantations:

> They have, as a rule, their own paddy fields, their own cows, bullocks, their own fruit-gardens; and the tending and managing of these occupy all their attention. Their wants are easily supplied, and unless they wish to present their wives with a new cloth, or to procure a gun or powder and shot for themselves, they really have no inducement to work on the coffee plantations.[8]

There were other reasons. A more perceptive observer commented:

> The [Kandyan] has such a reverence for his patrimonial lands, that were his gain to be quadrupled, he would not abandon their culture.... Besides, working for hire is repulsive to their national feelings, and is looked upon as almost slavery. They being obliged to obey orders and to do just what they are commanded is galling to them.[9]

The substantial immigration of Indian labourers to work on the coffee plantations of Sri Lanka began in the 1830s and increased to a regular flow in the early 1840s. These immigrant workers formed part of the general movement of Indians across the seas to man the plantations of the second British empire. In many ways—and largely because of the close proximity of the island to India—the movement of plantation workers to Sri Lanka differed considerably from that to the other tropical colonies, in that it was seasonal. The coffee plantations unlike the tea and rubber plantations of the future, did not require a large permanent labour force. The demand for labour reached its peak during the coffee-picking season, generally mid-August to November. Since this coincided with the slack season on the rice fields of south India, peasants from there were able to make an annual trip to Sri Lanka to work on the plantations and return to their homes in time for the next harvest.

At every stage the immigration from India to the West Indies and Mauritius was rigidly controlled and carefully supervised by the imperial government, the East India Company in India and the receiving territories. To a large extent this close supervision was the result of agitation in England and India by evangelical groups.[10] The gravity of the problems involved in the transition from slave to free labour compelled these governments to intervene in a sphere of activity which the conventional wisdom of the day placed outside the scope of the state's legitimate functions.

Faced with agitation from the planters on the island for the adoption of a policy of state-sponsored and state-subsidized immigration of plantation labour on the model of Mauritius and the West Indies, the government urged that there was a significant difference between those examples and the immigration of Indian labour to Sri Lanka. The latter, they insisted, was more akin to the seasonal immigration of Irish agricultural labourers to England. The government's policy was to leave the importation of labour to the planters themselves, who in their turn left the business in the capable but unscrupulous hands of Indian recruiting agents—the *kangānies*—from whom a system of private enterprise in the provision of immigrant labour, generally on a seasonal basis, developed. It was inefficient and, above all, led to a heavy death toll, not indeed from any unusual rapacity on the part of planters and recruiting agents but largely because of the perils of the trek from the coast to the plantations through malaria-infested country.

The rapid expansion of plantation agriculture created an unprecedented demand for wastelands. With several senior civil servants actively engaged in plantation agriculture and predisposed to help the planters, the urgency of the need to provide land for the expansion of capitalist agriculture was appreciated with greater alacrity than it otherwise may have been. Up to 1832, wastelands at the disposal of the Crown were allotted on the land grant system, the practice prevailing in all parts of the empire at this time.[11] The Crown lands in each colony were virtually at the disposal of the governor and through him of the administration in the colony. This system was inefficient and economically wasteful and it had in addition the disadvantage of breeding local vested interests which, in many colonies, resisted all attempts at reform. The Colonial Office was at this time intent on simplifying and systematizing land sales procedure in the colonies and on imposing a measure of uniformity in these matters in all parts of the empire. The guiding principles behind this uniformity were provided by the theories of Edward Gibbon Wakefield. In Sri Lanka, however, the applicability of Wakefieldian theory was limited by the fact that the island was never looked upon as a settlement colony proper. Nevertheless, on the initiative of the Colonial Office, Wakefieldian dogma was introduced into the island in the more limited sphere of land sales policy. By 1833, the principle of selling Crown lands by auction, as well as the idea of a minimum upset price were introduced and the land grant system was abolished. The minimum upset price was 5 shillings an acre as in the Australian colonies. The adherence to a precisely defined upset price generally applicable to all lands in the colony was prompted by faith in one of the cardinal tenants of Wakefieldian theory, namely, that the price of land should be a restriction sufficient to adjust the supply of land to the supply of labour. The minimum upset price was expected also to deter speculators and to afford encouragement to capitalists, usually with limited means, who were intent on immediate development.

Land sales policy in Sri Lanka was motivated by the need to create a land market for the purpose of plantation agriculture. But while the planters wanted land as cheaply as possible, they also wanted clarity of title, fixity of tenure and a precise definition of the rights of ownership, all of which were essential requirements for their commercial transactions, but which were alien to the traditional practice of the local population, who only understood the age-old 'rights' and practices of land use. Ordinance 12 of 1840 sought to provide some at least of those requirements of modern commerce and land tenure, above all to establish the point that the Crown had 'a Catholic right to all the lands not proved to have been granted at an earlier period'. This was no more than a projection into an oriental situation of contemporary European concepts of feudal society in general and Crown overproprietorship of land. That this theory was rather convenient—and profitable—was another of its attractions, for it must not be forgotten that every single official involved in the actual preparation and amendment of this ordinance had a stake in the coffee industry and some of them earned a measure of notoriety as land speculators. Ordinance 12 of 1840 was clumsily drafted and required amendment almost immediately. But the amending Ordinance 9 of 1841 did not succeed in clarifying all the ambiguities and by administrative order (which was not embodied in legislative enactment) the interpretation of the ordinance was modified to the benefit of inhabitants of the Kandyan districts, thus softening to some extent the impact of the original ordinance in which the advantages were overwhelmingly with the Crown in the definition of title to land. However defective it may have been as a legal instrument for the purposes which it was introduced to serve, this ordinance still did not prove an obstacle to the creation of a land market adequate for the purpose of a rapidly expanding plantation system. And this, for the planters, was the main point.

By 1843, the revitalizing effect of the coffee boom was evident in the marked improvement in the government's revenue. The increase in the receipts from customs dues,[12] though notable in itself, was clearly overshadowed by a phenomenal rise in the revenue derived from the sale of wastelands for plantation agriculture. With the colony fast outgrowing its revenue system, the Colonial Office by 1845 was in the mood for reforms in this sphere. But it was not till the end of 1846, and in the shadow of a devastating slump, that the first substantial changes in the revenue system after the extraordinary success of coffee culture in the island were planned by J. E. Tennent, the colonial secretary of British Ceylon, in his path-breaking *Report on the Finances and Commerce of Ceylon*. These were altogether more radical and systematic than those conceived in 1845 by the Colonial Office, or indeed by Colebrooke in 1833. They reflected also the new mood in Whitehall where Earl Grey, as Secretary of State for the Colonies (1846–52), was intent on removing 'restrictions from industry' and 'securely establishing a system of free trade throughout the empire'. The island's revenue system was dominated by indirect taxes (export and import duties); and, in sharp contrast to the position in British India, land taxes were of peripheral significance. What Tennent recommended was in effect a version of the British Indian revenue system with a land tax as its mainstay. Export and import duties were to be either totally abolished or sharply reduced and foreign imports were to come in on the same terms as British goods.

Tennent's report, however, could hardly have appeared at a worse possible time. The recession of 1846 had become by 1847 a severe depression. With the coffee industry facing a grave crisis and cinnamon seemingly irretrievably ruined, the new governor of the colony, George Byng, Viscount Torrington, chose more cautious and conventional measures than the introduction of a land tax. The government proceeded to impose a series of new taxes which bore heavily on the peasants and the rest of the local population. Of these, the most significant was the Road Ordinance which became what Tennent's land tax was to have been, the pivot of the colony's new revenue system. All these taxes were vexatious and irritating in their impact on the people, and save in the case of the Road Ordinance, did not even have the advantage of yielding a substantial income. The latter, however, was viewed by the people of the Kandyan areas as an attempt to revive rājakāriya in a most obnoxious form—compulsory labour for road construction—for the benefit of the planters.

A blend of the visionary and the practical, Tennent's reform proposals were formulated on the basis of a critical evaluation of available data and on the basis also of a coherent theoretical framework. Torrington's measures on the other hand, were ad hoc devices contrived not so much to reform the revenue system as to cope with the urgent problem of bridging a budget deficit. If one sees this change of focus and reordering of priorities as evidence of flagging reformist energies, these latter were totally exhausted in the political crisis of the minor rebellion that erupted in 1848. The parliamentary committee of inquiry that followed the 1848 rebellion saw the end of an era of reform which began with the Colebrooke–Cameron reforms.

THE 'REBELLION' OF 1848

There were two centres of disturbance in 1848, one—on a minor scale—in Colombo and the other in the Kandyan provinces at Mātale and Kurunegala. The fact that in the Kandyan provinces the 'rebellion' occurred in regions where plantation activity was widespread prompted many contemporary observers to suggest a causal connection between the spread of plantation agriculture and the outbreak of the 'rebellion'. As a result, the impact of the plantations on the Kandyan region (a theme which had hitherto been ignored) became—in the wake of the 'rebellion'—a matter of serious concern among officials, as also did the innovative tendencies inherent in a policy that placed so much emphasis on plantation agriculture to the neglect of peasant agriculture.

However, the stresses created by the rapid development of plantation agriculture could not by themselves have caused the eruption of 1848. It has been argued that the plantations and British land legislation of the 1840s resulted in the equivalent of an enclosure movement and their consequences—the disintegration of the peasant economy and landlessness among the peasantry—culminated in the events of 1848. This hypothesis has a facile plausibility which up to very recent times has given it a currency and standing which it hardly deserves. The impact of the plantations was less destructive of the traditional economy *at this time* than the 'orthodox' theory would have us believe, when the land legislation did not lead to any great expropriation of peasant landholdings and landlessness was not a serious problem.

If coffee had thrived on the mud lands required for paddy cultivation and if plantation agriculture had succeeded in establishing itself in the lowlands of the densely populated Southern and Western Provinces, the confrontation between the planters and the peasants might well have been both prolonged and violent. But coffee failed in the latter regions and established itself eventually in the hills of the more sparsely populated regions of the Central Province, where it was planted on the hillsides away from the mud lands in the valleys.

It is not that there was no friction between the peasants and the planters in the Kandyan region, especially with regard to village cattle trespassing on plantations and the use and sale of wastelands in the periphery of villages. Perceptive observers had noted the gradual disintegration of the traditional society in many parts of the old Kandyan kingdom after the consolidation of British rule there and undoubtedly the breakdown was accelerated after the 1830s with the juxtaposition of the commercial economy of the plantations and the traditional subsistence economy of the peasants. One of the symptoms of the resultant malaise was an increase in crime. Equally significant was the fact that much of the crime and lawlessness was due to low-country settlers (and to a much smaller extent, Indian immigrant labourers) who had been drawn there by the economic opportunities provided by the plantations. A contributory factor, and one which attracted considerable notice, was the excise policy of the British government which encouraged the opening of taverns in the Kandyan areas, especially in the plantation districts, a region noted for the social disapproval accorded to drunkenness. But the plantations did no more than aggravate more material grievances which accounts for the very significant fact that few plantations were attacked by the Kandyans in 1848 although they offered such tempting and vulnerable targets. Of these more substantial grievances, the Buddhist policy of the British government—the attempt to dissociate the state from its formal connection with Buddhism—served to alienate the aristocracy and the sangha, the two most influential groups in Kandyan society. As the natural leaders of Kandyan opinion they looked upon this as a gross betrayal of a solemn undertaking given at the cession of the Kandyan kingdom. The estrangement of the elite might have been less harmful to British interests at a time of crisis if the people at large had been satisfied with British rule; but the British had done little or nothing for the peasants in the Kandyan areas, a neglect which stemmed from an excessive concentration on plantation agriculture. The result was that every segment of the Kandyan population either nursed a sense of grievance against the British administration, or had no positive reason to give it their support.

A scare of rebellion in 1842–43 had brought these issues, and the Kandyan problem in general, into the limelight. A pretender (or pretenders) to the Kandyan throne had appeared on that occasion, but as a result of leakage of information the threatened outbreak was nipped in the bud. These incidents should have provided ample evidence of a widening gap between the administration and the people, but even if the alarming implications of this dawned on the more intelligent civil servants, little heed was paid to these symptoms. For one thing, the officials concentrated their attention too exclusively on the beneficial effects anticipated from the success of coffee cultivation. This was much more than a matter of self-interest on the part of civil servants with plantation investments to protect. The common assumption, even among those who had no such investments, was that the plantations would be the catalyst of modernization, the basis of a buoyant economy, and that these advantages far outweighed any unpleasant side effects. That the state had a reciprocal obligation to give some minimal protection to the interests of the peasants on the issue of land sales was not accepted. This would have served to create the impression among the Kandyans that the civil servants were hardly likely to be impartial arbiters in any confrontation that may have developed between the planters and the peasants.

The government had done little for the peasants. Peasant agriculture was on the decline and the bulk of the irrigation works, not merely in the Kandyan areas but in the Southern

Province too, were in a sad state of neglect and disrepair till the end of the 1850s. It was natural, therefore, for the peasants to conclude that they were faced with a most unsympathetic administration and one totally unconcerned with their welfare. It is important, however, to remember that the blame for the neglect of peasant interests in the question of land sales does not lie with the planters or with the government only. The Kandyan headmen were equally to blame. Without their connivance, if not support, land in the periphery of villages could not have been declared Crown property. The evidence suggests that the Kandyan peasants suffered as much from the machinations of corrupt Kandyan headmen, who were in the best position to understand and manipulate the new situation, as they did from the indifference and neglect of British officials.

The opportunity afforded by the events of 1842–43 for reappraisal and reassessment of current policies and attitudes was thus missed. When, in July and August 1848, widespread opposition emerged to Torrington's taxes, the administration was caught unawares. It confronted much the same combination of forces that had been at work in 1842–43. But now these forces were stronger and better organized and intent on channelling this widespread discontent into a foolhardy attempt to rid the Kandyan regions of the British presence. The leaders did not belong to the traditional elite but were of peasant stock, some of them hailing from the low country. Their aim was a return to the traditional Kandyan pattern of life, which they aspired to resuscitate by making one of their own king. The force that inspired these men was the traditionalist nationalism of the Kandyans, a form of nationalism poles apart from that of the twentieth century, but still nationalism for that.

Two points concerning the rebellion of 1848 need emphasis. One of these is the contrast with the Great Rebellion of 1817–18. This earlier rising was the nearest approach to a 'post-pacification' revolt that developed, a great crisis of commitment which affected the community at large. The 'rebellion' of 1848, on the other hand, was confined to a much narrower region of the country and never involved the community at large to anywhere near the same extent as the Great Rebellion. This might be explained partly at least by the swiftness with which it was put down, and this in turn was due to the roads which had been originally built for precisely such a contingency as this. The second point is even more interesting. The riots of 1848 were by no means confined to the Kandyan region. There was an urban disturbance in Colombo and here, for the first time, a deliberate attempt was made to introduce into Sri Lanka society the current ideas of European radicalism. It is curious, however, that precisely such a fusion—'Sinhalese traditionalism' and radical ideology borrowed from Europe—made the mass nationalism of the years around 1956 so potent a force. A century was to pass before the fusion was attempted and when it succeeded few turned back to memories of 1848, when the two forces had appeared together for the first time, as movements with some likeness but with no mutual connection.

One of the immediate consequences of the 'rebellion' of 1848 was the reappraisal by the British government of its Buddhist policy largely because it was recognized as having contributed to the alienation of the Kandyan aristocracy and the bhikkhus, the natural and traditional leaders of Kandyan opinion: their fears for the safety of Buddhism had affected other classes of Kandyan society. After the rebellion there was a reluctance to proceed further with that policy for fear of aggravating the sense of grievance that prevailed among the Kandyans. Further, the departure of Stephen no doubt facilitated the conversion of the Colonial Office to the view that the policy of complete dissociation from Buddhism was 'not consistent with the spirit of our engagements to the people of Ceylon...'. Thus after 1848 the Buddhist policy of the Colonial Office became noticeably less rigid and evangelical than it had been before. Although still insisting on a dissociation of the state from Buddhism, it conceded that there was an obligation to initiate and supervise the performance of specified legal functions, especially with regard to the Buddhist temporalities. The missionaries were dissatisfied with this compromise, but the Colonial Office backed Governor George Anderson, in his policy of moderation.

Although the compromise settlement of 1852–53 was unsatisfactory from the missionaries' point of view, it was nevertheless true that they had won a significant victory, for they had, through the controlled application of pressure, brought the age-long connection of Buddhism with the rulers of Sri Lanka to an end. Their triumph was the more significant for having been won in spite of the resolute opposition of the Sri Lankan government. It was also the only issue on which the missionary groups showed any sort of unity.

A Plantation Economy, 1850–1910

The consolidation and expansion of the plantation sector is the central theme of the economic history of Sri Lanka in the second half of the nineteenth century.[1] In the mid-nineteenth century, the ascendancy of the coffee industry—fully recovered from the depression of 1847–48—seemed to be so conspicuous as to present convincing evidence of a trend towards monoculture (either the cultivation or the export of one crop exclusively) in the plantation sector of the island's economy. But this was not to be. The coffee industry went through the normal succession of peaks and troughs, to which any plantation product is subject, over a period of four decades; but more dramatically it withered away never again to recover. Moreover, throughout these decades, there was the unobtrusive but steady expansion of coconut cultivation to the point where it offered a potential challenge to the pre-eminence of coffee in terms of the area covered by coconut plantations, if not in regard to the volume of revenue and profits from the industry. At the same time, from the late 1860s, tea and cinchona established footholds in the plantation districts and soon ceased to be merely experimental crops. Throughout this period they remained in the shadow of the giant coffee industry, but both demonstrated their viability as commercial ventures and their potential for future development. Nevertheless, in the period from 1850 to 1880 the coffee industry had such a preponderant position in the economy that this chapter is best introduced by a review of the main phases in the development of that industry in these decades. This is all the more necessary because the coffee industry was always the pacesetter in plantation agriculture and during the period of its ascendancy it was the catalyst of modernization. Almost every salient feature of modern Sri Lanka may be traced back to the coffee era.

In the course of the early 1850s coffee culture became once more a profitable commercial venture. We have seen in the previous chapter how scores of plantations had changed hands during the crisis of 1847–48 at very low prices and their new owners were able to start off without the crippling burden of their predecessors' debts. Although coffee prices never attained the heights they had reached in the early 1840s, there was an adequate if not substantial margin of profit because of improved techniques of production and management. The expansion set in motion by the stimulus of rising prices and increased demand might have been swifter in the five years (1850–55) of Sir George Anderson's administration, if he had not been so inhibited by his instructions to establish 'an equilibrium in the island finances'. There were three things that the planters sought from any colonial governor: first, generous government expenditure on the improvement of communications; second, state-sponsored immigration of Indian labourers and, along with this, increased welfare measures for these immigrants; and finally, the ready availability of Crown land for plantations. The order of priority they attached to these requirements depended on the circumstances of the day. Anderson's cautious financial policy was anathema to them. Backed by the unanimous support of the press, the planters launched a vigorous campaign against the stringent economies in government expenditure which was the keynote of his administration.[2] Anderson's prudence, however distasteful to the planters, was not entirely without benefit to the colony's economy, for the surpluses he accumulated enabled Sir Henry Ward, whose appointment as governor in 1855 marks the start of a period of remarkable prosperity and expansion in the coffee industry, to adopt a more confident note than had been possible for Anderson. It could also be said that 'the coffee industry' was in need of a period of quiet consolidation after the trauma of the depression of 1847–48, before being able to cope with another phase of expansion. Anderson's restraints on government expenditure on roads and bridges were conducive to this process of consolidation, even if the plantation community was in no mood to appreciate its benefits.

The crux of the problem in the planters' view was that communication between the interior and the coast had become uncertain, costly and inadequate. The existing roads formed part of the lines of communication developed by Barnes in the 1820s for strategic and security purposes. To these there had been a few haphazardly made additions, but there had been no attempt at a major overhaul of the roads, much less the construction of new roads into the more inaccessible plantation districts. Anderson himself had made one of the few noteworthy additions to the system—the road from the Ginigathena Gap to Yatiyantota, constructed in the hope of facilitating the transport of coffee from Ambagamuva and Kotmale to the Kelani River and thence by boat to Colombo. The road system as it then existed was totally inadequate to meet the needs of the plantations and a coffee industry poised on the verge of another period of expansion was in danger of being stifled as a result. This Ward understood. Taking advantage of an expanding revenue and the surpluses accumulated by his predecessor, he adopted energetic measures for the extension of the existing roads and the construction of new roads for the specific purpose of serving the plantations. Between 1855 and 1860 he spent over £1 million on the construction of roads and bridges. On his departure from the island he left 4,800 km of roads in good repair and all the major roads were adequately bridged. Nevertheless, the roads could barely keep pace with the pressures imposed on them in transporting increasingly larger quantities of coffee produced by a rapidly expanding coffee industry. A railway was clearly necessary. As early as 1845, there had been plans for a private company to finance the construction of a railway from the coast to the plantation districts, but this venture proved to be beyond the capacity of private investors on the island and was not sufficiently attractive to foreign (that is, British) capital. Ward took steps to make the railway a reality, as a state enterprise. Much of the essential preliminary work—the surveys, estimates and contracts—was in the process of preparation, if not completion, before he left the island.

In 1858 there occurred, under Ward's direction, a radical departure from the established policy on Indian immigration.

The principle of state supervision of the immigration of Indian labourers was at last accepted. The new policy was not the success it was expected to be. It did not end the seasonal shortages of labour on the estates. But to some extent this may be explained by the entry of a new factor which tended to upset all calculations—the laying of the railway line from Colombo to Kandy which offered another source of employment to the immigrant labourers. Again, under Ward, the surveyor general's department was able to secure its quota of competent surveyors at long last, with the result that Crown lands suitable for plantation agriculture were made more readily available to the planters than had been the practice in the past. Nevertheless, a cadastral survey of the island, the lack of which had greatly hampered the efficient sale of Crown lands in the previous decades, was still beyond the capacity of the surveyor general's department to provide, despite the increase in its cadre of surveyors (indeed this cadastral survey remained an aspiration which never materialized during the whole period of British rule on the island).

During Ward's administration the coffee industry enjoyed a period of expansion comparable to that in the years 1845–47. By 1857 the area under plantation coffee had increased to 32,739 hectares (it was 20,234 hectares in 1847) while there were over 19,440 hectares owned by peasant cultivators. Besides, cultivation was expanding into the forest-clad mountains of Dimbula, the region around Adam's Peak and into the forests of Haputale (in Uva). Although the coffee boom continued into the early years of the administration of Ward's successor, Sir Charles MacCarthy, there was a reversion to the stringent economies that characterized Anderson's regime and road construction and maintenance was reduced to a minimum, while a succession of droughts and unprecedented floods contributed to a swift deterioration of the roads serving the plantations. All the while under the stimulus offered by the consolidation of coffee prices at about 54 shillings a hundredweight for plantation coffee, and 40 shillings for peasant coffee, the area under coffee cultivation kept advancing steadily, thus increasing pressure on the existing roads and creating the need for further investment in road construction.

But MacCarthy's sights were set on the construction of the railway to Kandy and he would not be diverted from this to what he regarded as matters of lesser importance, such as investment on roads. He set about piling up surpluses to pay off the debts incurred in constructing the railway. The Colonial Office for its part was mainly interested in ensuring that the colony paid an enhanced military contribution. Accustomed to the spacious days of Ward's administration, the planters were exasperated by MacCarthy's policies and their frustration was aggravated by the Colonial Office's single-minded pursuit of an increase in the military contribution. A campaign was launched under the aegis of the plantation community, both within the Legislative Council and outside it, for enhanced government expenditure on roads. In the Legislative Council they dramatized their dissatisfaction by strenuously opposing the military payment to the imperial exchequer and by raising a demand for the control of the colony's finances by the unofficial members of the Legislative Council.

This review of the recovery and expansion of coffee cultivation in the two decades after 1847–48 emphasized the importance of the development of transport facilities as a factor in the process. The setback which occurred in 1866 drew attention to another vital element in plantation agriculture—capital. Techniques of cultivation had improved markedly since the first experimental phase of the early 1840s, but the financing of coffee cultivation and production was still as haphazard and speculative as it had ever been. Although very little foreign capital was invested in the island's plantations, the events of 1866 showed that it could nevertheless make the difference between viability and failure in lean years. In 1866, the plantations on the island suffered losses because of their dependence on the London money market at a time when investors were increasingly wary of plantation agriculture in the Indian subcontinent; and by the failure of banks whose losses elsewhere brought down their branches on the island. However, the depression of 1866 was much milder in its impact on the economy than that of 1847–48 and within a year the damage was repaired to the extent that between 1867 and

1871 the area under coffee increased by 14,175 hectares, chiefly in Uva and Sabaragamuva but in other regions as well. Coffee planters turned once more to the Southern Province, but this time to the mountainous Moravak kōralē within easy reach of Uva and Sabaragamuva. Because rail transport had led to a striking reduction in transport costs, a price generally around 54 shillings a hundredweight (cwt) was sufficient to sustain the momentum for expansion.

In the last years of Sir Hercules Robinson's administration, and in the whole period of Sir William Gregory's administration, coffee cultivation enjoyed its last and longest spell of unbroken prosperity.[3] In the 1870s it reached its zenith. The area under plantation coffee rose from about 79,380 hectares in 1871–72 to about 110,565 hectares in 1878 and dropped to around 103,680 hectares in 1881. The export crop had reached 1 million cwt for the first time in 1868. Similarly, prices reached unprecedented heights in this decade. In 1875–89, the annual average was around 109 shillings per cwt. Increased exports swelled the coffers of the state and budget surpluses were used to expand the network of roads and railways. In 1871, the railway was extended from Kandy to Navalapitiya through Peradeniya and in the late 1870s its continuation to Nanu Oya was planned, as well as the construction of a branch line from Kandy to Mātale. On the coast, a southward expansion to Kalutara was proposed. With the opening of the Suez Canal there was a noticeable increase in the number of ships calling at Galle and Colombo and faced with the choice of developing one of these as the island's main port, Gregory decided on Colombo. The development of the harbour there was the last link in the comprehensive communications network of the coffee era, but it is ironical that before work on Colombo harbour was completed the coffee age had come to an end.

A leaf disease—*Hemileia vastratrix*[4]—was the undoing of coffee culture in the island. It had first appeared at Madulsima as early as 1869; over the next decade it spread rapidly and relentlessly into every other coffee district. Soaring coffee prices encouraged planters to expand production even when it was obvious that the leaf disease had led to a perceptible reduction of production per acre. Coffee planters felt apprehensive that the industry was stricken by a mortal ailment. There was abundant faith in its resilience and hope that improved techniques of pruning and manuring and the introduction of more disease-resistant varieties of coffee would save the day. But these expectations proved too sanguine. From the beginning of the 1880s the decline was swift and almost total. The coffee plantations in Uva, seemingly more resistant to the disease than those elsewhere, survived into the 1890s but these too eventually succumbed.

The last quarter of the nineteenth century saw an astonishing recovery of the plantation economy from the near-bankruptcy to which it seemed destined when the coffee industry collapsed. The three decades from 1880 to 1910 mark a period of sustained growth in the plantation sector of the economy which matched, if it did not surpass, that achieved in the coffee era. It is in these years that the pattern of an overwhelming dominance of three major plantation crops (tea, rubber and coconut in descending order of importance) in the island's economy was established and which survived in the face of all efforts to diversify the economy and to reduce its dependence on them. Of these crops, tea and rubber (but more especially the latter) emerged into full bloom after the collapse of coffee.[5] Coconut, on the other hand, has a longer history as a plantation crop in British times.

Statistical information on all aspects of the island's economy in the nineteenth century is scanty and often unreliable as well. Those relating to the coconut industry are scantier and more unreliable than most others. Nevertheless, it would appear that in the second half of the nineteenth century the expansion of the area under coconut was as noteworthy as the establishment of the tea industry. The rapid expansion of the coconut industry had begun in the late 1850s, but the pace had been accelerated in the 1860s; the area under coffee went up from about 1,01,171 hectares in the 1860s to about 3,43,938 in the first decade of the twentieth century. Much of the expansion had occurred before the collapse of coffee, although the ruin of the coffee industry may well have contributed to this extension of the area under coconut. It is a point worth noting that the sale of Crown lands to Sri Lankans for coconut cultivation increased by over 200 to 300 per cent in the North-western Province during the 1880s, in complete contrast to trends elsewhere on the island. The area under coconut constituted 37 per cent of the total area under cultivation in 1871 (more than the area under coffee which accounted for about 21–23 per cent); it increased to 41 per cent of the total cultivated area in 1900 (when tea was 20 per cent and paddy 32 per cent). The main centre of coconut cultivation was the south-west littoral, especially the coconut triangle Colombo–Kurunegala and Chilaw. Coconut cultivation was of importance in the economies of all coastal districts, including the Jaffna Peninsula in the north and Batticaloa in the east. It was by far the most significant agricultural product in the Western Province and the North-western Province, and a major crop in the Southern Province.

There are four noteworthy points with regard to the coconut industry. Of these the first and most important was the dominance in it of local capitalists, principally low country Sinhalese, but with a sprinkling of indigenous Tamils. In the early 1880s, only about 12,140 hectares were under European ownership. While European planters became interested in coconut in the mid-1890s, their investment seldom rose above 5 per cent of the total. As with other plantation products, however, the processing and shipping of coconut products was largely controlled by British commercial houses. The predominance of the local capitalists in coconut cultivation is partly explained by the fact that it required much less capital investment than coffee or tea and the maintenance of coconut plantations was also simpler and cheaper. As a result—and this is the second point—the greater part of the area under coconut was under smallholdings, often at the expense of paddy. Third, coconut cultivation required much less labour than coffee and far less than tea (about one labourer for each 4 hectares of coconut on the larger plantations, whereas for tea the requirement was as much as one per hectare or indeed half a hectare). Besides, this labour was often indigenous—the coconut plantations were more closely intertwined with the economics of neighbouring villages than coffee or tea plantations. Both plantations and smallholdings—in coconut—afforded villagers part-time employment which could be conveniently fitted into the cultivation patterns on their paddy fields and chēnas. Fourth, as with other plantation crops, coconut cultivation also provided a stimulus to the extension of road and railway communications. The construction of the southern railway to Matara between 1877 and 1895, the line to Negombo (1907–9) and beyond to Chilaw and Puttalam later on, and the railway to Jaffna through Kurunegala (1894–1905) owed a great deal to agitation from coconut producers especially with regard to the Negombo–Chilaw–Puttalam extensions.

The planters turned to tea and cinchona to fill the void in the plantation sector caused by the collapse of coffee. Of these, cinchona appeared to prosper for a while but failed within a short time. Tea, on the other hand, survived to become the bedrock of the island's economy by the last decade of the nineteenth century, a position which held till well after the mid-twentieth century. It is important to note that neither the origin nor the early popularity of tea and cinchona had much connection with the demise of coffee culture. Tea cultivation in Sri Lanka, as distinguished from amateurish experimentation, had begun in the 1860s after the widespread impression that tea could not be grown on the island because of its proximity to the equator had been dispelled. The interest in tea cultivation was part of a wider attempt by coffee planters to introduce a variety of other crops which could be conveniently grown alongside coffee at no great additional cost. Interest in cinchona had much in common with that in tea and in contemporary eyes its future potential was virtually on a level with that of tea.[6]

In the 1870s, the prospects for coffee appeared to be so bright that conditions were not conducive to a major shift of enterprise from coffee to tea. And yet there was an extension of the area under tea at this time, so that by the 1880s there were 5,670 hectares under tea, of which 2,428 were in the Central Province. Economic conditions were rather more favourable for cinchona cultivation. Traditionally, cinchona was interplanted with coffee; it cost less to produce than coffee and so did not tax the capital resources of the planter unduly. Moreover, cinchona was a scarce commodity in the world market, where the island's product enjoyed a reputation for quality. By 1878, when the coffee disease had spread very extensively, the price of 1 ounce of cinchona had risen to 12s. 6d. By 1883, the area under cinchona rose, from a mere 202 hectares in the 1870s, to 26,305. But its potential for expansion was limited by two factors: the demand for it was inelastic and the tree grew best at elevations over 1,219.2 m. The first of these was a much more formidable constraint than the second, as was demonstrated when increased production in Sri Lanka and Java precipitated a disastrous drop in prices from to 12s. 6d. in 1878 to 1 shilling through the 1890s. The planters turned to other and more profitable crops. By 1900, cinchona was a minor crop with only 1,620 hectares standing. (It had been reduced to an even lower status than cocoa which was also tried in this period, unsuccessfully, as a substitute for coffee.)

Tea survived and prospered. Unlike cinchona and cocoa, it could be cultivated at a greater range of altitudes than coffee (from about 305 to 1,829 m, with the best growing at around 1,219.2 m), while the heavy tropical rainfall, which constantly endangered the coffee crop at critical stages of its growth, actually increased production of tea. Until about 1800, nearly four-fifths of the tea sold in the London market was obtained from a traditional source, China. Indian suppliers provided the rest. At this time there was an increasing demand for tea in the British markets as a stimulating non-alcoholic drink and its price kept rising in response. Within a decade, China's share of the tea market had dropped to what India's supply had once been and Sri Lanka benefited from this astonishing reversal of fortunes as much as India herself. In both Sri Lanka and India, there was a notable increase in the area planted in tea. The expansion in Sri Lanka was as much as 8,100 hectares a year up to about 1897. By 1890, the value of tea exports was far greater than that of any other crop; at the turn of the century tea accounted for Rs 53.7 million (and coconut products Rs 16.3 million) of the island's total export earnings of around Rs 90.8 million.

Tea was the plantation crop par excellence. Its efficient production and processing called for heavy capital investment in large factories and expensive machinery. As a result, smallholders played a much more restricted role in the cultivation of tea than in coffee or coconut and none at all in the processing of tea. The pattern of labour utilization on tea plantations was also notably different from that on coffee and coconut estates. On the coffee estates the demand for labour was seasonal and so the maintenance of a large permanent labour force was not warranted and the vast majority of the seasonal immigrants returned to their homes each year after the coffee harvest. In contrast, the labour requirements on tea plantations were more exacting and were continuous throughout the year. The maintenance of a permanent supply of labour was now a prime necessity. Since Sinhalese labour was just as averse to work on the tea plantations (perhaps more so in view of the year-round demand) as on the coffee estates, the reliance on immigrant Indian labour continued and was reinforced. More important, there was now a change in the pattern of immigration. In the two decades 1880–1900 (during which tea was successfully established as a commercial crop) the increase in migration far exceeded the natural increase of the island's population. The plantation workers were becoming permanent residents rather than seasonal migrants, thus introducing a new element of plurality into the island's multiracial society, one which was to have profound consequences for the future.

By the early 1890s profit margins in tea had begun to decline and prices as well. This latter was a reflection of a fall in the per capita consumption of tea in the United Kingdom at a time of worldwide depression. The decline in prices was accelerated by a rapid increase in tea production outside Sri Lanka. The fall in prices continued till 1905, but a crisis was reached by about 1897, in which year the planting of new acreages ceased altogether. The depression in prices was to have far-reaching consequences for the plantation economy in Sri Lanka. Of these consequences the first concerns the tea industry itself, in the organization of plantation activity. In the late 1890s, individual ownership of plantations was quite common if not the rule. But as a result of the slump, there was greater emphasis on better management of production to improve quality, as well as a significant increase in mechanization, all of which compelled an aggregation of individual plantations into units of large combinations controlled by companies. The number of individual estate proprietors was quite small by the end of the second decade of the twentieth century. The tea industry was better able to respond to the increase in prices after 1905. The market for tea remained buoyant till the outbreak of the First World War, as part of the general upward movement of commodity prices.

The area under tea was reduced as was the output, but the emphasis was on quality teas for which prices were high. Thus the recovery of the tea industry was due to two factors: the emphasis on quality in production and the economies of scale inherent in large plantations served by efficient management and increasing mechanization.

The second of the consequences of the depression in prices in the last decade of the nineteenth century was the search for alternative crops. Coconut was conveniently at hand and attracted British and European planters and investors to a much greater extent than in the past. But the most striking development in this search for alternative crops was the emergence of rubber as the third of the island's major plantation products. Rubber had been introduced on the island in 1877 and survived as an experimental crop, mainly on small plantations. By the 1890s, many British planters as well as enterprising Sri Lankans were impressed with the possibilities of growing rubber on a commercial basis. The area of cultivation, which was at first confined to the Kalutara district, began to spread in other parts of the low country (mainly below the 457.2 m contour) in the Western, Central and Southern Provinces. The swift rise in prices served as an incentive to expansion of cultivation. With the development of the motor industry the rapid growth of the rubber plantations was clearly assured

Smallholders took to rubber production from the beginning and by 1910 controlled about one-fifth of the plantations. The net effect of the introduction of rubber production was to bring large parts of the traditional sector in the Western Province, Southern Province and the Central Province into the export economy. The rubber booms of 1905–10 induced many smallholders to convert their properties into rubber plantations. Very little foreign capital was involved in the development of the island's rubber industry and the major participants in the establishment of rubber plantations were the tea companies and the indigenous capitalist class. Like the tea plantations, the rubber estates required a large permanent labour force although they were not so labour-intensive as the former. But in contrast to the tea plantations, rubber estates were able to attract local, village labour to a considerable extent.

While the expansion of the rubber industry in the period covered by this chapter and its capacity to attract capital helped to mitigate the effects of the slump in the tea industry, its real significance lay elsewhere and was not confined to a mere growth in volume. By 1910, rubber had replaced coconut as the largest export product of the island after tea. This change became a permanent feature of the economy under British rule and in the middle decades of the twentieth century.

TRANSFORMATION OF THE ECONOMY

Looking back from 1910 over the sixty years covered by this chapter, one is struck by the remarkable transformation of the island's economy. One aspect of this has been mentioned earlier, namely that the pattern of the island's economic development, with three major products dominating the modern plantation sector and the economy as a whole, was established. This survived to the mid-twentieth century despite all attempts at changing it. There is little doubt that the development of the plantations enabled the country to achieve a modest breakthrough towards prosperity in the nineteenth century. While this prosperity was not evenly distributed either geographically or through all strata of society, some of it did seep through to nearly all classes of the people. We have no reliable statistics for computing the growth rate over much of the period, especially in the coffee era, but all the evidence available indicates that economic growth was sustained at a substantial level throughout the period. The growth of the economy in the years 1880–1910 was probably much more solid.

The spectacular advance in communications by sea in the late nineteenth century brought down transport costs while at the same time speeding up the process of transport. The railway within the country had much the same effect. It has been shown that some of the tropical countries must undoubtedly have matched the per capita growth of the gross domestic product in western Europe (1.0 to 1.5 per cent) over these years and Sri Lanka was certainly one of these because of the rapidity with which the plantation sector expanded in the three decades after the collapse of the pioneering coffee industry. The modern sector of its economy was much larger in relation to the traditional sector than was the case in many other tropical colonies. Despite the rapid growth of population, both by natural increase and immigration (the rate of population growth was one of the highest in Asia in the nineteenth century), the ratio of population to available and potential land resources was more favourable than in British India or Egypt. The expansion of exports raised the national income per head of population between 1880 and 1910. It was a solid foundation which might have led to self-sustaining growth if tropical trade did not suffer a thirty-year depression after the First World War.[7] It was high enough at this stage to give Sri Lanka a standard of living well ahead of that in the rest of south Asia and most of south-east Asia, with the possible exception of Singapore and parts of the Federated Malay States.

If the plantation sector of Sri Lanka's economy was larger in relation to the traditional sector than in most tropical colonies, the interconnection between the two sectors was also much stronger. At every stage, segments of the indigenous population participated in plantation agriculture. Local capitalists had a share in coffee and tea, were rather more influential in rubber, and were, predominant in coconut. Smallholders (largely peasants) controlled up to one-third of the area under coffee at any given phase of that industry's development. Although their contribution to the growth and expansion of tea was on a more modest scale, they were influential in rubber and even more so in coconut. The point to be emphasized is that the indigenous planters—capitalists, smallholders and peasants—played a much more prominent role in plantation agriculture than their counterparts in most other tropical colonies in south-east Asia. While labour on the plantations was predominantly Indian, it was never exclusively so; indigenous labour on the plantations varied with the nature of the crop produced and the locality in which the plantation lay, being much greater in coconut and rubber than in coffee, far less in tea than in coffee and much more in the low country and parts of Sabaragamuva than in the Central Province and Uva. Again, some of the services on the plantations and specialized functions were performed almost entirely by the Sinhalese. These included clearing of the forests for plantations and the transport of produce from the plantations to the ports. Till the introduction of the railway, transport was a Sinhalese monopoly, both as regards the workers and the ownership of the carts. The planters made several efforts to bring the transport of coffee under their own control and to break the hold of the Sinhalese in this enterprise, but none of their ventures so much as got off to a start. (Sinhalese expertise in transport, developed through the carts in the coffee era, flourished in the first half of the twentieth century in the form of domination of road transport, both motor buses and lorries.) Government expenditure on roads, ports and railways was intended to benefit the planters mainly, but by their very nature these component elements of a modern transport network served to strengthen the connection between the plantation sector and the traditional sector of the economy.

Economic growth was steady and noticeable. But it was also lop-sided. British agency houses and banks had a dominant interest in the economy. Their control over the processing and export of plantation crops was all but total, even if they did not have a similarly comprehensive hold on production in the plantations, especially in coffee, rubber and coconut. The trend towards the increasing control of the agency houses over the plantation industry was accelerated with the extension of tea production and became even more pronounced in the years after the First World War. From the beginning, an intimate connection was established between the colonial government on the island and the British-controlled export sector of the economy. The corollary of this was a comparative neglect of the traditional sector, a theme which will be treated in a separate chapter.

One aspect of this lop-sided development has been referred to earlier—the dependence of the plantations on Indian labour. We have seen how the special labour requirements of the tea plantations led to a qualitative change in the nature of Indian immigration. But here again this was an acceleration of a trend which had emerged in the last phase of the coffee industry. In 1871 and 1881 there were respectively 123,000 and 195,000 'resident' workers on the plantations. By 1891 this had increased to 235,000. Many of these were now permanent settlers, that is to say they had ceased to be merely seasonal immigrants. It was not the plantations alone which relied on immigrant Indian labour. They were employed in road building, in the construction of the railways and in the harbour, as well as in much hard, unpleasant and tedious work in the towns. An urban and plantation proletariat had emerged. But it was confined to plantation 'ghettos' and the less desirable areas of the towns, cut off from the local population by language and culture. Sri Lanka's Indian problem in its modern form had emerged.

And finally, there is the complex question of land and population. The plantations and British land legislation of the coffee era are believed to have resulted in the equivalent of an enclosure movement, with its predictable consequences—the disintegration of the peasant economy, landlessness among the peasants and social discontent, especially in the Kandyan areas. Comprehensive studies of the economic history of Sri Lanka in the nineteenth century, through which these theories and hypotheses could be tested, have not been made. The, statistical information is meagre and far from reliable. Nevertheless, our knowledge of these processes has increased considerably in recent times. Up to the depression of 1847–48, 101,250 hectares of land had been sold, mostly to European coffee planters, in the Central Province, the heartland of the old Kandyan kingdom. Although a few Sinhalese did obtain some of this land, the vast bulk of it ended in British hands. Many of these British purchasers were speculators. But the crisis of 1847–48 put an end to this phase of development and land speculation.

Speculative purchases of Crown lands were much less after 1850, since much of the expansion of coffee culture was on lands that had been sold earlier. In the second half of the nineteenth century there was a remarkable change in regard to the purchase of wastelands from the Crown. During the period 1868–1906, 'non-Europeans' bought 72 per cent of the Crown lands sold in Sri Lanka. Although these 'non-Europeans' were not necessarily all Sinhalese or indigenous Tamils, these two groups—and especially the Sinhalese—were the main buyers.[8] Second, the largest number of sales were of small allotments. Third, sales of Crown lands were not confined to the Kandyan areas but covered all parts of the island. The Central Province and Uva apart, most of the Crown lands in other areas were sold to 'non-Europeans'. In this thriving land market planters were not the only buyers. Smallholders were a key element, even if they did not dominate the market. Nor were sales confined to Crown lands; peasant holdings in villages and the partition and sale of freehold property (paraveṇi pangu) became increasingly important. Indeed, a good deal of the expansion of plantations occurred on lands privately owned and freely sold for the purpose.

To what extent did land sales of plantations act as a constraint on peasant agriculture? If one were to confine one's answer to the coffee era proper and the Kandyan area and especially the Central Province, it would appear that there was an adequate supply of land in the periphery of the villages for the potential cultivation needs of the immediate future. The population of the Central Province in the mid-1850s has been estimated at 150,000. On this computation the peasants of the Central Province had quite adequate resources of land for paddy cultivation and for chēnas during the coffee era, that is, c. 1830 to c. 1880, despite the fact that the population more than doubled in the same period and despite the conversion of at least 20,250 hectares of chēna into 'native' coffee.[9] Nor must it be forgotten that much of the expansion of cultivation in coffee in the years from 1860 to 1880 was away from the Central Province, into Uva and Sabaragamuva where vast unbroken tracts of virgin forests (as in Haputale and the Wilderness of the Peak)[10] in mountainous regions, with little or no population, were brought into cultivation. When the coffee industry collapsed in these areas, tea and cinchona took its place.

It was with rubber and coconut that a new trend emerged, the expansion of plantation agriculture into the low country, relatively more densely populated than the Kandyan areas, into the Kalutara district, the south-west and north-west littoral, and parts of the interior bordering on Sabaragamuva. If at the end of the nineteenth century the land–population ratio was becoming unfavourable in any part of the country, it was not in the Central Province and Uva but in the plantation districts of the low country. One must remember too that Sri Lanka's population explosion is not a twentieth-century phenomenon. It had its beginnings in the middle of the nineteenth century. In 1824, the population was a mere 851,940; by 1911, it had reached 4,106,300. Undoubtedly the immigration of Indian labourers was one element in this increase, but the rate of natural increase was among the highest in Asia. This natural increase was greater in the low country than in the Kandyan areas. The increase by itself would have led to greater pressure on land resources, but these were generally adequate to absorb it without resort to any substantial movements of internal migration, Not that there was no internal migration: the plantations attracted not merely immigrant plantation workers from south India, but local people as well—traders, craftsmen, technicians of various sorts and carters to townships and market centres serving the plantations, not to mention others who came into newly opened plantation regions to secure a modest niche in traditional subsistence agriculture in the periphery of the plantations. In the Chilaw district in the late nineteenth century, the success of coconut cultivation led to a movement of population there and an internal migration took place away from Harispattuva, in the Central Province, to the adjacent district in the North-western Province with the opening up of land for coconut cultivation.

Thus the problems of land sales and population growth in the plantation districts are infinitely more complicated than the conventional views on these themes would have us believe. But much more research is necessary before we can come to firmer conclusions on these processes of social and economic change than the tentative ones outlined here.

Peasant Agriculture, 1850–1910

Till the beginning of Ward's administration, the colonial government in Sri Lanka had shown little concern for the welfare of the peasant population and the focus of interest and attention had always been the development of the plantations (a regrettable but understandable situation, given the fact that the higher bureaucracy itself was deeply involved in plantation agriculture). Unfortunately, this neglect of peasant agriculture has not been confined to the British administrators; it has affected the island's scholars as well. Their interest too has been concentrated on the plantations and peasant agriculture is one of the relatively unexplored fields in the social and economic history of nineteenth-century Sri Lanka. The present chapter does not pretend to redress the balance or to provide a comprehensive treatment of the subject in all its complexity, but it aims instead at concentrating on some broad themes, at posting a few questions and at framing answers to some of those questions. The state of our knowledge of many of these problems being what it is, the conclusions reached can be no more than tentative, provisional and conditional. Our three main themes will be irrigation policy, chēna cultivation and the grain taxes. All of them form part of the problem of peasant agriculture in our period. Other issues related to this main subject are discussed, but more briefly.

One distinguishing feature of this period is the sustained, though not unbroken, effort to rehabilitate the dry zone through a revival of the ancient irrigation network there. For the first time in several centuries a vigorous effort was made to repair and restore the dry zone's irrigation facilities.[1] But it is necessary to point out that in the first sixty years of British rule the irrigation network in the island had suffered a further deterioration. First of all, the scorched-earth tactics adopted during the Great Rebellion of 1817–18 destroyed the irrigation complexes in Uva, then a relatively prosperous region of the old Kandyan kingdom. Second, as a result of the collapse of the Urubokka and Kirama dams in the 1830s, nearly one-third of the rice lands of the Magam-pattu in the Southern Province went out of cultivation and the damage was not repaired for decades. Third, even the abolition of rājakāriya had its destructive aspect for it involved the sudden demolition of the traditional communal machinery which had kept the village irrigation facilities and the major tanks that were still in use functioning and in a state of repair. The 'rebellion' of 1848 did shake the lethargy of the British administration and brought home to it the neglect of the peasants in general and irrigation in particular. Tennent tried to amend the Road Ordinance of 1848, to permit the use of labour organized under it for irrigation works as well, but the Secretary of State for the Colonies, Earl Grey, although sympathetic to the object in view, nevertheless refused to allow the amendment which Tennent sought.

All this emphasized the value of Ward's initiatives in attempting to revive the ancient network of irrigation channels and tanks in the dry zone. His irrigation policy was characterized by a blend of humanitarianism and realism. If he regarded the restoration of irrigation facilities as a duty that the state owed to the people of the dry zone—a genuine humanitarian concern for the condition of the peasantry—there was beneath it a hard-headed realization that it was in the interest of the government to provide these facilities: it would contribute enormously to making the government popular and respected and, no less important, it would increase the government's grain revenues and make these a major source of income for the state, as they were in all parts of British India. Besides, the rehabilitation of the ancient irrigation network might be the means of making the island less dependent on imports of rice. The drive and vigour which alone made an irrigation programme of this nature possible was provided by Ward. His personal example served as a stimulus to the civil service which, fortunately, was at last an efficient instrument of government action. Men of the calibre of Bailey, Rawdon Power and Birch provided him with the data (and ideas) essential for the task, supplementing what he had gathered for himself on his numerous tours in the provinces.

The first venture undertaken was the restoration, under Bailey's direction, of the Uma Ela in Upper Uva. By July 1856, this had proved itself a financial success and it had also demonstrably been of benefit to the people of that area. The Uma Ela project served as unambiguous evidence of the industry of the peasants and their willingness to cooperate in ventures of this kind. As for the government, the success of this pioneering project helped to strengthen the conviction that such restorative schemes were practicable. One of the striking features of Ward's irrigation policy lay in the lingering influence on it of the theories of Edward Gibbon Wakefield.[2] The prerequisites of a coherent irrigation policy, in Ward's view, were land, capital, water and labour. Land and water were freely available on the island and it needed only government aid (in lieu of capital) for these resources to be utilized. But there was another equally important consideration, namely, the availability of labour. The existence of a reasonably large population, in short, made the projects viable. Most parts of the dry zone, however, were sparsely populated and it was largely because of this that Ward was compelled to abandon his efforts to develop the Kantalai Tank (in 1856–57) and the Yodavava (in 1853–59), along with his plans for the regeneration of the Tamankaduva district. The main impediments to the development of this latter region were sparseness of population, the prevalence of malaria and *parangi* (yaws) and the lack of roads, but the sparseness of population was considered the most formidable of these obstacles. As a solution to this, the idea of the colonization of the dry zone was revived. In 1847–48, Tennent had hopes of establishing colonies of Indian immigrant labourers in the present North-central Province. Ward, in contrast, thought in terms of settlements of peasants from the more densely populated regions of the Eastern Province (of which Tamankaduva was a part at this time). Kantalai was chosen as the site of the first such experiment in colonization, but the venture never really got started. Thus the focus of attention in the regeneration of irrigation facilities was shifted to the region around Batticaloa in the Eastern Province and the Magam-pattu of the Southern Province, where the financial prospects seemed brighter than in other parts of the dry zone and the general benefits anticipated from investments in irrigation appeared more promising than in the Anuradhapura and Polonnaruva districts, on the rehabilitation of which Ward had at first set his sights.

Ward's contribution to irrigation activity in nineteenth-century Sri Lanka was nevertheless of far-reaching significance. First, the indifference towards the peasantry and irrigation which had prevailed for so long was at last reversed. Second, the combination of financial assistance and technical supervision from the state with voluntary local labour at the grass-roots level (the 'grant-in-aid' system, as it was called), which was introduced in the restoration and improvement of minor irrigation works during his administration, was widely used by his successors in the expansion of the irrigation programme which he had pioneered. During his administration, no water rate was levied on the landowners who profited from such works. The government hoped to recoup most of its investment from the anticipated augmentation of the paddy tax and land sales. Third, there was the outstanding contribution made by his Irrigation Ordinance (Ordinance 9 of 1856) 'to facilitate the revival and enforcement of the ancient customs regarding the irrigation and cultivation of paddy lands'. This ordinance revived the traditional customs relating to paddy cultivation, in particular those relating to the peasants' access to water from irrigation channels and the communal machinery for the settling of disputes relating to the use of this water. Up to this time redress for infringements of these customs could only be obtained in the civil courts (the traditional machinery for the enforcement of these customs having fallen into disuse under British rule) at the cost of considerable delay and the near-certainty of the financial ruin of both plaintiff and defendant. Ward's Irrigation Ordinance was devised with certain interrelated objects which included elimination of the protracted and expensive process of litigation with regard to disputes of this nature and restoration of the traditional customs by means of communal machinery—generally the *gansabhāvas*—under the direct supervision of the government agents and their assistants. This ordinance was introduced as an experimental measure in a few places. The response from the people of these areas was so enthusiastic that it was regarded as sufficient justification for its extension to other parts of the dry zone and for its re-enactment in 1861 and 1867 (when its operation was made permanent) with an expansion of its scope. Originally, the powers of enforcement under this legislation were largely in the hands of British officials. In 1861 and 1867 provision was made for a greater use of native officials and gansabhāvas. The success of this measure led to its extension by Governor Sir Hercules Robinson, in 1871, in the Village Communities Ordinance of that year, to include other phases of village life, particularly the trial of minor offences through the same machinery.

One consequence of the renewal of interest in irrigation during Ward's administration was that there were exaggerated hopes of quick financial returns on investment in these projects. After Ward's departure from the island, his successor Sir Charles MacCarthy called for a searching examination of the financial implications of the irrigation works in the Batticaloa district. The review was initiated much too early (within three years of the inception of these projects) for a realistic assessment of their benefits to the country. MacCarthy in the meantime suspended further investment in irrigation and when the results of the review proved unfavourable, as might have been expected in the circumstances, this was treated as concrete evidence in support of his decision to call a halt to further investment on irrigation projects. The years 1860–65 were a period of retrenchment, of stringent cuts in government expenditure even though the economy was still buoyant. The Colonial Office was bent on using the surpluses obtained by these economies to extract a higher military contribution from the island, while MacCarthy gave the highest priority to financing the railway from Colombo to the coffee-producing regions.

There was a renewal of interest in irrigation during the administration of Sir Hercules Robinson and this was maintained over the next decade. At this stage, the Colonial Office was keenly interested in the restoration of irrigation works and two Secretaries of State, Lord Kimberley (1870–74) and Lord Carnarvon (1874–78), especially the latter, conscious of the neglect of irrigation in the past, encouraged Robinson and later Gregory to resume large-scale investment in irrigation projects. Robinson began on a more modest scale and a more cautious note than Ward. In the irrigation projects which he initiated, the beneficiaries were called on to repay the outlay to the government in ten annual instalments through a water rate. Thus the principle of directly recouping expenditure was introduced and became an integral part of British irrigation policy in Sri Lanka. But his successors did not apply this principle to minor irrigation works.

It was under Gregory that the renewal of interest in irrigation began to gather greater momentum and eventually had its most far-reaching effects in the regeneration of the heartland of the ancient irrigation civilization of the Sinhalese, the Anuradhapura and Polonnaruva regions. At the time, this huge territory was, as Gregory himself described it, in a 'wretched state' and lay 'totally neglected'. A half-century earlier the ruins of these cities had been rediscovered,[3] but the massive tropical forests which covered these regions and the malaria mosquitoes, which found congenial breeding grounds in the ruined tanks and channels, were insuperable obstacles to the regeneration of the old Rājarata. Appallingly poor communications accentuated their isolation from the rest of the country. The population was scattered, ill-nourished, disease-ridden and declining in numbers. These conditions had defeated Ward's endeavours to restore some of the main irrigation works in the region. Gregory resumed this effort with the full backing of the Colonial Office, which now gave higher priority to expanding the irrigation programme than to the improvement of transport facilities on the island. His approach to the problems of this region was characteristically decisive and innovative. The initiation of large-scale irrigation works and

the repair of irrigation channels there were preceded by a
'political' decision of great importance—the creation of a new
provincial unit incorporating Nuvarakalaviya (from the
Northern Province), Tamankaduva (from the Eastern Province)
and the Demala Hatpattu (from the North-western Province).
This was the North-central Province, the first new province
established since 1845 and the first departure from the political
principles which guided the demarcation of provincial
boundaries since Colebrooke's days.

The first phase of Gregory's irrigation programme for the
North-central Province was the repairing of village tanks. For
this purpose he made extensive use of a practice initiated by
Ward, of the villagers shifting the earth and the government
providing the sluice and masonry without charge. The
gansabhāvas provided the administrative machinery required
for this purpose at the grass-roots level, and in accordance with
custom the villagers were called upon to cooperate in the repair
and upkeep of the tanks. In 1878, Gregory reported that 'work
is now going on vigorously upon hundreds of tanks in the North-
central Province where the experiment was begun at the
suggestion of Mr Dickson [the first government agent of the
new province] and now applications for similar assistance are
coming in from the Western, North-western and Northern
Provinces'.[4] Emboldened by the success that had attended the
village tank project, Gregory moved on to the restoration of
the great tanks: the Kantalai Tank at the meagre cost of £ 6,000
and—a far greater undertaking—the Kalavava, which was
expected to irrigate 9,305.8 hectares of land. At the same time,
improved communications, the completion of the northern road
connecting Jaffna with Kandy and the road to Trincomalee
through Tamankaduva reduced the isolation of that region. Only
one obstacle remained, the most formidable of all: malaria.

Gregory was justifiably proud of the improvement that
these projects had effected in the North-central Province. When
he returned to the Kalavava region, he was impressed by the
remarkable change there. The 'wretched half-starved, dying-
out population' was now 'plump well-fed sleek, healthy and
well-to-do from the spread of irrigation...'.[5] Looking back on

this project, he remarked with understandable pride: 'Never was a great social experiment more speedily and entirely successful.'[6] Gregory's administration was indeed the high-water mark of British achievement in irrigation activity in the nineteenth century.

While the direct financial recouping of investment had gained acceptance as the guiding principle of British irrigation policy, it became evident by the late 1870s that the state could not recover most of its expenditure on these ventures. But this did not put an end to investment on village irrigation projects as well as major schemes. Loans were occasionally employed to finance irrigation projects, although the general revenue was normally adequate for the purpose. Sir Arthur Gordon, governor from 1883 to 1890, financed the completion of restoration work on the Kalavava through a loan. In 1893 the Legislative Council stipulated that loans should be resorted to for undertakings involving Rs 300,000 or more in estimated expenditure. The fact is that while the government was not reluctant to use general revenues for investment in irrigation, there was undisguised hostility to this from European planters, whose representatives often gave expression to this disapproval in the Legislative Council when the votes on irrigation, which were part of the annual budget, came up for debate. This spurred Gordon into devising an important innovation in the financing of irrigation works. In 1887, an Irrigation Fund was established by annually setting aside a quarter of the proceeds of the grain taxes for expenditure on irrigation projects. When the taxes were abolished in 1892, the money for the Irrigation Fund was obtained from the import duties on rice and paddy and Rs 200,000 was set aside annually for this purpose. With the abolition of the paddy tax much greater emphasis was placed on the collection of the water rate.

The establishment of a separate Irrigation Department in 1900 seemed to indicate that an even greater emphasis would be placed on the extension of irrigation facilities in the first decade of the twentieth century. But by 1905 investment of government revenues on irrigation projects declined or ceased altogether. Although the annual expenditure varied with the state of the export trade, it was seldom less than 1.5 per cent of the total revenue in the twenty years between 1885 and 1904. In the period 1855–1904, the total amount spent by the government on irrigation was around Rs 13.5 million. The principal achievement—and object—of this programme of irrigation activity was the conversion of irregular into regular cultivation. There was nevertheless an expansion of the area under cultivation, moderate and modest in comparison to the investment, but in historical perspective the first such expansion in the dry zone for several centuries.

It is convenient to discuss the impact of irrigation activity on peasant agriculture under two headings, village works and large-scale projects. As for the first of these categories it would appear that the North-central Province and the North-western Province benefited most from the restoration of village tanks. Undoubtedly, these village irrigation works contributed to an extension of the area under paddy cultivation in these two provinces. In general, since many of the village tanks had not yet been linked to major irrigation schemes and were dependent on rainfall for their water supply, their restoration did not necessarily afford an absolute insurance against crop failures. But such occasions of food scarcity were much less frequent than before, although they did not disappear altogether. As for the large-scale irrigation projects, their greatest impact was on the Batticaloa district of the Eastern Province and the Matara district and Magam-pattu in the Southern Province. In both these regions there was a notable increase in population and an impressive improvement in rice production, although not solely due to the irrigation works. There were other factors too. The Batticaloa district became an area with a rice surplus, exporting its excess production to the adjoining Uva Province by land and to Jaffna and other regions by sea. Population increase in the Magam-pattu was 46.5 and 48.5 per cent respectively in the decades 1881–90 and 1891–1901. In the decade 1871–80 it had been a meagre 3.9 per cent. There was a substantial increase in the area under paddy and in the value of paddy lands after the completion of the Kirindi Oya in 1876. Large-scale irrigation works benefited the North-central and Northern Provinces as well, but not to the same extent as the other regions mentioned earlier.

On the basis of the meagre statistical information available, it appears that between 1850 and 1900 the area under paddy expanded by about 80,920 hectares in the whole island. Most of this expansion was stimulated by the irrigation programme described earlier, but there was also a substantial expansion of rice cultivation in the wet zone where irrigation was unimportant or unnecessary—in the Western Province alone it was as much as 28,350 hectares.

Two important points in regard to peasant agriculture at this time need emphasis. First, the increase in the area under paddy and in the actual production of paddy in the latter half of the nineteenth century was not a response to market forces or a commercialization of paddy culture on an island-wide basis. Except in the Batticaloa district and a few other areas, very little paddy was produced for sale. Subsistence agriculture was the norm. Second, given the increase in population during the period, the per capita acreage under paddy remained more or less constant despite the extension of the area under cultivation. But the expansion of cultivation kept in step with the growth of population. Nevertheless, the apparent increase in the area under paddy represents a not so insignificant achievement considering the fact that at the same time there was an expansion of the area under cash crops, namely, coffee, coconut and tea mainly; but also rubber.

These problems can be viewed in a more realistic perspective if we ask the question in a different form: why was expansion of rice cultivation or production not more rapid in the island generally, especially in the dry zone, during this period? Paddy producers in all parts of the island, whether large landowners or peasant cultivators, made no attempt to change the traditional techniques of cultivation and few technical innovations were attempted, much less adopted, in the course of the nineteenth century. Crop rotation was not resorted to and cultivators sowed their seed paddy by broadcasting rather than the more productive technique of transplanting. It is true that capital resources for innovations in production techniques were limited (in the case of small landowners) or non-existent (in the case of peasants), but even the richer landowners who commanded capital were not more venturesome than the others. As a rule, paddy production did not attract the big capitalist or large commercial firms, since the profits seemed so much more limited than in the island's main commercial crops. No European or Indian entrepreneur sought to make a fortune through paddy cultivation—Colebrooke's hopes in this regard expressed in 1832 proved to have been visionary. A few Sri Lankans did make the attempt. There was the Jaffna and Batticaloa Agricultural and Commercial Company launched by a group of Sri Lankans and Chetties in the late 1870s and early 1880s. It failed badly, as did ventures launched by other Sri Lankans in the early twentieth century. Low yields per acre were a general feature of paddy production in Sri Lanka regardless of variations in tenurial practices. Productivity of paddy lands on the island was among the lowest in Asia and this persisted till the late 1930s at least.

In the whole of the dry zone only one region—the Jaffna Peninsula—supported an efficient and intensive system of agriculture, but it had certain natural and other advantages which served to delineate the factors operating as constraints on efficient agriculture in other parts of the dry zone. There was, first, a dependable water supply through wells sunk into the limestone which underlay much of the peninsula. Neither malaria (which was endemic in most parts of the dry zone and singularly debilitating in its effects on the health of the people) nor yaws, the two principal health hazards of the dry zone, were much of a problem in Jaffna. The peasants of the Jaffna Peninsula were rigorous and resourceful, their techniques of cultivation painstaking and scientific (heavy manuring of the soil was resorted to) and the yields there were much greater than in the rest of the dry zone. While rice was the main crop, tobacco (a coarse variety exported mainly to south India) and garden crops supplemented increases in agriculture. Fishing was an important source of additional earnings.

In the wet zone there were other constraints on rice production. Paddy cultivation came into direct competition with export crops for the available labour resources and there was no question that the latter were regarded as being more profitable. There agriculturists and peasant cultivators had a wide range of more profitable alternatives before them. They—and particularly the agriculturists—did invest in paddy lands as well, but these investments were often for personal prestige and profit was seldom the main consideration. The easy availability of inexpensive and high-quality rice from abroad was hardly conducive to the expansion of local production at a time when the government was not inclined to impose protective tariffs. But the dependence on imports had other causes as well. The immigrant plantation workers from India had a marked preference for imported rice and would not touch the local varieties just like the upper classes among the local population, who had developed a taste for imported rice. Moreover, the local rice was inefficiently produced, variable in quality and not always available because of poor marketing facilities. In contrast, Burmese rice was cheap, uniform in quality, efficiently marketed and obtainable throughout the island.

The upshot of this was that the island was not self-sufficient in rice. More important, the increasing demand for rice, both from the local population and from the immigrant workers from India, did not—as it should have done—change the peasant from a subsistence cultivator into a producer for the market, and transform, that is, modernize rice production. In short, it brought the paddy cultivator into the modern sector of the economy without resort to the discipline and rigours of plantation life which the Sinhalese peasant loathed. Some of the reasons for this have been discussed earlier, but one other point needs to be mentioned: had the colonial administration in Sri Lanka taken a more positive attitude towards peasant agriculture, such a transformation might have been possible. The revival of interest in irrigation did not amount to a formulation of a comprehensive policy on peasant agriculture. This irrigation programme, as has been pointed out, arose from a mixture of motives—humanitarian, political and economic. It did not touch the wet zone, the most productive region on the island, where peasant agriculture and plantation production were in unequal competition. There were sporadic attempts at a more emphatic attitude of support for peasant landholdings, but at no stage were the implications of this fully realized, nor was there any sustained attempt to weave a comprehensive policy on peasant agriculture.

One of the peculiarities of peasant agriculture in Sri Lanka was that, in contrast to several other countries, dry farming or swidden agriculture was generally practised by peasants who also participated in the cultivation of rice and garden crops on a perennial basis. Chēna cultivation was economically more important in the dry zone than in the wet zone. In both it was a subsidiary source of income to the peasants, although it might well have been the main source in parts of the dry zone. The British viewed this slash-and-burn cultivation as a primitive, economically wasteful, destructive (of valuable timber resources) and demoralizing form of agriculture which produced the seemingly less nutritious dry grains rather than paddy. As a general rule the British were no more sympathetic to and tolerant of chēna cultivation than the VOC. Their attempts at restraining it were pursued more rigorously and effectively in the wet zone than in the dry zone. In the maritime provinces all land which was not recognized as private property was treated as belonging to the Crown and all chēna and forests (potential chēna) was regarded as Crown land. It was thus easier to impose controls on chēna cultivation there than in other parts of the wet zone and in the dry zone. In the Kandyan provinces, on the other hand, the British accepted the possibility of private or village ownership of chēna. But there were regional variations in the legal status accorded to chēna lands within the Kandyan provinces. Thus in the dry zone lowland districts of Nuvarakalaviya, forest or scrub land which villagers used for chēna cultivation was regarded as Crown property.

In the years 1850–80 one sees a hardening of the official prejudice against chēna cultivation. In general chēna cultivators required a special permit from the government. From the 1860s onwards the conditions on which such permits were granted became progressively more rigorous and in the 1870s very few permits were issued for chēna cultivation on Crown lands in the wet zone districts of the maritime provinces and also in the Kandyan region. At times the issue of chēna permits was entirely prohibited. (These controls only applied to lands which were deemed Crown lands.) The conventional wisdom of the day accorded very high priority to the conversion of chēnas into paddy fields and other forms of regular cultivation. Since population was expanding much more rapidly in the wet-zone districts of the south-west littoral and the adjacent Kandyan regions than elsewhere on the island, the restraints on chēna were perhaps justified by economic necessity. The wet-zone chēnas were increasingly being converted into paddy fields and garden lands and were used for cash crop production on smallholdings and plantations for the cultivation of coffee and coconut during this period and, later, rubber. As a result, chēnas in their traditional form became much less important in the economy of the wet-zone village. But even within the wet zone, chēna was not totally eclipsed. Some proprietors of privately owned land preferred to continue the practice. Controls over chēna cultivation, which the government began to impose in the latter part of the nineteenth century, only applied to lands which were deemed Crown lands. Till the mid-twentieth century much of the chēna land in the wet zone of the hill country (a small proportion of the cultivated area anyway) was privately owned.

In the dry zone, on the other hand, the peasants' dependence on chēna was greater and for this reason chēna permits were issued on less stringent conditions, especially during periods of drought and food scarcity (not infrequent during the latter half of the nineteenth century), when chēna cultivation was the sole barrier against famine conditions. In parts of the Badulla district in Uva, droughts were so frequent during the 1860s that sometimes not a single crop of paddy could be sown for anything up to nine years. The interior regions of the North-western Province were notably susceptible to frequent crop failures, especially in the 1870s. The situation was not dissimilar in the Mannar and Mullaitivu divisions of the Northern Province in the same decade. Throughout the last quarter of the nineteenth century, there was great distress from frequent crop failures in lower Uva—

Vellavaya, Bibile, Buttala and Alutnuvara—and the Valapane division of the Nuwara Eliya district.

The most generous interpretation one can place on this opposition to chēna cultivation was that it sprang from a misplaced benevolence, a desire to wean the peasants away from a wasteful form of agriculture—believed to be converting them into feckless and improvident individuals—to more settled, productive and socially beneficial types of cultivation. There was at the same time an urge to protect the forests from encroachment. While chēna policy was on the whole unimaginative in conception and ineffectual in application, its one redeeming feature was that it led to the establishment of climatic reserves and village forests or pasture resources, primarily to check soil erosion but also to meet future requirements of lands for village expansion. Excluding the Northern Province, North-central Province and the Eastern Province, 139,766.31 hectares of reserved forest, 4,765.6 of village forest and 40,528 of communal reserves and pasture were demarcated in the rest of the island in the forty years after 1885. In many areas the reserves came too late to check soil erosion and even in their other role of a reserve for potential agricultural land for the needs of the future, their impact was severely limited.

Chēna cultivation in the dry zone was a wise concession to the natural limitations of that region and its prohibition was a harsh exercise in bureaucratic rigidity so long as the peasants were not offered a feasible alternative. This alternative came only with the provision of irrigation facilities in the dry zone despite the limitations of the latter programme.

THE GRAIN TAXES

The grain taxes,[7] the last major theme in this review of peasant agriculture in Sri Lanka in this period, were among the most controversial issues in the administration of the colony in the last quarter of the nineteenth century. Their discussion needs to be introduced with a brief historical outline without which it would be difficult to understand much that happened.

The first point to note is that the British did not inherit a land tax from either the VOC or the Kandyan kings. Land revenue on the island took the form of taxes on grain, both paddy and dry grains. The grain taxes in operation under the British were a perpetuation of a system of which the roots went back to the times of the Sinhalese kings and which had been continued with modifications to suit their own purposes by the Portuguese and the Dutch. In the same way the nature, incidence and methods of imposition and collection of the taxes underwent change under the British. In the Kandyan provinces the grain taxes were limited to lands sown with paddy. The headmen in the Kandyan provinces and the viharagam and dēvālēgam were exempt from these taxes. Exemptions were also granted to individuals for loyalty to the British during the Great Rebellion. The tax was also lighter (one-fourteenth of the produce) in those regions which had remained loyal during the Rebellion—the Kegalla and Ratnapura districts benefited substantially from this lighter tax—while the districts in which resistance was strongest paid a heavier tax (one-fifth of the produce). These exemptions, concessions and penalties apart, the tax was normally one-tenth of the gross produce. In the maritime provinces the taxes were also imposed on lands sown with grains other than paddy. These taxes on dry grains were limited to the littoral and within this region were of importance only in the Tamil districts of the north. As for the paddy tax, the Crown share ranged at first from one-fourteenth to a half, but the trend was to convert to one-tenth. Third, an import duty on rice and paddy was introduced in 1810 for revenue purposes rather than protection. The tendency was to link these duties to the paddy taxes as part of a common system of taxes. By 1840, the import duties grew progressively larger than the grain tax.

Originally, there were two methods of collecting the taxes: the *aumani* system, which prevailed under the Sinhalese kings, whereby the taxes were collected directly by state officials; and the renting system, the most widespread method of collection at the end of Dutch rule, where the right of collecting the tax was farmed out to the highest bidder. The British, while continuing these, introduced a third method in the 1830s, the commutation system under which the paddy grower had the option of paying the tax in cash at a rate fixed for each district by a commutation settlement.

The grain taxes in the period surveyed here were not by themselves particularly onerous—the land tax was so much higher in other parts of southern Asia—but the renting system, which was the predominant mode of collection, was widely regarded as harsh and oppressive and this brought the grain taxes as a whole under criticism. Colebrooke had urged the redemption of the grain tax by annual instalments spread over twenty years. This recommendation was accepted and owners were given the option of redemption either at a fixed rate in money or in kind, but the instalments were to be spread over eight and not twenty years. It would appear that from 1832 to 1842 redemption of the tax proceeded apace particularly in the Central Province, till in the early 1840s, at a time when the government's coffers were depleted, it was realized that redemption tended to diminish the state's resources, and from 1849 it was discouraged if not altogether prohibited. At the same time, the practices and regulations pertaining to the renting system were consolidated in Ordinance 14 of 1840, which sought to define and standardize the methods of collection and to establish some administrative machinery through which renters could use legal processes to recover taxes due from cultivators and producers and thus make tax evasion difficult.

In the late 1840s, Tennent excoriated the grain taxes in his *Report on the Finance and Commerce of Ceylon* and urged their abolition as part of his scheme of introducing an acreable land tax. The Colonial Office itself accepted this recommendation and the comments of a Whitehall committee which reviewed Tennent's principal recommendations were as strongly critical of the grain taxes as those of Tennent himself. But when the proposal to introduce a land tax was abandoned, all hopes of abolishing the grain taxes disappeared. Commutation, however, continued unevenly and sporadically. The discouragement of redemption from 1842 does not appear to have checked commutation. Indeed, if there was any consistency over the next four decades in the official attitude to the grain taxes, apart from a determination to maintain them, it lay in the marked preference for commutation as against the renting system. Despite the adverse effect it had on government revenues, commutation was free from the criticisms which were persistently levelled against the renting system—that it was oppressive and extortionate. It had the positive advantage of eliminating the middlemen—the renters—who were looked upon as the main beneficiaries of the renting system. Officials believed that the share of the tax which eventually reached the treasury did not form half the actual amount paid to the renters by the peasantry. Nevertheless, despite this official preference for commutation settlements, the renting system held its own in several districts. An island-wide commutation remained an objective beyond the capacity of the administration to achieve. The commutation system was not without its own disadvantages—of which a lack of flexibility was the most prominent—and these were aggravated by Ordinance 5 of 1866, which empowered the government to seize the lands of those who defaulted on their payments of the commuted paddy tax and to sell the lands to recover arrears of tax. For about ten years these powers were seldom used, but they were then employed with deadly effect, as we shall presently see.

How was it that these taxes survived for so long when their abolition, or supersession had been recommended at regular intervals? There are three main reasons. The first and most important was the purely economic reason, namely, that the colonial administration feared that their abolition would severely strain the government's financial strength. Between 1845 and 1868, the revenue from the import duty on rice with the yield of the grain tax together constituted a quarter of the government's revenue. In the 1870s, the proportion was slightly lower, around one-fifth. Second, the tendency was to connect the import duty with the paddy tax in computing the loss of revenue anticipated from the potential abolition of the grain taxes, although import duty had little or nothing to do with the paddy tax. Thus when the Colonial Office in the late 1860s suggested a reduction of the import duty on rice, Governor Sir Hercules Robinson rejected this advice on the grounds that 'the state of the revenue would not admit of the loss'. It was the same argument that Gregory had used for the retention of the grain tax. The government's renewed interest in irrigation at this time served to strengthen its resolve to maintain this tax, both because—as Gregory urged—a permanent supply of water

396. A History of Sri Lanka

was the best of all available means for weaning the peasants
from the renting system and because of the fear that investment
in irrigation would need to be curtailed, if not abandoned
altogether, if the government's revenues were reduced by the
abolition of the tax. Third, there was powerful support for the
status quo from an influential section of the Sinhalese elite who
feared that the probable alternative—a land tax—would be much
more unfavourable to their interests. James Alwis, as Sinhalese
representative in the Legislative Council, lent his support to
the administration in its efforts to retain the grain taxes.

Critics of the grain taxes made skilful use of the contemporary
distaste for food taxes in general to bring the former into
disrepute. They were encouraged in this by the fact that even
those who urged the maintenance of the status quo conceded
that the grain taxes were abhorrent in principle; second, these
critics focussed attention on the renting system and its abuses;
and third, they argued that the paddy tax as a whole was a
formidable restraint on the extension of paddy cultivation and
the reclamation of wastelands. Pressures for the modification
if not abolition of the grain taxes became too strong for the
government to ignore and a commission was appointed in
1878 to examine these questions. By posing the question whether
the people would prefer a land tax to one on paddy and dry
grain, the commission only succeeded in obscuring and confusing
the issues it was appointed to clarify. The answer to the question
was inevitable—no one, not least the Sinhalese elite, welcomed
the substitution of a land tax for the grain taxes. However,
the recommendations of the commission did at least lead to
one significant change. Through Ordinance 11 of 1878, a new
system of compulsory commutation was introduced, superseding
the prevailing system of commutation: under the new scheme
not only was commutation compulsory but assessments were
to be supervised by British civil servants and not by native
officials. One unforeseen but inescapable consequence of this
latter change was that a shortage of personnel prevented the
introduction of the new system to all parts of the island
simultaneously. The old system was thus superseded in stages;
it survived in Uva till 1887 and in the Central Province till 1888.

In 1888, a startling disclosure by C.J.R. Le Mesurier, assistant government agent of Nuwara Eliya, in his annual administration report that '[1048] villagers...died of starvation...within sight of [Nuwara Eliya,] the sanatorium where our governors and high officials resort for health and lawn tennis...' focussed attention once more on the grain taxes. Le Mesurier alleged that these deaths had occurred between 1882 and 1885 as the culmination of the process of enforcing the payment of the grain tax and implementing Ordinance 5 of 1866, with the utmost stringency, to seize the lands of those in arrears of tax, to evict such persons and to sell their land to recover the arrears of tax. He pointed out that at this time the peasants did not have the means of paying the tax.

Inevitably, the establishment closed ranks and Le Mesurier came under attack. His arguments, his statistics and his judgement were alike ridiculed or severely criticized. But even if the statistical information may have been flawed, his analysis has stood the test of critical examination by scholars.[8] It would appear that in the 1880s landowners and peasants had defaulted in the payment of the paddy tax and arrears of tax had accumulated on a large scale at Ratnapura, Galle, Batticaloa and the Kandyan region. The problem was most acute in some of the Kandyan areas where the collapse of the coffee industry had deprived the people of a ready source of money with which to pay these taxes, especially when, as often happened at this time, the paddy and chēna crops failed. At the same time there had also been a sharp fall in the government revenues and, as in similar circumstances in the past, the government turned its attention to the peasants as a source of taxation. No new tax was devised, but Ordinance 5 of 1866, which had been little used in the past, was implemented to the very letter. This caused acute distress, especially in the Valapane division of the Nuwara Eliya district and in Udakinda in Uva.

When these matters were ventilated in the House of Commons, Governor Gordon made a mild and half-hearted defence of the grain taxes. But privately he conceded the basic accuracy of Le Mesurier's disclosures. He informed Gregory, living in retirement in England, that 'as to the Grain Tax, I

would only add between ourselves, that the harsh enforcement
of the payment of arrears in parts of the Central Province and
Uva was unquestionably the direct cause of a large number of
deaths from want'.[9] The Valapane evictions and Le Mesurier's
disclosures discredited the entire system of grain taxes, created
an atmosphere adverse to their continuation and eventually
helped Sir Arthur Havelock (Gordon's successor as governor)
in 1892 to convince the Colonial Office of the need to abolish
them altogether. In this final phase of their campaign, the
abolitionists found Gordon's administration—and especially
Gordon himself—in a hesitant, defensive mood, and they made
the most of this. Critics of the grain taxes gained an ally with
the appointment of T.B. Panabokke as Kandyan member in the
enlarged Legislative Council in 1889. Together with Ponnambalam
Ramanathan, the Tamil representative, he used the legislature
as a forum for outspoken criticism of the taxes. In the past,
Sinhalese representatives in the Legislative Council had either
supported the maintenance of these taxes or had remained silent
when these issues came up for discussion. Besides, the campaign
against the taxes was taken up by the newly formed Ceylon
National Association and its contribution to the abolition was
its most constructive achievement in the whole of its existence.
The campaign for abolition owed much to the press over the
years, to George Wall and the *Ceylon Independent* within the
island, and to the Cobden Club and radical opinion in Britain
with the support of the *Manchester Guardian*. Ranged against them
had been A.M. Ferguson and John Ferguson and their newspaper,
the *Ceylon Observer*, with the assistance of the *Ceylon Patriot*.

It is perhaps appropriate that this survey of peasant agriculture
should end with this discussion of agrarian distress and rural
poverty in the Kandyan region. Throughout the last quarter
of the nineteenth century, and in the first decade of the
twentieth, there are frequent references in published official
documents to famines, conditions of near-famine, chronic rural
poverty, destitution and, above all, starvation in many parts of
the country, especially the dry zone. After a century of rule, the
British colonial administration had not succeeded in improving
the living standards of the rural population in most parts of
the country.[10]

The Consolidation of British Rule
The Triumph of Conservatism

The commitment to social change and the reformist attitudes, which were so marked in the second quarter of the nineteenth century, had given way to a more conservative mood by the beginning of the 1870s. This persisted till the end of the century and beyond it into the twentieth century. After the events of 1848, there developed, slowly at first but quite emphatically in time, a suspicion of social change and what began as a keener—and politic—appreciation of the religious sensibilities of the people, especially in regard to the Kandyan areas, now also became evident in other aspects of social policy. Except in education, there was a notable lack of innovation in all fields and the retreat from innovation, which had started in social policy, tended to affect administrative policies and emerging political attitudes as well.

There had been a far-reaching reappraisal of the policy on Buddhism almost immediately after the 'rebellion' of 1848. The British government recoiled from the evangelical zeal which had pervaded its Buddhist policy in the years preceding its outbreak and paid more heed to the sensibilities of the Kandyans when legislation affecting them was prepared. Thus the Colonial Office's reaction to an ordinance of 1852, which sought to assimilate the law of the Kandyan provinces 'so far as regards the persons and properties of all persons other than Kandyans' to that of the maritime regions, is worth noting. Sir John Pakington, the Secretary of State for the Colonies, gave his approval to this with a word of caution; he informed Governor Sir George Anderson: 'I have advised this confirmation in reliance on your judgement and that of the

Legislative Council in not hastily introducing legal changes which might shake the confidence of the people of the Kandyan provinces in the intention of the Government to maintain their rights and usages; and I have no doubt that you will attentively consider this point in undertaking such reforms as may affect them.'[1] The sensitivity to Kandyan feelings was further illustrated in the manner in which the abolition of Kandyan polyandry was handled. Despite the loathing in which British officials held polyandry, great pains were taken to show that the initiative in preparing Ordinance 13 of 1859 'to amend the laws of marriage in the Kandyan province' came not from the government but from a group of Kandyan chiefs.

When innovation was attempted, quite often it took the form of restoration of institutions, the value and utility of which had been disregarded in the earlier reformist era. The revival of the gansabhāvas illustrates this. The Irrigation Ordinance of 1856 made provision for the establishment of gansabhāvas with powers to make rules for the control of cultivation and the use of water in villages dependent on irrigation. In 1871, these powers were extended to cover other aspects of village life and the regulations framed for these purposes were enforceable by the gansabhāvas by effective legal sanctions. These tribunals also exercised a limited criminal and civil jurisdiction locally. This resuscitation of an indigenous institution, one of the most constructive achievements of this period, also marked the one notable— though far from decisive—deviation from the general trend towards 'anglicization' of the administration of justice. The reluctance to initiate change and reform became more pronounced in the 1860s and 1870s. Thus, when the question of service tenures within viharagam and dēvālēgam became a matter of public discussion again in 1869–70, Sir Hercules Robinson would agree to nothing more drastic than a purely permissive measure, despite the cogently argued case made mainly on humanitarian grounds by E.L. Mitford for the immediate and compulsory abolition of these tenures.[2] And the memory of 1848 lingered on even in matters relating to taxation policy: as late as 1877, Governor Gregory urged, as a serious objection to the introduction of a land tax, that it would be imposing a direct tax on the people—'a very serious matter the consequences of which no one can foretell.'

It will be shown in the discussion that follows that by the 1870s the retreat from innovation began to have its impact on administrative policy as well, especially in relation to the role of native headmen in the administration. Although there is evidence of a change in the government's attitude to the native chiefs within a decade of the 'rebellion' of 1848, it was Gregory who boldly reversed the trend, discernible since the Great Rebellion of 1817–18, of being wary of the Kandyan chiefs. He began a policy of resuscitation of aristocratic influence in the administration, continued by men like Gordon and McCallum and given added impetus in an attempt to build up a bloc of loyalists as a counterweight to the more assertive sections of the emerging elite, who were brashly demanding a share of political power in the country.

There was one other notable development under Gregory. Revision of provincial boundaries, hitherto used as an administrative device to keep Kandyan 'nationality' in check, was now utilized for the exactly opposite purpose. His reasons for the establishment of the North-central Province seem in retrospect a damning condemnation of the principles behind Colebrooke's redrawing of provincial boundaries in 1833. These reasons were: '[The] wretched state of this huge extent of territory; its totally neglected condition; the impossibility of a Government Agent residing at Jaffna, the northern part of the island being able to supervise the immediate improvement necessary; and last, but not least, that this portion of the Northern Province was Kandyan in its population whereas in the North it was Tamil, and generally ruled by a Government Agent who was more conversant with Tamils than with Singhalese [sic]...'.[3] Two more Kandyan provinces were carved out in the 1880s: Uva in 1886 and Sabaragamuva in 1889. These changes in provincial boundaries stretching over the years 1873–89 marked a distinct change of attitude to the Kandyan problem. The policy which had prevailed since 1833 was abandoned, because the political factor on which it was based—the fear that a 'traditional' nationalism guided by an aristocratic leadership was a threat to British rule—had lost its validity. It indicated a shrewd grasp of the realities of a changed political situation. Between the 1880s and the attainment of independence in the twentieth century, the Kandyans mostly took satisfaction in a new role—that of associates of the British and a counterweight to the reform and nationalist movements dominated by the emerging elite of the maritime districts. The leaders of Kandyan opinion seldom showed much sympathy for the political aspirations of these movements; when not positively hostile, they stood aloof and suspicious.

This discussion of the redrawing of provincial boundaries is an appropriate point of departure for a brief review of an important aspect of the process of consolidation of British rule in the last quarter of the nineteenth century—the increasingly effective control of the secretariat in Colombo over the provincial administration. During much of the nineteenth century, the main strength of British colonial administration on the island lay in its provincial organization. The provinces were divided into a varying number of districts, the total number being twenty-one, of which fourteen were administered by assistant government agents while the government agent who was in overall control of the province had sole charge of the principal district of his province. The government agent, as the chief government representative in his province, was vested with the executive authority of the state. The further away from the Centre and the more difficult the communications, the greater was the power wielded by the government agent and his subordinates. Although officials of the higher bureaucracy held judicial appointments too, their judicial and executive powers were separated except in some of the remoter districts— Anuradhapura, Trincomalee, Vavuniya and Mannar—where the assistant government agents were also district judges.

The network of roads constructed during the second quarter of the nineteenth century and expanded thereafter to keep pace with the growth of the plantations facilitated communications between Colombo and the provinces. The telegraph and, later, the railway brought the provincial administration under closer supervision from Colombo. A decision taken by Gregory in 1873 was a foretaste of the future: in that year the first of what was to be a series of annual conferences of government agents was held under his auspices. Its purpose was to promote uniformity in provincial administration. At this annual 'durbar' the government agents were 'enjoined to bring a list of works [they] required, and each had full time to give all necessary explanations...'. It was 'a general meeting to discuss various subjects of public interest on which the Agents had been invited to prepare themselves'. This annual 'durbar' marked the beginning of the decline of the government agents' powers vis-à-vis the secretariat in Colombo.

The consolidation of British rule has so far been discussed in terms of two problems—the Kandyan question and the relationship between the secretariat in Colombo and the provincial administration. The processes of consolidation comprised other features as well and all these latter had one common element—a conservative outlook. Three of these salient features are reviewed next: the erection of barriers to the entry of Sri Lankans to positions of influence in the higher bureaucracy; the reconciliation between the British and the traditional elite and a retreat from the policy of even-handed treatment of caste problems. In all these there was a distinct reversal of enlightened policies enunciated during the age of reforms in the decade following the publication of the Colebrooke–Cameron reports and the introduction of reforms based on them. To turn to the first of these problems, it was natural that appointment to the higher bureaucracy should become an object of ambition among educated Sri Lankans. Entry to the higher bureaucracy was cherished because it amounted to admission into the charmed circle of the ruling elite. The early policy of educating mostly young men from among the traditional elite tended to reduce considerably both the pressure for government employment and competition between different social groups, but the expansion of educational opportunities increased competition

Appointment to the civil service—as the closed division of the higher bureaucracy was called—was in the patronage jointly of the Secretary of State for the Colonies and the governor of the colony; from 1852 this patronage was equally divided. Since 1845 nominees of the Secretary of State had been required to pass the Haileybury entrance examination and from 1856 the open competitive examination instituted by the Macaulay Committee was applied to Sri Lanka. No such examination, however, was required for candidates nominated by the governor. Ward successfully resisted moves to establish a competitive examination for the governor's nominees, believing that it was possible to obtain more suitable men through the prevailing system of personal selection. In 1863, his successor, C.J. MacCarthy modified the policy, and thereafter the governor's candidates were required to pass a non-competitive examination on 'general attainments'. For a few years this examination was of a lower standard than that set by the British Civil Service Commission, but from 1870 they were required to sit for the same examination in Colombo as did the candidates in London. This system of simultaneous examinations for entry to the civil service was abolished in 1880 and thereafter all candidates were required to vie in open competition in London. The purpose of this change was quite explicitly to compel candidates to obtain their education in London. Governor Longden himself argued that 'it was impossible for any young man without leaving the island to shake himself free of local ties and local feelings of caste prejudice and insular narrowness as to acquire any independence of thought'.[4] The injustice of this requirement was hardly mitigated by the award—begun in 1870—of Queen's Scholarships for study in British universities. Within three years of making the comment quoted earlier, Longden was complaining that the unintentional effect of throwing open the cadetships to competition by public examination in England was the virtual exclusion of natives of the island from the civil service proper. In 1868 (well before Longden's administration), there had been seventy-four Britons and ten Sri Lankans including Burghers in the higher bureaucracy; by 1881 the proportion was reduced, the numbers being eighty-four to seven respectively.

This virtual exclusion of Sri Lankans from the higher bureaucracy was resented all the more because the public pronouncements in the 1870s and 1880s of successive governors of the colony, who had repeatedly and emphatically raised expectations regarding increased opportunities for Sri Lankans to enter the civil service, were so much at variance with the actual policy followed. These gubernatorial declarations were reduced to vacuous good intentions by the higher bureaucracy who justified their resistance to any large-scale addition of Sri Lankans to their ranks with the argument that it would lead to a lowering of standards and efficiency in administration. The rationale behind this virtual exclusion of Sri Lankans from the civil service was the contention that expatriate British officials were and would be more responsible and jealous trustees of the people's interests than their potential replacements from among the educated Sri Lankans. Total exclusion from the civil service was impossible, but those who secured admission were quickly diverted to the judicial side of the administration. In the 1870s, all the Sri Lankans in the higher bureaucracy were in judicial posts, a trend which continued unchanged till well into the twentieth century. Whereas in India, civil servants were entitled to a choice between the executive and judicial line, in Sri Lanka there was no choice and it was the less able—or those less socially acceptable—who were most often appointed judges. These judicial appointments were much less prestigious and desirable than administrative and revenue posts; judges had less chance to show initiative and to influence policy. It was precisely these latter posts to which nationally conscious or socially sensitive Sri Lankans aspired, but which they did not get. In this period, no Sri Lankan attained the status of assistant government agent, much less that of a government agent. The rationale for this restriction of Sri Lankans to judicial appointments was the argument that while they might have gained distinction in the fields of law and medicine, they had yet to demonstrate the qualities which were necessary in the more pragmatic field of administration where the ability to direct and control people was the key requirement.

In the last quarter of the nineteenth century and the first decade of the twentieth, it was the specialized 'technical' departments—such as the Medical, Education and Public Works Departments—which provided Sri Lankans with the widest choice and greatest opportunities for responsible if not remunerative employment. Even so, appointments in some technical departments such as the Railway,[5] Irrigation[6] and Survey Departments were for long the exclusive preserve of Europeans. Moreover, within the 'technical' departments which were open to Sri Lankans, the positions available to them were less influential and prestigious and were the least important in decision making. As a sop to the Sri Lankans who continuously agitated for entry to the civil service, a local division of the civil service was created—as in India—with allegedly similar prospects but undeniably inferior status. This was done in 1891 and six civil service positions were reserved for Sri Lankans in this local or subordinate division. Needless to say, it did not satisfy educated Sri Lankans, who continued to press for equality of treatment with Europeans in civil service appointments.

There was scant sympathy for these aspirations from Governors Gordon and Havelock. On the contrary, they urged that appointments to the subordinate civil service should be by the governor's nomination and not through competitive examination. Gordon argued that the examination system 'shut out from all hope of higher employment just those men most fitted for it, and entitled to it; those who have already served well as Presidents [of Village Tribunals], *Mudaliyārs, Rate Mahatmayas,* Acting Magistrates, or Acting Cadets...but who are too old to enter by competitive examination even if they would...'.[7] In writing thus in a private letter to his successor Havelock, Gordon was preaching to the converted. Havelock contended that the Sinhalese and Burghers best suited for service were the young men who had had a gentleman's education but who would be beaten in a competitive examination by those who were not gentlemen and were less fitted for the service than those whom they would have beaten. In a confidential despatch to Joseph Chamberlain, Secretary of State for the Colonies, Havelock expanded on this theme: 'If the Governor could exercise such a power of appointment in favour of the de Sarams, de Liveras, Bandaranaikes and de Soysas[8] etc., a much better class of officer would be obtained than the present system [of examinations] is likely to procure. I confess that I look to the future result of the present system with extreme apprehension...'.[9]

At the turn of the century, Governor Sir Joseph West Ridgeway sought to reverse these trends. He believed that the entry of Sri Lankans to the higher bureaucracy in increasing numbers was inevitable and that it was desirable to encourage it. Indeed, he foresaw the time when Europeans would be confined to a few key and sensitive posts in the civil service and would serve largely in a supervisory capacity. Once again, expectations were raised only to disappoint those who hoped for change. By the first decade of the twentieth century, the exclusion of Sri Lankans from the more important posts in the higher bureaucracy was maintained with renewed vigour. For example, an attempt was made to exclude them from employment in the higher ranks of the police. More significantly, Walter Pereira, a leading Sri Lankan lawyer, was not confirmed in the post of attorney general for which he was eminently qualified, although he had acted as attorney general with aplomb and distinction. In contrast, two Sri Lankans (both Burghers) had served as attorney general in the second half of the nineteenth century: Sir Richard Morgan and Sir Samuel Grenier. An official in Whitehall justified the decision to overlook Walter Pereira's claims by arguing that the man chosen to be attorney general 'must be a good lawyer and ought to be pure white...'.[10]

MUDALIYĀRS

A parallel development to the successful resistance of the British civil servants to a large-scale entry of educated Sri Lankans to the higher bureaucracy was a more sympathetic view of the native chiefs. Despite an avowed policy—pursued with greater conviction if not with any dogged persistence since the Colebrooke–Cameron reforms—of undermining their influence in Sri Lankan society, the chiefs were still indispensable in the administrative structure at the district level[11] and below. Many of these positions carried no remuneration and were held on a loose hereditary basis. They owed their survival within the administrative structure to a combination of factors—most of all, inertia: it was convenient to have them around in these subordinate posts, and in any case British officials felt more comfortable with them than with more educated Sri Lankans from lower strata of society. Second, they were indispensable because the alternative to their elimination was an increase in the number of British officials down to the chief headmen's division and even below, and this was prohibitively expensive even if so large a number of officials could have been found.

In the Kandyan areas, the British had, on the whole, failed in such attempts as they made—not that there was any consistent effort—to build up a group of loyal collaborators who could have been used as a countervailing force to the detriment of the chiefs. But in the maritime districts, the traditional elite—the mudaliyārs themselves—were evolving by the middle of the nineteenth century into precisely such a group of loyalists. By the 1850s one sees clear evidence of a tendency to rely on them as an auxiliary force of collaborators. The application of a similar policy to the Kandyan areas took longer, but with the revitalizing of the village communities and the creation of the village tribunals, there was a restoration of some of the powers lost by the chiefs in earlier decades. In 1871, the powers of the gansabhāvas, which originally had to do mainly with rules for the control of cultivation and the use of water in villages dependent on irrigation, were extended to cover other aspects of village life. The members of these bodies were chosen from among the principal landowners of the area. They were presided over by the chief headmen under the supervision of the government agents and had power to make rules for the regulation of village facilities. The village tribunals, it has been seen, were, in fact, local courts which not only tried breaches of village rules but also had jurisdiction in minor criminal and certain civil cases. These courts were at first presided over by the chief headmen, although presidents of village tribunals with some legal training were later appointed.

Under Gregory the growing reconciliation between the British and the Kandyan chiefs blossomed into a relationship of trust and mutual dependence. With Gordon this policy was extended to the low country as well. Where Gregory was impelled by sentiment, Gordon was purposeful in his policy of aristocratic resuscitation; he was after all the pioneer—while in Fiji—of the system of indirect rule in which the traditional elite were the key element. He extended the use of the 'durbar' by associating in it—for ceremonial purposes—the chief native headmen. This trend was continued and strengthened in the first decade of the twentieth century by Sir Henry McCallum who had the advantage of experience of similar gatherings of chiefs in Malaya, Nigeria and Natal, in a more formal, consultative and deliberative capacity. McCallum modelled his 'durbars' on the *indaba*s of Natal, at which the chiefs discussed the vital issues of the day with the governor and his principal officials. Thus McCallum took the policy of aristocratic resuscitation a stage further and once again the reasons behind it were political, the anxiety to build a counterweight to the more assertive sections of the educated elite who were demanding a share of power in the colony. Gordon himself had explained the advantages of this line of policy: 'It is my desire to preserve as long as possible a system which enlists all native local influences in support of authority, instead of arranging them against it; and which shields the government to a great degree from direct friction with those it governs...'.[12] 'The [office of] Ratemahatmaya', Sir James Robert Longden (Gordon's predecessor) declared, 'is one which demands for the efficient performance of its duties, not so much efficient training as that the occupant should have among the natives the sort of influence that pertains to high birth, landed property and experience in affairs.'[13] The hallmarks of the system were wealth, influence and social status. By the end of the nineteenth century, all posts of president of village tribunals were in the hands of the Kandyan chiefs and the mudaliyārs in the low country. There were six Sinhalese police magistrates in 1901, all members of the same traditional elite families.

The bond between the government and the traditional elite was destined to have far-reaching political consequences on

account of the caste problem. The policy of aristocratic
resuscitation brought with it, almost inevitably, a reversal of
the commitment to discourage caste privilege which had been
a striking feature of the era of reforms that followed the
introduction of the Colebrooke–Cameron reforms.

Appointment of Karāvas and Salāgamas to posts of
mudaliyār of kōralēs was not infrequent in the early and mid-
nineteenth century. Non-Goyigamas had even been raised to
the status of mahā mudaliyār in early British times. Adrian de
Abrew Rajapakse, a Salāgama scholar, was made mahā mudaliyār
and he held the post jointly with Conrad Peter Dias, a member
of the Goyigama establishment. At this time more mudaliyārs
of these castes secured appointment as kōralē mudaliyārs than
in previous decades and the greater frequency of their entry
to these posts marked a recognition of their equality with the
Goyigamas, even though the latter never entirely lost their
advantage for office or rank. Thus, till about the 1880s the policy
of administering the country with the cooperation of the
traditional Goyigama establishment had not necessarily implied
the exclusion of other caste groups from favour. Indeed by
the third quarter of the nineteenth century, the non-Goyigama
elite, increasingly self-assured and affluent, were not inclined
to accept the claims of the Goyigama elite—'the first-class'
Goyigamas, as they called themselves—to superiority in caste
status over others. The most aggressive critics and the most
formidable challengers of the Goyigama establishment were
the Karāvas. The government stayed aloof from these contests
and its neutrality, if not ostentatious, was seldom in doubt.

A change in policy came with Gordon, who intervened
decisively in support of the claims to caste privilege advanced
by standard-bearers of the Goyigama establishment, the Diases
and Dias-Bandaranaikes. He refused to appoint a successor to
Louis de Zoysa as mahā mudaliyār when he died in 1884, even
though the local press, English and Sinhalese, strongly backed
the claims of gate-mudaliyār Samson Rajapakse (Salāgama) and
C.H. de Soysa (Karāva) to the post. Contemporary critics
attributed Gordon's discrimination against the non-Goyigama
castes to the influence of his mahā mudaliyār (a Dias-

Bandaranaike), whose kinsfolk he favoured over better-qualified applicants. Gordon's actions provoked acrimonious pamphleteering campaigns in which the Goyigama claims to superiority were challenged and similar and conflicting claims on behalf of other castes were advanced. The recrimination directed at Gordon by the non-Goyigama castes, in particular by the Karāvas, was a reflection of their bitter disappointment that he had succeeded in emphasizing once more the relevance of caste as a determinant of elite status. Moreover, because of the feeling that government recognized caste distinctions, even minor officials began to discriminate against non-Goyigamas especially in selection to government posts. As for Gordon himself, his associations and instincts were essentially feudal; he revered the past and aspired to rule the Sinhalese in the spirit of the old rulers. But there were other reasons too for the decision to support the Goyigama establishment: the Goyigamas were by far the largest caste group, constituting nearly half the Sinhalese population and were the most contented section of the community. These more pragmatic considerations would have appealed to Gordon's successors, for the exacerbation of caste rivalries undoubtedly impeded the growth of a sense of unity and nationality among the Sinhalese. Goyigama support was essential for any political movement to make an impact; lacking it, minority castes could make little headway in their political agitation. When these minority castes led a demand for reform, it could always be dismissed as the agitation of a small clique not representative of the country at large.

REVIVAL OF BUDDHISM

An interesting aspect of the link between the consolidation of British rule and triumph of conservatism was the attempt to develop a more accommodating attitude towards Buddhism. In the 1870s, Buddhism was, if not on the crest of a wave of recovery, at least very much on the upgrade. A Buddhist revival had been gaining ground steadily in an atmosphere of covert and overt hostility from missionary organizations and government officials (the neutrality of the state did not ensure the neutrality of its officials). The Buddhist revival proved a spur to the growth of national consciousness and the recovery of national pride. But before any attempt could be made to direct this stream of religious 'nationalism' into 'political' channels—indeed, before anyone thought of such a possibility— Gregory and Gordon sought to guide it into a conservative mould. Gregory, a Protestant and Liberal Irish landlord, initiated a policy of active interest in and sympathy for the Buddhist movement. This he did by according a measure of judicious patronage to the movement as well as by consciously seeking to emphasize the government's neutrality in religious affairs. The fact that he was at the same time engaged in the attempt to disestablish the Anglican church appeared to demonstrate this neutrality in a manner which was at once vigorous and open (the disestablishment was actually achieved under Longden). Gordon not only continued this policy but also endeavoured to underscore the principle of a special obligation towards Buddhism: he hoped thereby to make the Buddhist movement a conservative force, something which would help to revitalize the traditional society in the face of the eroding effects of education and social change.

Both Gregory and Gordon viewed Buddhism as essentially conservative in the sense of being the bedrock of the traditional way of life. They valued it for its potential as a countervailing force against movements for change and reform which raised the prospect of disturbing the political balance which the British were seeking to maintain. But the forces behind the Buddhist revival were not necessarily conservative in a political sense. Gordon's assumption that religious revivalism and political conservatism were twin forces which would blend harmoniously was too facile and simplistic. The Buddhist revival could not be thus contained. By the turn of the century a sustained temperance agitation with which it was inevitably linked gave it added momentum. This temperance agitation became, as we shall see, at once an integral element in religious revival and an introduction—tentative but astutely restrained—to political activity, which, far from helping to consolidate the forces of conservatism in Sinhalese society, actually helped to undermine them.

Education and Social Change in the Late Nineteenth Century

Even for many who have not found it possible personally to visit Europe, education of a purely European type has become more easily accessible and has been sought with eagerness. This had led, in my opinion, not to the working of any marked transformation in the bulk of the population, but to the creation of, or, at any rate, to a great extension in the matter of numerical strength of, a class of natives which formerly was almost a negligible quantity.

[It] is precisely the acquisition of European ideas and the adoption of European in preference to Ceylonese civilisation that differentiates this class of Ceylonese from their countrymen...[and separates them] by a wide gulf from the majority of the native inhabitants of the Colony. Their ideas, their aspirations, their interests are distinctively their own, are all moulded upon European models, and are no longer those of the majority of their countrymen.

Thus wrote Governor Sir Henry McCallum in 1910, focussing attention on a very significant aspect of a half-century of rapid change, coinciding with the second half of the nineteenth century: the emergence of a new elite. He refers here to two of its most distinctive characteristics—that it was Western-educated, anglicized and hence alienated from the people. As an avowedly hostile critic of this elite, he caricatured it rather than drawing a true-to-life picture. It would have surprised him immensely to know that the three points he made about the elite—that it was a new elite, anglicized, Western-educated and alienated from the people—should have formed for decades the stock-in-trade of social scientists in their analysis of social and political change in Sri Lanka in the late nineteenth century and the first half of the twentieth century. (Not that these social scientists drew their inspiration from McCallum; they came to these conclusions on their own.) Yet, each of the points in this analysis was at best a half-truth.

In the years before 1832, the processes of social and economic change generated by the establishment of British rule had resulted in a renewal of the strength of the traditional elite as it adapted itself to the new environment. But in the second half of the nineteenth century, these same forces of change led, if not to the displacement of the traditional elite, at least to the emergence of challengers to their position who were mostly self-made men, eager to grasp the new economic opportunities open to Sri Lankans, and much more adept at doing so. If these self-made men emerged as challengers to the traditional elite, the British themselves attempted purposefully to dispense with the traditional elite. The establishment of a more bureaucratic form of government after the Colebrooke–Cameron reforms was motivated partly at least by a desire to reduce the influence and prestige of the mudaliyārs and the Kandyan aristocracy in the administrative structure; but, as we have seen, they continued to be an integral element in the administration and an essential channel of communication between the British government and the people. Their inherited advantages survived despite a deliberate reduction of their powers, and there appears to have been no falling-off in the deference shown to them by the people, or in their influence over the people. Eventually, by the 1870s, the British themselves reversed this policy and introduced the diametrically opposite one of aristocratic resuscitation.

The traditional elite found it more difficult to maintain an economic superiority over other segments of the local population. This had largely been a function of their advantageous position as the principal landholders. With the remarkable success of coffee culture, local entrepreneurs began to accumulate wealth on an unprecedented scale, but here too the traditional elite was not entirely displaced. However, its challengers could compete effectually in all spheres of social and economic activity which the traditional elite had hitherto dominated. This was especially so in regard to ownership of lands in which it was soon left far behind. This happened also, though not to the same extent, in education and professional training. As in most societies, the traditional elite resented the new men most of all for their ostentatious emulation of the lifestyle which had hitherto been an attribute of hereditary status. But the new men could not be denied their place in the ranks of the elite. The established men still formed part, though very much a subordinate part, of the 'governing elite'; their challengers grudgingly accommodated in the 'non-governing' sector of the elite, were aspirants for entry and acceptance in the lower rungs of the 'governing elite'. Together, both groups formed a tiny segment of indigenous society which claimed or aspired to a position of superiority and a measure of influence over the rest of the community. They all shared, in a greater or lesser degree, the three main notions commonly associated with elite status: superiority, prestige and power. Although the established men were compelled to accommodate themselves to an expansion of the elite by the absorption of the new rich, the latter were very soon the dominant section in terms of number, wealth and education, and were in effect a new elite in which hereditary status was only one, and not necessarily the most significant, attribute of elite ranking.

It has long been usual to treat education as the key factor in the development of this new elite. But the starting point of an understanding of these processes of social change is the realization that the role of education in it was as complex as it was basically limited.[1] It is important to remember that secondary education in Sri Lanka was a phenomenon of the late nineteenth century, beginning in 1869–70 with the implementation of some of the recommendations of the Morgan Committee's report.[2] From 1870, the formulation and, to a lesser extent, implementation of the education policy was in the hands of the Department of Public Instruction and its administrative head. Government resources were devoted largely to the spread of vernacular education, English education being left almost entirely to the missionaries. Elementary education itself was interpreted narrowly, on the lines envisaged for England by Lowe's Revised Education Code of 1862, as something suited to the rural child whose horizon was limited to the confines of the village. In the 1880s, Charles Bruce, who drafted the Revised Education Code for the island at that time, argued that government policy should be directed at the extension of primary education to equip the village child for the 'humble career which ordinarily lies before him'. The government's interest in English education was confined to the maintenance of a few superior English schools—the Central Schools—which the Central School Commission had set up. The English and Anglo-Vernacular schools run by the government were closed down wherever there were missionary schools teaching in English in close proximity to them. The aim quite clearly was to restrict if not discourage entry to these schools. Bruce's Revised Education Code made this quite explicit. The fees charged in these English schools were high enough to serve as an effective barrier to easy entry for most of those who aspired to such an education. These English secondary schools were nevertheless given pride of place in the island's education system.

The last quarter of the nineteenth century was the heyday of denominational missionary education on the island. While the Department of Public Instruction directed schools through its codes, the missionary interests were undoubtedly the determining influence in educational expansion. The introduction of the grants-in-aid system had the effect of strengthening the influence of these interests, for, in deference to their wishes, the requirement of a conscience clause was omitted and grants were given for secular instruction, while little or nothing was done to curb the use of the educational process by missionaries for proselytization and for sectarian purposes. As in Britain after the Forster Act in 1870, the practice adopted by the Department of Public Instruction was one of supplementing the educational enterprise of religious bodies, in this instance the missionaries.

Despite these restrictive tendencies and despite the retrenchment adopted after the coffee crash in the late 1870s and early 1880s, there was sustained progress in the extension of educational facilities, and the increase in the number of schools was the largest seen since the establishment of British rule. In 1869, the last year of the School Commission, there were 140 schools with 8,751 pupils; by 1874, there were 838 schools and 1,178 in 1878, and the number of pupils increased correspondingly to 47,278 and 67,750 respectively. Nevertheless, the development was lop-sided. In terms of numbers, the increase was largely in vernacular schools. The quality of education in these schools was generally poor and the teachers were incompetent. The situation was worst in the more remote and backward areas. In 1883, for instance, two-thirds of the boys and five-sixths of the girls on the island had no education at all. As for attendance at school, the average for the island was one in thirty, but the range was from one in twenty-one in the Western Province to one in 222 in the North-central Province. In the coastal districts of the south-west, the North-western Province and the Northern Province, there was a lively interest in education.

The government and the missionaries were by no means the only school builders; wealthy philanthropists, especially the new rich, vied with each other in building schools. Most of these were established in the low country—in both Sinhalese and Tamil areas—where there was already a comprehensive and expanding network of schools run by the missionaries and the government. As a result of this pattern of growth, the low-country Sinhalese and the Tamils left the Kandyans far behind in education. The number of educated Kandyans in proportion to the Kandyan population was a fraction of the corresponding figure for the low-country Sinhalese and Tamils. It is hardly surprising that the dominance of the missionaries in the field of education should have been reflected in the disproportionate number of Christians among the elite groups. In the late nineteenth and early twentieth centuries, the Christians were well ahead of all other groups in literacy.

Despite the increase in the number of schools and pupils in the last quarter of the nineteenth century, those who had had the benefits of an English education remained very small.

Nevertheless, their importance in society was far from negligible: by the middle of the nineteenth century there was already a small group of Sri Lankan civil servants and professional men, who came to enjoy higher salaries (and earnings) and greater prestige and were accorded higher precedence in official rankings than the mudaliyārs or the Kandyan aristocracy.[3] Within this group, the Burghers were disproportionate in their large numbers but by the last quarter of the nineteenth century they had begun to lose their predominance and were in the process of being overshadowed by the Sinhalese and Tamils.

As under the traditional Sinhalese system, government service carried status, prestige and authority, and for this reason the civil service—the higher bureaucracy—as the apex of the administrative structure was the object of ambition among the educated classes. Only slightly lower in terms of the status and the prestige they conferred were the professions—law, medicine and the (church) ministry, in that order. The greatest economic and social rewards were provided by the legal profession. At first it was the traditional elite—the Sinhalese establishment— which came to dominate it. A legal career became an attractive alternative for the sons of mudaliyārs who could not be accommodated in the ranks of the lower bureaucracy. But precisely because it was the only route to the highest posts in government service (as illustrated by the careers of several scions of mudaliyār families, but more appropriately by the success of the Burgher elite in the persons of Morgan and Grenier), the monopoly enjoyed by the mudaliyār families soon ended. The children of the rising affluent men worked their way into this charmed circle. For them wealth had opened the way to better educational facilities within the island, to higher education, mainly in British universities, and professional qualifications in law at the Inns of Court. Many also obtained university education in Calcutta and Madras.

The attractions of a legal career were, no doubt, enhanced by the stringent restrictions on the employment of Sri Lankans in the higher bureaucracy. The unbending zeal with which the Ceylon Civil Service was maintained as a British and European preserve was the most persistent grievance of educated Sri

Lankans. But the colonial administration on the island, as we have seen, resisted all pressures from the Colonial Office as well as from Sri Lankans to widen opportunities for the latter in the higher bureaucracy. It could be argued that these curbs on the entry of Sri Lankans into the civil service and the pattern of economic development on the island called for very limited facilities for higher and technical education. But, more important, both the colonial administration and the traditional elite viewed the expansion of educational facilities with little sympathy. If the British government's antipathy was largely to English education and post-secondary institutions, the traditional elite's opposition was much more comprehensive in scope. Thus J.P. Obeysekere, Sinhalese representative in the Legislative Council, who belonged to the hard core of the traditional elite, was among the strongest supporters of Bruce's Revised Education Code when it came up for discussion in the Legislative Council. He castigated ignorant villagers, who, in his opinion, got into debt because of the fastidious notions of their English-educated children. And he argued forcefully for the imposition of the severest restrictions for entry to all schools, so that the children of the rural poor would be forced 'to follow such avocations as they are fitted for by nature'. Obeysekere was giving candid expression to the views of his own social group and its fear that education, by widening intellectual horizons, would stimulate processes of social change which would almost certainly undermine their own privileged position in the country. The traditional elite realized that its challengers among the new rich had an enthusiasm for education which infected the rest of society. Moreover, the anglicized lifestyle of its members became an ideal of elite behaviour and one which was easily and readily emulated. The English schools were the nurseries of the anglicization process. The curricula of the public and grammar schools of nineteenth-century England were the models for the Colombo Academy and the prestigious English schools run by the missionaries, which concentrated mainly on the academic courses which were the prerequisite for higher education and entry to the professions. Thus, while access to English education was limited, it was nevertheless an important hallmark of elite status, although by no means its sole determinant. And as in all societies, the establishment was not inclined to welcome a broadening of the basis of the elite through an increase in its numbers.

From the point of view of the traditional elite and the government, the fact that there were only limited facilities for post-secondary and vocational education within the island had at least the advantage of keeping the number of aspirants to educated elite status small enough for them to be accommodated within the existing framework without much strain. Unemployment or even underemployment among men with a university or professional training was unheard of in late nineteenth-century Sri Lanka, and as we have seen, those who aspired to a university education needed to go to Britain or to India unless they were satisfied with the less attractive but less expensive alternative of an external degree of London University. The establishment of the Medical College and the Law College (in 1870 and 1874 respectively) helped to fill the gap somewhat, but there were no technical institutes on the island till well into the twentieth century. Thus, in striking contrast to the three presidencies in British India, education was not the prime determining factor in elite formation. The acquisition of an English education had the obvious advantage not only of enhancing an individual's status and bolstering his self-confidence, but also of giving him easier access to the rulers of the day. The values inculcated by this process of education included a critical interest in political issues, even though this did not then extend to organized political activity directed against the colonial government. The homogeneity of the elite, such as it was, was based partly at least on its anglicized lifestyle, of which English education was a fundamental characteristic. The 'insatiable anxiety to attain everything that is English' did give the elite a common outlook on many matters, but the adoption of English ways and 'luxuries and refinement of living', which were previously unknown, did not cut them off completely from the local milieu.

British administrators believed that a huge gulf separated the educated few from the illiterate many; they failed to see the personal and social ties that enabled the elite to bridge it.

An elite group is, by any standard of assessment, exclusive, but—as its critics among British officialdom seldom realized—the social influence of members of this elite, by which they set so much store, depended largely on the establishment and maintenance of close personal relations between them, as members of the elite, and the people among whom they lived, and their readiness or wish to communicate their values to them. The stronger such links, the greater the influence of the elite and the greater its ability to initiate—or thwart—change and to make new ideas acceptable to the community at large. Nor was communication of values always a one-way process, from the elite to the masses. On the contrary, the elite proved just as receptive to the pressure of traditional values immanent among the people as the latter themselves. Thus an English education and an anglicized lifestyle conferred no immunity against the virus of caste prejudice endemic in the country. Indeed, the English-educated were in the forefront of the acrimonious caste disputes that broke out among the Sinhalese in the late nineteenth century. Again, the leadership of the religious revival—Buddhist, Hindu and Muslim—in the same period was largely in the hands of a section of the English-educated and the wealthy if not affluent.

ELITE FORMATION AND ECONOMIC GROWTH

One of the most potent forces in elite formation in nineteenth-century Sri Lanka was the rapid economic growth which followed upon the successful establishment and expansion of coffee culture. The plantation sector of the Sri Lankan economy was larger in relation to the traditional sector than in most tropical colonies. At every stage in the development of plantation agriculture, segments of the indigenous population participated in it. Local capitalists, as we have seen, had a share in coffee and tea, were rather better represented in rubber, and were predominant in coconut and (overwhelmingly so) in cinnamon, which survived as a minor crop. Sri Lankans obtained a far larger share in the export trade than hitherto. In short, the indigenous planters, capitalists, smallholders and peasants played a much more prominent role in plantation agriculture than did their counterparts in most tropical colonies in Asia.

Again some of the services on the plantations and specialized functions were performed almost entirely by the Sinhalese. These included the clearing of the forests for the establishment of plantations and the transport of produce from the plantations to the ports. Till the introduction of the railway, transport was very much a Sinhalese monopoly as regards both the labour and the ownership of the carts. British planters and agency houses made several efforts to bring the transport of coffee under their control and to break the hold of the Sinhalese on this enterprise, but none of their ventures so much as got off to a start. Sinhalese expertise in transport, developed through the bullock carts in the coffee era, flourished in the first half of the twentieth century in a domination of road transport—both motor buses and lorries.

Several Sinhalese families made large fortunes in the mining, processing and export of graphite in the late nineteenth century. Two other profitable fields of investment were toll rents of bridges and ferries on the main highways (these rents declined in importance after the railway was built) and, most importantly, the arrack monopoly: entrepreneurship in the arrack trade was by far the most profitable of these ventures. Urban property was greatly sought after and must have helped consolidate the economic foundations of several families. John Ferguson, a perceptive observer of the contemporary scene, was struck by the increasing prosperity of the small and influential class of Ceylonese capitalists and the conspicuous consumption in which they indulged:

> There are a considerable number of wealthy native gentlemen enriched by trade and agriculture within British times and nearby all the property in large towns as well as extensive planted areas belong to them.... In nothing is the increase of wealth among the natives more seen in the Western, Central and Southern Provinces than in the number of horses and carriages, now owned by them. Thirty or forty years ago, to see a Ceylonese own a conveyance of his own was rare indeed; now the number of Burghers, Sinhalese and Tamils driving their own carriages in the towns especially, is very remarkable.[4]

There existed neither income tax, land tax nor death duties,[5] so that fortunes could be amassed without any effective fiscal restraints. The economic base expanded, the number of Ceylonese capitalists increased and the more affluent among them were eager and aggressive aspirants to elite status. As a result, the traditional elite's primacy as the most affluent group in indigenous society was at stake. The first area of competition was landownership and in this the traditional elite was able to hold its own for a while. In the years after 1832, with the abolition of the land grant system and the introduction of the sale of wastelands by the state through a system of auctions, land became accessible to all classes in society, thus effectively removing landownership as an exclusive attribute of elite status. In the early stages, a section of the Goyigama mudaliyārs emerged as the main beneficiaries of the new system when they converted their landholdings into commercially viable plantations and kept increasing the acreages they controlled. But their dominance in this sphere was short-lived for the Karāva of Moratuva soon overtook them and they—the Goyigama—were left far behind by other Sri Lankan landowners as well, as the acquisition of land became a channel of upward social mobility for the new rich. British policy on Crown land affected all land on the island and not merely the plantations and the villages in their neighbourhood. And for Sri Lanka as a whole, during much of the second half of the nineteenth century, a greater proportion of Crown land was purchased by Sri Lankans or non-Europeans than by European planters.

Within a decade or two of the successful establishment of coffee culture, the really extensive tracts of plantations in the hands of Sri Lankans were controlled by the new rich, among whom the Karāvas were the pacesetters.[6] To a great extent the fortunes of Moratuva could be traced directly to a single family group closely related to pioneers who had established themselves in the early years of the coffee industry. By the middle of the century the de Soysas of Moratuva were clearly the most affluent Sri Lankan family and over the next few decades their fortunes continued to expand. Even the collapse of the coffee industry hardly altered them, for their investments were spread over a wide range of interests, including the liquor trade and urban property. The Revd R.S. Spence-Hardy, writing in 1864, described the development of Moratuva thus:

> The description of the place given fifty years ago, 'wretchedly poor,' is no longer applicable. A young bride married a few months ago, was dowered with a richer portion than ever princess of Ceylon carried over to any of the courts of the continent. There is scarcely an estate in the island that has not contributed to the wealth of Morotto [Moratuva].... The profits of arrack farms have been greater, but more questionable sources of revenue; and much wealth has been gained by farming tolls and ferries.[7]

It has been estimated that in the period 1877–97, the profits from the arrack trade in the hands of the Moratuva Karāvas, who dominated this trade, was as much as Rs 30 million, unequally distributed among the renters.[8] Thus by the last quarter of the nineteenth century, the Karāvas were what the Salāgamas had been in the late eighteenth and early nineteenth centuries, the most dynamic and assertive of the non-Goyigama castes, except that the affluence of the Karāva leadership was on a scale that had no parallel in the past.

Three non-Goyigama castes, the Karāva, Salāgama and Durāva, provided a disproportionate number of men whose success in plantation agriculture, trade and commerce had left them far richer than the generality of the traditional elite. Unlike the latter, they had no contempt for trade, but, on the contrary, took it up with zest. More significantly, land was to them potential plantation property, or real estate—a commodity of trade to be bought and sold dispassionately like any other. They had no sentimental attachment to paddy cultivation, which carried status but brought very little in terms of economic returns on investment. Since the most assertive and affluent segments of the new capitalist class were members of these castes, in particular the Karāva caste, elite competition also became very much a matter of caste rivalry. The Karāvas, as the most affluent of them all and the largest non-Goyigama group numerically in the low country, grew sufficiently self-confident to set out a claim for the top position in the caste hierarchy displacing the Goyigamas. This claim they supported with elaborate and fanciful theories of caste origin based on myth and distorted historical tradition. They were followed in this by the Salāgamas and others, with equally extravagant claims to pride of place in the caste hierarchy. When this happened, the Goyigamas—the traditional elite as well as the rising men of wealth and education—closed ranks to defend their long-accepted status as the most 'honourable' of the castes (just as paddy cultivation was the most 'honourable' vocation) and their position at the apex of the caste structure.

In the last quarter of the century, the Goyigama elite received unexpected support from the colonial administration in Sri Lanka in the person of Governor Gordon. Although the latter was primarily interested in buttressing the traditional elite, he was not averse to extending this assistance on a caste basis to Goyigamas of all categories whenever they were challenged by competitors from other castes. This policy was continued by his successors, over the next two decades at least. One result of this, it must be emphasized, was the reassertion of caste as an element in elite status, but this succeeded only in preventing the elimination of the traditional elite in the administrative structure, particularly in its lower rungs. Its displacement in terms of wealth and education could not be checked by gubernatorial fiat. It was impossible to rebut a claim to elite status earned by wealth or education (or a combination of these) even when it was not based on caste privilege and hereditary position. Among the traditional elite, it was the Kandyan group whose displacement was almost total. They were far behind in education, and very few extended their modest landholdings substantially or converted them into plantations. Traditional agriculture was their forte, but there were no fortunes to be made in it and the returns on investment in this sphere were meagre. To a greater extent than the mudaliyārs of the low country, the Kandyan elite hankered after headmen's posts and the trappings of the past. Gregory did them more harm than good by bringing them in from the cold and into a junior partnership in the colonial administration, for in the long run this proved a dead end. Kandyan representation within the capitalist class was miniscule if not non-existent.

The fact that the colonial administration threw the weight of its influence into helping the traditional elite, in what appeared to be an unequal battle with more resourceful newcomers, did not put an end to caste-based elite competition in public life, but served to intensify this competition as the Karāvas campaigned to gain a position in public life commensurate with their remarkable, if new-found, affluence. There was still competition in education, philanthropy, for mudaliyārships (the title of mudaliyār divorced from the traditional system was used as an official 'honour' for other groups as well), for places in the higher bureaucracy as well as for all posts in government service. But the struggle was keenest in the periodic campaigns to catch the governor's eye for nomination to the Legislative Council. By the 1890s, on each occasion when the Sinhalese seat was vacant, the Karāvas would organize public campaigns to get their candidate nominated, but to no avail.

Thus by the end of the nineteenth century, the elite had expanded in numbers, but while still quite heterogeneous, neither the common outlook nurtured by an English education nor its anglicized lifestyle gave it much more than a superficial cohesion. Nevertheless, whatever their origins, once members of the elite had consolidated their fortunes as such, they became members of a single class, an elite representative of, but not synonymous with, the capitalist class. This class situation, much more than education or an anglicized lifestyle, provided for a degree of homogeneity in the elite. But the community of interest engendered by class was shattered by the divisive effects of caste loyalties. In the next chapter, another point of conflict, though not such an intense or deep-rooted one at this time as caste, will be discussed—namely religion. One divisive force had not yet emerged—ethnicity—and there were few signs of it. Elite conflict on a caste basis absorbed energies which might have been more profitably engaged in political organization and political activity on a national level.

Religion and the Rise of Nationalism, c. 1870–1900

By the last quarter of the nineteenth century, the long history of Kandyan resistance had come to an end. It was now the turn of the maritime regions, in particular the Western Province, where the resistance of the indigenous society to the impact of British rule took the form of religious revival, formation of political associations and incipient trade union activity. Together, these constituted a process of holding off the intrusive pressures of British rule and of accommodating change and absorbing it in forms seldom anticipated by those who initiated it in the first place. Above all, it was a complex and sophisticated response to Western rule which formed a half-way house between the traditionalist nationalism of the Kandyans and the ideologically coherent nationalism of the twentieth century. These 'secondary' resistance movements developed into a force of no little political significance. But they had no support from the Kandyans who, between the 1880s and the attainment of independence, mostly took satisfaction in a new role, that of associates of the British and a counterweight to the reform and nationalist movements dominated by elite groups from the maritime provinces. The leaders of Kandyan opinion seldom showed much sympathy for the political aspirations of these movements. They stood aloof and suspicious when not positively hostile. Nevertheless, the memory of Kandyan resistance and of the Kandyan kingdom, as the last independent Sinhalese kingdom, persisted in providing some inspiration for the more forward-looking 'reformers' and for those among the latter who came to form the nucleus of a genuine 'nationalist' movement.

It was in the form of a revival of Buddhism and a rejection of the efforts of missionary organizations to convert people to

Christianity that the secondary resistance movement manifested itself as its first and, in retrospect, most profoundly effective expression. Initially, the response of the people to evangelization had been one of polite indifference. By the late 1840s, there were signs that a more marked resistance to it was emerging— sporadic and localized, but resistance nevertheless. This resistance was originally more pronounced in the Kandyan region, where the missionaries had, in fact, made little headway. There the people demonstrated a more positive commitment to the traditional faith and the 'rebellion' of 1848 had its religious overtones to the extent that some of the rebel leaders articulated the resentment of the Kandyans at attempts by the British to abrogate their undertaking to maintain the traditional link between Buddhism and the state. More important, resistance to the spread of Christianity was discernible in the south-west, from the vicinity of Colombo to Kalutara and beyond, in regions that had not been affected by the 'rebellion'. The leadership in opposition to evangelization came largely from bhikkhus. Whether this resistance was systematically organized and how widespread it was are matters on which there is no firm evidence, but there was a perceptible change in the people's attitude to missionary enterprise from courteous indifference to positive though still somewhat muted opposition. There was now a more explicit commitment to their traditional faith.[1] Certainly, the indigenous religions, particularly Buddhism, had not declined to the point of becoming moribund, as some of the more sanguine prognostications of the missionaries and effusively hopeful Sinhalese Christians of the 1850s and 1860s would have had us believe; the more intelligent and realistic of the missionaries neither shared this belief nor underestimated the very real strength of the resistance to the missions.

By the 1860s, the Buddhists' opposition to Christianity was much more self-confident and vocal than it had been before and nothing illustrated the change in mood and tempo better than their response to challenges from missionaries to public debates—verbal confrontations, in which the tenets of Buddhism and Christianity were critically examined with a view to demonstrating the superiority of Christianity to the audience gathered for the occasion. Such disputations had been staged from the mid-1840s and in general the missionaries had used their debating skills to the obvious discomfiture of some diffident and not very erudite representatives of the traditional religions. In the 1860s, the technique of public debate, which the missionaries had used so effectively in the past, only succeeded in providing Buddhist spokesmen with a platform for a vigorous reassertion of the virtues of their own faith. Between 1865 and 1873, there were five debates between Christians and Buddhists and on every occasion the Buddhists faced up to their opponents with a verve and assurance that had seldom been evident before.[2] The Panadura debate of 1873 was the most notable of them all; there the Revd Migettuvatte Gunananda proved himself a debater of a very high order, mettlesome, witty and eloquent if not especially erudite. The emotions generated by this debate and the impact of Migettuvatte Gunananda's personality deeply affected the next generation of Buddhist activists. A contemporary described him as 'the terror of the missionaries...more wrangler than ascetic... the boldest, most brilliant and most powerful champion of Sinhalese Buddhism...the leader of the present revival'.[3]

Migettuvatte Gunananda's triumph at Panadura set the seal on a decade of quiet recovery of Buddhist confidence. In retrospect, the establishment of the 'Society for the Propagation of Buddhism' at Kotahena and of the Lankopakara Press at Galle (both in 1862) would seem to mark the first phase in this recovery. There was at the same time a parallel development, which, while independent of the theme of Buddhist–Christian confrontation, nevertheless contributed greatly to sustaining the self-assurance of Buddhists. This was the establishment in 1865 of the Ramanna Nikāya, an offshoot of the Amarapura Nikāya, and the foundation of the two centres of Oriental learning: the Vidyodaya Piriveṇa in 1872 and the Vidyalankara Piriveṇa in 1876. The Ramanna Nikāya laid even greater stress than the Amarapura on vows of poverty aṛd humility; its establishment was, in fact, a conscious attempt to cleanse the sangha and to return to a purer form of Buddhism free from the influence of Hinduism.

Newspaper reports of the Panadura debate reached the United States of America, where they attracted the attention of Colonel H.S. Olcott, the founder (in 1875) of the Theosophical Society. Olcott began a regular correspondence with Migettuvatte Gunananda and sent him a mass of pamphlets and tracts, all deeply critical of Christianity. Gunananda in turn translated these letters, as well as extracts from books, pamphlets and tracts into Sinhalese and distributed them throughout the island. Through these translations the names of Olcott and his Russian associate Madame Blavatsky became familiar to Buddhists. Their arrival on the island in 1880 caused great excitement and they were received amid extraordinary scenes of religious fervour. By this time the Buddhist revival was well under way. Because of their familiarity with the rationalist and scientific critique of Christianity, the Theosophists gave a more positive intellectual content to the movement against the Christian forces in Sri Lanka. Above all, they gave the Buddhists what they lacked most—a lesson in the techniques of modern organization to match the expertise of the missionaries in this sphere. In doing so they contributed enormously to the self-confidence and morale of the Buddhists. With the help of leading bhikkhus and laymen, Olcott started the Buddhist education movement. An education fund and Buddhist national fund (which were later, and significantly, merged into one) were established; the celebration of the *Vesak* festival (commemorating the birth, attainment of enlightenment and death of the Buddha) was revived and an agitation was begun (from 1881) to have Vesak Day declared an official holiday. He was also instrumental in the design and adoption (in 1885) of a distinctive Buddhist flag.[4]

The presence in Sri Lanka of a group of westerners openly championing Buddhism had a deeply significant psychological effect on the Buddhist movement. It was not force alone but the acceptance of the total superiority of European culture that held the non-European in awe and psychological subjection to western rule—and the prestigious position of Christianity was an aspect of this. For the Buddhist movement of this period, reliance on the 'charisma' of a westerner counterbalanced the limited vision and diffidence of the indigenous leadership of the day.

DISESTABLISHMENT OF THE ANGLICAN CHURCH

The missionary campaign of the 1840s for the dissociation of the state from Buddhism had attracted support from quarters which would normally have been repelled by the bigotry and intolerance demonstrated in it because it could be viewed as an aspect of a wider struggle for the principle of separation of church and state. Those who cherished this principle as an integral part of the liberal ideology gave the missionaries a degree of guarded support in their campaign.[5]

However, the liberal insistence on the separation of church and state was a double-edged weapon. If it could be used against the association of the state with Buddhism, it could also be directed against a similar connection with other religious organizations. Among the first to feel its keen edge was the Anglican establishment. In the eyes of the colonial government, the Christian missions on the island were equal and the Anglicans possessed no special privileges. The Colonial Office also let it be understood without actually making an explicit statement of policy, that it would not defend Anglican privileges in the colony and that the position of the Anglican establishment in Sri Lanka was in no way analogous to that of the parent body in England. By the 1850s, the one privilege which the Anglicans continued to possess, despite occasional but increasingly vociferous protests, was their connection with the state. However, neither the Colonial Office nor the Ceylon government would attempt the disestablishment of the local Anglican Church, although it was clearly the logical consequence of their own policies and even though influential voices urged that this next step be taken.

Over the next two decades, the defence of Anglican privileges became steadily more difficult and resentment of an established church grew increasingly vocal, especially because Anglicans, although powerful and influential, were nevertheless a tiny minority of the population. The expenditure of state funds on the Anglican establishment could not be justified either on the basis of the size of its flock (they were too few in number) or equity (they were generally among the richest and most powerful in the land). Besides, by the 1870s, the Anglican Church had been disestablished in many of the West Indian colonies. Gregory lent his gubernatorial support to the campaign for disestablishment in the years 1876–77. But his impetuosity and tactlessness nullified his efforts and it was left to Sir James Longden to effect the disestablishment in 1881, by which time even the Anglicans seemed to have realized the futility of resisting it. Bishop R. S. Copleston on their behalf did not 'on principle' oppose the withdrawal of subsidies, but only urged that it be done gradually. This dignified acceptance of a painful decision was in strong contrast to the truculence with which Anglicans, particularly high churchmen, were inclined to defend the Anglican position in the 1840s.

With the withdrawal of ecclesiastical subsidies in 1881, the separation of church and state was very nearly complete. But it soon became clear that a total separation could not be made, if for no more pressing reason than the fact that the revival of Buddhism in the late nineteenth century brought with it a persistent demand for state assistance in the maintenance and supervision of Buddhist temporalities.

THE BUDDHIST REVIVAL

The Buddhist revival of the second half of the nineteenth century was the first phase in the recovery of national pride on the island, the first step in the long process which culminated in the growth of nationalism in the twentieth century. Its massive and historic achievement becomes all the more astounding in the context of the limitations, most of them in a sense self-inflicted, within which it operated. The first of these was that the Buddhist revival of the late nineteenth century was basically a low-country (Western Province and Southern Province) movement. It had little influence and made little impression on the Buddhism of the Kandyan areas, which were under the tutelage of the Malvatta and Asgiriya chapters of the Siyam Nikāya. At issue was the wealth of the prestigious Kandyan viharas and dēvālēs, with the low country activists urging that some of these revenues be used for the establishment of schools.[6] Second, the leadership of the movement was largely in the hands of laymen—wealthy entrepreneurs and traders and men of property of average means generally, many if not most of whom were members of the Karāva, Salāgama and Durāva castes. Indeed the Buddhist movement was, in part at least, the religious expression of the improved economic and social status of the major non-Goyigama castes of the maritime districts.[7] Third, as regards participation by the sangha, support came from the Amarapura Nikāya rather than the Siyam Nikāya. Even in the low-country areas, the powerful Siyam Nikāya was inclined to stay aloof from this religious revival partly because of its mistrust of the enthusiasm of the Amarapura Nikāya. This brings us to the fourth limitation, the sectarianism of the sangha: all attempts to bring the rival Nikāyas together proved futile.

Two factors worked to the advantage of the Buddhist movement. The first of these was a change in the attitude of the government towards Buddhism which began with Gregory displaying an active interest in Buddhism and Oriental learning. This new conciliatory attitude also had a political motive: because the Buddhist movement did not formulate any precise demands on constitutional or administrative reform—the two main points of interest in the incipient formal political activity of the day—men like Gregory and Gordon felt they could accommodate its objectives insofar as those involved the government and its attitude to religious issues. They believed they could guide the movement into serving as a buttress for the traditional society in the transformation that was taking place, that in the Sri Lanka context religious—Buddhist—revival. could be the precursor of a national resurgence.

Whatever the motive there was no mistaking the advantage to the Buddhist movement. The first breakthrough came over establishing the crucial principle of the state's neutrality in religion. It came, seemingly, with studied deliberation, and moved from one precedent to another. First, there was a symbolic gesture: a contribution from the state for the repair of the Ruvanveli Dāgāba at Anuradhapura; this was followed by the gift of two lamps to the Daladā Maligāva. These appeared to demonstrate more than a courteous regard for Buddhism, for Gregory was, at the same time, actively engaged in the attempt to disestablish the Anglican Church, which gave credibility to the principle he was seeking to establish—the state's neutrality in religion. This principle Gordon underscored even though he balked at the idea of a formal declaration making explicit the state's neutrality in religious affairs, a declaration which, he felt, carried the insidious implication that the government had been partisan in the past. More important, it would stultify the other related principle in which Gordon believed, namely, that the state had a special obligation towards Buddhism. With this the breakthrough was consolidated. Gordon warmly concurred in Olcott's opinion that the British government had too hastily severed the state's association with Buddhism. He eagerly accepted Olcott's proposal that Vesak Day should be made a public holiday. It was on the basis of this principle of a special obligation towards Buddhism that Gordon endorsed the view that the state should interest itself in taking in hand the problem of Buddhist temporalities.

The second factor which worked to the advantage of the Buddhist movement was what happened on Easter Day 1883, although it is doubtful if Buddhist activists of the period would have regarded it as such. But its effect—as a review of the events of that day will show—was to give a powerful boost to the Buddhist revival. If these events helped to concentrate the minds of officials powerfully on the Buddhist revival, their aftermath was even more important—they led to a revitalization of the organizational structure of the Buddhist movement and a clearer definition of its objectives. Above all, they formed the background against which Gordon's reappraisal of government policy on Buddhism was effected.

On Easter Sunday 1883[8] came the first outbreak of physical violence directed against the Buddhist movement—the Kotahena riots. Kotahena, a suburb of Colombo, had for long been a Roman Catholic stronghold, but it had also become the scene of considerable Buddhist activity after Migettuvatte Gunananda took charge of the vihara there. The riots were precipitated by a *pinkama* (religious ceremony) organized by Migettuvatte Gunananda on a scale of unusual significance in honour of the completion of a large reclining figure of the

Buddha, as well as of other important additions and embellishments. Because of the proximity of the vihara to the Roman Catholic cathedral, 'the anger and jealousy of the Roman Catholics was gradually aroused by the long continuance of the festival, extending as it did to Easter week'.

The government's response to these events exasperated the Buddhist activists. A number of Roman Catholics were arrested on charges of complicity in the riots, but when it was realized that the evidence available was too unreliable to sustain a conviction in the courts they were released. Governor Longden appointed a commission of enquiry into the incident but its report was unsatisfactory to the Buddhists, for although it held that the Roman Catholics had indeed attacked the Buddhists, Gunananda's fiery speeches and 'the fervour with which the Buddhists were conducting their activities' were described as factors that had contributed to provoking the riots. Worse still, one result of these events was that government sought to place restrictions on all religious processions. This was especially hard on the Buddhists for whom *peraheras* and pinkamas accompanied by music were an essential feature of religious practice.

The Buddhists now set their sights on an official inquiry, to be conducted under the aegis of the Colonial Office. Olcott and Madame Blavatsky returned to the island on a second visit at the special invitation of the Buddhists to help organize the presentation of their case before Whitehall. Olcott arrived on 27 January 1884 and the following day a Buddhist Defence Committee was formed. It was decided that Olcott should make representations on behalf of the Ceylon Buddhists at the Colonial Office. But Olcott's visit to the Colonial Office accomplished very little in the way of redressing Buddhist grievances over the riots, although it was fruitful in other ways.

When Olcott returned to the island in 1886 (accompanied on this occasion by G.W. Leadbeater), he came to organize support for the cause of Buddhist education and to augment the financial resources of the Buddhist educational fund. The energies of the Buddhist movement were now diverted to a sustained effort to build up a network of schools. Education at this time was a minefield of administrative regulations devised to protect vested interests—mainly those of the Protestant missions—and the Buddhists could expect no consistent support from government officials in overcoming these obstacles (the neutrality of the state did not guarantee the neutrality of its officials). The first and most efficacious challenge to the superiority of the Protestant missions in the field of education came from the Roman Catholics under the leadership of Monsignor C.A. Bonjean. If the Roman Catholics found the administrative regulations governing the registration of schools irksome but not insuperable obstacles, Buddhists could justifiably complain that they were a positive hindrance to the progress of their educational activities. The result was that education, without quite ceasing to be the battleground of rival Christian groups, became one of the focal points of the growing 'nationalist' opposition to the missions. Indeed, the revival of the indigenous religions—and of Roman Catholicism—was inextricably bound up with the expansion of their own educational programmes. Apart from obstruction from officials and missionaries, the most formidable obstacles that Buddhist activists in the field of education had to contend with were the paucity of financial resources, skilled administrators and teachers and, above all, the apathy of the vast mass of Buddhists. By organizing a series of lecture tours throughout the country Olcott aroused genuine enthusiasm among the people for the establishment of a network of schools, but it was difficult to sustain this enthusiasm for long or to channel it to some constructive purpose without a more permanent administrative structure. This was provided largely by the Theosophical Society. By 1890, the society had established forty Buddhist schools, the efficient running of which, if not their continued existence, was due to the administrative skills and leadership of men like Leadbeater, A.R. Buultjens and Bowles Daly, the manager of Buddhist schools, and the financial support of a group of Sinhalese philanthropists.

The work of the pioneer Buddhist educationists proved to be more comprehensively performed than had previously seemed possible. The schools they left to their successors in the early twentieth century fulfilled an important historic function by breaking the monopoly of the Christian missions in the sphere of education. This by itself was no mean achievement, but, more important, the schools built up an enviable tradition and record of service. Their alumni made their influence felt in the twentieth century in politics and education, helping to quicken the pace of political agitation, generating more enlightened attitudes in social and economic issues and engendering a pride in Buddhism, the Sinhala language and the cultural heritage associated with these.

BUDDHIST TEMPORALITIES

Of the issues which agitated the Buddhists at this time none was more complex than the vexed one of temple lands— Buddhist temporalities. In the aftermath of the Kotahena riots, the government's attention was drawn to this issue and once more Gordon, reviving an initiative attempted by Gregory, broke through a barrier of bureaucratic inertia and missionary opposition to give the Buddhists some satisfaction with regard to a long-standing grievance. But first the background needs to be briefly sketched.[9] The crux of the problem lay in the government's failure to live up to the promise held out in 1852—as the price of the severance of the state's link with Buddhism—that some administrative machinery would be devised for the protection of Buddhist temporalities. In 1856, Ward had made a start by introducing legislation for the registration of temple lands. A commission was appointed to examine claims to land made by temples and to register those regarded as well founded. But registration of temple lands was only one feature (though an essential one) of the intricate problem of the administration of Buddhist temporalities. Although Ward had intended to legislate on other aspects of the question, nothing was done during his administration and its consideration was laid aside for twenty years until it was taken up again in the time of Gregory.

Buddhist activists were appalled by the steady deterioration in the condition of these temporalities brought about by a mixture of inefficiency in administration and corrupt diversion of revenue to the pockets of those entrusted with the control

438 of these properties. There were insistent demands for state

of these properties. There were insistent demands for state intervention as the only possible remedy for this relentlessly worsening situation, but missionary organizations made clever use of the prevailing sentiment in favour of cutting all links between the state and religious establishments to stop the government from considering any such move. The difficulties were compounded by the fact that charges of maladministration and peculation came largely from Buddhist activists of the low-country regions, where temples seldom had any extensive estates or wealth to administer. Those who controlled the wealthy Kandyan viharas and dēvālēs had a vested interest in the maintenance of the status quo and there were no complaints from them. On the contrary, they were perturbed by the proposals made by Buddhist activists that some of the revenues of these temples should be used to establish Buddhist schools. (This demand had a parallel in the 1840s, when missionaries and some influential officials had urged that part of the revenues of the viharas and dēvālēs should be used to support schools run by the missionaries.)

Not surprisingly, Ward's successors were reluctant to intervene in this question. There was, above all, a fear of rousing the opposition of the missionaries. However, Gregory was willing to grasp the nettle. He prepared an ordinance for the purpose of establishing an administrative machinery for the control of Buddhist temporalities, but the Colonial Office objected to some of its features, especially the provision allowing the use of any surplus revenues, left over after the costs of maintaining the temples had been met, for purposes related to Buddhist educational programmes. This the Colonial Office termed an 'arbitrary transfer' of temple endowment income for educational purposes and refused to approve the ordinance. Gregory's successor, Longden, shared this outlook. Indeed he was convinced that the government should confine itself to the establishment of an organization for the control of Buddhist temporalities and merely frame such laws and regulations as would enable the Buddhists themselves to check the evils that existed in the administration of those temporalities. Again, while he acknowledged the obligation to legislate for the maintenance of Buddhist endowments in the Kandyan region, he was opposed to extending the same principle to cover the lowlands where there was no such treaty obligation. Above all else, Longden was inhibited by the fear that intervention in these matters would be tantamount to official recognition of a continued connection with Buddhism. For the man who carried through the 'disestablishment' of the Anglican Church on the island, this was an overwhelmingly important consideration. Nevertheless, he did prepare legislation for the better administration of Buddhist temporalities, but it was not introduced in the Legislative Council.

Gordon, as Longden's successor, preferred to make a fresh start. For Longden, legislation on Buddhist temporalities was a somewhat disagreeable concession to agitation, whereas Gordon viewed it as a matter of conscience and as the fulfilment of an obligation which the British government owed to the Buddhists of the island, who constituted over two-thirds of the population. He took care, however, not to be diverted, as Gregory had been, to legislating for the use of revenues from temple endowments for education. The solution he outlined in 1888 was an ordinance of considerable complexity: the control of Buddhist temporalities in each district was transferred to a committee of Buddhist laymen, elected by the bhikkhus and by their own number in a particular area; the committee was in turn to elect the trustees of viharas and dēvālēs within its own area of authority. These district committees came under the supervision of larger provincial committees, with the further check of a strict audit of accounts under the direction of the courts. There was considerable opposition to this bill both within and outside the Legislative Council, but Gordon steered it through to Colonial Office approval in 1889, though not without some concessions to his critics.

The ordinance of 1889 was important because of the principles it embodied rather than for any impact it had on the problems it was devised to remedy. It proved too complicated and cumbersome in its working and it did not eliminate or for that matter even significantly reduce corruption and peculation among the trustees of these temporalities, especially in the Kandyan provinces. The Buddhist movement regarded this state of affairs as an intolerable scandal, a blot on the reputation of Buddhists in general and continued the agitation for stronger measures to eradicate it. In response to this pressure and in recognition of the validity of the charges levelled by Buddhist activists, the colonial government in the early years of the twentieth century took a careful look at Gordon's legislative enactment and decided that it should be replaced by a fresh bill, 'to prevent more effectively than in the past misappropriation of trust property'. Ordinance 8 of 1905 was introduced to consolidate and amend the law relating to Buddhist temporalities and was brought into operation in February 1907. The ineffectual provincial committees were abolished and the powers of the district committees were enlarged and strengthened. They were entrusted with the appointment and disciplinary control of trustees of viharas and basnayaka nilamēs of dēvālēs. These district committees too were elected bodies like those established under Gordon's ordinance.

By this time, however, the Buddhist movement was pitching its demands higher. What it wanted was that the state should assume direct responsibility for the administration of Buddhist temporalities. But the British government was reluctant to go so far.

RELIGION AND NATIONALISM

By the turn of the century the Buddhist movement had gained great self-confidence. Its leaders turned their attention to what was regarded as one of the great social evils of the day, and one associated with the process of westernization—intemperance. To the Buddhists the drawing, distilling and sale of arrack and toddy—in short, the use of spirituous liquors—was contrary to the precepts of their religion and the traditional usages of Sinhalese society. Nevertheless, the manufacture and distribution of arrack and toddy were controlled by Sinhalese capitalists, many if not most of whom were Karāva Christians, although there were also Buddhists of the same and other castes who had large investments in the liquor industry. To the British government excise duties were a legitimate source of state revenue, and while there was an increasing awareness of the evils attendant on excessive alcohol consumption, there was a reluctance to endanger a valuable source of revenue by the wholehearted pursuit of temperance objectives. The Buddhist movement, on the other hand, had no such inhibitions, and by the turn of the century temperance activity was a vitally important facet of the religious revival. Some of the money that went into the support of temperance agitation came from wealth amassed in the liquor trade, conscience money from Buddhists who thus repudiated a lucrative source of income—there were many prominent Buddhists in this category—or, as was more often the case, from those who had inherited fortunes wholly or partly based on the arrack trade.

By the first decade of the twentieth century, temperance agitation had spread far and wide especially in the Sinhalese areas of the Western Province and the Southern Province, and the response it evoked had sufficient passionate zeal in it to sustain the hope that it had potential for development into a political movement.[10] On occasions, temperance agitators indulged in criticism of the government by associating it with the evils of intemperance and diatribes against foreign vices and Christian values were cleverly scaled down into more restrained and subtle criticisms of a 'Christian' government. But while the temperance agitation gave added momentum to the Buddhist movement it afforded only a tentative and astutely restrained introduction to formal political activity. It is significant that no attempt was made to channel the mass emotion it generated into a sustained and organized political movement. The politicization of the movement, once its appeal to the people became evident, seemed the logical and inevitable next step, but this was never taken. Equally significant was the fact that the mass grass-roots support which the temperance agitation generated was achieved without the assistance, much less the association, of such political organizations as existed.

The colonial authorities on the island instinctively got their priorities right. They either ignored these political organizations, or where their aspirations were regarded as an affront or a mild threat to the British position on the island, they were treated with studied contempt. But many British administrators in Sri Lanka were perturbed from the beginning by temperance agitation and they viewed the proliferation of temperance societies with the utmost suspicion, in recognition of the fact that the Buddhist revival and the temperance movement had generated a feeling of hostility to the colonial regime which could, potentially, disturb the hitherto placid political life of the island. Christian missionaries had come to much the same conclusion. 'The political consciousness', they declared in 1919, 'is almost inevitably anti-British and pro-Hindu [in India], and in Ceylon pro-Buddhist.... The anti-British feeling becomes anti-Christian feeling: the pro-Hindu or pro-Buddhist feeling develops into a determination to uphold all that passes under the name of Hinduism or Buddhism...'.[11] With specific reference to the situation on the island the missionaries noted that 'one of the most serious aspects of the Buddhist revival is the attempt to identify Buddhism with patriotism, and to urge upon people that loyalty to the country implies loyalty to the religion... [The Buddhist revival] is hostile to Christianity, representing it as alien, and Buddhism as national and patriotic...'.[12]

The recovery of Hinduism in nineteenth-century Sri Lanka predated that of Buddhism by a whole generation. The Hindus were in a more advantageous position in relation to resistance to the intrusion of the Christian missions: it was possible to draw on the tremendous resources of Hinduism in India. And the Tamil elite, despite their eager acceptance of English education, eschewed the anglicized lifestyle which their Sinhalese counterparts of similar educational attainments adopted so enthusiastically. Hindu customs and culture permeated Tamil society and were kept alive in the face of the encroachments of Christianity and anglicization. Nevertheless, in the first half-century of British rule on the island—and for that matter even later—the missionary societies were much stronger in Jaffna and its environs than in most other parts of the island and their network of schools was run far more efficiently.

The Hindu recovery of the nineteenth century was dominated by a single personality, the remarkable Arumuga

Navalar, a man of enormous erudition and massive energy who left an indelible mark on the Hinduism of the indigenous Tamils of Sri Lanka.[13] Its strength as well as its flaws flow from his pioneering work, especially from his greatest contribution—the systematic compilation of an authoritative restatement of Saivite doctrine. The basis of his success as a religious reformer was his profound knowledge of the classical Tamil texts. The publication of his critical editions of these texts enabled Hinduism in northern and eastern Sri Lanka to meet and repel the pressures of Protestant Christianity. Through these texts his influence spread across the Palk Straits to south India as well. He had worked for well over a decade with Christian missionaries and although never a convert to Christianity, he had helped to translate the Bible into Tamil. From his association with the missionaries he absorbed much of their skill in organization and in the propagation of their faith. He used these to great effect in the resistance to Christian encroachment. For the first and by no means the last time in the Sri Lankan context the missionaries found that the techniques of proselytization which they had developed could be used with equal facility by their critics and opponents.

Navalar demonstrated the value of schools and education as instruments of religious recovery. In 1849–50, long before the first Buddhist schools were started, he founded the Vannarponnai Saiva Pragasa Vidyasalai. He was intent on establishing Saivite schools in every village in which education would be imparted in a Hindu environment with the aid of school textbooks specially prepared for the purpose. At the same time he was not unmindful of the value of an English education and the Saivangala Vidyasalai, which he launched in 1872, was later to become the Jaffna Hindu College, the premier Hindu English school on the island.

This emphasis on education, for all its importance, would have been no more than the stock response of a conservative mind to the challenge of a dynamic alien religion had Navalar's activities not gone well beyond this. He was a protean figure, a man of amazing versatility whose achievement in any one of the fields in which he performed so creatively would have placed him in the first rank among the unusual talents of his time. But he excelled in a number of fields. In 1849, he established a printing press at Vannarponnai and from this there poured forth a succession of tracts and pamphlets expounding Hindu doctrines and defending them against the strictures of the missionaries in lucid Tamil prose designed to be understood by the common people. This was a remarkable departure from convention for a man as steeped in the Tamil classics as he was, yet Navalar the pamphleteer and propagandist was also a great figure in modern Tamil literature both in Sri Lanka and in south India. At the same time, he was equally gifted in the art of platform speaking; here he modelled himself on the missionaries with their open-air lectures delivered in simple language. His lectures on Hinduism delivered on Fridays at the assembly hall of the Siva Temple at Vannarponnai attracted huge crowds. One other facet of Navalar's achievement deserves mention: his initiative in the formation of secular organizations devoted to the propagation of Hindu ideals—most notably the Saiva Pragasa Sabhai, which he established in 1853. He was instrumental also in the formation in 1888 of the Saiva Paripala Sabhai which, along with the Hindu College Board of Management, eventually came to control more than 150 schools, both primary and secondary.

If the positive achievements of the Hindu revival of the nineteenth century owed so much to Navalar's influence, so unfortunately did its shortcomings. Navalar was no social reformer; the Hindu revivalist movement strengthened orthodoxy and did little to soften the rigours of the caste system among the Tamils. The latter had much less flexibility than the Sinhalese counterpart, because caste distinctions among the Tamils had as their basis the religious sanction of the Hindu religion, which made them all the more rigid as a result. The consequence was that the hierarchical dominance of the Vellālas (the Tamil counterpart of the Goyigama), who also held a commanding numerical superiority over other Tamil castes, was never effectively challenged by those other castes. As it turned out, the Vellāla proved to be the main beneficiary of the new opportunities opened up by the British. The Vellālas used the sanctions of Saivite orthodoxy to maintain their caste privileges at the expense of those in the lower rungs of the caste hierarchy. Untouchability, which was almost non-existent among the Sinhalese, was and still is very much a problem in Hindu society in Jaffna. Temple entry was forbidden to some castes, the most conspicuous act of religious discrimination in Hindu society.

The recovery of Islam forms an interesting parallel development to that of Hinduism, which it followed a generation later.[14] The Muslims of Sri Lanka had been notable for their refusal to succumb to the blandishments of Christianity. The resistance to conversion had persisted throughout the nineteenth century, but the survival of Islam in Sri Lanka had, in a sense, been secured at the expense of the social and economic advancement of the Muslims. Since the education provided in the schools was primarily English, there was among the Muslims an attitude (natural to a conservative and cohesive community) tending to reject it because of the presumed danger of the impact on Islam of a foreign culture. Besides, education was not only in English but was also largely Christian in content, and for that reason many Muslims were prepared to sacrifice the material benefits of an English education because it supposedly endangered the faith of their children. This manifestation of zeal for their ancestral faith had some regrettable consequences, and by the third quarter of the nineteenth century the more enlightened Muslim leaders were profoundly disturbed to find their community sunk in ignorance and apathy, parochial in outlook and grossly materialistic.

The arresting of the decline in vitality of the Muslim community has long been associated with the 'charisma' of Arabi Pasha (Ahmed Arabi),[15] who is believed to have jolted it out of its conservative seclusion. Much more important, however, were the foresight and tactical skill of a local Muslim leader, M.C. Siddi Lebbe, a lawyer by profession and a social worker by inclination, who helped to bring his community to accept the need for a change of outlook. Like Arumuga Navalar, Siddi Lebbe saw the supreme importance of education as a means for the regeneration of his community. The revitalizing process initiated during this phase continued during the first half of the twentieth century. Despite the apathy of his co-religionists, he persisted in his campaigns for educational progress and prevailed upon Arabi Pasha to use his influence and prestige in the cause of Muslim education. The latter spent the rest of his days in Sri Lanka (even after Siddi Lebbe's death in 1898) in the cause of English education for the Muslims and in the advocacy and initiation of reforms in religious practice. Siddi Lebbe for his part established and organized the Muslim Educational Society, which endeavoured to create an elite, educated on modern lines, that would provide the leadership which the Muslims so badly needed.

Men like Siddi Lebbe faced tasks which were in every way more formidable than those which confronted Arumuga Navalar, but they adopted methods remarkably similar to those of Navalar—the establishment of schools and the improvisation of techniques of popular education for the community as a whole. One method adopted was the establishment of a Tamil language[16] newspaper *Muslim Naisen,* which appeared from 1882 to 1887. Through this newspaper he campaigned for the abandonment of customs which, though not inherently connected with Islam, were yet intimately associated in the minds of the people with their faith; and against the parochial outlook of his co-religionists. One of the most noteworthy aspects of his popular teaching was his emphasis on the worldwide interests of the Muslims and every development in the Muslim world found its way to the pages of this newspaper.

Although the stirrings in these indigenous religions had much in common with the processes of Buddhist resurgence, there were features in them which set them apart from the Buddhist experience. While the Islamic revival benefited greatly from the presence on the island of the charismatic figure of Arabi Pasha, the Hindu recovery was much more self-reliant and self-sufficient than the recovery of either Buddhism or Islam. Much more important was the fact that neither the Hindu nor the Islamic revival in Sri Lanka developed any political overtones in the sense of a potential anti-British or anti-imperialist attitude. There was an obvious contrast to the Buddhist recovery, which was never wholly without political overtones. Before the end of the century there were men who saw the possibilities of exploiting (Buddhist) religious sentiment for political purposes.

Politics and Constitutional Reform in the Late Nineteenth Century

In striking contrast to the vigorous resistance offered by the Buddhist movement to the encroachments of Christianity in the last quarter of the nineteenth century, the island's formal politics lacked any sense of purpose and animation. The present chapter and the next will review the characteristic features of the politics of this phase in the country's history and seek to analyse the causes of its tepidity. It is necessary first, however, to look briefly at the Legislative Council[1] in the second half of the nineteenth century, since it was the focal point of political activity.

From its inception in 1833, there were two conflicting points of view on the essential purposes of the Ceylon Legislative Council. The Colonial Office looked upon it as a check on the governor, in the sense that it was an independent and fairly reliable source of information on the affairs of the colony to the Secretary of State, who would otherwise have been dependent for this on the governor alone; thus it served as a means of making Whitehall's control over the colonial administration more effective. This indeed was what Colebrooke himself had in mind, but not what the Legislative Council was content to be. In retrospect it would seem that Colebrooke's concept of the Legislative Council's role was too restrictive; for the really remarkable feature of the Legislative Council was not so much the existence of an official majority as the presence of unofficials. The latter served to underline the validity of the comment that the 'essential purpose of establishing a legislature has always been to give representation to the inhabitants of the dependency'. Implicit in this was the assumption that the acceptance of the principle of representation necessarily involved the acknowledgement also of the concept of the legislature as a representative legislature in embryo.

In the period 1833–70, the Crown Colony of Ceylon was the 'constitutional pioneer' of the non-European dependencies of the British empire;[2] it had a more advanced constitution than all the others. From the outset the unofficial members of the Legislative Council and some of the newspapers of the day tended to look upon the Legislative Council as the local Parliament. The rapid development of representative institutions and, later, of responsible government in the settlement colonies seemed to indicate the future trend of events for Sri Lanka. The Colonial Office would not fundamentally change its view of the essential function of the Legislative Council; nevertheless, this did not stop the sporadic agitation within the colony for the transformation of the Legislative Council into a more representative body. During this period, its powers were enlarged on three separate occasions, but, neither singly nor together, did this amount to anything significant. There was no increase in the Council membership, nor was there a change in the mode of representation from nomination by the governor to election, direct or indirect. Unofficial representatives were appointed by the governor on a communal basis. This seemed both natural and logical because the whole point of the Council was to elicit knowledge of local conditions. The ratio was fixed by convention as three Europeans and one each from among the Sinhalese, Tamils and Burghers, although the nomination of Sri Lankans quite often deviated from this precise proportion. There was no nominee for the Muslims.

The constitutional practice in the empire was that as bodies capable of serving as electorates or constituencies developed, the system of sending unofficial members to the Legislative Council changed from nomination to election. This did not happen in Sri Lanka in the nineteenth century, but for the Europeans there was a limited advance in this direction with the governor consulting the Chamber of Commerce (established in 1839) and the Planters' Association (established in 1854) in selecting unofficial members for nomination (it is not clear when this practice began). Among the Sri Lankans it became the practice to send petitions to the governor recommending nominations, but even this does not appear to have had much effect since nomination to the Sinhalese and Tamil seats was so often made from among the members of the same families. In the 1840s, Dr Christopher Elliott, who combined the practice of medicine with some remarkably outspoken journalism, led the agitation for a reform of the council to make it genuinely representative of the people at large,[3] but the radicalism of his demands ensured their speedy rejection by the colonial authorities. Not till well into the twentieth century do we see again anything like the radical and democratic tones that Elliott so fearlessly demonstrated in the 1840s.

When pressure for a reform of the Legislative Council was revived in the 1850s, it came from the European merchants and planters on the island and from the Burghers—descendants of Dutch settlers and VOC officials who had made Sri Lanka their home. What they wanted above all else was an increase in unofficial representation in the Legislative Council. There was no enthusiasm for elected representation except on the basis of a very restricted franchise; in a Legislative Council reformed on this basis the planters and European merchants would gain an influential voice in the disbursement of the government's contingent expenditure, if not control over it.

Earl Grey in the early 1850s had stated the case against the establishment of representative institutions in a colony like Sri Lanka: 'If they were to be established in such a form as to confer power upon the great body of the people, it must be obvious that the experiment would be attended with great danger, or rather with the certainty of failure.'[4] This, no doubt, was his answer to the demands of men like Elliott. But his rejection of the claims of the planters was if anything more forthright:

> If...the system of representation were so contrived as to exclude the bulk of the native population from real power, in order to

vest it in the hands of the European minority, an exceedingly narrow oligarchy would be created.... Were a representative Assembly constituted in Ceylon, which should possess the powers usually entrusted to such a body, and in which the European merchants and planters and their agents had the ascendancy, it can hardly be supposed that narrow views of class interests would not exercise greater influence on the legislation of the colony than a comprehensive consideration of the general good....[5]

Successive Secretaries of State merely expanded on these themes, particularly the second one, when demands were made in the 1860s and 1870s for a reform of the Legislative Council. Nor were the colony's governors more receptive to demands for constitutional reform: they made much of the fact that there was no agitation from the people at large for an elective system of representation and argued that since it was impossible to establish any legislature representative of the mass of the population, the prevailing pattern of administration should remain unchanged. Governor Gregory, for example, despite his strong liberal inclinations and his initiation of reform in every other sphere, remained unenthusiastic over the liberalization of the constitution. He was, in fact, an unabashed advocate of the view that the powers of the governor needed to be conserved as they were and, if possible, strengthened. The implication was that these powers would be used not for the protection of any merely sectional interests but for the welfare of the people at large. There was, besides, the presumption that any political concessions by way of a reform of the constitution must be preceded by, and could only be justified by, a substantial improvement in education and literacy in the island's population.

The rationale for masterly inactivity in regard to the constitutional structure came under purposeful attack in two pamphlets published in 1876–77 in which the author William Digby, a British journalist resident on the island, made a cogently argued case for the introduction of representative institutions in Sri Lanka.[6] For the first time since the days of Elliott, the case for constitutional reform was securely based on liberal ideology, but without the radical flourishes which Elliott had engaged in. Digby's pamphlets proved enormously influential not indeed for any immediate consequences in the way of extracting concessions from the government, but because the main arguments he advanced were to be used again and again over the next four decades by political activists on the island in their agitation for constitutional reform. The point he made was that since 1833, when the constitution had been introduced, there had been a transformation of the economy through the astonishing success of coffee culture. This was reflected in the flourishing state of the island's revenue in rapid and far-reaching social change, especially in the expansion of the education system and literacy, and indeed in every sphere except the constitutional and political. The case for reform was thus the simple one of harmonizing the island's constitution with the advances achieved in its economy and revenue system and in education and literacy. Whitehall's insensitivity to a reform of Sri Lanka's constitution became even more illogical when some of Britain's other tropical colonies, smaller than Sri Lanka in area and population, and far behind it in regard to the economy, revenue, education and literacy, were granted constitutions well in advance of hers. Had Digby's arguments been set out by a Sri Lankan it would have marked the beginning of a new era; as it was, the fatal flaw was precisely the fact that they were not. There was no demand from Sri Lankans themselves for representative government and the colonial government of the day made the most of this.

CONSTITUTIONAL DEVELOPMENT

Sri Lanka's role as the constitutional pioneer of the non-European dependencies lasted less than fifty years after 1833. By the end of the nineteenth century, colonies like Jamaica, Mauritius and Trinidad were far ahead in constitutional development.

In the non-white dependencies a constitutional problem had emerged: the beginning of a conflict between Britain's willingness to meet local demands for greater political influence

and her determination to retain political control. To have fully
conceded the colonial demand for representative government
would have seriously weakened Crown control, yet the
complete rejection of such demands was difficult if not
impossible. Jamaica was the pioneer in constitutional growth
and by the early 1880s three concessions had been made there:
the introduction of elected members into the Legislative
Council; the grant of a provisional elected majority and a veto
on financial proposals which could be exercised by any six of
the elected members, subject to the overriding power of the
governor. Concessions based on the Jamaican model were
introduced in Mauritius, but over a much longer period. The
reforms in Jamaica had a more immediate impact on Trinidad,
where changes were introduced in the period 1887–93.

These changes were not a steady application of carefully
thought-out principles, nor were they part of a long-term
progress towards responsible government. The Colonial Office
favoured constitutional reform on the grounds of administrative
expediency as a response to the strength of local demand and
agitation. In its preoccupation with immediate administrative
problems, it tended to underestimate the full implications of
these changes and their effect on other colonies. Despite the
fact that in all these changes the basic principle (one of
expediency) of the Crown retaining the ultimate power not
only to veto but to pass legislation was maintained intact,
politicians in other colonies saw only the advances made, and
in the context of the Crown Colony system in the tropical
colonies of the period, these seemed substantial indeed. The
prevalent view was that the reforms introduced in Jamaica
and Mauritius had made the grant of similar concessions
elsewhere inevitable, but after 1886 attitudes at the Colonial
Office hardened against constitutional reform. When the
plantocracy of Trinidad succeeded in extracting similar reforms,
Lord Selborne, Joseph Chamberlain's parliamentary
undersecretary at the Colonial Office, declared in 1895 that
these would not be an example to 'the empire at large'. He
had been told that 'mutterings of a similar agitation [had] been
heard from Hong Kong and Ceylon' and he hastened to

warn that there were 'very grave objections to any divergence from the pure Crown Colony in the case of [these two Colonies]'.[7]

The contrast between Sri Lanka's static constitution and the reforms introduced in Jamaica, Mauritius and Trinidad led some contemporary observers of its political scene to attribute the difference to the absence there of a class of wealthy European settlers which had led the successful agitation in the West Indies and Mauritius. But this explanation is too facile, even though it was true that the European planters and merchants in Sri Lanka were all birds of passage and not permanent settlers with an abiding interest, that is, they were not a true plantocracy. More important, it overlooks some important distinctions between Mauritius and the West Indian islands of Jamaica and Trinidad, on the one hand, and British Sri Lanka on the other. The first three were plantation colonies proper and the last was not, even though its economy was dominated by the plantations. Moreover, the situation in Sri Lanka was far more complex because of its large indigenous population and its indigenous elite. Thus the comparative quiescence of the island's public life in the last quarter of the nineteenth century and the lack of a persistent agitation for reform of the constitution is to be explained by the diffidence of the indigenous elite, in particular the Sinhalese.

The Sinhalese representatives in the Legislative Council, far from taking the lead in the pressure for reform of the constitution, showed little interest in it, when they were not adamantly opposed to any change at all. Buddhist activists may have filled this void in leadership, but apart from a somewhat hesitant claim for a member to represent Buddhist interests— the Sinhalese members in the Legislative Council had invariably been Protestant Christians—they did not attach much importance to the wider problem of constitutional reform. They showed very little interest in the active opposition led by sections of the Sinhalese elite against the objectionable features of the system of representation for the Sinhalese in the Legislative Council, namely, that nominees to the Sinhalese seat came, with one exception, from one family group. In 1878, the first challenge to this 'family compact' appeared when it became necessary to fill the vacancy caused by the death of James Alwis. The contender on this occasion was William Goonetileke, a Goyigama scholar and lawyer, who made no claims to 'first-class' status, but the vacancy was filled by J.P. Obeysekere, yet another member of the family to which James Alwis belonged. When the position fell vacant again in 1881, the competition assumed a new dimension—a non-Goyigama challenge to the 'first-class' Goyigama monopoly of the Sinhalese seat. From now on, political activity became an aspect of the caste rivalry which was such a prominent feature in Sinhalese society at this time.

In 1882, the Ceylon Agricultural Association was formed at the instance of C.H. de Soysa, the wealthiest of the Karāva entrepreneurs, primarily to safeguard the interests of the indigenous planters, and in 1888, when the Sinhalese seat was vacant once again, it was converted into the Ceylon National Association. Political activity on this occasion was much more than the conventional and decorous jostling to catch the governor's eye for nomination. It was altogether more purposeful, with the emerging elite, spearheaded by the affluent Karāvas, seeking to give greater momentum to their pressure for recognition by institutionalizing it into a distinctly political organization which was something more than a merely temporary platform for advancing an individual's claims. The formation of the Ceylon National Association, and the agitation which it led for constitutional reform, appeared to herald the beginnings of political initiatives of a far-reaching nature. Gordon was sufficiently perturbed to set about devising a scheme to foil the activists. Two additional unofficial seats in the Legislative Council were created in 1889, thus seeming to acknowledge the strength and reasonableness of the pressure for the enlargement of the Legislative Council, but these were allotted for the representation of the Kandyans and Muslims—two groups that had shown no serious interest in the agitation for constitutional reform. The non-Goyigama Sinhalese, under the leadership of the Karāvas who had led the agitation, got nothing from it, but Gordon, anxious to conciliate another set of activists (the Buddhist movement), expressed the hope that the Kandyan member should be a Buddhist and a spokesman for Buddhist opinion.

Gordon's reforms of 1889 incorporated another innovation—all unofficials were henceforth to be nominated for a five-year term. Hitherto nomination had been for an undefined period, with the governor retaining the right of suspension or dismissal. This right was never exercised and nomination was effectively for life. The innovation of a fixed term was bound—and perhaps intended—to curb the independence of unofficial members, especially because there was the prospect of renomination for another term. What it did indicate was that the hostility to constitutional reforms was not confined to a desire to thwart the ambitions of the Karāvas. Nomination for a five-year term had one unexpected consequence. Aspirants to nomination had more—and regular—opportunities to advance their claims and a five-year cycle of political activity developed, rising to a crescendo just when a member's term of office was due to end. But there was no change in the nature of the agitation, so far as the Sinhalese were concerned, for these regular campaigns to catch the governor's eye for nomination to the legislature were no more than exercises in caste rivalry.

But these campaigns too made little impression on the colonial administration. Nor was there a more favourable outcome when the candidate whose claims were sponsored had very impressive credentials. Ever since his return from Cambridge and Lincoln's Inn in 1887, James Pieris had been regarded as a young man marked out by virtue of a brilliant academic career (a double-first and the presidency of the union at Cambridge) and marriage to an heiress (the daughter of Jacob de Mel) for a path-breaking career in politics. In 1900, his claims to represent the Sinhalese in the legislature were advocated through petitions and well-attended public meetings in many parts of the island. Similar public meetings were held in support of the claims of S.C. Obeysekere, who was nominated. The same process of agitation was repeated in 1905 when the seat fell vacant again, and again Pieris was a candidate, but S.C. Obeysekere was renominated. Both in 1900 and 1905, James

Pieris had been sponsored by Karāva interests as their candidate. By 1905, the Karāva challenge was not limited to an attempt to repudiate the claims of the 'first-class' Goyigamas to represent the Sinhalese in the Legislative Council. The conspicuous affluence of a wide and powerful section of the Karāva community made them sufficiently self-confident to question the claims of the Goyigama caste to superior status. They went on to stake a claim for a separate seat for the Karāva caste in the Legislative Council. Although numerically they were much smaller than the Goyigamas, they could see no basic contradiction between the pursuit of their sectional interests as a caste group and the identification of these interests with broadly democratic principles. They also saw no irony in the attempt to equate the advancement of Karāva caste interests with the progress and welfare of the wider Sri Lankan community. From 1905 onwards they became the driving force behind demands for the introduction of the elective principle to the colony. They must have realized that the Karāva lead in education and wealth could be converted into political influence of a substantial order if the elective principle were accepted with property and educational qualifications.[8] They could thus put an end to the domination of Sri Lankan public life by the 'first-class' Goyigama and yet at the same time lend an air of respectability to the pursuit of their own sectional interests by parading as the champions of political reform and enlightened social progress. Nevertheless, their political ambitions were almost as narrowly limited as those of the 'first-class' Goyigama establishment whom they sought to displace.

This diversion of political energies to caste competition was self-defeating. At a time when the British administration in the colony had embarked on a deliberate policy of propping up the Goyigama establishment, the Karāvas were engaged in a futile exercise. The passion and zeal their campaigns aroused were all to no purpose. In fact, their campaign had a negative effect for it resulted in dividing the Sinhalese elite rather than uniting it in a common struggle against the British. It would have been evident that Goyigama support was essential for any concerted political movement to make an impact. Without it the minority castes on their own could make little headway in their political agitation and their demands for reform could always be dismissed as the agitation of a small clique not representative of the people. The Karāva challengers of the goyigama establishment were men of some achievement if not distinction, most being lawyers, but the colonial government on the island would not depart from its practice of appointing 'first-class' Goyigamas to represent the Sinhalese. No doubt this practice had hardened almost to a convention, but there was more to it than that: what counted was a family tradition of loyal service to the British in the office of principal mudaliyār, notwithstanding mediocre intellectual talents. The traditional elite, because of greater willingness to serve as collaborators, would have its uses to the colonial administration as a counterweight to the brash and affluent Karāva-dominated capitalist groups organized in the Ceylon Agricultural Association and its successor, the Ceylon National Association.

In the last decade of the nineteenth century and the opening years of the twentieth century, formal politics in Sri Lanka were remarkably passive, even stagnant or immobile—of which the transformation which took place in the Ceylon National Association is an excellent illustration. By 1885, the early promise of political initiatives had withered away and the controlling influence within it was with men who had no interest in political or constitutional reform. When some of its younger members sought to convert it into an organization modelled on the Indian National Congress and indeed to adopt the title of Ceylon National Congress, they were thwarted with consummate ease by those in control of it. The Ceylon National Association, in fact, scrupulously avoided involvement in political activity. It would not associate itself with the temperance movement either. However, it had one solid achievement to its credit: its notable contribution to the successful campaign for the abolition of the grain taxes. One may cite even more striking evidence of the quiescence of the elite and in particular the Sinhalese elite. In 1902, on the occasion of King Edward

VII's coronation, John Ferguson, owner-editor of the *Ceylon Observer*[9] and one of the unofficial European representatives in the Legislative Council, took the lead in seeking to organize a public meeting or a conference to secure the adoption of a resolution or memorial on the reform of the constitution. He received little support from the prominent public figures of the day. 'The Sinhalese are our great difficulty', he complained. '[S.C.] Obeysekere objects to elections and James Pieris (as D[istrict] J[udge] in embryo) has not replied at all.... They would not trust power to their countrymen....' In 1904, he moved a resolution in the Legislative Council urging the creation of an additional seat for the low country Sinhalese, but this motion lapsed for want of a seconder. The Sinhalese representative at this time was S.C. Obeysekere and his hostility to this proposal was as implacable as it was undisguised.

Obeysekere at least was consistent. The reluctance of James Pieris to support Ferguson's initiative in 1902 seems inexplicable in view of the fact that just two years earlier he had staked a claim to the nomination to the Sinhalese seat. What his reasons were we do not, and may never, know, but Ferguson was apparently convinced that the diffidence sprang from his aspiration to an important post in the judiciary. If that was indeed true, Pieris was typical of the elite of his day which showed greater interest in pressing for Ceylonization of the higher bureaucracy and the judiciary than in constitutional reform as such. This was not a case of distorted priorities, as it would seem at first, for the higher bureaucracy was till very much the elective government of the island. James Pieris, the reluctant politician, typified the Sinhalese elite of his day in other ways as well, especially in the preference for commerce and plantation agriculture over politics. By the last quarter of the nineteenth century, its stake in plantation agriculture, trade and commerce was becoming increasingly substantial. Sinhalese entrepreneurs were making fortunes in liquor, plumbago, coconut and rubber. The wealthy and educated Sinhalese—those whose educational and social background fitted them for a role of leadership in politics (and who, in fact, resented the dominance of public life by the 'first-class'

Goyigamas)—were engrossed in commercial ventures, often
to the neglect of their professional activities. James Pieris, for
instance, practised as a lawyer, but his heart at this time was in
business and plantation agriculture. There was also the case of
Dr H.M. (later Sir Marcus) Fernando, who was to be in the
forefront of political activity in the early twentieth century. His
academic record as a medical student at London University
was exceptionally distinguished, but on his return to the island
his medical practice took second place to plantation agriculture,
before being abandoned altogether. No wonder then that there
was a lack of 'real downright earnestness in political agitation'
and that the more committed advocates of reform should have
deplored the fact that the potential leaders of the elite preferred
their economic interests to political activity. Indeed, a British
newspaper of the day commented: 'Ceylon is one of those happy
possessions of the British Crown.... While other countries make
a noise in the world, Ceylon makes money.'[10]

At this time, moreover, the economic interests of these
wealthy Sinhalese entrepreneurs were not in competition with
those of British commercial interests on the island and certainly
much less so than was the case with their Indian counterparts
in most parts of that subcontinent. In plantation agriculture, Sri
Lankan and European interests were complementary rather than
competitive. There were no influential and wealthy indigenous
groups with investments in banking or shipping; nor were there
any large industries controlled by Sinhalese entrepreneurs. As
for commerce, although the Sri Lankan share was on the increase,
it was still very much in the shadow of British and Indian business
houses and was never in strong competition with them. The
result was that when (in the first decade of the twentieth century)
these entrepreneurs did eventually make their way into the
political arena, they showed themselves to be very conservative
in outlook, deeply appreciative of the British connection and
quite concerned not to stir up the sort of agitation that had
erupted in parts of British India.

The only venturesome and articulate political organization
among the Sinhalese was a regional body, the Chilaw
Association, composed largely of wealthy landowners,

organized and led by the Corea brothers. The impetus to its
formation stemmed from an agitation to have the west coast
railway link extended from Negombo to Chilaw and Puttalam
in the north-west, the heart of the coconut triangle, where
plantation agriculture was dominated by the Sri Lanka elite.
The association spearheaded the opposition to the Wastelands
Ordinance of 1897, the avowed purpose in this campaign being
the defence of the interests of the Sinhalese peasants against
what were regarded as the reprehensible features of this item
of legislation. More important—unlike the moribund Ceylon
National Association—it made political agitation the central
feature of its activities in its attempt to focus attention on the
need to introduce the elective principle for the representation
of native interests in the Legislative Council. But even this
agitation was restrained and narrowly elitist in concept. It
bore no comparison to the broad-based temperance movement
which derived its remarkable vitality from its appeal to the
people at large.

With the disinclination of the Sinhalese to take the lead in
formal political agitation, it was left to men like Ferguson and,
more significantly, the Tamils, to assume the initiative. The
energy and enterprise displayed by the Tamil elite was a sharp
contrast to the political inertia of their Sinhalese counterparts.
'The intellectual and political activity noticeable among the
Tamils', a local newspaper commented in 1889, 'is a favourable
sign of the times.... The intellectual activity of Tamils of the
rising generation has reacted on those of other communities....
In matters political it is gratifying to notice their activity.'[11] The
Tamils had been admirably served by their representatives in
the Legislative Council since the days of Sir Muttu Coomaraswamy,
who was succeeded in the seat by his nephews, the brothers
Ramanathan and Coomaraswamy, while a third brother,
Arunachalam, was a distinguished career civil servant who
kept up a lively interest in political issues, though this position
prevented him from giving public expression to these views
or taking an initiative in politics. It was at Arunachalam's
urging that Ferguson endeavoured to call a meeting or
conference of public men to adopt a memorial on constitutional

reform in 1902, utilizing the occasion of Edward VII's coronation. Ferguson accommodated Arunachalam by publishing two pseudonymous letters written by him in his newspaper the *Ceylon Observer* in early June 1902, making out a clearly argued case for political reform. In an editorial note, Ferguson strongly supported the claims made in these letters. Arunachalam's letters were in a sense an expansion of the arguments Digby had set out in his pamphlets in 1876–77. Digby's influence on Arunachalam was unmistakable and strong—they were close friends and maintained a long and interesting correspondence on political reforms.

None of the Sinhalese representatives of this period—the last quarter of the nineteenth century—matched the intellectual dynamism, independence of outlook and political maturity of Ramanathan and his brother, Coomaraswamy. The one exception was James Alwis, but even he lacked vision in many spheres of activity, most notably religion. As a staunch Anglican he would do nothing for the Buddhists; this task fell by default on Ramanathan, and his services to the Buddhist cause elicited a fulsome tribute from the leading Buddhist journal of the day, the *Sarasavi Sandaresa* in 1899. '[Ramanathan]', it asserted, 'not only looks after the welfare of his own constituents, but also all matters connected with various interests on the island.... It might well be said, judging from the active part he has taken, and the amount of time and labour he has devoted to questions on Council affecting the Sinhalese alone, that he was their representative.... The Buddhists owe Mr Ramanathan a deep debt of gratitude. His interest in the question of the *Vesak* holiday and the Buddhist Temporalities Bill...and a host of other services towards Buddhism have endeared him immensely to the Buddhists of Ceylon.'[12] Then again there was the question of the grain taxes. James Alwis gave unstinted support in the Legislative Council to the perpetuation of these taxes. It required the entry of the first Kandyan member Panabokke to give expression to the views of the Sinhalese peasantry on this issue. But all along Ramanathan had been critical of these taxes and he played a leading role in the successful agitation for their abolition.

Coomaraswamy, his elder brother, and successor to the Tamil seat, had neither Ramanathan's flair for dramatic gesture nor his eloquence, but he was nevertheless a man of strong convictions and sturdy independence, qualities which the government of the day did not always appreciate. Coomaraswamy was the first of the nominees under the new system of fixed-term appointments to feel the sting of the gubernatorial whip. When his term of office ended in 1889, he was not renominated. Instead his place in the council went to W.G. Rockwood, a non-Vellāla, and lest this be regarded as a change of heart by the government on caste, the old family compact retained its hold on the Sinhalese seat. As we have seen, S.C. Obeyesekere was nominated in 1900 and then renominated in 1905 (and again thereafter as well). What Rockwood's nomination signified was that the essential condition for renomination was unstinted support for the status quo as seen by the British and that any hint of independence merited a reproof. With the appointment of Rockwood and subsequently of Kanagasabhai as Tamil representatives, the Sri Lankan unofficials in the Legislative Council all reached a comfortably even level of mediocrity in intellect and conservatism in outlook; all of them were unimaginative men who showed not the slightest interest in political reform. But until 1898, the Tamil representatives had taken an independent line within the Legislative Council and quite often the lead in national politics as well. The Tamils' penchant for political activism attracted unfriendly criticism at the Colonial Office as well. A senior official gave expression to this attitude by commenting that 'the Tamils in Ceylon are the most intriguing section of the population'.[13]

The economic resources of the Tamil areas were much more limited than those of the wet zone and although there were Tamils with investments in plantations and trade, in this they hardly matched low-country Sinhalese. The educated Tamils turned to the professions and to service in the bureaucracy, especially in the lower clerical grades. Literacy in English was higher in Jaffna than elsewhere on the island and educated Tamils found that positions in the bureaucracy were outnumbered by those who aspired to them. Emigration to Colombo for employment was an established feature of life in Jaffna, as too was the brain drain—the steady flow of educated Tamils to the Federated Malay States and the trickle to East Africa in search of clerical and technical posts and teaching assignments. But by the end of the nineteenth century this emigration was drawing to a close because such opportunities were becoming increasingly scarce. It came to an end in the 1920s. What remained was internal migration to the Sinhalese areas where the competition for clerical posts intensified the rivalry between the Tamils and the Burghers, who had for so long been dominant in this form of employment. Here there was no competition between the Tamils and the Sinhalese— unemployment among the educated was not yet a serious problem for the latter.

Tamil students had long been accustomed to going across to India, particularly the Madras Presidency, for their university education. They absorbed the political influences at work in India and on their return sought to stimulate political activity on the island on the lines of Indian political movements.[14] The receptivity of the Tamils to the stimulus of Indian nationalism was strengthened by the fact that the Tamil elite, despite its passion for an English education, was much less anglicized than its Sinhalese counterparts. This held true for Tamil Christians as much as for the Hindus. Besides, the Tamil lead in politics was sustained over the first two decades of the twentieth century.

One last point. At this stage in the island's development ethnicity was not a divisive factor. A local journal commented in 1899 that 'among the different races to be found in Ceylon, the existing relations are perhaps far more cordial than...in any other British dependency in the East'.[15] The divisive forces were religion and caste, especially the latter, and these caused divisions among the Sinhalese themselves rather than dividing the Sinhalese from the other ethnic and religious groups on the island.

Political Change in the
Early Twentieth Century

In the first decade of the twentieth century, there was a perceptible quickening in the pace of political activity on the island after the near-immobility in formal politics in the last quarter of the nineteenth century. This owed much to events outside the island. First, there was Japan's victory over Tsarist Russia, hailed with almost as much enthusiasm by sections of the elite in Sri Lanka (especially the Buddhist activists) as it was in other parts of Asia. Second, and perhaps more important in a practical sense, there was the great Liberal victory in the British general election of 1906, marking the end of nearly twenty years of Tory rule and arousing hopes of colonial reform, largely because of the 'pro-Boer' stand taken by an influential section of the Liberal Party. Third, there was the example of the Morley–Minto reforms in India. As a result of these developments, the years from around 1905 to 1919 were characterized by the growth of secondary movements in the low country in the forms of political associations (both regional and national), trade unions and welfare associations. The concept of secondary resistance was demonstrated most acutely in the resurgence of Buddhism and the sustained temperance agitation closely associated with it. One sees the Buddhist revival and this ancillary movement in retrospect as an integral part of the recovery of national pride. They too had their main centres of activity in the low country and within these confines they demonstrated some of the characteristics of modern mass nationalism.

While nationalist sentiment was deeply intertwined with the reassertion of Buddhist values, and despite a persistently anti-Christian tone, one of the most interesting features of the

Buddhist revival in the early twentieth century was the extent
to which the Buddhist movement in the hands of men like the
Anagarika Dharmapala was almost the mirror image of
Protestant Christianity in its organizational apparatus,[1] never
more than in its propaganda techniques and the *mores* it upheld
as an integral part of the current Buddhist culture.[2] The new
Buddhist revivalist movement was indeed old missionary writ
large. Dharmapala grasped, as few of his contemporaries did,
the political implications of the Buddhist resurgence and he
never lost sight of the need to set this within the wider
framework of the rise of nationalism in Asia. But he was, at
the same time, an unabashed advocate of a Sinhalese-Buddhist
domination of the island. His propaganda bore a remarkable
similarity to that of the great champion of the Hindu resurgence
in western India, Tilak. In this blend of religious fervour and
national pride, of a sophisticated internationalism with a coarse
insularity, Dharmapala was a model for the Buddhist activists
of post-independence Sri Lanka. For few parts of the ex-
colonial world is Anthony Low's comment that 'empire was
as much a religious as a political or economic or ideological
problem'[3] more valid than it is for Sri Lanka.

THE TEMPERANCE MOVEMENT

The first attacks on the reprehensible features of the
government's excise policy—the proliferation of taverns in all
parts of the country in a sordid pursuit of revenue without
heed to the social evil of drunkenness, which spread even
more rapidly than the taverns—had come from the missionaries
and other Christian organizations in the last quarter of the
nineteenth century. They were joined in this enterprise by
Buddhists, who by the beginning of the twentieth century
were the most vocal if not the most enthusiastic advocates of
temperance. Within a decade they had succeeded in taking
over the leadership of the movement and, more significantly,
in giving it a distinct Buddhist identity. Although Christian
groups continued their association with temperance agitation,
their role was now clearly that of a junior partner whose moral
position in the campaign was being cleverly undermined by the

success with which Buddhist temperance enthusiasts linked the consumption of liquor with westernization and 'Christianisation'.[4]

The temperance agitation of the first two decades of the twentieth century, which reached two distinct peaks, one in 1903–05 and a more important one in 1911–14, linked the elite, particularly its Buddhist segment, with the masses in a common purpose, which, though primarily religious in form and content, was never without political overtones. Disparagement of Christianity and attacks on Christian values could be, and were, adroitly extended to cover the British government as well. The fact that some influential officials were articulate Christians was deftly used to bring the government itself—as a 'Christian' administration—within the scope of these criticisms.[5] For the elite who moved into the leadership of the temperance agitation in the first decade of the twentieth century, this was a consolation prize, a surrogate for participation in the government of the country for which they yearned but which lay beyond their grasp. It introduced them to the mechanics of organizing public opinion through the network of temperance societies which sprang up in and around Colombo and other parts of the country. Again, with this temperance activity a stratum of society which had hitherto been quiescent if not inarticulate, namely, the lower rungs of the rural elite consisting largely of notaries, schoolteachers and small traders, made its presence felt as an indispensable link between the rural masses and the leadership of the movement. The, Hapitigam complex of temperance societies springs to mind as perhaps the most efficient and effective in the network built up in 1903–05. It drew crowds of 20,000 or more to its meetings in this rural area at a time when the population of the Colombo district (excluding the municipality of Colombo) was a little over 600,000. The man behind it was Don Spater Senanayake who had made his fortune in plumbago among other things and who was the father of F.R., D.S., and D.C. Senanayake, all of whom made their entry into public life through the temperance movement. It provided the take-off point into national politics for the Senanayake family.

When this first phase in temperance agitation petered out after 1905, its organizational apparatus was not dismantled but survived to be used for other purposes, mainly religious ones. With the revival—British administrators would have used the word recrudescence—of temperance agitation in 1911, this network of village and urban units was revamped and extended to cover most parts of the low country and beyond. Temperance work narrowly defined (which continued to be the main focus of activity) spread to the wider aspects of rural regeneration and welfare. Between the temperance agitation of 1903–05 and that of 1911–14 there were substantial differences. The campaigns of 1911–14 covered a much wider area and the response they evoked at the grass-roots level was, if anything, even more enthusiastic. There was greater sophistication in the organizational techniques adopted and, above all, it came as near as ever in the early twentieth century to a politicized movement. With the formation of the Total Abstinence Central Union, the temperance agitation grew in strength in 1913 and 1914 and assumed the proportions of a popular movement with distinct potential for transformation into a political struggle with wide mass support. Some temperance leaders, among them F.R. Senanayake and D.S. Senanayake, visualized the network of temperance societies as a viable basis for a nationwide political organization. But this promise, as we shall see, was to remain unfulfilled.

The temperance agitation of 1911–14 had one other special feature. It began primarily as a movement of resistance to reforms which the government proposed to make in the excise laws. Directed at protecting the government's revenue from this source, these reforms were also designed to break the hold which small elite groups (mainly capitalists of the Karāva caste) had on the liquor industry. Consequently, among the most vociferous critics of the government's projected reform of the excise laws were those who stood to lose financially if and when these reforms were introduced. One needs, therefore, to distinguish between the strident opposition of the vested interests to excise reforms and the more disinterested temperance agitation of the Buddhists. Between them there existed merely a common objective of opposition to the new excise policy, but no identity of interests or indeed a common purpose. These vested interests were as suspicious of, and perturbed by, the Buddhist temperance agitation as the government itself,[6] whose response to the temperance movement was one of unconcealed hostility. In the rural areas, this agitation posed a threat to the position and authority of the chief headmen, the government's men on the spot in the lower rungs of the administration, who were regarded as the natural leaders of the people. The confrontation that followed between the temperance leaders and these chief headmen, showed that the latter had lost their touch in grassroots 'politics'. The government was apprehensive of this for fear that it would also affect the position of British civil servants and reacted to the presumed dangers presented by the movement to its own position and interests with an ill-advised attempt to contain the infection by discouraging native officials in the administration, particularly the village-level headmen, from association with temperance activity. This was especially so in 1911–14, when the government viewed the revival of temperance societies with the utmost suspicion, especially because of the tendency to use temperance platforms for criticism—sardonic more than trenchant—of government policies on other issues as well. In the hope of checking the expansion—an exuberance—of temperance societies, an order was issued prohibiting village headmen from joining temperance societies. Other public servants wishing to join such societies were required to obtain prior permission from the government. These directives proved a costly blunder. They provoked public criticism both on the island and in Britain. It was especially because of the latter that the government was compelled to rescind them. The withdrawal of the orders was hailed as a notable success for the temperance movement and contributed greatly to boosting its leaders' morale and self-confidence.

It is remarkable, however, that such a powerful movement, which affected not merely the elite but the people at large, should not have had an invigorating influence on the formal political activities of the elite at this time. No consistent attempt, much less a systematic one, was made to channel the enthusiasm and discontent it generated into a political force of real significance. To explain this development by the fact that the most militant and charismatic of the 'nationalist' leaders, Anagarika Dharmapala, was out of the island for considerable periods, is to leave many questions unanswered. It does not explain why, even when he was on the island, the 'nationalists' diffused their energies over a whole range of religious, social, cultural and educational issues and made little effort to focus their attention consistently on any clearly defined political objective or objectives. Although Dharmapala and some of his close associates saw the political implications and potential of the forces that were emerging—Dharmapala was among the first to advocate Swaraj or national independence— they received no encouragement from those who played a prominent role in Buddhist activity in these attempts to politicize the Buddhist revival and the temperance movement. The temperance movement itself was not a monolith. Despite his missionary zeal in its support, Dharmapala was suspect to many of the Buddhist temperance leaders and they refused to accept his leadership. While the moves to outline a political objective for the Buddhist revival and the temperance movement had so little support from the Buddhists themselves, they were anathema to the bulk of the elite, especially the Christians and Burghers who dominated the political life of the country. They would have nothing to do with a political movement which showed so much potential for development into a vehicle for religious—Buddhist—'nationalism'.

The theosophical movement,[7] with its cosmopolitan outlook and comparative freedom from sectarian loyalties, could well have become the driving force behind the development of a Buddhist political organization to channel religious enthusiasm into more secular fields had it not lost a great deal of its influence with the Buddhist movement by the beginning of the twentieth century. The result was that the few efforts made to establish an ideological link between religion and political nationalism were doomed to failure.

NATIONALISTS AND REFORMERS

Buddhist activism, as we have seen, was distinctly more vigorous and volatile than the formal political movements of the day, not that they were separated from each other by any sharp distinction. Nor is it possible to divide the politicians of the age meaningfully into 'radicals' and 'conservatives'. There is, however, a more valid distinction and its basis was largely religio-cultural—the distinction between 'nationalists' and 'constitutionalists'. One needs to remember, however, that while these are useful ideal types, the actions of all individuals or groups reveal a mixture of both. While the 'constitutionalists' stood for a limited programme of political action which would leave undisturbed the constitutional and political structures introduced by the British, the 'nationalists' sought to give more coherence to political activity by according greater emphasis to the country's cultural patterns and religious traditions. Some of the more articulate 'nationalists' like Dharmapala demonstrated a precocious commitment to the cause of Swaraj, but they were not many and not representative even of the 'nationalists' in general. The temperance movement, for example, brought 'nationalists' and 'constitutionalists' together in a common cause, but large sections of the latter either stood aloof or gave very lukewarm support to the former in their campaigns against the missionary movement. Moreover, the bulk of the 'constitutionalist' elite, in striking contrast to the 'nationalists' and the temperance agitators, were suspicious of large public meetings and of demonstrations of zeal in political activity. They had nothing to compare with the network of temperance societies in the villages of the low country.

Formal political activity had to do mainly with the reform of the Legislative Council and the entry of Sri Lankans to the higher bureaucracy. Where these were concerned, the attitude of the Colonial Office and the colonial administration on the island was of decisive significance. Most Colonial Office officials in Whitehall were not averse to the grant of limited political concessions to Sri Lankans, but the absence of sustained agitation for reforms and the divisions in the ranks of the Sri Lankans on these issues, had the effect of convincing the Colonial Office that there was no serious dissatisfaction with the existing system. They were, therefore, reluctant to launch reforms on their own initiative, especially when there was the prospect that these might have a disquieting effect. With the Liberal victory of 1906 there was a feeling in the Colonial Office that some reform measures were imperative in Sri Lanka to prevent such dissatisfaction as existed from maturing into disaffection. Many of the more influential of these officials sympathized with the aspirations of the Sri Lankan reformers. But in the colony, Governor Sir Henry McCallum was an arch-conservative whose credo was firm opposition to the grant of any constitutional reform.

That the Colonial Office was not opposed to a reform of the constitution was well known on the island. It was also clear that the first moves would have to come from within the colony and in the form of agitation for reform. 'It is useless to hope to get political privileges without our first agitating for them', a local newspaper, the *Ceylon Morning Leader*, declared in its issue of 13 June 1908. It added: 'Even in England the people did not earn their enviable privileges by sitting quiet.' A Sri Lankan who had pressed the subject of constitutional reform on an official in Whitehall had received the blunt reply 'Why don't you agitate for it? The political history of England has been one long series of agitations.' But the only national political organization, the Ceylon National Association, was by this time nearly moribund. Nothing at all in the form of political agitation was possible with it, yet at the same time nothing could be achieved without it unless a newer and more energetic association were to emerge to fill the gap. The only other political bodies were either communal (that is, ethnic) ones like the Dutch Burgher Union and the Jaffna Association, which was also a regional body like the Chilaw Association, or commercial groups like the Low-Country Products Association and the Plumbago Merchants Union. Most of these were politically conservative and not inclined to lead an agitation for reform. The Jaffna Association and the Chilaw Association, especially the latter, were more liberal in outlook and not afraid to venture into political agitation, but they were hardly a substitute for a genuine national organization. The reformers, moreover, faced the obdurate hostility of the traditional elite, who denied the need for any reform at all. This elite was small in number but influential with the colonial administration. It also had the advantage of representation within the Legislative Council—a convenient platform for the expression of its conservative views.

Caste rivalry continued to divide the Sinhalese and was regarded as the main reason for the lack of unity and cooperation among them. Nevertheless, when political agitation did emerge, the main driving force behind it once again consisted of Karāva interests seeking political influence commensurate with their economic strength. At long last James Pieris took the lead. The main political demand was a claim for a greater but still very modest share for the educated elite in the administration of the colony.[8] But the British administration in Ceylon responded to these proposals for reform with heavy-handed opposition. Not only did it deny the need for any basic change in the constitution, but it also refused to acknowledge the claims of the educated elite to speak on behalf of the people. British administrators saw only the gulf that divided the educated few from the illiterate masses and disregarded the close personal and social ties that enabled them to bridge it. Thus, they neither acknowledged the claim of the elite to speak on behalf of the masses nor did they see the need to make constructive use of those members of the elite who were not part of the administrative machinery (and they were by far the greater part numerically) in a mediatory role between the administration and the people.

Indeed, the argument was advanced by Governor Sir Henry McCallum[9] that the 'real representatives' of the people in the Legislative Council were the senior and experienced civil servants '[whose] work for years at a time has brought them into daily and intimate touch with the peasantry.... Their advocacy of the claims of the native population are [sic] at once fearless and disinterested.' There were, too, the 'durbars of Native chiefs...[which] also afford to the native population, through their chiefs, an additional means of making their wishes and opinions known to the government.' McCallum did concede that the educated elite was 'a new factor in the political situation, [and] inasmuch as no special provision for its representation is contemplated by the existing constitution, in so much and in no other respect...the constitution is antiquated.' Despite this tardy recognition of the special position of the educated elite, McCallum was totally opposed to the concession to them of the principle of elected representation. When the elective principle, in a very limited form, was conceded to the educated Sri Lankans in 1910, it was on the initiative of Lord Crewe, then Secretary of State for the Colonies, and his parliamentary undersecretary, Colonel Seely, and in the face of the disapproval of the permanent officials at the Colonial Office and the stubborn hostility of the colonial administration in Colombo. Even after the concession was announced, McCallum and his advisers persisted in their opposition in the hope that it would be withdrawn under pressure from them; but it was not.[10]

The franchise was confined to a tiny segment of the people, the educated elite, and in particular the English-educated elite. When the reform proposals of 1910 were announced, the Buddhist press deplored the injustice of excluding literacy and education in Sinhalese from consideration in determining qualification for the franchise. Most of the 'constitutionalist' elite, however, soon pronounced themselves gratified with the gains achieved in 1910–12, in particular the concession of the elective principle. They had a deep commitment to the proprieties of colonial agitation, a faith in the soft tone and the sober memorandum, a refusal to be attracted by what they thought were merely rhetorical gestures. Behind it all there was a deep and abiding faith in the basic justice of British rule. It is a measure of the fervid hostility of British officials on the island to political and constitutional reform at this time that even the movement for constitutional reform led by men like James Pieris, H.J.C. Pereira and E.W. Perera, who were deeply attached by sentiment and political inclination to British institutions and the British empire, was only slightly less suspect in their eyes than the 'nationalist' agitation linked with the temperance movement and Buddhism. Every concession, even the most minor, was viewed as a diminution of authority of the government and its officials and was resisted for that reason. As for the elective principle in regard to entry to the legislature, the hostility to it sprang from a recognition of its real and immediate threat to the position of the native headmen and the likelihood of elected representatives enjoying a higher standing in public life than the former. Far from complacently watching the displacement of the traditional elite, McCallum (and his colonial secretary, Hugh Clifford) gave renewed strength to the policy of propping them up as a conservative countervailing force against the reform movement, an exercise that was as futile in the long run—the influence of the chief headmen had been too badly eroded for that—as it was self-defeating in view of the prodigious moderation of the bulk of those who sought entry to the legislature.

THE RIOTS OF 1915

In the first quarter of 1915 the two strands of agitation discussed earlier, the Buddhist and the 'constitutionalist', showed every sign of a fruitful convergence. British officials on the island, who only a few months earlier were basking in the genuine warmth of public support for Britain's cause with the declaration of war against Germany, were taken aback by the upsurge of nationalist sentiment in March and April 1915. The central event in this surprising transformation was the commemoration in March of the centenary of the Kandyan convention. The emotions it generated were sustained by the National Day celebrations in April, which on this occasion extended for the first time over the whole island. There was every indication at this point that 1915 would be a year of destiny, a turning point in the island's political evolution. But within a few weeks—by the end of May—the outbreak of communal disturbances shattered all these hopes.

The riots of 1915[11] were directed against the Muslims, but more especially at a section of the Muslim community called the Coast Moors who were mainly recent immigrants from the Malabar Coast in south India. The ubiquitous activities of the Coast Moors in retail trading brought them in contact with the people at their most indigent levels—they were reputed to be readier than their competitors to extend credit, but they also sold at higher prices. This earned them the hostility alike of the people at large and of their competitors among the Sinhalese traders (mainly low country Sinhalese), who had no compunctions about exploiting religious and racial sentiments to the detriment of their well-established rivals. Since the low-country Sinhalese traders were an influential group within the Buddhist movement, religious sentiment often gave a sharp ideological focus and a cloak of respectability to sordid commercial rivalry. The Coast Moors were not only tenacious in the protection of their trading interests, but they were also more vociferous than the indigenous Muslim community in the dogged and truculent assertion of their civic rights, which stemmed no doubt from their familiarity with such matters in India. This streak of obduracy and their insensitivity to traditional rites and customs of other religious groups brought them, at a time when there was a resurgence of Buddhism, inexorably into conflict with the Sinhalese-Buddhist masses.

It was only when the British authorities in Sri Lanka, after initially treating the riots as communal disturbances pure and simple, came to regard them as part of an organized conspiracy against the British by the Sinhalese that these events began to take on a different complexion. Although there was little or no evidence to support the sedition or conspiracy theory about the origins and nature of the riots, it nevertheless gained wide currency among British officials and triggered a series of panic measures of inexplicable harshness against the alleged leaders of the conspiracy—the Sinhalese-Buddhists. A situation which could easily have been handled by the bureaucracy and the police was dealt with by the military, who acted in a way which showed that they did not understand the distinction between civil commotion and war.

The British authorities came down hard on three sets of people, all of them Sinhalese and Buddhists. First of all, the close connection between temperance activity and nationalist sentiment had always aroused the government's suspicions. All the prominent temperance leaders were arrested and jailed, notwithstanding the fact that many of them had used their influence towards restoring order and in protecting the lives and property of Coast Moors. The detainees included the

Senanayake brothers, D.B. Jayatilaka, W.A. de Silva, C. Batuwantudawe and Edmund and Dr C.A. Hewavitharane (brothers of the Anagarika Dharmapala).[12] Second, a new and youthful political organization, the Young Lanka League, also came under suspicion and its active members, among whom A.E. Goonesinha was the most prominent, were arrested and detained. This organization had been established in 1915, the first 'radical' and 'nationalist' political association to be formed in Sri Lanka with a political programme which was overtly and defiantly opposed to the continuation of British rule on the island. It chose the centenary commemoration of the cession of the Kandyan kingdom to pledge themselves to securing national independence for Sri Lanka. Its formation was also significant because it was intended to demonstrate a lack of confidence in the political leadership of their day—the 'constitutionalists'—and its overwhelming conservatism. Instead they preferred to emulate the militant and radical wing of the Indian nationalist movement.

The third set were a group of railway workers, particularly some trade union activists in the locomotive workshops in Colombo. Twenty-eight of them (including nineteen from the locomotive workshops) were arrested at the end of June and 'deported' to the Eastern Province, then very much the 'Siberia' of the island. The first signs of 'trade union consciousness'[13] and agitation had appeared in the last decade of the nineteenth century. A spectacular carters' strike in 1906 had been regarded in official circles as presaging the transference of 'Indian sedition' to the island. (At that time bullock carts were, apart from the railways, the most popular means of commercial transport on the island and the only means of commercial transport within the city of Colombo.) By the beginning of the second decade of the twentieth century, there was considerable unrest and discontent among skilled workers in Colombo and its suburbs, a reaction to deplorably bad working conditions and poor living standards buffeted by inflationary pressures. This discontent and unrest were most pronounced on the railways, and especially the locomotive workshops in Colombo. British officials, accustomed to docility among workers, were alarmed by the frequency with which they now resorted to strike action in support of their claims. There were, besides, close links between the elite and these workers on such occasions. The leadership in these labour disputes was taken by the elite, especially those most active in the temperance movement and political agitation.

In the Legislative Council, Ponnambalam Ramanathan, with all the moral authority of the elected representative of the educated Sri Lankans,[14] rose to the defence of the Sinhalese leaders in a series of impassioned speeches notable alike for their fearless condemnation of the excesses committed by the British forces in suppressing the riots and the cogently argued refutation of the conspiracy theory. He opposed both the Act of Indemnity, which placed the civil and military authorities beyond the reach of the law, and the Riots Damages Ordinance which imposed collective retribution in the form of a levy of compensation on all Sinhalese residents of specified localities, with no regard to whether or not they were implicated in the riots. More important, for two years or more he persisted in a fruitless agitation to secure the appointment of a select committee of the Legislative Council to investigate charges of grave miscarriages of justice and needlessly harsh punitive measures láid against British officials, military and civil, as well as others, such as planters associated with them, by Sinhalese leaders. Ramanathan received strong support from Harry Creasy, one of the most respected English residents on the island, also the European representative in the Legislative Council, but their efforts to obtain redress for these grievances were undermined, if not totally nullified, by the intemperate opposition of the nominated Sinhalese representative, S.C. Obeysekere, who preferred to revel in the discomfiture of men whom he despised as his social inferiors and whose aspirations to political leadership were anathema to him.

In the meantime, E.W. Perera, a Sinhalese Christian, left for England immediately after the riots to attempt to rouse British public opinion in sympathy with the grievances of the Sinhalese and to secure the appointment of a body of commissioners from Britain to inquire into the incidents connected with the riots. For four years he (and D.B. Jayatilaka for three years) remained in England on this mission,[15] but they were no more successful than Ramanathan had been in his enterprise of securing the appointment of a select committee of the Legislative Council.

THE CEYLON NATIONAL CONGRESS

Surprisingly, the immediate effects of the riots of 1915 was to freeze an evolving political situation before its potential was fully realized and to postpone any fresh developments for some years. This change of mood reflected accurately the balance of forces among the elite, with the 'constitutionalists' emerging as more powerful than ever before and determined to dampen all enthusiasm for any political agitation other than their own decorous but futile, though long-sustained, campaign for a commission of inquiry into the riots.

Before the riots, the temperance movement was potentially the basis of a popular political movement with a genuine grass-roots appeal. The politicization of the movement appeared to be the next and most logical step. But the riots proved to be a setback to the temperance movement. This was partly the necessary consequence of the riots, as the elite leadership was bending over backwards to show the British government and public opinion in Britain that the movement was essentially a religious one. After the suppression of the riots, there was no serious attempt to revive the temperance movement on the scale and style of 1911–14.

The prevailing mood of restraint and excessive caution in politics affected other issues as well. The distrust of enthusiasm, which was one of its most notable characteristics, spilled over into the sphere of religious activity as well; the brand of militant Buddhism associated with Dharmapala receded into the background for over a generation and 'the constitutionalists' took charge of the Buddhist movement as well. F. R. Senanayake and D.B. Jayatilaka between them kept a tight rein on religious enthusiasm. Their approach to the religious problems of the day was in every way a contrast to Dharmapala's and they set the tone from about 1918 up to Jayatilaka's retirement from active politics in 1942.

With the Ceylon National Association still paralysed by its resolute respectability, there was greater need than ever before for a larger and more elective political organization. But the riots and their aftermath were a setback, if only a temporary one, to the movement—if such it could be called—for establishing a Sri Lankan counterpart to the Indian National Congress.[16] Not that this movement or restrained agitation had any strong support, even before the riots, from the 'constitutionalist' leadership in control of the Ceylon National Association, who were so deeply suspicious of the political techniques and political outlook of the Indian National Congress that many of them resisted the formation of a similar body in Sri Lanka. This resistance stemmed both from the conservatism of the 'constitutionalist' elite who were perturbed by the potential consequences of agitation politics and fearful of the radicalism inherent in the broadening of the bases of existing political associations and from the fears of minorities—racial, religious and caste—at the prospect of a strong challenge to their position and privileges which a National Congress, as the vehicle of Sinhalese-Buddhist nationalism, held out.

As a spur to the formation of a larger and more politically effective organization than the Ceylon National Association, developments in India—beginning with Edwin Montagu's (Secretary of State for India) celebrated declaration of 20 August 1917 on the future course of constitutional development there, his well-publicized visit to India and the publication of the Montagu–Chelmsford Report—were more significant than the riots of 1915. Their effect on politics on the island was immediate and dramatic. They seemed to give new meaning and spirit to political agitation in the island. The impact on Sri Lanka of Montagu's pronouncement on India's political evolution and his visit there was apparent at once in the 'constitutionalists' redefining the goals of political advancement as they envisaged them; but it was more important in that it broke down opposition to the creation of a larger national political organization than any which existed. For it became obvious that an organization of this sort was an essential prerequisite for any purposeful pressure for the grant of a substantial measure of constitutional reform. The strength of opposition to the creation of such an organization is shown by the fact that two more years were to pass before a Ceylon National Congress was established and this despite the stimulus of those Indian developments.

The first president of the Ceylon Reform League was Sir Ponnambalam Arunachalam, whose standing in the country made him the obvious choice for the post; the intention clearly was to give the post of president a prestige which only he could have conferred on it. Indeed in the years 1917 to 1921, the leadership in the agitation for constitutional reform was in Arunachalam's hands, as was the movement for the formation of a Ceylon National Congress. During this period his prestige was at its height; his leadership was ungrudgingly acknowledged by the most prominent Sinhalese of the day and was not seriously challenged till 1921.

What distinguished elite politics in Ceylon in the first two decades of the twentieth century from succeeding decades was the harmony that prevailed between the Sinhalese and Tamil leadership. In the political jargon of the day, there were two majority communities, the Sinhalese and Tamils, and the minorities were the smaller racial groups. The situation changed fundamentally after 1922 when instead of two majority communities and the minorities, there was one majority community—the Sinhalese—the Tamils now regarding themselves increasingly as a minority community. It has remained so ever since.

To Arunachalam, the inauguration of the Ceylon National Congress was the fulfilment of dreams cherished from the time he was an undergraduate at Cambridge. It was also the culmination of a resolute campaign conducted by him—if not single-handed, then at most with very little support from most of the leadership of the 'constitutionalist' elite, Sinhalese and Tamil alike. The task of overcoming the political myopia of his colleagues in the 'constitutionalist' leadership and of reconciling the conflicting claims of advocates of territorial representation and those who stood in defence of sectional interests, would have been beyond

the capacity of anyone lacking Arunachalam's personal prestige
and political vision. Those who shared his political outlook
saw in the newly formed Ceylon National Congress a symbol
of national unity and racial harmony. But there were many
among the leaders of the 'constitutionalist' elite who had deep
reservations about the Ceylon National Congress. Despite the
efforts of its more forward-looking members—and they were
very few—it converted itself almost from the outset into an
exclusive organization dominated by a conservative elite,
although the Young Lanka League played the role of a radical
gadfly within it. In its exuberance, this small group had hopes
of converting the larger organization into the vehicle of a
genuine nationalist movement on the lines of the Indian
National Congress, which at this time was coming increasingly
under the influence of Gandhi. They hoped to compel the
'constitutionalists' who dominated the Congress to come to
grips with the issue of national independence.

Thus, from the very inception of the Congress there were
two sharply opposed points of views within it. The more
influential of the two were the 'constitutionalists' who believed
in negotiation along properly constituted channels. Their
methods of agitation were the memorial and the deputation
and their political objective was 'to secure for the people of
Ceylon responsible government and the status of a self-
governing member of the British Empire'. This was to be
achieved by 'constitutional methods' and by 'a reform of the
existing system of government and administration'.[17] The
second point of view was represented by the radical
nationalism of A.E. Goonesinha and the Young Lanka League,
whose goal was the Gandhian ideal of Swaraj. They advocated
more forceful expressions of opposition to British rule in
imitation of the Indian National Congress. Their contribution
to the development of the nationalist movement in Sri Lanka
was the introduction to the country of the technique of mass
politics and the tactics of agitation based on the politicization
of the urban working class of Colombo.

It is from this time onwards that it becomes possible to
look at politics in the island in terms of 'conservatives' and

'radicals'. But the conservatism of the 'constitutionalists' in the Ceylon National Congress lay less in the declared political objectives which they adopted as the Congress platform than in their techniques of agitation, their reluctance to countenance the politicization of the masses, their neglect of the deeper social problems of the country and the economic problems which affected the people and in the elitist nature of the membership of the Congress.

Elite Conflict and the Ceylon National Congress, 1921–28

Elite competition in the late nineteenth century and early twentieth had been a matter of caste rivalry among the Sinhalese rather than a conflict between the Sinhalese and the ethnic minorities, in particular the Tamils. In the years covered in this chapter, these divisions among the Sinhalese persisted and caste was indeed as divisive a force in the early 1920s as it had been earlier.[1] It was a factor in the general elections to the Legislative Council in 1921 and 1924 and a rather embarrassed leadership of the Ceylon National Congress adopted a resolution urging its members to desist from raising caste issues at election time. The increase in the number of voters in the 1920s was sufficiently large to cause a momentous shift in the balance of caste influence. The Goyigamas were able to assert, for the first time, their majority status (it was not the 'first-class' Goyigamas of old who emerged as the dominant factor, but rising men of wealth, education and achievement) and the Karāva influence in politics and public life was reduced from a position of dominance to one merely of significance.

But two other problems manifested themselves. The first was a fresh point of division among the Sinhalese, with competition between the Kandyans and low-country Sinhalese revealed as a noteworthy ingredient in politics. Even more important, ethnicity became a decisive factor in elite competition in the form of rivalry and conflict between the Sinhalese and the Tamils. The present chapter surveys the unfolding of these various problems and issues in the political arena and national life.

THE CEYLON NATIONAL CONGRESS IN DISARRAY

The hopes of men like Arunachalam that the foundation of the Ceylon National Congress would mark a turning point in Sri Lanka's politics, were never fulfilled. There were two reasons for this. First, the 'constitutionalist' leadership who gained control committed the Congress to a narrow and unimaginative course of action, contriving that the Congress did not aspire to the role of a political party with a mass base. This was no more than a tactical adjustment of attitudes to political realities, but associated with it was a mixture of rigidity and overcaution which exasperated the more venturesome spirits like Arunachalam, for example, and alienated the younger radicals both within the Congress and outside it.

The second factor had to do with the arrival in 1919 of Sir William Manning, one of the most masterful British governors of the island. Despite the self-imposed limits on its political methods and ambitions, Manning regarded the Ceylon National Congress as an intolerable challenge and set about fashioning its discomfiture with a grim determination befitting a more formidable adversary. He was totally insensitive to the need for any substantial measure of constitutional reforms. Indeed, he believed that any readjustment of the constitutional structure was detrimental to the British position in Sri Lanka and should, therefore, be resisted at all costs. At the time of Manning's arrival, the Ceylon National Congress was in the throes of formation. He watched those proceedings with a jaundiced eye. The vistas of political change which the newly established organization seemed to presage jarred his conservative instincts, and even as the 'constitutionalists' were celebrating the success of their endeavours he was devising plans to upset them. That these plans bore fruit within two years owed as much to the intrinsic brittleness of the Ceylon National Congress as a political structure as to the skill with which Manning exploited its potential points of weakness.[2] It is most unlikely that it would have come apart so soon had he not stepped in with such zest to speed it on its way to self-destruction.

Very early he had decided that the Congress was more vulnerable on its right flank than its left, that is to say there was more to gain by pandering to the fears of the conservative groups to its right, who had suspicions about the Congress as an instrument of low country Sinhalese domination of the island's politics, than by hoping for advantages from the vocal criticisms of the 'constitutionalist' leadership from radicals on its left. He turned to the Kandyans.[3] The appearance early in 1920 of a pamphlet entitled *Present Politics and the Rights of the Kandyans* should have given the 'constitutionalist' leadership warning of the potentially divisive effect of Kandyan aspirations as embodied in that document. There the tradition of Kandyan 'resistance' was invoked not against the British but against the 'constitutionalist' leadership. The crux of the argument was that the 'lawful and just aspirations of the Kandyans' were threatened by the demands of the 'constitutionalists'. '[Where] the Kandyan heritage begins', the author of the pamphlet asserted, 'there the low-country Sinhalese claim for it ends'. The Kandyans were urged to regard the British as 'trustees of Kandyan nationality' under whose guidance and tutelage there should be a separate administrative structure for the Kandyan provinces with 'full control over internal management'.

The author of this pamphlet, J.A. Halangoda, was soon to be a member of a three-man delegation of Kandyan representatives (the others being T.B.L. Moonemalle and G.E. Madawala), all lawyers, who arrived in London and were received by the Secretary of State for the Colonies, Viscount Milner, on 22 June 1920. It was a command performance with Manning as the impresario.[4] This delegation urged that the Kandyans be allowed to elect their representatives through communal electorates. At the outset Milner was not inclined to extend the communal principle to the Kandyans, but eventually he conceded it in the face of unremitting pressure from Manning, who wanted it as part of a scheme of checks and balances in the readjustment of the constitutional structure in Sri Lanka. It was indeed far more than a matter of checks and balances, for Manning had succeeded in extending the principle of communal electorates to a section of the Sinhalese and in gaining Colonial Office endorsement of his extraordinary contention that the Kandyans were a minority community.

The Kandyan delegation had done their work extremely well and greatly impressed Milner. Their charge that the Congress politicians aimed at conserving 'the whole of the administrative power in their hands and [at] dominat[ing] the weaker minorities' seemed sufficiently convincing. This undoubtedly queered the pitch for the Congress delegates led by Arunachalam who met Milner the next day.

There were many reasons why the Kandyans took shelter under the colonial umbrella and offered collaboration in return for certain minimum requirements being met. The most important of these, it would appear, were the economic ones. Although the Kandyan region was the main centre of the plantation industry, fewer benefits from this process of economic development had accrued to the Kandyans themselves than to any other group among the Sri Lankans. In general, the Kandyans had been left far behind by the low country Sinhalese and the Tamils in the exploitation of the avenues of advancement available after the consolidation of British rule in the nineteenth century in trade, commerce and plantation activity, and in education and the professions. When a high level of education and property qualifications were laid down as conditions for the exercise of the vote under the reforms of 1910–12, the Kandyans had seen the low country Sinhalese and Tamil lead in these spheres converted into the hard reality of political advantage in the electorate (the educated Ceylonese electorate). They felt incapable of meeting unaided the challenge of the more enterprising segments of the Sri Lanka community and were willing to assist Manning in frustrating the expectations of the 'constitutionalist' elite.

Although he had won a section of the Kandyans over to his side in 1920, Manning had no intention of falling captive to a single collaborating group. When a rift between the Sinhalese and Tamils developed after the elections to the reformed Legislative Council in early 1921, he was presented with an opportunity for detaching the Tamils in the Ceylon National Congress from that organization and from their association with the low country Sinhalese in the common purpose of agitation for constitutional reform. The potential advantages of such a course of action were enormous: for the Tamils, though fewer in number than the Kandyans, were politically more sophisticated and articulate; besides, they were regarded, not least by Manning himself, as a majority community.

As with the Kandyans, it was the mechanism of representation that provided Manning with an exploitable opening. The first elections to the reformed Legislative Council had returned thirteen Sinhalese to territorial constituencies as against three Tamils, whereas in the old Legislative Council there had been a near equality in representation between the Sinhalese and Tamil unofficial members. Soon after the new Legislative Council met, influential Tamils began to campaign for the restoration of the proportion of Tamil to Sinhalese representation that had existed before 1920. It was against the background of this demand that a written undertaking given in December 1918 by James Pieris and E.J. Samarawickreme, in their respective capacities as presidents of the Ceylon National Association and Ceylon Reform League,[5] regarding the creation of a special seat for the Tamils in the Western Province, was revived. Surprisingly, Pieris and Samarawickreme asserted that their pledge involved no precise commitment to this peculiar concession, but was merely an agreement 'to accept any scheme which the Jaffna Association may put forward so long as, it is not inconsistent with the various principles contained in the resolutions [adopted at the constitutional conference of December 1918] the most important of which was that of territorial representation'. In a few months, this seemingly trivial issue assumed the proportions of a major controversy both within the Congress and without. Manning, in fact, had little to do but watch the 'constitutionalist' leadership shuffling from one costly blunder to another in coping with this problem. The dénouement—Arunachalam's departure from the Congress— was as shattering in its impact on that organization as it was unexpected.

Arunachalam indeed had been at odds, since the middle of 1920 and even earlier, with his colleagues in the Congress leadership on the tactics to be adopted to respond to Manning's initiatives and objectives. It was ironical, however, that he left the Congress in a dispute over the special communal seat for the Tamils in the Western Province. The written undertaking on this given by Pieris and Samarawickreme in December 1918 to the Jaffna Association had been crucial in winning the latter over to supporting the formation of the Ceylon National Congress. More to the point, Arunachalam had negotiated this settlement and thrown the full weight of his prestige behind it. It would thus seem that the public disavowal of this pledge shattered his confidence in the leadership of the Ceylon National Congress irretrievably. By the end of 1921 he was, if not an ally, at least the co-belligerent of his brother Ramanathan and men like Ambalavanar Kanagasabhai.[6] Their narrow outlook and conservative politics would have appalled him before he began his drift to their camp; a man with a radical outlook and a strong social conscience, he had remained a Gladstonian liberal throughout his public career. In contrast, Ramanathan had shed his liberalism well before the dawn of the century. His defiant condemnation of the repressive measures taken by the British authorities in Sri Lanka in the wake of the riots of 1915 was a spontaneous visceral reaction against injustice and not a political campaign with wider objectives. Shortly thereafter he made it clear that he was opposed to any far-reaching reform of the constitution—he was against the principle of an elected majority in the Legislative Council.[7] Arunachalam had been reluctant to associate himself too closely in political activity with his brother and yet the pressures of elite conflict drove him, in the twilight of his distinguished public career, into the camp of 'communal' politics though he was never comfortable in its ranks. The Tamils had by now begun to think of themselves as a minority community and Arunachalam himself was inclined to share this view. When, however, the Tamils in their new role of a minority community looked for leadership, they turned to Ramanathan rather than to Arunachalam. It was an astute choice since Arunachalam did not relish the transition from national to communal leadership and could not have filled the latter role with the conviction and panache which Ramanathan was to demonstrate.

The prime beneficiary of the shifts and changes in the political scene was Manning. The initiative was now unmistakably with him and he seized it with unconcealed pleasure to fashion the complete discomfiture of the Congress. In this he had Ramanathan as his collaborator. In mid-November 1921, two conferences were held in a desperate bid at reconciliation between the Sinhalese and Tamil leadership, but these broke down because of one crucial issue—the Tamils were not prepared to relinquish their claim to a special reserved seat in the Western Province. Manning's political instincts were as sharp as ever and throughout 1922 and 1923 he contrived to keep this issue alive with occasional but well-timed public expressions of support for the Tamils on it.[8] The support of other minority groups was more easily obtained. Their political survival depended on the continuation of communal representation and they viewed the Congress demand for a legislature in which a clear majority of members were to be representative of territorial electorates as a threat to their interests.

Despite Manning's formidable skills as a political manipulator, he would scarcely have achieved all he eventually did had the Sinhalese leaders of the Ceylon National Congress not contributed to their own discomfiture. Their tactics and strategy alike were woefully inadequate in this contest with a man of Manning's resourcefulness. For one thing, they allowed themselves to be embroiled in a needless conflict on an intrinsically unimportant issue—the reserved seat for the Tamils in the Western Province—when a timely concession generously made would have removed it from the arena of political controversy. Second, they rejected the appeal of radicals like A.E. Goonesinha within their organization that Congress should adopt more forceful techniques of agitation to demonstrate their antipathy to Manning's policies. Instead, they persisted with their conventional mode of agitation, which, without in any way disturbing Manning's composure, only drove the radicals to despair. Thus, although the constitutions introduced in 1920 and 1923 fell far short of their demands, Congress leaders would not resort to a policy of boycott and non-cooperation but preferred to help in working the new constitutional machinery. In doing so they enabled Manning to retain the initiative. It would be easy to argue that all this is evidence that they were more afraid of their radical critics than of Manning except that Congress leaders believed that the adoption of the tactics advocated by the radicals would be self-defeating because they would have contributed to the irrevocable alienation of the minorities. In this mood the 'constitutionalist' leadership in the Congress were easily outwitted by Manning.

By the beginning of 1925, Manning's triumph was complete when, in the aftermath of the elections of 1924, the rapprochement between the Congress leadership and the Kandyans was shattered. Under the 1920 constitution, the Kandyans had been given separate communal electorates; but in 1923 this concession was rescinded. Kandyan opinion acquiesced in this because of assurances given by the Congress leadership that 'seats in the Kandyan provinces would not be contested by low-country Sinhalese'. This was an undertaking which could never have been honoured, for Congress leaders had neither the party machinery nor party discipline which could have enforced this decision on their supporters. In the 1924 elections, only three Kandyan seats returned Kandyans to the Legislative Council. To explain the defeat of the Kandyans as being the result of their lack of sophistication in political matters, a consequence of their resistance to the liberalizing influences of western rule, as many did at that time,[9] afforded them little consolation. Indeed, after the elections of 1924, the prominent Kandyan members of the Congress—most notably A.F. Molamure, Dr T.B. Kobbakaduva and P.B. Ratnayake— joined in the demand that 'the Kandyan race should be separately represented in our Legislative Assembly, and that our entity as a separate and distinct community should otherwise too be recognised and maintained'.[10] A Kandyan communal organization, the Kandyan National Assembly, was formed in 1923 in opposition to the Congress. At its inaugural sessions, held in December that year, the Kandyan demand for separate representation was affirmed. By November 1927, the Kandyan National Assembly put forward a demand for a federal state with regional autonomy for the Kandyans.[11] The faith in federalism as the solution to the Kandyan problem remained a keynote of their demands for more than a decade thereafter. They found Manning and his successor, Sir Hugh Clifford, very sympathetic to their demands and indeed quite eager to support their claims to a special status, in the hope of using the Kandyans as a conservative buffer against the forces of political agitation and reform.

There were at this time other advocates of the federal solution: S. W. R. D. Bandaranaike, a Congressman himself and then in the earliest phase of his remarkable political career, came out in favour of a federal governmental structure as a means of bringing about better understanding among the several ethnic groups on the island.[12] It was for a time the main plank in the political platform of the youthful and far from influential political group, the Progressive Nationalist Party, which he headed at this time. But the more influential political leaders of the day, Sinhalese as well as Tamil, were not at all receptive to these demands for a federal constitutional structure for the island.

THE MAHĀJANA SABHĀS

One feature of the political life of this period has not received the attention it richly deserves. This was the Sinhala Mahājana Sabhā, established in 1919 under the auspices of the Ceylon National Congress with the prime objective of reaching the 'great masses of the people'. It soon established a network of local sabhās or associations,[13] a notable feature of whose membership was the presence in them of peasant cultivators, who formed a majority of the membership in many.

The aims of these societies were social reform and rural regeneration. There was, in general, an emphasis on religious and cultural activities, including temperance agitation. We have seen in the previous chapter how the temperance movement did not recover its original vitality after the riots of 1915, but interest in temperance activity survived, and more important than that the network of temperance societies established prior to 1915 did not become extinct. It remained dormant for a while and many of its component units were transformed into mahājana sabhās.

The link with the pre-1915 temperance movement was evident also in the leadership of the Sinhala Mahājana Sabhā: the Senanayake brothers and D.B. Jayatilaka were in control. F.R. Senanayake was the undisputed leader and he gave lavishly of his wealth to keep the movement going. He served as its president from its inception in 1919 to his untimely death in December 1925 when D.C. Senanayake took his place at the helm of affairs in the movement.

In regard to the main political objective of the movement— attainment of self-government for Sri Lanka—the Sinhala Mahājana Sabhā and its provincial units were affiliated to the Ceylon National Congress, within which it and these local sabhās retained their distinctive identity and considerable freedom of action. In the other spheres of activity the quite explicit aim was for the mahājana sabhās to pursue an independent role. Although it was originally intended that the political activities of these associations should be secondary to the social ones, gradually more emphasis was given to the former than was anticipated at the time of the movement's inauguration and political activity gained greater momentum with the rapid increase in the number of branches on the island.

Through the sabhās the 'constitutionalists' sought to bring the rural population into politics as auxiliaries of the elite. Characteristically, they refused to face up to the implications of this restrained exercise in politicization. In retrospect, it would seem that these sabhās existed not so much to mobilize popular support for the political objectives of the Ceylon National Congress as to demonstrate that such support was available if necessary, evidence once again of the rock-hewn moderation of the 'constitutionalists'. It was politicization without enthusiasm or a sense of commitment. The relationship between the leadership and the rank and file was basically deferential on the part of the latter.

From the start, the mahājana sabhās conducted their proceedings in Sinhalese, and their rules and regulations were printed in that language. This emphasis on Sinhalese had the inevitable effect of strengthening ethnicity, as a cohesive force within the sabhās, and from this it was but a short step to emphasizing ethnicity as a point of distinction or separation from rival groups. During the political squabbles of 1923, the Tamils accused F.R. Senanayake of rousing communal feelings against them (he had threatened a boycotting campaign) through the mahājana sabhā movement. Similarly, the mahājana sabhās emphasized a second point of distinction, religion: they sponsored the cause of Buddhist candidates and stood opposed to Christians. In this sense they were, under F.R. Senanayake, very much in the tradition of the religious nationalism of men like the Anagarika Dharmapala and precursors of the Sinhala Maha Sabhā of the 1930s and 1940s, and the Mahajana Eksath Peramuna (MEP) of the mid- and late 1950s. The same forces were at work: Buddhist activists (laymen[14] and bhikkhus), the rural sub-elite of ayurvedic physicians, traders, teachers, cultivators and the Sinhalese-speaking intelligentsia. The difference between the mahājana sabhās and their successors lay in the tight rein that F.R. Senanayake and D.B. Jayatilaka had on the movement, dampening excessive enthusiasm and zeal and keeping the incipient 'populist' tendencies very much under control. It was this populism and mass enthusiasm which distinguished the MEP of the 1950s from the mahājana sabhās and largely also from the Sinhala Mahā Sabhā.

The political initiative—such as it was—demonstrated in the mahājana sabhā movement received a serious setback with the untimely death, at the age of forty-four, of F.R. Senanayake. Deprived of his leadership, the movement survived fitfully for a few more years without a sense of purpose or direction. The strata of society to which it appealed did not lose their interest in politics, it took another ten years before a similar organization was set up to give them leadership. This was the Sinhala Mahā Sabhā of S.W.R.D. Bandaranaike, who in the mid-1920s served his apprenticeship in the mahājana sabhā movement in the Veyangoda area (the country home and subsequent political base of the Bandaranaikes) under the Senanayakes.

RADICALISM

While the mahājana sabhās were seeking to revitalize the rural areas and to politicize the peasantry, the Young Lanka League under the leadership of A.E. Goonesinha was engaged in an enterprising bid to politicize the urban working class of Colombo. Infinitely smaller in numbers than the peasantry who formed the natural constituency of the mahājana sabhās, the urban working class had a more restricted geographical base, but it was also much more cohesive and volatile as a political force. The most significant difference between the two lay in the fact that the radicalism of the Young Lanka League challenged— no doubt ineffectively but challenged nevertheless—the 'constitutionalist' leadership by setting out viable alternatives in terms of political objectives and methods of action.

The keynote of the new radicalism was its interest in trade unionism and labour activity. During the years following the end of the First World War, there was widespread unrest among the urban working class of Colombo as a result of the economic dislocation of that time; in particular, there was a shortage of rice and a consequent increase in its price when there was no corresponding rise in wages. In 1920, these conditions sparked off a series of industrial disputes, first among the railway workers and then the first major strike in the Colombo harbour. The existing workmen's organizations, sponsored if not run by the 'constitutionalists' in the Congress, proved to be totally incapable of meeting the situation created by this wave of labour unrest and significantly the workers themselves, particularly the dockers, preferred to rely on their own resources. The 'constitutionalists' had clearly failed and into the void created by their failure stepped the radicals led by A.E. Goonesinha, who supplied a new and more forceful leadership.[15]

The first major political initiative of the Young Lanka League in the post-war period was their organization of opposition to the poll tax under which all adult males were required to pay Rs 2 annually, or work six days on road construction in lieu. The really irksome and onerous part—road construction work—fell only on the very poor who could not afford the money payment. There was thus great resentment against this tax, which ran deep and strong among the urban poor of Colombo. Its abolition in 1922, largely as a result of a sustained campaign against it by Goonesinha and his associates in the

Young Lanka League, was a triumph for the radicals and a demonstrable vindication of the techniques of agitation which they had devised for the purpose.

They turned next to trade union activity. Clearly there was need for a trade union organization which would be something more than a mechanism for conciliation between employers and their workers in the event of labour disputes—the function performed by the Ceylon Workers Federation controlled by the 'constitutionalists'. Goonesinha's Ceylon Labour Union, formed on 10 September 1922, was the new model trade union. Its establishment was timely for in February and March 1923 it led Colombo's working class in a spectacular show of solidarity and strength—a general strike which dislocated the economic life of the city. Although the strike eventually collapsed, its message rang out clear: there was a new mood of militancy among the workers, who therefore would not tolerate a return to labour practices of the past to which the employers were accustomed. There was a political dimension to this message, directed at the 'constitutionalist' leadership of the Congress no less than at the colonial administration: the working class was making its entry into the political arena, bringing with it new styles of action, making novel demands and introducing a new and less deferential tone into politics.

By 1923 Goonesinha was already a popular figure, a folk hero and a politician of great promise who had emerged from the ordeal of these strikes with a keener appreciation of the political potential of the masses. The Ceylon Labour Union was by then at once the leading trade union in the country seeking to consolidate its position as the dominant influence on the urban working population and the most radical force in politics. In 1922, it affiliated with the Congress: the hope was that, with the Young Lanka League, it could influence the Congress' policies and transform its outlook to the point where its political objectives would take on a sharper and more radical focus by greater responsiveness to the social and economic problems of the masses. In short, it would oversee the transformation of the Ceylon National Congress into a dynamic mass organization on the lines of its Indian prototype. On the other hand, the energies of the 'constitutionalists' who effectively controlled the Congress were aimed at preventing just such a transformation.

When Goonesinha urged his colleagues in the Congress to adopt Gandhian tactics in their forlorn struggle against Manning's administration, he was recommending an extension of the scale and scope of political activity which would have undermined their own position even more than Manning's. More dispassionately, he was thinking in terms of the success the radicals had achieved in the agitation against the poll tax and no doubt hoping that similar tactics in national politics would bring better results than had been achieved so far by the indestructible moderation and respectability of the 'constitutionalists'. But they would not be shifted from the cosy orthodoxies of elitist politics. Certainly, few among them welcomed—as the radicals did—the politicization of the urban working class, or were anxious to channel its energies into the national political struggle. On the contrary, they were perturbed by the militancy of the labour movement as reflected in the strikes of 1920 and 1923. They regarded Goonesinha as a troublemaker and irresponsible agitator, and lent him no support during the general strike of 1923. (Significantly, the men who were most consistent in their support of Goonesinha and the strikers were C.E. Victor Corea, a militant nationalist at this stage and Anagarika Dharmapala, now in the last phase of his career, who consistently looked upon strikes by Sri Lankan workers as a manifestation of a spirit of nationalism.) The 'constitutionalist' leadership in the Congress demonstrated very little interest in the problems of the urban working class, although the industrial disputes of the 1920s had brought these increasingly to public attention. There was substantial justice in the charge laid against Congress members of the Legislative Council by radical critics that they had shown no initiative in securing the introduction and adoption of legislation on issues which vitally affected the working class—the right to form trade unions, the principle of a statutory minimum wage, unemployment relief and workmen's compensation through insurance against industrial hazards.

An even more significant point of divergence between the radicals and the 'constitutionalists' related to suffrage. The 'constitutionalist' leadership in the Congress had always been notably unenthusiastic about the extension of the franchise. Arunachalam had been one of the early advocates of manhood suffrage,[16] as early as 20 September 1919 in his address (in Sinhalese) at the inauguration of the Lankan Mahajana Sabha[17] and then—even more pointedly and emphatically—four days later at a public lecture in Colombo. But in this he had no support from the 'constitutionalists', whom he was at this point seeking to coax into establishing the Ceylon National Congress.

From 1923 onwards Goonesinha took up the cry for representative government based on manhood suffrage and repeatedly urged the Congress to accept that principle. But he found its leaders—now that Arunachalam was no longer one of their number—coldly unsympathetic on this issue. No doubt Goonesinha's advocacy of manhood suffrage stemmed from his realization of the political potential of the urban working class. Manhood suffrage would be the means for converting his influence and prestige in that quarter into a substantial base for his own political advancement and for an effective challenge to the position of the educated elite in the public life of the country— a consideration which must have made manhood suffrage all the more unpalatable to 'constitutionalists'. The differences between Goonesinha and the Congress leadership were brought into even sharper focus, before the public's gaze, in 1925–26. In June 1925, he had embarrassed them greatly by his vociferous opposition to a move, sponsored by them, to raise funds from the public to commemorate the award of a Knight Commander of the Order of St Michael and St George (KCMG) to the mahā mudaliyār, Sir Solomon Dias Bandaranaike. Late in 1926, they struck back by supporting the mahā mudaliyār's son, S.W.R.D. Bandaranaike, in a contest with him for election to the Maradana ward of the Colombo Municipal Council. Goonesinha's defeat on this occasion was a stunning but only temporary setback to his political career. It did little to detract from the substance of his achievement in politics in the dozen years from the foundation of the Young Lanka League. He had made a notable contribution to the growth of nationalism in Sri Lanka, first by giving leadership in the process of politicizing the working class and then by demonstrating the dynamic role of social and economic reform, both as essential ingredients in national regeneration.

Social and Economic Change in the Early Twentieth Century, 1910–28

PLANTATION AGRICULTURE

The two decades surveyed in this chapter were years of economic stagnation. This was the result of a contraction in world trade because of the World War of 1914–19 and then the economic dislocation in Europe in the 1920s, followed by the Great Depression of the late 1920s and early 1930s. Tropical trade, in general, had expanded in volume at an average annual rate of 3.6 per cent in the period 1883–1913; between 1913 and 1929 it dropped to 3.1 per cent (thereafter falling sharply to 1.5 per cent). Thus the whole of the interwar period was an unusually prolonged recession for the tropical colonies. The growth rate of their national income, as well that of the productive capacity of their economies, declined noticeably. The plantation sector of Sri Lanka's economy reflected this trend.[1]

Rubber fared better, with the outbreak of war and in wartime conditions, than tea and coconut.[2] Although the boom conditions of 1904–10 did not continue and prices fell from 5s 6d a pound in 1910 to 4s 6d in 1911 and 1s 11d at the outbreak of war, they were sufficiently remunerative to keep the industry buoyant. Indeed, there was a substantial increase in exports, which actually doubled between 1912 and 1914. Moreover, the restrictions on shipping, which adversely affected coconut and tea, did not affect rubber and there was no serious dislocation of market arrangements. As for tea, the market ceased to be buoyant with the outbreak of war, and in wartime conditions, especially because the British government imposed controls on tea exports from India and Sri Lanka, as well as fixing prices. But peace brought problems for both tea and rubber.

When the British government released the reserve stocks of tea which had been built up during the war, hopes that improved shipping conditions and removal of wartime restraints would result in a return of the prosperity the tea industry in Sri Lanka had enjoyed just before the war, were shown to have been too sanguine: by 1920, the prices of the commoner varieties of tea had dropped sharply. Similarly, while the rubber industry began to adjust itself to normal demand conditions, the stocks of rubber which had accumulated in the producing countries tended to depress prices. Under the stimulus of wartime conditions, the area under rubber had expanded between 1914 and 1918 by 10,117 hectares. This was sustained over the years 1918–20 when a further 12,950 hectares were added. Prices fell by 1921 to 7d a pound, which was well below the costs of production for most rubber producers. Worse still, as a result of the expansion in the area under rubber, production increased in the next decade, thus accentuating the fall in prices.

Tea producers in India and Sri Lanka, the main areas of tea production, responded to the hard times with voluntary restrictions on production and this almost immediately had the desired effect. Prices improved and indeed these new schemes of restriction worked so well that by 1926 the principle of restriction itself was abandoned. In the period 1920–30 the area under tea production expanded by 21,448 hectares, but this recovery proved to be shortlived. Teas from India and Sri Lanka lost the preferential duty they had enjoyed over competitors in the London market, to the great and immediate advantage of teas from the Dutch East Indies. The tea industry had hardly adjusted itself to this loss of its competitive edge when the Great Depression reduced demand and prices even more drastically. The situation was aggravated in the early 1930s when the new plantations that had been opened in the previous decade came into production. At this time the supply of tea was far outstripping demand.

Voluntary restriction of output in the rubber industry was less effective than the cognate process in tea. Only the bigger and more commercially viable producers were anxious for restrictions and the smaller firms and smallholders were reluctant to join in such schemes. Although the Colonial Office would not yield to insistent demands from the larger producers to have restrictions on production imposed on the whole industry, the British government nevertheless stirred itself to some action with regard to the formulation of a comprehensive scheme to restrict production, but the obstacle this time was that the Netherlands would not join in it. Eventually, a scheme applicable to British Malaya and Sri Lanka, the principal sources from which the empire obtained its supplies of rubber, was devised—the 'Stevenson Scheme'—and was in force from 1922 till 1928. This was the first attempt to regulate the production and supply of rubber. Its flexibility contributed to its success, and it certainly led to an increase in prices. By 1924–25 the price of a pound of rubber had risen to 2s 3d. But these improved prices did not survive the onslaught of the Great Depression, which had a more severe impact on rubber than on tea. (It would appear that under the stimulus of relatively attractive prices in the mid- and late 1920s there had been an extension of the area under rubber by 38 per cent, most of it in the Dutch East Indies.) By 1930, the price of rubber was a mere 5 $\frac{5}{16}$d. In 1932, it had sunk even lower—to 2 $\frac{5}{16}$d.

The coconut industry, was, if anything, worse off than either tea or rubber in these decades.

PEASANT AGRICULTURE AND COLONIZATION

If the interwar decades were a period of stagnation in plantation agriculture, they marked a revival of interest in peasant agriculture and irrigation. There was no link between these two developments. Indeed, at the beginning of the period of our survey it seemed as though stagnation would affect the peasant sector as well. The establishment of the Irrigation Department in 1900 was not the breakthrough to greater investment of resources in irrigation which it was expected to be. Instead, within a few years all investment in major new irrigation projects was suspended and the department restricted itself to the servicing of existing projects. Even the inauguration of the Department of Agriculture in 1912— established with the primary objective of introducing the peasant to more scientific agricultural practices—did not at first, or indeed for a long time, mark a significant new departure in the government's attitude to peasant agriculture. The wartime disruption of food imports and the massive food production drive organized as a result changed all that. There was now a distinct revival of interest in peasant agriculture and irrigation. It coincided too with a greater interest in peasant agriculture on the part of indigenous politicians.[3]

Inextricably linked with this was a renewal of interest in the development of the dry zone. For Sri Lankan politicians of the day the dry zone conjured up visions of a revival of past glories and—at a more practical and realistic level—of achieving 'a more even balance of population'. British officials had fewer illusions. They were all too aware of the enormous problems involved in developing the dry zone, but in the years after 1914, with food supplies from traditional sources drastically curtailed, they turned to the dry zone for an immediate solution to an urgent problem—an increased supply of food from within the island. One interesting feature of this renewed interest in the dry zone was the attempt to force the pace of development by resorting to commercial firms using techniques of production perfected in wet-zone plantation agriculture. Proprietors and managers of wet-zone plantations regarded increased production of rice through capitalist agriculture in the dry zone as a practical solution to the problem of breaking away from dependence on imported rice to feed their workers. They sought to use immigrant Indian labour on these projects, both as hired hands and prospective settlers. (Sri Lankan politicians were greatly perturbed by this and deeply resented it, for they looked upon the dry zone as the birthright of the Sinhalese.) In 1919, a group of Sri Lankan capitalists established the Minneriya Development Company in an effort to begin food production in the Polonnaruva district in the region served by the Minneriya Tank. When this venture collapsed, it was taken over by the Sinhala Mahājana Sabhā which sought to establish a colony at Nachchaduva. This latter project was as idealistic in outlook as it was practical in its objectives, but the resources available in terms of finance and of technical and managerial skills were totally inadequate for a pioneering venture of this size. None of these capitalist ventures, indigenous or British, showed any signs of success, and once conditions returned to normal, that is, when imports came in without difficulty, the interest of British capitalists in the dry zone evaporated. Indigenous capitalists did not persist either.

This revival of interest in the dry zone did have some immediate beneficial effects. First, after nearly two decades there was an expansion of the area under irrigation in the dry zone by about 8,094 hectares. Had the government of the day not pointedly ignored some of the more innovative recommendations of the Food Supply Committee of 1920, much more would have been achieved. This committee had recommended that the Irrigation Department should not in future be regarded as being primarily a revenue-earning branch of the administration and, more important, that its operations should no longer be assessed on the basis of commercial profit. It was also recommended that the improvement of means of communication should precede rather than follow the development of a district. (The most formidable obstacle to the development of the dry zone was malaria, and the North-central Province, for instance, consisted of isolated malaria-stricken villages with very little in the way of road or rail communication.) None of these proposals was adopted. Second, the wartime disruption of food imports and the post-war inflation (and food scarcities) concentrated the minds of politicians and officials as never before on the need to develop the island's food resources so as to make it self-sufficient in rice. From this stemmed an increasing willingness on the part of the government to liberalize the system of alienating Crown lands in order to accommodate the peasants: the prevailing land legislation and regulations governing the sale of Crown lands had been under regular attack from Sri Lankan politicians on the grounds that they benefited the capitalist developer at the expense of the peasantry. It is against this background that one needs to view the work of C.V. Brayne, an extraordinarily imaginative British official who began experimenting, in the

1920s, with a new tenurial system in the Batticaloa district. Under this scheme—the peasant proprietor system, as it was called—allottees of Crown lands were carefully selected and were granted a leasehold tenure. The crucial restriction on the right of ownership was the prohibition on alienation by sale or mortgage without official authority. This restricted tenure gave the leaseholder most of the advantages of ownership, but the government retained the right to eject those who proved unsatisfactory. Once its viability was successfully demonstrated in the Batticaloa district, it was introduced into the Matara district in 1925 and thereafter into the Hambantota district as well.

In 1927 came the most important decision of all—the appointment of an important Land Commission by the then governor of the colony, Sir Hugh Clifford. It was recognition that the time had come for a comprehensive reappraisal of land policy. Among its members were some of the more prominent unofficial elected Legislative Councillors, the most notable being D.S. Senanayake, now a rising star of the island's political leadership and beginning his association with a sphere of activity which he was to dominate from 1931 until his death in 1952. Brayne himself was a member of the commission. It sat for two years and after an exhaustive study of the subject, made detailed and far-reaching recommendations in a series of reports. It strongly endorsed Brayne's initiative in the new tenurial arrangements which formed the basis of the peasant proprietor system. It unhesitatingly adopted the then current notion—supported by Clifford and D.S. Senanayake alike—that the preservation of the peasantry as a social group should form the basis of the new land policy. Among the major recommendations was that in future the alienation of Crown lands should be centralized and regulated through a special officer, the commissioner of lands, and that allocations should be made according to the needs of the government and the people, with the peasants having priority. Perhaps the most far-reaching recommendations concerned the tenure of lands alienated by the government: outright grants, leases under the peasant proprietor system (which had already proved its worth) and a new tenurial system under which alienation by the grantee by sale or mortgage would be severely restricted, with lands passing on the death of the original grantee to a nominated successor or heir-at-law.

As for colonization, the commission recommended that prospective colonists should be carefully selected, and while some form of financial assistance would be provided, self-help should be made the guiding factor. Reflecting the views of the government, the commission concluded that on the whole the problem of land hunger and congestion could be solved within the wet zone in close proximity to the problem areas.[4] The almost total failure of attempts at colonization in the dry zone in this period appeared to justify the low priority which officials attached to the dry zone in their calculations. All in all, the recommendations of the Land Commission constituted a fundamental change in British land policy in Sri Lanka and a calculated reversal of trends that had been in force since the mid-nineteenth century.

POPULATION AND IMMIGRATION

There was a very close link between the reappraisal of land policy and the question of population pressure on existing resources of land. In 1927, Sir Hugh Clifford had quoted with relish Bacon's aphorism 'The true greatness of a state consisteth essentially in population and breed of men' to which he coupled a line of more recent provenance: 'An increasing population is one of the most certain signs of the well-being of a community'.[5] He went on to show that between the mid-nineteenth century and the census of 1921 there had been 'a truly phenomenal increase of population...in the space of seventy years' from 1.73 to 4.50 million. The point he was making was that 'nothing approaching it could conceivably have occurred had not the indigenous inhabitants of this island enjoyed during that period—which synchronises, be it noted, with the greatest expansion of its agricultural enterprises in its history—not only peace and security, but a very large measure of material prosperity'.[6] A truly extraordinary increase of population there had indeed been, even if one would not endorse Clifford's contention that there had been 'a very large measure of material prosperity' as well. According to the census of 1901, the island's population had reached 3.56 million. The rate of increase over the first decade of the century was thus 15.2 per cent (to 4.11 million); in the next decade it dropped to 9.6 per cent (4.50 million in 1921); but between 1921 and 1931 it accelerated again to 18 per cent (5.31 million). As a result, there were throughout these years expressions of concern (from Sri Lankan politicians and British officials alike, including Clifford himself) at overpopulation in parts of the wet zone, especially on the south-west coast.

That coast (that is, the Western Province and the Southern Province without the Hambantota district) retained its position as the most densely populated area containing, during much of this period, at least two-fifths of the country's whole population. Within that region, population density was greatest in the strip, extending about 11.3 km into the interior that covered the coastline from Negombo to Matara. The Colombo district proper accounted for nearly one-fifth and Colombo city one-twentieth of the island's population. The hill country plantation districts (the Central Province, Uva and Sabaragamuva) showed peaks and troughs in population growth corresponding to the fortunes of the tea and rubber industries.[7] The Central Province, for instance, showed a growth rate of 32.8 per cent between 1921 and 1931, the highest since the decade 1891–1901 when it had been 31.3 per cent. Uva and Sabaragamuva recorded high growth rates throughout the period, generally over 20 per cent per decade, with only a slight drop in 1911–21. The dry zone (excluding the Jaffna peninsula and the narrow east coast), covering more than half the land area of the island, was relatively sparsely populated. It contained less than one-fifth of the population and this did not significantly change in the early twentieth century. The Northern and Eastern Provinces recorded a growth rate of less than 10 per cent up to 1931, while the lowest rate was in the North-central Province, less than 1 per cent in the period 1921–31. The Kurunegala district of the North-western Province accounted for nearly 40 per cent of the population of the entire dry zone and the proportion was maintained if not increased during much of this period. This reflected its importance as one of the main coconut-producing areas of the island. In much of the dry zone, the most formidable constraint on economic development and population growth was malaria, especially in the North-central Province and the Vanni areas of the North-western Province and the Northern Province.

With increasing population growth, overall density of population rose from 54 per sq. km in 1901 to 102 in the mid-1940s, with marked regional variations in density, which ranged in 1901 from over 500 in the Colombo district to less than 50 in most of the dry zone areas. There was no significant change in this pattern in the early twentieth century. Despite this rapid growth in population it remained predominantly rural in all parts of the island, including the south-west coast and the Colombo district.

One important facet of this process of population growth attracted more attention than others at this time—population pressure had reached the point where the land resources of the wet zone were incapable of sustaining peasant agriculture against the competition of the plantations for land. This was most acutely felt in the rubber- and coconut-producing areas of the Western Province and the Southern Province. The coconut-producing areas of the Kurunegala district in the intermediate and dry zones were also beginning to feel the pressure, as indeed were the tea- and rubber-producing areas of the hill country. By this time the plantations were spreading in regions above the 1,066.8m contour where there was either no village population or only a very sparse and scattered one. But within a decade or so after the establishment of plantations there, pressure on land resources followed, on account of both the need for expansion of the plantations and the requirements of the villagers in the periphery of the plantations—some of whom were attracted to these remote areas because of the opportunities for work available on the estates.

One other feature of population growth needs to be mentioned. By the beginning of the twentieth century there was, in and around the city of Colombo, a mainly Sinhalese and Buddhist working class, small in comparison with the plantation proletariat (of Indian workers) but growing in numbers. Most of its members were employed in the transport industry and in the port of Colombo. Among them the most vocal and best-organized group consisted of the railway workers, especially those in the railway workshop in Colombo. There was also an important Indian element, but these Indian workers were largely unskilled, and performed the menial and unpleasant tasks of street cleaning, garbage collection and sanitation.[8] All of them—Sinhalese and Indian, skilled and unskilled—faced poor wages and hard working conditions without the benefit of the labour legislation that afforded a modicum of protection and security to the plantation workers. The rates of pay varied with the skills involved, but they were generally low, hours of work were long and conditions of work were hard and unpleasant, with little or no job security. The living standards of the working population, which were already deplorably poor, deteriorated still further with the steadily increasing inflationary pressures of the first decade of the twentieth century.

The clamour for better wages and improved working conditions which ensued provided a powerful stimulus to trade union activity and was the decisive breakthrough to the organization of a trade union movement and the politicization of Colombo's working class. The focal point of this agitation and discontent was the railway, with its solid core of skilled workers in its main workshops in the city, who could be organized for agitation and strike action with comparative ease, unlike the more dispersed and smaller groups elsewhere who were generally less well paid and who, more often than not, endured working conditions no less rigorous than those of the railway workers. Nevertheless, the unprecedented labour unrest of this period and the agitation for betterment of the working population's conditions of life reflected a heightening of trade union consciousness more than an awakening of any cohesive sense of class identity.[9]

In the last quarter of the nineteenth century, the colonial government had taken the initiative in adopting a variety of welfare measures on behalf of immigrant workers directed at improving working conditions on the plantations as well as facilitating their travel to the estates on their way from India and back after their spell of work was over for the year. One reason for these welfare measures was the need to conciliate the Indian government with regard to the well-being of these workers; in any case, it was politic to adopt them to ensure a regular supply of labour and encourage the immigrants to remain on the plantations as more or less permanent settlers. Among the rudimentary welfare measures adopted were free housing (never more than shacks, however) and medical facilities. Not that working conditions on the plantations were anything other than hard or wages much above subsistence level, but by the beginning of the twentieth century this trend towards welfare measures for the Indian plantation workers was well established, and it continued and was expanded in the early twentieth century. On the best estates the Indian workers and their families received free medical treatment and hospitalization; schools were established for their children and at these schools free meals were provided for the pupils.

In 1912, the Legislative Council approved an ordinance which permitted a greater degree of inspection, by government officials, of sanitary conditions on the plantations. At the same time, the process of recruiting Indian labour was made more efficient. A Ceylon Labour Commission had been established in 1904 to tap the labour potential of the districts of south India which traditionally supplied Sri Lanka with plantation workers. In 1923, provision was made through an ordinance for a common fund to meet the costs of recruiting unskilled labour. Moreover, immigrant plantation workers had been exempted from the unpopular and irksome poll tax, to which the local population was subject. Then in 1927 came a Minimum Wage Ordinance, the most notable of these welfare measures of the early twentieth century. Under its terms, the wages payable to the various categories of Indian plantation workers were set out and wage boards were established for that purpose. It was also made obligatory for planters to make specified quantities of rice available at subsidised rates to their Indian workers, thus converting an established practice into a statutory requirement.[10]

The colonial government's labour legislation was, in fact, exclusively concerned with immigrant Indian workers, in particular those on plantations, who in consequence received statutory benefits denied to their indigenous counterparts. One important trend in the agitation of the Sri Lankan working class in the 1920s was pressure to win for themselves the statutory benefits enjoyed by immigrant labour but from which they had been excluded. Sri Lankan politicians, 'constitutionalist' and radical alike, were resentful of the privileged position of Indian plantation workers in regard to the rudimentary welfare benefits that existed at that time. Thus in the debate on the Minimum Wage Ordinance in the Legislative Council, some of Sri Lanka's leading politicians, including D.S. Senanayake, pointedly referred to this and expressed their disappointment at the fact that the indigenous working class was deprived of the benefits of this measure. Faced with this charge of discrimination the controller of Indian immigrant labour stated that this ordinance had been introduced at the request of, and under pressure from, the Indian government. He added—and here he was either surprisingly oblivious to developments in and around Colombo, or cynically disingenuous—that the special treatment accorded to Indian plantation workers was because this sector of the working population alone was 'organised'.

Although in the early 1920s, immigrant workers joined the indigenous working class in trade union agitation under Goonesinha's leadership, this linkage was limited to Indian workers in and around Colombo and no consistent attempt .was made to unionize the plantation workers, much less to mobilize them in support of strike action by the more militant urban workers. Indeed, even this limited alliance between immigrant and indigenous urban labour groups did not blossom into unity of action sustained over any great length of time, for when conditions became harder in the late 1920s, the temptation to treat the former as competitors of the latter was too strong to resist, and the working class on the island remained divided into two separate and mutually suspicious if not hostile groups.[11]

In K. Natesa Iyer, an erstwhile colleague of Goonesinha's in trade union activity, the Indian workers soon found an effective leader. From organizing the Indian workers in Colombo, Natesa Iyer extended his activities into the much wider field of the plantations, where he played a pioneering role in organizing the plantation workers. But his success in both these areas of activity was achieved at the expense of widening the gulf between the indigenous and immigrant sectors of the working class.

EDUCATION

We turn next to the field of education.[12] By the first decade of the twentieth century the denominational system, still very much the dominant influence in education, was facing strong criticism from the Buddhist movement, from which there was now a demand that in education the state should assume the main responsibility. There was also agitation for the introduction of a 'conscience clause' to prevent Christian organizations from using schools as a convenient machinery for proselytization. The Wace Commission of 1905 did recommend a 'conscience clause', but missionary interests succeeded in weakening its effect when it was introduced by throwing the responsibility for invoking it on the individual student (and parent). Thus the 'conscience clause' became a negative measure rather than the positive one which critics of the missionaries demanded and about the merits of which the Wace Commission had been convinced.

However, among the missionaries themselves there was a perceptible weakening of support for the denominational system. The Methodists and Anglicans were lukewarm and were inclined to accept a less influential role for the state in education, but there was no general support for this from all missionary groups and especially from the Roman Catholics. They realized that the alternative to the denominational system would be state control of education and this they objected to most vehemently. Thus from the 1990s, the Roman Catholics took the lead in the defence of the status quo in education.

For a brief period in the early 1920s, the denominational system and the missionary interests in education seemed to be in danger from a most unlikely source—the colonial government under Governor Manning. First of all, the Education Ordinance of 1920 extended the negative conscience clause to English-medium schools. At the same time, Manning announced his intention of withdrawing grants from any denominational school in which the majority of students did not belong to the denomination that ran it. But this change of policy did not survive the end of Manning's tenure of office. However, Buddhists and Hindus, now better represented in the Legislative Council than before, continued their agitation for a positive conscience clause; in 1929 the MacRae Commission recommended its adoption but once more missionary organizations successfully resisted its implementation. Thus by 1931, the denominational system had survived without much change and the missionaries were still very much in control of education.

Nevertheless, there had been a significant increase in the number of government schools in the decade 1920–30: from 919 to 1,490, while proportionately the increase in the number of mission schools was much less—up to 2,502 from 2,122. This latter was an indication of a definite check to the expansion of the missionary school system and the beginning of a policy of consolidation in which the missionary interest concentrated on improvements to existing schools rather than building new ones.

The division between a privileged minority of English-medium schools and a mass of vernacular schools was perpetuated throughout this period. There were three types of schools: vernacular, Anglo-vernacular (bilingual) and English schools. The government's policy was one of promoting mass vernacular education—education was compulsory between the ages of five and fourteen—and with this in view the vernacular schools levied no fees. Vernacular education aimed at importing 'basic instruction for living in a community with very limited horizons' and any curricular innovations were directed towards this end. The number of students in schools increased to 4,41,372 in 1925 and 5,39,755 in 1930 or nearly half the school-age population. There was, as a result, a noticeable improvement in the rate of literacy in general,[13] and the gap in this regard between the Christian minority and the adherents of other religions narrowed quite considerably. At the same time, the proportion of children in school to the total population increased in each province. However, vernacular education was very much the poor relation: the abler and better-off students escaped from vernacular schools at the earliest opportunity, for social mobility and economic advancement were alike dependent on the acquisition of an English education.

The Anglo-vernacular schools sought to occupy the no-man's-land between the much sought after English-medium schools and the rather utilitarian vernacular ones. They taught in the local languages in the mornings and in English in the afternoons. These schools were no great success, as was evident from the very slow increase in their number—from twenty-eight schools in 1900 to forty-six in 1930.

The English-medium schools—the sector of the educational system with most prestige—were organized at two not very clearly demarcated levels, elementary and secondary. The former was rather restricted in scope and catered mainly to those in search of white-collar employment, while the latter offered a varied and much more sophisticated curriculum aimed at preparing students for higher education in British universities and for the professions. The English-medium schools were few in number and all of them levied fees. The content of education in almost all schools, but more particularly the English-medium ones, had a strong literary bias, the natural result on the one hand of the transfer of British educational practice to the colonies—and emulation of the British grammar school tradition—and on the other, of the more mundane business of finance. It was much cheaper to provide such an education than a technical or scientific training.

In the late nineteenth century, little or no progress had been made with regard to agricultural, technical and commercial education. Institutions established to teach these subjects had either all failed by the end of the century or barely survived, while attempts made to bring these subjects into the regular school curricula had failed too. In 1901, a school garden scheme was introduced into the vernacular schools in an avowed bid to give a more practical bias to teaching in them; these school gardens received a government grant in 1911 and elementary textbooks in agriculture were published. Yet at the end of our period, less than a third of the vernacular schools had school gardens and agricultural training had not been integrated into the general curriculum of the schools. The results of the efforts to introduce industrial training in some primary schools after 1916 were even more limited.

When a School of Tropical Agriculture was established at the Royal Botanical Gardens at Peradeniya in 1916, there were high hopes of a real breakthrough in tertiary education. But within six years this institution was downgraded and two farm schools were established, one at Peradeniya, as a successor to the School of Tropical Agriculture, and another in Jaffna: these provided a two-year agriculture course in English, and a one-year course in Sinhalese and Tamil. The Technical School (later, the Ceylon Technical College) established in Colombo in 1894 offered training in engineering and surveying to technical officers in government departments. Private firms gave practical technical and craft training schemes on their own. But all these together did not amount to anything like a sound basis for successful departure into a scheme of tertiary education, even in the restricted field of technical instruction; nor did they provide a really satisfactory counterweight to the predominantly literary bias of the general school curricula.

Projects for a general overhaul of the education system figured prominently in the early twentieth century. Before the First World War, there were two notable reports on education, the Bridge and the Macleod Reports. The first of these was the more avant-garde in outlook and in its recommendations, which were that (i) the mother tongue be the medium of education in elementary grades in all schools; (ii) that a local examination should replace the Cambridge examinations and a local university should be the apex of the educational system; (iii) that a departure from the overwhelming literary bias in curricula should be made; and that (iv) there should be very strict restrictions on entry to secondary education. Not all these recommendations were novel but those that were tended to arouse the suspicion and opposition of both the missionary interests and the leadership of the reform movement, for different reasons. Each of these sets of critics had, in its own way, much greater influence on the Macleod Report, which came out against both local languages and local examinations; its commitment to a university was less than wholehearted. The upshot was that the Education Code of 1914 reorganized education on more efficient lines but with as little disturbance as possible to the status quo. There were no major reforms in education over the next fifteen years.

One of the more constructive achievements of this period was in regard to higher education. In contrast to British India, Sri Lanka had no university and students needed to go abroad for a university education or to take the external examinations conducted by London University. By the last quarter of the nineteenth century there was pressure from the island's elite for the establishment of a university and by the 1900s this agitation had developed into what came to be known as the 'university movement'. The early 'nationalists' regarded a university as essential to 'national existence' and vital for the purpose of arresting the 'process of denationalization'. The two outstanding figures in the 'university movement' were the great Orientalist, Ananda Coomaraswamy and Sir Ponnambalam Arunachalam. The major premise of their case for a Sri Lankan university was that external examinations conducted by British universities were a poor substitute for a real university education in an indigenous university.

It was taken for granted that the initiative for the establishment of a university on the island should come from the state, which would also provide all or most of the finances, but the attitude of the British government to a university in Sri Lanka was lukewarm when it was not ambivalent. In the early stages it regarded the project as something which should be 'cautiously but firmly encouraged'.[14] However, when the pressures for the establishment of a university increased, there were second thoughts: 'We must avoid the dictates of noisy impetuosity and rhetorical exaggeration, and guard above all things against flooding the country with "failed BAs".'[15] But it was impolitic to oppose it openly and when a subcommittee of the Legislative Council—appointed to consider this question—

recommended in 1912 that a university be established in the new buildings of the Royal College in Colombo, the country's premier government secondary school, the recommendation received the endorsement of the government. Only in 1921, however, was it implemented. Partly, these delays were the inevitable consequences of the outbreak of the war; questions relating to the nature of the university and its site needed to be resolved; but in any case this was not treated as something warranting high priority. What emerged in 1921 was much less than the university for which Coomaraswamy and Arunachalam had agitated; it was a 'University College' affiliated to the University of London which would prepare students for the examinations of that university. From the beginning the University College in Colombo was treated as no more than a halfway house to a national university. The legislation necessary for this transformation was ready by 1925, when it was caught up in a prolonged controversy over the best possible site for the university, which was eventually resolved only in 1938. The choice was between a site (or sites) in Colombo and one in or near Kandy.[16] By 1927, the Legislative Council had decided in favour of a site in Kandy and resolved too that the university should be 'unitary and residential'. A draft constitution for it was ready by 1930, but a dozen more years were to pass before the University of Ceylon was established and nearly ten years after that till it was moved to Peradeniya near Kandy. In the meantime, the existence of the University College, established in 1921, was artificially prolonged till 1942.

The Donoughmore Commission and Its Recommendations, 1927–31

THE DONOUGHMORE COMMISSION

In late November 1926, Sir Hugh Clifford sent home a monumental despatch[1] outlining the defects of the island's constitution, as he saw them, and prescribing some rather radical remedies. The leitmotif of the despatch was that the 1923–24 constitution should be regarded as no more than a transitional one and that a greater measure of responsible government was the logical and almost inevitable next step. At the Colonial Office this despatch at first created a favourable impression and was considered a masterly analysis of the political and constitutional problems of the island. But this impression did not survive closer scrutiny and the despatch soon became something of an embarrassment largely because of what were then perceived as indiscreet and unsympathetic comments on the island's politicians and ethnic groups. Nevertheless, it must have prepared the Colonial Office for a closer look at the island's constitution and to devise ways and means of reforming such defects as Clifford had delineated.

Many of the senior officials at the Colonial Office would not endorse Clifford's views on the reform of the constitution, but William Ormsby-Gore, the undersecretary of state for the colonies, adopted a more conciliatory attitude. He saw Clifford's despatch as a 'masterly' document, a 'skilful diagnosis of the diseases of all democracies as illustrated in Ceylon' and 'worthy of study by all liberals of all countries'.[2] He took the view that 'a Royal or Parliamentary Commission appointed by the S[ecretary] of S[tate] *before* the next general election in this country is clearly the line'. This indeed was the line of policy eventually adopted. Thus the decision to appoint the Donoughmore Commission to review the constitution of the colony of Sri Lanka affords an exact parallel to the appointment of the Simon Commission for India—to make a gesture to Sri Lankan aspirations and to forestall the appointment of such a commission by what might turn out to be a Labour government after the general elections scheduled for 1929.

Clifford's announcement on the appointment of a special commission on constitutional reform in Sri Lanka, which was made early in April 1927, had the effect of galvanizing the island's politicians into action. E.W. Perera, then president of the Ceylon National Congress, called for the publication of Clifford's secret despatch of November 1926 to facilitate discussion of the problems of constitutional reform, but by this time the Colonial Office had decided that this long and rambling document would not be published. However, the Sri Lanka government on its own initiative revealed brief extracts from it in an official communication to the Ceylon National Congress.[3] The governor's categorical assertion that 'the present position [is]...eminently unsatisfactory' must no doubt have given Congress politicians a great deal of encouragement. The extracts that followed this were even more encouraging to Congress politicians, since they seemed to endorse their own line of thinking:

> It is reasonable to assume that His Majesty's Government in granting during the past fifteen years successive measures of constitutional reform and holding out hopes of still further reforms in 1929, has entertained the intention of conceding to Ceylonese politicians sooner or later some form of self-government and is persuaded that the adoption of this course at some future date at any rate is not only desirable but practicable.

From these premises the conclusion was reached that:

> A radical revision of the existing Government machinery in this island is urgently demanded in the interests of all concerned...designed as to place real and direct responsibility upon the unofficial members of the Legislative Council and strengthen and not weaken the Executive Government.... [The]

new measures [should be] designed to train the Ceylonese for
eventual self-government which is the object that all the reforms
granted up to now have conspicuously failed to achieve.

The news of the appointment of a special commission on
constitutional reform—with the Earl of Donoughmore as
chairman—from Britain almost exactly a century after the
arrival of the last such commission—the Colebrooke–Cameron
Commission—had the effect of exacerbating communal and
political tensions in the island, with individuals and groups
making exaggerated claims and demands in the hope of
influencing the commission's work and the political–
constitutional structure it would recommend. The stresses set
off by these pressures and counter-pressures led to a further
weakening of the Congress as a political body. First, there
was the acrimonious termination of the increasingly uneasy
association of A.E. Goonesinha and the radicals with the
Congress, and second, sharp differences of opinion erupted
among Congress leaders on the objectives of the next stage in
constitutional reform. The final break between Goonesinha
and the Ceylon National Congress came in 1927 over a
fundamental difference in the response to the process of
radicalization in politics. There was little doubt now that with
the appointment of the Donoughmore Commission, a further
and substantial measure of constitutional reform was about
to be conceded. But while Goonesinha was just as anxious as
the Congress leadership for the attainment of self-government,
he recognized—as they or most of them did not—the need
for far-reaching social and economic changes as the
concomitant of political reform. Congress leaders set their
sights on constitutional reform per se; Goonesinha raised the
issue of universal suffrage.

With the arrival of the Donoughmore Commission the
question of the suffrage became an important—and divisive—
issue in Sri Lankan politics. From 1923, Goonesinha had urged
the Congress to accept the principle of manhood suffrage, but
the Congress leadership was coldly unsympathetic on this issue.
As late as 5 November 1927, when the Congress delegation
was preparing its brief for presentation and argument before

members of the Donoughmore Commission, he exhorted them to accept manhood suffrage as part of the 'party' platform, but in this he was defeated. Congress politicians did not give it any high priority in their programme of constitutional advance. On 22 and 23 November 1927, the Congress deputation led by its president, E.W. Perera, a seasoned campaigner, with two of the bright young men of the day, S.W.R.D. Bandaranaike and R.S.S. Gunawardane, as its joint secretaries, appeared before the Commission to outline their demands for constitutional reform. In its written memorandum to the commission the Congress had taken the view that 'we advisedly refrain from making any suggestion on the question of the franchise or on the mode of allocating or distributing seats in the Legislative Council. We are concerned not so much with the details as with the principles of the constitution we want to see remodelled.' In its oral evidence, when the question of the franchise inevitably came up, the Congress deputation was quite emphatic that the franchise should be restricted to those earning at least Rs 50 a month, arguing that almost the entire adult population who were fitted for the exercise of the vote would thus be enfranchised. If they went a grade lower, the delegation asserted, there was the danger that they might get a class of person who would not use the vote with any sense of responsibility and whose votes might be at the disposal of the highest bidder. One concession the deputation was prepared to make was to extend the franchise to women over twenty-five years of age, but with either a rigid literacy test or a property qualification. The delegation went on to add, with disarming candour, that although its opposition to any further extension of the franchise might well lead to accusations that it was seeking to establish an oligarchy, it was not inclined to change its views, feeling that any precipitate extension of the franchise might jeopardize the gains the country had achieved so far. In striking contrast, Goonesinha was the one prominent political figure to advocate universal suffrage before the Donoughmore Commission.

The insensitivity of the official Congress delegation over universal suffrage served to alienate the commission (in particular its most active and effective member Dr Drummond

Shiels) and to confirm its impression of the Congress as a rigidly conservative, oligarchic body determined to maintain the sectional interests of a group of landowners and capitalists in preference to the larger interests of the people as a whole. Shiels soon developed a close association with Goonesinha, whom he regarded as the representative of the democratic and radical forces in the country and a politician whose views were all the more valuable on that account.

Equally embarrassing to the Congress was the revelation that an influential section of its leadership would not endorse the official Congress call for responsible government as the next stage in the country's political evolution. While men like E.W. Perera, D.B. Jayatilaka and Francis de Zoysa insisted that the Congress must demand responsible government without a further transitional phase, the 'old guard'—James Pieris and E.J. Samarawickreme in particular—argued that, on the contrary, Sri Lanka was not yet ready for so decisive a step forward. Support for this latter point of view also came from other quarters. Thus the newly formed Ceylon Unionist Association[4], a small group of Colombo-based native pukka sahibs with little or no connection with the political groups then in existence and much less with the people, but which was nevertheless influential through the esteem which some of its members enjoyed in official circles—came out with the opinion that Sri Lanka was not ready for self-government, especially because elected members of the legislature had little or no experience in the art of government. The Ceylon Unionist Association advocated a further period of training for Sri Lanka preparatory to the grant of self-government.

The demand for self-government received no support from minorities, or for that matter from the Kandyans.[5] The most influential Kandyan political organization, the Kandyan National Association, intent on keeping its distance from the Ceylon National Congress, pressed for a federal political structure for Sri Lanka[6] and urged in support of it the contention that: 'Most of the grievances under which [the Kandyans] labour at the present day are directly due to the amalgamation of Government in 1833...'.[7] They argued further that 'the fundamental error of British statesmanship has been to treat the subject of political advancement of the peoples of Ceylon as one of the homogeneous Ceylonese race'.

THE DONOUGHMORE REPORT

The Donoughmore Report has been described as 'the most remarkable state paper on Colonial affairs of the twentieth century'.[8] In the acuity of its analysis of the constitutional problems of the colony and its singular readiness to depart from convention and tradition in the solutions recommended, it has been compared to that path-breaking nineteenth-century document on colonial administration, the Durham Report on the Canadas, with the significant difference that while the latter 'found the solution of the problems of the Canadas in the model of the British Constitution, [the former] was remarking that western parliamentary systems are irrelevant to non-western communities....' [9]

Like the Durham Report in its day, the Donoughmore Report found the basic issue in Sri Lanka to be the divorce of power from responsibility,[10] and while rejecting the demands of the Ceylon National Congress for full responsible government, it nevertheless recommended semi-responsible government and conceded a very substantial measure of responsibility to the colonial politicians with—and this is the significant point—commensurate power. The central feature of the constitutional structure recommended for the colony was the departure from the conventional mode of advance to semi-responsible government: instead of the familiar cabinet or quasi-cabinet there was to be a system of executive committees modelled on those of the League of Nations and the London County Council. As a device in colonial constitutional practice, the executive committee system was at once novel and unusually complex. The members of the unicameral legislature, the State Council, were grouped into seven executive committees. The aim, quite explicitly, was to give the members not merely responsibility but administrative experience and political education as well. The constitutional structure was not only one based on committees, it was fundamentally dyarchical as well. While it was intended that the elected members should have a large measure of administrative responsibility for internal affairs, there were clearly marked limits to their power, and three of the most important executive departments were assigned to officers of state with responsibility for these to the governor alone. In addition, there were the governor's reserve powers: these powers had been a feature of the constitutions devised in 1920–24, but now they were more precisely defined and strengthened. The governor had at his disposal a larger variety of courses of action in matters of paramount importance and in periods of emergency.

The members of the Donoughmore Commission were quite unwilling to consider the conferment of semi-responsible status on the island without introducing at the same time a drastic widening of the franchise (under the constitution of 1923–24, only 4 per cent of the male population had the vote) to avoid the transfer of power to a small oligarchy at the expense of the poorer classes. They recommended that all males over twenty-one and females over thirty should be eligible to vote; in implementing this recommendation in 1931, the Colonial Office went further and brought the age limit for females down to twenty-one. Sri Lanka thus became the first British colony in Asia—and indeed the first Asian country—to enjoy the privilege of universal suffrage.

Just as radical in approach was the commissioners' attitude to the question of communal representation. Quite deliberately, no provision was made for communal representation, although the minorities were almost unanimous in urging that it be retained. 'It is our opinion', the report stated, 'that only by its abolition will it be possible for the diverse communities to develop together a true national unity.... Communal representation in Ceylon has no great antiquity to commend it, and its introduction into the constitution with good intentions has had unfortunate results...'.[11]

RESPONSES TO THE DONOUGHMORE REPORT

Despite all its attractive features, the Donoughmore Report satisfied none of the important political groups in Sri Lanka.

The leadership of the Ceylon National Congress was irked by the device of the executive committee, and the maintenance and strengthening of the governor's reserve powers. Indeed, for them the Donoughmore scheme was not 'a natural stage in the political evolution of the country'. At best it represented 'an outsider's view of what was good for Ceylon.' They had envisaged the grant of full-fledged parliamentary institutions—the orthodox cabinet form of government—as the logical goal of the slow process of constitutional evolution that had begun in 1910. They did not expect, and were unwilling to accept, a new model which appeared 'by reason of its very modifications, to be a counterfeit especially designed for their benefit'.

Another point gave the leaders of the Ceylon National Congress cause for concern, namely, the extension of the franchise to the immigrant Indian plantation workers on almost the same terms as for the indigenous population. Sinhalese politicians feared that this would lead to a potentially harmful increase in the political influence of the European planters, the employers of Indian labour. But these fears were nothing compared to the alarm they felt over the prospect of a political threat to the interests of the Sinhalese population in the plantation districts. The Indians were present in some districts in such large numbers that the Sinhalese, especially the Kandyans, were thoroughly disturbed at the possibility of an Indian domination of the central highlands of the island if permanent citizenship rights were conferred on the Indian population there without adequate safeguards for the interests of the indigenous population. The opposition to the unrestricted extension of the franchise to the Indians in Sri Lanka became one of the major political issues in the country in the aftermath of the Donoughmore Report, an issue on which there was an identity of interests between the Congress leadership and the Kandyan leaders.

On the other hand, the minorities were bitterly hostile to the Donoughmore Report on account of its forthright condemnation of communal electorates. Unlike the Montagu–Chelmsford Report on Indian constitutional reform, the Donoughmore Report took rejection of 'communalism' to its logical conclusion by devising an electoral structure which made no concession to 'communal' interests. Representatives of minority opinion complained that while a significant measure of political power had been transferred to Sri Lankans, safeguards for protecting the interests of minorities were surprisingly inadequate. Moreover, the minorities found universal suffrage just as unpalatable as the Sinhalese, who took a stand against it, and indeed even more so: for universal suffrage would result not only in the democratization of the electorates but would guarantee the permanent Sinhalese domination of politics. Sir Ponnambalam Ramanathan, for instance, came out strongly against it on behalf of the Tamils: he made a well-publicized but totally fruitless visit to Whitehall, seeking to persuade the Colonial Office to reject the Donoughmore proposals, while on behalf of the Muslims, T.B. Jayah (the Muslim representative in the Legislative Council) sent a memorandum entitled 'Muslims and Proposed Constitutional Changes in Ceylon' to the Colonial Office, complaining that the Muslims were 'aggrieved that they were forced to submit to a scheme wholly unacceptable to them'.[12]

Only two political groups on the island supported the Donoughmore proposals unreservedly, Goonesinha's Labour Union and the Unionist Association, a curious combination of radicals and arch-conservatives. In the Legislative Council the proposals were adopted by the slimmest of margins—19 to 17 (the vote was quite deliberately restricted by the governor, Sir Herbert Stanley, to the unofficial members[13])—after a long and acrimonious debate and they were only adopted at all because the Colonial Office, at the instance of the Ceylon government and in the face of vigorous opposition from the Indian government, imposed restrictions on the franchise for Indians resident in Ceylon in the modification of the Donoughmore proposals. All the minority representatives in the Legislative Council voted against acceptance of the Donoughmore proposals, as did two low-country Sinhalese, but the reasons which caused the latter to cast their votes against acceptance were totally different from those which guided the representatives of minority communities. E.W. Perera and the other Sinhalese who voted against the Donoughmore proposals did so because they felt that these did not go far enough in the direction of self-government.

What was the immediate effect of the Donoughmore Report on the politics of Ceylon? Undoubtedly, one of the most striking developments was A.E. Goonesinha's colourful prominence in national politics. His Labour Union had left the Congress before the Donoughmore Report was published and the breach between him and his erstwhile colleagues widened with its publication. The way seemed open for the labour movement in Ceylon to assume an independent role in politics. From being merely a close associate of Drummond Shiels, Goonesinha became a 'protégé' of the British Labour Party. He returned from a visit to Britain, where he had made a careful study of the political and trade union activity of the British Labour Party, to form the Ceylon Labour Party and the All Ceylon Trade Union Congress. The three years from 1928—the year of the foundation of the Ceylon Labour Party—to 1931, when the Donoughmore reforms were implemented, were the high-water mark of his influence in the country's politics and in the trade union movement. The latter was effectively demonstrated in the spate of major strikes that occurred between 1927 and 1929, beginning with one in Colombo harbour in 1927 and culminating in the Colombo tramways strike in 1929 and its sequel, the Maradana riot, a clash between the strikers and their sympathizers on one side and the police on the other, when the Colombo working class came out into the streets in support of Goonesinha and to demonstrate their defiance of the Colonial administration. Faced with this unparalleled exhibition of working class solidarity and militancy, the employers, who in the past had refused recognition of trade unions led by Goonesinha, came to terms with the unions. One result of this outbreak of industrial unrest was the formation of the Employers' Federation and the signing in June 1929 of the first collective agreement between this body and Goonesinha's Ceylon Trade Union Congress. For the first time, official recognition was given to the existing trade unions and to the right of workers to organize trade unions. The colonial administration in Sri Lanka was much less inclined to yield to militant trade unionism and attempted to introduce into the island the main restrictive provisions of the British Trade Unions and Trades Disputes Act of 1927—to which, however, Lord Passfield (Sidney Webb), Secretary of State for the Colonies in Ramsay MacDonald's Labour Government of 1929–31, refused to give his approval.

For Goonesinha the most encouraging feature of the arrival of the Labour Party to power in Britain was the appointment of Drummond Shiels as Passfield's undersecretary.[14] From this vantage point Shiels kept a protective watch over the interests of Sri Lanka's adolescent labour movement. It was confidently expected that with the implementation of the Donoughmore reforms the labour movement led by Goonesinha would achieve political influence on a scale never before seen in Sri Lanka. But the story of the years 1931–37, in part at least, is the story of how this did not happen.

Congress politicians were no doubt apprehensive of their position with the introduction of the new constitutional structure. But they found that the widening of the franchise made little immediate difference to their political fortunes, despite the fact that they fought the first general election to the State Council in 1931 as individuals and not as a group or political party. Their strength lay in the rural constituencies and the rural vote easily swamped the working class vote in the urban areas.

The confrontation between the official Congress delegation and the Donoughmore Commission had been, for the former, a chastening experience and its members emerged from it disheartened and more than a little embarrassed. Despite their misgivings about the recommendations of the Donoughmore Commission, they were in no position to indulge in spectacular demonstrations of their dissatisfaction. In an official memorandum to the commission the honorary secretaries of the Congress, S.W.R.D. Bandaranaike and R.S.S. Gunawardane, had emphasized the point that 'Ceylon is one of the few British possessions in which the demand for political reform has never passed from constitutional agitation to hostile demonstration. Our appeal has always been to reason and justice.'[15] More important, not only did the Congress have no support from other political groups and the minorities, but its leadership was sharply divided on the objectives to be aimed at in constitutional reform. After some initial hesitation, the Congress opted to accept the Donoughmore scheme. At the annual sessions of the Congress held on 20 and 21 December 1929, the following resolution was adopted: 'This Congress reaffirms its demand for full Responsible Government at the next revision of the Constitution, but pending such revision recommends the acceptance for a short period of the proposed Donoughmore Scheme of Constitutional Reforms as modified by the Secretary of State for the Colonies.'

The decision to cooperate in the implementation of these reforms led to the departure of yet another section from the ranks of the Congress. The most notable of the new dissidents was the redoubtable E.W. Perera who, as president of the Congress, had led the official delegation to the Donoughmore Commission. Among the senior Sinhalese political figures, he had been perhaps the most trenchant and outspoken critic of the Donoughmore scheme—on the ground that it did not go far enough in the way of responsible government. Indeed, he had voted against it in the Legislative Council. He now broke away from the Congress on this and other issues and, as was to become customary with dissident (and disgruntled) politicians in Sri Lanka, formed his own political organization, the All-Ceylon Liberal League. For a year or two it attracted to its ranks a remarkable array of political and legal talent and gave every impression (to Governor Sir Graeme Thomson,[16] among others) of developing into a formidable challenge to the Congress. Among the young politicians it attracted were S.W.R.D. Bandaranaike and G.G. Ponnambalam, the two outstanding orators of their day, soon to distinguish themselves as the most notable exponents of the divisive politics of ethnicity. But the All-Ceylon Liberal League, formed to agitate for a more significant advance to responsible government, was soon deflected, by the lawyers who came to dominate it, from this political objective to a concentrated opposition to the introduction of income tax and to the advocacy of the classical (and doctrinaire) laissez-faire attitudes in matters of economic policy.[17] Thus its early promise of new departures in political activity was never fulfilled.

In the Northern Province too the conservative leadership in politics seemed to be losing ground. The situation there was more complex and interesting than in the Sinhalese areas. The more prominent Tamil politicians had seen little to commend in the Donoughmore scheme—indeed the commissioners' unequivocal rejection of communal representation made them especially apprehensive of the future, since it involved the rejection of one of the basic principles of Tamil politics, the insistence on weightage for the minorities to compensate for the numerical superiority of the Sinhalese. But after the failure of Sir Ponnambalam Ramanathan's mission to the Colonial Office, Jaffna's political leaders acquiesced in the decision to give the new constitution a trial despite their initial misgivings. It was at this point that the Jaffna Youth League, composed 'chiefly of teachers and students', entered the picture. The League was opposed to the Donoughmore scheme because it fell short of self-government, and as an advocate of the immediate grant of Swaraj to the island it resolved on organizing a boycott of the elections to the State Council as the most effective expression of their dissatisfaction. This decision was taken just after the annual meeting of the Jaffna Youth League in April 1931, presided over by the Indian politician Kamaladevi Chattopadhyay. The League soon outmanoeuvred the senior politicians of their region. The move to boycott the elections in the Jaffna region and the Northern Province was in the nature of an amazingly successful coup d'état staged at almost the eleventh hour, on 4 May 1931, the last day for nominations, in the context of a situation where candidates had been nursing electorates in anticipation of keen contests in every constituency in the Northern Province. The only contest in the Northern Province was for the Mannar-Mullaitivu seat which the League was quite unable to prevent. The League was much less successful when it turned to organizing in Jaffna a boycott of imported necessities of life—such as sugar, kerosene and cigarettes. What mattered more, however, were the purely political aspects of its activities and here, for the moment at least, it was stunningly successful.[18]

At every stage the 'moderate' politicians of Jaffna sought to beat the boycott. They called a meeting at Manipay to repudiate it but had to concede defeat. Again, a number of chairmen of village committees attempted to pass resolutions against it but they either failed to secure a discussion of the resolution or, in many instances, the resolutions were rejected. The failure of the 'moderates' to beat the boycott may be attributed to two factors. One was the matter of personalities. The death of Sir Ponnambalam Ramanathan (in 1930) had deprived them of the only charismatic figure in the Tamil community—the one man who, if so minded, might have stood up to the Youth Leaguers and persuaded Jaffna to give the new constitution a trial. Waitialingam Duraiswamy's decision to endorse the action of the Youth League was just as important, for he was nearly as influential as Ramanathan had been in his last years. While Jaffna may not have endorsed the Youth Leaguers' decision to boycott the elections because the Donoughmore constitution did not grant Swaraj, a gesture of this sort was not without its attractions for others who objected to the Donoughmore constitution for less enlightened reasons.

Some sections of Sinhalese opinion—especially those desiring a more positive advance towards self-government than that conceded by the Donoughmore Commission[19]—warmly applauded the political initiative of the Jaffna Youth Leaguers. Their example also served as a fillip to the Youth League movement in other parts of the country. The Jaffna Youth League sought to establish an understanding with political groups in Colombo who shared the same outlook on the Donoughmore reforms and it is significant that their approach was made to the Liberal League rather than to the Congress leadership or the Labour Party. Jaffna seemed once more to be setting the pace in politics. But this favourable impression of the Jaffna boycott did not last very long. None of the major Sinhalese political figures supported it. What the politically conscious Sinhalese remembered were Sir Ponnambalam Ramanathan's well-publicized mission to Whitehall and the opposition of the more prominent Tamil leaders to any significant political advance for Sri Lanka which did not preserve the existing privileges of the minorities. H.A.P. Sandarasagara, for instance, made the melodramatic claim: 'I'll make Jaffna an Ulster' and 'I'll be its Lord Carson.'[20] Thus when the Jaffna Youth League initiated the boycott in imitation of the left wing of the Indian National Congress, most Sinhalese politicians preferred to look upon it as a parody of Ulster sectionalism rather than an emulation of Indian nationalism. Nor did the British officials on the island take a more generous view. An official telegram sent to Whitehall by the governor on 6 May 1931 stated that the 'ostensible reason [for the boycott] is that new constitution is no advance towards self-government. Real reason is no doubt dissatisfaction at what Tamils consider their inadequate representation.' Most of the candidates in the northern constituencies had not been in sympathy with the boycott and within a few months—despite the immediately favourable response it evoked among certain sections of the Tamil intelligentsia—the complaints against it became audible in the Jaffna Peninsula itself. But the governor was convinced that it 'would be a great mistake to make overtures to them', an attitude in which he was supported by the Colonial Office.

It took nearly two years for Tamil politicians to persuade the governor and the Colonial Office to relax their opposition to the holding of elections to the vacant seats.[21] When they eventually relented they were no doubt impressed by the Tamil Conference held in Jaffna on 2 January 1933 with representatives from all parts of the Jaffna district, which condemned the boycott movement in unequivocal terms. As regards Jaffna, this conference, at which some of the principal boycott leaders made an open confession of the blunder they had committed, gave the final blow to the boycott movement. At the Colonial Office it was argued that 'now [that] the Jaffna Tamils are anxious to secure representation in the State Council we should be well advised to meet their wishes and to involve them in a tacit acceptance of the provisions of the constitution. Further, addition of four Tamil members to the State Council will be a valuable counterpoise to the existing Sinhalese majority.'[22]

The elections to the Jaffna constituencies held in 1934 marked the entry into the State Council of G.G. Ponnambalam (elected from the Point Pedro constituency) who was soon to assume leadership of the Tamils in their political campaigns.

The Politics of the Transfer of Power: The First Phase, 1931–42

Congress politicians gained an easy domination over the new administration established under the Donoughmore constitution, although they had fought the first general elections to the State Council as individuals and not as a group or party. A duumvirate consisting of D.B. Jayatilaka and D.S. Senanayake was soon calling the tune. While Jayatilaka, as vice-chairman of the Board of Ministers and leader of the State Council, was the official leader, there was at his side the imposing if not yet dominant personality of D.S. Senanayake, whose influence on the members of the State Council was perhaps greater than Jayatilaka's. Both were prison graduates of the class of 1915 (see Chapter 28). D.B. Jayatilaka was at this time the better known and his position within the administration was strengthened by two factors. First, he enjoyed the confidence of British officialdom in Sri Lanka, to say nothing of the Colonial Office, and received unstinted support from them. This was partly at least because of the suspicion among British officials that D.S. Senanayake was anti-British and the feeling that he would not be quite so malleable as Jayatilaka. Second, Jayatilaka's prestige as a politician was enhanced by his position as the undisputed lay leader of the Buddhist movement whereas D.S. Senanayake, unlike his elder brother F.R. Senanayake, was rather less interested than Jayatilaka in Buddhist activity. But Jayatilaka, as early as 1931, was already an elder statesman and D. S. Senanayake, though still somewhat in his shadow, was regarded as his inevitable successor. As a result, the leadership in the State Council was shared between them. In most matters their policies and priorities were much the same and indeed there was no sphere of activity in which they tended to come into conflict.

During the period covered by this chapter, 1931–42, D.B. Jayatilaka was leader de jure and, at least till around 1939, de facto as well, but by 1940 his power, if not his influence, was distinctly waning and it came as no great surprise when, in 1942, he decided to retire from national politics and accepted the less demanding position of Ceylon's representative in New Delhi. The posts of vice-chairman of the Board of Ministers and Leader of the State Council which he vacated went as of right to D.S. Senanayake. There are other reasons too for treating 1942 as a convenient terminal point of the review of events in this chapter—the politics of the island in the first decade of the Donoughmore system—and these all relate to a single and overwhelming important theme: Second World War and its effects on the island's politics and constitutional structure. The economic and social problems of the period, which form the essential backdrop to the political and constitutional problems analysed here, are treated in detail in a separate chapter.[1]

THE FIRST STATE COUNCIL, 1931–35

The new administration, in which several prominent Congressmen secured election to the Board of Ministers, took office at a time when the country was in the throes of the Great Depression of 1929–31. And just when it seemed that the worse was over, an epidemic of malaria devastated the Kurunegala and Kegalla districts. This epidemic had been preceded by an unusually severe drought in most of the island.

The economic depression and the malaria epidemic were so cataclysmic in their impact that they baffled conventional wisdom of the day and the normal machinery of government in coping with the mass of misery they created.[2]

In the economic crisis, the Board of Ministers was no more imaginative in the solutions it offered than the more experienced politicians of democratic regimes in more advanced societies. The Donoughmore constitution placed the treasury under the financial secretary, one of the three British officers of state, and he was intent on the conventional exercise of balancing the budget by a vigorous policy of retrenchment. The fact, however, is that elected ministers did not show themselves ready to adopt more radical measures or unorthodox solutions; so it was easy for their critics to describe their response as one of helplessness bordering on indifference. This change appeared to derive such validity as it may have had from the higher priority they gave to constitutional reform.

The immediate effect of the introduction of universal suffrage, as demonstrated in the general election of 1931, had been to help the 'constitutionalists' consolidate their hold on power within the national legislature. A.E. Goonesinha, for instance, entered the State Council with great hopes of establishing himself and the Labour Party as a powerful influence within the legislature, but his role turned out to be altogether less distinguished than what he had in mind. To a large extent this was a reflection of the steady erosion of his power in the trade union field in the wake of the massive unemployment that followed the Depression. Besides, younger rivals, more doctrinaire in their radicalism, were in the process of replacing him in the leadership of the trade union movement and the politics of the urban working class. Fortunately for the 'constitutionalists', these radical forces had as yet no base in the State Council and so did not affect the balance of power within it. Moreover, because of the Jaffna boycott of elections, the Tamils were under-represented in the State Council and had no articulate spokesman till 1934 when G.G. Ponnambalam entered the legislature.

Although their sights were set on securing a revision of the Donoughmore constitution as early as possible—within a year or two of its introduction, in fact—the 'constitutionalist' leadership and their associates entered the State Council and secured election to the Board of Ministers not so much to show how flawed the new apparatus of government was or deliberately to wreck it, but to demonstrate their fitness for a further measure of self-government by making a system that they believed to be unusually complex and with built-in deficiencies, work as well as possible. Their tactics and strategies had the same self-imposed restraints as those of their predecessors in the Legislative Council of the 1920s in their strong commitment to constitutional methods of agitation.

Agitation for reform of the constitution had begun as early as July 1932 and it had been initiated by E.W. Perera, a senior politician and the leading spokesman of the Liberal League (though not a member of the Board of Ministers) with the introduction of a series of seven resolutions for debate in the State Council. These resolutions sought a reduction of the governor's reserve powers, the abolition of the Crown's power to legislate by Order in Council and the replacement of the novel machinery of executive committees by a form of cabinet government—in short, the orthodox constitutional machinery devised for colonies in transition to self-government. Of these resolutions only one, that on executive committees, failed to secure the endorsement of the State Council. In 1933, the Board of Ministers took the initiative in the negotiations for constitutional reform and thereafter kept these under their own control. If they sought the support of the State Council when it was thought necessary to strengthen their position in negotiations with the governor and the Colonial Office. Their demands were set within the framework established through the resolutions of 1932, but drafted with greater precision, and there was a renewed emphasis on the need to replace the executive committees by a cabinet or quasi-cabinet of ministers.[3]

Closely linked with the agitation for constitutional reform— indeed it was an integral part of it—was the continuing pressure for the Ceylonization of the higher bureaucracy. By 1931, the gains made were so substantial that the main issue was more or less settled. The ministers were now bent on achieving a drastic reduction, if not entire elimination, of the recruitment of European 'cadets' to the elite Ceylon Civil Service and on the abolition of privileges enjoyed by members of the higher bureaucracy by way of home leave with their passages paid by the government. The Colonial Office was inflexible in its opposition to both demands. Although the governor (Sir Edward Stubbs) himself supported the Board of Ministers in 1934 in seeking an end to the recruitment of European cadets to the Ceylon Civil Service, the Colonial Office refused to sanction such a change on the grounds that 'the maintenance of a European element [in the higher bureaucracy was] essential to the proper exercise by the Governor of the powers reserved to him by the constitution'.[4] Nor would they countenance any measure which could be regarded as curtailing existing emoluments and privileges of the Ceylon Civil Service.

As for a reform of the constitution, the Board of Ministers came up against the reluctance of the Colonial Office to consider amendments to a constitution which had taken nearly three years to devise and which by 1934 had been in operation for barely three years. They might have achieved greater success if they had won the support of the minorities for their proposals. This they did not have and it weakened their case substantially. Curiously, there was greater readiness to consider a change in the system of executive committees where the appointment of ministers was concerned, but this soon vanished in the face of persistent claims by the minorities that their position vis-à-vis the Sinhalese, weak as it was, would deteriorate further should the executive committees be abolished. The minorities had by now the same strong faith in the executive committee system as a buttress of their inherently weak political position as they once had in communal (and weighted) representation. They were, therefore, quite determined to resist any constitutional advance without a consolidation of such advantages as had accrued to them from the introduction of the executive committee system. And so the decision was made to postpone any consideration of a reform of the constitution till after the general elections of 1935–36, especially because there was the feeling in the Colonial Office that while there was indeed agitation among a political leadership for constitutional reform, there was no great urgency about it even among them. If this lack of urgency was a fact—there is no evidence to support it—it was because the State Council elected in 1931 had long since ceased to reflect the changes in the island's politics which occurred in the wake of the Depression, and the increasing radicalization of the trade union movement and militancy of the working class, because Goonesinha and his Labour Party were losing ground to the Marxists.

The entry of Marxists into politics had come through the *suriya mal* movement which had its origins in the dissatisfaction of some Sri Lankan war veterans over the proportion of funds collected by the sale of poppies on Remembrance Day which was to be retained for local use. With the support of the youth leagues in the city of Colombo, a Ceylon Ex-servicemen's Association was formed in 1926, which set about establishing a campaign to rival the sale of poppies. The suriya flower was chosen for this purpose and it was used to collect funds for Sri Lankan ex-servicemen. In the early 1930s, the youth leagues came under the control of Marxists who proceeded to take the leadership in the suriya mal campaign as well. The latter was continued up till the outbreak of the Second World War as an anti-imperialist campaign, pure and simple, with no reference any longer to the island's war veterans and disabled soldiers. Furthermore, during the malaria epidemic of 1934–35, the Marxists organized relief work in some of the most severely affected areas. Their vigorous response to the shattering effects of this great calamity, together with the medical and material aid they rendered, has been one of the enduring folk memories of the region (Kegalla district) in which they worked. There was the added bonus, in future years, of a secure political base (the Ruvanvella constituency) for one of the most prominent of the Marxist leaders, Dr N.M. Perera. But that was still to come.

In the wake of the Great Depression they made their presence felt in the trade unions in and around Colombo (their advances here were made—over several years—at the expense of Goonesinha and his Labour Party). In doing so, they gave the process of politicization of the urban working class greater cohesion by infusing it with a sense of class identity in place of Goonesinha's hazy populism. Despite all this they made no greater headway against the 'constitutionalists' other than Goonesinha himself. Up till then they had no political base from which to operate save the trade unions in Colombo and the indigenous working class which, despite its increasing militancy, was much the smaller section of the island's working population. The message they preached—the need for a sterner commitment to nationalist goals than the 'constitutionalists' demonstrated, with objectives clearly set out, and deriving their validity from an ideological framework and from a keener sensitivity to the problems of the people—had a limited audience compared with what they would have had if there had been a few articulate spokesmen in the State Council to exploit the publicity by attacking speeches there to disseminate these views.

Not surprisingly, Congress politicians were more concerned with the political agitation of communal organizations—the politics of ethnicity—rather than with the politics of radical Marxism. For the former, unlike the latter, the arena for confrontation with the 'constitutionalists' was the State Council and this conferred on it a legitimacy, so far as the 'constitutionalists' were concerned, which they were loath to concede to the fledgling Marxist movement.

THE SECOND STATE COUNCIL, 1936–47

The results of the general elections to the second State Council did not, at first glance, mark any significant shift of power away from the 'constitutionalists'. Both Jayatilaka and Senanayake were returned uncontested as they had been in 1931 and most, if not all, of their close associates had retained their seats while some of their most persistent critics, E.W. Perera, for instance, had been defeated. For politicians who had faced the hustings as individuals and not as candidates of a party, Congressmen had done well—remarkably so considering that they had been part of a political establishment which shared power and responsibility at a time of acute economic distress.

There were also changes in the air, evidence that universal suffrage and the pressures of a democratic electorate were beginning to have some effect on the country's politics. For one thing, the small group of aristocratic backwoodsmen who had won seats in the first State Council, some of them without the inconvenience of a contest, had almost all been defeated or had retired from the scene. Dr N.M. Perera, one of the leading lights of the Marxist Lanka Sama Samaja Party (LSSP), established on the eve of the general election of 1936,[5] was elected from Ruvanvella. In the neighbouring constituency of Avissavella, the most dynamic of the LSSP stalwarts, Philip Gunawardane, defeated a leading Congressman, a scion of the Obeysekere family. This was a significant if numerically meagre reward for an intelligent and vigorously conducted campaign in which they had come out strongly against the policies, methods and objectives of the Ceylon National Congress and the Labour Party.

Apart from the Marxist challenge to the 'constitutionalist' leadership in the State Council, there were two other noteworthy consequences of the impact of universal suffrage on the politics of the country. Universal suffrage was among the main determining factors in the revival of 'religious' nationalism, that is to say nationalism intertwined with Buddhist resurgence and the cultural heritage associated with Buddhism. In the perspective of the island's long history, this was a more significant development than the entry of the Marxists into national politics. The leadership in this was taken by S.W.R.D. Bandaranaike's Sinhala Mahā Sabhā, the lineal descendant of F.R. Senanayake's Sinhala Mahājana Sabhā and— in the politics of ethnicity, of religion and language—the progenitor of the Sri Lanka Freedom Party of today. Thus, it was inherently divisive in its impact, but no less democratic for that. Thirdly, and on a different level, universal suffrage was largely responsible for a broad impulse towards social welfare in the Donoughmore era, especially in the period of the second State Council (1936–47) when the 'constitutionalist' leadership became more responsive to the social and economic facts of the resurgence of nationalism.[6]

When Congress politicians and their sympathizers retained control of the State Council at the general elections of January 1936, they scarcely revealed any perception of a change in the political system. On the contrary, their first act was significant in underlining their belief that nothing had changed—this was the election of a homogeneous Sinhalese Board of Ministers by the device of disposing their supporters in the various executive committees according to plan. The 'Pan-Sinhalese' ministry established through these manoeuvres secured a show of unanimity for the demands of the Board of Ministers, but the immediate effect of this not too subtle move was to aggravate communal feelings on the island without the compensation of impressing on the Colonial Office the urgency of the need for a reform of the constitution or the genuineness of the new unanimity of views of the Board of Ministers.

The Board of Ministers treated its return to office as an endorsement of its demand for a further measure of constitutional reform and soon set about the business of outlining its proposals. In a memorandum which it eventually submitted to the governor, Sir Edward Stubbs, in March 1937,[7] it set out its priorities on constitutional reform: the curtailment of the governor's reserve powers and the abolition of the posts of officers of state; and the replacement of the executive committees by 'the ordinary form' of cabinet government 'with a Chief Minister either invited by the Governor to form a government or elected by the State Council itself'. This memorandum was issued by the Pan-Sinhalese ministry without consulting the State Council. While there was general support for the proposals regarding the officers of state and the governor's powers, the minorities expressed their fears that the cabinet system would deprive them of any chance of participating in the government. Although Stubbs himself felt constrained to agree that the Donoughmore constitution was now 'a proved failure', he was far from certain about what should take its place. He would not support the demand for a reduction of the governor's powers, at any rate for a long time to come, nor would he agree to abolish the posts of officers of state, since he believed that it was too soon to transfer their functions to elected ministers. He suggested that the only practicable course of action would be to appoint a commission to take a fresh look at the island's problems and determine whether a more satisfactory constitution could be devised.

The tempo of these exchanges on constitutional reform quickened with remarkable suddenness in the first quarter of 1937, the last months of Stubbs's term of office as governor. The change was precipitated by the intrusion of Marxist agitation into an issue relating to the balance of power in the constitution, through what came to be called the Bracegirdle incident. Mark Antony Bracegirdle, a young communist from Australia (and a recent immigrant there from Britain), had arrived in Sri Lanka in 1936 as an employee of a tea estate company. He outraged the plantation community by taking an interest in trade union activity among the plantation workers, and even more by appearing on LSSP platforms in plantation districts. He was dismissed from his post and his deportation from Sri Lanka was arranged mainly between the inspector general of police and the chief secretary on the basis of powers conferred on the government by an Order in Council of 1896.[8] The order of deportation was served on him on 22 April 1937, but before he could be deported he was successfully spirited away by the LSSP. In the meantime, legal action was taken against the police by the issue of a writ of habeas corpus. The validity of the deportation order was challenged before the chief justice and the senior puisne justice, who held that Bracegirdle could not be deported for exercising his right of free speech, which, in fact, was all he had done.[9]

The Bracegirdle incident provoked a constitutional crisis of the first magnitude.[10] The basic issue, in brief, was that of the relations between ministers and heads of government departments within their ministries. More specifically, from the point of view of members of the State Council, ever suspicious of the officers of state, one of the latter—the chief secretary— was seen to be encroaching on the functions of an elected minister, the minister of home affairs, vice-chairman of the Board of Ministers and leader of the State Council, D.B. Jayatilaka, no less. The uproar that ensued surprised Stubbs, and he saw it, quite correctly, as the direct result of the intervention of the LSSP, who had ensured that tempers would remain at fever heat for as long as possible by taking the issue to the wider public beyond the walls of the State Council, within which debates on such issues had been confined in the past. By doing so and securing the support of the Board of Ministers, of A.E. Goonesinha and of the majority of the members of the State Council, on this issue, the LSSP demonstrated that negotiations on the constitution conducted at the official level between Whitehall, the governor and the Board of Ministers were strangely remote from the realities of the political situation on the island.

The most notable political and constitutional crisis of the Donoughmore era, the Bracegirdle incident brought the LSSP into the limelight on a national scale and gave it substantial publicity and increased popularity. But there was more to it than met the eye in the support the party received from the established politicians of the day, who would normally not have associated themselves with a political move initiated by the LSSP. Stubbs was personally unpopular with the Sinhalese leaders (with D.S. Senanayake for one) for his role in 1915. He had never succeeded in erasing the bitter memories which this had left and therefore many of them enjoyed the prospect of embarrassing him by giving their covert support to the LSSP on this issue. S.W.R.D. Bandaranaike, minister for local government, appeared on the platform at a mass meeting organized by the LSSP to demonstrate popular feeling against the action of the colonial authorities. His Sinhala Mahā Sabhā was seeking its distinct identity as a political force and although it had little in common with the LSSP, it no doubt relished this opportunity of showing that it was no less anti-imperialist in outlook and political attitude than the Marxists. But there was no doubt that the main beneficiary in terms of the prestige and publicity derived from this imbroglio was the LSSP. Stubbs had received a decisive rebuff and Sir Baron Jayatilaka emerged with his reputation considerably tarnished as a result of his maladroit handling of this constitutional issue.

Significantly, however, neither the 'constitutionalist' leadership in the State Council nor the Colonial Office grasped the full significance of the Bracegirdle incident. The former did not see the need to change its political style to cope with the new dimension in the island's politics which the events relating to this crisis had revealed. The Colonial Office did not understand the point that the Board of Ministers was under attack in an altogether more systematic manner than before from another generation of politicians, for otherwise it would hardly have gone ahead as it did with a constitutional amendment strengthening the governor's reserve powers.

CONSTITUTIONAL REFORM, 1937–39

On 10 November 1937, the British Cabinet approved an Order in Council amending the Donoughmore constitution and bringing it, so far as the governor's reserve powers of legislation and the control of the civil service were concerned, more in line with the Government of India Act of 1935. The Order in Council was introduced in the island in January 1938. The governor was now authorized to legislate independently of the State Council in all matters that concerned 'public faith, public order, and the essentials of good government', in a manner vitally different from the practice of the past in regard to the exercise of his limited powers of 'certification'. He could proclaim his ordinances direct and needed only to communicate them to the clerk of the State Council; the council's right to discuss or delay such measures was thus removed. The Order in Council caused considerable public visitation and coming as it did in the wake of the Bracegirdle crisis, it was assumed that there was a connection between the two. But there was no such connection. Indeed, the permanent officials at the Colonial Office were very critical of Stubbs's actions on the Bracegirdle issue, arguing that he had precipitated the crisis by acting without due regard to constitutional practice and plain good sense.

But the political situation in Sri Lanka did affect the Colonial Office thinking on the amendment to Article 22. On 5 July 1937, the Colonial Office 'expert' on Sri Lanka, H.R. Cowell, noted: 'It must be borne in mind that Sir D.B. Jayatilaka is not physically strong, and if he is succeeded—as seems possible— by Mr Senanayake as Leader of the Council we must expect these attacks on the Governor's reserve powers to be intensified'.[11] Stubbs, who was personally hostile to D.S. Senanayake, had succeeded in convincing the Colonial Office that Senanayake was 'a great danger' to British interests and a man who was 'entirely anti-British'.[12] A constitutional amendment on these lines had been thought of as early as 1932 when there were fears (largely in the Colonial Office) of a potential breakdown of the constitution over a budgetary crisis. Such a breakdown had not occurred. Indeed, by the end of 1933, the Colonial Office was satisfied that the constitution was working as smoothly as could have been expected in a period of acute economic crisis and so the proposed amendment was shelved. By the middle of 1935, however, this proposal was revived. Not that there had been any constitutional crisis, much less a breakdown: there were few occasions when the governor resorted to the use of his reserve powers and most if not all such instances related to salaries and leave privileges of members of the Ceylon Civil Service, about which, as we have seen, Whitehall was especially sensitive. One of the disadvantages, as they saw it, of the machinery devised under Article 22 of the Donoughmore constitution for the use of the governor's reserve powers was that it permitted a debate in the State Council, inevitably long and acrimonious, on every occasion when the governor did use such powers. As most such debates related to conditions of service of public officers, this procedure was regarded with increasing distaste for its presumed demoralizing effect on the higher bureaucracy (especially the British and European element in it). The decision to proceed with the amendment to Article 22 was hastened by the delaying tactics adopted by the State Council, with the connivance of the deputy speaker, in 1936–37, over an increase in the salaries of police officers.

The experience of the years 1936–37 would seem to indicate that while the ministerial group on the island, especially the representatives of the Sinhalese, believed in the inevitability of progress from semi-responsible status to self-government on the model of the white dominions, the permanent officials in Whitehall held a diametrically opposed view. For them there was no such inevitability in constitutional development. They could point to the examples of Jamaica, British Guiana and, most recently and prominently, Malta, where semi-responsible status had not led to responsible government but to political crisis, constitutional breakdown and a reversion, if only temporarily, to colonial status. The concurrent constitutional crisis in Malta must, no doubt, have weighed heavily with the permanent officials in the Colonial Office as they viewed the situation in Sri Lanka and affected to notice signs of incipient crisis by focussing attention on one theme alone, the annual ritual demonstrations of the legislators' pique over the fringe benefits of the higher bureaucracy. But the starting point of a

clear understanding of events in the transfer of power in Sri
Lanka is a realization of the breakthrough that came in 1937–
38 when two men of liberal instincts, Malcolm MacDonald as
Secretary of State and Sir Andrew Caldecott as governor,
brought fresh and unorthodox minds to bear on the problems
of constitutional reform in the island.

Within days of his arrival on the island, Caldecott had to cope
with the political fallout from the Bracegirdle incident, an
unusually difficult if not inauspicious start. He found to his
advantage that the island's political establishment was intent
on bringing the dispute to an end in the certain knowledge that
the only beneficiary of its prolongation would be the LSSP. Besides,
there was the expectation that with a new governor there would
be a fresh start in the 'establishment's' campaign for constitutional
reform. For once, its attitude coincided with that of the Colonial
Office, except that they were unaware of the price they were
expected to pay for it—the amendment to Article 22 of the
Donoughmore constitution. Once the Order in Council embodying
this amendment had been approved by the Colonial Office, a
draft despatch was prepared informing the governor that the
constitution of the colony would be amended 'in certain directions
more acceptable to Ministers after examination by the Governor
and possibly by a further Commission of Enquiry'. This it believed
would 'lessen the criticism of the immediate amendment'.

A despatch from W. Ormsby-Gore (Secretary of State for the
Colonies) dated 25 November 1937 made no reference to a
commission, but asked Caldecott to review the constitutional
problems of the island to obtain the views of all sections of
opinion there and make a report as soon as he had time to form
his own conclusions. Caldecott himself was not in favour of a
commission of enquiry sent from Britain. He felt that the
governor of the colony was in a much better position than such
a commission to conduct the preliminary negotiations on the
reform of the constitution. He spent his first six months on the
island studying memoranda from the Board of Ministers, from
state councillors representing minority interests and from
numerous political and communal associations.

The initial response to the publication of the Order in
Council on the change in the machinery of the governor's

reserve powers had ranged from pained surprise on the part of the Board of Ministers to vociferous protests from the LSSP, but once the political establishment decided to treat it as a peripheral issue that could be conceded without too much protest, in the greater interest of a comprehensive reform of the constitution on which Caldecott was intent, the original tempo of the discussions initiated by him was sustained without any serious interruption. This Order in Council was regarded as a minor inconvenience rather than a serious setback by all except the LSSP.

Between January and May 1938 Caldecott received eleven formal delegations which placed before him a bewildering array of views and proposals for, inter alia, a limitation of the franchise, the establishment of a second chamber and the 'fifty–fifty' demand, then vociferously advanced by G.G. Ponnambalam, which envisaged the equal apportionment of seats in the State Council between the majority community and the minorities collectively.[13] Caldecott was firmly opposed to all these schemes and indeed to any attempt to deal with communal representation by a mathematical formula of whatever kind. He did, however, advise that a new committee be set up to revise the boundaries of electoral districts in order to create more seats, especially in parts of the country where there were large concentrations of minorities. But the distinguishing feature of his reforms despatch of 13 June 1938 to the new Secretary of State for the Colonies, Malcolm MacDonald, was his forthright but carefully considered rejection of the executive committee system.[14] He recommended that it be replaced by a cabinet form of government, headed by a chief minister chosen by the governor as the person most likely in his opinion to command the support of a majority in the legislature. The officers of state would not be members of such a cabinet, and many of their functions would be transferred to the appropriate ministries. Indeed, Caldecott came to attach as much importance to the introduction of a cabinet system as the Board of Ministers themselves; he went on to argue that the success of democracy in Sri Lanka would depend greatly on the discipline and drive which party loyalties alone could

A History of Sri Lanka

infuse into a democratic political system and that the development of a healthy party system could only be fostered by cabinet government. One link in the reforms he advocated placed him at odds with most sections of opinion in the State Council. This was his insistence that the advance to responsible government would have to be accompanied, as a temporary measure, by an increase instead of a substantial reduction in the governor's reserve powers.

On 10 November 1938, Malcolm MacDonald sent Caldecott a short formal reply to his reforms despatch and expressed general agreement with the principal recommendation it embodied, namely, the replacement of the executive committee system by a cabinet form of government. Caldecott was instructed to publish his reforms proposals and to submit them for discussion in the State Council. The next phase came when a series of resolutions embodying Caldecott's proposals was introduced in the State Council in 1939. These were all adopted after prolonged discussion but without substantial modification. Thus a consensus on constitutional reform had been successfully negotiated by Caldecott in 1939, a decisive breakthrough had been achieved and the stage was set for one more step forward in the island's constitutional evolution to responsible government. But very soon thereafter, with the outbreak of the Second World War, Britain's energies began to be concentrated on Europe; the constitutional problems of a small Asian colony took very low priority. How the Second World War affected the transfer of power in Sri Lanka forms the central theme in a separate chapter of this book. And for the present we turn to some of the critics of the 'constitutionalist' leadership, beginning with the most vocal of them, the LSSP.

Membership of the State Council, and the 'parliamentary' immunity it conferred, enabled the two LSSP members to exploit the publicity automatically attaching to speeches in the State Council for the propagation of their views, to set out in opposition to the political establishment of the day an alternative programme and techniques of action for the achievement of independence and to affirm their commitment to a more virile brand of nationalism than that of the 'constitutionalists' and their associates such as the Sinhala Mahā Sabhā. From the Bracegirdle incident to the incarceration of the LSSP leaders shortly after the outbreak of the war, the Sama Samajists sought to establish themselves in the vanguard of militant nationalism, the Sri Lanka counterpart of the socialist wing of the Indian National Congress. Their objective was national independence, 'purna Swaraj' rather than the seemingly inferior dominion status, with its implications of a constitutional link with the Crown, which was what the political leadership in the Board of Ministers aspired to. In the State Council, the LSSP members used every opportunity they had—and they had a great many—to proclaim their opposition to the link with the Crown and all its manifestations in the public life of the country: the eager acceptance by Sri Lankans of imperial honours, the enthusiastic celebration of royal birthdays and the coronation of George VI, and the votes of loyalty to the king.

Within the State Council, the executive committee system gave the LSSP members a disproportionate effectiveness by letting them in at the initial stage of policy making. It is certainly significant that they (and S.W.R.D. Bandaranaike later) always continued to see merits in the device of the executive committees when the bulk of the Congress leadership saw only its (very real) drawbacks.

Had the elections scheduled for 1940–41 been held, the new radicalism of the LSSP might have loomed larger than it did, at least to the extent that they may have captured a few more seats. But the outbreak of the war put an end to all that. For the LSSP, the year 1940, which might well have been a year of solid political achievement, proved to be one of anguish and reverses. First, there was the split, on ideological grounds, which occurred when the hardcore of Stalinists was expelled from the party and the LSSP proclaimed itself a Trotskyist party aligned to the Fourth International. Then in June 1940 came the arrest, under the Defence Regulations, of the LSSP leaders and their detention without trial. The party went underground for the duration of the war although its trade union activity continued till March 1942 when it was declared an illegal organization.

Before the incarceration of its leaders the LSSP had created considerable apprehension in plantation districts by sponsoring a series of strikes (accompanied by sporadic acts of violence) in the tea plantations of Uva. This was part of an attempt to break into the trade union monopoly in the plantations enjoyed by K. Natesa Iyer. Although they made little headway against Natesa Iyer's union, they nevertheless succeeded in disturbing the planters to a greater degree than the traditional leadership because of the nature of their propaganda and their techniques of agitation—their anti-imperialist slogans, their advocacy of class conflict and violence and the spectacular shows of strength they organized such as the May Day rally in Badulla in 1940. The planters and the British officials alike were perturbed and from the former came insistent demands for pre-emptive punitive action against the LSSP before it could establish a bridgehead in the plantation districts.

The Mool Oya incident,[15] with its attendant threat of a constitutional crisis, was the direct result of these developments. The LSSP moved in once more to seize the initiative in a bid to repeat its successful stage-managing of the Bracegirdle affair, but the Board of Ministers, with D.S. Senanayake assuming the leadership, handled the situation more astutely than it had done over the Bracegirdle affair, capitalizing on the intervention of the LSSP to extract concessions from the governor. These took the form of an interpretation of the rules regarding the working of the executive committee system, which really strengthened the position of the chairman (as against the body of the committee), particularly in the vitally important sphere of initiating action in directing administrative policy.

In retrospect, the most notable achievement of the LSSP in these years was to have compelled its opponents and critics to focus attention on issues which the latter would have preferred to ignore or to confront on their own terms and at moments of their own choosing. This was all the more remarkable when one considers the limited (in terms of both geographical area and social composition) political base they operated from—the urban areas of the south-west, the Sinhalese working class and a section of the intelligentsia. Their

links with the peasantry were tenuous at best, and at no stage
in this period did they have a mass organization to back their
political initiatives. The failure to build up a mass organization
could be explained, partly at least, by the political immaturity
of a largely illiterate, recently enfranchised and quite
unorganized rural population. But, equally important, they
did not offer—as Bandaranaike's Sinhala Maha Sabha sought
to do—anything that was intelligible to the peasantry such as,
for example, a social programme couched in the language of
religio-linguistic nationalism.

There were at the same time attempts to give renewed
vigour to more orthodox forms of nationalism, as was evident
in the establishment of S.W.R.D. Bandaranaike's Sinhala Mahā
Sabhā and not less significantly in the positive effort made to
infuse new life into the Ceylon National Congress and to make
it what it had never been before namely a real political party
with a well-defined political objective. The establishment in
1937 of the Sinhala Mahā Sabhā showed that within the
Congress fold there were many who were quite as responsive
as the Marxists to the forces of social and economic change in
the country and who posed solutions in terms no less radical
than theirs but rooted more securely in the traditional cultural
and religious patterns of the people. The policies of the Sinhala
Mahā Sabhā were directed at building a political programme
out of the religio-linguistic nationalism of the early twentieth
century, at a time when the Marxists remained dogmatically
unresponsive to the attractions of this brand of nationalism,
often dismissing it as mere chauvinism. There was no doubt
about the viability of religio-linguistic nationalism as a political
force or the validity of its appeal to a democratic electorate,
but its potentially divisive effect in a plural society such as Sri
Lanka deterred the moderate leadership in the Board of
Ministers from giving it their support with any enthusiasm.
For the members of the Sinhala Mahā Sabhā could not conceive
of a Sri Lanka polity that was not essentially Sinhalese or
Buddhist in character. As a result, every attempt at a precise
definition of its political programme provoked charges of
'communalism', especially—but by no means only—from the
Tamil politicians who followed G.G. Ponnambalam's lead in

the resistance to the grant of self-government without adequate safeguards for minority interests.

Such strength as the Sinhala Mahā Sabhā had within the State Council and among members of the Ceylon National Congress was because of its presumed utility as a platform for opposing the activities of G.G. Ponnambalam and his associates in the latter's own idiom, that of ethnic politics. Indeed, Bandaranaike and Ponnambalam had much more in common than either would have liked to admit. They were the outstanding orators of their day, but the language in which they expressed themselves with such fluency was English and not their own. In the early years of the Donoughmore era they had served an apprenticeship in the Liberal League but had gone their separate ways, especially after Ponnambalam entered the State Council in 1914. Both had their critics on the left of the political spectrum who despised their programmes but conceded a grudging admiration for their political skills. They were alike in rejecting the orthodoxies of laissez-faire economics and were advocates of social and economic reform. But for Bandaranaike, unlike Ponnambalam, religion was an intrinsic element in political activity as it was in his social and economic programmes; indeed, these latter programmes were vital to Bandaranaike's political initiatives. They did not have a similar importance in Ponnambalam's. More significantly, Ponnambalam—unlike Bandaranaike—represented the mainstream of the political activity of the ethnic group to which he belonged.

Indeed, Bandaranaike's politics were as suspect to Jayatilaka and D.S. Senanayake as they were to the Marxist left. The political programmes of Bandaranaike and Ponnambalam were intrinsically divisive in their impact, fed the worst fears of their opponents and thus helped consolidate each other's appeal to their own respective political bases just as they served to emphasize the differences among the ethnic (and, to a lesser extent, religious) groups on the island when the duumvirate of Jayatilaka and Senanayake, not to mention the LSSP, were intent on forging links between them in a nationalism which transcended ethnic and religious distinctions. Jayatilaka's influence was decisive in the reluctance, if not refusal, to countenance the policies advocated by the Sinhala Mahā Sabhā. His dual role of elder statesman in political and religious affairs gave him added prestige in both spheres, which he used to dampen excessive zeal and enthusiasm and to curb what he regarded as extremism. It required his retirement from the political scene and his death shortly thereafter to open the way for a new generation of militant nationalists (many of whom were members of the Sinhala Mahā Sabhā and the Buddhist Theosophical Society) to make their distinctive but divisive impact on the life of the country.

Ponnambalam's political programme was much more limited in scope than Bandaranaike's. His basic aim was to win political concessions for the Tamils as the price of their acquiescence in the grant of responsible government to Sri Lanka; his associates in these campaigns were the British business community on the island and the smaller minority groups, including the Muslims. The fatal flaws in his political campaign were the breadth of his demands—nothing less than an equal division of seats in the legislature in a situation where the main ethnic group represented just over two-thirds of the population—and the doggedness with which he pursued it. For all his eloquence, his adroitness came through as perverse rather than skilful; and he alienated the one man whose sympathy, if not support, was vital to the success of this cause, the governor of the island. Without Caldecott's support, Ponnambalam's occasional visits to England to lobby parliamentarians and officials in Whitehall were ineffective exercises in personal diplomacy. Unfortunately for him, his main opponents were men like Senanayake. He would have evoked a more sympathetic response from these sources had it been Bandaranaike and his associates in the Sinhala Maha Sabha.

In the course of 1939, a group of younger members of the Ceylon National Congress led by J.R. Jayewardene and Dudley Senanayake succeeded in formulating a party programme, comprehensive and forward-looking in content and outlook, and securing its adoption by the 'party'. At last the Congress had a distinctive social and economic programme. At the same time, an attempt was made to revamp its apparatus of party organization and to extend it to cover the whole country. The Congress had been for too long a Colombo-based organization with only the most rudimentary political structure in the provinces. As part of the effort at reorganization, an attempt was made to build up interest in the Congress in other parts of the country.[16] Thus in December 1940 the annual sessions of the Congress were held at Mirigama in a deliberate attempt at creating an interest in Congress in rural areas. The next two annual sessions were held at Dummaladeniya (a village in the Chilaw district) in December 1941 and at Kelaniya in December 1942. After the Dummaladeniya sessions the *Times of Ceylon*, a persistently hostile critic of the Congress, conceded in a political review that the Congress had 'Mass Appeal at Last'.[17] An editorial in the journal *Young Lanka* (December 1941) made much the same point. It declared:

> The Dummaladeniya sessions of the Ceylon National Congress was a remarkable success both from a spectacular point of view and also from the standpoint of the tremendous support it is receiving from the masses.... The Congress is at a turning point in its...[and] a distinct change has come over the Congress. It is seeking ideas not policies, it is pursuing the public good not sectional welfare, it is evolving a national consciousness not for the party or community but for the nation and the people.

The third feature of the revival of the Congress was the attempt made to impose party discipline on its members. It had remained for long, a mere collection of individuals without any semblance of the discipline and organization of a political party, and dual membership of Congress and other—even rival—organisations was looked upon with a tolerant eye. But now an attempt was made to refuse membership of the Congress to those belonging to communal organizations, eight such bodies being named. Although the Sinhala Mahā Sabhā was not included among them, there was nevertheless a bid to ban its members from holding membership and positions of responsibility in the Ceylon National Congress. As a result, the attempt to impose party discipline brought the Ceylon National Congress into a collision course with the Sinhala Mahā Sabhā.

The confrontation was averted because neither the new Congress leadership nor the Sinhala Mahā Sabhā was strong enough to impose its will on the other. Too many influential Congressmen had links with the Sinhala Mahā Sabhā[18] which they were not inclined to sever, while the latter for its own part lacked the confidence to branch out on its own in opposition to the Congress. The Sinhala Mahā Sabhā remained within the Congress, while retaining more than a semblance of its separate identity, insisting all the while that it was not a communal organization. The evidence it advanced in support of this last assertion was distinctly disingenuous, namely, that it did not advocate the representation of communal and special interests in the legislature. But even if it was not very convincing, it was adequate for the purpose of patching up a quarrel which could have ended in yet another rift within the Ceylon National Congress.

D.S. Senanayake and the Passage to Dominion Status, 1942–47

In the context of the British colonial experience in Asia and Africa, the transfer of power in Sri Lanka was unusual for a number of reasons. For one thing, it was a peaceful process, in striking contrast to what happened in the Indian subcontinent and Burma. Second, it provides a rare (indeed, till the Indian elections of 1977, unique) example of power being transferred through the electoral process, completely democratically and constitutionally, from the original legatee of the British to a successor.[1] Third, the final phase in the transfer of power, 1942–7, was dominated, so far as Sri Lanka was concerned, by one man, D.S. Senanayake.

In all his negotiations with Britain, Senanayake was guided by a strong belief in ordered constitutional evolution to dominion status on the analogy of the white dominions. In insisting that dominion status should remain the primary objective and that this should be attained in association with, rather than in opposition to, the British, he stood against the prevailing current of opinion in the Ceylon National Congress that independence rather than dominion status should be the goal for Sri Lanka's leaders. Second, he understood the implication of Sri Lanka being a plural society to a much greater extent than the majority of his colleagues and associates in the national leadership. His policies for the transfer of power and in the early years of independence were framed on that realistic basis. The guiding principles behind his policies were his conception of Sri Lanka as a multiracial democracy, a multiracial state without any special or elusive association with any ethnic group or any section of an ethnic group, and his commitment to the ideal of a secular state in which the lines between state and religion were scrupulously demarcated. Here again he placed himself in opposition to an increasingly influential current of opinion—represented by Bandaranaike and his Sinhala Maha Sabha—which viewed the Sri Lanka polity as being essentially Sinhalese and Buddhist in character and which rejected the concepts of a secular state and a multiracial polity.

But first we need to go back to 1942 for a brief look at the background at the time when D.S. Senanayake took over as leader of the ministerial group on the island. A robust personality and an astute politician, Senanayake came to dominate the State Council and the Board of Ministers, unlike his predecessor, the scholarly and ageing D.B. Jayatilaka. He took over at a time when the consensus on constitutional reform, negotiated in 1938–39 by Sir Andrew Caldecott, the governor of the island, and Malcolm MacDonald, Secretary of State for the Colonies, was undermined by the force of events on the island and in the world at large. The most important of these was of course the outbreak of the Second World War, which led first of all, to the Colonial Office's decision to let the Board of Ministers in Sri Lanka operate as a cabinet or at least a quasi-cabinet, and second, the decision of the Colonial Office (late in 1940) to postpone, till after the war, the consideration of constitutional reform on the island. Caldecott was unwilling to accept this latter decision and protested strongly against it, but to no avail; the decision was confirmed and announced as official policy at the end of 1941. At the beginning of 1942, the moderate wing—by far the most influential—of the nationalist movement no longer regarded itself as bound by the compromise of 1938–39 and was set on dominion status as its objective. Within a year, the younger policy makers, who were increasingly influential within the Ceylon National Congress, succeeded in getting that organization to reject dominion status for the more emotionally satisfying concept of independence.[2]

Senanayake's negotiations with Caldecott and through him with Whitehall began against the background of a deteriorating military situation in south and south-east Asia. Japan had

D.S. Senanayake

overrun Burma, Malaya, Singapore, the Dutch East Indies and the Philippines, and was threatening the north-east frontier of India. When in 1944 the headquarters of Lord Louis Mountbatten's south-east Asia command was established in Kandy, Sri Lanka's strategic importance in the Allies' war effort was underscored; she became the bridgehead for the destruction by Japanese power and a vital link in the supply line to the Soviet Union via the Persian Gulf.

On 5 March 1942, Admiral Sir Geoffrey Layton was appointed commander-in-chief of the British forces on the island. His authority was not restricted to the armed forces but

S.W.R.D. Bandaranaike

extended to the civil government as well—he was authorized to use the governor's reserve powers under the constitution to any extent he desired or thought fit. Indeed, Layton's powers were so wide-ranging that clashes with the civil government—the governor and the Board of Ministers— seemed inevitable and there were fears that friction between the Board of Ministers and the commander-in-chief could lead to a constitutional breakdown. For Senanayake, the powers conferred on Layton and the establishment of a War Council on the island on Layton's initiative and under his control were new and unpredictable complications that confronted him in his campaign for constitutional reform. There were fears, too, that the island's strategic importance in the struggle against Japan would be a further constraint. What happened, however, was that Senanayake soon established a cordial working relationship with Layton and Caldecott. The Board of Ministers gave its unstinting support to the war effort and as a result, Senanayake found that the island's strategic importance strengthened his bargaining powers.

Early in 1942, Caldecott and Layton between them took the initiative in reopening the question of constitutional reform for Sri Lanka by urging Whitehall to respond to the spirit of cooperation demonstrated by the Board of Ministers with a new declaration of policy on constitutional reforms that would 'meet the desires and aspirations of the more moderate elements in Ceylon'. The British government reciprocated in December 1942 with a fresh statement of views on the reform of the island's constitution, but Caldecott and Layton regarded it as falling well short of what was required to meet the wishes of Senanayake and the Board of Ministers. They warned the War Cabinet in Britain that unless a more positive declaration was forthcoming, they expected 'immediate and progressive loss of co-operation and decrease of war effort, coupled with the deflection of now moderate opinion towards intransigent nationalism and the demand for the right of secession'.[3] At the same time, they sent home a very carefully drafted document setting out a declaration of policy on constitutional reform in Ceylon for Whitehall's approval, which they hoped would be substituted for that sent by the Colonial Office in December 1942. The principles enunciated in this document were eventually endorsed by the Colonial Office and the War Cabinet and published on the island on 26 May 1943, using much the same phraseology used by Caldecott and Layton.

A comparison of the two declarations, those of December 1942 and 26 May 1943, is very revealing. In both, no hope is held out about any changes during the war. But the second declaration 'definitely committed [Great Britain] to a far-reaching reform after the war'. Where the first merely promised 'the fullest possible development of self-governing institutions within the Commonwealth', the second offered 'full responsibility for government under the Crown in all matters of civil administration'. The only matters to be reserved would be external relations and defence, 'while of course the proposals [did] not include the right of secession. Thus constitutionally, Ceylon while not attaining full Dominion Status, would be very much in the position occupied [then] by Southern Rhodesia.'[4]

In external affairs, a major concession had been made by 1943. This was with regard to the Indian question, the status of Indian workers in the Sri Lanka polity, specifically their right to the franchise. The original recommendations of the Donoughmore Commission on this point had led to a public outcry in Sri Lanka, and Governor Sir Herbert Stanley had taken the initiative in modifying these substantially in order to gain acceptance of the main recommendations of the commission. But Sinhalese politicians were unwilling to regard Stanley's compromise as a permanent settlement of this crucial issue. In November 1940, D.S. Senanayake led an official Sri Lankan government delegation (the other members included S.W.R.D. Bandaranaike, G.C.S. Corea and the financial secretary, H.J. Huxham) to New Delhi to discuss these questions, especially that of the franchise of the Indian plantation workers, with the Indian government. But little headway towards a settlement was made on this occasion, or in 1941 when a senior Indian official, Sir Girja Bajpai, led an Indian delegation to Colombo on the same issues.

An important aspect of D.S. Senanayake's mission to India needs to be mentioned at this stage. Under the Donoughmore constitution, external affairs came under the purview of the chief secretary. But the despatch of an official mission to India under D.S. Senanayake's leadership meant that, with regard to the crucial question of the Indians in Sri Lanka, the Board of Ministers was given the right to negotiate on behalf of the country. This was taken a stage further when a Sri Lanka government representative to New Delhi was appointed in the person of D.B. Jayatilaka, who took up the post early in 1943. Thus, at the time when D.S. Senanayake assumed the leadership in the negotiations on the transfer of power, the Board of Ministers had been conceded the right to speak on behalf of the country on one of the most crucial aspects of its external relations.

While a reform of the constitution was postponed till after the war and the Donoughmore structure was maintained formally intact, there was nevertheless a transformation in practice and by convention. The Board of Ministers became in all but name a quasi-cabinet and D.S. Senanayake himself very much a chief minister. There was correspondingly a reduction in the power and influence of the State Council and executive committees. The latter were soon dominated by their chairmen, who became de facto ministers, the committees being reduced to the status of advisory standing committees. If the exigencies of the war compelled this transformation, it was eased by the more ready availability of finances to support the welfare measures which became a feature of the last years of the second State Council. The Board of Ministers, in control of the finances, were able to reward their supporters by making provision for projects and ventures in which the latter were interested.

The resignation of D.S. Senanayake from the Ceylon National Congress in 1943, although no doubt precipitated by the entry of the communists into that body,[5] was also a carefully calculated move. First, it was an attempt to demonstrate his severance of ties with an organization which had still not regained the confidence of the minorities. Earlier, the election (masterminded by D.S. Senanayake) of a Tamil, A. Mahadeva (son of Sir Ponnambalam Arunachalam), as minister of home affairs in place of Sir D.B. Jayatilaka heralded a well-publicized abandonment of the principle of a pan-Sinhalese ministry. Besides, he wanted as free a hand as possible in the negotiations on constitutional reform and to keep these under his personal control, although he would of course consult his colleagues in the Board of Ministers and seek the support, when necessary, of the State Council. But, beyond this, he did not feel himself called upon to consult any political organizations, including the Congress, especially when he knew that their policies would run counter to those he advocated.

The first task that confronted him was to formulate a draft constitution on the basis of the conditions laid down in the Secretary of State's declaration of 26 May 1943, and the clarification of this given on 11 July 1943.[6] There were three points of importance in this declaration. First, that the Donoughmore system would be abandoned and there would be a return to the Westminster model in Sri Lanka's constitutional structure. Second, the semi-responsible status conferred in 1931 would be further strengthened although it would fall short of responsible government. The internal control of the imperial government—the governor's reserve powers and the officers of state—would be abandoned and there would be full responsible status in internal civil matters, while the Crown's reserve powers would be retained as the basis of the external control of the imperial government. Three important features of the Crown's reserve powers would be: the limitations set upon the scope of the Sri Lanka legislature in regard to legislation discriminating against religious or communal minorities; the Crown's constituent powers; and finally—most important of all—control of defence and external affairs. The new constitutional structure would guarantee the attainment of internal sovereignty, while external sovereignty would lag behind. The third important feature of the declaration was the requirement that a constitution framed on these lines had to be approved by a three-fourths majority of all members of the State Council, excluding the three British officers of state and the speaker, or any other presiding officer—a degree of support which was well beyond the reach of any draft constitution which did not incorporate meaningful concessions and guarantees to the minorities.

THE MINISTERS' DRAFT CONSTITUTION OF 1944 AND THE SOULBURY COMMISSION

The preparation of a draft constitution that would meet the requirements of the declaration of 1943 was a challenge to the statesmanship and political acumen of Senanayake and the Board of Ministers. They—and his advisers[7]—worked with remarkable speed and by the beginning of 1944 a draft—the Ministers' Draft Constitution[8] as it came to be called—was ready for submission to Whitehall. On the whole it bore the stamp of Senanayake's influence, especially in the concessions made to the minorities. The speed with which they had completed their work was due largely to the fact that nobody outside the Board of Ministers, not even members of the State Council, had been invited to participate in the preparation of the draft constitution. While this was not contrary to the terms of the declaration of 1943, it was nevertheless one of the criticisms of the draft constitution raised by the more vocal representatives of Tamil opinion and by British business interests on the island.

Under the terms of the declaration of May 1943, it was envisaged that this draft constitution would be examined by a 'suitable commission or conference' after victory over the Axis powers had been achieved. Once the draft was ready, Senanayake and the Board of Ministers pressed for an immediate consideration of their scheme. Senanayake argued that urgent local circumstances made an early decision on the constitution a matter of vital necessity. He was supported in this by Caldecott and Layton, but the most convincing case for the appointment of a constitutional commission before the ending of hostilities was made by Lord Louis Mountbatten who, as Supreme Allied Commander, South-east Asia Command, was consulted and whose views were largely responsible for overcoming the original reluctance of the Colonial Office and the War Cabinet to concede to Senanayake's request.[9] This reluctance was so strong that the decision could well have gone against Senanayake had Mountbatten not intervened.

The official announcement on the appointment of a commission to visit the island was made on 5 July 1944, but far from being received with cordiality and a sense of satisfaction at the extraction of an important concession, it was greeted in ministerial circles in Colombo with undisguised dismay. The point at issue was the widening of the scope of the commission's terms of reference well beyond that set out in the declaration of May 1943, from an examination of the draft constitution prepared by the Board of Ministers under the terms of that declaration, to include consultations with 'various interests, including the minority communities concerned with the subject of constitutional reform in Ceylon'. Senanayake and his colleagues in the Board of Ministers argued that this amounted to an abrogation of one of the terms of the declaration of 1943 and urged that the terms of reference of the commission should be restricted to the scope set out in that declaration which meant in effect that the commission's work would be limited to an examination of the Board of Ministers' draft constitution. They added that the requirement of a three-fourths majority in the State Council was quite adequate as protection for the minorities.

The ministers' protests were overruled and the terms of reference of the commission were not changed when the appointment of a chairman (Lord Soulbury) and members of the commission was announced on 20 September 1944. In view of the anxieties of the minorities over the protection of their legitimate rights in any new constitutional arrangements, Whitehall could hardly have come to any other decision. Contrary to the impression created in Sri Lanka that the widening of the commission's terms of reference was due mainly to pressure from Caldecott and his British advisers on the island, the initiative in this came from Whitehall, apparently in response to criticisms made by minority representatives (mostly Tamils) about the way in which the ministers' constitutional proposals had been prepared.

Senanayake believed that Caldecott had let him down over this and, as a result, relations between them were rather strained in the last few months of Caldecott's tour of duty as governor. Senanayake and the Board of Ministers resolved on an official boycott of the commission, as an expression of their disapproval at the widening of its terms of reference.[10] In practice, this meant merely that they did not appear before the commission at its public sittings. Intermediaries conveyed their views to the commission; Senanayake and the ministers had private meetings with the commissioners, whom they met at public gatherings at which the commissioners were guests of honour. Above all, although the ministers did not present their draft constitution before the commission, the latter regarded the examination of that document as its main task during its stay on the island.

Once the commission had left, Senanayake decided on his own course of action—to be in London in time for the publication of its report. If that document were favourable, he would ask for more—for dominion status, in fact; but if it was unsatisfactory, he would repudiate it and refuse to be bound any longer by the declaration of 1943, which the British government itself had disowned, regarding the commission's terms of reference. In a conciliatory gesture, the then Secretary of State, Oliver Stanley, readily consented to extend an invitation to Senanayake to visit London.

SENANAYAKE'S MISSION TO WHITEHALL, AUGUST–SEPTEMBER 1945

When Senanayake reached London in mid-July, he found that events were moving with remarkable rapidity. He met Stanley on 16 July for the first time, and was promised a copy of the Soulbury Report, but on 25 July, the Conservatives were swept out of power in the general election. This inevitably meant that no immediate response was likely from the new government to the Soulbury proposals. Senanayake met G.H. Hall, the new Secretary of State for the Colonies, on 9 August and was then given a copy of the Soulbury Report.

On the international scene, the war in the east was over with dramatic suddenness and this too contributed to the delay in the cabinet review of the Soulbury proposals, for its energies were now concentrated on the urgent task of formulating its policy in the face of the diplomatic and political consequences of Japan's defeat. The change in the international situation also affected Senanayake's attitude to the Soulbury proposals. Had circumstances been different, that is to say, had the war with Japan not come to so sudden an end, Senanayake would have been elated to find that the Soulbury commissioners had endorsed the main principles of the ministers' draft constitution of 1944. But the war was over and there was, therefore, no reason for accepting anything short of dominion status.

When Senanayake had met Hall on 9 August and been given a proof copy of the Soulbury Report, it was expected that the two sides would meet again soon to outline their respective attitudes to its proposals. They next met on 4 September. The cabinet was too preoccupied with the problems stemming from

Japan's surrender to have much time for the comparatively unimportant issue of constitutional reform in Sri Lanka. When it met on 3 September, it instructed Hall to inform Senanayake that the Labour government was not committed to the conclusions in the Soulbury Report and that these were to be regarded as merely the basis for discussion.[11] Senanayake took a completely different line. Hall summarized Senanayake's views to the Cabinet Colonial Affairs Committee thus:

> His principal plea was that Ceylon Ministers had originally accepted the 1943 Declaration as a basis for interim reforms which would enable them to increase the war effort of Ceylon, but now that the war is over, they were no longer prepared to proceed on the basis of the 1943 Declaration, but wished to press for the grant to Ceylon of Dominion Status.[12]

Senanayake explained to his colleagues in the Board of Ministers that:

> The recommendations of the Soulbury Commission are without doubt an advance on the existing constitution, but they cannot satisfy us now. The Commissioners' terms of reference confined it to the 1943 Declaration but the conditions on which we Ministers were prepared to frame and work a constitution within the Declaration no longer exist...the 1943 Declaration had been accepted...as adequate only in respect of war conditions then prevailing, and the conditions had now changed; opinion in Ceylon had hardened in favour of Dominion Status.[13]

In his discussions with Hall, he seized on the remaining obstacle to the attainment of dominion status by Sri Lanka: the limits on her external sovereignty in regard to defence and external affairs laid down in the 1943 Declaration and adhered to by both the Soulbury Commission and the ministers themselves in their draft constitution of 1944. The restrictions in these spheres incorporated in the ministers' draft constitution were elaborated in the Soulbury Report in a way which made them unworkable in practice and this became one of the main arguments in Senanayake's case for the immediate grant of dominion status without the intermediate stage envisaged in the Soulbury Report. Coupled with this was his most remarkable proposal: he urged that, if the legislation required to confer dominion status was likely to be time-consuming, the British government could resort to an Order in Council for the purpose of granting self-government immediately, together with an agreement for the purpose of safeguarding the defence of the island and providing the same relations in external affairs as in the case of a dominion. When he met Colonial Office officials on 7 and 10 September for a detailed review of the Soulbury[14] Report, he produced a 'comprehensive draft of a constitution...based on the fundamental assumption that, pending the conferment of Dominion Status on Ceylon by the amendment of the Statute of Westminster, full self-government would be established by Order-in-Council subject to an agreement about Defence and External Affairs and the general relations between the United Kingdom and Ceylon....'[15] His advisers prepared a draft of an Order in Council, and had it delivered to Hall on 12 September, together with an explanatory letter on 14 September.

The conferment of dominion status through an Order in Council and the insistence on agreements on defence and external affairs as a prior condition were the most controversial features of the transfer of power in Sri Lanka, and a good deal of the controversy arose from the belief that these had been devised by the Colonial Office and imposed in Sri Lanka in 1947. In fact, the proposals which first came from Senanayake in September 1945, were devised by his own advisers as a pragmatic solution to a complex problem, and the Colonial Office did not evince much interest in them when they were first proposed.

What, in the meantime, of the Labour government's response to the Soulbury proposals? On 11 September, the cabinet decided that it would accept the Soulbury Report as the basis on which the island's new constitution would be framed. But it was firmly opposed to the immediate grant of dominion status. Hall conveyed the gist of these decisions to Senanayake on 17 September. The latter returned home, disappointed that his main objective had not been attained, but convinced that it would not take long for the island to achieve self-government. Both he and his adviser A.G. (later Sir Arthur) Ranasinha believed that they had succeeded in extracting an oral promise of dominion status from Hall, who had been overruled by the cabinet.[16] They would have been surprised to learn that Hall was no more sympathetic to this proposal than his cabinet colleagues. In a memorandum to the Cabinet Colonial Affairs Committee on 12 October, Hall explained that there could be no possibility of Sri Lanka reaching self-government before India or Burma, but, realizing that Senanayake's support was essential to get the Soulbury proposals approved by the State Council by as large a majority as possible, he was willing to make one concession: to review this question once more and to consider the possibility of granting a form of dominion status six years after the adoption of the new constitution, that is, around 1953–54. A similar promise had been made to Burma, and Hall advanced this as one more argument for a revision of the new constitution based on the Soulbury Report after a period of six years.

This reference to a revision after six years was contained in the original draft of the British government's White Paper on the Soulbury constitution. It was eventually deleted by the cabinet in the final version of the White Paper but not because it was regarded as too long a period: rather it was felt to be impolitic to lay down a specific period of time.[17] The new governor of the colony, Sir Henry Monck-Mason-Moore, understood the position perfectly when he explained that he 'appreciated that His Majesty's Government may not be prepared to give Ceylon a blank cheque for self-government in six years' time'.[18] Instead, at the suggestion of Clement Attlee, the prime minister, a reference was made to the evolutionary character of constitutional development. The people of Sri Lanka were assured that the British government was in sympathy with their desire 'to advance towards Dominion Status and they are anxious to co-operate with them to that end'. It was added, even more reassuringly:

> It is, therefore, the hope of His Majesty's Government that the new constitution will be accepted by the people of Ceylon

with a determination so to work it that in a comparatively short space of time such Dominion Status will be evolved. The actual length of time occupied by this evolutionary process must depend upon the experience gained under the new constitution by the people of Ceylon.[19]

Senanayake and the Board of Ministers welcomed the White Paper as a clarification of the British government's attitude to the question of constitutional reform in Sri Lanka and were relieved to find that, while there was to be no immediate grant of dominion status, it was merely postponed pending the successful working of the new constitution. They would have been appalled to know that by 'a comparatively short space of time' the British cabinet meant 'not less than six years', and that the British prime minister held the view that even if Sri Lanka 'emerged successfully from the test', it could not be taken for granted that 'she would automatically attain full Dominion Status'. This they did not know. As it was, the White Paper strengthened Senanayake's position to the point where the State Council on 8–9 November 1945 endorsed his motion for the acceptance of the White Paper on Constitutional Reform by an overwhelming majority of 51 votes to 3, far above the three-fourths majority which the British government was reluctant to insist upon for fear that it could not be achieved.

In less than two years after this, Senanayake's objective was achieved. In early 1947, with general elections to the new parliament scheduled for August–September 1947, Senanayake pressed Whitehall for a more precise statement of policy on the attainment of dominion status. India's independence was announced by the British cabinet on 20 February 1947. With the partition of the Indian subcontinent into the states of India and Pakistan and the grant of independence to Burma, the way was clear for dominion status for Sri Lanka. Arthur Creech-Jones, Hall's successor at the Colonial Office, was much more receptive to the request for dominion status from Senanayake. The negotiations with Whitehall were handled by O.E. (later Sir Oliver) Goonetileke on Senanayake's behalf.[20] At Whitehall, there was a clear understanding that Senanayake and the moderates were facing increasing pressure from left-wing forces, apart from other critics, and that the immediate grant of dominion status was now an urgent necessity as a means of ensuring their political survival. In recognition of this, the British government made the official announcement on 18 June 1947 that the island would receive 'fully responsible status within the British Commonwealth of Nations'. The formula adopted on this occasion was precisely the one proposed by Senanayake in September 1945—an Order in Council and agreements on defence and external affairs.

This seemed to suggest a qualitative difference in the nature of the independence that was being conferred on Sri Lanka, in comparison to the cognate process in India, Pakistan and Burma, when no meaningful difference in status was either intended by Britain or accepted by Sri Lanka's leaders in the Board of Ministers prior to independence and later in the cabinet. But if the political leadership in Sri Lanka took pride in the fact that the transfer of power was smooth and peaceful, they seemed oblivious to the political perils involved in making the process so bland as to be virtually imperceptible to those not directly involved. Above all, the agreements on defence and external affairs appeared to give credibility to the argument that Sri Lanka's independence was flawed. They themselves were regarded as badges of inferiority and checks on full sovereignty in external affairs; moreover, fears were expressed about secret clauses not divulged, or a secret treaty even more detrimental to the island's status as an independent nation. Events were to prove that these fears and suspicions were without foundation in fact and certainly no secret undertaking had been given by Sri Lanka in 1947–48. Yet suspicions on this score persisted until 1956–57.

34

Social and Economic Change in the Donoughmore Era, 1931–47

One remarkable feature of the last phase of the transfer of power in Sri Lanka was the emergence of a rudimentary welfare state. In retrospect this would seem the inevitable effect of the pressures of a democratic electorate under universal suffrage and a system of semi-responsible government. But in the years of the Great Depression of 1928–32 and the malaria epidemic of 1934, although attention was focussed as never before on the condition of the people, a contracting economy combined with a treasury under a British civil servant as financial secretary bent on the conventional exercise of balancing the budget by a rigorous policy of retrenchment seemed insurmountable obstacles to any initiatives in social welfare. With the Second World War, however, the economy was at last in a more buoyant state than at any time in the inter-war period. Money was now more readily available for expenditure on social welfare. The politicians of the day confronted greater pressure for increased expenditure on social welfare and had a more realistic understanding than the British officers of state of the political importance of responding generously to these demands than they—the politicians—themselves had done in the 1930s.

1931–39

We need to begin this survey, however, with a look at the plantations, the bedrock of the island's economy.[1] The problem common to all the plantation industries in the early 1930s was how to cope with the Great Depression and its impact. The response to these problems was much the same in both the tea and the rubber industries, although the depression in the rubber market was far worse than that in tea.

In the tea industry, there was first of all an attempt to reduce costs by establishing more efficient and economically viable units by merging small and middle-sized plantations into larger ones, or absorbing them as units of a large complex of plantations ('groups', as they were called) under common management. The question, however, was essentially one of overproduction and this called for joint action by the major producers of tea in Asia. In 1933, an international restriction scheme for tea was successfully negotiated under which Sri Lanka, India and the then Dutch East Indies were each allocated export quotas based on a fixed percentage of the maximum quantity of tea exported in the period 1929–31. The Tea Control Ordinance of 1933, which gave effect to this agreement, introduced a system of export coupons which were allocated to individual tea producers. By permitting the sale of the coupons, the scheme was given a flexibility which guaranteed its survival and success. Partly as a result of these measures, but also because of the gradual recovery of the industrial countries from the Great Depression, tea prices began to recover by the mid-1930s. Although the prices fetched hardly matched those of 1922–30, the recovery was nevertheless substantial.

The same pattern was seen in the rubber industry too: first an attempt was made to reduce output and when it became evident that this was inadequate to ensure the survival of the industry, an international agreement was sought on the restriction of production. An International Rubber Agreement was negotiated between the main rubber-producing countries in 1934. Sri Lanka was an eager participant in this arrangement. A Rubber Control Ordinance was approved by the State Council under the terms of which the planting of new areas under rubber was prohibited. The effect on prices was entirely salutary and for the rest of the decade rubber prices rose moderately.

The coconut industry had been less influenced by external conditions than tea and rubber, although there was a pattern of troughs and peaks in prices and world demand in the period up to the Great Depression. There had been a steadily increasing world demand for coconut products, for the manufacture of soap and margarine, since the beginning of the twentieth century. But coconut—either in the form of copra or as an edible oil—was not only much less important than tea or rubber as a revenue earner, but also its price was determined by the international prices of fats and oil. Coconut products constituted just 9 per cent of the world resources of fats and oil. With the Depression the market for coconut products in the industrial countries was considerably reduced and prices declined sharply. Since the production of coconut was largely controlled by Sri Lankans (ranging from owners of large plantations to a motley group of smallholders), the near collapse of the industry gravely affected the economic well-being of the indigenous planting community. There was no resort to artificial restraints on production to improve prices and recovery of the industry was due entirely to improved demand for coconut products in the world market in the middle and late 1930s.

In general, the effects of the Great Depression were felt more severely in countries like Sri Lanka, producing primary commodities for export, than in industrial economies. The relevant statistics for Sri Lanka make dismal reading: the revenue from exports plunged from Rs 479 million in 1927 to Rs 189 million in 1932, reflecting the decline in prices of her main exports, while the price index fell from 169 in 1927 to 65 in 1932, even though there was a slight increase—from 97 to 102—in the volume of these exports. The terms of trade registered a sharp fall from 99 in 1927 to 61 in 1932, the drop being as much as 15 per cent per annum in the years 1929–32. The fall in the terms of trade contributed most to the decline in real incomes.[2]

Since the major part of the national income was derived from exports, the depression in the export trade spread to all sectors of the economy. Unemployment was the major problem. It is estimated that over 9,000 Sri Lankans and 84,000 Indians lost their jobs between 1929 and 1932. Over 1,00,000 immigrant plantation workers returned to their homes in India in the period 1930–33, the most significant large-scale emigration to India since the late nineteenth century. Unemployment in the plantations was not restricted to manual workers but affected managerial (least of all), technical and clerical staff as well, which was very largely Sri Lankan. Outside the plantations, about one-tenth of those employed in commercial firms belonging to the Employers' Federation were retrenched in the aftermath of the Depression, while the number employed in the state sector fell from 69,287 in 1930 to 60,553 in 1933. Temporary workers were discontinued in all sectors of the economy. Minimum wages of plantation workers were reduced and there was a temporary levy on the salaries and wages of permanent employees in the state service.

The village economy and traditional agriculture did not escape unscathed. On the contrary the sharp fall in prices of primary products affected locally produced rice as well, and with it there was an inevitable deterioration in the living standards of the peasantry. Again, although the tea and rubber plantations did not rely to any appreciable degree on indigenous labour, they did provide opportunities for casual work for peasants living in their vicinity. With the Depression this source of seasonal employment was lost. As a consequence, the meagre resources of the village economy were subjected to even greater strain.

The large-scale emigration of unemployed plantation workers relieved the government of its responsibility over the gravest aspect of the unemployment problem—it was exported to India. Even so, unemployment and underemployment among the indigenous population was serious enough. The government's response was lethargic and, as we shall see, riddled with contradictions. This was partly because finance was a matter in which the primary responsibility under the Donoughmore constitution lay with British officials who were more committed to the orthodoxies of laissez-faire economics than Sri Lankan ministers and more inclined than the latter to take a cold, hard look at proposals which involved the expenditure of large amounts of public funds in welfare measures. Retrenchment and curtailment, their standard remedies for the country's economic malaise, aggravated the unemployment problem when casual and temporary employees in the state service were laid off. The votes of the Public Works Department, the largest employer of casual labour in the state sector, were severely pruned, with an inevitable contraction of its capacity to employ casual or temporary workers.

Unemployment was viewed as part of the wider theme of population pressure in the wet zone, and the most appropriate strategy—as British officials and the most influential of the political leaders of the day saw it—was to encourage the opening of the dry zone to relieve this pressure. This was especially true of underemployment among peasants in the plantation areas, and it was seen as the most viable solution to the problem of urban unemployment as well. The problem of urban unemployment called for more immediate short-term ameliorative measures, and here the government's response was the provision of relief work. Ironically, the victims of unemployment for whom these measures were devised were often casual and temporary workers thrown out of work by the government's own policies of retrenchment and cuts in public expenditure. In the city of Colombo, the municipality began to organize unemployment relief measures on a modest scale, but these were subsequently expanded under the aegis of the Central government to the more constructive enterprise of building and repair of roads, canals, flood protection embankments and swamp reclamation work. Similar measures, but of an ad hoc nature and far less ambitious in scale and constructive in scope, were organized by the municipalities of Kandy and Galle.

The country had hardly recovered from the effects of the Depression when large areas of it were devastated by the worst malaria epidemic of the century. The stricken areas were in the wet and intermediate zones of the country where malaria was not endemic—the Kegalla and Kurunegala districts. Ad hoc emergency measures were all that was possible and these the government provided, with its resources spread thin and wide in the process. Small wonder then that left-wing groups organizing relief work in the stricken areas and bent on demonstrating the vigour of their response, in contrast to that of the government, were able to make a strong impression on the people among whom they worked. Imaginative medical programmes designed to keep the disease at bay (there was no prospect of eradicating it) called for much greater financial resources than were available at a time of economic depression. One long-term solution was the extension of preventive health facilities in rural areas and especially to the regions in which the disease was endemic. This was resorted to with considerable success in the late 1930s and early 1940s.

By the mid-1930s, with the rise in prices of tea (which went up steadily) and rubber (which moved upwards far more rapidly),[3] the terms of trade turned in Sri Lanka's favour again: by 30 per cent between 1935 and 1937, and as much as 100 per cent if the comparison was between 1932 and 1937. As a result, unemployment eased considerably. Thus the number of Indian workers in the plantations increased from 4,38,000 in 1933 to 4,77,000 in 1935, though it fell slightly again to an average of 4,57,000 in 1936 and 1937; while the number of persons employed in the public service increased from 61,000 in November 1933 to 66,000 in November 1937. By the mid-1930s, there was also a distinct improvement in real incomes.

It was not always possible to restrain the impulse to social welfare by preaching the tenets of laissez-faire, especially where legislation broadening the scope of the state's activity did not entail any heavy expenditure of revenue. There were instances, moreover, when the pressures of a democratic electorate were well-nigh irresistible because of the close connection of some aspects of social reform with religion. An example of this would be educational reform. Finally, there were spheres of activity in which powerful politicians were deeply interested and made it their special concern, such as D.S. Senanayake's interest in peasant colonization in the dry zone. Perhaps the best example of the first category discussed here would be legislation for the protection of workers and their rights. In 1934, a Workmen's Compensation Ordinance was passed, providing for benefits for certain categories of workers. A scheme of maternity benefits was introduced; although the actual financial benefits of the scheme were rather modest, it was nevertheless a landmark in welfare legislation. The Trade Union Ordinance of 1935 made registration of trade unions compulsory, devised means of securing trade union funds against defalcation by corrupt officials and, most important of all, protected trade unions from actions in tort. In 1938, an employment exchange was established in Colombo.

The Buddhist temporalities question, a problem over which the Buddhist activists had been agitating since the middle of the nineteenth century, was settled in 1931 with the passage of the Buddhist Temporalities Ordinance of that year. It conceded the demand for state intervention in, and supervision of, the administration of Buddhist temporalities. Significantly, this issue was settled long before the establishment of the Sinhala Mahā Sabhā. Unlike their predecessors in the Legislative Council, politicians of the first and second State Council were subject to the pressures of a popular electorate. Buddhist pressure groups could now work through the electoral process to influence elected state councillors. The ordinance which was passed in 1942 for the preservation of the sacred city of Anuradhapura was based on sober necessity, but lent itself to a reassertion of the link between religion and nationalism. While the government still prided itself on its neutrality in religious affairs, it had become more politic than ever before to underline the sense of special obligation towards Buddhism.

Once the problem of Buddhist temporalities was out of the way, Buddhist activists turned their attention to education. Educational reform was a special problem; it was part of the general trend towards social welfare and for that reason it had the support of radical groups that were pressing for greater equality of opportunity in education. The concept of 'free' education (which in reality meant no more than free tuition) had an irresistible appeal to the electorate because of its connotations of social justice and equality of opportunity. But it was also part of the wider theme of Buddhist–Christian confrontation and of the campaign of Buddhist activists against the Christian missions. For all these reasons it was much more controversial than other aspects of social welfare and aroused opposition not from Christians alone but also from some of the more powerful Sinhalese politicians. Educated in mission schools, attached to western concepts of secular government and the apparatus of political democracy, they were disinclined to yield to pressures from more vociferous Buddhist groups who agitated for state control over the mission schools.

In the late 1930s, the denominational system of education came increasingly under attack and the use of the educational process as a means of conversion to Christianity received an effective check. The Education Ordinance of 1939 was the harbinger of nearly a decade of radical and acutely controversial education reform in which the determination of the minister of education (C.W.W. Kannangara) to carry through a policy of far-reaching change was resisted by denominational interests and by influential colleagues in the Board of Ministers alike. When this ordinance was debated in the State Council, spokesmen for denominational interests opposed it with great vehemence and succeeded in securing the adoption by the State Council (by a vote of 27 to 26), despite the opposition of Kannangara, of an amending clause which read: 'This Ordinance is not designed to give effect to any policy aimed against denominational schools'.

The strength of the resistance can be explained thus: by the instinctive distrust of the changes envisaged, demonstrated by the more influential political leaders of the day (most notably D.S. Senanayake); and by the fact that many of the members of the State Council, although themselves Buddhists, were alumni of mission schools and were susceptible to missionary influence. There was more to this than a sentimental attachment to the 'old school tie', for they had a deep-seated regard for the positive achievements of the mission schools and were unwilling for these to be jeopardized by the precipitate introduction of radical reform. Finally, the defence of the denominational principle was by no means confined to the Christian missions; the managers and principals of denominational schools controlled by Buddhists and Hindus, many of whom were state councillors (some in the Board of Ministers and others as members of the Council of Education itself), recognized that their own vested interests in education could best be protected by the maintenance of the status quo. However, in the early 1940s, despite their opposition, the role of the state in education was considerably enlarged at the expense of the missions. In the State Council, the Executive Committee on Education formed itself into a special committee by co-opting educationists and after long deliberation it produced in 1943 a report which recommended radical changes in the education policy.

The impulse to social welfare manifested itself most prominently and with much less controversy in the establishment of peasant colonization schemes in the dry zone, with conditions of land tenure designed to prevent fragmentation of holdings.[4] D.S. Senanayake's schemes for the restoration of the irrigation works of ancient Sri Lanka were a continuation of policies which had their origins in the twilight of the last Legislative Council. Under the new constitution and holding the key post of minister of agriculture, he had greater influence than ever before on the initiation and implementation of irrigation policy, and he demonstrated a visionary zeal in peasant colonization of the dry zone—as a return to the heartland of the ancient irrigation civilization of the Sinhalese. Characteristically, there was no commitment to a theory, or a blueprint, but instead a refreshing practicality and common sense in the drive and vigour which he provided in eliminating legislative and bureaucratic obstacles to quick decisions. There was by now a much greater appreciation of the potential value of the undeveloped dry zone. Its colonization seemed the only way out of the economic crisis of the Great Depression; and even before the government moved to promote it, there was a steady but significant stream of migrants there with Minneriya as the special attraction—striking evidence of a spontaneous response to economic and population pressure. Senanayake shared with Clifford (who had appointed a Land Commission) and influential British officials a faith in the peasantry as the key to the regeneration of the malaria-infested dry zone.

The legislation required to give legal form to the recommendations of the Land Commission was delayed despite the pleas of the commissioners that this should be prepared and passed as early as possible. Before the demise of the Legislative Council, the Land Settlement Ordinance of 1931 was enacted, reversing in effect the colonial government's traditional policy on chēnas and chēna cultivation, and recognizing one-third of a century's possession and occupation of land—including what earlier was chēna—for the purpose of title against the claims of the crown. And the recommendations of the Land Commission had a strong influence on administrative decisions on land policy in the early years of the first State Council. When the Land Development Ordinance of 1935 was passed, it formalized most of the measures already taken in this way, or proposed in the reports of the Land Commission.

Before the introduction of this ordinance, the two focal points of land policy had been, first, village expansion schemes with settlements in rural areas and, second, colonization. When land was allotted for these purposes, the tenure adopted was based on the recommendations of the Land Commission. No direct financial assistance was given to settlers in colonization schemes, but the government did provide some of the services required to facilitate easy settlement. With the Minneriya scheme (1933) these services were expanded to include the entire cost of clearing the land, which practical experience had shown to be a great burden on settlers in the past, and colonists were exempted from payments of water rates for three years after settlement. Provision was also made for the settlement of 'middle class' colonists. Ownership of land in colonies was restricted to Sri Lankans and those possessing a Sri Lankan domicile of origin. Immigrant Indians, who had once been regarded as the ideal colonists for the development of the dry zone, found these settlements closed to them. The dry zone was to be the preserve of the indigenous peasant and to many the preserve only of the Sinhalese peasant.[5]

Indeed the establishment of colonization schemes in the dry zone had one far-reaching political consequence. The expanding frontier cut into the forests, which had stood for centuries as the barrier between the Tamil and Sinhalese areas of the island. Although this expansion did not go far at this time, there was a consciousness—especially among the Tamils, who were deeply suspicious of it—that an irreversible process had begun, and with it increasing prospects of a confrontation between the intruding colonists and the Tamil settlements in the Vanni, especially in the regions near the provincial boundary between the Northern Province and the North-central Province.

One other point needs emphasis. Although the establishment of viable colonization schemes in the dry zone and the economic development which they signified, were among the major achievements of the Donoughmore era, much more land was alienated in the village expansion schemes in the wet zone than in the colonization projects of the dry zone. The fact was that in the dry zone malaria was still a formidable problem, although no longer an insurmountable obstacle to the extension of the frontiers of settlement there.

The introduction of the Land Development Ordinance did not, for a few years at least, accelerate the rate of development of colonization. There were no new schemes established till 1939 when the decision was taken that the scale of aid given to the colonists should be rather more generous than it was. Experience had shown that the colonists had to face a grim struggle until their allotments yielded their first harvests. It was felt that the colonists were entitled to assistance from the state in money or services or both during this crucial period.[6]

1940–47

One of the consequences of the outbreak of the Second World War was the extension of the life of the second State Council beyond 1940–41, when dissolution was due, to 1947. During this period the 'constitutionalist' leadership in the Board of Ministers was much more responsive to the need for initiatives in social and economic reform while with wartime prosperity, money was at last available on a scale to match the ambitions of politicians committed to policies of social welfare. The outbreak of the Second World War gave a fillip to the plantation industries of the island, especially with regard to rubber with Sri Lanka as the main, if not the only, source of natural rubber for the Allied powers after the Japanese overran Malaya and the Dutch East Indies. The rubber restriction scheme was abandoned and producers were encouraged instead to increase their output to the maximum extent possible by resorting to 'slaughter-tapping'.[7] But because all her rubber and tea were made available to Britain at fixed prices, Sri Lanka did not receive the full benefits of increased demand for scarce commodities which would have accrued to her had normal market pressures prevailed.

With regard to tea, prices were revised from time to time as the costs of production increased, but it is significant that when the contract system was done away with, there was a very substantial increase in tea prices. As for rubber, the price of 11d per pound f.o.b., which had been decided on by Britain, was recognized as being far too little considering the increased costs of production, the enormous wartime demand for rubber and scarcities in world supplies. As a result of pressure from producers in Sri Lanka, the price was raised by 3d a pound, but thereafter no increase was made despite a continuing agitation for fairer prices. Instead, the British government offered to compensate producers who were willing to 'slaughter-tap' their rubber trees to increase output; this compensation would amount to the repayment of the costs of capital replacement. Despite the artificial restraints on prices resulting from the contract system imposed by Britain, the plantation industries were nevertheless in a far healthier condition than they had been since the 1920s.

With the establishment of the South-east Asia Command and its network of bases on the island, heavy military expenditure by the Allied powers had an invigorating effect on the island's economy. At its peak in 1944, this expenditure was estimated to be as much as Rs 435 million; in the previous year it was Rs 264 million. Both these were very large disbursements in relation to the size of the national income.[8] The active money supply in the island increased by 69 per cent between 1942 and 1945. While this wartime prosperity inevitably raised inflationary pressures and contributed to increasing discontent among the white-collar and urban workers, its immediate effect was to place much larger financial resources than ever before in the hands of the Board of Ministers.

The main contribution of D.S. Senanayake to the welfare programmes of this phase continued to be in the field of peasant colonization. The regeneration of the peasantry remained the keynote of his land policy, just as the resuscitation of the dry zone was the central theme in his irrigation policy. Together, his land and irrigation policies had as their basis the assumption that there was, if not an identity of interests between the elite and the peasantry, at least a potentially harmonious relationship between these two conservative social groups. He saw the peasantry as a stabilizing element in the social order which was now under increasing pressure from a politicized and radical urban working class and white-collar workers. There was a greater urgency now about peasant colonization in particular and food production in general, for the country still depended on imported food supplies and was a long way from self-sufficiency. Wartime conditions greatly aggravated the problem when the traditional sources of supply of imported food were overrun by the Japanese. Investment on peasant colonization schemes in the dry zone was increased and the range of free services given by government to the colonists expanded well beyond what had been envisaged in 1939. Far more important, malaria, the age-long scourge of the dry zone, was at last losing its grip.

Traditional agriculture in all parts of the island and not merely in the dry zone benefited from incentives for food production which were introduced at this time. In 1942, an Internal Purchase Scheme was set up with a guaranteed price for rice set well above the world market rate; originally Rs 2.50 a bushel, by October 1943 this had been increased substantially to Rs 6.00. Introduced as a wartime measure, this guaranteed price scheme was retained thereafter as an essential and permanent feature of government assistance to traditional agriculture. Despite these and other measures, however, the island was still as dependent as ever on imports of food. Although rice imports in wartime remained at about half of what Sri Lanka had imported in 1930, the return of normal peacetime conditions in 1945 saw a steady increase in the imports of rice. But if self-sufficiency remained a distant dream, active support of traditional agriculture became an established feature of post-war policy. And the rapid development of the dry zone came to be viewed as the principal means of achieving self-sufficiency.

While D.S. Senanayake supported many of the other social welfare measures of this period—for example, the substantial increase of expenditure on health services and food subsidies— there were aspects of social reform which he viewed with the utmost suspicion. He was opposed, for example, to J.R. Jayewardene's motion to make Sinhala the official language in place of English. The amendment—which was carried—to make Tamil and Sinhala together the official languages of the island had his support, as well as S.W.R.D. Bandaranaike's, and the problem was settled in 1943–44 on the basis of this compromise. To Kannangara's education reforms he was resolutely opposed, and here he was unable to have his way. The constitutional structure of the Donoughmore scheme left a great deal of the initiative in matters of social reform in the hands of individual members of the Board of Ministers and backbench pressure groups such as the younger members of the Ceylon National Congress, who carried these education reforms through despite his opposition.

The most controversial of Kannangara's proposals was the recommendation that tuition fees be abolished at all levels of education, from the primary schools to the university. Had this 'free' education scheme, as it came to be called, been confined to the state schools, there would have been little opposition from denominational interests, but Kannangara was determined to bring the denominational schools within its purview. For this purpose he proposed to revise the grants-in-aid provided by the state to these latter schools, without which the great majority of them could not have survived. These new financial arrangements were regarded by the Christian missions especially as a potent threat to their interests.[9]

When Kannangara's education proposals of 1943 were introduced for debate in the State Council in the latter half of 1944, there was a prolonged confrontation between the protagonists of the scheme and the advocates of denominationalism. The Board of Ministers was divided on this issue. G.C.S. Corea, the minister of labour, industry and commerce, led the opposition to these reforms in the State Council, while his colleague S.W.R.D. Bandaranaike[10] was among their most ardent advocates, as for that matter were the members of his Sinhala Mahā Sabhā, J.R. Jayewardene[11] and the younger Congressmen. It was in June 1945 that the State Council gave its endorsement to these reforms, significantly at a time when D.S. Senanayake was out of the island on his mission to Whitehall to discuss questions relating to the reform of the constitution.

D.S. Senanayake's opposition to these educational reforms was based on two main considerations. The first of these concerned the financial implications, for he believed that they would impose a severe strain on the economy and that expenditure would keep increasing. Second, his opposition sprang from the belief that they exacerbated the fears of the minorities. He was especially sensitive to the political implications of these tensions at a time when he was engaged in delicate negotiations to reach an understanding with the minorities on the terms of the transfer of power and when a new constitution for Sri Lanka was in the process of being drafted against the background of Whitehall's requirement that any new constitutional structure would need to be adopted by a majority of three-fourths of all members of the State Council save the presiding officer and the officers of state.

The preparation of legislation to give effect to the Kannangara reforms took place at a time when the main point of interest was in the new constitutional structure that was to replace the Donoughmore scheme. For D.S. Senanayake these education reforms were of peripheral interest, but the advocates of the scheme were bent on securing the passage of legislation before the State Council was dissolved, and early in 1947 an ordinance incorporating the Kannangara proposals was introduced in the State Council. Denominational interests led by the Roman Catholics were quite as determined to have the debate on the ordinance postponed, in the hope no doubt that with the dissolution of the State Council and elections to the new parliament, the delay might give them the opportunity of influencing the preparation of a more congenial piece of legislation by someone other than C.W.W. Kannangara. The bargaining powers of the Christian minority were at a premium at this time, when a new constitution had been drafted in which limitations on the power of the new parliament (which was to replace the State Council) to enact legislation discriminating against any religious or ethnic community were a special feature and requirement.

There was now a polarization of forces, with the Roman Catholics leading the resistance and a Central Free Education Defence Committee, representing Buddhist interests, taking the issue before the electorate in an island-wide campaign to put pressure on the members of the State Council (who were about to face an election to the new parliament) to have the education ordinance enacted before the dissolution of the State Council. Their pressure proved more effective than that of the Roman Catholics and the Education Ordinance of 1947 was eventually approved by the State Council. Assisted denominational schools which did not come into the 'free' education scheme were to receive grants-in-aid on the old basis till 30 September 1948, after which all aid would cease. [12]

This discussion of education reform would be incomplete without a reference to two of the most notable achievements of this period. First, there was the Central School Scheme, the establishment of large and well-equipped English secondary schools run by the state in rural areas. Originally, it was intended that these schools should provide a blend of the conventional academic education and more practical instruction in agriculture, commerce, handicrafts and domestic science; but in practice this latter aspect was neglected—when it was not forgotten completely—and education in Central Schools was modelled on the patterns of the prestigious urban secondary schools run by the Christian missions and other private organizations. Where previously the state had one such school—the Royal College in Colombo—by 1944 there were fifty. With the abolition of tuition fees after 1945, these Central Schools became 'one of the major avenues of advancement for the rural child'.

Second, there was the establishment of the University of Ceylon in 1942 as a culmination of a process which had begun in 1921 and been prolonged because of a controversy over the choice of a site for the university, among other reasons. The Ceylon University Ordinance of 1942 created an autonomous university incorporating the old Medical College as one of its faculties; it was envisaged that when it was transferred from Colombo to its site in Peradeniya near Kandy, it would become a residential institution. The physical transfer to Peradeniya began on a modest scale in the late 1940s but was accelerated in 1952 with the shift of the arts faculty. The shift to a site near Kandy was supported partly at least in the belief that the new university would be 'the focus of a cultural renaissance'. During the period surveyed in this chapter, the university continued to be in Colombo. Its student enrolment increased from 904 in 1942 to 1,554 in 1947 despite the competing attraction of external degrees of London University. Tuition fees were abolished with the educational reforms of 1945.

The unemployment problem eased considerably in the early 1940s and disappeared altogether in the period 1942–45, when the military bases established on the island under the southeast Asia Command provided employment opportunities for the local population as civilian workers and in ancillary services. By 1945, as many as 83,500 civilians were employed on these bases. The demand for labour was not confined to the defence services; all sectors of the economy were affected. In 1939, the Colombo Employment Exchange had 25,000 registered unemployed; in 1941, the number had dropped to 2,000 and this had fallen to a mere 1,000 in 1944. (By 1945, with the ending of hostilities, this figure had increased again to 10,000.[13]) If increased defence expenditure and the establishment of military bases provided a short-term solution to the unemployment problem, the increase in the active money supply led to inflation. The rise in the domestic price level in Sri Lanka during this period was much greater than the contemporary price inflation in Britain. Official statistics showed a 35 per cent increase in the working-class cost of living index between 1942 and 1945; but the actual increase in the domestic price level has been estimated at 69 per cent. Inflationary pressures might well have been more severe had export prices not been prevented from reaching their free market level by bulk purchase agreements and the lack of shipping space.[14]

The inevitable consequence of these inflationary pressures was increasing discontent among the working class and white-collar workers, which did not erupt into major strike activity only because of restrictions on strikes during wartime and from the lack of encouragement by the Communist Party, which became the most influential force among the urban working class after the LSSP had been proscribed.[15]

The government sought to cushion the effect of these pressures by raising wages and salaries. From March 1942, a special war allowance based on the Colombo working-class cost of living index was paid. And on the plantations the minimum wage of estate labour was increased. But none of these increases in wages kept pace with inflation. The government resorted also to a policy of controlling prices and rationing essential consumer goods, mainly food and textiles. From the middle of 1943 it went a stage further in freezing the prices of several important food items, as well as subsidizing others, and importing as well.[16] Much of the distribution of rice, wheat flour and sugar was taken over by the state in order to make price control and rationing more effective. These food subsidies, introduced in 1943 as a wartime measure to control inflation, were continued thereafter to become one of the island's social welfare services. No doubt, they were retained as a means of blunting the growing challenge of the Marxist left who were moving in after the end of the war to use working class and white-collar discontent over inflation in a campaign of trade union action directed against the government.

One other area of importance in social welfare needs to be mentioned. The last major malaria epidemic—that of 1934–35—underlined the inadequacies of the medical facilities in the country. The latter were concentrated in the principal towns, while the rural areas had little or nothing by comparison. A programme of investment in new hospitals in rural areas (called 'cottage hospitals') was initiated and there was increased emphasis on preventive medical facilities in all parts of the country. These had a notable impact on the living conditions of the people.

All in all, the social legislation of this period laid the foundations of a welfare state on the island. A high-calibre Social Service Commission was appointed in 1946 to review the progress that had been made and to suggest ways and means of expanding and financing social welfare. Although the commission stressed the importance of adopting a Health Insurance Scheme, an Unemployment Insurance Scheme, a National Provident Fund— to be financed partly by employers and partly by contributions from employees themselves—and an Old-age Pension Scheme, they were alive to the financial costs of such a programme. They pointed out that wartime prosperity was transitory and should not be regarded as the norm in discussions concerning the financial feasibility of a reasonably comprehensive social welfare scheme, a conclusion which 'ran counter to the rising expectations of the Ceylonese radicals'.

The demographic patterns of the early twentieth century continued through much of this period. Population growth reached the quite unprecedented rate of 25.4 per cent in the years between 1931 and 1946, reflecting a continued decline in the crude death rate and a fall in fertility as well. Immigration increase was a mere 69,552 as against a natural increase of 1,280,000. There was accelerated emigration of Indian workers to India in the wake of the Depression. Population increase was greatest on the south-west coast which by 1946 contained 40 per cent of the island's total population. The Western Province itself recorded an increase of 29.9 per cent. Overall population density for the whole island reached 102 per sq. km in 1946; that of Colombo district doubled from 855 in 1901 to 1,758 in 1946. The Jaffna region which comprised the peninsula and groups of islands was characterized by dense settlements throughout. The relative population of this region declined from 8.5 per cent in 1901 to 6.4 per cent in 1946.

One new demographic pattern emerged in this period— the rapid population growth in the main dry zone provinces.

The North-central Province recorded the highest growth rate of all—43.4 per cent—with the development there of peasant colonization schemes, the restoration of irrigation works and the conquest of malaria. The Northern Province and Eastern Province recorded growth rates of 20.2 and 31.4 per cent respectively for 1931–46.

One needs, however, to guard against exaggerating the importance of the DDT programme, which became well established in 1946, as a factor in bringing down the crude death rate. For one thing not all parts of the island were malaria-ridden: for example, the densely populated south-west and nearly all parts of the wet zone, as well as the Jaffna peninsula, were not. Besides, the fall in the crude death rate had already become perceptible in 1945. Nevertheless, once the spraying of DDT became standard practice it contributed greatly to sustaining—and accelerating—the decline in the crude death rate in the late 1940s. As a result, there was a phenomenal increase in population in the years after independence. Meanwhile, the expanded school system and the much greater access to education increased the number of students aspiring to white-collar jobs at a time when the economy was not expanding at the same pace as the population, in particular the school-going population. Thus an unprecedented increase in population growth and the rising expectations of an increasingly educated population created an almost unmanageable situation for Sri Lanka's leaders in the first decade after independence.

Literature and the Arts: The Nineteenth and Twentieth Centuries

THE NINETEENTH CENTURY

In the early part of the nineteenth century, the classical age in Sinhala literature came to an end in the Kandyan kingdom no less than in the littoral where the current spoken Sinhala had been enriched by the languages of the two Western powers that had ruled it in turn, the Portuguese and the Dutch. Neither of these languages was a substitute for the traditional sources of Sinhala culture, especially Sanskrit. (Portuguese had greater potential in this regard than Dutch for it survived well into the mid-nineteenth century as a spoken language on the littoral.) In the Kandyan kingdom, the ancient literary tradition still survived but its sterility was all too evident.

Because of the rapid shrinkage of the world in the nineteenth century, Sri Lanka would have faced westernization anyway, but the British, in fact, deliberately started the process in the 1830s after some hesitation in the early years of their rule on the island; the English language became a vehicle for the entry of new ideas and techniques from the West and revitalized the indigenous languages, Sinhala and Tamil alike, as profoundly as Sanskrit had done in the past, perhaps even more so. Its influence was seen first of all, and naturally enough, through translations into the indigenous languages of the authorized version of the Bible and such intrinsically religious works as *Pilgrim's Progress*. If this seemed a rather unpromising continuation of a pattern established under the Portuguese and the Dutch, translations of works of a more decidedly secular, if not utilitarian, nature heralded the beginnings of more far-reaching changes, the adoption of a new set of values and new attitudes to life and society, in short, a transition from an essentially religious ethos to an intrinsically secular literature.[1]

Journalism was the bridge to the new literature. At the core of this journalism were polemical essays, some of them on religious themes (controversies between Buddhists and Christians and between Buddhist nikāyas) but mostly on literary and caste controversies. By fostering a taste for fiction, the new journalism was the take-off point to a new phase in the evolution of indigenous literature which began in the early years of the twentieth century. The transition from journalism to a new Sinhalese literature took several decades to effect, the last quarter of the nineteenth century serving as a period of preparation. Indeed, the new genres, the novel and the short story, had a long struggle before gaining acceptance among a reading public whose tastes had been set by traditional literary forms. They were put off by themes such as romantic love—a puritanical streak in Sinhalese society reinforced now by the teachings of the missionaries—which was the stuff of novels and short stories. There was also a problem of evolving a style and developing a vocabulary suitable for the new genres and a new age. Some continuity in language was possible in Sinhala prose—classical Sinhala had been used for prose narratives although there had never been avowed narrative fiction—but not in poetry where the language of the classical tradition was too rigid, formal and conventional for easy adaptation to the new ideas in vogue.[2]

The same trends were perceptible in Tamil literature. Its prose and poetry alike were stylized, tediously conventional and suffused by a concern with Hindu doctrine and mythology and by an overpowering Sanskrit influence. On these as on their Sinhala equivalents, English had an invigorating effect, stimulating the adoption of new genres and a new outlook. On Tamil too the most immediate effect lay in the development of prose literature linked with journalism and polemics—some of it religious—Hindu ripostes to missionary criticism which modernized the language and rid it of much of its classicism. In Tamil as in Sinhala, the pioneer lexicographical works came from the Protestant missionaries based in Sri Lanka. A more

distinctive contribution of the missionaries working in Jaffna
was introductory textbooks in Tamil on modern sciences.[3]

Tamil literature was dominated by the protean figure of
Arumuga Navalar, the father of modern Tamil prose literature,
the one man of his day who could be described as a polymath
of oriental learning. His creativity ranged from contributing to
the production of a standard Tamil translation of the Bible to
the writing of scintillating polemical works and editions of the
Hindu classics many of which he rendered into a chaste modern
Tamil. This last was his greatest achievement and perhaps as a
result the link between modernity and tradition was stronger
in Tamil than it was in Sinhala. As with Sinhala literature, the
nineteenth century was for Tamil a period of preparation for
the acceptance of new literary genres rather than of any substantial
creative achievement in them. The few novels and short stories
that were produced were important as being the first of their
kind rather than for any intrinsic artistic merit. Nor was the
emerging modern Tamil literature of Sri Lanka so distinct in
style or content as to set it apart from the south Indian variety.

The English language stimulated a revitalization of literary
activity in Sinhala and Tamil in nineteenth-century Sri Lanka
but was curiously sterile when it came to producing a
distinctive Sri Lankan English literature. This is all the more
surprising because of the remarkable receptivity of the
educated elite, especially its Sinhalese segment, to anglicization
and the blandishments of the lifestyle of the upper classes in
the metropolitan country. For most of them English had a
utilitarian value; they spoke it fluently and communicated in it
in their professional work, but in creative writing they seemed
incapable of using it with any proficiency. They produced no
novels in English, no short stories, no memoirs, no biographies,
no literary essays and no poetry—in short, no indigenous
English literature. There was just one historical work in English
written by a Sinhalese, James Alwis's *History of Ceylon*, some
chapters of which appeared in instalments in one of the English
newspapers of the day. Its analysis and narration were
competent, as was the use of documents, but its language was
somewhat ponderous—it had nothing of the exciting style and

brittle eloquence of Tennent's classic work on Ceylon published in 1859–60, the model by which a nineteenth-century history of Ceylon would have to be judged. Had it been published in book form, as the author clearly intended, this would have been the first historical study by a Ceylonese in a western language. Thus, as with Sinhala and Tamil, such creativity as there was lay in journalism. There the performance was truly professional—the style clear and sharp, the comments incisive and, on political issues, often witty and iconoclastic.

In the early twentieth century, the indigenous tradition in the visual arts petered out, its vitality sapped by the lack of state support which had sustained it in the past. The adjustment to changed circumstances proved too difficult and, unlike in literature, the traditions of the new rulers in the visual arts, far from stimulating a revitalization, contributed to a swift decline.

The civic and domestic architecture of the early nineteenth century was a pleasing adaptation of Dutch styles; indeed, the Dutch achievement in tropical architecture was the most distinguished and successful in the long history of western rule on the island. When in the course of time the British broke away from this, the result was often an unsatisfactory mixture of European (predominantly British) styles which neither blended harmoniously with the landscape nor coped successfully with the rigours of a tropical climate. The public buildings, however, had at least a certain subdued grandeur which compensated for their more obvious aesthetic flaws. On the other hand, the Protestant churches and chapels, which proliferated in nineteenth-century Sri Lanka, were conspicuously English in design. Their clean lines conveyed an impression of blandness and austerity which enhanced their remoteness and alienation from the temple architecture of the island. There is not a single piece of sculpture, indigenous or British, produced at any time in the nineteenth century which could bear comparison with the best or even the less distinguished products of the past. As for painting, the new modes and outlook in vogue neither developed a fruitful creativity of their own nor became successfully integrated with the artistic traditions of the country. Only two artists of the nineteenth century deserve to be mentioned in this survey, namely, Andrew Nichol, an Englishman, and J.L.K. van Dort (1831–91), a Sri Lankan, from a small Burgher community. Nichol, the first serious painter in watercolours to work on the island, was in charge of the School of Design in the Colombo Academy in the 1840s. Van Dort was the sole superior talent thrown up in the new wave of popular painting launched by Nichol. Apart from these two, the record in painting in the nineteenth century was singularly barren; in painting, no less than in sculpture and architecture, the break with tradition was complete.

THE TWENTIETH CENTURY TILL 1947–48

In this phase of its history, Sinhala literature developed from the pioneering efforts of Piyadasa Sirisena and W.A. Silva in the early years of the twentieth century to the mature artistry of Martin Wickremesinghe (1891–1976), novelist and literary critic, whose prolific career spanned a half-century of distinguished creative achievement from the 1920s. Sirisena's novels reflected a passionate commitment to the threatened values of traditional society, a root-and-branch opposition to the pervasive anglicization to which the educated elite was succumbing so easily. As a novelist and poet, Sirisena was first and last a combative, argumentative and totally dedicated nationalist. This propagandist strain obtruded in all his work to the point of damaging its artistic quality. W.A. Silva placed greater stress on literature as entertainment and his most notable contribution was the clean break he effected in his novels from both the other-worldly orientation of classical prose narrative and Sirisena's turgid didacticism.[4]

If any one writer deserves the title of father of modern Sinhalese literature it is Martin Wickremesinghe. Like Sirisena, he came to literature from journalism and remained in journalism after his reputation as a novelist and literary critic had become securely established. His trilogy about the village of his birth, on the south coast of the island, is a deeply moving depiction of the human condition set against the background of a society in the throes of change. The first two parts of the trilogy, *Gamperaliya* (1944) and *Yuganthaya* (1948), appeared in this period. The third part of the trilogy, *Kali Yugaya*, appeared in 1957. With them the Sinhala novel came of age. In technique, theme and language he demonstrated a mastery and sophistication that Sirisena and W.A. Silva had lacked.

What Wickremesinghe was to the Sinhala novel, G.B. Senanayake was to the Sinhala short story and E.R. Sarachchandra—in the first phase of a remarkable career— to literary criticism. Wickremesinghe and Senanayake combined creative writing with literary criticism. While Wickremesinghe's criteria in evaluating the classical literary heritage were a synthesis of Indian and Western traditions of literary criticism, Sarachchandra's were those of the major figures in British and American literary criticisms.[5] As a literary critic Sarachchandra outshone his two rivals. All of them spoke English—Sarachchandra more fluently than the others—and an easy familiarity with Western (especially English) literature widened their intellectual horizons and buttressed their self-confidence. Through their literary criticism they contributed to the creation of a new Sinhalese literary elite capable of synthesizing and harmonizing the best features of the western indigenous literary traditions. As novelists and literary critics, they educated the Sinhalese reader to a more mature response to his environment.

Creative achievement in Sinhalese—prose, poetry and criticism alike—overshadowed that in Tamil. There didacticism and tradition were deeply entrenched and survived much longer against the efforts of the English-educated elite among the Tamils to do for Tamil literature what men like Wickremesinghe had accomplished in Sinhala. Although their efforts did enrich the Tamil of Sri Lanka and south India alike, it neither secured a breakthrough to greater refinement and modernity in literary tastes nor succeeded in conferring an individuality or distinctiveness on the island's Tamil which would differentiate it from the overpowering south Indian version.

In the works of two writers, S.J.K. Crowther and J. Vijayatunga, both journalists, Sri Lankan English at last showed signs of establishing itself as a creative force in its own right. In the hands of a lesser talent, Crowther's *The Knight Errant* might have been no more than a clever roman à clef on Sri Lanka's political elite of the 1920s, which he intended it to be. But what he had achieved was something more substantial: a political satire of considerable distinction. When Vijayatunga's *Grass for My Feet* was published in London in 1935, it came like a storm after a long drought, refreshing proof that a Sri Lankan could use the English language with the same sureness of touch as the major Indian and West Indian writers in English. Few Sri Lankan novelists and essayists— whatever their language—have evoked the island's rural scene with Vijayatunga's subtlety and sensitivity to mood. Like Wickremesinghe, he wrote of the rural south, but his vignettes and characterization alike are sharper and clearer, and the atmosphere is more authentic and less sentimental. Only Leonard Woolf's poignant tale of rural Sri Lanka—again the southern part—*Village in the Jungle*, the distilled essence of a British civil servant's sympathetic but acute observation of the people over whom he ruled as assistant government agent at the turn of the century, ranks above *Grass for My Feet* in literary skill. Vijayatunga and Crowther, however, proved to be two swallows who did not make a summer rather than the heralds of a new age in Sri Lankan literature. Neither of them produced another work of similar quality, nor did their contemporaries, writing in English, rise above an uninspiring vapidity of sentiment and mediocrity in technique.

Of Sri Lankan English poetry there is little to be said except to emphasize its singular lack of distinction. In Tamil poetry the dead hand of tradition crushed creativity just as completely—if not more so—than it had done in prose writing. Even though poetry was the most popular literary form in Sinhala in the years before independence, it did not seem set for a more promising start than its English and Tamil counterparts with the neoclassicism of men like Sirisena, Ananda Rajakaruna (1885–1957) and G.H. Perera (1886–1948). What they attempted to do was to resuscitate the narrative form and stylized idiom of classical poetry, but in their hands it regressed into jejune narrative verse or versified fiction more concerned with precision in grammar and an archaic poetic diction than with content, which was totally banal. When the reaction to this spiritless exercise in sustaining the archaic set in, the avant-garde adopted a more contemporary idiom, discounted precision in grammar, explored new forms and themes but still maintained the traditional prosodic form. Their works were distinguished by a restless experimentation rather than any substantial improvement, in terms of artistic merit, on the work of neoclassicists.

Very little by way of a dramatic literature had survived in Sri Lanka, and no tradition of the theatre, at least not of the kind that would have provided entertainment for the court and literati in the days of the Sri Lankan kings.[6] What had survived was a tradition of folk drama: *kōlam, sokari* and *nādagam.* Its vitality was revealed in the years after independence when Sarachchandra used it for a strikingly successful and innovative departure into a more sophisticated theatrical experience. In the last decade of the nineteenth century, this tradition of folk drama contributed to the growth of an urban theatre, but the greatest influence on the latter was exerted by the Parsi theatre companies from India which toured the island and attracted large and appreciative audiences. This urban theatre, symbolized by the Tower Hall in Colombo, flourished for two decades in the first quarter of the twentieth century before it began an unexpected but rapid decline. It left behind only a dim memory of a theatrical experience, of little value by way of dramatic literature, and a few melodies. John de Silva (1854–1932) and Charles Dias, the main playwrights in this theatre, went back into legend and history for their themes and to the repertory of the Parsi companies for their melodies. They were to drama what Sirisena was to literature, nationalists using the theatre as a platform for their political message.

The most notable feature in the history of the theatre in Sri Lanka in the 1940s was the role of the University of Ceylon as a disseminating centre for a more refined and discriminating taste in drama, and as a workshop for experiment in artistic expression in the theatre. E.F.C. Ludowyk as professor of English kept pace with his productions of some of the classics of western drama, in English, an exciting start which led to a reanimation of Sinhala drama in Sarachchandra's adaptations of these western classics. In Tamil drama too there was this same trend towards a more sophisticated theatrical taste, drawing its inspiration from western drama.

In music the search was on for a national idiom, identity and authenticity. Because traditional music had all but disappeared by the beginning of the twentieth century, its resuscitation and revival were altogether more difficult. The urban theatre of John de Silva and Charles Dias created a taste among the Sinhalese for the Hindustani music of northern India, which was soon adopted as the standard, or classical music of the Sinhalese. The emerging national musical tradition took on a distinct Indian form when the avant-garde adopted *nūrti* music, using north Indian classical ragas for their compositions. But by the 1940s, the search for a national identity in music took the form of a deliberate attempt to break free from the pervasive influence of this Indian tradition.[7]

Nowhere was the discontinuity between tradition and modernity sharper and more complete than in painting, sculpture and architecture. The only evidence that continuity was still possible and real was in the crafts of the island. There the indigenous tradition lived on. The civic and public architecture of this period was decidedly less successful than that of the nineteenth century. When it was not overwhelmingly utilitarian it was totally occidental in concept. Indeed, the British architectural legacy in Sri Lanka is extraordinarily uninspiring, without a single building or monument which could stand comparison with those of the past for originality in design and aesthetic appeal. Surprisingly, the Anglican Church led the way in the 1930s and 1940s in a fruitful fusion of western building technology and the indigenous architectural tradition in the construction of chapels and churches but not only were such new departures few but they hardly amounted to a determined reversal of the established pattern of an obtrusive occidentalism in public buildings, secular and religious.

In painting, however, the synthesis between east and west was both powerful and successful. The two outstanding painters of the day were Justin Daraniyagala and George Keyt. The latter fused together the tradition of Picasso and Hindu mythology with a virtuosity that established him as one of the greatest south Asian painters of the century—his reputation being even more securely established in India than in Sri Lanka. Keyt, in fact, is the one major artistic talent to emerge out of the encounter between east and west under British rule on the island.

Sri Lanka Since Independence: The Dominance of the UNP, 1947–56

THE END OF THE BRITISH RAJ

A perceptive observer watching the collapse of European empires in Asia after the Second World War would have been struck by the contrast between the situation in Sri Lanka and that in the rest of south Asia and Burma. It could hardly be expected that the transfer of power in the Indian subcontinent would be free of turmoil, but the violence that raged over British India on the eve of independence was on a scale which few but the most pessimistic could have anticipated. The dawn of Indian independence was marred by massacres and migrations in Punjab on a scale unparalleled in world history in a time of peace; these occurred also in eastern India. The subcontinent seemed on the verge of a calamitous civil war.[1] Aung San, the youthful leader of Burma's independence struggle, did not live to see the signing of the treaty (which he had negotiated) between Britain and Burma on 17 October 1947, which granted Burma her independence; he was assassinated along with a group of his closest associates on 19 June that year. If the civil war which at one stage seemed India's inevitable fate was avoided through the drastic device of partition, Burma was not so fortunate; violence erupted there almost from the very first week of the existence of the new Burmese republic.

Sri Lanka in 1948 was, in contrast, an oasis of stability, peace and order. Set against the contemporary catastrophes in the rest of the former British possessions in south Asia in the scale of violence involved, the industrial disputes and the general strike of the years 1945–47 paled into utter insignificance. The transfer of power in Sri Lanka was smooth and peaceful; little was seen of the divisions and bitterness which were tearing at the recent independence of the new nations of south Asia. Within a few months of independence in 1948, one of the most intractable political issues in the country—the Tamil problem— which had absorbed the energies of its politicians and the British themselves to an inordinate degree since the early 1920s, seemed on the way to amicable settlement. G.G. Ponnambalam, who had led the Tamils in their political campaigns since his entry into the State Council in 1934, became a member of the cabinet, bringing with him into the government most of the leadership and members of the Tamil Congress. In so doing, he helped convert the government into what was very much a consensus of moderate political opinion in the country. In Ponnambalam's decision to join Senanayake's government there was, as is usual in these matters, a mixture of motives. On a personal level, there was a realistic assessment of the undoubted advantages of working with an old rival whose political attitudes were so much like his own. There were also the attractions of office with all that it meant in terms of power, influence on policy and patronage. But above all, in responding thus to Senanayake's political initiative, Ponnambalam was acknowledging that the prime minister's sensitivity to minority interests was genuine.

For Senanayake, the Sri Lankan polity was one and indivisible. While his deep conviction of the need for generous concessions to the minorities was much more than a matter of political realism, he was nevertheless acutely aware that these were essential to ensure political stability in a plural society such as Sri Lanka in the vital last phase in the transfer of power. An analysis of his response to the political implications of minority anxiety on Sri Lanka's development as an independent state would need to emphasize three main points of interest.

First, there were the guarantees preventing legislation discriminating against minorities which were incorporated in the Soulbury Constitution. These guarantees had been borrowed from provisions in the Board of Ministers' draft constitution of 1944, which had been introduced on D.S. Senanayake's initiative as a gesture of generosity and reassurance to the minorities. In retrospect, it would seem that the rights of minorities had not received adequate protection in the Soulbury Constitution, but in 1946–47, the constitutional guarantees against discriminatory legislation seemed sufficiently reassuring to them largely because of their trust and confidence in D.S. Senanayake. Second, there was the initiative he took in forming the United National Party (UNP). This was designed to make a fresh start in politics in the direction of a consensus of moderate opinion in national politics. It was to be a political party necessarily representative of the majority community, but at the same time acceptable to the minorities. His own standing in the country was sufficient guarantee of its being acceptable to the majority, but its position among the Sinhalese was strengthened by S.W.R.D. Bandaranaike's decision to bring in his Sinhala Mahā Sabhā From the beginning it had the enthusiastic approval of the small but influential Christian minority. The Muslims, who in the past had given substantial support to the Tamils in their political campaigns, at last broke away and sought association with the new party. When the Tamil Congress crossed over to the government in 1948, the equilibrium of political forces which D.S. Senanayake had sought to establish was stabilized at a level which he found acceptable, even though the Tamil Congress did not lose its separate identity and despite the fact that a section broke away from it into a stubborn but, at that time, seemingly futile opposition. Only the Indian community, consisting mainly of plantation workers, was left out. But there was a special reason for that: it was regarded as an unassimilated group without roots in the country. The decision to leave the Indians out was deliberately taken on that account. To the extent that he shared the attitudes and prejudices of the great majority of Sinhalese politicians over the Indian question—the status of Indian plantation workers in the Sri Lankan polity and, more specifically, the denial to them of unrestricted rights to the franchise—his conception of a multiracial polity was flawed.

Third, D.S. Senanayake thwarted all efforts to abandon the concept of a secular state and the principle of the state's religious neutrality. He succeeded in this to the extent that in 1948, despite some Buddhist displeasure over the continued prestige and influence enjoyed by the Christians, there seemed little or no evidence of the religious turmoil and linguistic conflicts which were to burst to the surface in the mid-1950s.

The island's political leadership within the Board of Ministers and its successor, the new cabinet, took pride in the smooth and uneventful nature of the transfer of power. Thus, the last British governor of the colony became the first Governor General of the new dominion. If there was a parallel for this in the case of India and Mountbatten, there was also, as we have seen in a previous chapter, a notable difference between the constitutional and legal instruments which conferred independence on Sri Lanka and the cognate process in India, Pakistan and Burma. This created, for some time at least, the illusion of a qualitative difference in the political status conferred on Sri Lanka compared to that of the other successors to the British Raj in south Asia. The constitution under which the new dominion began its political existence was of British origin in contrast to the autochthonous constitution drafted for the Indian republic by a constituent assembly. Once again, there was an element of exaggeration in this criticism, for the new constitution of Sri Lanka was basically the Board of Ministers' draft constitution of 1944—approved subsequently by the State Council—modified to suit the needs of the changed circumstances of 1946–47. There was also an emphasis on the Commonwealth connection and the maintenance of the link with the Crown as head of the Commonwealth after India and Pakistan had opted for republican status. India's acceptance of membership of the Commonwealth went a long way towards demonstrating that dominion status had no connotation of constitutional subordination to Britain and, in fact, meant complete independence, with the advantages of membership of a worldwide Commonwealth. Above all, the agreements on defence and external affairs, negotiated before the transfer of power, helped to give an air of credibility to the argument that the independence achieved by Sri Lanka was flawed.

Thus the real worth of D.S. Senanayake's achievement over the transfer of power came to be denied because the means

adopted for the attainment of independence under his leadership
were not as robust and dramatic as they should have been.
By laying so much stress on the decorous and peaceful processes
of constitutional agitation, he and the Board of Ministers had
deprived themselves, perhaps consciously, of the opportunities
of exploiting the numerous chances they had of making a more
emotional and vigorous commitment to nationalism. Left wing
critics of the government were able to argue that the
independence achieved in 1947–48 was 'spurious'. The jibe of
'fake' independence, which they kept hurling at the government
evoked a response from a wider circle of the political nation
than the left wing alone, largely because the Indian experience
seemed to provide a more emotionally satisfying example than
the process by which power had been transferred in Sri Lanka.
Independence granted from above was regarded as much less
satisfying to the spirit of nationalism than if it had been won
after prolonged strife and unstinting sacrifice.

THE LEGATEES OF THE BRITISH

In the general elections of 1947, left-wing parties made
substantial if not spectacular, gains and held between
themselves and their fellow-travellers about a quarter of the
elected seats. Earlier they had organized a series of major
strikes culminating in the general strike of 1947. These strikes
had been the most noteworthy demonstrations of solidarity
of the working class and white-collar workers up to that time.
The strikes were as much political demonstrations as they were
trade disputes—one of the main demands was the rejection
of the Soulbury constitution. The strife generated by these
strikes served the purpose of underlining the difference in
approach between two concepts of nationalism. The 'moderates'
had come into their inheritance and the 'radicals'—in the sense
of the left-wing—had demonstrated their determination to
deprive them of it. They had taken a stand against the Soulbury
Constitution and they dismissed the grant of independence
in February 1948 as a cynical deal between the imperial power
and its pliant agents in Sri Lanka to preserve the old order
under a guise of independence.

If D.S. Senanayake was sanguine about the prospects of ethnic harmony and a fair balance of responsibility and duty between the majority and the minorities (religious and ethnic), he paid exaggerated importance to the presumed threat from the left and took extraordinary steps to meet it. There were, first of all, the advantages accruing to him from the demarcation, in which he had had no hand or influence, of constituencies to the new Parliament, where the electoral balance was heavily in favour of the rural areas, which were generally more conservative in outlook.[2] But more important were decisions in which the initiative was his. Of these, the most notable were, first, the Citizenship Act of 1948, the Indian and Pakistani Residents (Citizenship) Act of 1949 and the Parliamentary Elections (Amendment) Act of 1949, which deprived the great majority of the Indian Tamils resident in Sri Lanka of their citizenship rights and franchise. Sinhalese opinion, especially in the Kandyan areas, was deeply suspicious of the Indian Tamils and apprehensive of the prospect of Indian domination of the central highlands of the island. There was another fear as well—the Indian plantation workers as an additional source of political strength to the indigenous Tamils. More important, and this mattered most to Senanayake, left-wing groups began to look upon the Indian workers, if they could be weaned away from the Ceylon Indian Congress which controlled them, as a potentially powerful component of their own trade unions. In the general elections of 1947 the Indian vote was decidedly anti-UNP. Where there were no candidates of the Ceylon Indian Congress, the Indians had voted enthusiastically for the left-wing parties and left 'independents'. And within the new Parliament representatives of the Ceylon Indian Congress sat on the opposition benches and gave their support to the 'left'. Thus the new citizenship legislation not only served to assuage the fears and suspicions of the Sinhalese in general and the Kandyans in particular, but also to demolish a potentially powerful prop of the left-wing groups. The immediate effect of this was to distort the electoral balance even more markedly than before and to make the Sinhalese rural voter the arbiter of the country's politics: with each fresh delimitation of constituencies up to 1976, the Sinhalese rural voters' position was strengthened. This new electoral balance gave the UNP and its allies a decisive advantage in the general elections of 1952, and the left-wing parties were greatly handicapped. Second, the Public Security Act of 1947 and the Trade Union (Amendment) Act of 1948 were directed against the Marxist-dominated working class organizations and were the direct result of the working class agitation and industrial turmoil of 1945–47, when the LSSP leadership, recently released from prison, were flexing their muscles in anticipation of the general elections scheduled for 1947.

The left-wing challenge to the government appeared more formidable than it really was. At the general elections of 1947, the left-wing parties reaped the electoral rewards that were available to any credible opponents of the newly formed UNP, most of whose leaders had enjoyed power since the 1930s. Besides, while only the UNP presented itself to the electors as a party making a serious bid for power, its party organization was rudimentary at best, and UNP candidates cheerfully fought each other in many constituencies, sometimes with three or even four candidates standing as representatives of the party. Not surprisingly, their opponents did remarkably well. Never again were the Trotskyists and the communists so well represented in Parliament as they were after the general elections of 1947, when they and their fellow-travellers held about one-fifth of the membership. Indeed, in the heady aftermath of the elections there were sanguine expectations in some quarters of the possibility (admittedly somewhat remote) of the left wing forming the nucleus of an alternative government to one dominated by the UNP.

Within a year of independence, the UNP had stabilized its position, not least because of the patronage it had at its disposal. In contrast, the left-wing parties were as divided— by personality conflicts and ideological disputes—in 1950 as they had been in 1947 when the elections were held. For almost three years they could not agree among themselves on a leader of the Opposition. The LSSP, the largest opposition group, was in favour of its leader accepting this position, but the more doctrinaire Trotskyist group, the Bolshevik Samasamaja Party, was hostile to the suggestion, and so for that matter were the communists. It was in June 1950, after the two Trotskyist groups had merged, that the LSSP leader, Dr N.M. Perera, took office as leader of Opposition. The communists gave him no support in this.

In the meantime, the UNP had improved its parliamentary position quite substantially with the entry of G.G. Ponnambalam and most of the Tamil Congress members into the government. Not only were the ranks of the opposition depleted, but the government was able to acquire the formidable oratorical and forensic skills of the Tamil Congress leader. Those members of the Tamil Congress who opposed the new alignment of forces formed a rival Tamil organization, the Federal Party, in December 1948, but this latter organization was very much a voice in the wilderness until the general elections of 1956 when it emerged as by far the most influential of the Tamil parties.

The social welfare schemes of the Donoughmore era were continued beyond 1947, partly at least as a means of blunting the challenge of the Marxist left. Sri Lanka, poor though she was, enjoyed a much higher standard of living than India, Pakistan and Burma, and the national finances seemed adequate to maintain the welfare measures to which the country had grown accustomed in the last years of British rule. In 1947, the total expenditure on welfare absorbed 56.1 per cent of the government's resources; the corresponding figure for the late 1920s had been a mere 16.4 per cent. It was not yet evident that the burgeoning costs of these welfare measures were an unsupportable burden for a developing country and one which added a dimension of weakness to an economy of which the principal feature was its dependence on the vagaries of a world market.

Ironically, however, neither of the protagonists—the government led by D.S. Senanayake and its left-wing critics—showed much understanding of the Buddhists' sense of outrage and indignation at what they regarded as the historic injustices suffered by their religion under Western rule. The affront was to culture no less than to religion, and the resentment was felt even more strongly by the ayurvedic physician, the Sinhalese schoolmaster and the notary than by the bhikkhus. And as regards religion it was the withdrawal of the traditional patronage and the consequent precedence and prestige that was resented. Beneath the surface, these religious, cultural and linguistic issues were gathering momentum and developing into a force too powerful for the existing social and political set-up to accommodate or absorb. They were to tear the country apart within a decade of 1948 and to accomplish the discomfiture of both the UNP and its left-wing critics.

Indeed, the Marxists placed as much emphasis as did Senanayake himself on Sri Lanka as a multiracial polity, as a secular state and on a territorial concept of citizenship. (Their version of this polity was much more comprehensive because it also encompassed the Indian plantation workers, whom not even the most liberal of the 'constitutionalists' was willing to regard as an integral element of a Sri Lanka polity.) In this emphasis on a secular state there was much more in common between Senanayake with his supporters among the 'constitutionalists' and the Marxists than between the former and S.W.R.D. Bandaranaike's adherents within the 'constitutionalist' camp.

NATIONALISM

The political settlement established by D.S. Senanayake was less stable than it appeared to be. The forces that sought to upset it were as insidious as they were truly formidable. In order to grasp their significance we need to turn to the nature of nationalism in Sri Lanka. There was always a tendency on the part of the Sinhalese to equate their own ethnic nationalism with a wider all-island one, to assume that these—Sinhalese nationalism and Sri Lankan nationalism—were one and the same. In support of this they advanced arguments based on history and immemorial tradition. But this was a short-sighted and unrealistic attitude. The Tamils, the most numerous and articulate group among the minorities, passionately rejected this identification of the sectional interests of the majority with the wider all-island focus of Sri Lankan nationalism. The Christians (among the Sinhalese and Tamils), particularly the Roman Catholics, were equally apprehensive and resentful of the common tendency to equate Sinhalese nationalism with Buddhism. The Tamils, for their part, developed an inward-looking ethnic nationalism of their own, although this, like its Sinhalese counterpart, lacked cohesion or even the touch of authenticity till language became, after independence, the basis of these rival nationalisms.

The other version of nationalism, a Ceylon or Sri Lankan nationalism, emphasized the common interests of the island's various ethnic and religious groups. It had as its basis an acceptance of the reality of a plural society and sought the reconciliation of the legitimate interests of the majority and minorities within the context of an all-island polity. Its most influential advocate at the time of the transfer of power was D.S. Senanayake. In 1948, this version of nationalism seemed to be a viable alternative to the narrower sectionalisms described earlier, and held out the prospect of peace and stability in the vital first phase of independence. It was based on a double compromise: the softening of Sinhalese dominance by the establishment of an equilibrium of political forces, the keynote of which was moderation, and an emphasis on secularism, a refusal to mix state power and politics with religion, even though the concept of a special responsibility for Buddhism was tacitly accepted. This Sri Lankan nationalism had a crucial flaw. It was basically elitist in conception and it had little popular support extending beyond the political establishment. It required D.S. Senanayake's enormous personal prestige and consummate statecraft to make it viable.

The first major challenge to this system had appeared when S.W.R.D. Bandaranaike crossed over to the Opposition in July 1951 with a small group of his supporters. In September 1951, the Sri Lanka Freedom Party (SLFP) was inaugurated as a centrist political force which deliberately sought to become the focal point of all interest groups which were dissatisfied with the UNP and at the same time opposed to Marxist solutions to the country's problems. The nucleus of a democratic alternative

to the UNP had emerged. Its populist programme was directed
at the large protest vote that went to the Marxist parties for
want of an alternative, and to the rural areas which formed
the basis of the UNP's hold on political power in the country.
The Marxist left had failed to make much of an impact on the
rural areas and its perennial ideological disputes, its rifts and
shifts and realignments, which were incomprehensible to most
of the electors in the country, carried no meaning to any save
true believers. Besides, the left was just as unsympathetic as
the UNP leadership to the religious, linguistic and cultural
aspirations of the Buddhist activists, and it was to this group
with its deep sense of grievance, its social and economic
discontent, its resentment at being neglected by both the left
and the UNP, that the SLFP as the successors of the Sinhala
Mahā Sabhā turned.

In the years after independence one of the major
preoccupations of the government under D.S. Senanayake had
been with the need to establish securely a Sri Lankan
nationalism and during the time of his leadership there had
been a policy of subordinating communal differences to the
common goal of fostering parliamentary democratic
institutions and strengthening the foundations of nationhood.
The primary aim was the establishment of an equilibrium of
ethnic forces within a multiracial polity. For some time it
seemed as though these policies were succeeding, but under
the surface powerful forces were at work to upset the
equilibrium thus established. This shift was in tune with the
essence of democratic politics in which, given a common basis
of agreement, the numerically larger group can peacefully alter
the power structure. It was to this process that S.W.R.D.
Bandaranaike sought to give leadership, and the ideals of
communal reconciliation and harmony were soon to give way
before the stresses released by the divisive forces of language
and religion. The Sinhalese-Buddhist majority, long dormant,
was beginning once more to assert its national dominance.
The first casualties were the concepts of a multiracial polity, a
Sri Lankan nationalism and a secular state.

The prospect of a classic confrontation between
D.S. Senanayake and S.W.R.D. Bandaranaike as the advocates

of two diametrically opposed versions of nationalism vanished with the death of D.S. Senanayake on 22 March 1952. He was succeeded as prime minister by his son Dudley after a brief but bitter squabble for the leadership within the inner circles of the UNP. The younger Senanayake was forty years old at this time. While he shared his father's views on secularism, communal harmony and resistance to the demands of Buddhist activists, he was also more receptive to the winds of change that were blowing over the island. He was much more amenable to reasonable concessions to the Buddhist movement and the trade unions. In short, he had reservations about many aspects of the status quo. He, therefore, could not defend it with his father's sense of commitment.

It was no great surprise when he led the UNP and its allies to a remarkable electoral victory in July 1952 over a formidable array of opponents—S.W.R.D. Bandaranaike's SLFP, the Marxists and the Tamil Federal Party. The election took place in an atmosphere of emotionalism following the death of D.S. Senanayake. The massive victory won by Dudley Senanayake was in many ways a ringing endorsement given by the electorate to his father's life's work. The equilibrium of forces he had sought to establish was seemingly stabilized by the massive electoral support received by his successor. S.W.R.D. Bandaranaike did not make much of an impact on the rural areas. The left lost ground heavily and the Federal Party made no impression at all in the Tamil areas, with its leader S.J.V. Chelvanayakam losing his seat to a UNP candidate.

But the forces aligned against the new prime minister were formidable. The left gave him a taste of the problems he faced when they organized a massive demonstration just after the elections in protest against alleged electoral frauds. There was no evidence that any frauds had been perpetrated, S.W.R.D. Bandaranaike, for one, never gave any serious support to this canard. The government responded by organizing an equally massive counter-rally.

More significantly, the SLFP emerged from the election as a viable democratic alternative to the UNP and its leader took on the role of leader of the Opposition on the traditional

Westminster model. The Marxist groups within parliament and in the country were hopelessly divided and a section of them preferred to acknowledge Bandaranaike's leadership of the opposition within the parliament rather than that of the LSSP leader, Dr N.M. Perera. But even so, their attitude to Bandaranaike and his policies was at best ambivalent. They had much greater faith than he in strikes, mass action and extra-parliamentary struggles as forms of protest against the government. And in August 1953 they were offered precisely the opportunity of embarrassing the government that they had been waiting for.

The new government took office against the background of an emerging economic crisis. The boom conditions which Sri Lanka's exports had enjoyed during the Korean War were soon followed by a sharp worsening of the terms of trade and a fall in rubber prices. It was evident that Sri Lanka could no longer afford the massive expenditure on food subsidies to which the country had grown accustomed in the days of D.S. Senanayake's government. Acting on the advice of a visiting World Bank mission, Dudley Senanayake sought to reduce the crippling burden of the rice subsidy. This move was doubly provocative: the price rose from 25 cents a measure (0.908 kg) to 75 cents in spite of the fact that during the election campaign of 1952, government spokesmen had capitalized on the popularity of the rice subsidy and promised to maintain it at the same level.

When public protests rose against the increase in the price of rice, the Marxist unions, with the Trotskyist LSSP in the lead, were mobilized to stage a one-day hartal (a mass stoppage of work). S.W.R.D. Bandaranaike declined to let his party get involved in this hartal, but the Marxists proceeded with it undismayed. The turbulent demonstrations that followed in the wake of the hartal exceeded the expectations of the Marxist leadership and several demonstrators were killed when the police opened fire.

The hartal had fateful political consequences for the UNP in the sense that it was one of the factors contributing to the resignation of Dudley Senanayake in October 1953. His successor was Sir John Kotelawala, who had neither the former's political vision nor any substantial reserves of committed public support beyond the ranks of the urban elite. The parliamentary majority he inherited was large enough to enable him to stabilize his position and to cope successfully with the problems caused by his predecessor's resignation. He could even afford to exclude some members of his predecessor's cabinet when he formed his government, but his political judgement went astray when he dropped a man of G.G. Ponnambalam's ability and standing; a few disgruntled members of parliament (MP) maintained a sullen silence, while others drifted into the opposition—potential recruits for a broad-based movement that would bring down the UNP. But the prime minister's hold on Parliament grew stronger.

It was not in parliament, however, that the real opposition to Kotelawala and the UNP lay. Religion, language and culture were emerging as the central issues of the day, and with regard to these he was so patently unsympathetic and lacking in understanding that the position of his government and the UNP was successfully undermined.[3]

The Sinhala-educated intelligentsia found that rewarding careers were closed to them by the pervasive dominance of English as the language of administration. Although they were not without influence in the villages, they had seldom in the past been able to exert any influence on a national scale and they felt that they had been unjustly excluded from a share of power commensurate with their numbers by the Western-educated elite. More important, they felt that they were better able than the latter to speak for the villagers. They also felt that the Tamil community had taken an unfair share of power by virtue of its superior educational opportunities. In addition, they believed that in its spiritual home Theravada Buddhism and the culture associated with it were not receiving sufficient support or respect. The worldwide celebration of the 2500th anniversary of the parinibbāna of the Buddha was scheduled for 1956. This afforded Buddhist activists a marvellous opportunity for their campaigns. At the same time a report by a prestigious non-government commission (consisting of eminent Buddhist personalities) on the deplorable state of Buddhism in Sri Lanka heightened these fears—they levelled the charge that the value of independence was 'vitiated' by the fact that the ruling elite was 'completely dominated by an alien outlook and values, and estranged from their national history and culture'.

If religious fervour was the prime determinant of change, the language question was its sharp cutting edge. Indeed the two elements—Buddhism and Sinhala—were so closely intertwined that it was impossible to treat either one in isolation. The anxiety to preserve and strengthen the Sinhala language stemmed partly at least from a fear that if it fell into decay in Sri Lanka, its religious and cultural tradition would die with it. What occurred at this time was a profoundly significant transformation of nationalism with language becoming its basis. (The most appropriate analogy for this would be the linguistic nationalism which erupted in Central Europe in the mid-nineteenth century.) This transformation of nationalism affected both the Sinhalese and Tamil population.[4]

To the Buddhist activists the prime minister was both an anachronism and a philistine and they sought to replace him by a more representative figure. Their first choice, significantly, was Dudley Senanayake, then a backbencher, semi-retired from active politics. But he declined their offer, first because his health was troubling him and, second, because he saw the political implications of the programme he was being called upon to champion, and these disturbed him. It was at this point that they turned to Bandaranaike. He had fewer compunctions about accepting the programme because he had been advocating much the same policies for many years. The profound political consequences of the programme did not deter him from adopting it with enthusiasm, because he was confident of his ability to ride the storm and to control the forces he was being asked to lead.

The crucial issue was language. Sir John Kotelawala's maladroit handling of this issue converted it into a highly inflammable one. The problem that faced him was to satisfy the aspirations of the Sinhala, who were increasingly insistent on the immediate imposition of Sinhalese as the sole official language in breach of the compromise on language reached in 1944 and the fears of the Tamils, who realized that such a step would place them at a severe disadvantage in the competition for posts in government service. Late in 1955, the prime minister, while on an official visit to the Tamil north, made a public pronouncement that he would make constitutional provision for parity of status for the Sinhala and Tamil languages. The thunderstorm of protests against this that arose in the Sinhalese areas took every section of opinion by surprise. Nobody had anticipated such a profoundly hostile reaction. The SLFP which, like the UNP and all other national parties, stood for Sinhala and Tamil as the official language of the country, capitalized on the situation by declaring itself in favour of Sinhalese as the only official language—with a provision for the 'reasonable use', of the Tamil language. Within a few months of this the UNP too (in February 1956) reversed its position on language rights and adopted one that was even more thoroughgoing in its commitment to Sinhalese as the official language than that of the SLFP. But the patent insincerity of the conversion discredited both the prime minister and the UNP. They lost the support of the Tamils, and as events were to demonstrate so dramatically, made not the slightest headway among the Sinhalese.

Sir John Kotelawala completely misread the trends of the day in believing that this last-minute volte-face on language would enable him to return to power at the next general elections. Scheduled for 1957, these were now advanced to 1956 in the hope that the UNP could capitalize on its stand on language at a time when the left wing parties were handicapped by their commitment to the policy of parity of status for Sinhala and Tamil. Sir John's chances of pulling off the elections seemed good enough not merely to his own advisers, but also to some of Bandaranaike's close associates who chose this moment to cross over to the government, thus demonstrating that a position in the centre of the political arena is not often the best place from which to judge which way the wind is blowing. But the decision to hold the general elections in 1956 offended Buddhist activists who preferred to keep the year free of political agitation and partisan politics for the Buddha Jayanthi, the worldwide celebration in May of that year of the 2500th anniversary of the Buddha's parinibbāna or death. They exhorted the prime minister to postpone the elections until after the celebration, but he refused to do so. Instead he aggravated the offence by initiating the first phase of the Buddha Jayanthi celebrations before the elections, which the most articulate sections of the sangha—a majority, in fact—regarded as a blatant exploitation of religious sentiment by a man whom they believed to have neither a sense of occasion nor any genuine love for Buddhism.

The opposition parties were now better prepared than ever before for their encounter with the UNP. This time the forces ranged against the UNP were altogether more formidable and more united than they had been in 1952 or 1947. It was recognized that Bandaranaike's SLFP was the most viable alternative to the UNP and that it should be given all possible support in the prime objective of defeating the UNP. Bandaranaike had protected his left flank by arranging a no-contest pact with the two leading Marxist parties, the LSSP and the Communist Party, in September–October 1955. In the meantime, the SLFP had joined forces with a section of the LSSP (under Philip Gunawardane) and two smaller Sinhalese parties, in the Mahajana Eksath Peramuna (MEP) (the People's United Front), in which the common links were a commitment to Sinhala as the official language and to a populist programme of social and economic change.

The UNP went it alone. Its Tamil Congress allies in the north had left them long before the elections and there the way was clear for the Federal Party. Dudley Senanayake stood aloof from this contest and did not give the UNP any assistance. His absence and that of the Senanayake family in general was skilfully exploited to the UNP's disadvantage. For the leadership of the UNP the defeat they suffered was all the more stunning for being so totally unexpected; few people, whether politicians or publicists, had correctly predicted that the outcome of the elections would be the crushing defeat of the UNP under Sir John Kotelawala. Not even the victors of this electoral struggle had gauged the real strength of the grass-roots movement which welled up under the direction of an army of concerned bhikkhus under the banner of an improvised organization, the Eksath Bhikkhu Peramuna[5] which transcended the traditional nikāya divisions. Buddhist activists succeeded in converting what might have been a conventional election campaign into a symbolic struggle between the forces of evil—the UNP—and righteousness.

In retrospect, the formation of the UNP and the strong government it provided for eight vitally important years were positive, even essential, achievements of the first decade of Sri Lanka's post-independence history.[6] The party ensured order and an orderly transition to democratic politics under a two-party system. S.W.R.D. Bandaranaike, for one, was well aware of the symbiotic relationship between the founding of the UNP and the stability of democracy in Sri Lanka in the early years of independence. The UNP gave Sri Lanka, he said, 'the stability of government which was needed, particularly at the beginning of a new era of freedom'.[7]

After the election of 1952, especially the overwhelming dominance of the UNP appeared to be leading inevitably towards the institutionalization of a monolithic party system as was happening elsewhere among new states. The victory of the MEP in 1956 and the smooth transfer of power from the UNP to that new force were a watershed in Sri Lanka's political evolution. They marked a change from a political structure in which one party was in a position of clear predominance to a multiparty system in which two major parties are in constant competition for power and each is joined at one time or another in coalition by smaller groups. This was also the coming of age of Sri Lanka's system of parliamentary democracy.

THE ECONOMY

Concerning the economy, even more than the political structure, the mood at the time of the transfer of power was singularly sober and realistic though not unduly pessimistic. There were on the contrary, high hopes of economic achievement. The country's assets were not unimpressive; although the population was increasing rapidly, it was, compared with other countries in south Asia, well fed and literate; the government of Sri Lanka was the largest landholder in the country, controlling no less than 1,315,228 hectares (mostly waste forest which needed the provision of roads and electricity to be made productive); the administration was competent, and above all, there were large sterling balances accumulated during the war.

Nevertheless, the economic legacy left behind by the British was just as ambiguous as the political one—perhaps even more so. The crux of the problem was that foreign income which 'directly or indirectly constituted the bulk of the national income began to fall rapidly', while at the same time there was a rise in the cost of imports. This was reflected in the country's balance of payments which fell consistently from 'a handsome surplus in 1945 to a heavy deficit in 1947'. For a country which practically lives by foreign trade, a contemporary economic survey pointed out,[7] 'no economic indices could be more significant. It represented a fall in national income and a march towards greater poverty and insecurity'.[8]

D.S. Senanayake's government inherited an undiversified export economy dependent principally on the three crops, namely, tea (the most important in terms of export earnings), rubber and coconut. The weakness of the economy lay in the wide fluctuations to which the revenues from these exports were subject, a reflex of world economic conditions. This was quite apart from the dominant, if not controlling, position of foreign commercial firms—largely British—in the plantations, especially tea and rubber, and in the export of plantation products. One of the most striking features of this economic structure was the absence of an industrial sector independent of the processing of tea, rubber and coconut for export and the related engineering and mechanical requirements. Nevertheless, there had been since 1931, and particularly since the outbreak of the Second World War, some state-sponsored industrial ventures. None of these was of more than marginal significance and on the whole little progress had been made. Private enterprise was reluctant to embark on industrial ventures in the absence of firm support from the government. Although the new government declared that the country cannot 'depend on agriculture alone to provide the minimum standard we are aiming at for our rapidly increasing people', this was merely lip service to the almost religious faith among the intelligentsia in industrialization as the panacea for Sri Lanka's economic problems.

Traditional agriculture—subsistence farming—lagged far behind the efficient plantation sector in productivity because of the long-term impact of a multiplicity of factors. Sri Lanka could not produce all the rice needed to feed a growing population: most of the country's requirements in rice and subsidiary foodstuffs were imported and accounted for more than half the imports.

Looking ahead to the years after independence, the Senanayake regime placed its hopes on the achievement of self-sufficiency in rice and subsidiary foodstuffs: 'Increased production, particularly in the matter of home-grown food', it declared, 'will be given a place of supreme importance in the policy of the Government'.[9] The principal means of achieving this objective was the rapid development of the dry zone, the heartland of the ancient irrigation civilization of Sri Lanka. Thus, in this enterprise one discerned too the search for inspiration from the past and the traditional sources of legitimacy of Sri Lanka's rulers.

All in all, however, there was no great emphasis on far-reaching changes in the economic structure inherited from the British. This latter had taken firm root in the period of British rule and the process of introducing changes in it was more difficult than it seemed to be, while any hope of dismantling it was beyond the realms of practical politics. For 'the export of estate products enabled the people of [Sri Lanka], or a large part of them, to be fed and clothed'.[10] Besides, the system itself was still viable and its potential for expansion was, if not undiminished, at least reasonably good. And it was also true that the political leadership of the day was reluctant to make changes in an economic system with which their own interests were identified. The result was that in the economic structure,

as in the political, there was an emphasis on the maintenance
of the status quo.

The first decade of independence was a period of significant
if not sustainable economic growth, stimulated by two boom
periods for the island's exports in the years 1950–55 and a
remarkable expansion in paddy production.[11] The first strong
upsurge of the gross national product (GNP) was in 1950–51,
the Korean War boom. Export earnings increased by 79 per
cent between 1949 and 1951, largely as a result of a 65 per cent
increase in export prices. In 1950, the country enjoyed a record
trade surplus of Rs 396 million, or 10 per cent of the gross
national output for the year; this represented an increase of
Rs 362 million over the previous year. The improvement in
the terms of trade from 1949 to 1951 was as much as 35 per
cent. With the collapse of the Korean boom in April 1951, the
demand for exports declined considerably and the terms of
trade turned adverse with a sharp drop in the GNP, although
disposable income still grew at a steady and fairly rapid rate.

One of the most dynamic sectors of the island's economy
in the 1950s—in terms of output, productivity and, certainly,
employment growth—was peasant agriculture. At the end of
the Second World War, it was still on the whole both backward
and stagnant. Its rapid transformation in the post-war period
is, therefore, all the more impressive. D.S. Senanayake was
passionately interested in the development of peasant
agriculture and under his leadership the UNP in its early years
of power stressed the building up of traditional agriculture,
especially its extension in area through land development and
irrigation schemes such as the massive Gal Oya Scheme, the
first major project since the days of the Polonnaruva kings.

Paddy production increased from 16.7 million bushels in
1947 and 22 million in 1950 and 1951 to 37.7 million in 1955.
This steady progress in paddy production, at a rate unsurpassed
even by the most modern sectors of the economy, was especially
remarkable since it was mainly a peasant activity. Most of the
progress can be attributed to government policies directed
towards regeneration of the peasant sector. One of these
policies was the extension of the area under paddy cultivation

by means of irrigation projects and peasant colonization schemes. But basically, the astonishing growth of peasant agriculture in this decade could be attributed to the sheer strength of market incentives; paddy output grew so fast because cultivators were rewarded for their production by guaranteed purchase at prices which were not only unprecedented but represented a subsidy of approximately 50 per cent over world market prices.

The UNP governments of this period are liable to criticism for having allowed the economy to drift for too long without putting a workable long-term development strategy into operation. The UNP's approach to development was partly a product of party ideology and partly a natural, if short-sighted, reaction to the fact that the early 1950s were good years for Sri Lanka's economic well-being. One characteristic of the economy in the 1950s was an exceedingly buoyant consumption level: both private and public current account expenditure tended to increase rapidly—in retrospect, far too rapidly—throughout most of the decade. The strong upsurge of the GNP in 1950-51 had been followed by an equally strong rise in consumption. In 1952, when the export boom came to its sudden end, consumption was still rising and indeed the consumption ratio increased sharply. It remained fairly stable at its higher post-boom level in 1953-54 and rose again in response to the boom conditions of 1955. When the boom of 1955-56 came to an end, consumption fell very little from its new higher boom-inspired level. Although after 1952 there was heightened concern for the economy's future and the UNP began to act with increasing boldness (as in the Six-Year Programme of Investment), investment remained below 10 per cent of GNP till 1956.

In contrast to the solid achievement in traditional agriculture was the lack of any substantial progress in refurbishing existing export industries or channelling investment into new industrial ventures. The failure to achieve rapid industrial development meant that the substitution of local production for imports (with the notable exception of rice) proceeded very slowly. So the structure of production changed little as population grew and when the foreign exchange problem had worsened rapidly after 1955.

There was, in this period, a sharp increase in population growth. From 2.5 per cent in 1946, it reached a peak of 3.0 per cent in 1950 and remained between 2.7 and 2.9 per cent throughout the 1950s. The crude death rate had been halved by 1953 and fell to 8.6 in 1960, while the birth rate of 39.6 in 1946 declined much more slowly to around 36.5 in the period 1955–60. Sir Ivor Jennings, commenting on the island's affairs in 1949, warned of the economic implications of the island's astonishing rate of population increase which had reached 3.0 per annum that year and he asserted with uncharacteristic exaggeration that this 'was the fundamental problem, of [Sri Lanka's] economy'.[12] If it was not quite that, this was because the increase in population was not concentrated in the under-25 group but spread through all age groups; in the decade 1950–59 the under-25 age group rose from 56 to 60 per cent of the gross population, a rate of growth which did not pose any insuperable problems as long as the expanding economy could cope with an annual addition to the labour force of around 54,000, as it did between 1946 and 1953. Thus the political system was not much disturbed by population pressure. Nevertheless, this rapid growth of population had the immediate effect of pushing up private and public consumption needs and reducing the surplus available for investment.

FOREIGN AFFAIRS

At the time of the transfer of power, scant attention was paid to external policy and the external environment. There was a consciousness of the island's strategic position in the Indian Ocean and its inability to defend itself. D.S. Senanayake had willingly signed the agreements on defence and external affairs with the United Kingdom before the grant of dominion status to Sri Lanka, for on these matters there was substantial identity of views between D.S. Senanayake and Whitehall. These agreements, as we have seen, were subjected to severe criticism both within and outside parliament in Sri Lanka, especially but not exclusively from Marxist groups.

Senanayake feared that with the British withdrawal the British empire in Asia in the familiar form in which it had existed would have ended and the political prospects in Asia would be hardly encouraging. A profound suspicion of India was the dominant strand in his external policy. Accordingly, it was as a policy of reinsurance for the country during the early years of independence, when it was not impossible that there might be a political vacuum in south Asia, that he viewed the agreements. Similarly, in the early years of independence, he claimed that membership of the Commonwealth would provide a 'counter-force' against any possibility of aggression from India in the future.

In these circumstances there is a natural tendency to overlook the fact that the first prime minister was also the original protagonist of non-alignment and neutralism'.[13] In 1948, D.S. Senanayake's government, along with other Asian powers, came out in forthright opposition to the Dutch police action against the republic of Indonesia. His was also one of the first governments to recognize the People's Republic of China and to sever diplomatic relations with the Kuomintang regime in Taiwan. More important, in 1951, speaking over the BBC in London, he emphasized the point that he wished his country to follow a 'middle path' in international politics and not entangle itself in the power and ideological conflicts of the cold war. This was indeed the very first time that a Sri Lankan statesman had articulated a definite guideline on foreign policy.

Thus the trend towards non-alignment had begun under D.S. Senanayake himself, a fact which has not received much attention for two reasons. First, it was a gradual development emerging from dramatic considerations without any semblance of ideological commitment. Second, Sri Lanka was embroiled in the ideological conflicts of the cold war and the Soviet Union regularly vetoed Sri Lanka's membership of the United Nations, urging in support of this, the argument that she was too much in the shadow of British power, a contention which dovetailed into the political battles in the island, where the local Marxist parties which were in direct opposition to the UNP and Senanayake's government in turn adopted a completely negative attitude towards communist countries and consistently refused to establish diplomatic or cultural links with any of them. Apart from fears that communist embassies in Colombo would inevitably strengthen local Marxist parties, there was, more logically, the view that it would not be to Sri Lanka's advantage to establish diplomatic links with countries which refused to acknowledge her status as an independent state.

Under his successors, his son Dudley (1952–53) and Sir John Kotelawala (1953–56), however, relations with communist states expanded, although these did not develop into firm diplomatic links. First there was the rubber–rice trade agreement with China in 1952; and then under Kotelawala, trade relations were established with Poland and Czechoslovakia in 1955 and Romania in 1956. The rubber–rice trade agreement with China was greeted with considerable dismay in the United States and the Sri Lanka government came under strong pressure from that quarter once it became known that such an agreement was being negotiated. Thus this agreement was at once a vigorous demonstration of Sri Lanka's independence in external relations and of her capacity to withstand pressures from Western powers.

Kotelawala, however, carried Sri Lanka well into the western camp, choosing the United States rather than Britain as the main ally. The commitment to Britain of course remained and British assistance continued to be the mainstay of Sri Lanka's defence, although by now she had begun to build up her own armed forces. His alignment with the west was best demonstrated when he permitted landing rights in Sri Lanka for United States airforce planes ferrying French troops to Indo-China.

Kotelawala's strong pro-western bias was a reflection of his anti-communist position in international affairs. He was responsible for initiating the Colombo Conference of 1954, at which Asian powers discussed the Indo-China problem. His ideological commitment was manifest here when he advocated the adoption of a resolution condemning 'aggressive communism', in addition to one critical of 'colonialism' favoured by a majority of the delegation. Again, at the path-breaking Bandung Conference held the following year, in which not only Asian but also African nations were represented, Kotelawala took up the same position. There were indeed fears that Sri Lanka would seek membership of South-East Asia Treaty Organization (SEATO); but despite his strong anti-communist outlook, he recognized that there would be strong opposition within the country—and not from opposition groups alone—to any move in that direction. And more than once he asserted that he had no intention of guiding Sri Lanka into joining any power bloc.

It was during his premiership that Sri Lanka was admitted to the United Nations in 1955 with the withdrawal of the Soviet veto. Trade links were established with some communist countries in 1955 and 1956. While this was a significant new development, Kotelawala, did not establish any diplomatic links with communist powers. However, such links were being contemplated by his government in its last months in office and when the country went to the polls in 1956 the decision to establish them had already been taken. Once more, pragmatic considerations governed a major diplomatic initiative.

Linguistic Nationalism and a Socialist Experiment, 1956–1977

THE BANDARANAIKES IN POWER: THE FIRST PHASE

Bandaranaike's electoral triumph[1] of 1956 marked a watershed in Sri Lanka's history in the rejection of so much that had come to be accepted as part of the normal order of things in post-colonial Sri Lanka.

Such elements of continuity with the policies of the UNP as there were, were clearly overshadowed by Bandaranaike's purposeful demolition of the balance of political forces which D.S. Senanayake had endeavoured to establish and sustain as the basis of Sri Lanka's post-colonial polity. What this amounted to was a rejection of the concept of a Sri Lankan nationalism which D.S. Senanayake had striven to nurture and the substitution for it of a more democratic and populist form of nationalism—linguistic nationalism—which was at the same time fundamentally divisive in its impact on the country.

One of the immediate consequences of the transformation of nationalism was that the concept of a multiracial polity was no longer politically viable. In Sinhala, the words for *nation, race* and *people* are practically synonymous and a multiracial or multi-communal nation or state is incomprehensible to the popular mind. The emphasis on the sense of uniqueness of the Sinhalese past and the focus on Sri Lanka as the land of the Sinhalese and the country in which Buddhism stood forth in its purest form, carried an emotional appeal compared with which a multiracial polity was a meaningless abstraction.

Second, the abandonment of the concept of a multiracial polity was justified by laying stress on the notion of a democratic sanction deriving its validity from the clear numerical superiority of the Sinhala-speaking group. At the same time, the focus continued to be an all-island one, and Sinhalese nationalism was consciously or unconsciously treated as being identical with a Sri Lanka nationalism. The minorities, and in particular the indigenous Tamils, refused to endorse the assumption that Sinhalese nationalism was interchangeable with the larger Sri Lankan nationalism. As early as 1951, at its first national convention, the Federal Party asserted that 'the Tamil-speaking people in Ceylon constitute[d] a nation distinct from that of the Sinhalese by every fundamental test of nationhood', and in particular stressed the 'separate historical past' of the Tamils and their linguistic unity and distinctiveness. This view has been consistently emphasized by the Federal Party and by other Sri Lanka Tamils in recent years and it is the foundation of their claim for a measure of regional autonomy (ranging from a unit or units in a federal structure to the more recent agitation for a separate state).

Up to the early 1950s, the Tamils' concept of nationalism lacked coherence and cohesion despite all their talk of a linguistic, religious and cultural separateness from the Sinhalese. As with the Sinhalese, it was language which provided the sharp cutting edge of a new national self-consciousness. Indeed, the Federal Party's crucial contribution to Tamil politics was its emphasis on the role of language as the determinant of nationhood.

Bandaranaike's main concern at the time he became prime minister in 1956 was about limitations and curbs on Sri Lanka's sovereignty, and these he was anxious to eliminate; but he was thinking less about the independence (Soulbury) constitution itself than about the defence agreements with Britain signed at the time of the transfer of power. Very soon he was able to satisfy himself that these agreements were not detrimental to the country's status as a free and sovereign state—and it is significant that these agreements, for all the criticisms to which they have been subjected from time to time, were never abrogated.

The survival of the Soulbury constitution for two decades without fundamental change can be explained partly by the flexibility of the constitution and the lack of a bill of fundamental rights: these enabled the political structure to accommodate itself to a series of far-reaching changes, most if not all of which adversely affected ethnic and religious minorities. As early as 1948, the Ceylon Citizenship Act eliminated the vast majority of the Indian plantation workers from the electoral registers by the simple device of defining the right to citizenship far more rigidly than under the Donoughmore constitution. It was thus demonstrated that the constitutional obstacle of Section 29(2)(b)[2] would not operate provided that legislation was so framed that there might be a restriction in fact but not in legal form. The restriction was made applicable to all sections of the community and not to a specific group. When Bandaranaike's Official Language Act was introduced in the House of Representatives in 1956, the speaker ruled that it was not a constitutional amendment and therefore required only a simple majority. (In 1960 the Roman Catholics found to their dismay that the constitution afforded them no protection in their campaign to preserve the status quo in education.)

Equally important, the nationalization of local and foreign business ventures was facilitated by the lack of any provision in the constitution for just and expeditious payment of compensation. Thus there was no constitutional protection for property rights in general.

While Bandaranaike had ridden to office on a massive wave of Sinhalese-Buddhist emotion, the sobering realities of political power compelled him to impose restraints. The riots which broke out in the wake of the introduction of the 'Sinhala Only' bill in 1956 had underlined the combustible nature of linguistic nationalism in a plural society. Thus, although this legislation was introduced and piloted through the legislature, its full implementation was postponed to January 1961. In the meantime, the Tamil Federal Party, at a convention held in Trincomalee in August 1956, outlined what they regarded as the main demands of the Tamils: autonomy for the Northern Province and the Eastern Province under a federal constitution, parity of status for the Sinhala and Tamil languages and a satisfactory settlement of the problem of the Indian Tamil plantation workers on the island.

In 1925–26, when Bandaranaike, who had just returned from Oxford, set out the case for a federal political structure for Sri Lanka he had received no support for it from the Tamils. His ardour for federalism cooled somewhat over the years, but it was a grim irony that he should be called upon, at the moment of his greatest political triumph, to articulate the strong opposition of the Sinhalese to any attempt to establish a federal constitution. The Sinhalese viewed the Tamils' demand for a federal constitution as nothing less than the thin end of the wedge of a separatist movement. The fact is that the Sinhalese, although an overwhelming majority of the population of the island, nevertheless have a minority complex vis-à-vis the Tamils. They feel encircled by the more than sixty million Tamil-speaking people who inhabit the present-day Tamil Nadu and Sri Lanka. Within Sri Lanka the Sinhalese outnumber the Tamils by more than six to one; but they in turn are outnumbered by nearly four to one by the Tamil-speaking people of south Asia.

Historical tradition and geography separate the Tamils of Sri Lanka and Tamil Nadu from each other. In the early years of Sri Lanka's independence, the Tamils of the north and east of the island had showed little inclination to identify themselves with the Tamils of Tamil Nadu. The only link between the two groups was language. Nevertheless, the Sinhalese feared this possibility and the campaign for federalism aggravated these fears. There was suspicion too of the attempt by the Federal Party to make the settlement of the problem of Indian plantation workers on the island a plank in their political platform; the programme of action outlined by the Federal Party in August 1956 was regarded as having ominous long-term dangers.

While the extremists in the ranks of the coalition he led could think only in terms of maintaining pressure on the Tamils in a policy of confrontation, Bandaranaike was devising schemes for a statesmanlike settlement with them, and with this in view he conducted negotiations with the Federal Party. The terms of this compromise were made public in July 1957; first, the Tamil language was to be an official language for administrative purposes in the Northern Province and the Eastern Province; second, as a concession to the federal demand, Bandaranaike agreed to establish a scheme of devolving administrative powers to regional councils[3] and third, he agreed to restrict settlement of Sinhalese colonists in irrigation schemes in the Northern Province and the Eastern Province so that the indigenous Tamils could maintain their majority position there. The moment the terms of the settlement were made public, there was a storm of protest, chiefly from the extremists in Bandaranaike's own camp. And the UNP, looking for a means of staging a recovery, came out in opposition to the settlement. It was thus provided with an ideal opportunity to embarrass the prime minister on a politically sensitive issue, and to establish its commitment to the 'Sinhala Only' policy before an electorate sceptical of their motives. Confronted with mounting opposition to this compromise, the prime minister played for time, but the pressures against it were too strong for him to resist. Led by a group of bhikkhus who performed satyagraha on the lawn of his private residence in Colombo, the extremists in his own party compelled the prime minister to abrogate the pact.

The tensions generated by these pressures and counter-pressures erupted once again in riots in May 1958. To assuage the feelings of the Tamils, in August 1958, Bandaranaike secured parliamentary approval of the Tamil Language (Special Provisions) Act to permit the 'reasonable' use of Tamil in administration. It was a significant concession, but it did not mollify the Tamils. In any case, although the bill was approved by Parliament, the regulations necessary for its implementation were not passed till 1966 when Dudley Senanayake was prime minister. An important point about Bandaranaike's abortive settlement with the Federal Party which needs to be mentioned was that despite its abrogation in 1958 it continued for about ten years thereafter to be the basis for negotiations on solutions to the Sinhalese–Tamil problem on the island.

Since the linguistic nationalism of the Sinhalese was so closely intertwined with the Buddhist resurgence, it was inevitable that there would be intensified pressure for a closer association of the state with Buddhism and for the declaration of Buddhism as the state religion. It was inevitable too that the Christian minority would come under attack because of

Buddhist displeasure at its continued prestige and influence, the most conspicuous evidence of which lay in the impressive network of mission schools; also because of the sense of outrage and indignation of the Buddhists at the humiliations— and worse—inflicted on them under western rule. Yet, legislation for the declaration of Buddhism as the state religion would meet the formidable and almost insuperable obstacle of Section 29(2)(b) of the constitution. It would have taxed the ingenuity of the most skilled legal draftsman to devise legislation for this purpose which would not be ultra vires to the constitution; and it was far from certain that the legislature would provide the special majority necessary for a constitutional amendment if that were required. Bringing the mission schools under state control was an entirely different proposition, for here the Marxist and radical groups were at one with Buddhist activists, and the constitution, as we have seen, afforded no certain protection to the Christians.

On the whole, S.W.R.D. Bandaranaike's government was much more cautious in handling matters relating to the interests of the Christian minority than over the language issue. It was a matter of prudence and priorities. The language struggle took precedence over all else and there was no desire to add to the government's problems by taking on an issue which was potentially just as explosive. While Bandaranaike was all in favour of restoring the traditional patronage accorded to Buddhism, he stopped well short of endorsing the demand that Buddhism be declared the state religion. His minister of education[4] put up a stout resistance to the heavy pressure from Buddhist activists to bring all schools under state control; those applying the pressure received little encouragement and certainly no overt support from Bandaranaike himself. In February 1957, he appointed the Buddha Sāsana Commission to examine questions relating to a reform of the sangha, and to make proposals regarding the general principle of 'according to Buddhism its rightful place in the country' to which the government was committed. The commission was soon embroiled in the complexities of a sensitive set of problems and in the inevitable interplay of pressures and counter-pressures from reformist groups and vested interests. Its recommendation, although far from radical, upset too many powerful groups in the sangha to stand any chance of implementation. One other decision—and this had nothing to do with the Buddha Sasana Commission and its recommendations—gave satisfaction to Buddhist activists, namely, that the two premier seats of Buddhist learning, the Vidyalankara and Vidyodaya Piriveṇas should be raised to the status of universities.

A Ministry of Cultural Affairs and a Department of Official Language Affairs were established, the former to channel state patronage for literature and the arts and the latter to organize the implementation of the government's language policy. In the revivalist atmosphere of the mid-1950s—with the millennial expectations of the Buddha Jayanthi and the nativistic urge to guard and preserve the Sinhala language and the Buddhist religion from the presumed 'threats' of the Tamils and the Christians—there was a general efflorescence of the arts. The year 1956, by a remarkable coincidence with the victory of the MEP, saw several memorable achievements in the arts. First, there was Martin Wickremesinghe's novel *Virāgaya* which in terms of significance of theme and sophistication of technique is perhaps the most outstanding work in modern Sinhala fiction. Then came E.R. Sarachchandra's unforgettable *Maname*, a theoretical tour de force which breathed new life into the folk tradition in Sinhala drama and is by far the greatest achievement in the history of the Sinhala theatre. Finally, there was Lester James Peiris's film, *Rekava*, a bold attempt to escape from the melodramatic stereotype which thrived under the shadow of the south Indian cinema and to bring the Sinhala film up to standards comparable with the best in world cinema.

Although none of these literary landmarks owed anything to the patronage of the state, the argument that the breakthrough they marked could be only stabilized and consolidated by active state support for the arts and literature became part of the conventional wisdom of the day. The institutional apparatus established for this purpose by the Bandaranaike government—a Ministry of Cultural Affairs—

was expected to give official patronage and financial assistance to the zeal for renewal then manifest in all spheres of the arts. And almost from the beginning it was confronted with the need to hold a balance between the two main and conflicting tendencies in aesthetic ideology: one oriented towards westernization and the other going back to indigenous traditions. It became obvious that westernization in the arts and literature, for all its attractions, could hardly hold its own against the powerful forces of traditionalism.[5]

The linguistic nationalism of the mid-1950s helped establish a popular government, in contrast to the elitist constitutionalism of the early years after independence. This popular quality, despite its seeming novelty at the time when it first appeared in the mid-1950s, had its roots in the recent past, especially in the temperance movement in the early twentieth century, when a similar mixture of religious fervour and commitment to national culture had captured the imagination of the Sinhalese people, especially in the rural areas of the low country. But in the mid-1950s it was present on a wider scale and its appeal was deeper. The SLFP accommodated itself—as the UNP clearly did not—to an expanding 'political nation' in which a Sinhalese-Buddhist intermediary elite sought an influence commensurate with its numbers. Ideologically hazy and politically opportunistic, Bandaranaike's 'middle way' promised people social change, social justice, economic independence from foreign powers and the completion of political sovereignty. It gave a sense of dignity to the common people and fortified their self-respect.

One of the notable consequences of the triumph of Sinhalese-Buddhist populism was the unexpected setback it caused to the Marxist movement. In the early months of the new administration, the LSSP was regarded—not least by itself—as a potential successor in office to Bandaranaike, should he falter and fail. Indeed, with Bandaranaike's coalition then enmeshed in the coils of the language problem and engaged in a desperate but futile bid to reconcile the intrinsically irreconcilable—the Federal Party now taking to extra-parliamentary forms of struggle and the forces of Sinhalese extremism which had spearheaded the government's bid for power in 1956—the

LSSP was engaged in the exercise of alerting the country to the divisive effects of Bandaranaike's language policies. But this was to no avail. The LSSP and the Communist Party had completely underestimated the strength of linguistic nationalism. As advocates at this time of parity of status for Sinhala and Tamil as national languages, their views were treated with suspicion if not distaste. Moreover, the LSSP's trade unions launched a series of massive strikes through the years 1956–59, many of which were politically inspired and aimed at embarrassing the government. In so doing they were exploiting the greater leeway which the trade union movement enjoyed after 1956. But the effect of this irresponsible resort to trade union action was to discredit the LSSP in the country at large.

It had always aspired to the status of the alternative government, and it was this aspiration which was thwarted by the eruption of linguistic nationalism and the populist form it took in the mid-1950s. It watched the gains of the past disappear and the prospects of the future become much more limited. It found to its dismay and discomfiture that linguistic nationalism had an appeal which cut across class interests and that it evoked as deep a response from the Sinhalese working class as among the peasantry and the Sinhala-educated elite. The cosmopolitan outlook of the Marxists and their enlightened advocacy of a multiracial secular polity proved to be profoundly disadvantageous and they were compelled to compromise on these issues, but without reaping any substantial political benefits. From being an alternative government they were reduced—after 1960—to the status of an appendage of the populist SLFP.

Although the Buddhist movement was generally hostile to Marxist ideology, it had no strong opposition to the adoption of a socialist programme. Since plantation enterprise, nascent industry and the island's trade were dominated by foreign capitalists, and the minorities were disproportionately influential within the indigenous capitalist class, Buddhist pressure groups viewed socialism as a means of redressing the balance in favour of the majority group. Every extension of state control over trade and industry could be justified on the ground that it helped to curtail the influence of foreigners and the minorities. The Sinhalese-Buddhist section of the capitalist class was not averse to socialism so long as its own economic interests were not affected. The result was that the SLFP has been able to reconcile a commitment to socialism with an advocacy of the interests of a section of the indigenous capitalist class, namely, its Sinhalese Buddhist section.

Bandaranaike has been acclaimed as the architect of neutralism in Sri Lanka's foreign policy and the man whose initiatives in this sphere turned Sri Lanka decisively in the direction of non-alignment as the guiding principle of its external relations. But there is a striking continuity between the foreign policy of the Senanayakes in the early years of independence and that of Bandaranaike. The latter's distinctive contribution lay in the greater emphasis he placed on aspects of the foreign policy of his predecessors than any significant departure from it. For, as A.J. Wilson has pointed out, 'the system, the outputs, the explanation for behaviour patterns and the forms of interaction available with neighbours as well as friendly powers leaves Sri Lanka's prime ministers little option but to operate along the only *continuum* of action available'.[6] Almost immediately after he came to power, he established diplomatic relations with the communist states, beginning with the Soviet Union and China. What would appear at first glance to be a major initiative was less path-breaking that it really was. There had been no diplomatic relations with the Soviet Union under the UNP governments because the Soviet Union had consistently vetoed Sri Lanka's application for membership of the United Nations and taken up the position that she was too much under Britain's tutelage to be regarded as an independent state. Once Sri Lanka gained admission to the United Nations, in 1955, this particular obstacle to friendly relations with the Soviet Union had been removed and Sir John Kotelawala himself, an archetypical anti-communist of the early years of the cold war, had decided on an exchange of diplomatic representatives between the two countries in 1956, the year the island went to the polls. It is doubtful, however, if a UNP regime under Sir John Kotelawala would have handled the establishment of diplomatic ties with these communist governments with Bandaranaike's panache.

In the same way, Bandaranaike used the Suez crisis as an opportunity to make known his neutralism in international affairs to the country and to the world at large. His expression of displeasure at the invasion of Egypt was as forthright as that made by other Commonwealth leaders who ranged themselves against Eden's government on this issue. But it is almost certain that the UNP government would have acted just as vigorously on this issue had it been in power in view of the strength of public opinion in the country against an act of aggression of these dimensions.

At the time of the transfer of power in south Asia in 1947–48, British politicians and publicists still believed in Great Britain's role as leader of a Commonwealth and empire and as a power with global interests and responsibilities. In these early post-war years, complete awareness of Britain's rapid international decline was delayed. But evidence of it came with dramatic suddenness with the Suez episode of 1956, the last occasion on which Britain was to act in its customary role as a great power, and the first and most telling demonstration of the fact that she was no longer one. It is in this context that one needs to view the transfer of Britain's military and naval bases on the island to the Sri Lankan government in 1957. Bandaranaike himself preferred to treat it as a major concession to his initiatives and pressure and as a symbolic gesture—the completion of the island's independence from British rule. In fact Britain, engaged in a reappraisal of her commitments east of Suez, was glad to be rid of a potential irritant in relations between the two countries. As for the defence agreements with Britain, he had been a prominent member of the Board of Ministers when these were negotiated and accepted and there is no record of his having raised any serious objections to them at that stage or later as a member of D.S. Senanayake's cabinet. In the Opposition benches he had been vehemently critical of them, thus lending greater credence to the view popular in left-wing circles that these were limitations on the country's sovereignty. Besides, Bandaranaike argued that they neither afforded the country any credible assurance of security nor ensured her neutrality in a potential confrontation between the rival power blocs in the cold war—indeed he asserted that they could lead to Sri Lanka's involvement in such a confrontation, against her wishes and interests. D.S. Senanayake had always insisted that there was nothing irrevocable or coercive about the agreements and that they were based on the mutual interests of the two parties; the transfer of the bases in 1957 had proved him right. But significantly, once in power, Bandaranaike made no move to abrogate them, although there was considerable political advantage in so doing.

As part of the Opposition, Bandaranaike was inclined to be critical of ties with the Commonwealth; in office he was as firm as the Senanayakes in support of the Commonwealth connection. Like them, he stressed the importance of the material benefits accruing from it and the common inheritance of democratic institutions as the cornerstone of the Commonwealth bond; unlike them, he chose to emphasize the Commonwealth's potential for development into a viable 'third force' distinct from the two main power blocs.

The UNP prime ministers of the period 1947–56, most notably D.S. Senanayake himself, hardly concealed their suspicions of India, which they viewed as a potential threat to the island's independence. Bandaranaike himself shared these suspicions and fears, but was readier than the UNP prime ministers to work with Nehru in international and regional affairs and more willing to follow his lead. He was at one with his UNP predecessors in office in maintaining the friendliest relations with Pakistan, which was viewed as a counterbalance to Indian domination of the south Asian region.

Bandaranaike repeatedly emphasized the point that his neutralism should not be construed as being directed against the West; more than once he declared that their shared democratic way of life drew Sri Lanka closer to the United States than to other countries. Nevertheless, in common with a number of Afro-Asian leaders who were emerging as neutralists at this time and feeling their way towards establishing friendly relations with the Soviet Union and the People's Republic of China, he was especially careful not to give the slightest offence to them as was illustrated by his attitude to the Soviet intervention in Hungary and China's in Tibet. His criticisms of the Soviet Union vis-à-vis the Hungarian episode were in the nature of a mild censure, while his attack on Britain and her allies in the Suez venture was unmistakably forthright, even bitter. The contrast was all the more marked because the events in question occurred at the same time. As for the Tibet affair, he preferred to view it as a purely internal matter of China's. Tibet was an issue on which the sensibilities of a large section of Sri Lanka's Buddhists were aroused. As a result, he drew heavy criticism from among both his supporters in the Buddhist movement and his opponents who stood to the right of his regime in the island's political spectrum.

Bandaranaike's great advantage was to have come to power at a time of rapid changes in the country's political life and in its external political environment. These changes lent themselves to dramatic symbolic acts which appeared to indicate a totally new approach and the emergence of a new international order. Thus his main achievement in Sri Lanka's foreign policy—to have securely established non-alignment as its central theme—has taken on an exaggerated importance as a dramatic new departure, which it was not. He had one other advantage, namely, the contrast between his handling of foreign affairs and, on the one hand, his predecessor's characteristically strident and extravagant attitudes at international conferences at home and abroad, and on the other hand, the rather dogmatic and doctrinaire views of the left—communists and Trotskyites—on international affairs. In the following years the positions taken on either side of Bandaranaike were less rigid: the Marxists became less doctrinaire, especially when associated with the SLFP in coalitions, while the UNP became more strongly committed to non-alignment and was no longer, as under Sir John Kotelawala, unequivocally pro-western. In short, there came about a broad consensus between all the major political parties in the country with regard to some major areas in external relations.

ECONOMIC POLICIES

In economic policy Bandaranaike's assumption of power marked a change from the previous near-laissez-faire economic doctrine of optimum opportunity for private commercial interests in the direction of a mixed economy, with greater emphasis on state controls.[7] The political turmoil that characterized his period of office as prime minister prevented concentration of attention on major structural changes in the economy. In any case, Bandaranaike was not inclined to encourage hopes of nationalizing the plantations, the bedrock of the island's economy, one of the main points in left-wing agitation. Thus the commanding heights of the economy continued to be in the hands of British and local commercial organizations.

Two important measures of nationalization were introduced—bus transport and the port of Colombo—and in 1958 Philip Gunawardane, Bandaranaike's minister of food and agriculture, successfully piloted through parliament his Paddy Lands Act, which offered tenant cultivators greater security of tenure. These measures marked the beginning of a process of state control over the economy which came to be accelerated under the aegis of the SLFP in the 1960s and after. Under Bandaranaike the principle of planned economic development came to be accepted. A National Planning Council was set up soon after he assumed office and by 1958 a Ten-Year Plan of Economic Development had been formulated and published in which industrial development received higher priority than it had in the past.

Bandaranaike's handling of the economy was one of his administration's weak spots. The euphoria that followed his entry to power built up exaggerated hopes of redistribution of wealth and in that unrealistic atmosphere no great attention was paid to economic growth, which was necessary to sustain a policy of redistribution. At most it was assumed that structural changes such as nationalization would automatically generate additional revenues. Population growth, by itself, had increased private and consumption needs. At the same time, under pressure from the trade unions, expenditure on salaries and wages kept expanding without heed to any corresponding improvements in productivity. These two processes resulted in a steady expansion of imports and correspondingly a steady decline in the island's external assets at a time when there was a strong and persistent tendency towards basic external imbalance. Besides, the export booms which had previously replenished the stock of foreign assets ceased to recur. As the payments position weakened, ever more stringent measures were resorted to by the government to arrest the deterioration. Thus the development effort of the late 1950s not only failed to provide a reasonably satisfactory rate of real growth in output, but also in the insufficiency of its response to the depletion of external assets.

The economic travails that beset the country in the 1960s could have been averted only if the deficits in the basic balance of payments had been corrected well before the depletion of foreign assets took place. External assets dropped from Rs 1,275 million in 1956 to Rs 541 million four years later. In 1946, the island's external assets had been the equivalent of twenty-one months' imports; at the height of the Korean boom this had been reduced to about twelve months and by 1954 it had declined to less than ten. But by the end of the 1960s it had fallen to just over three months. Some planned reduction of these assets from their high post-war levels would have been both inevitable and defensible, but such an exercise called for a careful assessment of a tolerable minimum level at which the depletion would be halted to hold the growth of imports within limits consistent with a basic balance in the external accounts—if not on a year-by-year basis, at least over a series of three or four years. But this was not done during the late 1950s. As a result, it was forced on the government by necessity during the early 1960s, years later than it should have been done by choice.

Bandaranaike was a visionary but no idealogue. He gave leadership to forces, the strength of which he failed to grasp and which he sought unsuccessfully to bring under control. For both these reasons, despite all the dramatic changes he initiated and all the new directions in policy he charted, his years in office have left behind the impression of a regime drifting along without much sense of priorities. His administrative skills never matched the demands imposed on him by his ambitions as a statesman. Throughout his career he demonstrated a remarkable buoyancy in the face of political difficulties, but swift, decisive moves were not his forte. Although resilience is a tremendous asset to a politician, it was often accompanied in Bandaranaike by an almost masochistic tolerance of indiscipline and turmoil. One of the main themes of his public addresses during his term of office was that the country was going through a period of transition and that so long as there was some control over the direction in which it was moving there was no need to be too anxious about the resulting tensions and turmoil. And his term of office saw a plethora of strikes, administrative breakdowns and, more important, race riots. It was as though Sri Lanka was paying, on deferred payment terms and at a tearfully high rate of interest, for the peace and stability which she had enjoyed in the first decade of independence.

During the not infrequent periods of turmoil, the administration of the country was often in the hands of Governor General Sir Oliver Goonetileke, who took control of the situation at the behest of the prime minister and in contravention of the conventions governing the role of the head of state in a parliamentary democracy. In this role of trouble-shooter Sir Oliver served Bandaranaike as devotedly as he had served D.S. Senanayake. It was a working relationship in which Sir Oliver's long experience of public affairs and undoubted administrative skills were used with great benefit to the country and the government, however unconventional and unusual this may have been. It was a relationship based on mutual trust, confidence and respect for each other's special skills in statecraft. This reliance on Sir Oliver was a reflection of the paucity of administrative talent and experience among the SLFP members of the cabinet; in this sense the burdens imposed on the prime minister would have been intolerable had he not been able to call upon Sir Oliver to assist him in moments of acute crisis.

Bandaranaike's hold on parliament was more impressive than his control of the cabinet and the coalition which he led.

Pressures and counter-pressures were pulling his cabinet apart within a short time of his victory in 1956, and it needed all his resources of prestige and influence to keep it together as an effective instrument of social reform. It was evident that his sympathizers were with the left-wing members of his cabinet, three of whom—Philip Gunawardane, William Silva and M.W.H. de Silva—did not belong to the SLFP. He respected their intellectual ability, their administrative skills, their sense of priorities, their purposeful approach and, above all, their integrity. But they were a minority, and the prime minister was compelled, in response to mounting and relentless pressure from the majority (who belonged to his party), to impose restraints on this innovative and reformist minority. By the beginning of 1959 the coalition was coming apart, although in Parliament the SLFP was strong enough, thanks to the disarray in the ranks of the Opposition, to continue its dominance. The first phase of the political crisis ended with the resignation of the left-wing group in the cabinet, but the prime minister was now left with a cabinet of mediocrities and a party in which the more liberal and reformist groups were becoming less influential. This bitter struggle for power within the governing party culminated in Bandaranaike's assassination on 26 September 1959. The instrument of his assassination was a bhikkhu and the conspiracy was hatched by the most powerful political bhikkhu of the day, who had contributed greatly to Bandaranaike's triumph in 1956 and who had engineered the elimination of the left-wing ministers from the cabinet early in 1958. In this murder conspiracy, the most sordid commercial considerations were mixed with the zest for control over the government. At the time of his assassination, Bandaranaike was no longer the masterful politician he had been in 1956–57, since when his hold on the electorate had weakened. But his murder dramatically changed the political situation. After a few months of drift and regrouping, the SLFP, under the leadership of Bandaranaike's widow, Sirimavo, emerged more powerful than ever before. Death is the essence of myth-making and the party had before it the inestimable advantage of the Bandaranaike myth with which to face the electorate and to fashion the discomfiture of its rivals on the political scene.

The general election of 1956 marked the beginning of two decades of SLFP primacy in Sri Lanka's politics. Except for the period 1965–70, it either formed the government on its own, or was the dominant element in a coalition government. With the break-up of the MEP coalition and Bandaranaike's assassination in 1959, there was, for a few months, a highly confused political situation. The first of the two general elections of 1960 held in March was a throwback to the pre-1956 system in that a revived UNP faced a multiplicity of warring rivals with no electoral agreement against it. In March 1960, the LSSP had made a highly publicized but totally futile bid for electoral power on its own. The result of the general election was inconclusive. The UNP emerged as the largest single group and formed a short-lived minority government, but its recovery led to a renewal of the old combination of forces devised to keep it out of power. Within parliament, a grand coalition of parties brought down the government, and in the general election of July 1960 the SLFP had the advantage of yet another no-contest pact with the left. This had the desired effect of bringing it back to power, this time on its own, riding on the emotional wave generated by Bandaranaike's assassination.

The SLFP's main rival, the UNP, was kept in the political wilderness by the peculiarities of an electoral system (which gave it, when defeated, far fewer seats than it would be entitled to on the basis of the wide support it had in the country) and the device of electoral agreements and no-contest pacts among its rivals during general elections and by-elections. The new demarcation of constituencies effected in 1959 worked on the principle of counting the total population of a province in computing the number of seats to which it was entitled, without regard to the fact that in the plantation districts the resident Indian workers had largely been excluded from the franchise. This anomalous situation worked in favour of the Kandyans, who with 26 per cent of the total population of the island had 44 per cent of the seats. Thus the electoral balance was distorted even more markedly than before and the Sinhalese rural voter became very much the arbiter of the country's politics. Since the rural vote shifted away from the UNP to the SLFP in 1956, the latter had succeeded in retaining its hold on it till 1977 and the electoral balance thus shifted against the UNP.

While the dominance of the SLFP has meant a corresponding decline in the electoral fortunes of the left-wing parties, nevertheless the apertura a sinistra was a necessary condition for keeping the UNP out of power. After the election of July 1960, the SLFP enjoyed for a brief period the support of the left, but this was soon dissipated. However, its parliamentary majority was adequate to ensure its survival. But a major challenge appeared to be emerging when the United Left Front (ULF) of the LSSP, Philip Gunawardane's MEP and the Community Party was formed in 1963. The ULF had hardly stabilized itself when the SLFP, largely because of the manifest incompetence of its own ministerial ranks, decided to seek a coalition with the left—an initiative which resulted only in a coalition with the LSSP in June 1964. The immediate effect was the collapse of the ULF; but it also led to deep misgivings among a section of the SLFP led by Mrs Bandaranaike's own deputy C.P. de Silva, who crossed over to the Opposition with a group of his followers and as a result brought down the government at the end of 1964.

In retrospect, it would seem that the two Bandaranaikes between them had established a new equilibrium of political forces within the country, to which their supporters and associates as well as their opponents were compelled to accommodate themselves. Its primary features were the acceptance of Sinhala as the national language, Buddhist predominance within the Sri Lankan polity and a sharp decline in the status of the ethnic and religious minorities.

The settlement reached by S.W.R.D. Bandaranaike in 1957 with the Federal Party remained the basis for future negotiations on solutions to the problem of the indigenous Tamils in a Sri Lankan polity, and it was on the assurance that it would be implemented by the SLFP under Mrs Bandaranaike that the Federal Party voted to defeat Dudley Senanayake's minority government early in 1960. But it became politically impossible to keep this pledge, not least because the UNP had made it an election issue, and although the verdict of the electorate went substantially in favour of the SLFP, its leadership nonetheless felt obliged to rethink its position on this issue under pressure from Sinhalese extremists in its ranks and outside. Within six months of Mrs Bandaranaike's assumption of office as prime minister, the Federal Party was totally alienated from her government, largely because of her insistence on Sinhala becoming the language of administration throughout the island from 1 January 1961, as envisaged in the 'Sinhala Only' bill of 1956, without any substantial concessions to the Tamils, despite the understanding reached with the Federal Party before and during the general election of July 1960. Once more there was the familiar pattern of a civil disobedience campaign in the north and east of the island in March–April 1961, the government responding with the imposition of a state of emergency in the Northern Province and the Eastern Province. Within parliament, the Federal Party moved from responsive cooperation with the government into staunch opposition. It did not change its position over the next two years and became increasingly receptive to overtures from the UNP.

Mrs Bandaranaike, unlike her husband, was not reluctant to take on two inflammable issues at the same time. She was not interested at this stage in the more complicated issue of the status of Buddhism vis-à-vis the state, but antagonism to the Tamils on the language question was accompanied by a policy of calculated opposition to the Roman Catholic minority over the mission schools. On this issue, unlike the language question, the Buddhists were supported by Marxist and radical groups. All of them welcomed state control of education: the Marxists and radicals welcomed it because they viewed it as a matter of social justice and secularization of education as an end itself; the Buddhists welcomed it because it would redress for them a long-standing grievance and eliminate what they continued to regard as the main instrument of conversion to Christianity under western rule and the basis of Christian privilege in modern Sri Lanka. There was also a more practical consideration. Implicit in state control was the prospect of increasing Buddhist influence on education both at the national and the grass-roots level. The fact that most of the mission schools depended almost

Sirimavo Dias Bandaranaike

entirely on government financing, while in all but a handful of them the majority of students were Buddhists, made it nearly impossible to meet the arguments of the advocates of state control. There was also the zealous care with which all denominations of Christians avoided recruitment of non-Christians to the teaching staff in their schools, although the salaries were provided largely if not entirely by the state. There were very few exceptions in the secondary schools, and even in the village schools where employment of Buddhists and Hindus could not be avoided, there was a distinct preference shown for Christians.

Once again it was the Roman Catholics who led the resistance and bore the brunt of the attack. Although all religious groups—including the Hindus and Muslims, not to mention the Buddhists themselves[8]—were affected by the decision to bring the state-aided secondary schools directly under state control, the Roman Catholics were the biggest losers. Most of the state-aided mission schools accepted the painful decision to be absorbed by the state, but a few big schools, mostly Roman Catholic ones in the urban areas, decided to retain their independence by becoming private institutions without the benefit of state aid. Deprived by law of the right to levy fees from their students, they maintained a precarious existence under the severest financial handicaps. Thus the Buddhist agitation for state control achieved its objective under Mrs Bandaranaike's SLFP government, but at great cost to the country in terms of the bitterness and tension it generated between the Buddhists and the powerful Roman Catholic minority. The Roman Catholics, like the Tamils, smouldered with resentment.

The government's relations with the Roman Catholics reached their nadir in the wake of an abortive coup d'état in January 1962, in which the leadership was assumed by some Roman Catholics and Protestant Christians. The armed services and the police had so often been called upon to wield emergency powers in the maintenance of law and order in periods of communal tension since 1956 that it was almost inevitable that some groups among them would begin to entertain ideas of taking control. Besides, the reality of administrative incompetence and economic failure was eating into the government's popularity. But the effect of the abortive coup was to revive the government's political fortunes and to provide the rationale for government patronage to Buddhist activists in their propaganda campaigns in a war of nerves against the Roman Catholic minority.

Among the most notable achievements of Mrs Bandaranaike's first government was the understanding she reached with Lal Bahadur Shastri, the Indian prime minister, in October 1964 on the question of the Indian minority in Sri Lanka. The citizenship legislation of 1948–49 had created as many problems as it solved. While most of the Indians in Sri Lanka had been deprived of citizenship rights, they were still physically present in Sri Lanka and the Indian government could not be persuaded to accept the position that they were Indian citizens, much less agree to their repatriation to India. The Nehru–Kotelawala pact of 1954 came nowhere near solving these issues; indeed they were aggravated by the controversies that arose in the interpretation of some of its clauses. S.W.R.D. Bandaranaike never had the time to devise a solution to these problems, and by the early 1960s the whole issue had become an intractable one. Neither government was prepared to allow the position taken by the other on it. Significantly, nothing could be achieved so long as Nehru was alive, but his successor, Lal Bahadur Shastri, was prepared to make a fresh start because he was not a party to any earlier commitment. The agreement[9] he reached with Mrs Bandaranaike provided for the repatriation over a fifteen-year period of 5,25,000 Indian residents in Sri Lanka to India, along with their natural increase, and the absorption of 3,00,000 as citizens of Sri Lanka; the future of the remaining 1,50,000 was to be negotiated later by the two countries.

Mrs Bandaranaike was justified in claiming that the agreement reached with the Indian government in 1964 marked a great advance, for the Indian government had been persuaded to recognize its obligations to persons of Indian origin in the island by undertaking to confer Indian citizenship on those who were to be repatriated and by accepting the principle of compulsory repatriation. But very soon her government's decision to place all persons of Indian origin— those who had already obtained Sri Lanka citizenship, as well as those who were entitled to it under the agreement of 1964— on a separate communal electoral register, antagonized all sections of the Indian minority resident on the island. They condemned this as patently discriminatory, since it established two categories of voters, one of which was distinctly inferior because its basis was ethnic and communal. The result was that the Ceylon Workers' Congress, the most powerful trade union-cum-political party among the plantation workers, led by S. Thondaman, its president, withdrew its support from the government and in a surprising volte-face swung over to support the UNP for the first time since 1947. The reconciliation was based on the understanding that the UNP would repudiate the policy of a separate register enunciated by Mrs Bandaranaike and examine afresh the implications of the principle of compulsory repatriation.

Thus by the end of 1964, acts of commission on the part of Mrs Bandaranaike's regime had converted erstwhile allies like the Federal Party and the Ceylon Workers' Congress into opponents, while the Roman Catholics, who had never been allies of the SLFP, were so aggrieved that they returned to the policy, which they had abandoned since 1956, of open and energetic support of the UNP. At the same time, the Muslims whom the government wooed with great ardour did not sever their traditional links with the UNP; indeed these links were strengthened by acts of omission by the government, in particular the failure to pass legislation conferring judicial status on the *quasis*[10] after the courts had ruled that they were not legally entitled to such powers. The outcome was that in the general election of 1965, the minorities voted overwhelmingly with the UNP, and along with a substantial shift of the Sinhalese vote from the SLFP, this was enough to bring the UNP back to power as the solid core of a coalition government, of which the Federal Party was a significant element.

S.W.R.D. Bandaranaike's agreement with the Federal Party in 1957 became the basis for securing the latter's support in the formation of a coalition government with the UNP. But the new government was placed on the defensive from the moment the Federal Party opted to join it. When the new prime minister made ethnic and religious reconciliation the keynote of his policy, he was confronted with the most virulent campaign of ethnic hostility ever waged in Sri Lanka in recent times. The Opposition unleashed a sustained barrage of racialist propaganda in which the SLFP, as the unabashed advocate of the Sinhalese-Buddhist domination of the Sri Lankan polity, was joined by the Communist Party and the LSSP. The left-wing leadership demonstrated all the ardour of recent converts in espousing a cause which they had once spurned.

Legislation introduced by the new UNP-led coalition in January 1966 implemented what were, in fact, the language provisions of Bandaranaike's agreement with the Federal Party. But this was done against the background of massive demonstrations against it led by the SLFP and its left-wing allies who argued, despite all the evidence to the contrary, that the regulations introduced by Dudley Senanayake's government in January 1966 violated the spirit if not the letter of Bandaranaike's language legislation of the 1950s. Once more a state of emergency was imposed, but any prospect of racial riots was nipped in the bud by decisive government action. A pledge to the Federal Party had been honoured at great cost in terms of the resulting erosion of public support.

But the limits of a policy of ethnic reconciliation were demonstrated most dramatically when Dudley Senanayake was forced in mid-1968 to abandon a bill which envisaged the setting up of district councils 'under the control and direction of the central government' a key feature in the Bandaranaike–Federal Party agreement of 1957 to which the UNP was now pledged. Once again, Sinhalese pressure groups organized a campaign against it which was successful, the crucial factor being the opposition to it within the government parliamentary party. Popular opposition to this bill was based on the suspicion that district councils would pave the way for a fully fledged federal structure, which in turn would be the precursor of a separation of the Tamil units of such a federation from the Sri Lankan polity.

The UNP's recently established links with the Ceylon Workers' Congress and the plantation workers were consolidated by the abandonment of the principle of a separate electoral register for persons of Indian origin, which Mrs Bandaranaike had sought to introduce, and by relaxation of the element of compulsion in repatriation to India. The prime minister found that concessions to the plantation workers were more manageable politically, despite opposition to this from Kandyan spokesmen, than similar concessions to the Federal Party.

It was evident that there were clear limits to the policy of ethnic and religious reconciliation to which Dudley Senanayake's government was committed and that these limits were set by the new balance of forces established by the Bandaranaikes, husband and wife, in the decade 1956–65. The first and still the most important of these limits was acceptance of the language policy established by S.W.R.D. Bandaranaike. When the Federal Party joined Dudley Senanayake's UNP in a coalition, it was itself tacitly accepting the consensus on language established between 1956 and 1965. Second, there would be no tampering with the country's unitary constitutional structure. Bandaranaike's district councils lost their political viability once the Federal Party became a force to be reckoned with, and even Dudley Senanayake's assurance that the district councils he had in mind would be directly under the control of the government was inadequate to win any support for such a scheme from the Sinhalese. Third, the primacy of Buddhism had to be accepted as a hard reality and it was necessary for the government to reassure the electorate that the protection of Buddhism as the national religion was a special obligation of the state.

The UNP was always suspect to Buddhist activists as a party having links with the Roman Catholics. It is for this reason it became impossible for Dudley Senanayake's government to make any concessions to them on the schools issue, despite the fact that the UNP had voted against the SLFP's legislation on the takeover of schools when it came before parliament in 1960. When Dudley Senanayake's government was formed in 1965, the Roman Catholics had expected a relaxation of some of the restrictive measures adopted by the SLFP government, but despite a formal pledge on this point in mid-1967, there was no change of policy. What is more, the Roman Catholics were aggrieved when the government introduced the *poya* holiday scheme under which the weekly holiday was based on the phases of the moon. Quite apart from the inconvenience of the irregularity of the weekly holiday under this scheme, the usual sabbath holiday was abandoned. In opting for the poya scheme, the government was bending over backwards to reassure the Buddhist movement about its bona fides on religion, but the effect was to cause dissatisfaction if not resentment among the Roman Catholics (despite 'official' acceptance of the change by the Roman Catholic hierarchy), without any substantial advantage in terms of gaining Buddhist support for the government.

FOREIGN AFFAIRS

In foreign policy, the national consensus established in this decade was obscured by occasional gusts of controversy over specific issues, especially whenever non-alignment, the core of the consensus, seemed to be threatened. Within the limits set by this consensus there could be, and was, a special emphasis in regard to relations with the two major power blocs, or major powers within them, and there was a choice between activism in foreign affairs and a low-profile approach.

Mrs Bandaranaike's first government illustrated one variation of policies possible within this consensus: an activist foreign policy with a distinct anti-western, and more particularly an anti-American, tilt. Although anti-Americanism was discernible from the beginning of her prime ministership, it was with the nationalization in late 1963 of the distribution of petroleum products, which had been controlled up to that time by Western oil companies, that relations between the two countries were quite obviously strained. When negotiations over compensation for the assets of the nationalized companies broke down, the United States government, acting under the guidelines established under the Hickenlooper amendment to the Foreign Aid Act,[11] stopped its programme of aid to Sri Lanka.

While relations between Sri Lanka and the United States steadily deteriorated, those with the People's Republic of China—the bête noire of the United States—reached a peak of cordiality. Indeed, these friendly ties with China survived the tricky diplomatic initiatives over the Sino-Indian crisis of 1962, when Mrs Bandaranaike remained doggedly neutral despite the pressures from within her party and outside it—especially from the UNP—to come out in support of India. Then in 1963 came a maritime agreement with China conferring reciprocal most favoured nation treatment in relation to seaborne traffic. This decision proved to be just as controversial as Mrs Bandaranaike's stand on the Sino-Indian crisis. Critics of the agreement—especially the UNP—contended that through it Sri Lanka was in danger of being drawn unwillingly into China's sphere of geopolitical influence at a time when her closest neighbour, India, was under severe pressure, both diplomatic and military, from China. Thus on the question of relations with China the SLFP and UNP were sharply divided.

There was no such divergence of views on Mrs Bandaranaike's commitment to the emerging unity of action among the non-aligned states of Asia and Africa and their search for a distinct identity as a third force in international affairs. Her years as prime minister of Sri Lanka coincided with a remarkably creative phase in the diplomacy of the non-aligned states. The conference of non-aligned states held at Belgrade in 1961 was a landmark in the history of what may be called the Third World identity. It was followed three years later by a conference at Cairo. At both, Mrs Bandaranaike was an enthusiastic participant, identifying herself and Sri Lanka unreservedly with the diplomatic initiatives which followed from the conference. For Sri Lanka herself there was one immediate benefit: stronger trade ties with the Third World, quite often on the basis of barter agreements, and through this a greater diversity in her pattern of external trade. Nothing demonstrated the activist flavour of Sri Lanka's foreign policy better than the conference held in Colombo on Mrs Bandaranaike's initiative in 1962 to mediate in the Sino-Indian dispute. But this one conspicuous intervention in the role of a mediator in international disputes did not achieve any significant results.

With the change of government came a new interpretation of non-alignment—away from the pro-China, anti-western stress of Mrs Bandaranaike's regime, and much less activist in expression. Indeed, the new prime minister regarded an active foreign policy as an expensive luxury for a small country like Sri Lanka, especially one which faced such severe economic pressures.

One of the first diplomatic moves of the new government was to negotiate a settlement of the question of compensation for the nationalized oil companies. Once this was done, the United States government resumed its economic assistance programme in Sri Lanka. If Dudley Senanayake's government regarded this as essential to the creation of a favourable climate for an increase in the flow of economic assistance from western nations, the Opposition—especially the Marxist parties—viewed it as fresh evidence of the UNP's incorrigible subservience to the west. Few foreign policy decisions of the new government evoked as much controversy as this one.

Relations with China became distinctly less cordial than under the SLFP, although there was no change either in the unequivocal support given by Sri Lanka on the question of China's admission to the United Nations or in the pattern of trade between the two countries, nor for that matter was there any substantial reduction of Chinese economic aid. Nevertheless, the UNP was instinctively suspicious of Chinese policies in Asia and this apprehension clouded Dudley Senanayake's judgement in decisions involving relations with China. It was an attitude which the Indian government especially appreciated because of its concern over the nature of Sri Lanka's ties with China in the early 1960s in the context of the crisis in Sino-Indian relations at that time, and also because of the importance of Sri Lanka in India's defence strategy. As a result, relations between Sri Lanka and India were greatly strengthened under Dudley Senanayake's government. The Soviet Union also viewed this new attitude to China with some satisfaction.

Links with Third World states established under the Bandaranaikes were maintained at the United Nations and elsewhere. On the critical issues of the day—Vietnam, Rhodesia, Namibia, the Soviet invasion of Czechoslovakia and the Arab–Israel conflict—the Senanayake government's policies were consistent with a continuing commitment to non-alignment. Its political instincts were more liberal and humanitarian than socialist, and its natural allies were the less assertive and more moderate states of the Third World. The prime minister recoiled from any assertive role in international relations and the views of his government were expressed with a moderation that was a sharp contrast to the fervour and intensity with which his predecessor in office had chosen to demonstrate her commitment to a Third World identity. Now in Opposition, she and her political allies and associates on the left were devising a new strategy on foreign policy to be introduced if or when they returned to power. This strategy was seemingly more dynamic, more abrasively anti-western in tone and more emphatically radical in content.

THE ECONOMY IN CRISIS

It was in the 1960s that Sri Lanka confronted in full measure the economic crisis that had been building up ever since the collapse of the tea boom of 1954–55. The crux of the problem lay in the continued decline in the price of tea, which provided nearly two-thirds of the country's foreign exchange. Between 1947 and 1970, the quantity of tea exported rose by over 60 per cent but the yield in foreign exchange increased by a mere 10 per cent. Rubber and coconut, the two other major sources of foreign exchange, had not fared much better either.[12]

The terms of trade steadily deteriorated since 1960 and over the years covered in this chapter, Sri Lanka's current payments to the rest of the world often exceeded her current receipts with the sole exception of 1965. Between 1962 and 1964, the index of the terms of trade (base 1947=100 per cent) fell from 142 to 105, a decline of 26 per cent. The slide continued over the years 1965–69 from 112 to 88, a fall of 21 per cent and in 1970 the terms of trade deteriorated by 3.6 per cent.

The first signs of this malaise had been evident in the mid-1950s, but in the exhilarating and turbulent days of S.W.R.D. Bandaranaike's government, few people were inclined to regard the sharp drop in tea prices as anything more than a temporary phase, a trough before the next crest of the wave and a return to more prosperous times. Thus the country's external assets, which stood at Rs 1,275 million at the end of 1956, were used to cushion it against the serious economic consequences of this fall in foreign exchange earnings and to finance imports on the same expansive scale as in the prosperous years of the Korean boom. By 1960, external assets had dropped to Rs 541 million, very little of which had been used to finance investment to sustain some growth in the economy. Most if not all of it had been spent on imports of consumer goods. The result was that controls on foreign exchange, which were imposed in 1960–61, were more severe than they need have been if these unpalatable measures had been taken earlier. All luxury goods and then, increasingly, more essential goods were eliminated from the country's import bill in the early 1960s, but despite this the decline in gross foreign receipts could not be reversed or indeed even halted and Sri Lanka confronted what was clearly a permanent foreign exchange crisis. The import bill was trimmed almost to the bone and this too was sustained by international borrowing.

The acute shortage of foreign exchange confronting the government acted as a great stimulus to the extension of state control over vital segments of the economy, which had begun during S.W.R.D. Bandaranaike's administration and indeed, in some fields, much earlier. Thus the import of rice, wheat and wheat flour, sugar and other foodstuffs had been under government control since the early 1940s, as were most of the wholesale and a great deal of the retail distribution of these items within the country. Now a much wider range of consumer articles was distributed through the network of government-sponsored cooperatives and through the state-controlled Cooperative Wholesale Establishment. Life insurance and general insurance were made a state monopoly, state control over banking was extended by the nationalization of the Bank of Ceylon, the only locally owned bank on the island, and—as we have seen in a different context in this chapter—the distribution of petroleum and kerosene was nationalized, and the assets of the oil companies operating in Sri Lanka were taken over by the state.[13]

However, this extension of state control over some sectors of the economy did nothing to increase production. It is production that ultimately matters and there, apart from a few bright patches in the field of industrial development and some improvement in rice production in 1960–61, not much progress was made. With the capacity to import so severely restrained, the need to develop means of earning or saving foreign exchange became more urgent after 1960 than before; yet progress on these lines continued to be slow. In part, at least, this was because export industries and import-substitution industries established in the early 1960s and expanded thereafter were, and have continued to be, heavily dependent on imported intermediate and capital goods.

The change of government in 1965 did not lead to any improvement on the economic front. On the contrary, 1966 saw a fall in the production—as well as in the prices—of tea and coconut, and receipts from exports declined by 12 per cent compared with the previous year. More ominously, there was a significant rise in the level of import prices—the inflationary trends in the industrial world were being imported to Sri Lanka—and the terms of trade for 1966 were the worst since 1962. The stagnation in the economy was reflected in the following figures: real increase in the GNP in 1965 was a mere 1.8 per cent; in 1966, it sank even further to 1.6 per cent.

Yet in 1967 there began a remarkable breakthrough in economic growth, the consequence of a fresh approach to economic development and social welfare.[14] Welfare had been taken hitherto to mean the provision of goods and services free or at subsidized rates; the major premise of the new government's reappraisal of policy was that the redistribution of money incomes was a self-defeating exercise so long as real resources were scarce. The most obvious means of rearranging patterns of consumption to the benefit of the poor was to increase incomes in the countryside where the minority of the population lived. This, the government proceeded to do by launching the Sri Lankan version of a 'green revolution', in the hope and belief that 'equity and growth [would go] hand in hand; wider dispersal of the distribution of new assets would lead to higher GNP growth and to greater equality in personal income'.[15] Dudley Senanayake, like his father, had a passion for traditional agriculture and regarded it as the key to the economic regeneration of the country. In such success as it achieved, his personal role in organizing and encouraging the national food drive was crucial.

By 1969, there had been a notable improvement in the production of paddy. Annual production had reached 68 million bushels that year, compared with the best previous achievement of 50.1 million bushels in 1964. In 1970, it reached 77 million bushels. Rice production had reached an all-time high level of 75 per cent of self-sufficiency in May 1970, when the government went to the polls. Industrial production rose from Rs 70 million to Rs 262 million between 1965 and 1968, and more significantly, there was a perceptible shift in emphasis from the production of consumer goods to intermediate goods.

The breakthrough in production was reflected in the rise of the GNP from 4.4 per cent in 1967 to 8.3 per cent in 1968.

In the end, however, the political advantages anticipated from this very considerable achievement in economic development eluded the government. For one thing, by its very nature the benefits of a programme of this kind would take many years before they became evident to the electorate, and by the time of the elections of 1970, such benefits as were so far evident seemed to have accrued to the affluent, the landholders, the middlemen and the employed. While these were a substantial section of the rural population, they were a minority; there were no benefits for the landless and the unemployed, and this at a time of inflationary pressures. It was easy, therefore, for the vociferous left wing to exploit consumers' fears of higher prices and to attribute these to the government's agricultural programmes. Inflationary pressures and the balance of payments crisis persisted, the first because of a substantial increase in the price of imports and successive devaluations of the rupee since 1967, the second because of slack demand and falling prices for the country's main exports. Net foreign debt more than doubled between 1964 and 1968—the government incurred substantial overseas debts to meet the import costs of its agricultural programme—and repayments to the International Monetary Fund rose sharply after 1968. On the domestic front, the government's expenditure exceeded its income for the entire period of its administration. Above all, the expansion of the economy had not made any noticeable dent in that most intractable of all the problems that confronted governments in this decade—unemployment.

The full force of population growth over the period 1946–60 hit the labour market in the 1960s. Those between fifteen and sixty-five years of age, roughly the working group, increased from 5.25 million to over 7.5 million in this decade. More significant was the increase in the number of those aged twenty-five and less: while their proportion to the total population did not show any significant rise, they had doubled in twenty-two years from 3.8 million in 1946 to 4.9 million in 1955, 6.5 million in 1963 and 7.2 million in mid-1968. In the period 1960–70 the growth in the number of those seeking employment far outran the demand for labour being generated by the basically stagnant economy. Estimated open unemployment climbed from 3,70,000 in 1959 to 5,50,000 in 1969–70, about 14 per cent of the workforce or one twentieth of the island's population. The immediate effect of population growth had been to push up private and public consumption needs, thus diminishing the investable surplus. This process was continued and even accelerated in the 1960s because of the whole range of welfare services, unequalled in most parts of Asia, to which the governments of the day were committed and which the country's diminishing resources could hardly sustain: education, irrigation projects, land redistribution schemes, health services, subsidized public transport in the form of cheap bus and rail fares, and above all food subsidies.

After 1960–61 primary and secondary education became, for all practical purposes, a state monopoly. University education had always been entirely state-financed, as for that matter were most aspects of technical education. State expenditure on primary and secondary education was one of the highest in Asia, constituting on an average a little more than 4.5 per cent of the GNP between 1959 and 1968. The literacy rate, if the 0–4 age group is excluded, was as high as 85 per cent of the total population. But as a result of its long-standing commitment to free education (in the sense of free tuition) at all levels—primary, secondary and tertiary—Sri Lanka in the 1960s became an outstanding example of the growing global phenomenon of educated unemployed.

In devising its economic strategy, Dudley Senanayake's government had the employment potential of the programme very much in mind. Indeed his agricultural programme was regarded as a means of absorbing the growing number of unemployed into productive employment—intensive smallholder food production and related activities. But this aspect of his strategy for economic growth did not yield the results expected of it or at least not at a speed which would have benefited the government politically. Nor were these the sort of jobs in which the most articulate and volatile sector of the unemployed—the

university graduates and the better-qualified school leavers—
were interested. The result was that the unemployed young
were enthusiastically receptive to the Opposition's criticisms
of the government's economic and social policies.

For the government the political implications of this were
ominous. Sri Lanka had been one of the first countries in the
world to lower its voting age to eighteen. Although this had
been done in 1959, the two elections of 1960 had been contested
using the previous system of votes at twenty-one. In the general
election of 1965, the voters between the ages of eighteen and
twenty-one cast their ballots for the first time. Political observers
were convinced that most of their votes went to the then
Opposition. In 1970, their numbers were much larger, their
alienation from the government was more pronounced and their
commitment to the Opposition was correspondingly stronger.

During their years in Opposition Mrs Bandaranaike and
her allies put together a broader coalition than that negotiated
in June 1964. The two major Marxist parties in the country, the
LSSP and the Communist Party (Moscow wing), formed a
United Front (UF) with the SLFP, under Mrs Bandaranaike's
leadership. In early June 1968, a common programme was
agreed upon by all three parties as their joint platform for the
elections scheduled for 1970; this was in the nature of a set of
alternative strategies radical in design and socialist in outlook.

In preparation for the elections, the Opposition seized upon
the government's seemingly strongest point, its food
production programme, for their most vitriolic criticisms, intent
on highlighting its flaws and failures so that the government's
blaze of publicity for the programme would become
counterproductive. These were good and intelligent tactics
against a government which seemed eminently vulnerable at
the polls; but there was also a whiff of ideological conflict in
it, for the left-wing parties viewed the high priority given to
agriculture in economic development with a distaste bordering
on contempt. For them and the intelligentsia the key to
economic development and the most effective means of solving
the unemployment problem was industrialization. It was not
yet evident—as it was to become in the years ahead—that

industry could not provide the impetus for the growth of the economy as a whole, nor was geared—because most of the island's new factories were capital-intensive—to the provision of productive employment. Hence the argument carried conviction in an atmosphere of uncertainty about the economic benefits of the government's programme in terms of the unemployment problem and inflation. Besides, the government's new strategy on agricultural development had been preceded in 1966 by a cut in the rice subsidy and thus its initiative was shown to the electorate as being no more than part of a concerted attack on the welfare system. In the final stages of the campaign, the Opposition concentrated on this almost to the exclusion of other issues. After his party suffered a landslide defeat[16] in the elections of May 1970, Dudley Senanayake ruefully commented that for the second time in his political career he had paid the penalty for disturbing the most cherished of the sacred cows of Sri Lanka's welfare system—the rice subsidy.

In their election campaign of 1970, the parties of the United Front (UF)—the SLFP, the LSSP and the Communist Party (Moscow wing)—had held out, through their manifesto and speeches, the assurance of purposeful, systematic and fundamental changes in every sphere of activity. The euphoria, reminiscent of 1956, which greeted the UF's decisive victory, seemed to suggest that it was a just reward for the skill with which its leadership had responded and given expression to the inchoate desires and feelings of the people.

Almost the first decision of the UF was to honour its election promise to make good the cuts in the rice ration imposed in 1966. This set the tone for much that happened in those early weeks, a plethora of decisions, some more important than others but all designed to dramatize a change of course and a new style of government. There was a new emphasis in the island's foreign policy, a distinct tilt to the left. In rapid succession, North Korea and the German Democratic Republic were given diplomatic recognition, while diplomatic links with Israel, which had been tenuous at the best, were severed.

These were in the nature of easy decisions, within the government's control. But the rhetorical flourishes indulged in during the acrimonious election campaign proved acutely embarrassing when economic conditions showed no sign of improvement and it became increasingly evident that there were no easy solutions to the problem of unemployment. Indeed, the size of the government's parliamentary majority (over 120 seats out of a total of 157) created and sustained the illusion that nothing was impossible if the government only had the will to attempt it.

JANATHA VIMUKTHI PERAMUNA (JVP)

Confronted by the same combination of factors that had brought down its predecessor—unemployment, rising prices and scarcities of essential items of consumption—the government, within a few months of coming to power, was floundering just as badly as Dudley Senanayake's had done in the first phase of his rule in the mid-1960s. Well before the end of 1970, its early popularity was being eroded and with great rapidity. If the government consoled itself with the thought that the UNP was too badly demoralized by its comprehensive electoral defeat and the open rift between its leader Dudley Senanayake and the leader of its parliamentary group and also leader of the Opposition, J.R. Jayewardene, to offer much of a challenge, it soon faced one from a different but not entirely unexpected quarter. The pace of change and reform in the first ten months of the government's tenure of office proved altogether inadequate to satisfy the aspirations of the more militant and articulate young people whose political appetites had been whetted by their zeal in working to bring the government to power. By the middle of March 1971 it was evident that the government faced a deadly threat from the Janatha Vimukthi Peramuna (JVP), an ultra-left organization dominated by educated youths, unemployed or disadvantageously employed.

This organization had made its presence felt in the violent and threatening demonstrations—which the government had condoned—that followed in the wake of the UF victory. Within a few months it had the field to itself as the most vocal critic of the government, with the UNP totally unable to function as the major political force it was. A series of mass meetings held by the JVP all over the country was at once a stern warning to the UF and a challenge to its credibility as a genuinely socialist government. The JVP made plain its feeling that the government seemed incapable of fulfilling its election promises and made no secret of its readiness and determination to overthrow the government if the changes it desired were not introduced. Thus the insurrection that broke out in April 1971[17] could hardly have been more openly proclaimed. If it took the government by surprise this was because intelligence reports were either disbelieved or misread. This arose from a refusal to believe that erstwhile supporters would react so violently against a regime they had helped bring to power and which shared their socialist aspirations.

The insurrection was from beginning to end a revolt of youth, the first large-scale revolt against the government by youth in the country and also perhaps the biggest revolt by young people in any part of the world in recorded history, the first instance of tension between generations becoming military conflict on a national scale. The creed of generational war was linked to the eradication of a colonial status which had ended two decades previously but was presumed to be still in existence. It was a movement of the new and ultra-left against the established left—the populist SLFP and the traditional parties of the left, the LSSP and the Communist Party. Although the most tenacious and defiant acts of the insurgents and the most serious centres of revolt accurately matched the large concentrations of some of the depressed castes, the *Vahumpura* and *Batgama,* caste was not the sole or even a major determinant of the insurrection. It was secondary to the class factor. The insurgents were, in general, the children of the rural poor, Sinhalese and Buddhist, and the ethnic and religious minorities played no significant role in the insurrection.

In analysing the critical factors in the outbreak of the insurrection, emphasis is generally given to the eminently exploitable social problems—the economic inequalities, exacerbated by one of the highest birth rates in Asia, creating a poverty-stricken, unemployed and frustrated element ranging from articulate university graduates to the landless unemployed. But equally important was the catalyst of the revolutionary

664 A History of Sri Lanka

violence, the JVP, which instilled a group consciousness, fashioned an ideology, planned a strategy, built up an organization and provided the leadership. Without this driving force, the unemployed and poor youth to whom the JVP appealed would have been far less conscious of the situation they were in and would very probably have put up with their deprivation, alienation and frustration without resort to armed insurrection.

In the immediate sense the 1971 insurgency failed. The rebels were not the spearhead of a popular outburst against a tyrannical or repressive regime, nor did they have the advantage of a dominating foreign presence against which they could have stirred up nationalist sentiment. There was no substantial support from either the rural areas or the urban working class. Besides, it was an inadequately trained and poorly equipped force that set out to do battle with the state. Once the momentum of their original thrust had been absorbed and repelled, they were unable to sustain their attack although they had the numbers to do so. The rebellion was put down with considerable ruthlessness.

The insurrection of 1971 left an indelible mark on Sri Lanka. The rebels, although defeated, played a part in shaping the future. Sri Lanka was pushed more rapidly towards being a socialist society: the moves begun under the UF in 1970 for an autochthonous constitution for Sri Lanka were hastened; a powerful impetus was given to the adoption of a series of radical economic and social changes, the most far-reaching of which were the Land Reform Law of 1972 and the nationalization of the plantations in 1975; state control in trade and industry was accelerated and expanded to the point where the state has established a dominance over the commanding heights of the economy. But there were three other consequences with which the rebels would have had less cause to be satisfied. First, the insurrection tested the army and police, whose success over the rebels gave them added prestige and, more important, put them in an immeasurably better position in terms of training, experience and equipment to face a similar threat in the future. Second, at the outbreak of the insurrection a quite incredible combination of countries came to the assistance of the government: India first and foremost, but also Britain and the United States, the Soviet Union, Egypt, Yugoslavia and Pakistan. The government insisted that there was no foreign involvement in the insurrection, but significantly the one foreign embassy that came under suspicion and was asked to close down was that of North Korea. The government's foreign policy now came round to a more even-handed neutralism: gradually, relations with the United States became very cordial and ties with the Commonwealth were strengthened. Third, and perhaps the most significant of all, the government tended to become increasingly authoritarian. What began as an inevitable after-effect of the rebellion was continued long after the rebels had been routed and the threat to the security of the state had diminished substantially. To many of these themes we shall return later in this chapter.

By the beginning of 1972, the UF government had long since lost the air of self-assurance and confidence it had exuded in its early days in office. The insurrection contributed to this in large measure, but a more powerful but insidious corrosive force was the rapidly worsening economic situation. The UF government had inherited a serious balance of payments problem but in the years after 1971 it deteriorated further and took on the proportions of a grave crisis partly, but by no means entirely, through the operation of external forces beyond its control. The crux of the problem was that the prices of the country's principal imports, particularly its food, rose to unprecedented heights, especially in 1973–74, with no corresponding rise in the price of its exports.

The gravity of the problem compelled the government to take a critical look at its import bill and at the food subsidies.[18] The people of Sri Lanka were over-dependent on imported food, which included much of its rice, made available to them at subsidized rates. Food imports not only absorbed far too much foreign exchange, but food subsidies also constituted one-tenth of all the services and goods produced on the island. Thus any reduction in food imports would bring immediate, substantial and lasting relief to the balance of payments, just as direct cuts in subsidies would help bridge the deficit in the budget. The irony of a government, which had made a political issue of the cuts in food subsidies introduced by its predecessor and had begun its administration by restoring them, being driven to adopt precisely the same policy was not lost on an increasingly sceptical electorate.

Trimming of food subsidies and cuts in welfare expenditure actually began with the second budget of the UF government in November 1971 and continued through 1972 and 1973. Stringent austerity measures for the rich, announced in the five-year plan introduced in the last quarter of 1971 and implemented subsequently—a ceiling on incomes, land reform and limits on the ownership of houses and apartments—did little to reduce the unpopularity of the government's new policy over food subsidies and welfare expenditure.

A second and equally notable reversal of policy was forced on the government by the foreign exchange crisis and this was an emphasis on agricultural development and self-sufficiency in food as the basis of economic recovery. This new strategy had long been preached by the government's main challenger, the UNP, and practised by them with much greater sureness of touch. The left was ideologically committed to industrialization as the solution to the country's problems and always believed that the UNP's commitment to agriculture as the key to Sri Lanka's economic regeneration was a misguided policy which only helped to perpetuate the country's economic backwardness and its subordination to the industrial economies of the West. The left—and the SLFP—had looked with disdain on the vigorous campaign of food production which Dudley Senanayake had led during his last spell in office.

The central issue was rice production. At the end of the previous government's term of office it had reached a record level of three-quarters of the country's requirements of rice. Had this pace of development been sustained, dependence on imports of rice from abroad would have been marginal one-tenth by 1974 and by 1975–76 the island would have been totally independent in this respect. Instead, there was a sharp fall in production in 1971 and a precipitous decline in 1972 which continued into 1973–74. The government had contributed to this by its short-sighted dismantling of the administrative machinery and dispersal of the scientific and administrative personnel associated with its predecessor's food production programme. It took two years to rebuild this administrative structure. In a bid to encourage rice production, the guaranteed price for paddy was raised substantially. The harvests of 1974–75 and 1975–76 were a distinct improvement on those of the three previous years, but they were still well below the levels reached in 1969–70.

The successive increases in the guaranteed price of rice might have generated a more substantial expansion of production but for two factors. The first—which was beyond the control of the government—was inflation, especially the sharp rise in the cost of fertilizers and other agricultural chemicals which were essential to boost production. The second was the government's own decision to establish a state monopoly for the purchase of locally produced rice. Viewed through ideologically tinted glasses, this was an incentive to production, but in reality it was an artificial check on prices. It was unpopular with producers and consumers alike—producers because they could get a much higher price in the free market, and consumers because off-ration rice was less easily available in the market and the price of rice rose as a result. The strong measures of compulsion required to protect this monopoly were greatly resented by the peasants, who formed the solid core of the electoral support of the SLFP.

The most popular substitute for rice was bread, but because wheat is not cultivated locally, and the parlous state of the country's foreign exchange resources permitted no increase in imports because of a steep rise in the price of wheat in the world market, a ceiling was imposed on imports of wheat and wheat flour. The country was treated to the novel spectacle of queues for bread in the city of Colombo and its suburbs, where demand for it was greatest. In desperation the government turned to the popularization of indigenous rice substitutes—tapioca, yams and dry grains—none of which, however, was produced in adequate quantities. This appeal to people to cut down on the consumption of rice and to resort to indigenous substitutes was nothing less than a call for a reorientation of food habits, a delicate operation requiring a degree of public support well beyond the capacity of the government to generate because of its lack of credibility. The government had, after all, come to power on—among other things—promises to increase the weekly ration of rice, to provide a plentiful supply of food and even to abolish the existing system of rationing 'subsidiary' foodstuff. The economic situation was all the more dismal because of the severe inflationary pressures of the years 1973–74, much of it reflecting the upward movement of prices for some primary products—wheat, sugar and rice, all essential import items for Sri Lanka—to be followed by the hardest blow of all, the unprecedented rise in the price of oil. The average person had little understanding of foreign exchange and balance of payments problems, or the imperatives of a harsh economic crisis all of which led to the shortages of food that confronted him and to the tightening of the rationing system. Instead, he could only see the increasing inability of the government to supply him with his essential food requirements in adequate quantities and at prices he could afford.

The new constitution adopted in May 1972 on the initiative of the UF government captured the mood and set the trend for a departure from the established pattern of government to a more authoritarian or less liberal one. Its salient feature was the establishment of a unicameral republican structure, a centralized democracy in which the dominant element was the political executive.[19] The conception of the National State Assembly as the vehicle of the sovereignty of the people found its final expression in the provisions of the constitution which denied to the courts the power or jurisdiction to pronounce on the validity of the laws enacted by the Assembly. While the National State Assembly was described as the supreme instrument of the state power of the republic, the most notable feature of the constitution was the dominance of the executive and the absence of meaningful institutional or constitutional checks on the exercise of its powers. Moreover, through the process of constitution-making the ruling coalition used its overwhelming majority in the Constituent Assembly to give itself an extended term of two years (to May 1977) beyond the original period of five for which it had been elected in May 1970. In taking this action—probably unprecedented in the annals of constitution-making in democratic states—the government showed scant regard for any sense of public integrity.

The expansion of executive authority was not limited to the advantages that came with the new constitutional structure. There were two other powerful weapons in the government's armoury. One of these was not new, namely emergency powers, which have been the stock-in-trade of all Sri Lanka's governments since independence, but they have been used more frequently since 1956 than before. Under the UF government, emergency powers were invoked in dealing with the insurgency, but they were retained long after it had been crushed, and were extended from month to month, not because they were really necessary but because they were convenient in dealing with dissent. These emergency regulations in effect suspended normal political processes, if not the constitution as a whole, and conferred extraordinary powers on the government. More significant and reprehensible was the second of the government's weapons. With the passage (and subsequent amendment) of the Interpretation Ordinance of 1972, the power of the courts to hear appeals against mala fide administrative decisions was drastically curtailed, thus removing a meaningful restraint upon the misuse of administrative power for political purposes by the government against its opponents. Once this judicial check was removed, the government had little hesitation in using the machinery of the state and administrative regulations to harass and intimidate its political opponents. One particularly vicious manifestation of this was in the acquisition of immovable property—land, factories, houses, shops and all sorts of buildings—as well as movable property such as vehicles, ostensibly for public purposes but, in fact, to deter known opponents of the government from political activity.

Freedom of the press was severely curtailed. First, the Associated Newspapers of Ceylon, the main newspaper group on the island, was converted by a special law into a government-controlled press. Next, emergency legislation was used to keep the Independent Newspapers group—which by 1973–74 had emerged as the main critic of the government—closed for nearly three years from April 1974. No such drastic measures were required to establish government influence over the Times group of newspapers: it succumbed without firing a shot. Once this happened, and with broadcasting entirely under government control, expression of critical opinion and dissent was limited to party newspapers and news-sheets, most of them maintaining a fitful existence on limited funds and circulation in a hostile environment of government controls over the allocation of newsprint, the withholding of advertisements by the government and the reluctance of business houses to advertise in Opposition newspapers for fear of offending the government thereby. With the media so completely under government control, only one other channel was available for the expression of dissent—public meetings. Here the problem was the state of emergency in the country in the wake of the insurrection. For security reasons, no public meetings were permitted except with government approval until September 1972. These restraints affected Opposition parties, but not meetings sponsored by the government parties. The first relaxation of the restrictions came with the by-elections of 1972.

By the middle of 1972 the UNP had recovered from its debacle at the polls in May 1970, and was at last in a position to mount a challenge to a government which was visibly losing public support. Its re-emergence as a viable democratic alternative was demonstrated in October 1972, when it won three out of four seats (a net gain of two) in the first set of by-elections to the Parliament elected in 1970.

Thereafter the usual pattern of Opposition meetings was resumed, with the UNP making all the running after its success at the by-elections. In the first quarter of 1973, the UNP staged a series of very successful propaganda meetings throughout the country, which attracted large crowds. Then on 13 April 1973, the UNP leader Dudley Senanayake died after a short illness. This led to unprecedented scenes of spontaneous grief and mourning throughout the island. Nearly half the entire population filed past his bier during the week beginning 14 April and the cremation of his body on 21 April attracted the largest crowd ever gathered together for any occasion in the island's history. The millions who braved the elements and underwent great physical discomfort, standing for hours in endless queues that stretched for miles along Colombo's streets, were doing something more than paying tribute to a much-loved national figure. It was a neat and expressive demonstration by a politically sophisticated people, who were unable at that time—because all local government elections had been postponed, among other reasons—to articulate their feelings over the problems they faced. The degree of popular participation in the funeral ceremonies and the depth of grief displayed (which bordered on mass hysteria) were almost without precedent, even in a country where the organization of political funerals was a well-developed art. It was a week that shook Sri Lanka—and frightened the government.

Its immediate effect, in fact, was to strengthen those forces within the government which pressed for increasingly authoritarian attitudes towards its political opponents. This trend was originally an after-effect of the suppression of the insurgency of 1971, but it persisted throughout the government's tenure of office long after the threat to the security of the state had disappeared. Indeed, this authoritarianism was one of the most distinctive characteristics of Mrs Bandaranaike's UF government, and for that reason is described in some detail in the next section of this chapter.

Encouraged by the response it had evoked and the astounding demonstration of grief at the death of its leader, the UNP surged ahead in 1973 and 1974 with a number of by-election victories to give it greater momentum and a sense of purpose. But when its campaign was leading to a crescendo, with a large number of rallies scheduled to be held simultaneously in all parts of the island in late April 1974 in what was to be the beginning of a civil disobedience movement, the government stepped in to demonstrate the limits of political action available to the Opposition. A curfew was imposed, emergency regulations of the utmost severity were introduced, and a ban which remained in force for almost a year was imposed on UNP meetings.[20]

With its main political opponents hamstrung by these restrictions, the government now had the field to itself, even in the matter of public meetings. In June 1974, it staged the first of what was to be a series of such meetings. They were, in fact, the first government political rallies after the insurgency but, more important, they had two novel features: the full resources of the state were used to organize them and compulsion was used to gather crowds for these demonstrations. This set the pattern for the rest of the government's period of office. There was also a flagrant misuse of state resources, including radio, newspapers, vehicles and personnel for party purposes, whether for propaganda rallies or for by-elections to the National State Assembly. State employees (especially in the lower rungs of the administration), teachers, workers in the state sector of the economy in distribution, services and manufacture and plantation workers in nationalized plantations were compelled to participate in government party rallies on threat of dismissal of temporary workers or transfer of permanent employees to uncongenial stations. The severe restrictions which had been imposed on the political activity of the Opposition parties served to emphasize the flagrancy of the discrimination in favour of the government.

One other point needs elaboration, namely, discrimination on political grounds. This form of discrimination is a comparatively novel one in the context of the liberal political traditions of Sri Lanka. Preferential treatment of supporters of the government in recruitment and promotion within the state service had always been a feature of the process of governance in Sri Lanka since independence, but now, for the first time, preferential treatment of government supporters was 'institutionalized'. This was facilitated by the government's repudiation of the British colonial type of administration and its basic idea of an impartial civil service. Politicization of public service was not restricted to key appointments at the policy-making levels, but extended throughout the service and intruded into the judiciary as well, although not to the same extent.[21] The bases of appointment were political affiliation, personal connection, or still more dubious considerations. It led to both inefficiency and corruption, with the latter serving the function of mitigating the worst effects of this system of open discrimination against employment of children and close relatives of Opposition activists and supporters, and the former serving the equally important one of softening the harsher and more repressive features of the authoritarianism which the UF established and encouraged.

With no local government elections since May 1971, electoral activity was limited to by-elections to parliament. In these, the government's record was dismal, indeed the worst of any since 1947. Only twice in its period of seven years in power did the government successfully defend a seat in a by-election, once in October 1972 and on the other occasion in August 1976. In the same period it had lost four seats in by-elections and failed to capture a single seat from the Opposition although more than a dozen opportunities came its way.

MINORITY PROBLEMS

The new balance of forces, of which the principal feature was the dominance of the Sinhalese and Buddhists in the Sri Lanka polity, was effectively consolidated with the victory of the UF coalition in May 1970. Although an undercurrent of hostility to the Tamils, indigenous and Indian, was discernible from the outset, the adoption of the new constitution in 1972 was the critical starting point of a new phase in communal antagonism on the island, especially in regard to relations between the Sinhalese and the indigenous Tamils. Indeed, the new constitution accurately reflected this new balance of forces.

The two main points at issue were language rights and religion. In regard to the latter, Chapter II of the constitution laid down that 'the Republic of Sri Lanka shall give to Buddhism the foremost place and accordingly it shall be the duty of the state to protect and foster Buddhism while assuring to all religions the rights secured by Section 18(i)(d)'. With this Sri Lanka ceased to be a secular state, pure and simple, even if it did not become the theocratic state which Buddhist pressure groups would have liked it to be.

The wide support for this clause in the Constituent Assembly—the government had the support of the UNP on it—was just as notable as the fact that the Christian minority did not oppose it. Indeed, one of the remarkable new developments of the years after 1970 was the improvement in relations between the Roman Catholics and the SLFP. This was partly because the Roman Catholics themselves had come to accept the new balance of forces as a political reality. And while the government made no attempt to change its education policy, which had been the point of divergence between the SLFP and the Roman Catholics since 1960, it nevertheless became much more conciliatory.

The Tamils, however, claimed that the new constitution gave validity and confirmation to their second-class citizenship by according the 'foremost place to Buddhism as the state religion', and by recognizing Sinhala as the state language, with a distinctly inferior and hazy position accorded to Tamil. They regarded the special status accorded to Buddhism as a clear act of discrimination.

Opposition to the new constitution brought the two main Tamil political parties, the Federal Party and the Tamil Congress, together for the first time since 1949. Along with the leadership of the Ceylon Workers' Congress and other Tamil politicians, they established the Tamil United Liberation Front (TULF), which was the main political organization of the Tamils. Previously, all attempts to bring the Indian plantation workers to the point of coordinating their political activities with those of the indigenous Tamils had failed.[22] A by-product of the increasing alienation of the Tamils from the Sinhalese since the adoption of the new constitution was the conversion of a large section of the Tamils of the north to the idea of a separate state: it is an indication of the intensity of feeling in the Tamil areas at what they saw as a deliberate attempt to reduce them to subordinate status. The Federal Party itself was a recent, but not entirely reluctant, convert to this policy, and the Tamil United Liberation Front of which it was the dominant partner came out in support of a separate state for the Tamil-speaking areas of the Northern Province and the Eastern Province.

Worsening relations with the Sinhalese-dominated government tended to make a link with Tamil Nadu more attractive to the Sri Lanka Tamils, if not yet politically viable. This trend has been strengthened by the decline of the Indian National Congress in Tamil Nadu and the emergence to power of the Dravida Munnethra Kazhagam (DMK), more conscious of the rights of Tamils in the Indian subcontinent and much less inhibited in expressing its concern.

The most militant agitators for separatism were the educated unemployed, now a very substantial and very volatile element in Tamil society. They served as the link between the Tamil parliamentarians and the Tamil people. Their support of the TULF campaign was an expression of their frustration at the bleak prospects of employment that faced Tamil youth. Nothing contributed more to the alienation of the latter than the changes introduced by the UF government on admission to universities. Academic ability per se was no longer sufficient to secure admission. They regarded these changes—introduced in 1970 and continued thereafter—as patently and deliberately discriminatory.[23]

In 1974, Mrs Bandaranaike negotiated the settlement, on a firm and amicable basis, of the vexed question of the status of the Indians in Sri Lanka. Nearly half a million of them would eventually be integrated into the Sri Lanka polity[24] and Sri Lanka citizenship will confer on them the political legitimacy which, as an ethnic group, they have not had since 1948. But relations between the government and the leadership of the Ceylon Workers' Congress, the most powerful trade union-cum-political party of Indians in Sri Lanka, were as unfriendly as those with the leadership of the indigenous Tamils. As a result, the government was oblivious to the plight of the plantation workers on the island who, during the early 1970s, were undoubtedly the most economically depressed group. While all sections of the population felt the impact of the inflationary pressures of the 1970s, their effect on the plantation workers was devastating—a precipitous decline from a bare subsistence to grinding poverty.

The UF and in particular the SLFP had good reason for elation at detaching a substantial section of the Muslims from their traditional links with the UNP into supporting the SLFP and the UF. This was masterminded by Badiuddin Mahmud, who had held cabinet office—including the post of minister of education—in Mrs Bandaranaike's first administration in the early 1960s. He was again given the crucial post of minister of education in the UF government. In his hands this cabinet post became at once a political base and a fountain of patronage, to be used to strengthen the ties between his community and the party to which he belonged, the SLFP. Such success as he achieved in this was by its very nature transient. He soon became a controversial figure; his education policy was one of the major points of divergence between the government and the Tamils. More significantly, by 1973 anti-Muslim sentiment was kindled among the Sinhalese by charges of favoured treatment of Muslims in the sphere of education. In 1974–75, there were sporadic Sinhalese–Muslim clashes in various parts of the island, with a dangerous confrontation at Gampola in the last week of 1975. The timely intervention of the police prevented widespread violence at Gampola. The clash that occurred in early 1975 at Puttalam, a Muslim stronghold in the north-west of the island, was—up to that time—the worst episode of communal violence since the Sinhalese–Tamil riots of the late 1950s.

This recrudescence of ethnic and religious tensions seemed menacing enough on its own, but there were other events which made the last weeks of 1975 especially sombre for the government. In the last quarter of 1975, the political alliance between the SLFP and the LSSP which had lasted, in opposition and government, since 1964 came to an end. It was always an uneasy alliance and it had lasted much longer than expected. A serious rift within the ruling coalition became public knowledge in mid-August, when a sharp difference of opinion over the mechanics of the nationalization of foreign-owned plantations on the island triggered off acrimonious bickering between the two major component units of the UF. All attempts to heal the rift proved futile and the LSSP was expelled from the government in October 1975.

THE BREAK-UP OF THE UNITED FRONT, 1975–77

On reflection, the break-up of the alliance seems to have been inevitable, because the programme of action for which it had been formed was completed with the nationalization of the plantations. Both parties regarded this as a landmark achievement, the LSSP saw it as the fulfilment of a campaign it had waged since its very inception, and the SLFP—reflecting Kandyan interests—saw it as redressing a historic grievance. Both were intent on claiming the credit for it. But with state dominance of the economy securely established, the SLFP was now intent on calling a halt to any further measures of socialization. As the SLFP saw it, the range of activities allowed to private enterprise was so limited that there was no further need for the extension of government control. As a party, the SLFP was itself a coalition of interests: from trade unionists, peasants and small traders to landowners, flourishing businessmen and industrialists; from a pragmatic right-wing to a populist centre and a vocal left. What happened now was that the pragmatic right became the dominant influence and was instrumental in a series of decisions, all of them unpalatable to the left-wing of the party and all indicative of an assumption that private enterprise still had a distinct role to play in the economy.

The first decision was perhaps the easiest to take because it immediately benefited the peasants who formed the solid core of SLFP support in the country. This was the restoration of the free market in paddy and rice and the government's role in this sphere was reduced from that of monopoly purchaser to a competitor with private traders. The range of interests which benefited from the second were more restricted, but also more influential. The ceiling on incomes was removed, taxes were reduced substantially from the levels they had reached through the budgets of the LSSP finance minister, Dr N.M. Perera, and Perera's proposals for heavier taxes on wealth were jettisoned.

This change of course coincided with a distinct improvement in relations between Sri Lanka and the United States. It was a trend which had begun in the aftermath of the insurrection of 1971, but it reached its peak in the months before the break-up between the SLFP and LSSP.

In the last quarter of 1975, the government—or at least its dominant SLFP partner in what remained of the coalition—appeared to be confident of its capacity to cope with the political consequences of dismissing the LSSP from the coalition. It was anticipated that some left-wing SLFP MPs would defect to the Opposition in sympathy with the LSSP, but this did not happen. On the contrary, the LSSP lost two of its MPs to the SLFP and one SLFP MP who did cross over to the Opposition joined the UNP.

Yet, the break-up of the SLFP–Communist Party alliance came less than eighteen months after the expulsion of the LSSP from the government. For one thing, with the departure of the LSSP to the Opposition, the government lost its ablest debaters and, what was to be more sufficient, its two-thirds majority in the National State Assembly as well. Second, the drift to the right within the SLFP placed the left wing of the party and the Communist Party in the position of an ineffective brake on a vehicle set on a course they viewed with apprehension. Their position and influence within the government was weak and growing weaker; their votes were essential to maintain the stability of the regime, but once that was achieved their own isolation within it was more pronounced. Nevertheless, their immediate and instinctive reaction was to close ranks in support of the government.

In the first half of 1976, the government's attention and energies were concentrated on the conference of non-aligned nations, which was scheduled for July–August 1976 and for which Colombo had been chosen as the venue. Within the country there was considerable criticism of the massive financial outlay involved in staging an important international conference of this nature, but all left wing groups (including the LSSP) backed the government's decision to hold the conference in Colombo. For the government, the anticipated benefits lay in the prestige likely to accrue to the prime minister from the international publicity for the conference and from her position as its president. The hope was that some of this would rub off on the government itself and buttress its position in the country. As if to give credence to this, in August 1976, the government retained a parliamentary seat in a by-election, its first such success after a string of defeats stretching back to October 1972. Instead of being a morale booster to sustain its self-confidence at the general elections due in mid-1977, this victory actually strengthened moves begun during the period of the conference to secure a postponement of the elections by an amendment of the constitution. Despite the losses sustained by the departure of the LSSP, the government had the support of nearly two-thirds of the MPs in the National State Assembly. Thus, if just two or three Opposition MPs could be won over— if necessary by offers of ministerial appointments—a constitutional amendment was within its reach.[25]

In September 1976, in the aftermath of the non-aligned nations conference and the by-election victory, the SLFP staged a series of public meetings at which one of the most persistent themes and vocal demands was the postponement of elections. For some months several senior cabinet ministers had advocated this and when in September 1976 F.R. Dias Bandaranaike, the most powerful of the SLFP cabinet ministers, joined the chorus of voices, these moves assumed the proportions of a well-organized campaign. Although the prime minister herself did not publicly support them, significantly she did not repudiate them either.

The campaign received an unexpected but serious setback when, in early October, all six Communist Party MPs (including their representative in the cabinet) and five SLFP cabinet ministers declared themselves opposed to any move to postpone the elections, striking evidence of a split in the cabinet on this issue and a sharp difference of opinion between the two coalition partners, the SLFP and the Communist Party. Nevertheless, the strategy was not immediately abandoned; only the tactics were changed and took the form of negotiations with the TULF in a bid to seek a resolution of differences between them and the government. The negotiations began in late 1976 and continued into the first quarter of 1977. Among the benefits which the SLFPs negotiators hoped for in their discussions with the TULF was the latter's support to extend the life of the Parliament elected in 1970. This they did not get, but at least there was the bonus of substantial progress in improving relations between the two parties to the negotiations.[26]

There was an air of unreality in the negotiations between the government and the TULF for they took place against a background of trade union agitation which culminated in a series of strikes, including some in key areas of the public sector such as the railways and the health services. The government was confronted at the beginning of 1977 with precisely the problem it had most feared, namely strikes sponsored by the LSSP. There had always been the hope that in such a confrontation the trade unions controlled by the SLFP and Communist Party would remain loyal to the government. In the event severe inflationary pressures and falling living standards led the rank and file of the pro-government trade unions to join the strike. Their sense of grievance was aggravated by the stern measures taken by the government to bring the situation under control. Although the immediate effect of the government's action which included the jailing of some of the strikers, led to an escalation of the strikes, eventually the strikers returned to work. Nevertheless, the government paid a stiff political price for its victory over the strikers. Its tactics alienated a section of its own MPs in the left wing of the party and the Communist Party as well. The Opposition, sensing the prospect of precipitating the fall of the government through defections from its ranks, laid down a vote of 'no confidence' on the government's handling of the strike situation. The debate was fixed for 19 February, but a week before this date parliament was prorogued till 19 May, only three days before 22 May when it was scheduled to be dissolved prior to the holding of the general election. This surprising move did not prevent defections from the ranks of the government to the Opposition. These came thick and fast: first five left wing SLFP MPs, followed by a SLFP cabinet minister and then, more important, the Communist Party MPs under strong pressure from the rank and file of the party. By the end of February the UF coalition was over and there was instead a SLFP government, discredited, dispirited and soon to face the general election which many members of the government had sought so desperately to avoid.

A Change of Regime, 1977–94

When the Sri Lankan electorate is in one of its not very infrequent moods of disenchantment with the regime in power it gives vent to its displeasure with an exuberance and vehemence which all but obliterates the governing party—in terms of parliamentary seats. No defeat in the annals of the island's volatile parliamentary history has been quite as comprehensive as that suffered by the rivals of the UNP in July 1977.[1] The SLFP was reduced to a rump of eight seats (it had 90 in the previous Parliament), while every candidate of the Marxist left was defeated. The UNP won 140 out of 168 seats securing absolute majorities in 126 of these; and for the first time the winning party at a Sri Lankan general election obtained a clear majority of the popular vote. The TULF won 18 seats.

This general election marked the compulsory retirement from parliamentary politics of several dominant figures in Sri Lanka's political elite whose careers had spanned the last years of British rule and the three decades since independence. All left-wing parliamentarians of that generation were rejected by the electorate, many of them quite decisively, while all the prominent politicians who had been swept to power in the victories of the Bandaranaikes in 1956 and 1960 lost their seats, with the exception of Mrs Bandaranaike herself and her deputy. The latter retained his seat by the narrowest of margins. It was as though some massive collective will was at work, sitting in judgement over those who had set the pace in politics since 1956, finding them wanting and sternly dismissing them. The election result could be, and was also, viewed as a decisive rejection of the undemocratic excesses of Mrs Bandaranaike's regimes.

Jayewardene who was seventy-one when he won the elections of 1977, and had twice rebuilt the UNP from the ashes of defeat, once in 1956 and again after he took control of the party in 1973, appeared to be wearing the mantle of victory right through the last months of Mrs Bandaranaike's UF regime, particularly throughout the election campaign.

J.R. Jayewardene

The island's electoral system was such that when a major shift of political power occurred through the ballot, a new regime was returned to power with a far higher proportion of seats in the legislature than was warranted by the popular vote it received. Since 1959–60 the distortions of the electoral system had worked to the disadvantage of the UNP, but in 1977 the SLFP found itself with a mere 4.8 per cent of the seats though it obtained 29 per cent of the vote.

More extraordinary still, the TULF emerged as the main parliamentary opposition to the UNP. As a result of the peculiar demographic profile of the island, with a concentration of Tamils in the north and, to a smaller extent, in the east of the island, the TULF with about one-fifth of the popular vote secured by the SLFP had more than double the number of seats, namely 18 as against eight for the SLFP. For the first time since independence a Tamil became leader of the Opposition.

This distortion of the electoral process would by itself have given an unusually sharp focus to minority rights over the life of the new parliament, but the minds of politicians and the intelligentsia alike became concentrated on these issues much earlier and more urgently than would normally have happened when a minor incident in Jaffna town—a clash between the police and a section of the people there—precipitated a ferocious outbreak of communal violence between the Sinhalese and Tamils in mid-August 1977 on a scale comparable with the riots of the mid-1950s. These incidents were the direct result of causes whose roots lay in the atmosphere of communal mistrust stemming from the political attitudes and policies of the SLFP-dominated UF regime. The new government stopped the conflagration with a mixture of firmness and restraint, and more significantly, without resort to emergency rule. At the height of the disturbances it announced that a commission of inquiry would be appointed to examine the circumstances that had led to that outbreak of violence. A former chief justice was subsequently appointed as a one-man commission. On a more practical basis, a series of administrative measures were taken to meet some of the long-standing grievances of the Tamils.[2]

If these ethnic conflicts deflected the government's attention from more pressing issues, they did not do so for very long. High among its priorities was a fresh and searching look at Sri Lanka's constitutional framework. The far-reaching constitutional changes envisaged had been incorporated in the UNP's election manifesto and had been a major point of controversy in the election campaign. The UNP treated its decisive victory at the polls as an unmistakably positive endorsement of its proposals for a major overhaul of the constitutional structure. The first steps in implementing these changes came in August–September 1977 in the appointment of a parliamentary select committee on constitutional reform and the adoption by the National State Assembly of a constitutional amendment establishing a presidential system of government. Under the terms of this amendment the prime minister, J.R. Jayewardene, assumed office as the first elected executive president of the country on 4 February 1978.[3]

The government, in fact, deliberately set out to introduce a new tone in political life, altogether quieter and more relaxed, and with more respect than was shown by Mrs Bandaranaike's regime for the delicate and intricate balance of forces which has ensured the survival of democracy in Sri Lanka. In October 1977, the Criminal Justice Commissions Law, perhaps the most controversial piece of legislation introduced by the UF government, which in its working had led to gross abuse of human rights and the harassment of political opponents of the government, was repealed.[4] The most notable beneficiary of this decision was Rohana Wijeweera, the leader of the JVP, who had been jailed since early 1971 for his role in the insurrection of that year and was now released. Early in 1978 came a far-reaching amendment of the Public Security Act. This amendment ensured that, contrary to recent practice, the imposition of emergency rule would be debated and voted upon by the national legislature, the National State Assembly, on the first available occasion, while the extension of emergency rule beyond a period of ninety days in the aggregate would require a special majority of two-thirds of the membership of the house.[5]

The new constitution, which came into effect on 7 September 1978, was a blend of some of the functional aspects of Sri Lanka's previous constitutions and features of the American, French and British systems of government—a presidential system designed to meet Sri Lanka's own special requirements in the light of past experience in the working of previous constitutions. An underlying theme was the rejection of many of the authoritarian features of the constitution of 1972: by imposing more effective restraints on the powers of the executive and the state, by sustaining the rule of law and by strengthening the independence of the judiciary, the rights of the individual as against the state and—most significant in the context of the current crisis in relations between the Sinhalese and Tamils—the rights of the minorities. Among other important innovations was the introduction of proportional representation on the list system, in place of the 'first-past-the-post' principle of representation based on the British model.

The concessions made to the Tamil minority regarding the status of their language in the Sri Lanka polity were a fulfilment of a pledge given in the government's first statement of policy in the National State Assembly on 4 August 1977, well before the outbreak of the communal disturbances later in that month. Two articles in the new constitution set the tone. Article 19 declared that Sinhala and Tamil shall be the national languages of Sri Lanka (with Sinhala remaining the sole official language), a major departure from the established language policy since the mid-1950s. Equally important, Article 26 abolished the distinction between citizens by descent and citizens by registration—an irritant to the Indian Tamils—and this removed the stigma of second-class citizenship attaching to the latter. Combined with the elimination, in December 1977, of the bar, in force since the 1930s, on plantation workers resident on estates voting in local government elections, this ensured that persons of recent Indian origin were treated on a par with Sri Lankan citizens by descent. The position of Indians resident in Sri Lanka was further improved by affording to 'stateless' persons the same civil rights as are guaranteed by the constitution to citizens of the country. No previous constitution, not even that of 1947, offered the minorities a more secure position within the Sri Lanka polity than does the present one.

The Indian Tamils responded more positively to these conciliatory gestures than the TULF. When S. Thondaman—leader of the Ceylon Workers' Congress, the main political party-cum-trade union of the Indian plantation workers—entered the cabinet with the introduction of the new constitution in September 1978, it marked a major breakthrough in Sri

Lanka's politics, for it brought the Indian Tamils within Sri Lanka's 'political nation' for the first time since the 1930s. The TULF, now very much a party of the indigenous Tamils, ostentatiously dissociated itself from the processes of constitution-making in its anxiety to underline a commitment to Eelam, a separate state for the Tamils. They appeared to lack the political strength for the bold initiatives which a policy of reconciliation called for. Above all, they seemed to be all too conscious of the challenge from a youth wing of the party and especially violent extremist groups who were the most committed adherents of separatism. Thus for the second time since the 1930s the pacesetters in Tamil politics were youth groups.

Jayewardene's government inherited a stagnant economy and one in which, with the nationalization of the plantations, the state sector was in a position of overwhelming dominance. Unemployment was high and the country was affected by severe inflation. The first budget of the new government, introduced on 15 November 1977, announced the principal theme of the government's economic policy—the establishment of a free economy after two decades of controls and restrictions. The second and third budgets in November 1978 and November 1979 were consistent with the first. Together they marked a purposeful bid to move sharply away from the conventional budgetary wisdom of the last twenty years. A free economy has remained part of Sri Lanka's political system ever since, despite a change of leadership in the UNP in 1989–90, when Jayewardene's second term as president came to an end and the victory of an SLFP-led coalition in 1994.

In 1976, during the last phase of Mrs Bandaranaike's regime, tea and rubber prices had registered their first substantial improvement in the world market since the mid-1950s. This continued throughout most of 1977 and, even though tea prices declined somewhat in 1978 and 1979, they were still well above those of the early 1970s. Rubber prices, on the other hand, continued to rise steadily. In 1977, Sri Lanka enjoyed a favourable balance of trade for the first time in about fifteen years and the country's foreign exchange reserve was at its highest level since the days of the Korean War boom. The remarkable transformation in the position of the foreign exchange reserve was sustained over 1978-79, even though the balance of trade had returned to its pre-1977 pattern of being an adverse one. The country's economy was growing much faster (an 8 per cent increase in the GNP in 1978, 6 per cent in 1979 and 5.5 per cent in 1980) than for a decade past.

Although the government's adherence to a mixed economy remained firm, its economic strategy was also avowedly designed to breathe new life into private enterprise. This strategy bore fruit in an expansion of both economic activity and employment opportunities in the private sector. The government's initiative in establishing an industrial processing zone in an area of approximately 518 sq. km to the north of the city of Colombo designed to attract industries manufacturing for export was one of the key features of the new economic policy.

There was no strong urge to reverse the process of state control over large areas of the economy—not indeed because it could not be done but because, especially with regard to the plantations, it was perceived as something for which there is no compelling need. Both productivity and managerial efficiency in the plantations had declined with nationalization, but while the government treated the rehabilitation of the plantations as a matter of the highest priority, the results of its efforts in this regard were, in the initial stages, decidedly meagre. In other areas of the state sector, a change of management and new managerial techniques did result in a marked improvement in productivity. In some of the large state-owned textile mills management was handed over to private-sector firms, and this experiment—the private sector acting as a leaven to reinvigorate the proverbially sluggish and inefficient public sector of the economy—was seen to hold out hope of success.

In regard to unemployment, however, it was to the resuscitation of traditional agriculture and the revitalizing of industry in that order that the government looked for effective solutions. One invaluable result of the economic and political bankruptcy of the early 1970s was the new respectability conferred on traditional agriculture. At that time a realism born of desperation triumphed over ideological preconceptions and sterile rhetoric, which had long relegated agriculture to the status of a poor relation of industry. Support for traditional agriculture was thus no longer a matter of controversy. In the agricultural policy of the new government there was an obvious continuity with that of the previous UNP government of 1965–70 and nowhere more than in the pride of place given in this sphere of activity to the development of the irrigation and power resources of the Mahaveli Basin.

The gigantic Mahaveli Project was by far the largest and most intricate irrigation enterprise attempted in the island's history—the most complex irrigation project since the days of the Polonnaruva kings. The government sought to force the pace of development by accelerating the completion of some of the key projects of this scheme in five to six years instead of twenty as originally envisaged and J.R. Jayewardene succeeded in doing so.

By their very nature these initiatives in industry and irrigation would bring results only on a long-term basis. On the other hand, the removal of import controls on most items of consumption and some capital goods which the government introduced with its first budget in November 1977 had immediate benefits. Its impact on unemployment has been referred to earlier in this chapter. There were other beneficial consequences as well. It has served to dispel the air of austerity, to eliminate scarcities of food and other consumer goods and the queues that were endemic over the two decades of the 1950s and 1960s in Sri Lanka. In addition, this change, as remarkable as it was unexpected before November 1977, had mitigated considerably the effects of rising prices which were the inevitable consequence of a devaluation of the Sri Lanka rupee in November 1977, the escalation of oil prices which came in 1978–79 and the inflationary impact of the government's development programmes in industry, housing and irrigation. Bumper paddy harvests in 1977–78, 1978–79, and 1979–80 also helped to keep the prices of locally grown food items relatively low. These favourable economic conditions largely explained the government's success in the

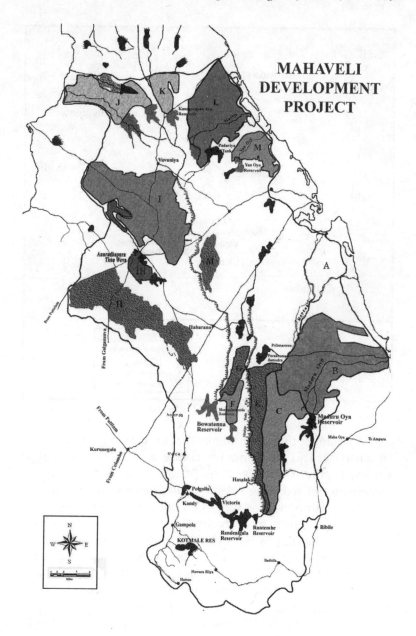

MAHAVELI
DEVELOPMENT
PROJECT

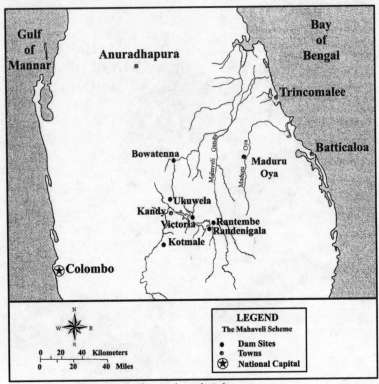

The Mahaveli Scheme

management of the 'political market', in retaining the initiative in politics and keeping its rivals at bay despite high unemployment and severe inflation and a policy of systematically reducing subsidies on food and other essential items of consumption, as well as on public transport.

In the elections to municipalities and urban councils in mid-May 1979 (the first to be held since 1969–70) the government won as decisive a victory as it had achieved in the general elections of July 1977. The SLFP came a very poor second while the 'old' left were routed once again. Only the TULF and, to a lesser extent, the 'new' left had cause for satisfaction.

By the middle of 1979 the activities of an extremist youth group among the Tamils of the north brought the country to the brink of another round of communal violence which was averted by the same blend of firmness and conciliation used in quelling the race riots of August 1977. Special legislation modelled on the British Prevention of Terrorism Act was rushed through parliament, a state of emergency was declared in the north of the island with a military commander to coordinate security arrangements and to stamp out terrorism there. These measures had the desired effect of restoring law and order and in paving the way for political initiatives designed to restore communal harmony on the island. The most notable of these conciliatory political initiatives was the appointment of a ten-member Presidential Commission to report on the decentralization of administration through district development councils. The commission completed its work in mid-February 1980 by which time the state of emergency imposed in the north of the island had been lifted. In August 1980, legislation based on the commission's report was approved by parliament thus paving the way for the establishment of development councils as a measure of democratic decentralization, which were expected to help blunt the edges of separatist aspirations among the Tamils and give the restive Jaffna Peninsula a durable peace.

The government benefited substantially from the continuing and total disarray of its opponents. The decline of the 'old' left was a notable factor in Sri Lanka's political scene. The 'new' left with the factionalized JVP in the vanguard was as hostile to the traditional left and the SLFP as it was to the government. It was thus vocal and vigorous but politically ineffective as an anti-government force. Its dismal electoral performance, both at the parliamentary and local government levels, seemed to indicate that the SLFP was not yet in a position to mount a serious political challenge to the government. With Mrs Bandaranaike's expulsion from Parliament on 16 October 1980 after a Presidential Commission of Enquiry had found her guilty of 'abuse of power', the party faced a long and debilitating leadership struggle in which Mrs Bandaranaike skilfully retained her power as the effective leader of the party. In this situation the government had much greater room for manoeuvre to deal with economic problems such as severe inflation and high unemployment than it would have had if it had confronted a cohesive opposition under a leadership with a reputation untarnished by association with the events of the early and mid-1970s.

Had economic growth provided more jobs, the growing unrest among Tamil youths may not have made separatist groups so attractive to them and they may not have turned so readily to violence. Among the Sinhalese the ultra-left and ardently nationalist JVP may not have become the deadly threat to state and society they turned out to be, first in 1971, and then again in the years from 1986 to 1989.[6] It was the JVP that led the first attempts at a violent overthrow of the government which they did in 1971. Although the attempt was a dismal failure, the example they set won them imitators among the radicalized youth in the Tamil separatist parties in later years, including most notably the Liberation Tigers of Tamil Eelam (LTTE), when they began their campaign of violence.

Sri Lanka's rural areas are free of the grim poverty seen in many parts of South Asia, and caste oppression seen in many parts of India. Agrarian reform has been more of a success in Sri Lanka than in other parts of south Asia. Yet, the Sri Lankan countryside has spawned the JVP and LTTE, two of the most ferocious radical movements in any part of the world in recent times.

ETHNIC CONFLICT

Our main concern in this part of the present chapter is with Sri Lanka's ethnic conflict, not with the JVP. With regard to the country's ethnic conflict a decisively important fact in the late 1960s and early 1970s needs special emphasis:the conversion of many political groups in the north of the country to the advocacy of separatism. The leadership in this came first from the Federal Party which, in a deliberate attempt to bring the rival Tamil parties together, converted itself to the core of the Tamil United Front (TUF), and later the Tamil United Liberation Front (TULF) to give the separatist cause a powerful political institution. By the late 1970s, however, the

TULF's dominance in the politics of the Tamil areas in the north of the country had become more apparent than real. As with similar movements in other parts of the world the 'moderates' cultivated radicalized youths, who were treated as foot soldiers in their separatist campaigns. In just over five years, these roles were being reversed with the foot soldiers now setting the pace and controlling the agenda of the separatist movement and driving their mentors, the TULF, to exasperation and, by 1986–87, to a more restricted role in Tamil politics than in the mid-1970s— not exactly as foot soldiers but something close to that. A similar life cycle in the leadership of separatist movements could be observed in many parts of the world and in India as well.

The general election of 1977 was a major landmark in the country's history, not merely because of the UNPs overwhelming victory in the Sinhalese areas of the country but also because of the equally emphatic victory in the Tamil areas in the north of the island for the TULF,[7] a victory that celebrated Tamil separatist aspirations. Efforts of the UNP government to reverse many of the policies associated with the SLFP did result in a period of quiescence in relations between the two main ethnic groups. In the late 1970s and up to 1983 significant changes were made in language policy: the controversial university admissions policy of the previous SLFP-dominated government was modified to make it more equitable for the Sri Lankan Tamil minority; above all, a second tier of government between the Centre and local government bodies was introduced in 1980, something previous governments had been unable or unwilling to do, a policy initiative which came fifty-two years after such a scheme of devolution had first been mooted and one which Tamil groups had insisted on since the mid-1950s. The economic policies of the 1960s and early 1970s were abandoned and a more liberal policy adopted in its place. This led to an immediate revival and rapid expansion of the economy.

But it became clear very soon, that the response to these changes from the Tamils was determined more by the radical activists than the moderate leadership of the parliamentary party, the TULF. The latter were being rapidly overtaken by separatist groups bent on violence against the state. The state responded to this with violence of its own. These confrontations became more frequent and increasingly more violent. Youth groups soon saw themselves and persuaded others to regard them as more committed and credible adherents of the separatist cause than the TULF. The latter's presence in parliament—indeed, the fact that its leader was leader of the Opposition—placed them in a position of great ambivalence, balancing the need to adhere to the norms and practices of parliamentary life while in the legislature, with the compulsion of recognizing the pressures of political change in the electorates in order to retain their continuing commitment to the separatist cause. By the early 1980s, the separatist cause had been taken over by youth groups belonging to various small and bickering political parties.[8] In time that bickering became explosively destructive and internecine conflicts among separatist groups became one of the principal features of politics in the Jaffna Peninsula. These conflicts persisted despite a common opposition to the state's security forces stationed in the Jaffna Peninsula. One such attack by the LTTE, a relatively minor one in retrospect, triggered the most ferocious episode of ethnic violence in Sri Lanka's recent history, the anti-Tamil riots of July 1983.

The Indian mediation/intervention which is dealt with in later pages of this chapter had a profoundly disturbing effect on Sri Lankan politics during Jayewardene's second term as president. One aspect of this was the second JVP insurrection (1987–89).

Acts of commission on the part of Jayewardene himself contributed to the problems of this period. One of these was undoubtedly his decision to substitute a referendum for a general election to parliament in 1982. This gave him a continuation of the massive five-sixths majority he had in parliament since 1977. But there was no mistaking the fact that while the referendum was constitutional, it was no genuine substitute for an election to parliament.

Despite all the disturbing features of the politics of the 1980s, the national economy still reflected some of the buoyancy seen in Jayewardene's first term as president. All the headworks of the Mahaveli irrigation system were completed during his second term as president. This would have been a substantial achievement even in the less disturbed times. It became much more substantial in the context of a very disturbed decade.

During Jayewardene's first term as president there were signs of a change in the structure of the economy which has continued to the present day. In 1977, at the time Jayewardene came to power, the traditional sources of foreign exchange for Sri Lanka—dominated by plantation products—were as much as 81.3 per cent of local exports. By 1996, this had decreased to 23.5 per cent. Non-traditional exports had increased from 18.7 per cent to 76.5 per cent. Textiles and garments accounted for 63.2 per cent of industrial exports.[9]

It is largely because of this transformation of the economy that the Jayewardene regime could finance heavy defence expenditure and the completion of the Mahaveli head works without too much of a strain.

In his last years in office, Jayewardene piloted the legislation required for the establishment of provincial councils through parliament. The elections to these councils were held during his presidency.

In 1989, he presided over the transfer of power to R. Premadasa, the new head of the UNP. The latter won the presidential election of 1989 defeating Mrs Bandaranaike. Under Premadasa the UNP won a comfortable victory to parliament, in the first general election under proportional representation.

INDIAN CONCERN, INDIAN INTERVENTION
AND MEDIATION

With the anti-Tamil riots and disturbances of 1983 a qualitative change transformed Sri Lanka's ethnic conflict, from a relatively low-intensity one to an increasingly violent one and from being a generally localized business to a conflict with regional ramifications. There was a more emphatic radicalization of politics in the Tamil areas in the north of the country. While the TULF remained in the political arena, the principal actors were the radicalized political groups and factions whose

Ranasinghe Premadasa

demands were expressed with an intensity and urgency that the TULF could not show. These militant or activist separatist groups sought to enter the political bargaining process on their own as the authentic representatives of Tamil opinion and were eventually accommodated in that process under Indian auspices in the mid-1980s. However, the most important factor, by far, in the transformation of the conflict was the unilateral intrusion of a regional actor, India, into the politics of Sri Lanka. India sought to manipulate if not dominate, the processes of negotiation, as a mediator, over the next seven years from 1983, with its own political objectives in these negotiations.[10] This botched intervention had incalculable adverse consequences for Sri Lanka and the governments of the country have had to struggle since 1990 to deal with them.

India's interest in the problems of Sri Lanka's Tamil minority—the Sri Lankan Tamils—emerged and grew in the 1970s and 1980s with India reaching into her neighbourhood in the role of regional hegemon, especially after her dramatically successful intervention in the separatist campaign in what is now Bangladesh.[11] The separatist agitation in Bangladesh had a profound influence on the thinking of Tamil separatist groups in Sri Lanka in terms of their political objectives as well as the process through which it could be achieved.

India had three roles in Sri Lanka's ethnic conflict. The first, which was intensified with Mrs Gandhi's return to power in 1980, was that of a covert supporter of Tamil separatism; several groups of separatists were operating in Tamil Nadu. This covert support continued until 1987. The second, the Tamil Nadu factor, forms an important aspect of India's role in Sri Lanka's affairs. The third of India's roles, that of mediator, began under Mrs Gandhi as a calculated political response to the anti-Tamil riots of July 1983 and continued under her son and successor, Rajiv Gandhi. A version of that third role, that of active participant, began late in 1987 and continued to the middle of 1990 by which time J.R. Jayewardene had given up the presidency.

The Indian intervention of 1983 was an exercise in realpolitik. Despite the fact that similar violent ethnic conflicts were a familiar feature in many parts of India at that time, in Punjab, for instance, and particularly in India's north-east, India sought to intervene in Sri Lanka's ethnic conflict invoking the political strengths of a regional hegemon. During the years of the Indian intervention/mediation, the Indian governments sought, desperately, to prop up the TULF as the principal spokespersons for the Sri Lankan Tamils, although most of their leadership who lived in Tamil Nadu—after 1983—no longer retained the support of the electorates they once dominated. The struggle for the control of these electorates was being conducted by the more radical and more violent separatist groups. The eventual winners of this conflict were the LTTE who had clearly established their position of primacy among them by 1986.

Through a ruthless resort to force, the LTTE killed virtually all their rivals to leadership among such groups, and had reduced its mentor, the TULF, to a merely marginal role in Tamil politics in Sri Lanka. From 1986 onwards, the LTTE was a powerful influence on negotiating processes in regard to Sri Lanka, even if the Indian government preferred to sustain the TULF in an unrealistic leadership role.

Throughout the period 1983–90, India never abandoned her role of being a principal in the dispute, as the presumed protector of the interests of the Tamil minorities on the island. The result was that India was at once a negotiator and an advocate. After the signing of the Indo-Sri Lanka Accord of 1987, the mediator found itself in the role of an active participant and continued in that role to the middle of 1990, during which it fought the LTTE in the north-east of Sri Lanka, a unique example in the history of mediation in ethnic conflict where the mediator took on the role of combatant and the presumed guardian of an ethnic minority waged an eventually unsuccessful military campaign against the principal political group of that minority and its military wing which India and Tamil Nadu had helped to build. Attempts at management and settlement went awry, in an unpredicted and unpredictable succession of blunders.

India had other roles as well, one of which was in internationalizing the conflict through the use of her diplomatic missions in the more important capital cities of the Western world and in initiating or lending support to moves at the United Nations and in subcommittees of the United Nations to espouse the cause of Sri Lanka's Tamils. There was, above all, the Tamil Nadu factor. Seldom has a constituent unit (a province or a state) of one country influenced the relationship between it and a neighboring country with the same intensity and persistence and to the same extent that Tamil Nadu did in the case of India's relations with Sri Lanka in the 1970s and 1980s. The India–Tamil Nadu–Sri Lanka relationship was thus a unique one in international affairs. Admittedly, the Indian Central government's own role in regard to the Tamil problem in Sri Lanka, from the 1980s to the present day, is more complex than merely reacting to the pressures of domestic politics in Tamil Nadu. Nevertheless, concerns about the latter have always been an important consideration. The state governments in Tamil Nadu have provided Sri Lankan Tamil separatist activists with overt support by way of sanctuaries, training and bases. These were apart from financial support, moral support and political pressure on behalf of Tamil separatists in Sri Lanka, within the national political system in India. Not only did the Central government—under Indira Gandhi and her son and successor Rajiv Gandhi—connive in the provision of such facilities by Tamil Nadu, it also tolerated the provision of training facilities and the existence of camps and bases in other parts of the country. This began with Indira Gandhi in the early 1980s, that is to say, well before the riots of July 1983 in Sri Lanka. The extent of that support dropped sharply in the late 1980s when the Indian army moved to the Tamil areas in the north and east of Sri Lanka during 1987–90 under the terms of the Indo-Sri Lanka Accord of 1987, but so far as Tamil Nadu was concerned it did not disappear entirely.

In the mid-1980s, the Sri Lankan government resorted to a two-pronged policy in dealing with the threat posed by the Tamil separatist activists. A military response was often accompanied by political negotiations, while the priority given to one or the other of these depended on the success achieved or the political pressures exerted by and from India. Throughout the period 1984 to 1986, negotiations for a political settlement continued sporadically against the background of regular outbursts of ethnic violence, especially in the north and east of the island, and conflicts between the security forces and Tamil guerrillas and terrorist groups.

Just prior to the eventual signing of an accord in Colombo in July 1987 by the president of Sri Lanka and the Indian prime minister, there was a brief period of a few months during which the two governments were at loggerheads when the Sri Lankan government attempted to re-establish control over the Jaffna Peninsula. The Sri Lankan army inflicted a number of defeats on the LTTE and had them on the run. At this stage the Indian government threatened direct intervention, that is, an invasion, in the event the Sri Lankan forces attempted to enter Jaffna, the administrative capital of the Northern Province. This threat sufficed to save the LTTE from an emphatic defeat at the hands of the Sri Lankan army, but restraint on the part of Sri Lanka did not prevent Indian intervention, shortly afterwards, in the form of a deliberate violation of Sri Lankan air space by Indian military aircraft which engaged in dropping food in Jaffna town and its neighbourhood in an unmistakable demonstration of India's sympathy for Sri Lanka's Tamil minority.

The Indo-Sri Lanka accord of July 1987 was signed in Colombo by President Jayewardene and Prime Minister Rajiv Gandhi. This, the most prominent of the diplomatic occasions in Indo-Sri Lankan relations after the Indian intervention in 1983, soon lost much of its aura when it began to look so much like the other well-publicized accords negotiated by Rajiv Gandhi in Punjab and Assam, both of which failed in nearly all their objectives. The Indo-Sri Lanka Accord did not fare better as was evident in the consequences that flowed from it, both immediately and on a relatively long-term basis: the failure to pacify the Tamil areas in the north of the island, stretched over two years or more; a more immediate flaw was that it precipitated a serious political crisis in the Sinhalese areas of the country. The signing of the accord led to violent protests, in and around Colombo and parts of the south-west coast, riots that were among the most serious episodes of anti-government violence seen since independence. The government forces took three days to a week to quell the riots and they were able to do so only because of the rapid transport by air (by the Indian air force) of several thousand Sri Lankan troops from Jaffna. Rajiv Gandhi himself narrowly escaped serious injury, if not death itself, at a guard of honour prior to his departure from the island. He had come to Colombo for the signing of the accord. Although the Indian Peace Keeping Force (IPKF) was never seen outside the north and east of the island (save perhaps in the North-central Province on its way to the east coast) its shadow lay across the country's political landscape. Its presence in the country was exploited, politically, against the government by a combination of the SLFP and the now revived JVP but most of all by the JVP, for whom opposition to the IPKF became the catalyst for violent political agitation and sporadic but calculated acts of violence in the Sinhalese areas of the country.[12]

With the signing of the Indo-Sri Lanka accord on 29 July 1987, the IPKF arrived on the island. They came, in the earliest phase, as peacekeepers but soon became combatants, against the LTTE forces and their allies, when the latter sought to resist the IPKF and actually engaged in violent confrontations against it. These confrontations saw the IPKF growing from a small peacekeeping force of 5,000–7,000 men which it was initially, into an Indian army of around 1,00,000 men, almost as large as the Soviet army then in Afghanistan and bigger than the British content of the Indian army of the Raj in its heyday in the late nineteenth century and early twentieth century. The Indian army had intervened in the Bangladeshi independence struggle in the late 1960s and early 1970s to secure the success of separatism; it initially intervened in Sri Lanka in 1987 to prevent the Sri Lankan armed forces from inflicting a decisive defeat on the Tamil separatists, principally the LTTE, and regaining control of the disaffected areas in the north and east of the island, at a time when the LTTE itself had suffered a number of defeats and were fleeing in disorder. Having secured the immediate objective of thwarting the Sri Lankan forces, the IPKF then found itself fighting the LTTE for a little over two years as part of the Indian government's own political agenda of opposition to the establishment of a separate Tamil state, for fear of its ripple effects on India itself, then engaged in struggles against separatist movements in Kashmir, Punjab and the north-east. Over a period of two years the IPKF drove the LTTE out of Jaffna and the Jaffna Peninsula but did not achieve its objective of weakening the LTTE to the point of making it more receptive and subservient to India's regional strategic objectives.

New Delhi's eight-year involvement thus provides a classic study of the flawed performance of a regional power seeking to manage and exploit ethnic conflict in a neighboring state to its own advantage; the principal flaw, and here the Indian intervention was unique in the history of external interventions by regional superpowers in ethnic conflicts in small states, was the external mediator's unintended transformation into a combatant. It entered the dispute with the avowed objective of protecting the interests of Sri Lanka's Tamil minority, but the Indian army soon began fighting the LTTE, the principal representatives of Tamil separatism, on Sri Lankan soil in the north and east of the island. Coercive intervention, with its ambiguous and eventually contradictory objectives, failed in almost all of its aims. Far from resolving the island's ethnic conflict, the failure of the Indian enterprise greatly aggravated it and Sri Lankan governments of the future have had to cope with the consequences of this. As a result of its two-year conflict with the LTTE, the Indian intervention elevated that organization to an unquestioned leadership role among the Tamil separatist forces.

J.R. Jayewardene's government was called upon to pay a heavy price in the erosion of its bases of support in the country. He had arrived in power in 1977 on a massive wave of popularity. He had lost much of this latter at the time he left office in 1989.[13] India's intervention in Sri Lanka's ethnic conflict was the cause of much of this change in his fortunes.

Epilogue: 1994 and After

THE BANDARANAIKES IN POWER: THE SECOND PHASE

Seventeen years after the decisive electoral defeat they suffered in 1977, the Bandaranaikes returned to power in 1994 under Chandrika Kumaratunga, the second daughter of S.W.R.D. and Sirimavo Bandaranaike. Given all the turmoil in the country in the 1980s, and particularly after the Indian intervention, it was inevitable that the electoral pendulum would swing against the UNP in the 1990s. As it was, the swing was not significant enough for Mrs Bandaranaike to make a comeback in 1989. Five years later she was in poor health and unable, therefore, to make a bid for power. But she had skilfully kept the SLFP under her control. This enabled her to oversee another spell of power for the family although her daughter Chandrika had left the SLFP some years before she came to power in 1994.

Two factors helped to swing the pendulum in her favour; one had to do with President Premadasa's failures as a political manager and the other had to do with the LTTE. While Premadasa had consolidated his power in 1989–90, his failures in the mechanics of party management saw a split in the UNP in 1991. This was seen in an attempt by two very able politicians to move a motion of impeachment on him. They were L. Athulathmudali[1] and G. Dissanayake. While the impeachment attempt failed, the expulsion of Athulathmudali and Dissanayake from the party along with about a dozen parliamentarians marked a new stage in the eventual weakening of the UNP's hold on the electorate.

At this stage, the LTTE entered the picture by organizing the assassination of some key UNP politicians, beginning with Ranjan Wijeratne, foreign minister and deputy minister of defence in March 1991. Wijeratne was also secretary of the

Chandrika Kumaratunga Bandaranaike

UNP and a potential successor to Premadasa. L. Athulathmudali was assassinated in April 1993 and Premadasa himself on 1 May 1993. G. Dissanayake, one of the principal figures in negotiating the Indo-Sri Lanka Accord was killed in October 1994. He was the UNP's presidential candidate at that time. His assassination, a week or so before the election, left the UNP demoralized. The party organization for the election virtually collapsed. It paved the way for Chandrika Kumaratunga to secure a facile victory at that presidential election.

NEGOTIATIONS

India's failed involvement left successive Sri Lankan governments, those of R. Premadasa and Chandrika Kumaratunga, to negotiate with a reinvigorated LTTE, and to resume a military struggle once the negotiations failed. The levels of violence and the intensity of the conflict were much higher than they were before the Indian intervention. The Sri Lankan situation provides insights into the difficulties faced by democratically elected governments in dealing with a separatist movement whose violent leadership has systematically marginalized its rivals and driven traditional democratic forces (among the Tamils) to the perimeter of the political system. This radicalization of Tamil separatism makes the search for a negotiated settlement[2] a much more difficult exercise than it was before the Indian intervention and before the LTTE established its dominance in Tamil politics in Sri Lanka, that is, before 1985–86.[3] Such is the troubled inheritance of the Norwegian government now (2003–04) 'facilitating' a new phase of negotiations in the Sri Lankan conflict, an exercise limited to bringing the two sides, recently in conflict, to the negotiating table.

Through much of the years 2000 and 2001, the Sri Lanka government was poised to resume talks with the LTTE[4] but the talks began only in 2002 after the election of the Ranil Wickremesinghe government of the UNP and continued into 2003 when the LTTE broke away from the talks. Even if the talks were to resume there is little room for optimism that there would be an easy, much less early, resolution of the conflict.

For the Sri Lanka political leadership, at the highest level, negotiations with the LTTE carry a lethal danger, the prospect of assassination. Three years after the failure of his talks with the LTTE, President R. Premadasa was assassinated in Colombo on 1 May 1993; just over five years after the failure of her talks with the LTTE, Chandrika Kumaratunga narrowly escaped death on 18 December 1999 in a botched LTTE assassination attempt which left her blind in one eye. No head of state/head of government negotiating a resolution of a deep-rooted conflict, in any part of the world, faces such personal dangers. All these were apart from the LTTE's assassination of Rajiv Gandhi in 1991.[5] The LTTE had stretched across to Tamil Nadu to accomplish this.

The Sri Lanka dispute in its current violent form has lasted for over twenty years. As we have seen in the previous chapter, one of the factors in the prolongation of the conflict has been the ill-fated Indian intervention. At the outset, India provided raw separatist cadres from Sri Lanka with arms and military training. Ironically, the LTTE who were not the special favourites of the Indians benefited most from this. Next, the Indians saved the LTTE in early 1987 from an overwhelming defeat at the hands of the Sri Lankan army. Then the LTTE gained additional experience and prestige in leading the Tamil resistance to the IPKF. Yet the IPKF had weakened the LTTE by the time it was recalled although not to the extent intended by the Indian government. Had the Premadasa government (1989–93) moved in to the Jaffna Peninsula to replace the IPKF in 1990 the LTTE could have resisted that move but did not have the capacity to prevent it. In the event the LTTE were permitted by the Sri Lankan government to replace the IPKF. Eventually, the LTTE's hold on Jaffna and the Jaffna Peninsula was broken by October 1995 by the Chandrika Kumaratunga government. But having driven the LTTE out of the Jaffna peninsula and on to the Mullaitivu area, the Sri Lankan forces let the LTTE off the hook through their attempt to take control of a route between Jaffna and rest of the Northern Province, through the middle of that territory, a strategic blunder which the LTTE exploited to its advantage in a long-drawn-out campaign of resistance.

Briefly then, despite the LTTE's undoubted proficiency as a guerrilla force, and indeed despite its sophistication as a guerrilla force with international links, its survival owes as much if not more to the follies of its opponents as to its own well-honed skills. There were at least three occasions or periods between 1987 and the present day, when the LTTE could have been decisively defeated. The Indian government saved them in 1987 from the Sri Lankan army; the Premadasa government saved them from the IPKF in its final phase when it seemed intent on delivering a coup de grâce; and the Kumaratunga government deprived itself of an excellent opportunity for a telling defeat of the LTTE in 1995.

After July 1987, negotiations have had little or no effect on the conflict till 2001. In early 1990, it was the LTTE which initiated moves for negotiations with the Premadasa government. Yet discussions took place over fourteen months without any progress at all on substantive issues, indeed without discussing such issues at all. In 1994–95, the initiatives came from the Kumaratunga government. [6] For the first time the talks were held in Jaffna itself. The search for practical measures to help solve some of the problems relating to the Tamils have been initiated by Sri Lankan governments, under Premadasa, and later under Kumaratunga. In 1993, a consensus was reached between the government (the UNP) and the principal opposition party (the SLFP) on constitutional and administrative measures for a settlement of the conflict. But the Tamil parties were reluctant to accept it. The LTTE showed no interest. Reaching a consensus between the government (the SLFP-led People's Alliance) and the principal opposition party (the UNP) proved to be more difficult in 2000, but even if such a consensus had been reached, the LTTE had shown no interest in anything other than a separate state despite all its talk, occasionally, of a federation or even a confederation. The moral of the story, so far as the Sri Lankan case is concerned, is that radicalization of Tamil politics makes the search for a negotiated settlement a much more difficult exercise than it was in the years before the LTTE established its dominance in Tamil politics in Sri Lanka.

CONTINUITY OF POLICIES

There were three points of continuity between the Kumaratunga government's policies and those of its predecessors. First, she followed her parents in organizing a left-of-centre coalition in 1994 to face the UNP. After she won power, she extended her left-of-centre coalition (the People's Alliance which was, in effect, a continuation of her mother's United Front) to a collation with the JVP in 2004. With this coalition's victory in the parliamentary election in April 2004 a new left-of-centre coalition with the JVP was established.

The second point of continuity, the attempts of negotiations with the LTTE, was with the UNP governments and Jayewardene and Premadasa.

Third, apart from attempts at negotiations with the LTTE there were other points of continuity in policies between Chandrika Kumaratunga and the UNP under Premadasa and Jayewardene. She repudiated many of the policies associated with her parents in the heyday of their political power and ascendancy in national politics—in language policy, the devolution of power—and finally, and no less decisively, there was a rejection of her parents' commitment to a recognition of the dominance of the Sri Lanka polity by the Sinhalese-Buddhist majority. And as though to cap it all, the daughter has cast aside her left-wing views on economic policy and enthusiastically adopted liberalization policies which she had once disdainfully dismissed, indeed excoriated, and has even begun to preach the virtues of privatization; she has kept on emphasizing the role of the private sector as the engine of economic growth.

Notes

CHAPTER 1

1. Deraniyagala, *The Pre-history of Sri Lanka*, Vol. I, p. 167.
2. Kulke and Rothermund, *A History of India*; Burton Stein, *A History of India.*
3. Weerakkody, *Taprobanê.*
4. On the geography of the island, see Peiris G.H., *Development and Change in Sri Lanka.*
5. The *Dīpavaṁsa* is a fourth-century work and the *Mahāvaṁsa* a sixth-century compilation. Some scholars believe it was a work of the fifth century. The *Cūlavaṁsa* is believed to have been written in the twelfth century. G.C. Mendis, 'Pali Chronicles of Ceylon', provides an excellent introductory survey. *See also*, S. Kiribamune, 'The Mahāvaṁsa' pp. 126–36.
6. The one exception is the *Rajatarangini* or The Kashmir Chronicle, composed in the twelfth century.
7. Two volumes published in 2001 and 2003 were the first to use these epigraphical sources in the writing of the history of Sri Lanka. These are Lakshman S. Perera, *The Institutions of Ancient Ceylon from Inscriptions* Vol. I (from the 3rd century to AD 830) and *The Institutions of Ancient Ceylon from Institutions*, Vol. II, Part I (from AD 831 to AD 1016). Volume II, Part II of this treatise is forthcoming in late 2005.
8. *See* particularly Deraniyagala, *The Pre-History of Sri Lanka.* This present brief survey of the island's prehistory is based primarily on Deraniyagala's two volumes and other essays by him. *See also* Senaratne, *Prehistoric Archaeology in Ceylon.*
9. *See* Seneviratne, 'The Ecology and Archeology of the Seruvila Copper-Magnetite Prospect', pp. 114–45.
10. On the Vijaya legend, *see* Basham, 'Prince Vijaya and the Aryanisation of Ceylon', pp. 172–91 and Mendis, 'Pali Chronicles', pp. 56–71.
11. *The Mahāvaṃsa*, Chapter VII verses 1–4, in Wilhelm Geiger, *The Mahāvaṁsa or the Great Chronicle of Sri Lanka*, p. 55.
12. There were several clans or families of the nobility in ancient Sri Lanka: the Lambakannas, Moriyas, Kalingas, Tarachchas, Balibhojakas and others. It is generally believed that these clan names had a totemistic origin—for instance, the emblem of the Moriyas was a peacock.
13. For a demolition of this myth as regards India, *see* Srinivas and Shah, 'The Myth of Self-sufficiency of the Indian Village,' pp. 1375–78.

14. *See* Deraniyagala, *The Pre-History of Sri Lanka*, Vol. II, pp. 739–50.
15. For a brief introduction to Buddhism, *see* Bhikkhu Rahula, *What the Buddha Taught*. *See also* Armstrong, *Buddha*. The Indian background to the emergence of Buddhism is reviewed in Thapar, *A History of India*, Chapter IV.
16. *See* Thapar, *A History of India*, pp. 85ff and *Asoka and the Decline of the Mauryas*.
17. *Ficus religioso*.
18. On the Pomparippu excavations and their significance *see* S. P. F. Senaratne, *Prehistoric Archaesology in Ceylon*; pp. 29–31; Indrapala, 'Early Tamil Settlements in Ceylon', pp. 15–33.
19. Since the Adichchanallur finds have been dated at around 300 BC, the same date is tentatively assigned to the Pomparippu complex which is regarded as being roughly contemporary with them.
20. Indrapala, 'Early Tamil Settlements in Ceylon', pp. 23ff; Kiribamune, 'Tamils in Ancient and Medieval Sri Lanka', pp. 9–23. *See also* P. Raghupathy, *Early Settlements in Jaffna*, pp. 179–87.
21. Indrapala, 'Early Tamil Settlements in Ceylon', p. 20.
22. This was made very clear by Lakshman S. Perera, in his chapter 'The Early Kings of Ceylon up to Mutasiva', pp. 98–111. *See also* Gunawardana's 'Prelude to the State', pp. 83–122.
23. As the titles of the early Sinhalese rulers, *gāmani* and *abhaya*, show, leadership in the country in the remote past was of a military character. The gāmani abhayas or 'warrior leaders' of early settlements known as *gama or janapada* later evolved into formal rulers who assumed pretentious titles such as raja or maharaja.
24. The central highlands.
25. There is less written on the southern kingdoms in the *Mahāvaṁsa* than should have been; indeed, it could be described as a blindspot of the author or authors of the *Mahāvaṁsa*. Recently attempts have been made to re-examine the role of Rohana in Sri Lanka's ancient history, using for the purpose the archaeological, literary and numismatic evidence now available. *See* particularly, Bopearachchi and Wickremesinhe, *Ruhuna*.
26. Deraniyagala, *The Pre-History of Sri Lanka*, Vol. II, pp. 712–50; Coningham and Allchin, 'The Rise of Cities in Sri Lanka', pp. 152–83.
27. On Mahatittha (Māntota), *see* Kiribamune, 'The Role of the Port City of Mahatittha (Māntota) in the Trade Networks of the Indian Ocean', pp. 435–54.

CHAPTER 2

1. For the history of the Anuradhapura kingdom, Nicholas and Paranavitana, *A Concise History of Ceylon*, is still a good source. The book is a study of ancient Sri Lanka. The authors' proclivity for fanciful theories in the later chapters of the book vitiates its usefulness. Fortunately, its chapters on the Anuradhapura kingdom are authoritative. Two earlier books, Codrington, *A Short History of Ceylon* and Mendis, *Early History of Ceylon*, can still be read with profit.
2. According to tradition, the Lambakannas had come to the island in the time of Devānampiya Tissa with the sacred bo-tree. The Tarachchas and Kaliṅgas, two less important clans, apparently came to the island at much the same time as the Lambakannas.

3. During much of this period, their rivals, the Moriyas, were on the retreat, quite often scattered over various parts of the island and occasionally—for instance, during the rule of Sabha (AD 120–27)—as refugees from Lambakanna persecution.
4. On the law of succession to the throne, or the lack of one, see Hettiarachchy, *History of Kingship in Ceylon*, pp. 172–74.
5. As early as the first century AD Illanāga (AD 33–43) had used south Indian mercenaries to capture the throne. The next such episode came two centuries later with Abhayanāga (231–40). The Moggallāna episode came two-and-a-half centuries later. See Kiribamune, 'Tamils in Ancient and Medieval Sri Lanka', p. 14.
6. Kiribamune, 'Tamils in Ancient and Medieval Sri Lanka,' pp. 14–15.
7. Ibid, pp. 14–15.
8. This theme is discussed in some detail in Perera, *The Institutions of Ancient Ceylon from Inscriptions*, Vol. I, pp. 34–44.
9. In the sixth century AD, a separate administrative division called Purathimadesa was created and placed directly in charge of the heir apparent. (This is evidence of the increasing economic importance of the Polonnaruva region.) But this administrative innovation appears to have been short-lived.
10. The smallest unit of administration was the gama or village which was under the authority of a gamika or village headman. There were also institutions of a more democratic character like the *niyamatana* which regulated the public life of the village.
11. On the Cōḷas see Nilakanta Sastri, *A History of South India from Prehistoric Times to the Fall of Vijayanagar*, and *The Cōḷas*; Spencer, *The Politics of Expansion*; Stein, *Peasant State and Society in Medieval South India*.
12. Spencer in his *The Politics of Expansion*, lays great emphasis on this point especially in regard to the Cōḷas and Sri Lanka.
13. Between the seventh and eighth centuries, four Sinhalese kings ruled from Polonnaruva in preference to Anuradhapura.
14. Kiribamune, 'Trade Patterns of the Indian Ocean', pp. 179–90.

CHAPTER 3

1. Murphey, 'The Ruin of Ancient Ceylon', p. 185.
2. Nicholas, 'A Short Account of the History of Irrigation Works', pp. 43–69. The reference to Vasabha is on p. 48.
3. Parker, *Ancient Ceylon*, p. 379. The bisokotuva, a square enclosure built of stone slabs, facilitated the control of the pressure and the quantity of the outflow of water when it was released from a reservoir or tank into the canals.
4. Ibid.
5. See Nicholas, 'A Short Account of the History of Irrigation Works'. See also Gunawardana, 'Irrigation and Hydraulic Society in Early Medieval Ceylon', pp. 3–27. The outstanding history of Sri Lanka's irrigation system, Brohier's *Ancient Irrigation Works in Ceylon*, discusses these works in great detail.
6. On this canal, see Brohier, *The History of Irrigation and Agricultural Colonisation in Ceylon*, pp. 6–8.

7.   The fact that the chronicles credit a king with the construction of certain public works does not necessarily imply that they were all begun and completed in his reign. The actual building operations would have lasted more than one reign or even one generation and utilized the labour of farmers during the slack season of the agricultural cycle. Instances are known of the chronicles giving a king credit for a project which he only initiated or completed.

8.   One of the themes neglected in the *Mahāvaṁsa* and *Cūlavaṁsa*, in the emphasis given to major irrigation works, is the contribution made by village tanks. It is only very recently that a serious study of village tanks has been made. *See* Panabokke, *The Small Tank Cascade Systems of the Rājarata*.

9.   Brohier, 'The Inter-relation of Groups of Ancient Reservoirs and Channels in Sri Lanka,' pp. 64–85. The quotation is from p. 70.

10.   Gunawardana, 'Irrigation and Hydraulic Society', p. 9.

11.   Brohier, 'The Inter-relation of Groups of Ancient Reservoirs and Channels in Sri Lanka'.

12.   *See* Chapter 2.

13.   Nicholas, 'A Short Account of the History of Irrigation Works', p. 57.

14.   Gunawardana, 'Total Power or Shared Power?', pp. 73–80.

15.   Nicholas, 'A Short Account of the History of Irrigation Works', p. 60.

16.   Murphey, 'The Ruin of Ancient Ceylon', p. 184.

17.   *See* Wittfogel, *Oriental Despotism*, pp. 569–611. Wittfogel was an unrepentant believer in the 'Asiatic Mode of Production' as propounded by Marx in the mid-nineteenth century.

18.   *See* Gunawardane, 'Irrigation and Hydraulic Society', and Leach, 'Hydraulic Society in Ceylon', pp. 2–26.

19.   An excellent index to the public perception of irrigation works among the literati of those times is the assessment of a king's contribution to public life in the *Māhavaṁsa* and *the Cūlavaṁsa* and the prominence given to irrigation in such assessments.

20.   *See* Panabokke, *The Small Tank Cascade Systems of the Rājarata*, for a discussion on this. *See also* Nicholas, 'A Short Account of the History of Irrigation Works', pp. 46–7.

CHAPTER 4

1.   Prickett, 'Sri Lanka's Foreign Trade Before AD 600'; Bopearachchi, 'Seafaring in the Indian Ocean', pp. 59–77.

2.   Kiribamune, 'The Role of the Port City of Mahatittha', pp. 435–54; 'Muslims and the Trade of the Arabian Sea', pp. 89–108; 'Trade Patterns of the Indian Ocean', pp. 67–78; Sirisena, 'Sri Lanka's Commercial Relations with the Outside World', pp. 12–21; 'Maritime Commerce', pp. 1–33.

3.   B.J. Perera, 'Foreign Trade and Commerce of Ancient Ceylon: The Ports of Ancient Ceylon', pp. 109–19; 'Foreign Trade and Commerce of Ancient Ceylon: Ancient Ceylon and Its Trade with India', pp. 192–204; 'Foreign Trade and Commerce of Ancient Ceylon: Ancient Ceylon's Trade with the Empires of the Eastern and Western Worlds', pp. 301–20.

4.   Chaudhuri, *Trade and Civilisation in the Indian Ocean*, is an excellent general study of the subject.

5. Bopearachchi and Wickremesinhe, *Ruhuna*, p. 42.
6. Weerakkody, *Taprobanê*, p. 1.
7. Bopearachchi and Wickremesinhe, *Ruhuna*, p. 42.
8. Ibid., Introduction, p. 7.
9. On south India's flourishing trade with Rome, see Kulke and Rothermund, *A History of India*, pp. 99–102.
10. Kiribamune, 'The Role of the Port City of Mahatittha' pp. 435–54.
11. See Kulke and Rothermund, *A History of India*, pp. 105–06, 146, 148 on the Pallavas.
12. Kiribamune, 'Trade Patterns of the Indian Ocean', p. 68. *See also* Sirisena, 'Maritime Commerce' pp. 1–33.
13. On the Palas, see Kulke and Rothermund, *A History of India*, pp. 111–13.
14. Many chapters in Bandaranayake et al. (eds), *Sri Lanka and the Silk Road of the Sea*, provide glimpses of Sri Lankan naval craft, shipbuilding and traders and sailors, engaged in external trade. *See* particularly, Gunawardana, 'Seaways to Seiladiba', pp. 25–44, and Gunawardana and Sakura, 'Sri Lankan Ships in China', pp. 277–80.
15. *See* Hornell, *Water Transport*, pp. 254, 258.
16. For the substance of this paragraph and the next, I have relied on Bopearachchi and Wickremesinhe, *Ruhuna*, pp. 15–30, and Bopearachchi, 'Ancient Coins in Sri Lanka', pp. 21–26.
17. The discussion here is based on the publications of Lakshman S. Perera, in particular his *The Institutions of Ancient Ceylon from Inscriptions*, Vol. 1. There is also his 'Proprietary and Tenurial Rights', pp. 1–32.
18. Perera, *The Institutions of Ancient Ceylon from Inscriptions*, Vol. 1, pp. 69–75, 149.
19. Ibid., *see* pp. 179–83 for a definition of *bojakapathi*.
20. The inscriptions refer to the owners of tanks (*vapi-hamika*) as well as to the practice of donating water charges from tanks to the sangha.
21. Perera, *The Institutions of Ancient Ceylon from Inscriptions*, Vol. 1, pp. 183–88 for a definition of *dakapathi*.
22. Gunawardana, 'Hydraulic Society in Medieval Ceylon', pp. 19–20.
23. Gunawardana, 'Some Economic Aspects of Monastic Life', pp. 71–72.
24. Karunatilaka, 'Early Sri Lankan Society', pp. 108–43.

CHAPTER 5

1. Kiribamune, 'The State and Sangha in Pre-Modern Sri Lanka', pp. 201–16; Liyanagamage, 'Conflicts in State-Sangha Relations', pp. 165–201. The most comprehensive work on Buddhism in Sri Lanka in the Anuradhapura period is the Revd Walpola Rahula's *History of Buddhism in Ceylon*. I have relied on it greatly in this chapter, as well as on Paranavitana's two chapters on Buddhism in the *University of Ceylon*, Vol. 1(I) (hereafter *UCHC*), pp. 125–44 and 241–68. *See also* Adikaram, *Early History of Buddhism in Ceylon*, and Paranavitana, *Sinhalayo*.
2. Paranavitana, 'Civilisation of the Early Period', p. 241.
3. Ibid., pp. 250–5.
4. Rahula, *History of Buddhism in Ceylon*, p. 58.

5. Ibid., pp. 73–4, 96–7.
6. There were in Sri Lanka, apart from the tooth relic, the collarbone, hair relics and the alms bowl of the Buddha.
7. *See* Paranavitana, 'Mahayanism in Ceylon', pp. 35–71.
8. In this section of the present chapter I have relied on the following authorities: Coomaraswamy, *History of Indian and Indonesian Art*; Ludowyk, *Footprint of the Buddha*; Paranavitana, *Sinhalayo*, and his contributions on religion and art in *UCHC*, Vol. I, pp. 241–67 and pp. 378–409; Rowland, *The Art and Architecture of India*.
9. There is no evidence of stupas in Sri Lanka before the introduction of Buddhism. No stupa built in this period is preserved today without alteration in shape or addition. The form of the oldest stupas was the same as that of the monument at Sanchi, the oldest preserved example of the type in India. There are six types of stupas in Sri Lanka, all described by reference to their shape: a bell, a pot, a bubble, a heap of paddy, a lotus and an *amalaka* fruit.
10. Under a load comparable to that of an Egyptian pyramid, the foundations have shown no signs of settlement after 2,000 years.
11. This was higher than the present St Paul's Cathedral in London and slightly lower than St Peter's in Rome.
12. Terraces of beams were added to the hemispherical dome of the dāgäba at its base; the larger stupas had more elaborate terraces than the smaller ones.
13. Moonstones are semicircular slabs richly decorated in low relief and placed at the foot of a stairway leading to a major shrine, with a standard pattern consisting of several concentric bands of ornament, beginning with an outer zone of luxuriant foliage followed by a spirited procession of animals—the horse, elephant, ox and lion—remarkable for their poise and probably symbolizing the four quarters of the world. This band of animals is followed by a belt of stylized vegetation and then a row of *hamsa* (sacred geese) dangling flowers in their beaks. The innermost bands are all inspired by the lotus plant and culminating in stylized lotus petals of great delicacy. The vitality of the carving is matched by an extraordinary restraint.
14. On the Buddha images we now have the works of Ulrich von Schroeder, the truly monumental *Buddhist Sculptures of Sri Lanka* and *The Golden Age of Sculpture in Sri Lanka*. *See also* Dohanian, *The Mahayana Buddhist Sculpture of Ceylon*.
15. Ulrich von Schroeder, *The Golden Age of Sculpture in Sri Lanka*, p. 51.
16. A seven-headed cobra forms a halo above the rich tiara of the nāga king and in his upraised hand he holds a vase of plenty, sprouting forth prosperity and abundance.
17. For a discussion of this, *see* Bandaranayake's *Sigiriya: City, Palace and Royal Gardens*, pp. 112–35. This sumptuous publication contains a number of essays by reputed scholars, but unfortunately it has no editor.
18. The Pali commentaries of Buddhaghosa and Dhammapala were based on the old Sinhalese exegetical texts which were preserved in the Mahāvihara as late as the tenth century.

19.   He was a Brahman (probably south Indian) convert to Buddhism.
20.   Paranavitana, *Sigiri Graffiti, Being Sinhalese Verses of the Eighth, Ninth, and Tenth Centuries.*

CHAPTER 6

1.   See *UCHC*, 1(2), Book IV, Chapters I–V, pp. 411–87, 507–25; Book V, Chapter I, pp. 613–34; and *CHJ*, IV, 1954–55, special number on the Polonnaruva period.
2.   *Culavaṁsa*, LXXX, verses 54–59, p. 132.
3.   Ibid., LXXX, verses 61–70, pp. 132–33.
4.   Ibid., verses 75–79, pp. 133–34.
5.   Parākramabāhu and Sri Vallabha were direct descendants of Mitta, a sister of Vijayabāhu I. The former was her grandson and the latter her great-grandson (the son of Mānabharana, Parākramabāhu's cousin).
6.   See Sirisena, *Ceylon and South-east Asia*; Taylor, 'The Early Kingdoms', pp. 137–81; Hall, 'Economic History of Early South-east Asia', pp. 137–81, 240–59; de Casparis and Mabbett, 'Religion and Popular Beliefs of Southeast Asia', pp. 281–321; de Casparis, 'Senarat Paranavitana Memorial Lecture', pp. 229–40; Frasch, 'The Buddhist Connection', pp. 85–98.
7.   Frasch, 'The Buddhist Connection', pp. 89–92; de Casparis and Mabbett, 'Religion and Popular Beliefs of Southeast Asia', pp. 295–96.
8.   Hall, 'Economic History of Early Southeast Asia', p. 249.
9.   Ibid., p. 250.
10.   Ibid.
11.   On Chandrabhānu's invasion p. 250. see Sirisena, *Ceylon and South-east Asia*, pp. 36–57.
12.   Paranavitana, 'The Arya Kingdom in North Ceylon', pp. 174–224.
13.   See *UCHC*, 1(2), pp. 553–57; Nicholas, 'The Irrigation Works of King Parākramabāhu I', pp. 52–68.
14.   Gunawardana, 'Irrigation and Hydraulic Society in Medieval Ceylon', pp. 12 ff.
15.   Ibid.
16.   Tennent, *Ceylon*, p. 432.
17.   Siriweera, 'Land Tenure and Revenue in Medieval Ceylon', pp. 2–3.
18.   Ibid., pp. 5–49; see also Siriweera, *History of Sri Lanka: From Earliest Times up to the Sixteenth Century*, pp. 146–67.
19.   See Gunawardana, *Robe and Plough*, pp. 282–312.
20.   Frasch, 'A Buddhist Network', pp. 69–92.
21.   Wijesekera, 'Pāli and Sanskrit in the Polonnaruva Period', pp. 91–97; Saparamadu, 'The Sinhalese Language and Literature of the Polonnaruva Period', pp. 98–112.
22.   Rowland, *The Art and Architecture of India*, p. 375.
23.   Ibid., p. 378.
24.   The vatadāgē, the most remarkable architectural monument to be seen at Polonnaruva, is of the same type as the circular shrines enclosing stupas at the Thūpārāma and Lankārama at Anuradhapura. This architectural

type is a development from the circular cetiya-ghara of India. The vatadāgē is the most developed example of this type.

25.   This is the view of Paranavitana, 'The Art and Architecture of the Polonnaruva Period', p. 75. *See also* Sirisena, *Ceylon and South-east Asia*, pp. 110–43.
26.   Rowland, *The Art and Architecture of India*, p. 375, is a supporter of the view that this monument was evidence of the affinity between the architecture of Polonnaruva and that of Cambodia and Burma. *See also* Guruge, 'The Sri Lankan Factor', pp. 245–52.
27.   *See* Prematilake and Karunaratna, 'Polonnaruva', pp. 86–111. This collection of essays does not have an editor.

CHAPTER 7

1.   *See* Indrapala (ed.), *The Collapse of the Rājarata Civilization*.
2.   *See*, Liyanagamage, *The Decline of Polonnaruva*.
3.   Murphey, 'The Ruin of Ancient Ceylon', pp. 181–200.
4.   p. 83.
5.   Ibid., pp. 198–200.
6.   On the Gampola kings, *see* Abeyasinghe, 'The History of the Kandyan Kingdom', pp. 429–47.
7.   On Senādhilankāra and the Alagakkōnāras, *see* Kulasuriya, 'Regional Independence', pp. 136–55.
8.   On Zheng He's naval activities, *see* Ma Huan, *Ying-yai Sheny-lan*; Levathes, *When China Ruled the Seas*. On the Sri Lankan episode, see Somaratne, 'Grand Eunuch Ho and Ceylon', pp. 36–47.
9.   The Kublai Khan mission sought the bowl and hair relics as well.
10.   On the history of the Kotte kingdom, *see* Somaratne, *Political History of the Kingdom of Kotte*.
11.   There is even less information on the economy of the Tamil kingdom.
12.   See C.R. de Silva, 'Trade in Ceylon Cinnamon', pp. 14–27, especially pp. 15–16.
13.   C.R. de Silva, 'The First Portuguese Revenue Register', pp. 1–83, especially pp. 22–34.
14.   There appears to have been no restrictions over the practice of their religion and they no doubt built mosques at the more important of their settlements. No mosque dating from this period has survived.
15.   See *UCHC*, 1(2), Book V, Chapter IV, pp. 770–76; Hettiarachchi and Paranavitana, *UCHC*, 1 (2), Chapter IV, pp. 778–93.
16.   Generally, a message in verse carried by a bird and addressed to a deity asking for a benediction on a king or some important personage.

CHAPTER 8

1.   *See* Abeyasinghe, 'The History of the Kandyan Kingdom', pp. 429–47.
2.   Indrapala, 'Dravidian Settlements in Ceylon'; 'Early Tamil Settlements in Ceylon', Chapter 2 in Gunawardana et al., *Reflections on a Heritage*, pp. 15–33; 'Early Tamil Settlements in Ceylon', pp. 1–28.
3.   Kiribamune, 'Tamils in Ancient and Medieval Sri Lanka', pp. 9–23.

4. Paranavitana, 'The Arya Kingdom in North Ceylon', pp. 174–224.
5. Indrapala, 'Dravidian Settlements in Ceylon', pp. 6–7.
6. Indrapala, 'Early Tamil Settlements in Ceylon', p. 18.
7. Ibid., p. 18.
8. Ibid., p. 19.
9. Ibid.
10. Ibid., p. 24.
11. Indrapala, 'Early Tamil Settlements in Ceylon', p. 44.
12. Ibid, pp. 54–55.
13. Ibid, p. 60.
14. Ibid.
15. Ibid., pp. 61–62.
16. Ibid., p. 62.
17. For a study of these problems the reader could consult Gunasinghe, *The Tamils of Sri Lanka*. Gunasinghe was a civil servant with a deep and abiding interest in historical research. He was awarded a PhD in 1980 by the University of Peradeniya on his dissertation entitled 'The Political History of Yapahuva, Kurunegala and Gampola'. See also C.R. Liyanagamage, *The Decline of Polonnaruva*, and Pathmanathan, *The Kingdom of Jaffna*.
18. For discussion of the theme of the Portuguese conquest of Jaffna, see Abeyasinghe, *Jaffna Under the Portuguese*. See also C.R. de Silva, *The Portuguese in Ceylon*. The map which serves as the frontispiece to the latter book shows the boundaries of the Jaffna kingdom as they were at the time of the Portuguese conquest of Jaffna.
19. On the Vanni districts and their history in the centuries after the collapse of the Polonnaruva kingdom, see Indrapala, 'Dravidian Settlements in Ceylon', Chapter V, pp. 306–16. See also his 'The Origin of the Tamil Vanni Chieftaincies of Ceylon', pp. 111–40; Pathmanathan, 'Feudal Polity in Medieval Ceylon', pp. 118–30.
20. See Abeyasinghe, 'The History of the Kandyan Kingdom', pp. 429–71.
21. Kulasuriya, 'Regional Independence and Elite Change', pp. 136–55.
22. See Liyanagamage, 'Kerelas in Medieval Sri Lankan History', pp. 76–93.

CHAPTER 9

1. See C.R. de Silva, 'The First Portuguese Revenue Register', pp. 1–83, especially pp. 22–34.
2. See Abeyasinghe, 'The History of the Kandyan Kingdom', pp. 433–34.
3. See MacGregor's chapter 'Europe and the East' in the *New Cambridge Modern History III*.
4. The fort built by the Portuguese at Colombo in 1519 was dismantled in 1524. Between 1520 and 1550, they had a great degree of control if not monopoly over the cinnamon trade without the need for a fort.
5. The most comprehensive study of the Sītāvaka kingdom is by C.R. de Silva, first of all his, 'The Rise and Fall of the Kingdom of Sītāvaka', pp. 1–43 followed by his 'The Rise and Fall of the Kingdom of Sītāvaka (1521-1593)', Chapter III, pp. 61–104.
6. At the time Bhuvenakabāhu was killed, de Noronha had left the island; he returned on hearing of the king's death.

7. Perhaps the most important of all, de Noronha had news that some of the petty rulers of Malabar, who had control of the region's pepper supplies, were planning a boycott of the Portuguese. One of the Portuguese viceroy's prime responsibilities was to see that a cargo of pepper was despatched annually to Lisbon. Noronha returned to his headquarters and with a show of force cajoled these recalcitrant Malabaris into supplying the Portuguese with pepper.

8. Rājasimha's conversion to Hinduism is regarded as having alienated the people from him, or at least weakened their enthusiasm for his cause. There is reason to doubt this. A strong commitment to Hinduism was nothing unusual in Sinhalese rulers. As we have seen, some of the Kotte kings and the elite in Kotte had been distinctly more favourable to Hinduism than to Buddhism.

CHAPTER 10

1. *See* Abeyasinghe, 'The Myth of the Malwana Convention', pp. 67–72.
2. The last major rebellion against the Portuguese was in 1630 in Badulla.
3. The rebellions of Kuruvita Rāla and Nikapitiyē Bandāra were in the Two and Seven Kōralēs respectively.
4. Abeyasinghe, *Portuguese Rule in Ceylon*, pp. 12–28.
5. Senarat married the widowed Kusumāsana Devi after the death of Vimala Dharma Sūriya.
6. C.R. de Silva, *The Portuguese in Ceylon*, Chapters II, III and IV.
7. For a discussion on this treaty, *see* Goonewardena, *The Foundation of Dutch Power in Ceylon*, pp. 17–19, 32–36.
8. During the period 1629–36 Dutch cruisers destroyed nearly 150 Portuguese ships, most of them in the straits of Malacca or off the Malabar coast. There were also several blockades of the principal Iberian naval bases at Goa, Malacca and Manila. Goa was blockaded nine times between 1637 and 1644.
9. Goonewardena, *The Foundation of Dutch Power in Ceylon*, pp. 32–36.
10. See Boxer, 'The Portuguese in the East', pp. 232–44, and 'Portuguese and Dutch Colonial Rivalry', on which this discussion is based.
11. Nevertheless the indifference or incompetence of the Spanish government in Madrid was not the primary cause of the defeat of the Portuguese in Sri Lanka and south India. The decline of the Portuguese Asian empire continued apace under the rule of the native dynasty of Braganza which was restored in 1640 under Joao IV. In brief, it was Portugal rather than Spain which must bear the responsibility for the debacle in south Asia in the mid-seventeenth century.
12. There were attempts to establish 'colonies' of Portuguese settlers on the island. Though they made some progress, they came nowhere near being a steady source of supply of manpower for the Portuguese army.
13. *See* Winius, *The Fatal History of Portuguese Ceylon*.
14. The rulers of Kotte had revenue records of their own, and it would appear that the first Portuguese thōmbo was based in part at least on these.
15. Abeyasinghe, *Portuguese Rule in Ceylon*, pp. 120–21.

16. Ibid., p. 119.
17. Many of the gabadāgam given out on quitrent lost their character as villages reserved for the king. This transformation was partly the result of land-grabbing in the chaotic conditions of the last decade of the sixteenth century, but most grants of gabadāgam were made as a matter of policy as rewards for loyal supporters.
18. C.R. de Silva, *The Portuguese in Ceylon*, pp. 215–35.
19. Ibid., pp. 221 ff.
20. Ibid., p. 224.
21. Ibid., pp. 226–35.
22. Ibid., p. 235
23. On the cinnamon trade, *see* particularly de Silva, Ibid, pp. 190–201. and his article, 'Trade in Ceylon Cinnamon in the Sixteenth Century', pp. 14–27.
24. On Portuguese missionary methods, *see* Boxer, 'Christians and Spices', pp. 346–54 and 'A Note on Portuguese Missionary Methods', pp. 77–90.
25. Quoted in Boxer, 'The Portuguese in the East', p. 244.

CHAPTER 11

1.   The analysis in this section of the present chapter is based largely on Arasaratnam, *Dutch Power in Ceylon*.
2.   To the west and south-west, Rājasimha II had annexed large parts of the territories under Portuguese control including the vitally important Seven Kōralēs, the greater part of the Sabaragamuva and the eastern half of the Four Kōralēs. On the east, Rājasimha obtained control over the ports of Trincomalee, Kottiyār and Batticaloa.
3.   One of these captives was Robert Knox who later wrote a celebrated book on the Kandyan kingdom, *An Historical Relation of Ceylon*.
4.   Ryklof van Goens participated in these deliberations at Batavia as a member of the council there. But, strongly opposed to this resolution, he did not sign the instructions sent to Sri Lanka.

CHAPTER 12

1.   Dewaraja, *A Study of the Political, Administrative and Social Structure of the Kandyan Kingdom; see also* Roberts, *Sinhala Consciousness in the Kandyan Period*.
2.   Up to the time of Rājasimha II there had been only one adigār. He added a second, and in the early years of the nineteenth century, the last Kandyan king appointed a third—perhaps as a means of dividing the authority of the adigārs and reducing their powers.
3.   Although bhikkhus had no official position in this council, the most influential among them could be summoned when required to participate in its discussions.
4.   These were Udunuvara, Yatinuwara, Tumpane, Harispattuwa, Dumbara, Hevaheta, Kotmale, Uda Bulatgama and Pata Bulatgama.
5.   By the end of the eighteenth century there were twelve disāvonies. The ratas and disāvonies were generally of equal status.
6.   The only towns of note were Senkadagala (modern Kandy), Nilambe, Alutnuvara, Badulla and Hanguranketa, all of which were royal residences at one time or another.

7. On the secularization of caste in Sri Lanka, *see* R. Pieris, *Sinhalese Social Organisation*, especially Part V, and Hocart, *Caste: A Comparative Study*.
8. Derived from the Sinhalese *hēn* or *hēna*.
9. A plot of land cleared for chēna cultivation was generally abandoned after two crops were taken from it.
10. Wickremasekara, 'The Social and Political Organisation of the Kandyan Kingdom', p. 90.
11. Certain castes of people paid miscellaneous duties to the king in iron, steel, salt, oil, ghee, betel and jaggery.
12. The organization and superintendence of these compulsory services, which could include service in the militia, lay with the disāvas, with the king retaining the right to exempt anyone from these services.
13. This tax was abolished by Kīrti Śrī Rājasimha, but it was revived in the early nineteenth century by the last king of Kandy, Śrī Vikrama Rājasimha.
14. Arasaratnam, 'Vimala Dharma Sūriya II', pp. 59–70.
15. For discussions on this, *see* Arasaratnam, 'Introduction: The Dutch in Ceylon and South India', especially pp. 1–36.
16. *See* Fernando, 'An Account of the Kandyan Mission sent to Siam', pp. 37–83; Jayatilaka, 'Sinhalese Embassies to Arakan', pp. 1–6; P.E.Pieris, 'An Account of Kīrti Śrī's Embassy to Siam', pp. 17–41; *see also* Malalgoda, *Buddhism in Sinhalese Society*.
17. *See* Chapter 14, this volume, for a discussion on this.
18. The theme of peasant unrest in the littoral is reviewed in Chapter 13, this volume.
19. Dewaraja, *The Kandyan Kingdom of Sri Lanka* pp. 26–91.
20. This was especially so with the accession of Kīrti Śrī Rājasimha to the Kandyan throne in 1747. He sought and obtained a bride of the Nāyakkar lineage from south India. Subsequently he married two other Nāyakkar princesses. There were thus from this time a number of Nāyakkar chiefs in court in positions of power and influence.
21. On the Dutch wars with Kandy, *see* Paulusz, 'The Outbreak of the Kandyan–Dutch War', pp. 29–52; Paulusz (ed.), *Secret Minutes of the Dutch Political Council*, pp. 1–19, Paulusz's introduction; Raven-Hart, *The Dutch Wars with Kandy*.
22. On the treaty of 1766, see Arasaratnam, 'Dutch Sovereignty in Ceylon', pp. 105–21.

CHAPTER 13

1. Sales in Asia were kept down to one-fifth of that in the more lucrative European market. In this way prices were maintained at an artificially high level so that it would be unprofitable for the company's competitors to buy cinnamon in Asia for sale in Europe.
2. Because of the monopoly imposed by the VOC, the Kandyan kingdom could not sell cinnamon through its ports to traders who called there. As a result, its economy was deprived of a valuable item of exchange with which to finance imports.

3. The destruction of a cinnamon plant, the unauthorized peeling of its bark, private trade in cinnamon and the transport of cinnamon were all placed in the category of offences for which the death penalty could be imposed. To enforce these draconian measures the jungles were systematically patrolled.

4. In an attempt to protect their children from these oppressive tenurial obligations, the Salāgamas often avoided registering their children with the Mahabadda.

5. Kotelawele, 'Agrarian Policies of the Dutch', pp. 3–33; see particularly p. 16ff.

6. Ibid., pp. 19–32.

7. In 1753 he placed a ban on chēnas but this was lifted within a year and in 1754 the clearing of land for chēnas was permitted under rigorous controls though the conversion of chēnas into gardens was strictly prohibited. This remained the basis of Dutch land policy, such as it was, till 1767.

8. Where they had legal title they were provided with title deeds which, apart from other considerations, was viewed as a useful method of introducing the indigenous population to the practice of land surveys previously attempted without much success during the administration of van Gollenesse.

9. We have little reliable information on the demographic trends of this period. The Dutch records refer to an increase in population and attribute this without much explanation to an excess of births over deaths.

10. Kanapathypillai, 'Dutch Rule in Maritime Ceylon', pp. 250–53.

11. Ibid., pp. 298–307.

12. Mattau, 'Governor van Imhoff', pp. 55–67.

13. See Kanapathypillai, 'Dutch Rule in Maritime Ceylon', pp. 272–73.

14. See Chapter 14, this volume.

15. On the thōmbos see Chapter 15, this volume.

16. Kanapathypillai, 'Dutch Rule in Maritime Ceylon', pp. 275–79.

17. See Arasaratnam (ed.), Memoir of Julius Stein van Gollenesse, pp. 28–35; Arasaratnam, 'Dutch Commercial Policies in Ceylon', pp. 109–30, and 'Baron van Imhoff and Dutch Policy in Ceylon, 1736-1740', pp. 454–66.

18. The trade was conducted on his behalf by the merchants of Quilon. The entire harvest in Jaffna was taken to Quilon and sold to the raja, who in turn released it for sale within his kingdom at a fixed price. He closely guarded this monopoly, and neither the merchants of Jaffna nor the Dutch had any share in these transactions. This trade continued well into the nineteenth century.

19. For further discussion on this, see Chapter 11, this volume.

CHAPTER 14

1. See Colgate, 'The Royal Navy and Trincomalee', pp. 1–6.

2. On the impact of the treaty of 1766 on relations between the VOC and the Kandyans, see Kanapathypillai, 'Dutch Rule in Maritime Ceylon', pp. 74–138.

3. See Mendis, 'The Advent of the British to Ceylon'; Boxer, The Dutch Seaborne Empire; Harlow, The Founding of the Second British Empire; Toussaint, A History of the Indian Ocean.

4.   Kanapathypillai, 'Dutch Rule in Maritime Ceylon', pp. 144–49.
5.   Ibid., pp. 158–203.

CHAPTER 15

1.   On the VOC's administrative structure in Sri Lanka, see Arasaratnam, 'The Administrative Organisation of the Dutch East India Company in Ceylon', pp. 1–13.
2.   Ibid., p. 5.
3.   Ibid., p. 1.
4.   See P.E. Pieris, The Ceylon Littoral-1593, pp. 27–8.
5.   When these restrictions were set aside by the British we find a significant number of Muslim entering the business of revenue farming in the early nineteenth century.
6.   Kotelawele, 'Agrarian Policies of the Dutch', pp. 28–9.
7.   In the first few decades after the establishment of Dutch rule, high-ranking officials of the VOC appropriated the best lands to their private use and this abuse was so widespread that Governor Pyl was obliged to step in and take back the land so alienated.
8.   Nadaraja, The Legal System of Ceylon, pp. 3–56.
9.   Cited in Nadaraja, Ibid., p. 13.
10. Nadaraja, Ibid., pp. 12–16.
11. For discussion on this see Nadaraja, 'The Law', pp. 327–42.
12. See Kotelawele, 'Nature of Class Relations', particularly p. 11.
13. Kotelawele, 'Agrarian Policies of the Dutch', pp. 1–12, pp. 3–33.
14. See Boudens, The Catholic Church in Ceylon', pp. 1–266.
15. There was a measure of force used to see that baptized Christians though not others conformed to and practised their faith regularly.
16. Arasaratnam, Memoir of Julius Stein van Gollenesse, p. 38.
17. Ibid., p. 38.
18. Ibid., pp. 38–39.
19. Boxer, The Dutch Seaborne Empire, pp. 147–49.
20. The Rt Revd Bishop Edmund Pieris, 'Sinhalese Christian Literature', pp. 163–81 and 'Tamil Catholic Literature', pp. 229–44.
21. On Gonçalves, see Fr S.G. Perera, Life of Father Jacome Gonçalves.
22. These anti-Buddhist polemics were among the main reasons why King Śrī Vijaya Rājasimha ordered the Roman Catholic priests out of the Kandyan kingdom at the beginning of his reign.
23. An even more remarkable example of this was the canals constructed by the VOC in Sri Lanka. See Chapter 13, this volume.
24. See Brohier, 'Ceylon-Dutch Domestic Art', pp. 75–79.
25. Brohier, Furniture of the Dutch Period in Ceylon. See also Pearson, 'European Chairs in Ceylon'. pp. 77–101.
26. This is seen in many Dutch words absorbed into the Sinhalese language to describe parts of a house and the furniture in it.

CHAPTER 16

1.   On this theme, see Malalgoda, Buddhism in Sinhalese Society, especially pp. 57–58.

2. Ibid., pp. 58–60.
3. Ibid., p. 61ff.
4. Ibid., p. 64.
5. Dewaraja, *A Study of the Political, Administrative and Social Structure of the Kandyan Kingdom*, p. 130.
6. Malalgoda, *Buddhism in Sinhalese Society*, pp. 87–105.
7. The basis of the classical tradition was a sound knowledge of Pali and Sanskrit. Its poetry adhered to the tenets of the Sanskrit mahākāvya, and its prose works were based on the Buddhist scriptures, or important elements in Buddhist worship such as the tooth relic or the sacred bo-tree.
8. This poetry was lacking in any fine sensibility, its language was coarse rather than merely bawdy, and a good many of the verses were more pornographic than elegantly Rabelaisian.
9. Malalgoda, *Buddhism in Sinhalese Society*, p. 64.
10. Coomaraswamy, *Medieval Sinhalese Art*, p. 12, quoted in Malalgoda, Ibid., p. 64.
11. MacDougall, 'Domestic Architecture Among the Kandyan Sinhalese'.

CHAPTER 17

1. *See* Brynn, 'The Marquess Wellesley', pp. 1–13; *see also* Adler, 'Britain and the Defence of India'.
2. Brynn, 'The Marquess Wellesley'. *See also* Ingram (ed.), *Two Views of British India*.
3. Dutch judges refused to continue in service beyond the time stipulated in the Articles of Capitulation, although they were urged to do so by the new administration. Dutch clergymen were even more reluctant.
4. Wickremeratne, 'The English East India Company', pp. 131–55.
5. An important aspect of this, relations with the Kandyan kingdom, is treated in Chapter 18, this volume.
6. Uliyam—the residence taxes on Muslims and Chetties; also the obligation to enumerated service in Jaffna, as well as its partial or total commutation.
7. Capitation taxes were paid by the *Nallava*s and *Palla*s, two castes of slaves in Jaffna.
8. On the rebellion of 1817–18, *see* Chapter 18, this volume.
9. The decision to establish the system of dual control had little to do with the rebellion of 1797–98. This had been decided upon before news of the rebellion reached Britain.
10. For discussion of North's attitude to the Muslims, *see* Wickremeratne, 'The English East India Company', pp. 140–55.
11. Dundas, private letter to Wellesley, 11 September 1800, in Ingram (ed.), *Two Views of British India*, pp. 297–98.
12. Brynn, 'The Marquess Wellesley', pp. 4–13.

CHAPTER 18

1. This is a revised version of my chapter of the same title in *UCHC*, III. For further reading, *see* P.E. Pieris, *Tri Sinhala; Sinhale and the Patriots*; and R. Pieris, *Sinhalese Social Organisation*.

2. Wickremeratne, 'Lord North and the Kandyan Kingdom', pp. 30–42.
3. On the Kandyan wars of the nineteenth century, *see* Powell, *The Kandyan Wars*.
4. *See* Powell, 'The Fall of Kandy 1815', pp. 114–22.

CHAPTER 19

1. *See* Samaraweera, 'The Cinnamon Trade of Ceylon', pp. 415-42. On the economy of the colony in the early nineteenth century, *see* the same author's chapter 'Land Policy and Peasant Colonisation, 1914–1948', in *UCHC*, III, pp. 446–60.
2. The new contract guaranteed the colony an income of £101,000 per annum. In contrast, the contracts of 1802 and 1806 had brought the colony a return of above £60,000 annually.
3. Arasaratnam, 'Dutch Commercial Policies in Ceylon', pp. 109–30.
4. Samaraweera, 'Land Policy and Peasant Colonisation', *UCHC*, III, pp. 50–54.
5. On the Colebrooke–Cameron reforms, *see* Samaraweera, 'Governor Sir Robert Wilmot Horton', pp. 209–28; *see also* the same author's chapter on the Colebrooke–Cameron Reforms in *UCHC*, III, pp. 77–88; K.M. de Silva, 'The Colebrooke-Cameron Reforms', pp. 245–56.
6. *See* Malalgoda, *Buddhism in Sinhalese Society*, pp. 87–105.
7. K.M. de Silva, 'Religion and the State in the Early Nineteenth Century', pp. 66–76.
8. *See* K.M. de Silva, 'Influence of the English Evangelical Movement', pp. 375–85.

CHAPTER 20

1. For a review of the administration of the colony in the early nineteenth century, *see* Samaraweera, 'The Development of the Administrative System from 1802 to 1832', *UCHC*, III, pp. 34–47.
2. For discussion on this, *see* K.M. de Silva, 'The Legislative Council in the Nineteenth Century', pp. 226–48.

CHAPTER 21

1. For discussion on these themes, *see* K.M. de Silva, *Social Policy and Missionary Organisations*, pp. 29–137.
2. Gate or guard mudaliyārs were attached to the governor's office and served as translators and interpreters.
3. K.M. de Silva, *Social Policy and Missionary Organisations*, pp. 64–137.
4. Boyd, 'Ceylon and its Pioneers', pp. 217–82.; Breckenridge, *The Hills of Paradise*, particularly Chapter V, pp. 31–38; Webb Jr, *Tropical Pioneers*, pp. 69–71.
5. Nearly half these plantations were formed between 1844 and 1846.
6. Successive reductions in the import duty on coffee had seen an increase in its consumption in Britain from 1 ounce per person per annum in 1801 to 1 lb 5¼ oz in 1831. The consumption of colonial coffee more than doubled between 1840 and 1848.

7. During the second half of the nineteenth century, the volume of cinnamon annually exported was actually larger than the average annual export in the first half, but since the quality was markedly inferior and the prices generally low, increased production did not yield a corresponding increase in revenue to the state or to the producer.
8. Boyd, 'Autobiography', p. 249ff.
9. Rigg, On 'Coffee Planting in Ceylon', pp. 123–42.
10. Tinker, *A New System of Slavery*.
11. *See* K.M. de Silva, 'The Third Earl Grey', pp. 5–20.
12. The customs revenue rose from £78,000 in 1843 to £100,000 in 1845; the revenue from land sales increased from £19,914 in 1840 (being more than double that of 1839) to £94,000 in 1845.

CHAPTER 22

1. See Roberts and Wickremeratne, 'Export Agriculture in the Nineteenth Century', *UCHC*, III, pp. 89–118; Breckenridge, *The Hills of Paradise*.
2. In 1854, they formed the Ceylon Planters' Association. Its motto was 'Agitate, agitate, agitate'.
3. On the worldwide expansion of coffee cultivation, *see* Pendergrast, *Uncommon Grounds*.
4. *See* Webb, *Tropical Pioneers*, pp. 108–116.
5. Breckenridge, *The Hills of Paradise*.
6. On the early years of the tea industry, *see* Wickremeratne, 'The Establishment of the Tea Industry in Ceylon', pp. 131–55.
7. Lewis (ed.), *Tropical Development*, particularly the editor's introduction.
8. Peebles, 'The Transformation of a Colonial Elite', particularly Chapter VI, pp. 236–38. *See also* his *Social Change in Nineteenth Century Ceylon*, pp. 197–230.
9. L.R. Jayawardena, 'The Supply of Sinhalese Labour to Ceylon Plantations'.
10. Named after the extensive hilly area in Derbyshire, England, which it was supposed to resemble.

CHAPTER 23

1. On irrigation in this period, *see* Roberts, 'Aspects of Ceylon's Agrarian Economy', pp. 146–66, and 'Irrigation Policy in British Ceylon', pp. 47–63.
2. Henry Ward had been one of the earliest converts to these theories. In 1836, he had served as chairman of a House of Commons Committee on colonial land which had given Wakefield a respectful hearing even though it would not commit itself to accepting his theories in their entirety.
3. Anuradhapura was visited for the first time by a British official (Thomas Ralph Backhouse, Collector of Mannar, 1820–23) in 1823, and Polonnaruva was visited by a young soldier, Lieutenant Fagan, in 1820.
4. Sessional Paper (hereafter SP) XXIV of 1878, *Paper Relating to the Grain Tax*, p. 10.
5. Gregory, *Autobiography*, p. 329.
6. Ibid., pp. 311–12.

7.   *See* Wesumperuma, 'The History of the Grain Tax in British Ceylon'. *See also* Roberts, 'Grain Taxes in British Ceylon, 1832-1878: Problems in the Field', pp. 809–34, and 'Grain Tax in British Ceylon, 1832-1878: Theories, Prejudices and Controversies', pp. 115–46.

8.   Wesumperuma, 'The Evictions Under the Paddy Tax', pp. 131–48, and 'Land Sales Under the Paddy Tax', pp. 19–35.

9.   Gregory MSS, Gordon's private letter to Gregory, 2 June 1893.

10. For a discussion on this theme, *see* Wickremaratne, 'Grain Consumption and Famine Conditions', pp. 28–53.

CHAPTER 24

1.   Colonial Office (hereafter CO) despatches, Series 54, Vol. 291, CO 54/291ff/ Pakington to Anderson, 9 of 6 January 1853. Dispatches may be accessed at the Public Record office in Kew, London.

2.   See SP XVIII of 1869, containing E.L. Mitford's memoranda on serfdom, I (December 1868) and II (January 1869), and Robinson's minute of 24 August 1869.

3.   Gregory, *Autobiography*, pp. 309–10.

4.   CO despatch 54/528, Longden to Kimberley, 15 October 1880.

5.   In the railway, for instance, nearly all the locomotive drivers, nearly all the guards and all the mechanical and track engineers were recruited from Britain till the 1920s.

6.   The Irrigation Department was established in 1900.

7.   Stanmore MSS, Series A, Vol. IX (49207), Gordon to Havelock, 6 May 1892.

8.   A curious inclusion this, for the de Soysas did not belong to the Goyigama mudaliyār establishment unlike the others in the list.

9.   CO despatch 54/625, Havelock to Chamberlain, confidential, 20 October 1895.

10. R.E. Stubbs's minute on MacCallum to Crewe, telegram of 27 January 1911, in CO 54/741.

11. Districts were divided into chief headmen's division (110 in all) and these in turn into 613 subdivisions under superior headmen and 4,000 or so villages under village headmen.

12. CO despatch 54/584, Gordon to Knutsfard, 426 of 31 October 1889.

13. CO despatch 54/541, Longden to Kimberley, 456 of 26 October 1882.

CHAPTER 25

1.   Roberts, 'A New Marriage, An Old Dichotomy', pp. 32–63.

2.   Wickremaratne, '1865 and the Changes in Educational Policies', pp. 84–93.

3.   On elite formation in nineteenth-century Sri Lanka, *see* Roberts, 'Problems of Social Stratification', pp. 549–77.

4.   Ferguson, *Ceylon in 1883*, p. 64.

5.   Estate duty was first introduced in Sri Lanka in 1919 (Ordinance No. 8 of 1919). It was not in force for a few years and was reintroduced with slight modifications (Ordinance No. 1 of 1938).

6.   Roberts, 'The Rise of the Karāvas'.

7.   Spence-Hardy, *The Jubilee Memorials of the Wesleyan Mission*, p. 192.

8.   K.M. Peebles, 'The Transformation of a Colonial Elite', pp. 185–200.

CHAPTER 26

1.   K.M. de Silva, 'The Government and Religion', pp. 187–212, particularly pp. 197–98.
2.   K.M. de Silva, 'The Government and Religion', pp. 199ff; 'Religion and Nationalism', pp. 103–38; Malalgoda, *Buddhism in Sinhalese Society*, pp. 191–231; 'Buddhist-Christian Confrontation in Ceylon', pp. 171–200.
3.   Olcott, *Old Diary Leaves*, p. 157.
4.   Prothero, *The White Buddhist*, pp. 85–115.
5.   K.M. de Silva, 'The Government and Religion', p. 191–93.
6.   *See* Malalgoda, *Buddhism in Sinhalese Society*, and Jayasekera, 'Social and Political Change in Ceylon', pp. 82–7.
7.   Wickremaratne, 'Religion, Nationalism and Social Change in Ceylon', pp. 123–50, especially pp. 137–38.
8.   K.M. de Silva, 'Religion and Nationalism', pp. 187–212.
9.   K.M. de Silva, 'The Government and Religion', pp. 205–07.
10.   On the temperance movement *see* Jayasekera, 'Social and Political Change in Ceylon', Chapter III; V. Kumari Jayawardena, *The Rise of the Labour Movement*.
11.   An extract from the reports of the World Missionary Congress of 1910 quoted in M.T. Price, *Christian Missions and Oriental Civilisations*, pp. 152–53.
12.   Ibid., pp. 152–53.
13.   Young and Jebanesan, *The Bible Trembled*, pp. 127–43.
14.   On the Islamic recovery of this period, *see* Azeez, *The West Reappraised*, and Samaraweera, 'Arabi Pasha in Ceylon', pp. 219–27.
15.   Arabi Pasha, the leader of the abortive Egyptian uprising of 1882, was exiled to Sri Lanka and spent nineteen years there (1883–1901). The Muslims of the island welcomed him with great enthusiasm. His role in Egyptian politics is reviewed in al-Sayyid, *Egypt and Cromer*.
16.   The Muslims of Sri Lanka were, and to a large extent, are still a Tamil-speaking community.

CHAPTER 27

1.   On this theme, *see* K.M. de Silva, 'The Legislative Council in the Nineteenth Century', pp. 226–48.
2.   Wight, *The Development of the Legislative Council*, p. 14.
3.   *See* K.M. de Silva, 'The Legislative Council in the Nineteenth Century', p. 237.
4.   Grey, *The Colonial Policy of Lord John Russell's Administration*, p. 14.
5.   Ibid., p. 14.
6.   Digby, *Representative Government*; *see also, An Oriental Crown Colony*.
7.   Selborne's minute of 3 August 1895, in CO despatch 295/563, Broom to Ripon, 186 of 15 May 1895, quoted in Will, 'Problems of Constitutional Reform', pp. 693–716, *see* p. 714.

8. The strength of their case lay in the fact that a fairly high qualification was assumed to be essential by the British, who had not quite done away with property qualification for their own voters at home.

9. John Ferguson's interest in constitutional reform went back at least to 1893. In his book *Ceylon in 1893* he made a plea for a reform of the island's constitution, especially for an increase in the number of unofficial representatives with some of them to be elected on the basis of a restricted franchise. This appeal drew no response from the government.

10. *Daily Graphic,* 10 January 1905.

11. *Ceylon Standard,* 14 September 1899.

12. *Sarasavi Sandaresa,* 28 May 1899.

13. CO despatch 54/682, Lucas's minute on Ridgeway to Chamberlain, 241 of 17 June 1903; *see also* his minute on Ridgeway to Chamberlain, 8 May 1898, CO despatch 54/626.

14. This point is made in LaBrooy, 'The Movement Towards Constitutional Reform', p. 192 ff.

15. *Ceylon Standard,* 8 June 1899.

CHAPTER 28

1. Obeyesekere, 'Religious Symbolism and Political Change in Ceylon', pp. 43–63.

2. This was especially so with regard to attitudes on monogamy, divorce and sexual morality in general.

3. Low, *Lion Rampant,* p. 114.

4. *See* Gunawardena, 'The Reform Movement and Political Organisations in Ceylon', pp. 14–73.

5. Ibid.

6. For discussion on these points, *see* Jayasekera, 'Social and Political Change in Ceylon', Chapter III.

7. Relations between the theosophists and the indigenous Buddhist leadership had never been consistently friendly even in the late nineteenth century. *See* Malalgoda, *Buddhism in Sinhalese Society,* pp. 250–55.

8. *See* de Mel, 'Reform of the Ceylon Legislative Council', pp. 32–38; *see also* SP II of 1910, Despatches Relating to the Constitution of the Ceylon Legislative Council, Crewe to Officer Administering Ceylon Government, 9 February 1909, enclosing memorandum by James Pieris, 12 December 1908.

9. SP II of 1910, MacCallum's despatch to the Earl of Crewe, 346 of 26 May 1909.

10. K.M. de Silva, 'The Reform and Nationalist Movements in the Early Twentieth Century', pp. 381–95.

11. The effective peak period of the riots was 28 May–5 June 1915. For discussion on the riots of 1915 and their historical significance, *see* Blackton, 'The 1915 Riots in Ceylon', pp. 219–66; and Robert (ed.), *A Symposium on the 1915 Communal Riots.* There is a more comprehensive review of these events in Jayasekera, 'Social and Political Change in Ceylon', pp. 247–424.

12. When the First World War broke out, Dharmapala was in Calcutta. He was accused of being engaged in intrigues with disaffected Indians—the

close ties between him and the Bengali nationalists did not pass unnoticed by the police—and the Sri Lanka government refused to let him return home. He was not allowed back till 1920.

13. *See* Roberts, 'Labour and the Politics of Labour', pp. 179–208, for a very perceptive and comprehensively researched study of this problem.

14. He was elected to the 'Educated Ceylonese' constituency in a contest with Dr Marcus Fernando in 1911.

15. *See* Fernando, 'The Post-Riots Campaign for Justice', pp. 255–66.

16. On the formation of the Ceylon National Congress, *see* K.M. de Silva, 'The Formation and Character of the Ceylon National Congress', pp. 70–102.

17. Article I of the constitution of the Ceylon National Congress.

CHAPTER 29

1. It had been in fact a major factor in the celebrated contest for the 'Educated Ceylonese' seat in 1911 between Ramanathan and Dr Marcus Fernando.

2. For discussions on this, *see* K.M. de Silva, 'The Ceylon National Congress in Disarray I', pp. 97–117, and 'The Ceylon National Congress in Disarray, II', pp. 16–35.

3. For a detailed discussion on Manning's relations with the Kandyans, *see* Ariyaratne, 'Communal Conflict in Ceylon Politics', pp. 70–75, 92–110.

4. Manning candidly stated that he had encouraged the Kandyans to go to London to make representations and the Kandyan delegation in their evidence before Milner confirmed this. *See* K.M. de Silva, 'The Ceylon National Congress in Disarray I', pp. 99–100.

5. For discussions on this, *see* K.M. de Silva, 'The Formation and Character of the Ceylon National Congress', p. 93ff.

6. *See* K.M. de Silva, 'The Ceylon National Congress in Disarray I', p. 114.

7. *See Ceylon Morning Leader,* 28 October 1916.

8. For Manning's adroit handling of this issue, *see* K.M. de Silva, 'The Ceylon National Congress in Disarray, II', pp. 16–35.

9. *Ceylon Independent,* editorial of 13 November 1924.

10. *Ceylon Independent,* 28 February 1925.

11. *See Ceylon Independent,* 7 December 1925, 31 January 1927, 17 November 1927.

12. *See* a series of six articles by S.W.R.D. Bandaranaike on federation in the *Ceylon Morning Leader,* 19 May to 30 June 1926. The federal structure he outlined was based on the existing provincial administrative divisions in the country and was more elaborate than the three units the Kandyans had in mind.

13. On the mahājana sabhās and their role in the politics of this period, *see* Gunawardena, 'The Reform Movement and Political Organisation in Ceylon', pp. 74–156.

14. F.R. Senanayake and D.B. Jayatilaka were the lay leaders of the Buddhist movement at this time.

15. For a comprehensive study of Goonesinha's impact on the politics of the 1920s, *see* V. Kumari Jayawardena, *The Rise of the Labour Movement in Ceylon,* pp. 191–310. *See also* Roberts, 'Fissures and Solidarities', pp. 1–31, and 'Labour and the Politics of Labour', pp. 179–208.

16. On 24–25 April 1919, the Revd A.G. Fraser, the dynamic principal of Trinity College, Kandy, had made what was in effect the first call for manhood suffrage. This was an article in the *Times of Ceylon* making out a case for responsible government for Sri Lanka (he was struck by the 'moderation of the proposals of the Ceylonese Reformers') in the course of which he argued that an essential prelude was 'to have a broad franchise. Personally I would like to see manhood suffrage.'

17. Arunachalam was, in fact, endorsing Fraser's view on this occasion.

CHAPTER 30

1. Lewis (ed.), *Tropical Development*. See the editor's introductory essay.
2. On Sri Lanka's plantation industry in the early twentieth century, *see* L.A. Wickremaratne, 'Economic Development in the Plantation Sector', pp. 428–45.
3. For a discussion on these problems in greater detail, *see* Samaraweera, 'Land Policy and Peasant Colonisation', pp. 446–60.
4. *See* Clifford, *Some Reflections on the Ceylon Land Question*, p. 27 for an authoritative statement of this view.
5. Ibid., p. 23.
6. Ibid., p. 2.
7. One notable feature in the pattern of population growth in the early twentieth century was that migration increase (through Indian plantation labour) was not an important factor in it.
8. Another section recruited from India consisted of the 'coal coolies' in the port (the coal wharves of Mutwal in Colombo), who handled loads heavier than the Sinhalese were inclined to shoulder—quite apart from the griminess, they regarded such work with distaste. The coal wharf in due course forced the elite Anglican secondary school situated there—St Thomas' College—to seek another and more salubrious site in Mount Lavinia.
9. Roberts, 'Fissures and Solidarities', pp. 1–31, and 'Labour and the Politics of Labour', pp. 177–208.
10. *See* Wickremaratne, 'Emergence of a Welfare Policy', p. 477.
11. Goonesinha himself came to share the outlook of his more conservative contemporaries in national politics in regard to the apparently privileged position of Indian plantation workers.
12. See Jayaweera, 'Education Policy in the Early Twentieth Century', pp. 461–75.
13. In 1900, the overall rate of literacy in the island was 21.7 per cent; by 1921, it had reached 34.2 per cent. Female literacy rose from 6.9 to 18 per cent in the same period.
14. Administration Report, Director of Public Instruction (1900), cited in R. Pieris, 'Universities, Politics and Public Opinion', p. 442.
15. Administration Report, Director of Public Instruction (1903), quoted in R. Pieris, 'Universities, Politics and Public Opinion', p. 443.
16. On the establishment of the University of Ceylon, *see* the authoritative article by Jennings (its first Vice-Chancellor), 'The Foundation of the University of Ceylon', pp. 147–67.

CHAPTER 31

1. CO despatch 537/692, Clifford to Amery, secret despatch of 20 November 1926.
2. Ibid., W. Ormsby-Gore's minute of 28 February 1927.
3. CO despatch 54/889, file 53266, letter of W.L. Murphy (for colonial secretary, Ceylon), 29 April 1927, to E.W. Perera, president, Ceylon National Congress.
4. Marcus Fernando, Donald Obeysckera and Tudor Rajapakse were among its leading lights.
5. On the Kandyan attitudes of this period, *see* Wickremaratne, 'Kandyans and Nationalism', pp. 49–68.
6. Kandyan National Assembly, *The Rights and Claims of the Kandyan People* p. 37.
7. Ibid., p. 34.
8. Wight, *The Development of the Legislative Council*, p. 94.
9. Ibid., p. 95.
10. *Donoughmore Report*, pp. 18–22.
11. *Donoughmore Report*, pp. 99–100.
12. CO despatch 51/900, file 73230/10, T.B. Jayah's memorandum of 27 July 1930.
13. There was for some time considerable doubt about the outcome of the vote in the Legislative Council. The Ceylon government and the Colonial Office were under great pressure from two sources—A.E. Goonesinha and the Unionist Association—to have the governor use the official bloc to carry the Donoughmore proposals through the Legislative Council. But the governor was firmly opposed to this and was supported in this by the Colonial Office.
14. Drummond Shiels came to the Colonial Office on 1 December 1929 and served in this capacity till the formation of Ramsay MacDonald's National Government on 31 August 1931 when he went into Opposition. For a brief period from 11 June 1929 to 30 November 1929 he had been undersecretary at the India Office.
15. Bandaranaike, *The Handbook of the Ceylon National Congress*, p. 814.
16. CO despatch 54/911, file 93011, Thomson to Cunliffe-Lister, confidential despatch of 24 May 1932.
17. *See* particularly the *Liberal Gazette* (an organ of the All-Ceylon Liberal League), Vol. I, Nos 1–3, December 1931.
18. On the Jaffna boycott see Russell, 'The Ceylon Tamils Under the Donoughmore Constitution', pp. 57–80. A revised version of this thesis was published with the title *Communal Politics Under the Donoughmore Constitutions, 1931-1947*. It contains the substance of the material on the '50-50' campaign and remains the definitive study of this issue.
19. *See*, for instance, the editorial in the *Ceylon Daily News*, 5 May 1931; also *Ceylon Independent*, 12 May 1931 and *Ceylon Daily News*, 13, 18, 23 and 26 May 1931.
20. *Ceylon Daily News*, 7 May 1931.

21. On the Jaffna boycott, *see* Russell, 'The Dance of the Turkey-Cock', pp. 47–67.
22. CO despatch 54/916, file 14233, H.R. Cowell's minute of 30 May 1933.

CHAPTER 32

1. Chapter 35.
2. Meyer, 'L'impact de la dépression des années 1930', pp. 31–66.
3. CO despatch 54/916, file 14264/2, memorandum of the Board of Ministers to Thomson, 29 July 1933.
4. CO despatch 54/960, file 34227/2, Cunliffe-Lister's secret despatch to Stubbs, 14 December 1934.
5. On the formation of the LSSP, *see* Lerski, *Origins of Trotskyism. See also* Leslie Gunawardana, *A Short History of the Lanka Sama Samaja Party*, and L. Jayawardena, 'Origins of the Left Movement in Ceylon', pp. 195–221.
6. *See* Chapter 35, this volume.
7. SP XI of 1937.
8. These powers should have lapsed with the termination of hostilities in 1919, but they were renewed in 1924 by a secret despatch from L.S. Amery to Manning of 10 November 1924 (CO despatch 54/872).
9. On the Bracegirdle question despatch, *see* SP XVIII of 1938. For the relative official correspondence, *see* CO despatch 54/948, files 55878 and 55878/1.
10. On the constitutional questions at issue, the best source is Governor Caldecott's secret minute of 26 October 1937 in CO despatch 54/948, file 55878.
11. CO despatch 54/943, file 55541, H.R. Cowell's minute of 31 August 1937.
12. Ibid.
13. SP XXVII of 1938, pp. 3–16.
14. Ibid., pp. 5–6, particularly paragraphs 13–15.
15. For the Mool Oya incident, *see* SP XV of 1940; for discussion on its constitutional implications see Namasivayam, *The Legislatures of Ceylon*, pp. 35–36, 85, 106 and 127. The incident arose out of the shooting of a plantation worker—an Indian—by a policeman, one of a small 'force' sent to quell a disturbance at Mool Oya Estate in Hevaheta near Kandy.
16. On the reorganisation of the Congress, *see* particularly the manuscript minutes of the executive committee of the Ceylon National Congress, 27 January 1940 and 25 July 1940.
17. *Times of Ceylon*, 30 December 1941.
18. In December 1938 it was estimated that apart from Bandaranaike, two other members of the Board of Ministers, C.W.W. Kannangara and J.L. Kotalawala, and thirteen members of the State Council belonged to the Sinhala Mahā Sabhā (see *The Times*, London, 10 December 1938).

CHAPTER 33

1. *See* Chapter 37, this volume.
2. On the transfer of power in Sri Lanka, *see* K.M. de Silva (ed.), *Sri Lanka in British Documents*. Apart from the editor's Introduction in Part I, the volumes contain selected documents.

3.   CO despatch 54/980, 580/5/1 No. 53, Caldecott's 'personal and secret' despatches to Oliver Stanley, Secretary of State for the Colonies, 27 January 1943 and CO despatch 54/580/5/1 No. 57, 17 February 1943.

4.   CO despatch 54/982/6 No. 89, Stanley, secret cabinet paper on 'The Ceylon Constitution', WP (43) 129 of 27 March 1943.

5.   From 1942, the Communist Party followed a policy of close association with the Ceylon National Congress as the 'official' nationalist party on the island. In 1943, the communists working through the Congress branch organizations urged the rejection of the declaration of May 1943 and advocated instead a demand for the attainment of independence without the intervening stage envisaged in that declaration.

They had the sympathy and support of the great bulk of the younger Congressmen, who succeeded at the annual sessions of December 1943 in changing the provision in the Congress constitution which forbade political parties to join the Congress and admitted the Communist Party to membership. The old guard of Congress leaders were greatly agitated at the admission of the communists to membership and D.S. Senanayake resigned in protest.

6.   SP XVII of 1943.

7.   His principal adviser on constitutional affairs was W.I. (later Sir Ivor) Jennings, then vice chancellor of the University of Ceylon.

8.   SP XIV of 1944.

9.   *See* WO 203/5412 Mountbatten's telegram No. SAC 2636 of 22 May 1944 (marked 'top secret') to the Chiefs of Staff, CO despatch 54/986, file 55541/5, War Cabinet 77(44), conclusions of meeting of 13 June 1944.

10. In September 1944, the Ceylon National Congress, rejecting the July 1944 declaration, came out in support of an all-party conference and resolved to boycott the Soulbury Commission.

11. CO despatch 54/986, file 5554/5 'secret', cabinet meeting 27(45), 3 September 1945.

12. CO 54/986, file 55541/5, 'secret', Cabinet C(45)3, memorandum by the Secretary of State for the Colonies, subtitled 'Ceylon Constitution', dated 12 October 1945. This document was prepared for the Cabinet Colonial Affairs Committee. *See* K.M. de Silva (ed.), *Towards Independence*, pp. 113–14.

13. Senanayake's report to the Board of Ministers, on his discussions with the Secretary of State for the Colonies, 9 October 1945. A copy of this paper is available in the Bernard Aluvihara manuscript at the University of Peradeniya.

14. The minutes of the discussions he had with Hall and with the Colonial Office officials are in CO despatch 54/986, file 55541/5.

15. Senanayake's report to the Board of Ministers, 9 October 1945.

16. Ranasinha, *Memories and Musings*, pp. 187–232; *see* particularly p. 230.

17. CO despatch 54/986, file 55541/5, minutes of Cabinet Colonial Affairs Committee, 15 October C(45) and minutes of cabinet meeting of 26 October (CM[45]46) and 29 October (GEN 99/1st meeting).

18. CO despatch 54/986, file 55541/5, secret and personal telegram from Monck-Mason-Moore to Hall, 17 October 1945.

19. CO despatch 54/986, file 55541/5, minutes of cabinet meeting of 29 October 1945.

20. For these negotiations, *see* Jeffries, *O.E.G.: A Biography of Oliver Ernest Goonetilleke*, pp. 65–97. *See also* Duncan Hall, *Commonwealth*, pp. 801–10.

CHAPTER 34

1. For a discussion on this, *see* Wickremaratne, 'Economic Development in the Plantation Sector', pp. 428–45.
2. *See* Das Gupta, *A Short Economic Survey of Ceylon*, and Indraratna, *The Ceylon Economy*. Neither of these is a comprehensive or inspiring work but they are still all we have. The reader could also consult Oliver's monograph, *Economic Opinion and Policy in Ceylon*.
3. Rubber prices had increased by 66.6 per cent over those of 1935 and the volume of exports rose by 30 per cent in the same period.
4. For further discussion on this, *see* Samaraweera, 'Land Policy and Peasant Colonisation', pp. 446–60.
5. Samaraweera, 'Land as "Patrimony"', pp. 341–62.
6. The free services available to them were now extended through government departments concerned with land and agriculture while marketing facilities were provided through a government department established for this purpose, the Marketing Department. Equally important was the provision of communal buildings, hospitals and schools.
7. The tapping of rubber trees for latex was generally a carefully controlled exercise. Under 'slaughter-tapping,' these controls were eliminated.
8. Das Gupta, *A Short Economic Survey of Ceylon*, p. 65; Indraratna, *The Ceylon Economy*, pp. 34–37.
9. 'Free' education was, in fact, less revolutionary than both its advocates and its critics thought it was. None of the state schools teaching in the local languages charged fees. All that happened was that this principle was extended from 1945 to fee-levying English secondary schools.
10. *See* his speech in *Hansard* (State Council), 13 July 1944, col. 1227.
11. Jayewardene's speech in *Hansard* (State Council), 24 January 1945, col. 492.
12. Kannangara was defeated at the general elections to the new parliament and the new minister of education extended the deadline beyond this date. Nevertheless, the vast majority of schools opted to join the 'free education' scheme.
13. Indraratna, *The Ceylon Economy*, p. 38.
14. Ibid., p. 36.
15. The Defence Regulations and the Avoidance of Strikes and Lockouts Act had severely curbed the activities of the trade unions. The communists replaced the banned LSSP as the chief political influence on the working class in Colombo and its periphery, but although they helped organize several trade unions, they were not inclined to encourage or support strike action
16. Earlier prices had been revised regularly in response to costs of imports.

CHAPTER 35

1. Sarachchandra, 'Sinhala Language and Literature', pp. 343–55.
2. Ibid., pp. 345–46.

3. Indrapala, 'Tamil Language and Literature', pp. 356–57.
4. Sarachchandra, 'Sinhala Language and Literature', pp. 349–50.
5. *See* Sarachchandra, *Modern Sinhalese Fiction* and *The Sinhalese Novel*.
6. Sarachchandra, *The Folk Drama of Ceylon*.
7. Dharmadasa, 'Drama, Film and Music', pp. 454–60.

CHAPTER 36

1. *See* Campbell-Johnson, *Mission with Mountbatten*; Moon, *Divide and Quit*; and Tuker, *While Memory Serves*.
2. Among the objectives of this demarcation was to provide weightage in representation to the backward and sparsely populated areas in some of which minority groups—Tamils and Muslims—were concentrated. The voting strength in the constituencies varied from province to province and within provinces to the point where the resulting distortions appeared to vitiate the principle of one man, one vote.
3. For the background to this, see Wriggins, *Ceylon: Dilemmas of a New Nation*.
4. *See* K.M. de Silva, 'Nationalism and its Impact', pp. 62–72.
5. On the Eksath Bhikkhu Peramuna, *see* Wriggins, *Ceylon: Dilemmas of a New Nation*; and Smith (ed.), *South Asian Politics and Religion*, especially pp. 453–88.
6. See Woodward, *The Growth of a Party System,* and his article, 'The Party System in Comparative Perspective', pp. 144–53.
7. Cited in Woodward, 'The Party System in Comparative Perspective', p. 146.
8. Das Gupta, *A Short Economic Survey of Ceylon*, p. 9.
9. Quoted in Oliver, *Economic Opinion and Policy in Ceylon*, p. 50.
10. W.I. Jennings, *The Economy of Ceylon*, p. 40.
11. *See* Snodgrass, *Ceylon: An Export Economy*, and his article, 'Sri Lanka's Economic Development', pp. 119–25.
12. W.I. Jennings, *The Economy of Ceylon*, p. 4; Wilson, 'Sri Lanka's Foreign Policy', p. 57.
13. Wilson, 'Sri Lanka's Foreign Policy', p. 57.

CHAPTER 37

1. The standard work on this theme is Wriggins, *Ceylon: Dilemmas of a New Nation*.
2. Section 29(2)(b) and (c) of the Soulbury Constitution provided that no law enacted by parliament could '(b) make persons of any community or religion liable to disabilities or restrictions to which persons of other communities or religions are not made liable; or (c) confer on persons of any community or religion, any privilege or advantage which is not conferred on persons of other communities or religions....'
3. In the 1940s, as minister of local government, Bandaranaike had advocated the establishment of a system of provincial councils as the apex of the local government system. But the legislation required for this purpose was never prepared.
4. W. Dahanayake.
5. *See* Dharmadasa, 'Literary Activity in the Indigenous Languages', pp. 434–46.

6.   Wilson, 'Sri Lanka's Foreign Policy', p. 53.

7.   On the economic policies of this period, *see* Snodgrass, *Ceylon*.

8.   The schools belonging to the Buddhist Theosophical Society (BTS) were also affected, but this was not regarded as any great hardship. An attempt by a faction within the BTS to retain control of some of the more prestigious schools as independent private schools was easily squashed by a threat of a strike by teachers and students in those schools.

9.   *See*, Jayasinghe, *The Indo-Ceylon Problem*, particularly pp. 205–93.

10. Quasis presided over a system of domestic relations courts for the Muslims. They had exclusive jurisdiction in respect of marriage and divorce.

11. This amendment provided for the termination of aid to countries which paid no compensation for property taken over from American companies.

12. For a discussion on this, *see* Snodgrass, *Ceylon*. *See also* his article 'Sri Lanka, Economic Development during Twenty-Five Years of Independence'.

13. The oil companies were limited thereafter to the supply of bunkers to ships and aviation fuel at airports. These functions too were nationalized in 1970.

14. Jiggins, 'Dismantling Welfarism in Sri Lanka', pp. 84–104. *See also* Jayawardena, 'Sri Lanka', pp. 273–79.

15. Jiggins, 'Dismantling Welfarism', p. 90.

16. More in terms of seats in parliament than votes in the country.

17. On the insurrection, *see* Blackton, 'The Ceylon Insurgency', pp. 4–7; Halliday, 'The Ceylonese Insurrection', pp. 55–91; Kearney and Jiggins, 'The Ceylon Insurrection', pp. 40–65.

18. Jiggins, 'Dismantling Welfarism'. *See also* Mervyn de Silva, 'Sri Lanka: The End of Welfare Politics', pp. 91–109.

19. On the 1972 constitution, *see* Wilson, *Politics in Sri Lanka*, Chapter V, pp. 189–225. *See also* K.M. de Silva, 'The Constitution and Constitutional Reform', pp. 312–29.

20. On the political situation in Sri Lanka at this time, *see* Saul Rose, 'Sri Lanka at the Turning Point', pp. 411–22.

21. *See* Samaraweera, 'The Role of the Bureaucracy', pp. 31–39, and 'The Administration and Judicial System', pp. 86–107.

22. The CWC's ties with the TULF were never particularly strong, and by the last quarter of 1976 there was increasing evidence of a conflict of interests between them. The crux of the matter was that the CWC saw no advantage to its members from the 'separate' Tamil state which the other sections of the TULF were advocating.

23. The most comprehensive and objective study of this problem is C.R. de Silva, 'Weightage in University Admissions', pp. 152–78.

24. No attempt was made by Mrs Bandaranaike to revive the scheme of a separate electoral register for them.

25. The advocates of this move were clearly influenced by developments in India; they called on the Sri Lanka prime minister to emulate her Indian counterpart who had secured parliamentary approval of a postponement of the general elections scheduled for 1976.

26. These negotiations never made much progress in the way of a settlement of the main points of division between the government and the TULF. They had, in fact, collapsed before the TULF leader fell seriously ill in March 1977. He died in April 1977.

CHAPTER 38

1. On the general election of 1977, see Samaraweera, 'Sri Lanka's 1977 General Election', pp. 1195–206; Russell, 'Sri Lanka's Election Turning Point', pp. 79–97.
2. Among the first such was a change in the mechanics of securing admission to the universities. The change was announced almost immediately after the new government took office, and well before the outbreak of the communal riots.
3. On the new constitution see CJHSS, 7(2), June–December 1977, a special issue 'A Tale of Three Constitutions, 1946–48, 1972 and 1978'.
4. Those convicted under the terms of the Criminal Justice Commissions Law were released from jail, or their fines and other penalties were quashed.
5. This was later reduced to a simple majority.
6. The JVP insurgency of 1971 is reviewed in Alles, Insurgency 1971. See also G.H. Peiris's article 'Insurrection and Youth Unrest in Sri Lanka', pp. 165–200.
7. In the Tamil areas of the Eastern Province the UNP pushed the TULF to second place.
8. For a very perceptive study of the Tamil separatist groups and the early years of the LTTE, see Narayan Swamy, Tigers of Sri Lanka; see also O'Ballance, The Cyanide War.
9. See Kelegama, Economic Development in Sri Lanka, p. 28.
10. On the Indian intervention in Sri Lanka, see K.M. de Silva, Regional Powers and Small State Security; Muni, Pangs of Proximity; Bullion, India, Sri Lanka and the Tamil Crisis; Sankaran, Postcolonial Insecurities.
11. Sisson and Rose, War and Secession.
12. On the JVP's second insurrection, the best study is Chandraprema, Sri Lanka: The Years of Terror.
13. On J.R. Jayewardene's last months in office, see K.M. de Silva and Wriggins, J.R. Jayewardene of Sri Lanka, Chapters 34–37.

EPILOGUE

1. As minister of national security he had led the campaign against the Tamil separatist forces in the 1980s.
2. See K.M. de Silva and Peiris (eds), Pursuit of Peace in Sri Lanka.
3. On these negotiations, see K.M. de Silva, 'Sri Lanka's Prolonged Ethnic Conflict', pp. 437–69.
4. On the LTTE and its current policies and objectives, see K.M. de Silva, 'Separatism and Political Violence', pp. 379–430.
5. See Kaarthikeyan and Raju, The Rajiv Gandhi Assassination.
6. K.M. de Silva, 'Sri Lanka's Prolonged Ethnic Conflict', pp. 437–69.

Sri Lanka's Rulers:
A Chronological List

ANCIENT AND MEDIEVAL SRI LANKA
250–210 BC

The following list is based substantially on that provided in Vol. I, Part II of *History of Ceylon*, pp. 843-47. The editor of that volume warns that the dates up to Sena I (833–53) are only approximate. One other point should be mentioned: not all the rulers listed here had effective control over the whole island.

Vijaya
Upatissa
Panduvāsudeva (Panduvasdev)
Abhaya
Pandukābhaya
Mutasiva

		BC
Devānampiya Tissa (Devanapä Tis)		250–210
Uttiya		
Mahāsiva		
Sūratissa		
Sena and Guttika (Aśvācāri)		
Asela		
Elāra (Elāla)		
Dutthagāmanī (Dutugämunu)		161–137
Saddhātissa (Sädätis)		137–119
Thūlatthana		119
Lañjatissa (Lämäni Tis)		119–109
Khallātanāga		109–103
Vattagāmanī Abhaya (Valagam Abā)		103
Pulahattha ⎫		
Bāhiya ⎪		
Panayamāra ⎬ Pañca-Drāvida	103–89
Pilayamāra ⎪		
Dāthika ⎭		
Vattagāmanī (restored)		89–77

Mahācūli Mahātissa	77–63
Coranāga	63–51
Tissa (Kudā Tissa)	51–48
Siva	
Vatuka	
Dārubhatika Tissa	
Niliya (Purohita Bamunā, Vāsukhi)	
Queen Anulā	48–44
Kutakanna Tissa	44–22
Bhātika Abhaya (also called Bhātika Tissa or Bhātiya Tissa)	22 BC–AD 7

	AD
Mahādāthika Mahānāga	7–19
Āmanda-gāmanī Abhaya	19–29
Kanirajānu Tissa	29–32
Cūlābhaya	32–33
Queen Sīvalī	33
Ilanāga	33–43
Candamukha Siva	43–52
Yasalālaka Tissa	52–60
Sabha (Subha)	60–67
Vasabha	67–111
Vankanāsika Tissa	111–14
Gajabāhuka-gāmanī (Gajabāhu I; Gajabā)	114–36
Mahallaka Nāga	136–43
Bhātika Tissa (Bātiya)	143–67
Kanittha Tissa	167–86
Khujjanāga	186–87
Kuncanāga	187–89
Sirināga I	189–209
Vohārika Tissa (Vēra Tissa)	209–31
Abhayanāga	231–40
Sirināga II	240–42
Vijaya-kumāra	242–43
Samghatissa I	243–47
Sirisamghabodhi (Dāhämi Sirisangabō)	247–49
Gothābhaya or Meghavanna Abhaya (Golu Abā)	249–62
Jetthatissa I	263–73
Mahāsena (Mahasen)	274–301
Sirimeghavanna (Kit Sirimevan)	301–28
Jetthatissa II	328–37
Buddhadāsa	337–65
Upatissa I	365–406
Mahānāma	406–28
Chattagāhaka Jantu	428
Mittasena (Mitsen)	428–29

Kassapa IV		898–914
Kassapa V		914–23
Dappula III		923–24
Dappula IV		924–35
Udaya III		935–38
Sena III		938–46
Udaya IV		946–54
Sena IV		954–56
Mahinda IV		956–72
Sena V		972–82
Mahinda V (Mihindu)		982–1029
Kassapa VI		1029–40
Mahālāna-Kitti		1040–42
Vikrama Pandu		1042–43
Jagatipala (Jagatpala)	(ruled in Rohana)	1043–46
Parakrama Pandu		1046–48
Loka (Lokissara, Lokesvara)		1048–54
Kassapa VII		1054–55
Vijayabāhu I (Vijaya-bā)		1055–1110
Jayabāhu I		1110–11
Vikramabāhu I		1111–32
Gajabāhu II		1132–53
Parākramabāhu I (Parakkamabāhu; Pärakumba)		1153–86
Vijayabāhu II		1186–87
Niśśaṅka Malla		1187–96
Vikramabāhu II		1196
Codaganga		1196–97
Queen Lilāvatī (first period of rule)		1197–1200
Sāhassa Malla		1200–02
Queen Kalyānavatī		1202–08
Dharmāśoka		1208–09
Anikanga, Mahādipāda		1209
Queen Lilāvatī (second period of rule)		1209–10
Lokeśvara		1210–11
Queen Lilāvatī (third period of rule)		1211–12
Parākrama Pandu		1212–15
Māgha (Kaliṅga Vijayabāhu)		1215–32
Vijayabāhu III (ruled at Dambadeniya)		1232–36
Parākramabāhu II (Pandita Parākramabāhu I)		1236–70
Vijayabāhu IV (Bōsat Vijayabā)		1270–72
Bhuvanekabāhu (ruled at Dambadeniya and Yapahuva)		1272–84
Interregnum		1285–86
Parākramabāhu III (ruled at Polonnaruva)		1287–93
Bhuvanekabāhu II		1293–1302
Parākramabāhu IV (Pandita Parākramabāhu II)		1302–26
Bhuvanekabāhu III(?) (Vanni Bhuvanekabāhu)		
Vijayabāhu V		1335–41
Bhuvanekabāhu IV (ruled at Gampola)		1341–51

Parākramabāhu V (ruled at Gampola and Dadigama)   1344–59
Vikramabāhu III (ruled at Gampola)   1357–74

KINGS OF KOTTE

Source: G.P.V. Somaratne, Political History of the Kingdom of Kotte, pp. 232–33.

Bhuvanekabāhu V (King of Gampola in the early part of his reign) 1371–1408
Parākramabāhu VI   1411–66
Jayavīra Parākramabāhu   1466–69
Bhuvanekabāhu VI   1469–77
Pandita Parākramabāhu VII   1477
Vīra Parākramabāhu VIII   1477–89
Dharma Parākramabāhu IX   1489–1513
Vijayabāhu VI   1513–21
Bhuvanekabāhu VII   1521–51
Dharmapala   1551–97

KINGS OF SĪTĀVAKA

Māyādunnē   1521–81
Rājasimha I   1581–93
Rājasūriya   1593–94

KINGS OF THE UDARATA (THE KANDYAN KINGDOM)

Sēnāsammata Vikramabāhu   1469–1511
Jayavīra   1511–52
Karaliyaddē Bandāra   1552–82
Vimala Dharma Sūriya I   1591–1604
Senarat   1604–35
Rājasimha II   1635–87
Vimala Dharma Sūriya II   1687–1707
Narendrasimha   1707–39
Śrī Vijaya Rājasimha   1739–47
Kīrti Śrī Rājasimha   1747–82
Rājādhi Rājasimha   1782–98
Śrī Vikrama Rājasimha   1798–1815

KINGS OF JAFFNA

The compilation of a reasonably accurate chronological list of the rulers of this
northern kingdom presents enormous difficulties. Who ruled this kingdom and
the regnal years of those identified as rulers are matters of scholarly controversy.
From the last quarter of the fifteenth century up to the subjugation of the kingdom
by the Portuguese we have more accurate information for the compilation of a
list of rulers but even in this phase there are problems with regard to regnal
dates.

Vijaya Kūlankaic Cakravartti
Kulasekara Ciṅkaiyārīyan
Kulottunga Ciṅkaiyārīyan
Vikkirama Ciṅkaiyārīyan
Varotaya Ciṅkaiyārīyan
Marttanda Ciṅkaiyārīyan
Kunapūsana Ciṅkaiyārīyan
Virotaya Ciṅkaiyārīyan
Jayavīra Ciṅkaiyārīyan
Kunavira Ciṅkaiyārīyan
Kanakacūriya Ciṅkaiyārīyan

Pararājaśekaram	1478–1519
Caṅkili I	1519–61
Puvirāja Pandāram	1561–65, 1582–91
Periyapillai	1565–82
Ethirimanna Ciṅkam	1591–1616
Caṅkili II	1616–20

PORTUGUESE CAPTAINS-GENERAL

Pedro Lopes de Sousa	1594
Jeronimo de Azevedo	1594–1612
Francisco de Meneses	1612–14
Manuel Mascarenhas Homem	1614–16
Nuno Alvares Pereira	1616–18
Constantino de Sa de Noronha (first term)	1618–20
Jorge de Albuquerque	1620–23
Constantino de Sa de Noronha (second term)	1623–30
Filipe Mascarenhas (first term)	1630–31
Jorge de Almeida (first term)	1631–33
Diego de Mello de Castro (first term)	1633–35
Jorge de Almeida (second term)	1635–36
Diego de Mello de Castro (second term)	1636–38
Antonio Mascarenhas	1638–40
Filipe Mascarenhas (second term)	1640–45
Manuel Mascarenhas Homem	1645–53
Francisco de Mello de Castro	1653–55
Antonio de Sousa Coutinho	1655–56
Antonio de Amaral de Menezes (Jaffna)	1656–58

DUTCH GOVERNORS

Willem J. Coster	1640
Jan Thyszoon (Payart)	1640–46
Jan Maatzuyker	1646–50
Jacob van Kittensteyn	1650–53
Adriaan van der Meijden (first term)	1653–60
Ryklof van Goens (first term)	1660–61
Adriaan van der Meijden (second term)	1661–63
Ryklof van Goens (second term)	1663
Jacob Hustaart	1663–64

Ryklof van Goens (third term)	1664–75
Ryklof van Goens Jr	1675–80
Laurens Pyl	1680–92
Thomas van Rhee	1693–97
Gerrit de Heere	1697–1703
Cornelis Jan Simons	1703–07
Hendrik Becker	1707–16
Isaac Augustin Rumpf	1716–23
Johannes Hertenberg	1723–26
Petrus Vuyst	1726–29
Stephanus Versluys	1729–32
Jacob Christiaan Pielat	1732–34
Diederik van Domburg	1734–36
Gustaaf Willem Baron van Imhoff	1736–39
Willem Maurits Bruyninek	1739–42
Daniel Overbeek	1742–43
Julius V.S. van Gollenesse	1743–51
Gerard Jan Vreelandt	1751–52
Johan Gideon Loten	1752–57
Jan Schreuder	1757–62
L.J. Baron van Eck	1762–65
Iman Willem Falck	1765–85
Willem J. van de Graaf	1785–94
J.G. van Angelbeek	1794–96

BRITISH GOVERNORS

The Hon. Frederick North	1798–1805
Sir Thomas Maitland	1805–11
Sir Robert Brownrigg, Bart.	1812–20
The Hon. Sir Edward Paget	1822–23
Sir Edward Barnes	1824–31
Sir Robert W. Horton, Bart.	1831–37
J.A.S Mackenzie	1837–41
Sir Colin Campbell	1841–47
Viscount Torrington	1847–50
Sir G.W. Anderson	1850–55
Sir Henry G. Ward	1855–60
Sir Charles Justin MacCarthy	1860–63
Sir Hercules G.R. Robinson	1865–72
Sir William H. Gregory	1872–77
Sir James R. Longden	1877–83
The Hon. Sir Arthur H. Gordon	1883–90
Sir Arthur E. Havelock	1890–96
Sir J. West Ridgeway	1896–1903
Sir Henry Arthur Blake	1903–07
Sir Henry E. McCallum	1907–13
Sir Robert Chalmers	1913–16
Sir John Anderson	1916–18

Sir William H. Manning	1918–25
Sir Hugh Clifford	1925–27
Sir Herbert J. Stanley	1927–31
Sir Graeme Thomson	1931–33
Sir Edward Stubbs	1933–37
Sir Andrew Caldecott	1937–44
Sir Henry Monck-Mason-Moore	1944–48

GOVERNORS GENERAL

Sir Henry Monck-Mason-Moore	1948–49
Viscount Soulbury	1949–54
Sir Oliver E. Goonetileke	1954–62
William Gopallawa	1962–72

PRESIDENT

William Gopallawa	1972–78

PRIME MINISTERS

The Rt Hon D.S. Senanayake	September 1947–March 1952
Dudley S. Senanayake	March 1952–October 1953
The Rt Hon Sir John Kotelawala	October 1953–April 1956
S.W.R.D. Bandaranaike	April 1956–September 1959
W. Dahanayake	September 1959–March 1960
Dudley S. Senanayake	March 1960–July 1960
Mrs Sirimavo R.D. Bandaranaike	July 1960–March 1965
Dudley S. Senanayake	March 1965–May 1970
Mrs Sirimavo R.D. Bandaranaike	May 1970–July 1977
J.R. Jayewardene	July 1977–February 1978

EXECUTIVE PRESIDENTS

J.R. Jayewardene	February 1978–February 1989
R. Premadasa	February 1989–May 1993
D.B. Wijetunga	May 1993–November 1994
Mrs Chandrika Bandaranaike Kumaratunga	November 1994–

PRIME MINISTERS UNDER THE EXECUTIVE PRESIDENCY SINCE 1978

R. Premadasa	February 1978–February 1989
D.B. Wijetunga	February 1989–May 1993
Ranil Wickremesinghe	May 1993–August 1994
Mrs Chandrika Bandaranaike Kumaratunga	August 1994–November 1994
Mrs Sirimavo Bandaranaike	November 1994–August 2000
Ratnasiri Wickremanayake	August 2000–December 2001
Ranil Wickremesinghe*	December 2001–April 2004
Mahinda Rajapakse	April 2004–

* He was head of government while Mrs Kumaratunga remained executive president

Bibliography

Abeyasinghe, T.B.H., 'The Myth of the Malwana Convention', *CJHSS*, 7(1), 1964.
_____, *Portuguese Rule in Ceylon, 1594–1612*, Colombo, 1966.
_____, 'The History of the Kandyan Kingdom', *The Sinhalese Encyclopedia*, III, Colombo, 1971.
_____, *Jaffna Under the Portuguese*, Colombo, 1986.
Adikaram, E.W., *Early History of Buddhism in Ceylon*, Colombo, 1946.
Adler, C.J., 'Britain and the Defence of India: The Origins of the Problem, 1798–1815', *Journal of Asian History*, I, 1972.
Alles, A.C., *Insurgency 1971*, Colombo, 1976.
al-Sayyid, Abet Latif, *Egypt and Cromer: A Study in Anglo-Egyptian Relations*, London, 1968.
Arasaratnam, S., *Dutch Power in Ceylon, 1658–1687*, Amsterdam, 1958.
_____, 'Dutch Sovereignty in Ceylon: A Historical Analysis of its Problems', *CJHSS*, 1(1), 1958.
_____, 'Vimala Dharma Sūriya II (1687–1707) and His Relations with the Dutch', *CJHSS*, 6(1), 1963.
_____, 'Baron van Imhoff and Dutch Policy in Ceylon, 1736–1740', in *Bijdra, Taal-, Land-en Volken*, 118(4), 1963.
_____, 'The Administrative Organisation of the Dutch East India Company in Ceylon', *CJHSS*, 8(2), 1965.
_____, 'Dutch Commercial Policies in Ceylon and its Effects on the Indo-Ceylon Trade (1690–1750)', *The Indian Economic and Social History Review (IESHR)*, 4(2), 1967.
_____, 'Introduction: The Dutch in Ceylon and South India, 1700–1750', in *Memoir of Julius Stein van Gollenesse, Governor of Ceylon, 1743–1751*, Colombo, 1974.
_____, *Memoir of Julius Stein van Gollenesse, Governor of Ceylon, 1743–1751*, Colombo, 1974.
Ariyaratne, R.A., 'Communal Conflict in Ceylon Politics and the Advance Towards Self-Government, 1917–1932, unpublished Ph.D. thesis, University of Cambridge, 1972.
Armstrong, Karen, *Buddha*, New York, 2001.
Azeez, A.M.A., *The West Reappraised*, Colombo, 1964.
Bandaranaike, S.W.R.D. (Compiler), *The Handbook of the Ceylon National Congress, 1919-1928*, Colombo, 1928.
Bandaranayake, Senake, *Sigiriya: City, Palace and Royal Gardens*, Paris and Colombo, 1993.

_____, Lorna Dewaraja, Roland Silva and K.D.G. Wimalaratne (eds), *Sri Lanka and the Silk Road of the Sea*, Colombo, 1990.

Basham, A.L. 'Prince Vijaya and the Aryanisation of Ceylon', *Ceylon Historical Journal (CHJ)*, 1(3), 1952.

Blackton, C.S., 'The 1915 Riots in Ceylon: A Symposium', in *Ceylon Studies Seminar*, 1969–70.

_____, 'The Ceylon Insurgency, 1971', *Australia's Neighbours*, 4th series, 76, July–August, 1971.

Bopearachchi, Osmund, 'Seafaring in the Indian Ocean: Archaeological Evidence from Sri Lanka', in H.P. Ray and J.F. Salles (eds), *Tradition and Archaeology: Early Maritime Contacts in the Indian Ocean*, New Delhi, 1996.

_____, 'Ancient Coins in Sri Lanka', *Economic Review*, October–November, 1997.

_____, and R.M. Wickremesinhe, *Ruhuna: An Ancient Civilisation Revisited*, Colombo, 1990.

Boudens, R., *The Catholic Church in Ceylon under Dutch Rule*, Rome, 1957.

Boxer, C.R., 'The Portuguese in the East, 1500–1800', in H.V. Livermore (ed.), *Portugal and Brazil*, London, 1953.

_____, 'Christians and Spices: Portuguese Missionaries in Ceylon, 1515–1658', *History Today*, 8(5), 1958.

_____, 'Portuguese and Dutch Colonial Rivalry, 1641–1661', *Studia*, 2, July 1958.

_____, 'A Note on Portuguese Missionary Methods in the East: 16th–18th Centuries', *CHJ*, 10(4-1), 1960–61.

_____, *The Dutch Seaborne Empire*, London, 1965.

Boyd, William, 'Ceylon and its Pioneers', *Ceylon Literary Register*, 2, 1888.

_____, 'Autobiography', *Ceylon Literary Register*, First series, 11, 1889.

Breckenridge, S.N., *The Hills of Paradise: The Story of Plantation Growth in Sri Lanka*, Colombo, 2001.

Brohier, R.L., 'European Chairs in Ceylon in the 17th and 18th Centuries', *JRAS(CB)*, 31(81), 1928.

_____, *Ancient Irrigation Works in Ceylon*, 3 vols, Colombo, 1934–35.

_____, 'The Inter-relation of Groups of Ancient Reservoirs and Channels in Ceylon, *JRAS(CB)*, 34 (90), 1937.

_____, 'Ceylon–Dutch Domestic Art', *Kalamanjari*, 1(1), 1950–51.

_____, *Furniture of the Dutch Period in Ceylon*, Colombo, 1970.

_____, *The History of Irrigation and Agricultural Colonisation in Ceylon: Tamankaduwa District and the Elahera–Minneriya Canal*, Colombo, 1998. (First edn 1941.)

Brynn, E., 'The Marquess Wellesley and Ceylon, 1798–1803: A Plan for Imperial Consideration', *CJHSS*, 3(2), 1973.

Bullion, A.J., *India, Sri Lanka and the Tamil Crisis, 1976–1994*, London, 1995.

Campbell–Johnson, Allen, *Mission with Mountbatten*, London, 1951.

Casparis, J.G. de, 'Senarat Paranavitana Memorial Lecture: Sri Lanka and Maritime South East Asia', *JRAS(CB)*, 41 (special number), 1996.

_____ and I.W. Mabbett, 'Religion and Popular Beliefs of Southeast Asia before c. 1500', in Nicholas Tarling (ed.), *The Cambridge History of South East Asia*, Vol. I: *From Early Times to c. 1800*, Cambridge, 1994.

Chandraprema, C.A., *Sri Lanka: The Years of Terror—The JVP Insurrection, 1987-1989*, Colombo, 1991.

Chaudhuri, K.N., *Trade and Civilisation in the Indian Ocean: An Economic History from the Rise of Islam to 1750*, Cambridge, 1985.

Clifford, Sir Hugh, *Some Reflections on the Ceylon Land Question*, Colombo, 1927.

Codrington, H.W. *A Short History of Ceylon*, Revised edn, London, 1947.

Colgate, H.A., 'The Royal Navy and Trincomalee: The History of Their Connection, c. 1750-1958', *CJHSS*, 7, 1964.

Coningham, R.A.E. and F.R. Allchin, 'The Rise of Cities in Sri Lanka', in F.R.. Allchin (ed.), *The Archeology of Early Historic South Asia: The Emergence of Cities and States*, Cambridge, 1995.

Coomaraswamy, A. K., *Medieval Sinhalese Art*, 2nd edn, New York, 1956.

———, *History of Indian and Indonesian Art*, London, 1965.

Crowther, S.J.K., *The Knight Errant*.

Das Gupta, B.B., *A Short Economic Survey of Ceylon*, Colombo, 1949.

de Mel, F.J., 'Reform of the Ceylon Legislative Council', *Ceylon National Review*, 44, July 1907.

Deraniyagala, S.U., *The Pre-history of Sri Lanka: An Ecological Perspective*, 2 Vols, Department of Archaeological Survey, Colombo, 1992.

de Silva, C.R., *The Portuguese in Ceylon, 1617–1638*, Colombo, 1972.

———, 'Trade in Ceylon Cinnamon in the Sixteenth Century', *CJHSS*, NS, 3(2), 1973.

———, 'Weightage in University Admissions: Standardisation and District Quotas in Sri Lanka, 1970–75', *MCS*, 5(2), July 1974.

———, 'The First Portuguese Revenue Register of the Kingdom of Kotte—1599', *CJHSS*, NS, 5(1 & 2), 1975.

———, 'The Rise and Fall of the Kingdom of Sītāvaka', *CJHSS*, NS, 7(1), 1977.

———, 'The Rise and Fall of the Kingdom of Sītāvaka (1521-1593)', *History of Ceylon*, Vol. II, University of Peradeniya, 1995.

de Silva, K.M., 'The Colebrooke–Cameron Reforms', *CJHSS*, 2(2), 1959.

———, *Social Policy and Missionary Organisations in Ceylon, 1840–1855*, London, 1965.

———, 'The Third Earl Grey and the Maintenance of an Imperial Policy on the Sale of Crown Lands in Ceylon, c. 1831–1852', *Journal of Asian Studies (JAS)*, 27(1), 1967.

———, 'The Formation and Character of the Ceylon National Congress, 1917–1919', *CJHSS*, 10, 1967.

———, 'The Influence of the English Evangelical Movement on Education in Ceylon', in *Centenary Volume of the Department of Education*, Colombo, 1969.

———, 'The Ceylon National Congress in Disarray I, 1920-21: Sir Ponnambalam Arunachalam Leaves the Congress', *CJHSS*, NS, 2(1), 1972.

———, 'The Ceylon National Congress in Disarray II: The Triumph of Sir William Manning, 1921-24', *CJHSS*, NS, 3(2), 1973.

———, 'The Government and Religion: Problems and Policies c. 1832 to c. 1910', *UCHC*, III, 1973.

———, 'The Legislative Council in the Nineteenth Century', *UCHC*, III, 1973.

———, 'The Reform and Nationalist Movements in the Early Twentieth Century', *UCHC*, III, 1973.

———, 'Religion and the State in the Early Nineteenth Century', *UCHC*, III, 1973.

———, 'Nationalism and its Impact', *CJHSS*, NS, 4(1 & 2), 1974.

_____, 'The Constitution and Constitutional Reforms since 1948', in K.M. de Silva (ed.), *Sri Lanka: A Survey*, London, 1977.

_____, *Regional Powers and Small State Security: India and Sri Lanka, 1977-1990*, Washington DC, 1995.

_____, *Sri Lanka in British Documents on the End of the Empire*, Series B, Vols 1 & 2: Part I, The Second World War and the Soulbury Commission 1939-1945; Part II, Towards Independence, 1945-1948, London, 1997.

_____, *Towards Independence: 1945–1948*, Part II, British Documents on the End of Empire Series, London, 1997.

_____, 'Religion and Nationalism in Nineteenth Century Sri Lanka: Christian Missionaries and Their Critics', *ESR*, 16(1), 1998.

_____, 'Separatism and Political Violence in Sri Lanka', in K.M. de Silva (ed.), *Conflict and Violence in South Asia: Bangladesh, India, Pakistan and Sri Lanka*, Kandy, 2000.

_____, 'Sri Lanka's Prolonged Ethnic Conflict: Negotiating a Settlement', *International Negotiation*, 6, 2001.

_____ and G.H. Peiris (eds), *Pursuit of Peace in Sri Lanka: Past Failures and Future Prospects*, Kandy, 2000.

_____ and Howard Wriggins, *J.R. Jayawardene of Sri Lanka: A Political Biography*, Vol. II, London, 1994.

de Silva, Mervyn, 'Sri Lanka: The End of Welfare Politics', *South Asian Review*, 1973.

Dewaraja, L.S., *A Study of the Political, Administrative and Social Structure of the Kandyan Kingdom of Ceylon, 1707–1760*, Colombo, 1972. (Revised edn published as *The Kandyan Kingdom of Sri Lanka, 1707–1782*, Colombo, 1988.)

Dharmadasa, K.N.O., 'Drama, Film and Music', in K.M. de Silva (ed.), *Sri Lanka: A Survey*, London, 1977.

_____, 'Literary Activity in the Indigenous Languages', in K.M. de Silva (ed.), *Sri Lanka: A Survey*, London, 1977.

Digby, W., *Representative Government, Elective and Broad, Not Nominated and Narrow*, Calcutta, 1876.

_____, *An Oriental Crown Colony Ripe for Representative Government*, Calcutta, 1877.

Dohanian, Diran K., *The Mahayana Buddhist Sculpture of Ceylon*, New York, 1977.

Donoughmore Commission, *The Donoughmore Report*, London, 1928.

Ferguson, J., *Ceylon in 1883*, Colombo, 1883.

Fernando, P.E.E., 'An Account of the Kandyan Mission Sent to Siam in 1750 AD', *CJHSS*, 2(1), 1959.

Fernando, P.T.M, 'The Post-Riots Campaign for Justice', *JAS*, 29(2), 1970.

Frasch, Tilman, 'A Buddhist Network in the Bay of Bengal: Relations between Bodhgaya, Burma and Sri Lanka, c. 300–1300', in Claude Guillot et al. (eds), *From the Mediterranean to the China Sea: Miscellaneous Notes*, Wiesbaden, 1998.

_____, 'The Buddhist Connection: Sinhalese-Burmese Intercourse in the Middle Ages', in Georg Berkemer, Tilman Frasch, Hermann Kulke and Jurgen Lutt (eds), *Explorations in the History of South Asia*, New Delhi, 2001.

Geiger, Wilhelm, *Culavamsa*, 2 vols, London, 1925 and 1927.

_____, *The Mahāvamsa or the Great Chronicle of Sri Lanka*, London, 1950.

Goonewardena, K.W., *The Foundation of Dutch Power in Ceylon*, Amsterdam, 1958.

Gregory, W., *Autobiography* (edited by Lady Gregory), London, 1894.

Grey, Earl, *The Colonial Policy of Lord John Russell's Administration*, 2 vols, 2nd edn, London, 1853.

Gunasinghe, P.A.T., *The Tamils of Sri Lanka*, Colombo, 1985.

Gunawardana, Leslie, *A Short History of the Lanka Sama Samaja Party*, Colombo, 1960.

Gunawardana, R.A.L.H., 'Hydraulic Engineering in Ancient Sri Lanka: The Cistern Sluices', *Past and Present*, 53, 1971.

———, 'Irrigation and Hydraulic Society in Medieval Ceylon', *Past and Present*, 53, 1971.

———, 'Irrigation and Hydraulic Society in Early Medieval Ceylon', *Past and Present*, 53, November 1971.

———, 'Some Economic Aspects of Monastic Life in the Later Anuradhapura Period', *CJHSS*, NS, 2(1) 1972.

———, *Robe and Plough: Monasticism and Economic Interest in Early Medieval Sri Lanka*, Tucson, 1979.

———, 'Total Power or Shared Power?: A Study of the Hydraulic State and its Transformations in Sri Lanka from the Third to the Ninth Century AD', *Indian Historical Review*, 7(1 & 2), 1980-81.

———, 'Seaways to Sieladiba: Changing Patterns of Navigation in the Indian Ocean and their Impact on Precolonial Sri Lanka', in S. Bandarnayake et al. (eds), *Sri Lanka and the Silk Road of the Sea*, Colombo, 1990.

———, 'Prelude to the State: An Early Phase in the Evolution of Political Institutions in Ancient Sri Lanka', in R.A.L.H. Gunawardana et al. (eds), *Reflections on a Heritage: Historical Scholarship in Pre-Modern Sri Lanka*, Part I, Colombo, 2000.

——— and Yumio Sakura, 'Sri Lankan Ships in China', in S. Bandarnayake et al. (eds), *Sri Lanka and the Silk Road of the Sea*, Colombo, 1990.

———, S. Pathmanathan and M. Rohanadeera (eds), *Reflections on a Heritage: Historical Scholarship in Pre-Modern Sri Lanka*, Part I, Colombo, 2000.

Gunawardena, R.D., 'The Reform Movement and Political Organisation in Ceylon with Special Reference to the Temperance Movement and Regional Association, 1930-1960', unpublished Ph.D. thesis, University of Sri Lanka, Peradeniya, 1976.

Guruge, A.W.P., 'The Sri Lankan Factor in the Development of the Art of Sukothai and Lanna Tai, in S. Bandarnayake et al. (eds), *Sri Lanka and the Silk Road of the Sea*, Colombo, 1990.

Hall, H. Duncan, *Commonwealth: A History of the British Commonwealth of Nations*, London, 1971.

Hall, Kenneth, 'Economic History of Early Southeast Asia', in Nicholas Tarling (ed.), *The Cambridge History of South East Asia, Vol. I: From Early Times to c. 1800*, Cambridge, 1994.

Halliday, F., 'The Ceylonese Insurrection', *New Left Review*, 64, September–October 1971.

Halpe, Ashley and K.N.O. Dharmadasa, 'Literature and the Arts, in K.M. de Silva (ed.), *Sri Lanka: A Survey*, London, 1977.

Harlow, V., *The Founding of the Second British Empire, 1763–1793*, 2 vols, London, 1952 and 1964.

Hettiarachchy, T., *History of Kingship in Ceylon up to the Fourth Century AD*, Colombo, 1973.

Hocart, A.M., *Caste: A Comparative Study*, London, 1950.

Hornell, James, *Water Transport: Origins and Early Evolution*, Cambridge, 1946.

Huan, Ma, *Ying-yai Sheny-lan* ('The Overall Survey of the Oceans Shores'), translated from the Chinese with introduction, notes and appendices by J.V.G. Mills, Cambridge, 1970.

Indrapala, K., (ed.), *The Collapse of the Rājarata Civilization in Ceylon and the Drift to the South West*, Ceylon Studies Seminar, Peridiniya, 1971.

——, 'Dravidian Settlements in Ceylon and the Beginning of the Kingdom of Jaffna', unpublished Ph.D. thesis, University of London, 1966.

——, 'Early Tamil Settlements in Ceylon', *JRAS(CB)*, 10, 1969.

——, 'The Origin of the Tamil Vanni Chieftaincies of Ceylon', *The Ceylon Journal of the Humanities*, 1(2), July 1970.

——, 'Tamil Language and Literature', *UCHC*, III, 1973.

——, 'Early Tamil Settlements in Ceylon', in R.A.L.H. Gunawardana et al. (eds), *Reflections on a Heritage: Historical Scholarship in Pre-Modern Sri Lanka*, Part I, Colombo, 2000.

Indraratna, A.D.V. de S., *The Ceylon Economy: From the Great epression ot eh Great Boom—An Analysis of Cyclical Fluctuations and their Impact 91930–1952)*, Colombo, 1966.

Ingram, E. (ed.), *Two Views of British India: The Private Correspondence of Mr Dundas and Lord Wellesley, 1798–1801*, Bath, 1970.

Jayasekera, P.V.J., 'Social and Political Change in Ceylon in 1900-1919', unpublished Ph. D. thesis, University of London, 1970.

Jayasinghe, W.T., *The Indo-Ceylon Problem: The Politics of Immigrant Labour*, Colombo, 2002.

Jayatilaka, D.B., 'Sinhalese Embassies to Arakan', *JRAS(CB)*, 35, 1940.

Jayawardena, V. Kumari, *The Rise of the Labour Movement in Ceylon, 1892–1933*, Durham, NC, 1972.

Jayawardena, L., 'Origins of the Left Movement in Ceylon', *MCS*, 2(2), 1971.

——, 'Sri Lanka', in Hollis Chenery, John H. Duloy and Richard Jolly (eds), *Redistribution with Growth*, London, 1974.

Jayawardena, L.R., 'The Supply of Sinhalese Labour to Ceylon Plantations, 1830-1930', unpublished Ph. D. thesis, University of Cambridge, 1963.

Jayaweera, Swarna, 'Education Policy in the Early Twentieth Century', *UCHC*, III, 1973.

Jeffries, Sir Charles, *O.E.G.: A Biography of Sir Oliver Ernest Goonetilleke*, London, 1969.

Jennings, Sir Ivor, 'The Foundation of the University of Ceylon', *UCR*, 9, 1951.

Jennings, W.I., *The Economy of Ceylon*, 2nd edn, London, 1951.

Jiggins, Janice, 'Dismantling Welfarism in Sri Lanka', *Overseas Development Review*, 2, 1976.

Kaarthikeyan, D.R. and R. Raju, *The Rajiv Gandhi Assassination: The Investigation*, Delhi, 2004.

Kanapathypillai, V., 'Dutch Rule in Maritime Ceylon, 1766–1796', unpublished Ph.D. thesis, University of London, 1969.

Kandyan National Assembly, *The Rights and Claims of the Kandyan People*, Kandy, 1928.

Karunatilaka, P.V.B., 'Early Sri Lankan Society: Some Reflections on Caste, Social Groups and Ranking', *The Sri Lanka Journal of the Humanities*, 9(1&2), 1983.

Kearney, R. and J. Jiggins, 'The Ceylon Insurrection of 1971', *Journal of Commonwealth and Comparative Politics*, 13(1), March 1975.

Kelegama, Saman, *Economic Development in Sri Lanka during the 50 Years of Independence: What Went Wrong*, Delhi, 1998.

Kiribamune, S. 'The Mahāvamsa: A Study of the Ancient Historiography of Sri Lanka', in P.L. Prematillaka, K. Indrapala and Lohuizen de Leeuw (eds), *Senarat Paranavitana Commemoration Volume*, Studies in South Asian Culture, Vol. III, Leiden, 1978.

_____, 'Muslims and the Trade of the Arabian Sea with Special Reference to Sri Lanka from the Birth of Islam to the 15 th Century', in M.A.M. Shukri (ed.), *The Muslims of Sri Lanka: Avenues to Antiquity*, Beruwala, 1985.

_____, 'Tamils in Ancient and Medieval Sri Lanka: The Historical Roots of Ethnic Identities', *Ethnic Studies Report (ESR)*, 4 (1), 1986.

_____, 'Trade Patterns of the Indian Ocean and their Impact on the Politics of Medieval Sri Lanka', in C.R. de Silva and S. Kiribamune (eds), *K.W. Goonerwardena Felicitation Volume*, Peradeniya, 1989.

_____, 'The State and the Sangha in Pre-modern Sri Lanka', in G.H. Peiris and S.W.R. de A. Somarasinghe (eds), *History and Politics: Millennial Perspectives*, Colombo, 1999.

_____, 'The Role of the Port City of Mahatittha (Mantota) in the Trade Networks of the Indian Ocean', in R.A.L.H. Gunawardana et al. (eds), *Reflections on a Heritage: Historical Scholarship in Pre-Modern Sri Lanka*, Part I, Colombo, 2000.

Knox, Robert, *An Historical Relation of Ceylon*, 1st edn, London, 1681. (Edited by James Ryan, Glasgow, 1911.)

Kotelawele, D.A., 'Agrarian Policies of the Dutch in South-West Ceylon, 1743–1767', *Afdeling Agrarische Geschiedenis Bijdragen (AAGB)*, 14, 1967.

Kulasuriya, A.S., 'Regional Independence and Elite Change in the Politics of 14th Century Sri Lanka', *JRAS (GR&I)*, 2, 1976.

Kulke, Herman and Dietmar Rothermund, *A History of India*, 3rd edn, New York, 1998.

LaBrooy, N.N., 'The Movement Towards Constitutional Reform in Ceylon, 1880–1910', unpublished D. Phil. thesis, Oxford University, 1973.

Levathes, Louise, *When China Ruled the Seas: The Treasure Fleet of the Dragon Throne, 1405–33*, Oxford, 1994.

Leach, E.R., 'Hydraulic Society in Ceylon', *Past and Present*, 15, 1959.

Lerski, G., *Origins of Trotskyism in Ceylon*, Stanford, 1968.

Lewis, W. Arthur (ed.), 'A Short History of Irrigation Works upto the 11th Century, *JRAS(CB)*, 7(1), 1960.

_____, *Tropical Development, 1880–1913: Studies in Economic Progress*, London, 1970.

Liyanagamage, A., *The Decline of Polonnaruva and the Rise of Dambadeniya*, Colombo, 1968.

_____, 'Conflicts in State-Sangha Relations in the Early History of Sri Lanka', in R.A.L.H. Gunawardana et al. (eds), *Reflections on a Heritage: Modern Scholarship on Pre-modern Sri Lanka*, Colombo, 2000.

————, 'Kerelas in Medieval Sri Lankan History: A Study of Two Contesting Roles', in R.A.L.H. Gunawardana et al. (eds), *Reflections on a Heritage: Modern Scholarship on Pre-modern Sri Lanka*, Colombo, 2000.

Low, D.A., *Lion Rampant: Essays in the Study of British Imperialism*, London, 1973.

Ludowyk, K.E.F.C., *Footprint of the Buddha*, London, 1958.

————, 'Native of Class Relations in the South-West of Ceylon, c. 1700–1833: A Review of Long Term Changes', *Vidyalankara Faculty Seminar*, Series 3, 1974.

MacDougall, R.D., 'Domestic Architecture Among the Kandyan Sinhalese', unpublished Ph.D. thesis, Cornell University, 1971.

MacGregor, Ian, 'Europe and the East', in *New Cambridge Modern History, III: The Reformation, 1520–1559*, Cambridge, 1958.

Malalgoda, K., 'Buddhist-Christian Confrontation in Ceylon, 1800–1880', *Social Compass*, 20, 1974.

————, *Buddhism in Sinhalese Society, 1750–1900*, Berkeley, 1976.

Mattau, S.A.W., 'Governor van Imhoff and His Scheme of Inland River Communications in the Colombo Disavony', *UCR*, 5(1), 1947.

Mendis, G.C., *The Early History of Ceylon*, Calcutta, 1932.

————, 'Pali Chronicles of Ceylon', *UCR*, IV(2), October 1946.

Mendis, V.L.B., 'The Advent of the British to Ceylon, 1762–11803', *CHJ*, 18, 1971.

Meyer, E. 'L'impact de la dépression des années 1930 sur l'economie et la societé rurale de Sri Lanka', *Purusärtha*, 2, 1975.

Moon, P. *Divide and Quit*, London, 1962.

Muni, S.D., *Pangs of Proximity: India and Sri Lanka's Ethnic Crisis*, Oslo, 1993.

Murphey, R., 'The Ruin of Ancient Ceylon', *Journal of Asian Studies*, 16(2), 1957.

Nadaraja, T., *The Legal System of Ceylon in its Historical Setting*, Lieden, 1972.

————, 'The Law', *UCHC*, III, 1973.

Namasivayam, S., *The Legislatures of Ceylon*, London, 1951.

Narayan Swamy, M.R., *Tigers of Lanka: From Boys to Guerrillas*, Delhi, 1994.

Nicholas, C.W., 'The Irrigation Works of King Parākramabāhu I', *CHJ*, 4(1-4), 1954–55.

————, 'A Short Account of the History of Irrigation Works up to the 11th Century', *JRASCB*, NS, 7(1), 1960.

———— and S. Paranavitana, *A Concise History of Ceylon*, Colombo, 1961.

O'Ballance, Edgar, *The Cyanide War: Tamil Insurrection in Sri Lanka, 1973-88*, London, 1989.

Obeyesekere, G., 'Religious Symbolism and Political Change in Ceylon', *MCS*, 1(1), 1970.

Olcott, H.S., *Old Diary Leaves: The True History of the Theosophical Society*, 2nd series, Madras, 1928.

Oliver, H.M., *Economic Opinion and Policy in Ceylon*, Durham, NC, 1957.

Panabokke, C.R., *The Small Tank Cascade Systems of the Rājarata: Their Settings, Distribution Patterns and Hydrography*, Colombo, 1999.

Paranavitana, S., 'Mahayanism in Ceylon', *Ceylon Journal of Science (G)*, 2(1), 1928.

————, 'The Art and Architecture of the Polonnaruva Period', *CHJ*, 4, 1954–55.

————, *Sigiri Graffiti, Being Sinhalese Verses of the Eighth, Ninth and Tenth Centuries*, Ceylon, 1956.

————, 'Civilisation of the Early Period: Religion and Art', in *UCHC*, I, 1959.

_____, (ed.), *History of Ceylon (UCHC)*, Colombo, 1959–60.

_____, 'The Arya Kingdom in North Ceylon', *JRAS(CB)*, NS, 7(2), 1961.

_____, *Sinhalayo*, Colombo, 1967.

Parker, H., *Ancient Ceylon*, London, 1909.

Pathmanathan, S., 'Feudal Policy in Medieval Ceylon: An Examination of the Chieftaincies of the Vanni', *CJHSS*, NS, 2(2), July-December 1972.

_____, *The Kingdom of Jaffna*, Part 1 (circa AD 1250–1450), Colombo, 1978.

Paulusz, J.H.O., 'The Outbreak of the Kandyan–Dutch War in 1761 and the Great Rebellion', *JRAS(CB)*, NS, 3, 1953.

_____ (ed.), *Secret Minutes of the Dutch Political Council, 1762*, Colombo, 1954.

Pearson, Joseph, 'European Chairs in Ceylon in the 17th and 18th Centuries', *JRAS(CB)*, 31(81), 1928.

Peebles, P. 'The Transformation of a Colonial Elite: The Mudaliyars of Nineteenth Century Ceylon', unpublished Ph.D. thesis, University of Chicago, 1973.

_____, *Social Change in Nineteenth Century Ceylon*, Delhi, 1995.

Peiris, G.H., *Development and Change in Sri Lanka*, New Delhi, 1996.

_____, 'Insurrection and Youth Unrest in Sri Lanka', in G.H. Peiris and S.W.R. de A. Samarasinghe (eds), *History and Politics: Millennial Perspectives*, Essays in Honour of Kingsley de Silva, Colombo, 1999.

Peiris, Rt Revd Bishop Edmund, 'Sinhalese Christian Literature of the XVIIth and XVIIIth Centuries', *JRAS(CB)*, 35, 1943.

_____, 'Tamil Catholic Literature in Ceylon from the 16th to the 18th Century', *Tamil Culture*, II, 1953.

Pendergrast, M., *Uncommon Grounds: The History of Coffee and How it Transformed Our World*, New York, 1999.

Perera, B.J., 'The Foreign Trade and Commerce of Ancient Ceylon: The Ports of Ancient Ceylon', *CHJ*, 1(2), 1951.

_____, 'Foreign Trade and Commerce of Ancient, Ceylon: Ancient Ceylon and Its Trade with India', *CHJ*, 1(3), 1952.

_____, 'Foreign Trade and Commerce of Ancient Ceylon: Ancient Ceylon's Trade with the Empires of the Eastern and Western Worlds', *CHJ*, 1(4), 1952.

Perera, Fr S.G., *Life of Father Jacome Gonçalves*, Madura, 1942.

Perera, Lakshman S., 'Proprietary and Tenurial Rights in Ancient Ceylon', *CJHSS*, 2, 1959.

_____, 'The Early Kings of Ceylon up to Mutasiva', in S. Paranavitana (ed.), *History of Ceylon*, Vol. I, Colombo, 1959.

_____, *The Institutions of Ancient Ceylon from Inscriptions (from the 3rd Century to 830 AD)*, Vol. I, Kandy, 2001.

_____, *The Institutions of Ancient Ceylon from Inscriptions (from 831 to 1016 AD): Political Institutions*, Vol. II, Part I, Kandy, 2003.

_____, *The Institutions of Ancient Ceylon from Inscriptions (from 831 to 1016 AD): Economic Institutions*, Vol. II, Part II, Kandy, 2005.

Pieris, P.E., 'An Account of King Kīrti Śri's Embassy to Siam', *JRAS(CB)*, 18, 1903.

_____, *Tri Sinhala: The Last Phase, 1796–1815*, 2nd edn, Colombo, 1939.

_____, *The Ceylon Littoral—1593*, Colombo, 1949.

_____, *Sinhale and the Patriots, 1815–1818*, Colombo, 1950.

Pieris, R., *Sinhalese Social Organisation: The Kandyan Period*, Colombo, 1956.

_____, 'Universities, Politics and Public Opinion in Ceylon', *Minerva II* (Summer), 1964.

Powell, G., 'The Fall of Kandy 1815: The Willerman Letters', *CJHSS*, NS, 1(2), 1971.

_____, *The Kandyan Wars: The British Army in Ceylon, 1803–1818*, London 1973.

Prematilleke P.L. and L.K. Karunaratna, 'Polonnaruva: The Medieval Capital', in *The Cultural Triangle of Sri Lanka* (a UNESCO publication), Colombo, 1993.

Price, M.T., *Christian Missions and Oriental Civilisations*, Shanghai, 1924.

Prickett, Martha, 'Sri Lanka's Foreign Trade Before AD 600: Archaeological Evidence', in K.M. de Silva, Sirima Kiribamune and C.R. de Silva (eds), *Asian Panorama: Essays in Asian History, Past and Present*, Delhi, 1990.

Prothero, Stephen, *The White Buddhist: The Asian Odyssey of Henry Steel Olcott*, Indiana, 1996.

Raghupathy, P., *Early Settlement in Jaffna: Archaeological Survey*, Chennai, 1987.

Rahula, Revd Walpola, *What the Buddha Taught*, London, 1959.

_____, *History of Buddhism in Ceylon*, 2nd edn, Colombo, 1966.

Ranasinha, A.G., *Memories and Musings*, Colombo, 1972.

Raven-Hart, R., *The Dutch Wars with Kandy, 1764–1766*, Ceylon Historical Manuscripts Commission, Bulletin No. 6, Colombo, 1964.

Rigg, C.R., 'On Coffee Planting in Ceylon', *The Journal of Indian Archipelago and Eastern Asia (Singapore)*, 6, 1852, 16 and 23 June 1846.

Roberts, Michael, 'Grain Taxes in British Ceylon, 1832-1878: Problems in the Field', *JAS*, 27(4), 1968.

_____, 'The Rise of the Kārāvas', *Ceylon Studies Seminar*, Series 5, 1968-69.

_____, 'Grain Taxes in British Ceylon, 1832-1878: Theories, Prejudices and Controversies', *Modern Ceylon Studies*, 1(1), 1970.

_____ (ed.), *A Symposium on the 1915 Communal Riots*, Ceylon Studies Seminar 1969/70 Series, 1970.

_____, 'Irrigation Policy in British Ceylon during the Nineteenth Century', *South Asia*, 2, 1972.

_____, 'Aspects of Ceylon's Agrarian Economy in the Nineteenth Century', *UCHC*, III, 1973.

_____, 'Fissures and Solidarities: Weakness within the Working Class Movement in the Early Twentieth Century', *MCS*, 5(1), 1974.

_____, 'Labour and Politics of Labour in the Late Nineteenth and Early Twentieth Century', *MCS*, 5(2), 1974.

_____, 'Problems of Social Stratification and the Demarcation of National and Local Elites in British Ceylon', *JAS*, 33(4), 1974.

_____, 'A New Marriage, An Old Dichotomy: The "Middle Class" in British Ceylon', in K. Indrapala (ed.), *J.T. Rutnam Felicitation Volume*, Jaffna, 1975.

_____, *Sinhala Consciousness in the Kandyan Period 1590s–1815*, Colombo, 2003.

_____ and L.A. Wickremeratne, 'Export Agriculture in the Nineteenth Century', *UCHC*, III, 1973.

Rose, Saul, 'Sri Lanka at the Turning Point: The Future of Parliamentary Democracy', *The Round Table*, 256, October 1974.

Rowland, B., *The Art and Architecture of India*, 3rd revised edn, Harmondsworth, 1967.

Russell, Jane, 'Sri Lanka's Election Turning Point', *The Journal of Commonwealth and Comparative Politics*, 16(1), 1978.

———, 'The Ceylon Tamils Under the Donoughmore Constitution (1931–1847)', unpublished Ph.D. thesis, University of Sri Lanka, Peradeniya, 1976. (Later published as *Communal Politics Under the Donoughmore Constitution, 1931-1947*, Dehiwala, 1982.)

———, 'The Dance of the Turkey-Cock: The Jaffna Boycott', *CJHSS*, 8(1), 1978.

Samaraweera, Vijaya, 'Governor Sir Robert Wilmot Horton and the Reforms of 1833 in Ceylon', *The Historical Journal*, 15(2), 1972.

———, 'The Cinnamon Trade of Ceylon in the Early Nineteenth Century' *IESHR*, 8(4), 1971.

———, 'Arabi Pasha in Ceylon, 1883–1901', *Islamic Culture*, 49, October 1976.

———, 'Land as "Patrimony": Nationalist Response to Immigrant Labour Demands for Land in the Early Twentieth Century Sri Lanka', *IESHR*, 14(3), 1977.

———, 'Land Policy and Peasant Colonisation, 1914–1948, *UCHC*, III, 1973.

———, 'The Development of the Administrative System from 1802 to 1832', *UCHC*, III, 1973.

———, 'Sri Lanka's 1977 General Election: The Resurgence of the UNP', *Asian Survey*, 17(2), December 1977.

———, 'The Role of the Bureaucracy', *CJHSS*, NS, 4(1&2), 1974.

———, 'The Administration and the Judicial System' in K.M. de Silva (ed.), *Sri Lanka: A Survey*, London, 1977.

Sankaran, S., *Postcolonial Insecurities: India, Sri Lanka and the Question of Nationhood*, Delhi, 2000.

Saparamadu, S. 'The Sinhalese Language and Literature of the Polonnaruva Period', *CHJ*, 4(1–4), 1954–55.

Sarachchandra, E.R., 'Sinhala Language and Literature', *UCHC*, III, 1973.

———, *Modern Sinhalese Fiction*, Mount Lavinia, 1943.

———, *The Folk Drama of Ceylon*, Colombo, 1946.

———, *The Sinhalese Novel*, Colombo, 1950.

Sastri, K.A. Nilakanta, *A History of South India from Prehistoric Times to the Fall of Vijayanagar*, Madras, 1955.

———, *The Cōlas*, 2nd edn, Madras, 1955.

Schroeder, Ulrich von, *Buddhist Sculptures of Sri Lanka*, Hong Kong, 1990.

———, *The Golden Age of Sculpture in Sri Lanka*, Hong Kong, 1990.

Senaratne, S.P.F., *Prehistoric Archaeology in Ceylon*, Colombo, 1969.

Seneviratne, S., 'The Ecology and Archaeology of the Seruwila Copper-Magnetite Prospect, Northeast Sri Lanka', *The Sri Lanka Journal of the Humanities*, 21(1 & 2) 1995.

Sirisena, W.M., *Ceylon and South-East Asia: Political, Religious and Cultural Relations, AD c. 1000 to c. 1500*, Leiden, 1978.

———, 'Sri Lanka's Commercial Relations with the Outside World from Earliest Times to the 8th Century AD', *The Sri Lanka Journal of South Asian Studies*, 2(1), 1980.

———, 'Maritime Commerce of Sri Lanka in Medieval Times', *The Sri Lanka Journal of the Humanities*, 11(1 & 2), 1983.

Siriweera, W.I., 'Land Tenure and Revenue in Medieval Ceylon (AD 1000–1500)', *CJHSS*, NS, 2(1), January–July, 1972.

_____, *History of Sri Lanka: From Earliest Times up to the Sixteenth Century*, Colombo, 2002.

Sisson, Richard and Leo E. Rose, *War and Secession: Pakistan, India and the Creation of Bangladesh*, Berkeley, 1990.

Smith, D.E. (ed.), *South Asian Politics and Religion*, Princeton, 1966.

Snodgrass, Donald R., *Ceylon: An Export Economy in Transition*, Homewood, IL, 1966.

_____, 'Sri Lanka's Economic Development during Twenty-Five Years of Independence', *CJHSS*, NS, 4(1 & 2), 1974.

Somaratne, G.P.V., 'Grand Eunuch Ho and Ceylon', *JRAS(CB)*, NS, 1971.

_____, *The Political History of the Kingdom of Kotte*, Colombo, 1975.

Spence-Hardy, R., *The Jubilee Memorials of the Wesleyan Mission, South Ceylon, 1814–64*, Colombo, 1864.

Spencer, G.W. *The Politics of Expansion: The Chola Conquest of Sri Lanka and Sri Vijaya*, Madras, 1983.

Srinivas, M.N. and Arsind Shah, 'The Myth of Self-sufficiency of the Indian Village', *Economic Weekly*, 12, 1960.

Stein, Burton, *Peasant State and Society in Medieval South India*, New Delhi, 1980.

_____, *A History of India*, The Blackwell History of the World, Oxford, 1998.

Taylor, Keith W., 'The Early Kingdoms', in Nicholas Tarling (ed.), *The Cambridge History of South East Asia, Vol. I: From Early Times to c. 1800*, Cambridge, 1994.

Tennent, James Emerson, *Ceylon: An Account of the Island—Physical, Historical and Topographical with Notices of its Natural History, Antiquities and Productions*, London, 1859.

Thapar, Romila, *Asoka and the Decline of the Mauryas*, Oxford, 1961.

_____, *A History of India*, Harmondsworth, 1966.

Tinker, H., *A New System of Slavery: The Export of Indian Labour Overseas, 1830–1920*, London, 1974.

Toussaint, A., *History of the Indian Ocean*, London, 1966.

Tuker, F., *While Memory Serves*, London, 1950.

Vijayatuaga, J., *Grass for My Feet*, Edward Arnold & Co., 1935.

Webb Jr, L.A. James, *Tropical Pioneers: Human Agency and Ecological Change in the Highlands of Sri Lanka, 1800–1900*, Athens, Ohio, 2002.

Weerakkody, D.P.M., *Taprobanê: Ancient Sri Lanka as Known to Greeks and Romans*, Brepolis, 1997.

Wesumperuma, D., 'The History of the Grain Tax in British Ceylon with Special Reference to the Period from 1878 to 1892', unpublished MA thesis, Vidyodaya University, 1968.

_____, 'Land Sales Under the Paddy Tax in Ceylon', *Vidyodaya Journal of Arts, Science and Letters*, (1), 1969.

_____, 'The Evictions Under the Paddy Tax, and Their Impact on the Peasantry of Walapane, 1882–1885', *CJHSS*, 10, 1970.

Wickremaratne, L.A., '1865 and the Changes in Educational Policies', *MCS*, 1970.

_____, 'Economic Development in the Plantation Sector, c. 1900 to 1947', *UCHC*, III, 1973.

_____, 'The Emergence of a Welfare Policy, 1931–1948', *UCHC*, III, 1973.

_____, 'Grain Consumption and Famine Conditions in Late Nineteenth Century Ceylon', *CJHSS*, NS, 3(2), 1973.

_____, 'Kandyans and Nationalism in Sri Lanka: Some Reflections', *CJHSS*, NS, 5(1&2), 1975.

_____, 'Religion, Nationalism and Social Change in Ceylon, 1865–1885', *JRAS(GB &LVI)*, 2, 1969.

_____, 'The Establishment of the Tea Industry in Ceylon: The First Phase, c. 1870 to c. 1900, *CJHSS*, NS, 2(2), 1972.

Wickremeratne, U.C., 'Lord North and the Kandyan Kingdom, 1798–1805', *JRAS(GB & I)*, I, 1973.

_____, 'The English East India Company and Society in the Maritime Provinces of Ceylon, 1796–1802', *JRAS(GB & I)*, 2, 1971.

Wickremasekara, S.B.W., 'The Social and Political Organisation of the Kandyan Kingdom', unpublished MA thesis, University of London, 1961.

Wickremesinghe, Martin, *Gamperaliya*, Colombo, 1944.

_____, *Yuganthaya*, Colombo, 1948.

_____, *Kali Yugaya*, Colombo, 1957.

Wight, M., *The Development of the Legislative Council, 1906–1945*, London, 1946.

Wijesekera, O.H. de A., 'Pāli and Sanskrit in the Polonnaruva Period', *CHJ*, 4, 1945–55.

Will, H.A., 'Problems of Constitutional Reform in Jamaica, Mauritius and Trinidad, 1880–1895', *English Historical Review*, 321, October 1966.

Wilson, A.J., 'Sri Lanka's Foreign Policy: Change and Continuity', *CJHSS*, NS, 4(1&2), 1974.

_____, *Politics in Sri Lanka, 1947–79*, London, 1979.

Winius, G.D., *The Fatal History of Portuguese Ceylon: Transition to Dutch Rule*, Cambridge, MA, 1971.

Wittfogel, K.A., *Oriental Despotism*, New Haven, Connecticut, 1957.

Woodward, Calvin, *The Growth of a Party System in Ceylon*, Providence, RI, 1969.

_____, 'The Party System in Comparative Perspective: An Assessment', *CJHSS*, NS, 4(1&2), 1974.

Wriggins, W. Howard, *Ceylon: Dilemmas of a New Nation*, Princeton, NJ, 1960.

Young, P.F. and S. Jebanesan, The Bible Trembled: The Hindu-Christian Controversy of Nineteenth Century Ceylon, Nobili Research Library, Vol. 22, Vienna, 1995.

Further Reading

1. BIBLIOGRAPHICAL WORKS

With H.A.I. Goonetileke's massive *A Bibliography of Ceylon: A Systematic Guide to the Literature on the Land, People, History and Culture Published in the Western Languages from the Sixteenth Century to the Present Day*, Switzerland, 1970–1983, of which five volumes have been published, researchers and the general reader alike have a reliable and self-sufficient source of reference on historical writings on Sri Lanka. Some short bibliographies by others including specialist historians might also be mentioned. They include Vijaya Samaraweera's bibliography in K.M. de Silva (ed.), *History of Ceylon*, Vol. III, University of Ceylon, Colombo, 1973, pp. 534–58 and the bibliography in K.M. de Silva (ed.), *History of Sri Lanka*, Vol. II (from c. 1500 to c. 1800), Peradeniya, 1995, pp. 567–94, compiled by the editor.

See also Vijaya Samaraweera, *Sri Lanka*, World Bibliographical Series, Vol. 20, London, 1987.

2. GENERAL

The following are short introductory surveys of the island's history and politics:

S. Arasaratnam, *Ceylon*, Englewood Cliffs, NJ, 1964.
H. W. Codrington, *A Short History of Ceylon*, revised edn, London, 1947.
K.M. de Silva, 'Historical Survey', in K.M. de Silva (ed.), *Sri Lanka: A Survey*, London, 1976, pp. 31–85.
C.R. de Silva, *Sri Lanka: A History*, Delhi, 1983.
B.H. Farmer, *Ceylon: A Divided Nation*, London, 1963.
E.F.C. Ludowyk, *The Story of Ceylon*, London, 1962.
E. Meyer, *Ceylon (Sri Lanka)* (in French), Paris, 1977.
S.A. Pakeman, *Ceylon*, London, 1964.
U. Phadnis, *Sri Lanka*, Delhi, 1973.

3. ANCIENT SRI LANKA

S. Paranavitana (ed.), *History of Ceylon*, Vol. I (Parts I and II), The University of Ceylon, published in 1959–60. This work, now out of print and out of date, still remains the most wide-ranging study of ancient Sri Lanka. The scope of C.W. Nicholas and S. Paranavitana, *A Concise History of Ceylon*, Colombo, 1961, is much narrower than its title suggests: it is, in fact, a study of ancient Sri Lanka. Its usefulness is vitiated by the authors' proclivity for fanciful theories on some aspects of the island's history. Two earlier works—H.W. Codrington, *A Short History of Ceylon* and G.C. Mendis, *Early History of Ceylon*, Calcutta, 1932, (several editions)—may still be read with profit.

A great deal of work has been done on several aspects of the history of ancient Sri Lanka; most of it is published in learned journals, or remain as unpublished doctoral dissertations. But there are several valuable monographs, many of them analysing aspects of the history of this period in considerable depth. Some of these are listed below. Those marked with an asterisk contain useful bibliographies.

E.W. Adikaram, *The Early History of Buddhism in Ceylon**, Colombo, 1953.

M.B. Ariyapala, *Society in Medieval Ceylon*, Colombo, 1956.

S. Bandarnayake, *Sinhalese Monastic Architecture: Viharas of Anuradhapura*, Leiden, 1974.

R. Brohier, *Ancient Irrigation Works in Ceylon**, 3 Vols, Colombo, 1933.

A. Coomaraswamy, *Medieval Sinhalese Art**, 2nd edn, New York, 1951.

W. Geiger (ed. H. Bechert), *Culture of Ceylon in Medieval Times**, Wiesbaden, 1960.

R.A.L.H. Gunawardana, *Robe and Plough: Monasticism and Economic Interest in Early Medieval Sri Lanka**, Tucson, Arizona, 1979.

T. Hettiarachchy, *History of Kingship in Ceylon up to the Fourth Century AD**, Colombo, 1973.

John C. Holt, *Buddha in the Crown: Avalokitesvara in the Buddhist Traditions of Sri Lanka*, New York, 1991.

K. Indrapala (ed.), *The Collapse of the Rājarata Civilization in Ceylon and the Drift to the South West**, Peradeniya, 1971.

A. Liyanagamage, *The Decline of Polonnaruva and the Rise of Dambadeniya**, Colombo, 1968.

_____, *Society, State and Religion in Pre-Modern Sri Lanka*, Colombo, 2001.

S. Pathmanathan, *The Kingdom of Jaffna*, Part 1, Colombo, 1978.

Lakshman S. Perera, *The Institutions of Ancient Ceylon from Inscriptions (from the 3rd century BC to 830 AD)**, Vol. I, ICES, Kandy, 2001.

_____, *The Institutions of Ancient Ceylon from Inscriptions—Political Institutions (from 831 to 1016 AD)**, Vol. II, Part I, ICES, Kandy, 2003.

_____, *The Institutions of Ancient Ceylon from Inscriptions—Economic Institutions (from 831 to 1016 AD)* Vol. II, Part II, ICES, Kandy, forthcoming 2005.

W. Rahula, *The History of Buddhism in Ceylon**, Colombo, 1956.

W.M. Sirisena, *Sri Lanka and South-east Asia**, Leiden, 1978.

Ulrich von Schroeder, *Buddhist Sculptures of Sri Lanka**, Hong Kong, 1990.

_____, *The Golden Age of Sculpture in Sri Lanka: Masterpieces of Buddhist and Hindu Bronzes from Museums in Sri Lanka**, Hong Kong, 1992.

4. SRI LANKA AND THE WESTERN POWERS

See particularly, K.M. de Silva (ed.), *History of Ceylon** (from the beginning of the 19th century to 1948), Vol. III, 1973, University of Ceylon, and K.M. de Silva (ed.), *History of Sri Lanka** (from c. 1500 to c. 1800), Vol. II, University of Peradeniya, 1995.*

Two very comprehensively researched monographs provide a splendid introduction to Portuguese rule in Sri Lanka: T.B.H. Abeyasinghe, *Portuguese Rule* *in Ceylon, 1594–1612**, Colombo, 1966 and C.R. de Silva, *The Portuguese in Ceylon, 1617–1638**, Colombo, 1972.

The expulsion of the Portuguese from Sri Lanka and the establishment of the Dutch on the island's coastal regions is surveyed in detail in G.D. Winius, *The Fatal History of Portuguese Ceylon**, Cambridge, MA, 1971 and K.W. Goonewardena, *The Foundation of Dutch Power in Ceylon**, Amsterdam, 1958.

S. Arasaratnam, *Dutch Power in Ceylon**, Amsterdam, 1958 is a study of the consolidation of Dutch power in the island in the second half of the seventeenth century. J. van Goor, *Jan Kompenie as Schoolmaster,* Groningen, 1978, briefly reviews Dutch education in Sri Lanka over the period 1690–1795.

R. Pieris, *Sinhalese Social Organisation**, Colombo, 1956 is a scholarly introduction to the Kandyan kingdom; H.L. Seneviratne, *Rituals of the Kandyan State*, Cambridge, 1978, deals with an interesting aspect of Kandyan life and covers a longer period than Pieris's book. L. Dewaraja, *The Kandyan Kingdom of Ceylon, 1707–1760**, Colombo, 1972, surveys the politics of the kingdom, in important phases in its history. Two books by Sir Paulus Pieris provide a graphic account of the last years of the Kandyan kingdom: *Tri-Sinhala*, Colombo, 1939 and *Sinhale and the Patriots*, Colombo, 1956, a study of the great rebellion of 1817–18. Buddhism in Kandyan times is a major theme in K. Malalgoda, *Buddhism in Sinhalese Society, 1750–1900**, Berkeley, 1976, while G. Powell, *The Kandyan Wars: The British Army in Ceylon, 1803–1818*, London, 1973, provides a balanced and objective account of the British military campaigns in the Kandyan kingdom.

See also Michael Roberts, *Sinhala Consciousness in the Kandyan Period 1590s to 1815*, Colombo, 2004.

On British rule, see G.C. Mendis, *Ceylon Under the British*, 3rd edn, Colombo, 1952 and L.A. Mills, *Ceylon Under British Rule, 1795–1932*, Oxford, 1933.

The following books and monographs deal with the period c. 1800–1948:

Colvin R. de Silva, *Ceylon Under the British Occupation, 1795–1832*, 2 Vols, Colombo, 1941–42.

K.M. de Silva, *Social Policy and Missionary Organizations in Ceylon, 1840-1855**, London, 1965.

K.M. de Silva (ed.), *Sri Lanka*—Part I, *The Second World War and the Soulbury Commission, 1939–1945*, London, 1997; Part II, *Towards Independence, 1945–1948*, London, 1997. British Documents on End of Empire Series.

V.K. Jayawardena, *The Rise of the Labour Movement in Ceylon*, Durham, NC, 1972.

Sir Charles Jeffries, *Ceylon: The Path to Independence*, London, 1962.

G.C. Mendis (ed.), *The Colebrooke–Cameron Papers*, 2 Vols, Oxford, 1959.

S. Namasivayam, *The Legislatures of Ceylon*, London, 1951.

M.W. Roberts (ed.), *Documents of the Ceylon National Congress and Nationalist Politics in Ceylon, 1929-1950*, 4 Vols, Colombo, 1978.

I.D.S. Weerawardene, *Government and Politics in Ceylon (1931-1946)*, Colombo, 1951.

5. SRI LANKA SINCE INDEPENDENCE

Four volumes provide a wealth of information on the island in this period, each containing material not available in the others:

762   A History of Sri Lanka

K.M. de Silva (ed.), *Sri Lanka: A Survey*, London, 1976.

T. Fernando and R.N. Kearney, *Modern Sri Lanka: A Society in Transition*, Syracuse, 1978.

Russell, Ross R., Andrea Matles Savada et al. (eds.), *An Area Handbook for Ceylon*, 2nd edn, Washington DC, 1990.

On the island's politics in the years since independence there are several introductory surveys:

K.M. de Silva (ed.), *Sri Lanka: The Problems of Governance*, Delhi, 1993.

J. Jupp, *Sri Lanka: Third World Democracy*, London, 1978.

R.N. Kearney, *The Politics of Ceylon (Sri Lanka)*, Ithaca, NY, 1973.

A.J. Wilson, *Politics in Sri Lanka, 1947-1979**, London, 1979.

The following are more specialized works on this period.

K.M. de Silva, *Regional Powers and Small State Security: India and Sri Lanka*, Washington DC, 1995.

_____, *Reaping the Whirlwind: Ethnic Conflict and Ethnic Politics in Sri Lanka*, Delhi, 1998.

K.N.O. Dharmadasa, *Language, Religion and Ethnic Awareness: The Growth of Sinhalese Nationalism*, Ann Arbor, 1992.

B.H. Farmer, *Pioneer Peasant Colonization in Ceylon*, Oxford, 1957.

Sir Ivor Jennings, *The Constitution of Ceylon*, 3rd edn, London, 1953.

_____, *The Economy of Ceylon*, 2nd edn, London, 1951.

Sir Ivor Jennings and H.W. Tambiah, *The Dominion of Ceylon*, London, 1952.

J. Jiggins, *Caste and Family in the Politics of the Sinhalese, 1947-1976*, Cambridge, 1979.

R.N. Kearney, *Communalism and Language in the Politics of Ceylon*, Durham, NC, 1967.

_____,*Trade Unions and Politics in Ceylon*, Berkeley, 1971.

W.D. Lakshman (ed.), *Dilemmas of Development: Fifty Years of Economic Change in Sri Lanka*, 1997.

G. Lerski, *Origins of Trotskyism in Ceylon*, Stanford, 1968.

Mick Moore, *The State and Peasant Politics in Sri Lanka*, Cambridge, 1985.

U. Phadnis, *Religion and Politics in Sri Lanka*, New Delhi, 1976.

Marshall R. Singer, *The Emerging Elite: A Study of Political Leadership in Ceylon*, Cambridge, MA, 1964.

D.R. Snodgrass, *Ceylon: An Export Economy in Transition*, Homewood, IL, 1966.

A.J. Wilson, *Electoral Politics in an Emergent State: The Ceylon General Election of May 1970*, Cambridge, 1975.

W. Howard Wriggins, *Ceylon: Dilemmas of a New Nation*, Princeton, NJ, 1960.

Calvin Woodward, *Growth of a Party System in Ceylon*, Providence, RI, 1969.

Index

Abhaya, Vattagāmani (c. 103 BC), 62
Abhayagiri sect, 62–65, 69–71, 77
absenteeism, 218
accomodessans, 176, 278
adhyaksas, 27
Adichchanallur, 13
adigārs, 199
administration, administrative structure, 21, 27,
  82,112, 117, 161, 198–202, 320, 325–37,
  394–96, 407, 437–38, 468, 472, 672;
  breakdown, 641; under British rule, 279, 282–
  86, 302, 306, 399, 401, 407–08, 414, 418, 452,
  548; costs, 327; under Dutch, 250–54, 276–
  77; hierarchy, 202, 251–52, 318; powers, 669;
  under VOC, 224
agency houses, role in plantation agriculture,
  347, 349
Aggabodhi I, king of Anuradhapura, (571–604),
  21, 24
Aggabodhi II, king of Anuradhapura, (604–14),
  21
Aggabodhi III, king of Anuradhapura, (628,
  629–39), 22
Aggabodhi IV, king of Polonnaruva (667–83),
  48, 71
Aggabodhi VII, king of Polonnaruva (727–77),
  48
agitation and discontent, 476, 479, 507–09
agrarian, agriculture, agricultural economy, 5,
  9, 12, 40, 43, 119, 121, 177, 203, 226, 315,
  344, 618, 620, 660; education in, 512–13;
  policy, 659, 688; reforms, 692; resources, 42,
  230; stagnation, 315; surplus, 2, 34, 38, 42,
  43; traditional, 226–32, 573, 582, 619, 621,
  657, 687–88; under VOC, 217–36
Agriculture Department, 500
Āhālēpola family, 202, 295–97, 299, 303–04
Akbo Vehera, 137
Alagakkōnāras, 114–15, 137
Alagiyavanna, 269
Älahära: Buddha images, 74
Älahära Canal, 35, 41
Alakeśvara, Vīra, Sinhalese king, 114, 115–16,
  122, 137–9
Alawwa: Dutch power, 189
All Ceylon Trade Union Congress, 525
All-Ceylon Liberal League, 527, 529

allied powers, allies, 556, 580–81
Aluntuwara inscriptions, 140
Alutkuru Kōralēs, 143, 185, 226
Alutnuvara, 392
Aluvihara, 77
Alwis, James, 396, 453, 461, 592
Amarapura Nikāya, 268, 320, 429, 433
Amaravati: Buddha images, 73
Amaravati school, 71, 73–74
ämati pajaha, 27
amātya mandalaya, 198
Ambagamuva, 362
Ambaganga, 35
Ambanvala Rāla, 188
American War of Independence, 240–41
Amogharajra, 67
anachronism, 614
Anderson, George, 340, 358, 361–63, 399
Andrews, Robert, 246–47, 278, 282, 287, 313
Anglican Church, Anglicans, 338–39, 510, 598;
  disestablishment, 412, 431–32, 439
Anglicization process, 325, 400, 419–21, 426,
  442, 594
Anglo-Dutch relations, conflict, 215, 237–38,
  243–44
Anstruther, Philip, Colonial Secretary, 331, 346
anti-Americanism, 652
Anuradhapura, Anuradhapura kings, 12, 15–
  17, 271, 402, 576; Cōla conquest 82;
  instability in politics, 23, 28–29; irrigation
  system, 28, 32–42; Lambakanna dynasty, 20;
  language and literature, 61; law of
  succession, 22; Moriyas, 21; political
  structure, 21, 28–29; political economy, 43–
  59; political struggle, 28; regeneration of
  irrigation facilities, 381; Sinhalese power/
  rulers, 20, 29–31, 42, 48, 109; south Indian/
  Dravidian invasion, 13, 19, 24, 28–31;
  succession disputes, 197; topography, 33, 36;
  trade settlements, 113, 129; village
  institutions, 112
Appuhamy, Akaragama, 165
Arabi Pasha (Ahmed Arabi), 445–46
Arabian peninsula, Arabs, 47–48, 120–21;
  Israel conflict, 654; Sri Lanka trade, 44
arahānt, 61
Arandara, 191

Chetties, 120, 220, 233, 388
chief headmen and temperance leaders, confrontation, 468
chiefdoms, chiefs, 243, 268, 333, 335; see also Kandyan chiefs, Vanni chiefs
Chilaw, 120, 178, 223, 229, 272; coconut cultivation, 367, 377; railways, 368
Chilaw Association, 459, 471
China and Sri Lanka, relations (ancient), 116; Chinese immigrants, 315; diplomatic relations, 623–24, 635, 638, 652–53; economic assistance, 654; Kuo-mintang, 623; Ming emperors, 89; religious links, 68; trade and commercial relations, 31, 38, 40, 44, 47, 49, 50, 119
Christians, Christianity, 48, 166, 167, 168, 259–61, 284, 320–23, 338–39, 342, 417, 428–29, 441–42, 445, 447, 466, 471, 493, 510–1, 576–77, 584, 591, 602–03, 609, 630, 632, 645–46; Buddhists, 321; and language issue, 631
Church and state, separation, 431
Church of England, 284
Church Missionary Society, 323
cinchona, 360, 368–69
cinnamon trade, 115, 119, 121, 143, 149, 145, 161, 275, 307–8, 311–12, 314, 317, 319, 331, 344–45, 421; Dutch control, 172–73, 184, 186, 189–90, 194, 210–11, 255, 257; export duty, 345; Portuguese control, 178–80; under VOC, 217–24, 227, 234, 238, 242
Cinnamon Department, 319, 331
citizenship, 675, 685; legislation, 647; rights, 523, 605, 628, 647–48; territorial concept, 608
Citizenship Act, 1948, 605
civil and military authorities, clashes, 330
civil disobedience movement, 645, 671
civil services, 327–28, 403–05; decline, 346; reforms, 1844–45, 346; exclusion of Sri Lankans, 404–07
civil war, 112, 246, 341, 475, 600
clans, 8–9, 20
class identity, 507, 663
Clifford, Sir Hugh, 474, 491, 503–05, 516–17, 578
coastal regions, 112; Moors, 474–75; trade, 309
Cochin: European settlers, 309
coconut industry, cultivation, trade, 143, 459, 498, 506, 458, 571–72, 618, 655, 657; British control, 346, 360, 366–68, 371, 373–74, 377, 391, 421; cultivation, 219, 221, 223
coexistence policy of Dutch, 209–13
coffee industry, coffee culture, 217, 220, 224–26, 310–12, 316, 342–44, 346–47, 350, 352–53, 355–56, 360–77, 382, 391, 397, 421, 422, 423, 451; collapse 1870s and 1880s, 416–17, 424; export, 310; export duty, 311; prices, 343, 365
Cōḷas, 1, 23, 48, 67, 68, 81–83, 85, 88–91; conquest of Anuradhapura, 18–19, 30–31, 42; invasions, 109; and Pāṇḍyas, relations, 87–89
Colebrooke, W.M.G., 306, 318, 324, 335–37, 338, 346, 353, 384, 388, 394, 401, 447

Colebrooke–Cameron Commission see Commission of Eastern Inquiry
Colombo, Colombo Disāvony, 120, 189, 291, 293, 304; Academy, 419; cinnamon trade, 179; customs revenue, 331; under Dutch rule, 187, 190, 253–54, 257, 260, 264, 279; Municipal Council, 497; Portuguese invasion/trading, 145, 149, 157–60; rebellion of 1848, 354–59; urban unrest, 458
colonial administration, 262, 313, 317, 325, 331, 336, 402, 419, 425–26, 447, 455, 470, 495, 525–26
colonial economy, 307–09, 331
Colonial Office, 307, 311, 316, 335, 339, 342, 351, 353, 358, 364, 382–83, 394–95, 398, 419, 431, 435, 438–39, 447–48, 452, 462, 470–71, 473, 500, 516–17, 522, 524, 530–31, 534–35, 539, 541–44, 555, 558, 562, 566, 568
colonization, 116, 232, 315, 380, 500–04, 579–80
commercial credit, 343
commercial crisis, 1847–48, 343–45
Commission of Eastern Inquiry (Colebrooke–Cameron Commission), Colebrooke–Cameron reforms, 306, 317, 318, 324, 335–37, 338, 345, 354, 384, 388, 394, 401, 407, 410, 414, 447, 518, 683
Committee of Investigation, 279–80
Commonwealth connection, 569, 603, 623, 636–37, 665
communal, communalism, 523–24, 549; disturbances and violence, 474, 610, 673, 676, 685, 690; electorate, 490, 523; harmony, 611, 691; organizations, 537; politics, 488; representation, 522
communication, communication network, 330, 335, 365, 384, 402; and plantation economy, reciprocal relationship, 347, 362; by sea, 373
communism, communists, 606–07, 624, 638
Communist Party, 587, 616, 634, 644, 649, 663, 678–80
Communist Party (Moscow wing), 660, 661
commutation system, 395–97
competition, competitors, 236, 308, 403, 423, 463, 615
compromise settlement 1852–53, 358–59
compulsory service system, 313–14, 318, 353
conscience clause, 510
consciousness, 335
conservatism, conservatives, 399, 411–12, 462, 470, 476, 479, 481, 486, 488, 491, 564
Constitution of Sri Lanka, 1923–24, 516, 522; 1944, 561–64, 603; 1972, 664, 668, 673; 1978, 684–85
constitutional crisis, 543, 548
constitutional development, 451–63
constitutional framework, structure, 450, 532, 651, 669, 683–84
constitutional reform, 1921–28, 484, 486; 1937–39, 533–35, 539, 541–53; 1942–47, 557–59, 562

Pybus, John, 213–14
Pyl, Laurens, 193–94

race, racial minorities, 7, 479, 626
race riots, 1966, 650; 1977, 690
radicalism, radical forces, 449, 470, 481, 488,
   493–97, 518, 520, 533, 547, 604, 645, 692–
   93, 697
Rāhula Maha Sthavira, 126
railways, 362–65, 373–75, 382, 402, 422; and
   damage to coconut plantation, 368; workers,
   507
rain forests, 6
rainfall, 2, 33
Rājādhi Rājasimha, 241, 271, 272, 288–89
Rājādhirāja 82
Rājagrha, 11
rājakāriya, 54–55, 139, 200, 203, 278, 280–81, 290,
   312–15, 317–19, 325, 332, 335, 353; abolition,
   340, 379
Rajakaruna, Ananda (1885–1957), 596
Rajapakse, Adrian de Abrew, 410
Rajapakse, Samson, 410
Rājarāja the Great (983–1014), 30–31, 109
Rājarata, 24, 30–31, 37, 40, 48, 67, 69, 81–85,
   110, 117, 135, 383
Rājaratnākāraya, 269
Rājasimha I, king of Sītāvaka, 156–62, 169,
   171–72
Rājasimha II, Kandyan king, 30, 171–73, 184–
   86, 188–89, 191–95, 196–97, 199, 202, 206,
   271, 272
Rajāvaliya, 136, 139, 140, 269
Rājendra, son of Rājarāja the Great, 31
Rājendra I, 82
Rājendra II, 82
Rāmanna Nikāya, 68, 429
Ranasingh, A.G., 566
Ratanāvalī, 86
rate ātto, 200
rate-rālas, 198
rationing, 587, 668
Ratnākaraya, 126
Ratnapura: exemption from grain tax, 393;
   grain tax, 397
Ratnayake, P.B., 490
Rayigam Bandara, 141
Rayigama, 116, 149–50, 185, 279; rebellion, 165
realism, 379
rebellion, 1757–60, 221–22, 1789–90, 226;
   1817–18, 301, 306, 313, 333, 357, 379, 392,
   401; 1848, 354–59, 399, 401
receptivity, 320
reconciliation policy, 686
redistribution policy, 639, 657
regional autonomy, 627
regional councils, power, 630
Rekava, 632
relics, relic worship cult, 65, 69, 83, 86, 306
religion, religious, 24, 58, 82, 113, 122, 124, 126,
   197–98, 277, 338, 341, 399, 426, 461, 471,

493, 538, 575, 607–10, 613–14; edifices, 17,
   43; under British, 283–84; from 1250 to end
   of fifteenth century, 121–26; bias, 7, 445;
   conflicts, 11, 63, 320–22, 603; policy under
   Dutch rule, 256–61; devotional aspect, 65, 67;
   establishments' property, 55–56; freedom,
   321; in Kadayan kingdom, 265–68; minorities,
   479; and identity, 8; and nationalism, 440–
   46, 538, 549; policies, 295; and politics, 471,
   550; impact of Portuguese rule, 181–83;
   revivalism, 269, 412; sanctions, 203; and
   state, 555
renting system, 393–96
repatriation, 648–50
representation mechanism, 487–88
representation principle, 448–50, 453–58
reservoirs, 3, 9, 33–35, 41, 43, 52, 379
resistance movements, 196, 427–28; against
   Portuguese, 165–66; see also rebellion, riots
retrenchment policy, 416, 533, 570, 573–74
revenue system, 330–31, 352–53
rice, rice trade, 32, 190, 226–27, 230, 233, 235,
   388–90, 619, 656, 666–67; import, 314–15,
   379, 389; import duty, 395
Ridgeway, Joseph West, 407
Ridī Vihāra, Kurunegala, 274
rights, 685
riots of 1915, 474–78, 488, 491
ritual elements, 65
Road Ordinance, 353
road system, roads network, 316, 347, 362, 375,
   384, 402
Robinson, Hercules, 365, 382–83, 395, 400
Rockwood, W.G., 462
Rodney, John, 330–31
Rohana, 8, 14–16, 24–25, 81–84, 110, 113, 135;
   agricultural development, 40–42; and
   Anuradhapura, relationship, 27; resistance
   against Cōlas, 31; irrigation network, 37
Roman Catholics, 148, 151, 154–55, 165, 169,
   176–77, 181–82, 250, 257–61, 277, 283, 321,
   434–36, 510, 584–85, 609, 628, 645–47, 649,
   651, 674
Roman coins, 50
Roman-Dutch law, 256–57
Roman maritime trade, 46
Royal Botanical Gardens, Peradeniya, 312, 316, 513
Royal College of Colombo, 515
rubber, rubber indutry, 366, 371–74, 421, 458,
   498–500, 506, 571–73, 580, 618, 655, 575,
   581; prices, 686
rural masses and the leadership, 466
rural poverty, 398
rural regeneration and welfare, 467
Ruvanvälisäya, 69, 77
Ruvanveli Dāgäbba, Anuradhapura, 433
Ruvanvella, 537; Dutch control, 189

Sabaragamuva, 6, 153, 296–97, 304, 401; coffee,
   365, 374, 376; Dutch control, 186, 191;
   population, 505

778   A History of Sri Lanka

Saddarma Ratnāvaliya, 125
Saddhātissa, 18–32
Sagama, 136
Sailabimbārāmaya, 274
Saiva Pragasa Sabhai, 444
Saivangala Vidyasalai, 443
Salāgamas, 121, 143, 178–80, 210–11, 218–19,
    221, 223, 251–52, 282, 312, 314, 318–20, 410,
    424, 433
Sälalihini sandeśa, 126
Salāvata, 120, 272
Salpiti, 165, 185, 279
salt, 314; prices, 312
salvation, 62
samādhi, 73
Saman, 67, 122–23
Samarawickreme, E.J., 487–88, 520
Samudra Devi, 151
Sandarasagara, H.A.P., 529
sandeśa kāvya, 124–26
sangha, 52, 60–61, 122, 433, 198
Sanghamittā, 12
sangharāja, 122
Sanghatissa II (614), 21
sanitary conditions, 508
Sanskrit, 79–80, 269, 591
Sapumal Kumāraya, king of Jaffna, 117–18
Sarachchandra, E.R., 595, 597; *Maname*, 632
saramāru nindagam lands, 204
Saranankara, 266–70
Saranankara, Välivita, 319
Sarasavi Sandaresa, 461
sāsana, 265, 267
Sassanian period, 48
School Commission, 339, 417
School garden scheme, 512
School of Tropical Agriculture, 513
school system, schools, 322–24, 339
Schreuder, Governor (1757–62), 212, 220–22,
    225, 253, 255–57, 260
sea routes, 45
seclusion, 445
secondary resistance, concept of, 464
sectarian disputes, sectarianism, 63–64, 433, 471
secularism, 555, 611
security forces and Tamil guerrillas, conflicts,
    699
Seely, Colonel, 473
Selborne, Lord, 452
self-consciousness, 627
self-respect, 633
Sena I, king of Polonnaruva (833–53), 29, 48, 67
Sena IV (954–56), 79
Senādhilankāra, 114, 122, 135–37
Senākadagala Nuvara, 111, 140, 134, 270–1
Senanayake, D.C., 466, 492
Senanayake, D.S., 446, 467, 503, 531–32, 537, 541,
    542, 548, 550–1, 554–64, 575, 577–78, 581,
    583–84, 601–3, 605, 607–12, 618–20, 622–
    23, 626, 635–37, 641; mission to Whitehall,
    564–69

Senanayake, Dudley, 551, 611–12, 614, 616, 624,
    630, 635, 650–51, 653–54, 657, 659, 661–62,
    666, 670–1
Senanayake, F.R., 466, 467, 478, 493, 492, 531,
    538
Senanayake, G.B., 595
Senanayakes, 476, 492, 493
senāpati (the chief of army), 27
Senārat, (1604–35) Kandyan king, 168, 171
separatism, separatist movement, 675, 686,
    692–96, 701, 705,
Seven Kōralēs, 159; Dutch control, 186, 189, 199,
    211; revolt (1616), 165, 304
Seven Years War, 238
Shiels, Drummond, 519–20, 525
ship-building, 49
shipping conditions, 365, 498–99
Shore, Sir John, 245, 275
Siavite Hinduism, 82
Siddi Lebbe, M.C., 445–46
Sigiri, 75–77, 79, 124
Sīhabāhu, 6, 7
Sīhapura, 6
Silākāla (518–31), 24–25
Silva, W.A., 594–95
Silva, William, 642
Silvat Samāgama, 266, 268
Simon Commission, 517
Singuruvana, 137
Sinhala language, 77–80, 590, 628; as national
    language, 644; as official language, 583,
    614–15; and Tamil, parity status, 615, 634
Sinhala Mahā Sabhā, 491–93, 501, 538, 541,
    546–47, 549–53, 555, 576, 584, 602, 610
Sinhala Only, 614, 628, 630, 645
Sinhalese, Sinhalese kings, kingdom, 7–8, 18–
    19, 22, 29–30, 68, 81, 85, 86, 89, 110, 115,
    120, 129, 143, 162, 196, 256, 258–59, 264–
    65, 268, 282, 289, 332–33, 340, 375–76, 406,
    411, 418, 419, 421–23, 427, 436, 440–41,
    444–45, 448–49, 453–59, 460–63, 477, 490–
    93, 501, 506, 524, 528, 534, 555, 605, 607,
    609, 613, 630, 633, 643, 649, 651, 663, 683,
    692, 693; architecture, 71–72; and Buddhist
    numerical superiority, domination, 79, 429,
    465, 475, 609–10, 614, 627, 629, 673; caste
    system, 121, 179; Christians, 250; clan
    structure, 27; crisis, 700; disintegration and
    disorder, 127; education, 417, 473; and ethnic
    minorities, conflict, 483; extremism, 681;
    labour, 370; *lascarin* troops, 166; linguistic
    nationalism, 609, 627, 630; literary tradition,
    literature, 126, 590–91, 594–95, 597, 632–
    33; merchants, 48–49; music, 598;
    nationalism, 358, 479; peasant, 389, 461;
    politicians, 523, 527, 530, 559, 577, 602;
    power, 110–3; Portuguese influence, 181;
    religious beliefs, 66; resistance, 165; rural
    voters, 605–06; sculpture, 73; and Tamils
    clashes, 16, 137–38, 480, 483, 487, 674, 685;
    —reconciliation, 489; taxation system, 393;